THE BEST PLAYS OF 1975–1976

THE
BURNS MANTLE
YEARBOOK

THE
BEST PLAYS
OF 1975-1976

EDITED BY OTIS L. GUERNSEY JR.

Illustrated with photographs and
with drawings by HIRSCHFELD

○○○○○○

DODD, MEAD & COMPANY
NEW YORK • TORONTO

~~by David F~~reeman. Copyright © 1976 by David Freeman. Reprinted by permission of International Creative Management. See CAUTION notice below. Inquiries concerning amateur acting rights should be addressed to: Samuel French, Inc., 25 West 45th Street, New York, N.Y. 10036. All other inquiries should be addressed to the author's agent: Bridget Aschenberg, International Creative Management, 40 West 57th Street, New York, N.Y. 10019.

"Pacific Overtures": by Stephen Sondheim and John Weidman. Copyright © 1976 by John Weidman, Stephen Sondheim, Harold S. Prince and Hugh Wheeler. Lyrics Copyright © 1975 by Revelation Music Publishing Corporation and Rilting Music, Inc. All rights reserved. Reprinted by permission of the copyright owners and Dodd, Mead and Company, Inc., publishers of the complete play. See CAUTION notice below. All inquiries should be addressed to the authors' agents: Flora Roberts, Inc. (for Stephen Sondheim and Harold S. Prince), 65 East 55th Street, New York, N.Y. 10022; Harold Freedman, Brandt & Brandt Dramatic Department, Inc. (for John Weidman), 101 Park Avenue, New York, N.Y. 10017 and William Morris Agency, Inc. (for Hugh Wheeler), attention: Mr. Jerome Talbert, 1350 Avenue of the Americas, New York, N.Y. 10019.

"Chicago": book by Fred Ebb and Bob Fosse; music by John Kander; lyrics by Fred Ebb; based on the play by Maurine Dallas Watkins. Book Copyright © 1976 by Fred Ebb and Bob Fosse. Reprinted by permission of International Creative Management, agents for the authors. Lyrics for "And All That Jazz" and "My Own Best Friend" Copyright © 1973 & 1975 by Kander-Ebb, Inc. & Unichappell Music, Inc. Lyrics for "All I Care About," "Mister Cellophane," "Class," and "Nowadays" Copyright © 1975 by Kander-Ebb, Inc. & Unichappell Music, Inc. Lyrics for "Roxie" Copyright © 1974 & 1975 by Kander-Ebb, Inc. & Unichappell Music, Inc. (For all lyrics contained herein: International Copyright Secured. Made in U.S.A. ALL RIGHTS RESERVED including public performance for profit. Any copying, arranging or adapting of these works without the written consent of the owners is an infringement of copyright. Used by permission of Unichappell Music, Inc., Administrator.) See CAUTION notice below. All inquiries concerning the use of the lyrics should be addressed to: Unichappell Music, Inc., 810 Seventh Avenue, New York, N.Y. 10019. All other inquiries should be addressed to: Bridget Aschenberg, International Creative Management, 40 West 57th Street, New York, N.Y. 10019.

"Travesties": by Tom Stoppard. Copyright © 1975 by Tom Stoppard. All rights reserved. Reprinted by permission of Grove Press, Inc. See CAUTION notice below. All inquiries should be addressed to the publisher: Grove Press, Inc., 196 West Houston Street, New York, N.Y. 10014.

"The Norman Conquests": by Alan Ayckbourn. Copyright © Alan Ayckbourn, 1975. Reprinted by permission of the author and publisher, Chatto and Windus Ltd. See CAUTION notice below. All inquiries should be addressed to the publisher: Chatto and Windus Ltd., 40-42 William IV Street, London WC2N 4DF, England.

EDITOR'S NOTE

THIS Bicentennial year we look back over where we've been and see that the theater's wake, instead of broadening behind it, is broadening as we go, with the wide range of American play production getting ever wider. No longer pressed between the narrow banks of Broadway as it was when this *Best Plays* series of yearbooks began in 1919–20, the professional American theater is gathering tributaries into a mighty river of hundreds and hundreds of productions from Broadway to Vandam Street, all around the town and across one river to Brooklyn and Queens and across the other to Seattle and Houston and Minneapolis and elsewhere in hundreds more productions by regional theater groups across the country.

The *Best Plays* series will follow and record this development of the American theater, wherever it leads. In the past nine volumes we've steadily increased our coverage of regional theater in Ella A. Malin's city-by-city Directory of Professional Regional Theater, and more recently of the mushrooming off-off-Broadway movement in Camille Croce's comprehensive listing of 135+ OOB groups which has passed 600 program entries and still counting. We can assure our readers that our record of 1975–76 theater activity in these two important areas includes all available information about major programs. These sections of our coverage gain added distinction from special articles and comments by Richard L. Coe on highlights of the theater's participation in the Bicentennial, by Marion Fredi Towbin on major off-off-Broadway events, by Rick Talcove on the Los Angeles theater year and by David Richards on the year in Washington, D.C.

In New York, the importance of revivals to this 1975–76 theater season, particularly on Broadway, has persuaded us to take extra notice by adding a new category to our list of selections of the year's "bests"—that of "best revival" under both the straight-play and musical headings. In this connection, the remarkable achievement of bringing the Brecht-Weill *Threepenny Opera* back in a new translation that panders not at all to the sweet tooth of Broadway audiences but instead restores the bitter irony of the original has prompted us to give it a special citation and a script synopsis exactly similar to those of the ten Best Plays.

Unlike the theater itself, the *Best Plays* volume isn't infinitely expandable, and there's a point beyond which an increase in its physical size begins to become counterproductive. Therefore, in order to make room for expanding coverage of the American theater, we've had to discontinue our London reports and listings. We thus sever our British ties with the same mixed feelings of regret and determination that must have filled the hearts of our forefathers 200 years ago, knowing however that our first responsibility, like theirs, is to our own. Major work of the London theater turns up in this volume anyway in the Broadway and off-Broadway listings, which are compiled as always to include every important detail.

The continuity as well as the immediate substance of information in the *Best Plays* volumes owe themselves in great part to the continued dedication and know-how of a team of diligent shepherds including Jonathan Dodd of Dodd, Mead & Company, publishers of this series, and the editor's persevering wife; compilers including Rue Canvin (necrology, books and records listing and other coverage), Stanley Green (cast replacements and touring companies), Jeff Sweet (a Best Play synopsis) and Bernard Simon of *Simon's Directory* (bus and truck tours); and informants/advisers including Henry Hewes of *Saturday Review,* Mimi Horowitz of *Playbill,* Hobe Morrison of *Variety,* Clara Rotter of the New York *Times,* Ralph Newman of the Drama Book Shop, the Off-Off-Broadway Alliance and the many, many patient and forbearing staff members of theater production offices who supply so many of the facts.

We are exceedingly grateful also for such invaluable embellishments as Al Hirschfeld's drawings, the photo-section illustrations of outstanding theater designs by Boris Aronson and Patricia Zipprodt and the photographs of theater in New York and across the country by Martha Swope, Sy Friedman, Inge Morath, David H. Fishman, Barry Kramer-Joseph Abeles, Gerry Goodstein, Sophie Baker, Frederic Ohringer, George E. Joseph, Ken Howard, Bert Andrews and Robert Galbraith.

And of course it's the authors of the plays and musicals both best and worst —the playwrights, composers, lyricists and librettists who have borne the essential burden of this theater season and this volume—to whom we offer our last and loudest applause. We owe their talented and persistent kind 200 years of American theater from Royall Tyler's *The Contrast* to Jules Feiffer's *Knock Knock.* As we look back from our 1976 vantage point we see clearly that the theater they created has been one of the cultural wonders of the ages, and we look forward confidently to more of the same, beginning this month with Neil Simon's *California Suite* and moving into and across the next two centuries.

OTIS L. GUERNSEY Jr.

June 1, 1976

CONTENTS

Drawings by HIRSCHFELD

SUMMARIES
OF THE
SEASONS

THE SEASON IN NEW YORK

By Otis L. Guernsey Jr.

LIKE any fine performance, the New York theater year of 1975–76 was largely a triumph of illusion. The impression of a crowded, brilliant season was as convincing as a great stage setting—and as fabricated. Grand new musicals and plays paraded through the theaters, flaunting their tip of the stage's massive creative effort—except that this season was a prop iceberg in a cardboard sea, all tip and no mass. There were enough leading attractions to break box office records, but there was no solid base of new shows underneath them on which the exception of a *Pacific Overtures* or *Streamers* or *Knock Knock* could stand tall.

Fortunately for everyone on both sides of the footlights, the illusion worked like magic, as it was supposed to. The smash hit, multi-prizewinning *A Chorus Line* stirred up so much excitement that for the first time in years there were rumors of ticket scalping (and never mind that this wonderful musical was last year's show, and a transfer from off Broadway). Star performances ranged from admirable (George C. Scott in *Death of a Salesman*) to heart-stopping (Irene Worth's in *Sweet Bird of Youth*)—and if you didn't look too closely you might not notice that, say, two-thirds of the Tony acting nominations were for roles in revivals, imports or transfers, not in new Broadway shows.

The illusion of a busy Broadway year was sustained by opening wide the doors of the theater libraries. Of 1975–76's total of 65 productions, 28—close to half the total effort—were revivals. New musical production seemed to be holding its own with 12 new entries, one transfer and three sizeable revues; but the production of new American plays was attenuated to next to nothing: three transfers from off Broadway and seven new scripts—seven which together played a total of only about 200 performances the whole season. The total Broadway playing weeks (if ten shows play ten weeks, that's 100 playing weeks) rose slightly to 1,136 as compared with 1,101 last year, well above the historic low of 852 the year before. The total was padded, however, with shows mounted elsewhere and brought in, like the five distinguished productions generated in Washington, D.C. as part of the Kennedy Center American Bicentennial Theater schedule produced by Roger L. Stevens and Richmond Crinkley with the help of a special grant from Xerox; or the year's outstanding Broadway drama, *The Runner Stumbles*.

Nowhere was the illusion more disarming than in the Broadway box office summaries. 1975–76 shattered the record for a season's total Broadway gross, amassing $70,841,738 as compared with the previous historical high of $58.9

3

The 1975–76 Season on Broadway

PLAYS (10)

The First Breeze of Summer (transfer)
Lamppost Reunion
The Leaf People
Yentl (transfer)
Kennedy's Children
Murder Among Friends
The Poison Tree
KNOCK KNOCK (transfer)
Legend
THE RUNNER STUMBLES

SPECIALTIES (3)

Monty Python Live!
Shirley MacLaine
The Belle of Amherst

MUSICALS (13)

CHICAGO
A Chorus Line (transfer)
The Robber Bridegroom
The 5th Season
Treemonisha
Boccaccio
Home Sweet Homer
PACIFIC OVERTURES
Rockabye Hamlet
Rex
So Long, 174th Street
1600 Pennsylvania Avenue
Something's Afoot

REVUES (3)

Me and Bessie
A Musical Jubilee
Bubbling Brown Sugar

FOREIGN PLAYS IN ENGLISH (7)

TRAVESTIES
Habeas Corpus
THE NORMAN CONQUESTS
Table Manners
Living Together
Round and Round the Garden
A Matter of Gravity
Zalmen or the Madness of God

FOREIGN PLAY (1)

Des Journées Entières Dans les Arbres

REVIVALS (28)

Circle in Square 1975:
Death of a Salesman
Bicentennial Theater:
The Skin of Our Teeth
Summer Brave
Sweet Bird of Youth
The Royal Family
The Heiress
Circle in Square 1976:
Ah, Wilderness!
The Glass Menagerie
The Lady From the Sea
Acting Company:
Edward II
The Time of Your Life
Three Sisters
Vivian Beaumont:
Trelawny of the "Wells"
Hamlet
Mrs. Warren's Profession
THREEPENNY OPERA
Hello, Dolly!
Very Good Eddie

Angel Street
Phoenix Theater:
27 Wagons Full of Cotton & A Memory of Two Mondays
They Knew What They Wanted
Secret Service
Boy Meets Girl
My Fair Lady
Who's Afraid of *Virginia Woolf?*
D'Oyly Carte:
The Mikado
The Pirates of Penzance
H.M.S. Pinafore

Categorized above are all the plays listed in the "Plays Produced on Broadway" section of this volume.
Plays listed in CAPITAL LETTERS have been designated Best Plays of 1975–76.
Plays listed in *italics* were still running June 1, 1976.
Plays listed in **bold face type** were classified as hits in *Variety's* annual list of hits and flops published June 2, 1976.

million in 1967–68. This was a whopping increase of 20 per cent in the record and 23 per cent over last season's $57.4 million—and this highest gross ever was attained in spite of the fact that it was a short year for the musicals: only 48½ weeks long, as a musicians' strike shut them down for three and a half weeks in October, reducing the year's total income by an estimated $3.5 million. The season included the first $2 million week in Broadway history, the week of Jan. 4. With the road enjoying its second-best year ever with a $52.6 million gross, the total take for Broadway shows in 1975–76 rose to an un-unprecedented $123 million-plus.

Audiences thronged Broadway's side streets in 1975–76, with many who couldn't quite afford the price of a ticket lining up at the TKTS booth on Duffy Square looking for a bargain (TKTS distributed more than half a million Broadway and almost a hundred thousand off-Broadway cut-rate tickets during the twelve months). The box office bonanza was achieved by a large increase in attendance, not by any significant increase in prices. According to an estimate prepared by Hobe Morrison in *Variety,* Broadway's attendance for the year was around 6,000,000—the importance of which to New York City may be judged in comparison to, say, the 4,000,000 drawn by all the New York baseball and football teams combined.

The top price for a Saturday night ticket to a hit Broadway musical moved upward last season from the previous $15 to $17.50, but only at *Chicago* in June and *Rex* in April, with the *My Fair Lady* revival priced at $16. Even with some upward ticket-pricing movement at other levels, inflation has made the once-shocking price of a Broadway show seem less forbidding. With attendance stimulated by a host of popular revivals like *The Royal Family,* a record gross resulted.

No one dares to suggest that the record was set because the shows were more attractive. Until someone can, even financial success must be viewed as somewhat illusory. For example, in this year of record theater prosperity there were, paradoxically, very few individually profitable shows. The handful of productions showing a profit, according to *Variety* estimate (see the one-page summary of the season accompanying this report), included last season's phenomenal *Same Time, Next Year* which by this season's end had grossed $5.3 million and was showing a $1.2 million profit on its relatively modest $230,000 investment.

The "star system," presumed burned out in the theater, flickered and then blazed back to temporary glory this season. In an engagement limited to ten weeks, Katharine Hepburn drew audiences to the admittedly second-rate *A Matter of Gravity* to the tune of a $350,000 profit on its $160,000 investment. Richard Burton took over the role of the doctor in the admittedly first-rate *Equus* which thereupon raised the price of its top ticket to $15 and packed them in with standees, doing 102 per cent of seating capacity for the 12 weeks.

Music concert stars visited Broadway theaters and could do no wrong. One event billed as "The Concert," with Count Basie, Ella Fitzgerald and Frank Sinatra in a two-week, 16-performance engagement at the Uris Theater priced at a $40 top, took in a higher two-week gross than ever dreamed of by a single

"Broadway" attraction: $1,080,000. Shirley MacLaine with her "gypsies" made a two-week visit to the Palace in a song-and-dance revue which had scored a big hit in London and broke the Palace's record, taking in $329,000 for the 14 performances.

At the same time, failures were ever more conspicuous. Last season's shows which were drawing their bottom lines in 1975–76 included *All Over Town,* a 1975 Best Play which nevertheless lost $300,000 on its $275,000 investment. David Merrick folded Tennessee Williams's *The Red Devil Battery Sign* out of town to the tune of an estimated $360,000. The short-lived Broadway transfer of *Knock Knock* set its producers back an estimated $250,000. Even pre-packaged revivals could be costly if they didn't happen to catch on; American Bicentennial Theater's *The Skin of Our Teeth* and *Summer Brave* did fine in Washington but dropped $144,000 and $175,000 respectively on Broadway, according to *Variety* estimate. A pre-tested foreign script was no talisman against failure, either. A *Habeas Corpus* full of stars and seemingly doing business dropped $225,000 on $200,000; *Zalmen or the Madness of God* went for $300,000. Even *The Norman Conquests,* a hit in every respect except at the box office, ended up in the red, dropping $235,000 of its investment of $275,000.

The New York *Times* quoted Stephen Sondheim in an interview: "It takes . . . . . guts to do a show on Broadway these days. A man like Joseph Papp, who is funded by the government, puts on a show in a theater workshop, and when he deems that show worthy of transferring to Broadway, he brings it uptown. Well, where's the courage in that? The courageous guys are the ones who lay themselves on the line for a million dollars." Translated into the facts of 1975–76, this means some courageous guys named Roger L. Stevens and Kennedy Center productions dropped an estimated $1.2 million on the Yul Brynner musical *Home Sweet Homer* which lasted only one performance on Broadway after a long cross-country tour. Other such courageous guys and dolls included Stevens again, with Robert Whitehead and Coca-Cola Company financial backing ($1.3 million for *1600 Pennsylvania Avenue*), Richard Adler with Roger Berlind and Edward R. Downe Jr. ($750,000 for *Rex*), Lester Osterman with Joseph Kipness and associates ($800,000 for *Rockabye Hamlet*), Frederick Brisson with The Harkness Organization and Wyatt Dickerson ($500,000) for *So Long, 174th Street*), Adela Holzer ($500,000 for *Truckload* and another $500,000 with associates for *Treemonisha*) and even Harold Prince whose highly-acclaimed *Candide* ended its run $310,000 in the red and whose *Pacific Overtures* was a long way ($1.13 million) from the black when it closed in June.

In such an economic context, the survival of Broadway as an arena for the exploration and development of the theater art is as illusory as a paper moon. It is impossible—or at the very least, foolhardy—to mount an untried script on Broadway these days. Simply, it costs too much and the chances of success are too small. Joseph Papp himself couldn't hack it with new plays at the Vivian Beaumont and lapsed this season into a revival schedule there. His plan to invade the West Forties with a series of new plays at the Booth Theater

KENNETH WAISSMAN AND MAXINE FOX, PRODUCERS
OF THE LONG-RUN MUSICAL "GREASE"

began and ended with the first one, Dennis J. Reardon's *The Leaf People* about a strange jungle culture, which ran only 8 performances, cost an estimated $400,000 (which Papp could probably afford, with his *A Chorus Line* a smash hit at the Shubert) and sent New York Shakespeare's experimental new-play-production program back downtown to the auditoria of the Public Theater where it belongs.

In such a context, Broadway has become no longer an arena but a showcase, a glamorous shop window for the display of all the items that caught on back in the recesses of the store. The pure theater artists of the cross-country and back-alley stages may turn up their noses at Broadway's exorbitant economy and crass commercialism, but Broadway is nevertheless the goal of their developmental efforts and the eventual destination of all their major successes. Off-Broadway hits move to uptown theaters faster than a speeding bullet; with regional theater hits and West End attractions it sometimes takes a little longer, but they all know where the big time is.

So do the interpretive artists who vie with each other for a place in the showcase—actors, directors and actors who served this year as directors both on and off Broadway: George C. Scott (*Death of a Salesman*), Douglas Turner Ward (*The First Breeze of Summer*), Joseph Buloff (*The 5th Sea-*

son), Charles Nelson Reilly (*The Belle of Amherst*), John Lithgow (*Boy Meets Girl*), Robert Drivas (*Legend*), Austin Pendleton (*The Runner Stumbles* and *Benito Cereno*), Alan Arkin (*The Soft Touch,* which closed in Boston), Brian Murray (*Endecott and the Red Cross* and *My Kinsman, Major Molineaux*) as well as Jason Robards (*Long Day's Journey Into Night*). The direction of musicals was often in the hands of choreographers: Bob Fosse (*Chicago*), Michael Bennett (*A Chorus Line*), Gower Champion (*Rockabye Baby*) and Patricia Birch (*Truckload,* which closed in previews). Among the busiest of the year's directors were Marshall W. Mason (who staged two Best Plays, *Knock Knock* and *Serenading Louie*), Arvin Brown (*27 Wagons Full of Cotton, A Memory of Two Mondays* and *Ah, Wilderness!*), Ellis Rabb (*Edward II* and *A Royal Family*), Edwin Sherin (*Sweet Bird of Youth, The Red Devil Battery Sign* and *Rex*) and José Quintero (*The Skin of Our Teeth* and the restaged *Knock Knock*).

Still the most viable of Broadway productions, apparently, is the most expensive: the big, brassy ebullient Broadway musical. As Sondheim said, it takes guts and a million dollars to produce one; but a hit can run for years at a $15 top, and it seems there are producers still brave enough and rich enough to turn out ten or a dozen annually. It's not surprising, therefore, to find two of these shows, made on and for Broadway, appearing on the Best Plays list this year: the handsome and innovative Stephen Sondheim-John Weidman-Hugh Wheeler-Harold Prince show *Pacific Overtures* and the jazzy, bittersweet Fred Ebb-John Kander-Bob Fosse adaptation of the 1920s Best Play *Chicago.*

Of the eight non-musical Best Plays, not one originated as a Broadway production. Two of them transferred from the New York theater's principal tryout town, London: Tom Stoppard's sparkling *Travesties* and Alan Ayckbourn's trilogy *The Norman Conquests,* a unique concept which on balance we judge to be 1975–76's best work. Four more emerged from Eastern regional productions: David Freeman's *Jesse and the Bandit Queen* tried out at the Eugene O'Neill Memorial Theater in Waterford, Conn. and David Rabe's *Streamers* (the year's best American script) at the Long Wharf Theater in New Haven before they both reached off-Broadway playhouses under Joseph Papp's banner; Milan Stitt's *The Runner Stumbles* moved to West 44th Street in the virtually intact Hartman Theater production from Stamford, Conn.; and Lanford Wilson's *Serenading Louie* had been produced at Stage West in Springfield, Mass. before appearing in New York on the Circle Repertory Company schedule. Joseph Papp produced still a third Best Play this season, Thomas Babe's *Rebel Women,* and Marshall W. Mason's Circle Repertory a second, Jules Feiffer's *Knock Knock* which later moved uptown. These last two off-Broadway productions were the only ones of the eight straight-play Bests which actually originated in New York, but far from Broadway.

The authorship of the ten 1975–76 Best Plays includes three professional New York debuts (David Freeman, John Weidman and Milan Stitt), two British dramatists (Tom Stoppard and Alan Ayckbourn) and four playwrights previously acclaimed for off-Broadway successes (Jules Feiffer, David Rabe,

Lanford Wilson and Thomas Babe). Only the authorship credits of the two musicals included Broadway veterans. The Best Plays list is balanced in tone, with *Streamers, Serenading Louie, The Runner Stumbles* clearly in the category of what used to be called "serious" drama, *Knock Knock* and the British plays keeping the franchise for comedy and *Jesse and the Bandit Queen* and *Rebel Women* somewhere in between. Other shows which came very close to making the Best Plays list included *The Primary English Class, Rich & Famous, Every Night When the Sun Goes Down, Medal of Honor Rag, The Shortchanged Review, Eden* and *Vanities* off Broadway and *Kennedy's Children, Lamppost Reunion* and *The Robber Bridegroom* on. In other seasons, this pinnacle of effort would have been founded on a broad pedestal of new, creative theater. Not so in 1975–76, most of whose major productions were vehicles not for creative but for interpretive artists. An exceptionally effective combination of the two was the Joseph Papp production of *Threepenny Opera* which is specially cited and represented in this volume as the best revival of the season.

The ultimate insignia of New York professional theater achievement (we insist) is selection as a Best Play in these volumes, a designation which is 16 years older than the Critics Award and only three years younger than the Pulitzer. Our Best Play selection is made with the script itself as the first consideration, for the reason (as we've stated in previous volumes) that the script is the very spirit of the theater, the soul in its physical body. The script is not only the quintessence of the present, it is most of what endures into the future. So the Best Plays are the best scripts, with as little weight as humanly possible given to comparative production values. The choice is made without any regard whatever to a play's type—musical, comedy or drama—or origin on or off Broadway, or popularity at the box office or lack of same.

If a script of above-average quality influences the very character of a season by its extreme popularity, or if by some means of consensus it wins the Critics, Pulitzer or Tony awards, we take into account its future historical as well as present esthetic importance to the season as a whole. This is the only special consideration we give, and we don't always tilt in its direction, as the record shows.

On the other hand, we don't take the scripts of other eras into consideration for a Best Play citation in this one, however good they may be or whatever their technical qualifications as "American premieres" of classics that don't happen to have had a previous production of record in New York. As far as we're concerned, they're still revivals, which aren't eligible for regular Best Play designation. We've never conceded that revived material can be "revised into newness," a rationale used to justify the Drama Critics Circle Award to the revived and revised *Candide* as best musical of the 1973-74 season. We sometimes join the applause for special achievement in this and other categories, however, with a special Best Play citation, as we have done in this volume in the case of the new Manheim-Willett translation of *Threepenny Opera*.

The ten Best Plays of 1975–76 plus one special citation were the following, as named previously in this report but listed here for visual convenience in the order in which they opened in New York (a plus sign + with the performance number signifies that the play was still running on June 1, 1976):

Chicago
(Broadway; 388+ perfs.)

Travesties
(Broadway; 155 perfs.)

Jesse and the Bandit Queen
(Off Broadway; 155 perfs.)

The Norman Conquests
(Broadway; 205+ perfs.)

Pacific Overtures
(Broadway; 161+ perfs.)

Knock Knock
(Off B'way & B'way; 104+ perfs.)

Streamers
(Off Broadway; 39+ perfs.)

Serenading Louie
(Off Broadway; 33 perfs.)

Rebel Women
(Off Broadway; 40+ perfs.)

The Runner Stumbles
(Broadway; 16+ perfs.)

Threepenny Opera (special citation as best revival)
(Broadway; 35+ perfs.)

Broadway

Broadway in 1975–76 was a feast of revivals and a famine of new American plays. The pitiful list of ten new American plays was padded with transfers, two from last year's off-Broadway season: Negro Ensemble Company's *The First Breeze of Summer* by Leslie Lee, dramatizing a black matriarch's memories of three generations of her family's upwardly mobile struggle, a strong play which came close to last year's Best Plays list; and Chelsea Theater Center's *Yentl the Yeshiva Boy* by Leah Napolin from an Isaac Bashevis Singer story, with Tony nominee Tovah Feldshuh as a Jewish girl who disguises herself as a boy to qualify for male prerogatives.

Still another transfer, Jules Feiffer's *Knock Knock,* arrived there in its off-Broadway Circle Repertory Company production (though later re-cast and re-staged; see the off-Broadway section of this report).

Milan Stitt's *The Runner Stumbles* came to Broadway late in the season, pre-packaged in a production mounted at the new Hartman Theater in Stamford, Conn. under Austin Pendleton's direction. The play itself (previously seen in stagings at Yale, the Berkshire Festival and OOB) is a darkly-lit drama whose tortured characters grope among religious tenets and human longings for some solid truth to steady themselves. Its study of a nonconformist priest and a life-loving nun drawn together irresistibly—and tragically—was based on a 1911 episode in Michigan that ended in the priest's trial for the nun's murder. The play flashes back from the priest (Stephen Joyce) in his jail cell to the arrival of the cheerful young nun (Nancy Donohue) in his small parish, under the watchful eye of his dogmatically religious housekeeper (Sloane Shelton). These three collide with each other in powerful variations on the theme of loneliness.

On Broadway as well as off, the 1975–76 theater seems to be shedding its heavy clown makeup of recent years and giving more attention to dramatic themes and subjects, even stark ones like *The Runner Stumbles*. Louis LaRusso II's *Lamppost Reunion* was a late-night encounter in a Hoboken bar where a singing superstar, played by Gabriel Dell, pays a post-concert visit to cronies in the neighborhood where he grew up. The reunion is not a happy one, since the singer had once found it necessary to step on friends in reaching for the first rungs of the success ladder. There was flavor added: Frank Sinatra is also a singing superstar who grew up on the Jersey side of the Hudson, and the play was talked of as a drama *à clef* (Sinatra has a sidekick named "Jilly" whereas the star in the play has one named "Jobby").

Among other Broadway dramas was Ronald Ribman's *The Poison Tree,* originally produced in Philadelphia and pointing the finger at prisons as incubators, not of rehabilitation but of inhumanity. It was a strong play, forcefully acted by Moses Gunn in the role of a stoolie in spite of himself, tragic in spirit but not in size and therefore a little too heavy even for this year's Broadway. The reverse was true of Robert Patrick's *Kennedy's Children,* a non-play made up of alternating monologues by 1960s types crying out in pain at the evaporation of their fondest dreams in the heat of the 1970s. The characters—a kill-crazy Vietnam veteran, a suicidal sex goddess, a JFK-idolizer, etc.—might have attained tragic stature except that their vehicle, a concert of soliloquys, didn't have the shape of a real play, even though it survived a long journey through OOB and London in order to reach the West Forties.

In a somewhat lighter vein there was *Murder Among Friends* by Bob Barry, with Jack Cassidy playing and having fun with the role of a stage star whose coterie of friends all seem to be both villains and victims of their murderous intentions toward each other. In still another American entry, Samuel Taylor's effort to use the Western motif in a novel way in *Legend* didn't come off, even with Elizabeth Ashley doing the honors in the leading role.

However enthusiastically and widely a certain rebellion is being celebrated this year, the British are slowly repossessing their lost American colony, or at least that part of it running between 45th and 54th Streets on the West Side of Manhattan. For still another year British plays stole the Broadway scene. For example, there was Alan Ayckbourn's *The Norman Conquests,* three full-length comedies with the same set of characters and the same situation but not exactly the same events, presented like rotating repertory in successive performances. These plays interlock in time but not in space during a single family weekend at a British country house. That is to say, each play takes place in a different "part of the forest," showing what was going on in the dining room (*Table Manners*), the living room (*Living Together*) and the terrace (*Round and Round the Garden*) as the characters drifted from one room to another, in the same weekend's time frame.

What was going on mostly was that the others were accusing Norman (Richard Benjamin) of romantic dalliance, or trying to lure him into it, while he was managing to make "conquests" of his two sisters-in-law and his own wife. An all-star cast of Paula Prentiss, Ken Howard, Estelle Parsons, Barry Nelson and Carole Shelley occupied the other places at this family party, which could be joined at any point in the trilogy. We single out the first play, *Table Manners,* for a complete synopsis in the Best Plays section of this volume, but it is *The Norman Conquests* as a whole that we cite, and therefore we've included excerpts from the other two plays. The performances were even more clearly unified efforts, with the same actors playing the same characters in the same vein throughout the three plays. In our opinion, Carole Shelley deserves top 1976 acting honors in a secondary role, particularly for the scene in which she is trying to impart to a left-footed young veterinarian (Ken Howard) some information about the ways of love at levels higher than that of the birds and the bees. We also designate *The Norman Conquests* as the best of bests for 1976—not only because it's an unusual if not unique triple-play concept, but also because each of its three parts is an example of playmaking the equal of any other script on this season's Best Plays list.

And then there was *Travesties,* Tom Stoppard's Critics and Tony Award-winning comic travesty of an old man fumbling among dim memories of his service at the British Consulate in Zurich during World War II. Mostly for his own ego-gratification, he acts out a boastful and almost totally false acquaintanceship with great personages living in Zurich at that time: Lenin planning revolution, James Joyce writing *Ulysses,* and the Dadaists. *Travesties* is constructed like the *Alice in Wonderland* "Eat Me" episode, flashing forward and backward between muddled old age and immaculate youth, in Alice's rhythm of growing taller and shorter by turns. To borrow still another image from Alice, Stoppard's play is the grin without the cat: a preposterous concept worked out in dialogue that is in itself clever to the threshold of brilliance, with puns, limericks, literary and political allusions, double entendres—a shameless revel of language conducted by a master. Still, there's not quite as much of the cat visible as there was even in Stoppard's verbally acrobatic *Jumpers;* the outline of any sort of working play has all but disappeared. As theater, *Travesties* leaned very heavily on John Wood's memorable, kaleidoscopic acting of the scatterbrained fogey and featherbrained youth. But it also holds out a promise of a great play or plays to come if and when Stoppard can produce both grin and cat in a single context.

Lest we begin to think of British playwrights as infallible, we should pause briefly to consider two more of their contributions to the 1976 New York theater season. Alan Bennett's *Habeas Corpus* was an object lesson in vulgarity with jokes about falsies, drooling middle-aged desire, etc. etc. The presence in the cast of such notable performers as Jean Marsh (the Rose of *Upstairs, Downstairs*), June Havoc, Celeste Holm, Rachel Roberts, Kristoffer Tabori and Paxton Whitehead was no help; the only thing that helped was Donald Sinden's decision to give up on the play from time to time and chat informally with the audience.

The other British entry was Enid Bagnold's unsatisfactory *A Matter of Gravity,* an attempt to characterize the decline of our society and devise an appropriate response to it—commit yourself to an asylum to take refuge from the crazy people outside—which not even charming, witty, supremely poised and skillful Katharine Hepburn could levitate off the stage floor. Still another foreign entry, a translation from the French of Elie Wiesel's *Zalmen or the Madness of God,* also took on more weight than strength in its clash between a modern Russian community of Jews and the Soviet authorities. The year's only foreign-language production on Broadway was a Bicentennial gift to the New York theatergoer from the French government: an 11-performance limited engagement of the Renaud-Barrault company's production of Marguerite Duras's *Des Journées Entières Dans les Arbres* (Days in the Trees), directed by Jean-Louis Barrault, with Madeleine Renaud and Jean-Pierre Aumont as mother and son trying to perceive outlines of meaning in the strange twilight of their lives and perhaps of their form of civilization.

It was an active year for musicals, with the successes not quite balancing out the heavy disappointments. The year's outstanding show followed in the footsteps of *Company, Follies* and *A Little Night Music* as an innovative brainchild of composer-lyricist Stephen Sondheim, and producer-director Harold Prince: *Pacific Overtures,* an adventure among Japanese sights, sounds and styles. The imaginative book about Commodore Perry's arrival in the mid-1800s and impact on a Japan which had been isolated for 250 years was written by John Weidman (Jerome's son) in his professional stage debut, with additional material by Hugh Wheeler. The script, score and production viewed their subject through the "wrong," or Japanese, end of the telescope as compared with the "right," or American-musical end. All characters, including Americans, were played by Oriental actors, with men playing the women and Commodore Perry, for example, portrayed as a lion-devil, Kabuki-style. Exotic instruments and strange harmonies and cadences permeated the score, which avoided conventional Broadway show tunes. The lyrics soared into rich poetic fancies (see examples in the synopsis of the script in the Best Plays section of this volume) or sparkled with pidgin-English humor. The styling in Prince's direction was flawless, of Boris Aronson's scenery fantastic, and of the cast seamless (with a standout performance by Mako in various roles including that of narrator).

Why this total trip into traditional Japan and its theater styles—why so much Kabuki and so little Broadway? *Pacific Overtures* never entirely or finally answered this question. If it was to make a contrast with the modern industrial Japanese nation, the contrast was dismissed rather perfunctorily at the end of the show with a quick change from traditional costumes to modern dress. Thus it sometimes risked presenting itself as an exercise for the participants rather than a show aimed to move its viewers. Otherwise, though, it was a major accomplishment of musical theater right across the board.

The most popular new musical of the season was *Chicago,* a show in the *Carousel* tradition of transposing the characters and atmosphere of a strong play into the larger context of a full-scale Broadway musical. The play by Maurine Watkins had the same title, was described as a "satirical comedy," played 172 performances and was named a Best Play of 1926–27. Its tale of a 1920s love nest murderess in the midst of all the gangsters, molls and shysters of her era was as jazzier-than-life as the score, book and lyrics by John Kander, Fred Ebb and Bob Fosse could make it, enhanced by Patricia Zipprodt's costumes and Tony Walton's sets. Since its heroine was after all a killer—albeit an appealing one in the person of Gwen Verdon—*Chicago* stretched our sympathies perilously close to the breaking-point. It was a black musical whose production concept (not overlooking standout performances by Jerry Orbach, Gwen Verdon and Chita Rivera) was so stylishly colorful that the show merits a 1976 Best Plays designation for its new musical self, even with the borrowed finery of its original script.

Smaller in scale but immensely likeable was *The Robber Bridegroom,* a new musical wedged into the revival repertory of John Houseman's Acting Company. "Legendary Mississippi" was its setting for a pleasantly folksy folk tale about a gentleman highwayman and the women in his life, with book and lyrics by Alfred Uhry based on a Eudora Welty story, and with a sprightly and equally folksy score by Robert Waldman. Patti LuPone and Kevin Kline cut handsome figures as the romantic leads, but Mary Lou Rosato stole the show with her portrayal of a jealous, grasping witch.

And then there were three latecomers—*Rex, 1600 Pennsylvania Avenue* and *So Long, 174th Street*—of which much was expected and much too little realized. The first was a maximum effort by Richard Rodgers with a new lyricist, Sheldon Harnick, and a new librettist, Sherman Yellen, to bring Henry VIII into focus as a father-figure, both as ruler and parent. The book just barely managed to touch on the paradoxical love-hate relationship between daughter Elizabeth and her royal father, but it never got a firm grip on this promising subject, even though Nicol Williamson was a formidable Henry. Viewed in perspective, it's an achievement for *Rex* to have brought Rodgers and Harnick together in a new collaboration and evoked another memorable Rodgers number, "No Song More Pleasing." As a show, it accomplished little else.

1600 Pennsylvania Avenue produced still another promising new collaboration, with Alan Jay Lerner and Leonard Bernstein teaming up to portray American heads of state from George Washington to Theodore Roosevelt as householders—White House-holders, that is—thanks to the black people performing the menial chores downstairs, with Ken Howard playing all the presidents and Gilbert Price all the butlers. *1600 Pennsylvania Avenue* came into town so close upon the heels of *Rex* that it invited comparison. The team of Lerner & Bernstein made considerably less headway than the team of Rodgers & Harnick; in fact, this was one confrontation that Washington lost and a British king won.

A much nearer miss than either of these two majestic musicals was *So Long, 174th Street,* directed by Burt Shevelove and therefore, happily, a *funny* musical for once. Also for once, Joseph Stein's book based on his comedy *Enter Laughing,* about a high school boy headed for pharmacy school but full of ego and longing to become an actor, held its own with the musical elements provided by Stan Daniels, delivered by an enthusiastic and willing cast. The Shevelove "a funny thing happened" kind of humor broke out all over the place in the clowning of Robert Morse assisted by George S. Irving, many of the scenes having a life of their own like revue skits.

Even among the other 1976 Broadway musicals, nobody was cutting to a pattern. *The 5th Season* was a bilingual (Yiddish and English) musicalization by Luba Kadison and Dick Manning of Sylvia Regan's hit 1953 comedy about the New York City dress business. *Treemonisha* was a distinguished folk opera by the late, great Scott Joplin about an orphan girl's magical impact on her black community. Written in 1907, it had never been able to find a home on Broadway and wasn't comfortable there this season, its unique musical qualities notwithstanding. In *Boccaccio,* Kenneth Cavander and Richard Peaslee musicalized a set of stories from *The Decameron,* with the winsome D'Jamin Bartlett helping to interpret the romantic ironies. And then there was *Rockabye Hamlet,* in which the events of the celebrated tragedy were exposed to the heat and noise of a full-volume rock treatment. It was the rock style that broke under the weight of the play rather than the reverse, with only Alan Weeks managing to carry both successfully in his portrayal of an arrogant, dictatorial Claudius.

Punctuating the end of the Broadway musical season like an italicized exclamation point was *Something's Afoot,* a jolly take-off of a mystery-story situation in which ten guests and servants marooned on an island estate at a British house party are killed off one by one, much as in Agatha Christie's *Ten Little Indians* (the characters were different but the concept identical). The show was a broad spoof, with Tessie O'Shea kicking up her still almost agile heels as an Agatha Christie type of nosy and indomitable white-haired lady sleuth. Gary Beach, Liz Sheridan and others under Tony Tanner's direction prowled comically among pieces of gloomy Victorian furniture rigged to murder them in a number of heavy-handed ways. It was a proper treat, once you got with it. The collaborators—James McDonald, David Vos and Robert Gerlach—credited their source in a show-stopping number entitled "I Owe It All to Agatha Christie." To a large extent, allowing for an extra degree of suspension of disbelief and an extra step of pleasant outrage, they did.

The 1975–76 revues were outstanding, with clear-cut themes and/or stylistic traits and inexhaustible energy in the performances. *Me and Bessie* was an outline of the life and career of the celebrated blues singer Bessie Smith. She wasn't directly impersonated, but her memory was clearly evoked by Linda Hopkins as the "Me" of the title. Miss Hopkins rendered Miss Smith's best-known songs with power and emotion, and at the same time narrated her life with a light touch, affectionate and appealing, in the year's best musical performance by an actress. *A Musical Jubilee* contained an abundance of noteworthy performances, with an all-star cast (Lillian Gish, Tammy Grimes, Larry Kert, Patrice Munsel, John Raitt, Cyril Ritchard and Dick Shawn) in a nostalgic history of the American musical with a continuity by Max Wilk and a collection of memorable numbers from shows. *Bubbling Brown Sugar* was also nostalgic and affectionate in its view of the glory days of Harlem in a lively reminiscence written by Loften Mitchell, strung with glorious song numbers of the 1920s and 1930s and performed effervescently by Vivian Reed, Avon Long, Joseph Attles and many others in a superbly accomplished musical ensemble under Robert M. Cooper's direction.

A charming addition to the 1975–76 Broadway scene was Julie Harris's impersonation of Emily Dickinson in the one-woman drama *The Belle of Amherst* by William Luce. Another appealing specialty was *Monty Python Live!,* a zany multimedia romp by the visiting British troupe whose antics are familiar to millions in the TV series *Monty Python's Flying Circus* shown here on Public Broadcasting.

The starring role played by revivals in the great Broadway 1975–76 illusion is the subject of another section of this report. Meanwhile, here's where we list the *Best Plays* choices for the top individual achievements of the season. In the acting categories, clear distinctions among "starring," "featured" or "supporting" players can't be made on the basis of official billing, in which an actor may appear as a "star" following the title (not true star billing) or as an "also starring" star, or any of the other typographical career-building gimmicks. Here in these volumes we divide acting into "primary" and "secondary" roles, a primary role being one which carries a major responsibility for the play; a role which might some day cause a star to inspire a revival in order to appear in that character. All others, be they as vivid as Mercutio, are classed as secondary (and of course there are a few plays that don't have any primary roles at all, like *The Norman Conquests,* acted by an ensemble).

Our problem isn't definition but an embarrassment of riches as we proceed to name the single best in each category. Here, then, are the *Best Plays* bests of 1975–76:

PLAYS

BEST PLAY: *The Norman Conquests (Table Manners, Living Together* and *Round and Round the Garden)* by Alan Ayckbourn

BEST AMERICAN PLAY: *Streamers* by David Rabe

BEST REVIVAL: *The Royal Family* by George S. Kaufman and Edna Ferber in the American Bicentennial Theater production

BEST ACTOR IN A PRIMARY ROLE: John Wood as Henry Carr in *Travesties*

BEST ACTRESS IN A PRIMARY ROLE: Irene Worth as Princess Kosmonopolis in *Sweet Bird of Youth*

BEST ACTOR IN A SECONDARY ROLE: Ron Leibman as various characters in *Rich & Famous*

BEST ACTRESS IN A SECONDARY ROLE: Carole Shelley as Ruth in *The Norman Conquests*

BEST DIRECTOR: Ellis Rabb for *The Royal Family*

BEST SCENERY: Santo Loquasto for *Hamlet*

BEST COSTUMES: Theoni V. Aldredge for *Trelawny of the "Wells"*

MUSICALS

BEST MUSICAL: *Pacific Overtures*
BEST BOOK: John Weidman and Hugh Wheeler for *Pacific Overtures*
BEST SCORE: Stephen Sondheim for *Pacific Overtures*
BEST REVIVAL: *Threepenny Opera* by Bertolt Brecht and Kurt Weill, translated
    by Ralph Manheim and John Willett, produced by Joseph Papp
BEST ACTOR IN A PRIMARY ROLE: Raul Julia as Mack the Knife in *Threepenny
    Opera*
BEST ACTRESS IN A PRIMARY ROLE: Linda Hopkins as Bessie Smith in *Me and
    Bessie*
BEST ACTOR IN A SECONDARY ROLE: Mako as Reciter, Shogun and Jonathan
    Goble in *Pacific Overtures*
BEST ACTRESS IN A SECONDARY ROLE: Chita Rivera as Velma Kelly in *Chicago*
BEST DIRECTOR: Harold Prince for *Pacific Overtures*
BEST CHOREOGRAPHER: Bob Fosse for *Chicago*
BEST SCENERY: Boris Aronson for *Pacific Overtures*
BEST COSTUMES: Patricia Zipprodt for *Chicago*

Off Broadway

Where did all the new plays go this year? Most of those that surfaced in
the New York professional theater in 1975–76 did so in the area we call "off
Broadway"—which was preserving a marvellous illusion of life all through
the season, despite the fact that Joseph Papp pronounced it finally and thor-
oughly dead more than a year ago. In this year of illusions, off-Broadway
mounted what seemed to be a real season of 26 new American plays, five of
which achieved Best Play status. This total of new American plays produced
in a single season is down from off-Broadway's peak, but it holds its own
fairly well with the totals of other years in the 1970s: 30 in 1975, 27 in 1974,
28 in 1973, 43 in 1972, 39 in 1971, 21 in 1970.

Certainly this continued vitality is illusory to the extent that the very great
majority of these new plays, and all the five Bests, were produced in the
shelter of subsidized organizational schedules. As Broadway built its illusion
of a 1975–76 season out of revivals, off Broadway built one out of an Establishment with outside support (outside the box office, that is) of such production groups as New York Shakespeare, American Place, Circle Repertory,
Chelsea and Negro Ensemble. When Joseph Papp says that off Broadway is
dead, what he probably means is that it's a marionette without an economic
life of its own, creating an illusion of life by means of strings pulled by
benefactors.

If so, public money was never better spent, private support never affected
an art form so directly and purposefully since the days of the Medicis. Off

The 1975–76 Season off Broadway

PLAYS (26)

Finn MacKool
Public Theater:
JESSE AND THE BANDIT QUEEN
Rich & Famous
So Nice, They Named It Twice
For Colored Girls Who Have Considered Suicide, etc.
REBEL WOMEN
American Place:
Gorky
Every Night When the Sun Goes Down
Circle Repertory:
The Elephant in the House
Dancing for the Kaiser
KNOCK KNOCK
Who Killed Richard Cory?
SERENADING LOUIE
Dear Mr. G
Jinxs Bridge
Newhouse Theater:
The Shortchanged Review
STREAMERS
Cracks
The Primary English Class
Negro Ensemble:
Eden
A Season-Within-a-Season
The Hound of the Baskervilles
Vanities
Medal of Honor Rag
Caprice
Titanic

RETURN ENGAGEMENT (1)

Women Behind Bars

FOREIGN PLAYS IN ENGLISH (3)

The Collected Works of Billy the Kid
The Family (Parts 1 & 2)
Ice Age

FOREIGN PLAY (1)

Phèdre

MUSICALS (6)

Boy Meets Boy
Christy
By Bernstein
Gift of the Magi
Apple Pie
Fire of Flowers

SPECIALTIES (7)

Conversations With an Irish Rascal
Baird Marionettes:
Alice in Wonderland
Winnie the Pooh
From Sholom Aleichem With Love
The Polish Mime Theater
Szajna's Studio Theater:
Dante
Replika

REVIVALS (29)

Delacorte:
Hamlet
The Comedy of Errors
Roundabout:
Summer and Smoke
Clarence
The Cherry Orchard
Classic Stage:
Measure for Measure
Hedda Gabler
A Country Scandal
Antigone
And So to Bed
Light Opera:
Iolanthe
Naughty Marietta
The Mikado
The Vagabond King
The Pirates of Penzance
H.M.S. Pinafore
The Gondoliers
Patience
The Student Prince
The Homecoming
Brooklyn Academy:
Sweet Bird of Youth
The Royal Family
Long Day's Journey Into Night
Henry V
The Hollow Crown
The Boss
Woyzeck
American Place:
Endecott and the Red Cross & My Kinsman, Major Molineux
Benito Cereno

REVUES (3)

Tuscaloosa's Calling Me ...but I'm Not Going
Dear Piaf
Tickles by Tucholsky

Categorized above are all the plays listed in the "Plays Produced off Broadway" section of this volume.

Plays listed in CAPITAL LETTERS have been designated Best Plays of 1975–76.

Plays listed in *italics* were still running June 1, 1976.

Broadway isn't necessarily or even usually the source of its own best work, which is often drawn in from experimental programs elsewhere. But it seems to be the major showcase open to American straight-play dramatists at the center of the American stage, which is still New York. Five of the six American Best Plays were produced off Broadway this season. In the theater's "two planks and a passion," the planks are essential to the passion, and off Broadway is sustaining a platform where otherwise none at all would exist.

No one puts private and public subsidy to better use than the abovementioned, esteemed Joseph Papp and his New York Shakespeare Festival. Activity in his many nooks and crannies uptown and downtown, indoors and outdoors, ranges from workshop-experimental to the most striking finished productions include three of the Best Plays, among them the Critics best-American-play award winning *Streamers* by David Rabe. Papp has produced all of Rabe's plays in New York: *The Basic Training of Pavlo Hummel, Sticks and Bones* (a Best Play plus a special Critics citation) and *Boom Boom Room,* both the original and the rewrite. He produced *Streamers,* too, in Lincoln Center's little Newhouse Theater uptown, but not before it had been tried out in front of New Haven audiences at the Long Wharf. We note this as symptomatic of the soft and changing state of the New York stage, in that a Papp playwright—perhaps *the* Papp playwright—would find it necessary to try out his script in regional theater prior to even an off-Broadway production by a group whose very specialty is generating new material.

Rabe's newest, the best American script of the year, attempted to delineate the American way of violence. Its characters are soldiers, but *Streamers* isn't a play about war. Most of its 1965 Virginia army Barracks inhabitants haven't seen combat yet. Their stresses are personal: the idealist (Paul Rudd) secure in his identity with middle America, the black (Terry Alexander) who has made a separate peace with society, the barracks gadfly (Peter Evans) alternately mocking and inviting homosexual behavior. Into this tense but not yet explosive situation is thrust an angry, deprived black (Dorian Harewood) who has *not* made peace with anyone including himself. He is a selfish, self-pitying misfit wracked by contempt for his peers and fear of loneliness. This barracks, a social microcosm, must purge him at once or suffer the inevitable consequences of his hostile presence. They don't purge him so they do suffer when his arrogance is detonated by rejection and explodes at knife-point into mindless acts of brutal, very bloody violence.

The characters were well developed and the action explicit to the point of shock under Mike Nichols's carefully thought-out direction. This was a strong play, albeit somewhat impulsive, with a confusion of imagery. When a middle-aged sergeant tells the young privates how, in Vietnam, he threw a grenade into the foxhole of an enemy sniper and held a lid down over him until the grenade exploded, the anecdote is obviously an analogy of the intrusion of the black killer into this closed barracks society. But the title image of a "streamer" —a parachute which fails to open—was never quite connected up with the play, just as the final violence seemed in a way disconnected because it was hugely out of proportion to its immediate cause, like an insane paroxysm.

Perhaps, though, this was Rabe's point: a "streamer" and a senseless knifing are accidents indigenous to American life and could happen to anyone at any time. Anyhow, Rabe did again what he did with *Sticks and Bones,* reinforce a whole season with an arresting drama.

Another of Papp's Best Plays was a Western of sorts, *Jesse and the Bandit Queen,* whose two characters, Jesse James and Belle Starr, wrap their legends and emotions around and around each other until they look exactly alike: part criminal and part hero, part man and part woman, part fiction and part fact. This was not a true history, but a series of metaphors in which only the deaths of Belle and Jesse were acted out literally. The two outlaws in the play are being used as symbols (a fact which they resent heartily). America invented them, stuffed them with the straw of romantic cliches and dangles them as a charm to ward off historical doubt and guilt. This Jesse and this Belle are both themselves and characters in a *Police Gazette* adventure, both vulnerable and violent, incestuous, cruel, selfish and never adequately loved, dangerous to the very admirers who place them on a pedestal, dangerous especially to themselves. As played by Kevin O'Connor and Pamela Payton-Wright (and her accomplished replacement Dixie Carter after she left the cast early in the run), they were as unforgettable in David Freeman's play as they seem to be elsewhere in American story and song.

New York Shakespeare Festival's third Best Play, *Rebel Women,* was the work of another of Papp's "own" playwrights: Thomas Babe, who made his professional debut last year at the Public Theater with the well-received *Kid Champion,* about the downfall of a rock music star. His second play turned backward to the past for a warts-and-all snapshot-in-transit of another sort of hero, Gen. William Tecumseh Sherman, larger than life and as sure-footed as death on his march to the sea over the helpless body of the defeated South. The sickness of war is well advanced upon Sherman and his men as they camp for the night in a Georgia mansion occupied by four Southern women. These soldiers and their leader welcome the brief escape of love or its semblance, any way they can and in any form available, to sweeten the bitterness of their duty. The script was overweight here and there, but Sherman himself was solid muscle, viewed as a military pragmatist whose convictions are like laser beams melting all illusions and—strangely —one "enemy" heart, at least for a night. The role vibrated with the power of David Dukes's performance, and Kathryn Walker, Leora Dana and Deborah Offner reflected some of it back at him as Southern belles of greatly differing character and standards. The direction by Jack Hofsiss held the focus on the conqueror, while Babe's script succeeded admirably in cutting down one of the heroic statues of American history to the size and proportions of a human being.

Papp's season of new plays up and downtown included a batch of other interesting works. Preceding *Streamers* at the Newhouse was *The Short-changed Review* by Michael Dorn Moody, reflecting the troubles of our times in the bloodshot eyes of a middle-aged, liberal pop-music radio station owner, whose friends and relations let him down and weigh him down in numbers of ways. Following *Jesse and the Bandit Queen* into the Public Theater was John Guare's collection of inside show biz jokes in *Rich & Famous,* with the season's most effective comedy teaming of William Atherton, Ron Leibman and Anita Gillette acting out a fledgling playwright's fantasies on the occasion of his first opening night under the expert direction of Mel Shapiro. Then there was the Myrna Lamb-Nicholas Meyers opera-style musical *Apple Pie,* about a woman who escapes from Nazi Germany only to be persecuted in America by anti-feminists, this show directed by Papp himself. In addition to this distinguished collection of new work there were the outstanding revivals in Central Park and at the Vivian Beaumont, about which more in the next section of this report. Debatable as some of Papp's most authoritative pronouncements may be ("Off Broadway is dead" indeed!), there's never been anything to compare with the consistent interest and versatility of his 1975–76 production schedules all around the town.

Violence, whether overt as in a *Streamers* or implicit as in a *Jesse and the Bandit Queen,* is now a preoccupation of our stage as it has been of our screen. Violence as we know it was invented by Jules Feiffer in a play called *Little Murders,* and it provided a sort of counterpoint to the hilarious absurdities of Feiffer's new *Knock Knock,* produced by Circle Repertory Company and then moved uptown to Broadway. This comedic Best Play was about two middle-aged recluses (played in the off-Broadway cast by Daniel Seltzer and Neil Flanagan) living in a cottage in the deep woods, passing the time by quarreling, until suddenly their lives are touched and transformed by magic. They rub a lamp, and lo! not a genie but Joan of Arc in person (the blonde and comely person of Nancy Snyder) knocks on their door, is greeted by a shotgun blast but stays anyway and manages to loosen the bonds tying the two men to their preconceived attitudes toward reality and fantasy. This mixture of old and new jokes, acrobatic language, an exploding kitchen, constantly lurking violence, etc., was stirred and seasoned to amuse by its director, Marshall W. Mason, and amuse it certainly did, with a touch of Feiffer bemusement for extra flavor. After the move to Broadway, *Knock Knock* was refurbished with a new cast (Charles Durning, John Heffernan and Lynn Redgrave) and new direction by José Quintero, but there was no way to make it more hilarious—in its perplexing Jules Feiffer fashion—than it was downtown.

Like Joseph Papp, Mason and his Circle Repertory Company didn't rest on the laurels of a single Best Play this season. Their second was Lanford Wilson's *Serenading Louie,* still another brown study of developing violence, this time with marriage as its breeding ground. The play was about two youngish couples ten years out of college and nine years married, the ex-quarterback (Edward J. Moore) to the ex-homecoming queen (Tanya Berezin) and his best friend (Michael Storm) to a self-possessed creature (Trish Hawkins) who demands such order in her marriage that she can hardly believe it when she discovers that her husband is spending a lot of time and emotion on a teen-ager. The other marriage is on the rocks, too, and here's where the greatest danger lurks. The quarterback can't stop adoring his college sweetheart even though he knows she's lavishing her favors on another man. *Serenading Louie* was a controlled, orchestrated series of revelations and reactions, with the characters sometimes cutting through the underbrush of suggestion, turning away from the play and speaking directly to the audience. Both homes were represented by the same stage setting, with the two families inhabiting it simultaneously, helping to make the play's statement that though these people may be individuals, neither their situation nor their problems are unique. The play moved smoothly through this unusual space-time arrangement under Mason's direction, which was as appropriately fluid for *Serenading Louie* as it was punchy for *Knock Knock.*

Circle Repertory's season also took in *The Elephant in the House* by Berrilla Kerr, a rewrite of a former Circle workshop production of a play about a bedridden New York woman who opens her house to peculiar strangers; *Dancing for the Kaiser* by Andrew Colmar, a London 1918 period piece; and A. R. Gurney Jr.'s *Who Killed Richard Corey?*, a further exploration of the subject of the poem by Edward Arlington Robinson. Circle Repertory is one of those emergent groups hard to classify as to its technical status—off Broadway or off off? Generally, our declared definition of "off Broadway" is a show with an Equity cast giving a regular schedule of 8 performances a week following opening night or nights at which the show invites public comment by critics, in an off-Broadway theater (and according to Paul Libin, president of the League of Off-Broadway Theaters, an off-Broadway theater is defined as a house seating 499 or fewer and situated in Manhattan outside the area bounded by Fifth and Ninth Avenues between 34th and 56th Streets, and by Fifth Avenue and the Hudson River between 56th and 72nd Streets).

Obviously, in the Best Plays volumes we sometimes stretch this complicated, confining definition to include, say, the Chelsea Theater in Brooklyn, or a show which has a regular schedule of only 7 or in very rare exceptions 6 performances (which is the Thursday-through Sunday schedule of some of the more ambitious OOB groups). Technically, Circle Repertory falls somewhere between the two categories, sometimes showing perfect off-Broadway conformation, but sometimes with the character of an OOB "showcase" in which Equity actors have special permission to appear under certain prescribed conditions. Having noted this, we hasten to add that Marshall W. Mason and his Circle are every inch professional. They've defined their own status with the quality of their shows, and whatever their dimensions may be, the rest of our theater, Broadway included, could do worse than measure up to them.

In its theaters in Brooklyn and Manhattan, Chelsea Theater Center put on an eclectic schedule of new, foreign, musical and revived shows. Chelsea's best this season was *Vanities* by Jack Heifner in his professional playwriting debut with a sweet-and-sour study of three women friends at crucial stages of their interwoven lives: as high school cheerleaders, as college seniors important in their campus roles and finally a half dozen years later

with their potentialities frozen into adult characteristics, most of them unattractive. Their youthful absorption with self was clearly portrayed by the
three-actress ensemble—Jane Galloway, Susan Merson and Kathy Bates—
and not allowed to let up under Garland Wright's direction, even during
intermissions when the performers remained visible at their vanity tables
upstage, making up for the next scene.

Other 1975-76 productions at Chelsea Manhattan were a translation of
the first half of Lodewijk de Boer's *The Family,* a Dutch play about life's
tribulations on the outskirts of Amsterdam; and the cabaret musical *By
Bernstein,* an assemblage of Leonard Bernstein show tunes which for one
reason or another had been cast overboard in the course of production. In
Brooklyn there was *Ice Age,* a translation of Tankred Dorst's lumpy indictment of a Norwegian author (played by Roberts Blossom) who supported
the Nazis and now, as an old man, is reviewing his actions; and, finally, a
Chelsea bow to the Bicentennial with Edward Sheldon's *The Boss,* a 1911
drama about industrial corruption which hasn't been revived professionally
in New York before. With shows like these, Chelsea held firmly to its artistic franchise in both boroughs, though it was less than a banner year.

The Negro Ensemble Company has made a habit of starting late but
coming on strong season after season down at St. Marks Place. *Ceremonies
in Dark Old Men, The River Niger* and *The First Breeze of Summer* were
some of its past accomplishments. This year it was *Eden* by Steve Carter,
a careful, intimate examination of intra-racial prejudice in the friction between a vain and disdainful West Indian immigrant patriarch and the sec-
ond-generation American black family living next door in the Harlem of the
late 1920s. Samm-Art (he is Samm when he writes plays, Samm-Art when
he acts) Williams and Shirley Brown acted the appealing young lovers star-
crossed by Montague-Capulet strife, and Graham Brown played the austere
and ferociously prejudiced West Indian parent who worships Marcus Garvey
as the messiah to lead them all back in glory to Africa, where he believes
they belong. This was a long but rewarding script, precisely directed by
Edmund Cambridge. The NEC also staged their customary "Season-Within-
a-Season" schedule of one-week showcase productions including *A Love
Play* by the abovementioned Samm Williams.

American Place came up with a pair of strong new scripts in 1976. Steve
Tesich's *Gorky* introduced the aging Russian dramatist and revolutionary on
the eve of a surgical "operation" ordered by Stalin and guaranteed to be
fatal. It then flashed back in Gorky's memory to his boyhood, his youth
and his loves in episodes of both character development and historical interest. The other was Phillip Hayes Dean's *Every Night When the Sun Goes
Down,* whose group of barroom escapists a la *The Time of Your Life* realize that even for them the time has come for social and evnironmental
renewal. In a rare example of homage to the Bicentennial on the part of
a New York theater, American Place brought back its famous Robert Lowell
trilogy *The Old Glory* in a distinguished two-program revival, with *Benito
Cereno* (about black slaves rebelling and capturing the Spanish ship on

which they're being transported) playing by itself and *Endecott and the Red Cross* (the massacre of a white settlement by the white governor at Merry Mount, Mass.) and *My Kinsman, Major Molineux* (the first days of the Revolution in Boston) playing together.

All off-Broadway productions cited so far in this report took place in the shelter of organizations. Independent production was scarce this season, increasingly inhibited by ever higher costs, with returns limited by the size of the auditoria. Even so, two remarkable scripts were independently mounted: Israel Horovitz's *The Primary English Class* and Tom Cole's drama *Medal of Honor Rag,* both of them plays of increasing pressure performed in one seamless piece, without intermission. The Horovitz comedy created the world's most frustrating English language class of pupils, each of whom speaks a different native tongue and not one word of any other, and their night-school teacher (Diane Keaton), a neurotic who patronizes and scorns her class. This adventure in non-communication was cleverly conceived and firmly pushed to a hectic conclusion.

The pressure of *Medal of Honor Rag* builds dramatically and inexorably toward disaster, in a session with an Army psychiatrist (David Clennon) and his patient (Howard E. Rollins Jr.), a black Vietnam veteran who went berserk when he saw his buddies killed. He attacked and decimated the enemy single-handed and cannot now always control the memory of his rage. The Cole and Horovitz scripts were small packages of exceptional theater, in a modern context that seems to have room for large packages only.

Most of the year's off-Broadway musicals were produced independently and to the sorrow of those backing them. The single exception was *Boy Meets Boy,* with a special appeal accurately represented by its title. One of the revues won a place deep in the hearts of New York theatergoers: *Tuscaloosa's Calling Me . . . but I'm Not Going,* a winning collection of songs and sketches making the case for living in New York City, written by a talented trio of young aficionados: Bill Heyer, Hank Beebe and Sam Dawn.

Among the year's specialty attractions were two visiting troupes from Poland, the Polish Mime Theater and Josef Szajna's stark, pantomimic images of World War II horrors. In a lighter, sweeter vein, the Bil Baird marionettes were a standout as usual, with their two fanciful 1975–76 offerings, *Alice in Wonderland* and *Winnie the Pooh.*

With 26 new American plays (including five Best Plays), the off-Broadway season wasn't as illusory as Broadway's. It was enhanced by the continued very long-run presence of *The Fantasticks,* Tom Jones's and Harvey Schmidt's fantastic musical, the longest-running professional New York production of all time, now in its 17th year having started the new 1977 season June 1 with its 6,700th performance. Combine Broadway's two all-time longest runs—*Fiddler on the Roof* and *Life With Father*—and their total still falls short of *The Fantasticks* by more than 100 performances. Before this indigenous off-Broadway phenomenon calls it quits, it may very well add the runs of *Tobacco Road* and *Hello, Dolly!* too. The supremely distinguished Joseph Papp to the contrary notwithstanding, and whatever else happens or fails to happen, off Broadway can never be pronounced dead while *The Fantasticks* lives on.

Revivals on and off Broadway

This was the season of the New York theater's center of gravity shifting markedly toward revival production, particularly on Broadway. Over the last two or three seasons, revivals have been on the increase, until in 1975–76 they were preponderant. On Broadway, 28 of the year's programs were revivals (there were "only" 18 last year), as compared with a total of 23 new American plays and musicals, including transfers.

Revivals were not only numerous in 1975–76, they were exceptionally successful. They provided the biggest new straight-play hit—*The Royal Family*—and three of the year's sizable musical hits—*Very Good Eddie, My Fair Lady* and *Threepenny Opera*. Revival casts, directors and designers received 19 Tony nominations, four of them winners: Irene Worth (best actress for *Sweet Bird of Youth*), George Rose (best musical actor for *My Fair Lady*), Edward Herrmann (best featured actor for *Mrs. Warren's Profession*) and Ellis Rabb (best director for *The Royal Family*).

Why this shift toward the theatrical past? The explanation must lie with the dismal science of economics, not with the glorious art of the stage. An already-proven script doesn't guarantee success, but it reduces the element of risk at a time when risks are becoming ever more expensive in failure and not all that much more lucrative in success. Audiences are increasing, and so production is stimulated. But new work is more dangerous, and so all the extra thrust is placed behind revival production.

The Bicentennial accounts for a small percentage of the increased revival activity. Six plays of the American Bicentennial Theater at Kennedy Center in Washington, sponsored in part by Xerox, were brought to New York by various producers: *Long Day's Journey Into Night* with Jason Robards starring and directing at the Brooklyn Academy of Music; *The Skin of Our Teeth* with Alfred Drake, *Summer Brave* with Alexis Smith and *The Heiress* with Richard Kiley and Jane Alexander (a memorable acting team, at least as effective as their original counterparts, Basil Rathbone and Wendy Hiller) to Broadway; and *Sweet Bird of Youth* and *The Royal Family* to both Brooklyn and Broadway. These programs are the subject of comment by Richard L. Coe of the Washington *Post* and David Richards of the Washington *Star* in "The Season Around the United States" section of this report. In New York, Miss Worth's performance as a faded movie queen in the Williams play was a towering one but did not entirely eclipse Christopher Walken as her doomed lover, under Edward Sherin's direction. And not enough gratitude can be expressed for the presence in New York this season of Ellis Rabb's re-launching of the 1927 George S. Kaufman-Edna Ferber comedy about a theatrical "royal family" reminiscent of the Barrymores, living in the grand manner of their performances. The acting ensemble of Eva Le Gallienne as the matriarch, Rosemary Harris as the Broadway star, George Grizzard as her movie-hating movie star brother, Sam Levene as the Broadway producer and others of equal importance in lesser roles outshone even *The Norman Conquests* company as a coordinated group.

In this connection, since just about half Broadway's production this season and a large chunk of off Broadway's was revivals, we've decided it's time we added a new category to our "best" list: best revival under both the straight-play and musical headings in the honor roll which appears at the end of the Broadway chapter of this report. Our 1975–76 choices are *The Royal Family,* of course, for best play revival. There were strong contenders in the musical section: a charming new *My Fair Lady* and an inventive re-staging of *Very Good Eddie,* an ice-cream-suit Jerome Kern musical with boys and girls, led by Charles Repole, romancing on the Albany night boat in an updated book by Guy Bolton, perfectly stylized by Bill Gile's direction. In the face of these superb productions, our choice for the best musical revival of 1975–76 is the Joseph Papp *Threepenny Opera,* the last in a four-program season of revivals at the Vivian Beaumont in Lincoln Center that was as admirable as Papp's new-play program was distinguished. These Beaumont shows may have been designed at least in part as audience-pleasers for the subscription set, but each of them had a little something extra, a little something challenging to flavor the experience for any more adventurous theatergoer who might happen along. The sentimental journey of Pinero's *Trelawny of the "Wells"* became a lively abrasion of high society and low-living theater folk under A. J. Antoon's direction, with a carefully color-blended ensemble of character actors: John Lithgow, Marybeth Hurt, Walter Abel and Aline MacMahon among them. Even *Hamlet* seemed almost newly-minted, with an imaginatively flexible design by Santo Loquasto and a pixillated Hamlet (Sam Waterston) who was no match for his stern Uncle Claudius (Charles Cioffi). *Mrs. Warren's Profession* became a collection of cameo performances by Lynn Redgrave, Ruth Gordon, Milo O'Shea, Edward Herrmann (the featured-player Tony Award winner) and others trying to capture the emerging feminism of the young century by characterizing various attitudes toward it.

Even more ambitiously, Papp decided to restore the Bertolt Brecht-Kurt Weill *Threepenny Opera* to something approaching its original design by producing, not the smoothed-over Marc Blitzstein translation so popular off Broadway in the 1950s and 1960s, but a new translation by Ralph Manheim and John Willett more faithful to its abrasive source. Papp's own program note described his aspirations in part as follows:

In comparing the lyrics and text of Blitzstein to the original, we discovered to our surprise that the Blitzstein adaptation excised much of the political and sexual thrust which is contained in our present translation and which gives the original German work its relentless power.

It is clear that the intention of Brecht in this now-classic work was to assault the audience with his irony and views of life. By neatly fitting his abrasive words into conventional musical pattern, the 1954 adaptation had the effect of neutralizing much of the bite of Bertolt Brecht. While the lyrics of Blitzstein may be more "singable" than Brecht's rugged, gutter lyrics, they quite clearly are at odds with the dramatist's purpose and dramatic sensibilities.

An example to demonstrate how Brecht's intent was softened by the 1954 adaptation:

Blitzstein:	*Brecht:*
Instead of, instead of	No they can't, no, they cant.
Goin' about their business and behavin'	See what's good for them And set their minds on it.
They make love, they make love;	It's fun they want, it's fun they want
Til the man is through	So they end up on their arses in the shit.
And then she's sorry that she gave in.	

It is our hope that this remarkable new translation of *Threepenny Opera,* in its original and uncensored form, will give our audiences knowledge of the true power of one of the great works of our 20th century.

Raul Julia's bold-faced portrayal of Mack the Knife was a finishing master-stroke in a masterly revival further informed by Richard Foreman's direction, with echoes of Peter Brook's *Marat/Sade.* When, a year ago, the Beaumont's audiences failed to support Papp's kind of new plays produced there, the producer was forced to try to give them what they apparently want: distinguished occasions of conventional theater. His 1975–76 set of revivals has served them better than anyone could have presumed to hope, punctuated by this provocative and brilliant *Threepenny Opera.* It was more than a revival, it was a thrilling restoration, which we recognize in this volume with a special "best" citation in addition to the usual ten, with the new translation appearing in abridgement and synopsis in the Best Plays section.

Another challenger at the musical peak was *My Fair Lady,* a captivatingly faithful copy of the original, tracing every line of the Moss Hart direction and Cecil Beaton design, produced by the show's original producer, Herman Levin, and with Robert Coote again treating Broadway to his interpretation of Henry Higgins's friend Colonel Pickering. Ian Richardson played Higgins differently than Rex Harrison but as validly: a little more force, a little less charm. Christine Andreas was in good voice as his fair flower girl, George Rose clowned all over the place as her father Alfred P. Doolittle, and Jerry Lanning was so good as Eliza's vapid young man Freddy that he stopped the show with his rendition of "On the Street Where You Live." Having *My Fair Lady* back in all its enduring glory of music, comedy and romance was indeed a joyful reunion, one of the year's most satisfying events.

Circle in the Square also produced a vintage season, beginning in June with *Death of a Salesman,* in which George C. Scott directed himself in the part of Willy Loman. Scott is an actor of such power that his Willy acquired a strength of character somewhat at odds with his other weaknesses—a contradiction reminiscent of Richard Burton's Hamlet of a few years back and with its same audience-shaking strength taking up some of the strain it placed on the play. The 1976 series of revivals by this Theodore Mann-Paul Libin group began with O'Neill in his front-porch, Fourth-of-July mood of nostalgic Americana in *Ah, Wilderness!* under the direction of the Long Wharf Theater's exceptionally accomplished Arvin Brown, who lent himself generously to Broadway projects this season. Mann himself directed a luminescent revival of *The Glass Menagerie* with Maureen Stapleton as Amanda, Pamela Payton-Wright as her daughter, Paul Rudd as the gentleman caller and Rip Torn playing son and brother with a wild-animal ferocity that brought a new and perfectly appropriate cutting-edge to his role in this wonderful, enduring play. The Circle in the Square season then provided the mystery and glamor of Vanessa Redgrave as Ibsen's *The Lady From the Sea* in the atmosphere of Rouben Ter-Arutunian's craggily spare Norwegian-fjord design. At season's end, this group was struggling forward toward a late-June premiere of a problematical effort to revive the Rodgers-Hart musical *Pal Joey,* with a successful season already emblazoned in the record, whatever might happen next.

Arvin Brown's directorial mastery was at work again on behalf of T. Edward Hambleton's Phoenix Theater in its outstanding program of two hardy one-acters: Tennessee Williams's *27 Wagons Full of Cotton,* with Meryl Streep in an unforgettable portrayal of a bored and seduceable wife, and Arthur Miller's *A Memory of Two Mondays,* with John Lithgow, Roy Poole and others rising painfully above the depressing anonymity of the daily grind in an auto-parts warehouse. The Phoenix's *They Knew What They Wanted* was another standout 1976 revival, with Barry Bostwick (Joe), Louis Zorich (Tony) and Lois Nettleton as the emotionally storm-tossed trio, with Stephen Porter directing. The second half of the Phoenix's schedule was of lighter weight, with William Gillette's *Secret Service* playing in repertory with Sam and Bella Spewack's *Boy Meets Girl.*

In addition to the new musical *The Robber Bridegroom,* John Houseman's Acting Company presented a varied revival repertory. Besides *Three Sisters* and *The Time of Your Life,* they did Christopher Marlowe's seldom-seen *Edward II,* about a politically and sexually troubled English king who met a violent end at the hands of brutal subjects. This was Ellis Rabb's second distinguished directorial stint of the season, with the first professional New York production of record of this challenging play.

Finally in group production of Broadway revivals there was London's visiting D'Oyly Carte Opera Company with its meticulous, historically correct versions of Gilbert and Sullivan operettas. Among individual productions, Ben Gazzara and Colleen Dewhurst delivered the powerful impact of

Edward Albee's *Who's Afraid of Virginia Woolf?* with full force under the author's own direction. Pearl Bailey returned for what she said was a farewell to Broadway in a limited engagement of *Hello, Dolly! Angel Street* brought back its melodrama, with Dina Merrill and Michael Allinson as husband and wife and Christine Andreas playing the maid Nancy just prior to her taking on the title role of *My Fair Lady*.

Off Broadway, the revival scene was important, but not yet quite predominant, with 29 revivals (a total somewhat inflated this year by the inclusion of nine Light Opera of Manhattan and four Classic Stage Company productions, two groups not listed in previous seasons) as compared with 32 new American plays and musicals. Among producing organizations the standout was Gene Feist's and Michael Fried's Roundabout, a going and ongoing New York theater concern now expanded into two theaters and broadening the scope not only of its production but its very name from Roundabout Theater Company to Roundabout Theater Center. The eclectic, high-quality programs of this, its tenth, season included a Bicentennial re-viewing of Booth Tarkington's *Clarence* (about a wounded World War I soldier's romantic conquests upon his return), as well as *Summer and Smoke, The Cherry Orchard* and the Roundabout's customary one new play, *Dear Mr. G,* a gangland comedy by Donna de Matteo.

The Classic Stage Company (CSC), like the Circle, moved up this season from OOB to full professional status, bringing with it the expertise with which Christopher Martin has put on so many programs over the past few years. Its 1975–76 repertory consisted of *Measure for Measure, Hedda Gabler, A Country Scandal* and Anouilh's *Antigone* (a list which provides some idea of its versatility and grasp), plus a new adaptation of *The Hound of the Baskervilles* and a few other productions which were mounted in the course of the CSC's season but were withdrawn before being formally presented to critics and public.

The Light Opera of Manhattan was and is firmly established at the Eastside Playhouse on East 74th St. Under the direction of William Mount-Burke, this company of gifted enthusiasts offered a musical repertory of six perennial Gilbert and Sullivan favorites, plus three operettas from the golden romantic age: Victor Herbert's *Naughty Marietta,* Rudolf Friml's *The Vagabond King* and Sigmund Romberg's *The Student Prince,* thereby assuring New York theatergoers a close and immensely rewarding acquaintance with what is probably the sweetest segment of its theater heritage.

The Brooklyn Academy of Music played host to the Royal Shakespeare Company's *Henry V* and *The Hollow Crown*. At the Delacorte in Central Park, Joseph Papp put on the summer *Hamlet,* later moved to winter quarters at the Beaumont, plus a production of *The Comedy of Errors;* and downtown he provided house room for Shaliko's version of *Woyzeck*. Of independent revival production off Broadway there was less than a smattering this season: a 7-performance production of J. B. Fagan's 1926 play about Samuel Pepys *And So to Bed* and a 9-performance *The Homecoming* brought up from OOB.

The most important function of New York's broad 1975–76 spectrum of 28 revival productions on Broadway and 29 off is to provide new insights into our theater's past and deepen our perspective. This it has done, to an extent which no single repertory company anywhere in the world could possibly aspire. To show off the New York theater's achievement in this regard, here are this season's 49 full-length and 4 one-act revivals listed in alphabetical order of their authors:

Edward Albee
Who's Afraid of Virginia Woolf?

Jean Anouilh
Antigone

Anthology (various authors)
The Hollow Crown

Guy Bolton (with Jerome Kern and Schuyler Greene)
Very Good Eddie

Bertolt Brecht (with Kurt Weill, translated by Manheim & Willett)
Threepenny Opera

Georg Buechner
Woyzeck

Anton Chekhov
The Cherry Orchard
Three Sisters
A Country Scandal

Dorothy Donnelly (with Sigmund Romberg)
The Student Prince

J. B. Fagan
And So to Bed

W. S. Gilbert and Arthur Sullivan
The Gondoliers
H.M.S. Pinafore (two productions)
Iolanthe
The Mikado (two productions)
Patience
The Pirates of Penzance (two productions)

William Gillette
Secret Service

Ruth and Augustus Goetz
The Heiress

Patrick Hamilton
Angel Street

Brian Hooker and W. H. Post (with Rudolf Friml)
The Vagabond King

Sidney Howard
They Knew What They Wanted

Henrik Ibsen
Hedda Gabler
The Lady From the Sea

William Inge
Summer Brave (*Picnic*)

George S. Kaufman and Edna Ferber
The Royal Family (two theaters)

Alan Jay Lerner and Frederick Loewe
My Fair Lady

Robert Lowell
Benito Cereno
Endecott and the Red Cross
My Kinsman, Major Molineux

Christopher Marlowe
Edward II

Arthur Miller
Death of a Salesman
A Memory of Two Mondays

Eugene O'Neill
Ah, Wilderness!
Long Day's Journey Into Night

Arthur Wing Pinero
Trelawny of the "Wells"

Harold Pinter
The Homecoming

William Saroyan
The Time of Your Life

William Shakespeare
The Comedy of Errors
Hamlet (two theaters)
Henry V
Measure for Measure

George Bernard Shaw
Mrs. Warren's Profession

Edward Sheldon
The Boss

Samuel and Bella Spewack
Boy Meets Girl

Michael Stewart (with Jerry Herman)
Hello, Dolly!

Booth Tarkington
Clarence

Thornton Wilder
The Skin of Our Teeth

Tennessee Williams
The Glass Menagerie
Summer and Smoke
Sweet Bird of Youth (two theaters)
27 Wagons Full of Cotton

Rida Johnson Young (with Victor Herbert)
Naughty Marietta

Offstage

The 1975–76 New York theater season was just beginning to take on its autumn momentum when the Broadway musicians struck, darkening all the big musicals. Local 802 was contending for an increase in pay, plus various other benefits. The strike started Sept. 18, and its issues were soon obscured as far as the public was concerned by its impact on New York City's already hard-pressed restaurants, hotels and other entertainment support facilities whose health depends on the theater much more than they know or realize in ordinary times. When the strike was settled (it lasted Sept. 18-Oct. 12, inclusive) the musicians had won a raise from $290 a week to $350-380. The estimated cost to the New York City economy was $1 million a day for the duration of the strike, proof expensive and positive of the theater's huge importance to the community's economic as well as cultural life.

A summer controversy over the Equity showcase code had lesser economic but perhaps greater artistic ramifications. With the rising importance of off off Broadway, Equity leadership proposed new rules that would have mandated a vested interest for actors in the future of workshop scripts in whose experimental productions they appeared: 2 per cent of profits from all subsequent productions if they rehearsed four weeks, 8 per cent if they rehearsed longer, with the showcase producer and author responsible for future reimbursements. It should be pointed out that actors more often than not receive no pay for showcase appearances and sometimes not even carfare; on the other hand the author gets no return either except the attention of critics, agents and producers to his work—and a showcase for the author is a showcase for the actor too. In any case, the Dramatists Guild (the professional association of stage authors) and the Off-Off-Broadway Association vigorously opposed the Equity Showcase Committee's proposed new code, the Guild circularizing its members and some other dramatists advising them not to sign any such agreement to share future royalties. Many Equity members also disagreed with their leadership's proposals, on the grounds that they would curtail the very OOB activity which offers a major, ongoing opportunity for training and exposure. At a special Equity membership meeting Aug. 25, a motion was adopted recommending to the Equity Council that the old code be reinstated pending further discussions. This was done, ending the acute phase of this controversy at least for the duration of the season. The New York *Times* commented in an editorial: "The off-off-Broadway scene is a remarkable phenomenon. It is home for innovation, for trying new wings and themes, for learning and dreaming. Equity's members have done their union and the community a service by recognizing that this delicate blossom could be killed by too much regimentation."

In other group activity offstage, the League of New York theaters decided to assess all its member Broadway and touring productions an aggregate $500,000 or more a year for the purposes of promotion, lobbying, marketing, theater district improvement, etc. The League also acquired the services of Harvey B. Sabinson as director of special projects such as its supervision of the Tony Award balloting and ceremonies. At the beginning of the season (prior to Mr. Sabinson's affiliation) the League's Tony administration, in consultation with the American Theater Wing which co-administers the Tonys, decided on a new nominating procedure. There would still be a Nominating Committee of ten critics, but they would no longer meet as a group to make the decisions about the eligibility and classification of candidates for Tony Awards (for example, was *The Norman Conquests* one play or three?). An Eligibility Committee of the League and Wing would present the nominating critics with a list of already-categorized candidates from which they would make their selections—and they'd make their choices individually, alone, instead of in a meeting. *Variety* reported the reasoning behind this isolation-booth system as follows: "It's figured that by having the nominator members make their selections privately, in writing, there may be less chance of electioneering and persuading, as well as less hurry."

Those of us who served on the 1976 Tony Nominating Committee would have to admit that the new system worked fairly well, avoiding the arguments and confrontations that used to take place in the group selection process. The new system turned up almost all the year's outstanding work on the nominations list, too. The few missing exceptions, in the opinion of the *Best Plays* editor, were Katharine Hepburn's capable performance in *A Matter of Gravity,* the three plays of *The Norman Conquests* (correctly classified as three separate plays by the eligibility committee and therefore unlikely to amass enough votes for any one of the plays to win a nomination) and Carole Shelley's and other performances in the same comedies (incorrectly classified as separate performances and therefore unnominated for the same reason). The best-musical-actor Tony to George Rose's admittedly appealing performance as Alfred P. Doolittle over Ian Richardson's memorable starring turn as Henry Higgins in *My Fair Lady* demonstrates that the Tonys have a long way to go in making clear and fair distinctions between leading and supporting performances. Classifying according to the billing terms "starring" and "featured" just doesn't do the job.

In other organizational developments, an ad hoc committee of theater journalists organized the New Drama Forum for the purpose of holding discussion meetings on various theater problems and subjects. The new group, which held several sessions during the season, was set up along lines similar to Drama Desk by former members of that organization: John Beaufort, William Glover, Henry Hewes, Stuart W. Little, Hugh Southern, Marilyn Stasio, Edwin Wilson and others.

The dream of establishing a Songwriters Hall of Fame in the Broadway area became a reality when the Academy of Popular Music, whose president is Sammy Cahn, took space at One Times Square (the angular building with the moving news sign) for the permanent establishment of a songwriters' showplace. Its facilities will include a small theater and such historical exhibits as Victor Herbert's piano and a first edition of "The Star Spangled Banner." In another area of activity, the Independent Booking Office bestowed its presidency upon Alexander H. Cohen, with Richard Barr as secretary and Samuel Schwartz treasurer.

The year's only audible critical hassle took place in hottest midsummer over the right to review the performance of a temporary replacement for an ailing star. When Gwen Verdon had to leave *Chicago* for a few weeks for a throat operation, Liza Minnelli was brought in to replace her so that the show would have a continuity of star quality at its center. The show's producers didn't want the critics to review Miss Minnelli's performance, however, on the grounds that comparisons between her and Miss Verdon could only be odious whichever way they pointed. Clive Barnes and the New York *Times* editors insisted that the appearance of Miss Minnelli on a New York stage was a news event demanding coverage as soon as her performance was set. The *Times* won its point. The critics came to praise Miss Minnelli without any consequent reflection on Miss Verdon, whose performance was later nominated for a Tony. Other replacement "events" such as the uptown move of *A Chorus Line,* Richard Burton for Anthony Perkins in *Equus* and the new cast and direction of *Knock Knock* were routinely covered, without objection.

The economic strictures of the late 1970s have been an ill wind blowing some good to the theater in delaying demolition of its precious Broadway-area housing. The planned razing of the Morosco and Ethel Barrymore to make way for a hotel-office block hasn't taken place (although the Morosco, which housed *The Norman Conquests* all season, looks as though it were crumbling of its own accord). The new theaters in skyscrapers, the Minskoff and the Uris, have turned out as inhospitable to legitimate theater production as was predicted and were mostly used as concert halls. On the plus side, the newly-refurbished Harkness Theater on Broadway across from Lincoln Center has become a comfortable setting for both shows and audiences. Its Broadway bookings this season were the Acting Company repertory, *Sweet Bird of Youth* and *So Long, 174th Street*. The Nederlander interests expanded their New York theater ownership, adding the Alvin to their Uris, Palace and Brooks Atkinson. They also reportedly bid $4 million for the McKnight theaters including the St. James and the Martin Beck in New York.

The importance of subsidy to the live performing arts was increasing faster than the sums allotted to it in 1975–76. The White House asked Congress for $82 million for the National Endowment for the Arts and was lucky to get $79.5 million ($6.3 million of which was the portion of theater groups in the form of matching funds), almost $5 million more than in 1974–75. The New York State Council on the Arts, under its new chairman Joan K. Davidson, had its subsidy reduced slightly in 1976 to $33 million from $34.1 million the year before and is expected to be cut again to $27.3 million in 1977. Discouraging as this trend may be, New York is still way ahead of the rest of the country in supporting its arts institutions, according to a state-by-state estimate published by *Variety* early in the year. New York's arts allotment is incomparably (and perhaps not surprisingly) the largest; Michigan is in second place with a mere $2.3 million for the year. New York's per capita contribution from state revenues is also tops: $1.96 per person. Only Alaska ($1.47), Hawaii ($1.30) and maybe Colorado ($.86) are in the same ball park. Sample per capita arts subsidies by other large states are California $.05, Illinois $.08, Pennsylvania $.13, Texas $.01, Connecticut $.13, Massachusetts $.28, New Jersey $.11, Ohio $.09.

At these pitiful levels of support, government aid to the arts in this richest and among the most creative of all countries is more promise than performance, a mere token of things we hope are soon to come. The money itself was of real help as far as it went ($121,000 to Chelsea, $125,000 to Negro Ensemble, $150,000 to New York Shakespeare Festival at the Public and the same at the Beaumont, $125,000 to Theater Development Fund, etc., etc.) which was nevertheless only a very short distance on the long, long uphill road stretching in front of the live performing arts through the end of the 1970s on into the 1980s.

So the 1975–76 theater season in New York can take any number of curtain calls for its performance—its illusion of a booming year—in which, to be sure, superb entertainment was sometimes a reality. The *Best Plays* series of theater yearbooks has always used May 31 and June 1 as the official dates on which one season ends and another begins, and of course we do the same in this volume. Show-wise, however, 1975–76 can be said to have been bounded in the beginning by the off-Broadway production of 1975's wonderfully imaginative *A Chorus Line* and at the end by the wonderfully reliable Neil Simon's *California Suite* which began the 1977 season so auspiciously in June.

No, we didn't come up with a musical as popular as *A Chorus Line* in 1975–76, but we had *A Chorus Line* itself on Broadway all year, plus the popular *Chicago,* the brilliantly innovative *Pacific Overtures,* the smashing *Threepenny Opera* and a glorious *My Fair Lady.* We didn't come up with a well-made play as entertaining as a new vintage Simon, but *The Norman Conquests* came triply close; we didn't have a stunner like *Equus,* but we did have one like *Streamers.*

One memorable event of the 1975–76 New York season wasn't visible on any stage except by reflection: the venturing into theater sponsorship of two large corporations scarcely connected with show business. Xerox gave American Bicentennial Theater its initial impetus with a grant of $400,000 and Coca-Cola backed *1600 Pennsylvania Avenue* for $1 million plus or minus, events whose importance towers above their immediate results.

In the former case, outstanding productions of *The Royal Family* and *Sweet Bird of Youth* reflect great credit, prestige and *attention* upon Xerox, just as the TV episodes of *Upstairs, Downstairs* have made many if not most of us aware for the first time in our lives that there is such a thing as Mobil Oil Corporation. As for the expensive demise of *1600 Pennsylvania Avenue,* even though the show fell far short of hopes and expectations the Coca-Cola Company deserves our most hearty applause for helping bring it into being. We commiserate with Coca-Cola on the insidious uncertainties of show business which, like a football, is of a peculiar shape and can bounce in any direction no matter how skillfully it is set into motion—by an Alan Jay Lerner or a Leonard Bernstein or even, ideally, an Alan Jay Lerner *and* a Leonard Bernstein.

We believe that in the case of the professional theater the game is worth the candle, however, and our personal respect and admiration goes out to anyone like Coca-Cola who dares to play it. The subsidy of first-class stage productions by non-entertainment corporate institutions is an idea whose time is long overdue. The possible advantages are obvious and so are the possible disadvantages—you can't win them all, and in the theater not even half of them. We hope and believe that both Coca-Cola and Xerox will discern that the former outweigh the latter in the long run, which is the only run that should concern the institutions of American arts and economics. They are made for each other, and the times are pushing them closer and closer together, in the live performing arts' need for additional sources of support and the corporations' need for some kind of public-service identity to sweeten the public's perception of their ever-increasing profitability. We expect that other large corporations will avail themselves of this new opportunity, now that Xerox and Coca-Cola have blazed the trail.

In 1975–76, the New York theater paid little attention to its country's Bicentennial celebrations of the past. Thanks to the efforts of unnamed corporate deciders, though, it may have started something this season that will materially brighten its future.

THE 1975–76 SEASON OFF OFF BROADWAY

By Marion Fredi Towbin

Playwright and critic, author of *What! and Leave Bloomingdale's?* and *Bed & Breakfast*

REMEMBER the late 1950s when off off Broadway meant an insufferably long Becketesque drama, badly performed in an insufferably hot backroom of a Greenwich Village cafe? Times have changed!

A Chorus Line, Yentl, Bubbling Brown Sugar, Knock Knock, Kennedy's Children, Godspell. These Broadway shows were nurtured off off. So were three productions in this season's WNET-TV's prestigious *Theater in America* series: Lanford Wilson's *The Mound Builders,* Leslie Lee's *The First Breeze of Summer* and Gardner McKay's *Sea Marks.*

Off off Broadway is the identifying banner of professional, non-profit theater in New York City, and is respected around the world as a significant cultural force. Off off has matured dramatically the past few seasons and is today New York's own regional theater: non-commercial, institutional and developmental in nature. Theaters are located in lofts, storefronts, basements, prisons, Y's and church naves from Battery Park to the Cloisters, and although most actors/actresses and off-off-Broadway production staffs still work without pay, there is a growing tendency toward small honorariums (say $20 per production) and living wages are forseeable in the future.

Off off Broadway is still, as it was in the very beginning, the performing artist's roots, showcase and laboratory. Increasingly, actors/actresses, playwrights, designers and directors are moving fluidly from Broadway to television to film to off off, back and forth. No commercial media could ever hope for OOB's tremendous range: experimental, classical, avant-garde, ethnic, political, musical. Off off is the source—the lifeline—of American theater.

It was the best of times and the worst of times OOB this season; the best, because it brought to light a number of new and exciting works—David Mamet's *Sexual Perversity in Chicago,* John Bishop's *The Trip Back Down,* Gardner McKay's *Sea Marks*—and some outstanding revivals. It was the worst because Equity negotiations to replace the outmoded Showcase Code dragged on and on (still without resolution), and the national economic crunch—on top of New York's own fiscal difficulties—forced one OOB theater to close and forced all others to tighten their already proverbially tight belts.

The keynote OOB this season was survival through improved, professional arts management, and it was to this crucial issue that two major East Coast conferences spoke. One, organized by Theater Communications Group (TCG), was held at the end of the season, June 13-17, 1976, in New Haven, Conn. and confronted the issue of arts subsidy. The conference resulted in a mandate that TCG explore an advocacy program at Federal,

state and municipal levels and that a lobbyist in Washington work on behalf of non-profit arts institutions.

Another conference was concerned solely with OOB and was organized
by the Off-Off-Broadway Alliance (OOBA), a highly visible cooperative
organization formed five years ago under the leadership of executive director Virginia Kahn. Originally, OOBA planned an outdoor theater festival,
like the celebration which brought OOB tremendous publicity in 1974. But
OOBA's funds were also slim, and sound judgment opted for the marathon
conference which lasted from sunrise to midnight at the Henry Street Settlement. Nearly 200 OOB professionals—producers, directors, public relations
and management personel—participated in the day-long seminars. Keynote
speaker for the event was the distinguished critic and director, Harold
Clurman. Panel discussions focused on the need for professional OOB management, with topics such as "Fund Raising," "New York City's Relationship to OOB," "Press Relations, Marketing and Audience Development."

OOBA is a purely administrative organization—it makes no artistic judg-
ments on member-theater productions—and is concerned primarily with
publicity and fund-raising. Of the 150-200 OOB theaters in New York City,
53 are OOBA members. Theaters are eligible for membership if they are
legally incorporated as a not-for-profit institution, are professional (voca-
tional, not avocational) and have been in operation at least two years.

The 1975–76 season off off Broadway began well enough, but by mid-
season all OOB theaters faced a severe budgetary crisis. One theater closed,
and the New York *Times* predicted the probable demise of three others.
Fortunately, the Jean Cocteau Theater, WPA and CSC did survive, the latter changing its status to off Broadway. It became glaringly apparent that
though OOB is non-profit, it doesn't exist in an economic vacuum, and the
mid-season crisis was a direct reflection of the city/state economic quandary
and the general retrenchment of stock, bond and investment portfolios.
Corporations which had begun nibbling OOB in 1974 had stopped, and no
one had taken their place. The juggling of Ma Bell and Con Ed bills—an
OOB fact of life—was replaced with another fact of life: the arts in general,
and non-profit theater in particular, cannot and should not be expected to
exist without considerable outside funding. One OOB producer noted, "If
every OOB theater sold every seat for every performance, it still couldn't
meet basic operating costs."

In a dramatic move, the Off Off Broadway Alliance took the first bold
step in establishing a large-scale endowment fund. The source? Major American corporations.

"The corporations are extremely conservative," says Virginia Kahn, "and
it's very difficult for them to understand the laboratory value of off off
Broadway—that this is the greatest theater laboratory in this country and
probably in the world. What we want is for two or three of these corporations to make a one-shot grant of $500,000 or $1 million to establish a
fund for the theaters of off off Broadway. Part of the money would be lent
to those theaters in dire need and the rest invested in short-term Treasury
notes and an interest-bearing savings account, and would thus grow for the

future. When the Heart Fund knocks on a corporation's door they never say 'Sorry, I can't give to you. I don't like the mistakes you made in the lab.' "

OOB got a boost from the Theater Development Fund (TDF) which invested $150,000 in its voucher program, the same amount as last season. Vouchers are purchased by individuals for $1 and are redeemed by participating theaters for $2.50. Vouchers provide theaters not only with necessary subsidy, but also with background information on their audience, and a method for measuring audience support and involvement, which is extremely useful when applying for grants. The New York State Council on the Arts, a major source of OOB funds, granted $990,000 to member theaters in 1975–1976, an increase of $15,000 over last season.

Among OOB's outstanding 1975–76 productions were David Mamet's *Sexual Perversity in Chicago* and *American Buffalo,* which began off off, moved off, and were awarded an Obie; Richard Foreman's funny and evocative *Rhoda in Potatoland: Her Fall Starts,* also an Obie winner; and Terry Schreiber's production of John Bishop's *The Trip Back Down.* Schreiber did his share of moving too this season: when his East Side theater was destroyed by fire, he found a temporary home at Mama Gail's, SoHo's beautiful restaurant-cabaret.

OOB's only Bicentennial fare was provided by The American Theater Company, located near historic Union Square, which presented *The Fall of British Tyranny,* written in 1776 by John Leacock. Equal time was given to the British with *The Battle of Brooklyn,* written in the same year by an anonymous Redcoat. The Joseph Jefferson Theater Company, housed in the landmark Little-Church-Around-the-Corner, entered its fourth season of first-rate American revivals with Robert Ardrey's haunting 1938 drama *Thunder Rock,* directed by William Koch, and a production of Philip Barry's early and enigmatic *John,* last seen in New York in 1921. Brendan Gill, whose Profile of Barry appeared in *The New Yorker,* spoke on opening night.

The Manhattan Theater Club presented the American debut of another David Storey play, this one *Life Class,* directed by Robert Mandel, and Sam Shepard's *Geography of a Horse Dreamer,* Jacques Levy directing. Proof that theater is a matter more of soul than geography, and proof that critics are people too, was the Iowa Theater Lab's *Sweetbird,* a non-verbal exploration of erotic feeling, presented by Playwrights Horizons. During the show's limited run, PH discovered its usual requests for press "comps" had tripled.

Playwrights working in OOB theater workshops and university writing programs were given a boost when the Double Image Theater and Samuel French co-sponsored a two-week short-play (or work-in-progress) competition, with the winner being published between those world famous yellow covers. And on the subject of awards, a special Obie was given this year to one of OOB's most versatile actor-directors, Neil Flanagan.

A century ago, the poet and critic Matthew Arnold wrote "The theater is irresistible; organize the theater." This season, off off Broadway did just that.

THE SEASON AROUND THE UNITED STATES

with

A DIRECTORY OF PROFESSIONAL REGIONAL THEATER

○
○
○

*Including casts and credits of new plays, selected
Canadian programs, selected programs for children and
extended coverage of the Los Angeles, Washington and
dinner theater seasons*

INTRODUCTION: THE BICENTENNIAL ONSTAGE

By Richard L. Coe

Drama critic of the Washington *Post*

WHILE the year of greatly unreal expectations is but half over, the Bicentennial has been one more broken illusion to those who expected stirring reflections of our American theater. Nonetheless, the 1975–76 season symbolizes a stirring period in our theater's development.

Not that people weren't trying for 200th birthday magic. There has been tremendous scurrying about for "American Classics." Though George Washington's step-grandson G. W. P. Custis was one of our earliest playwrights there are no early classics. Of the colonial period, *Ye Beare and Ye Cubb,* presented in Virginia in 1665, has had its revivals, especially in the South. David Garrick's *Miss in Her Teens* of 1747 (sometimes known as *A Medley for Lovers*) reappeared in Williamsburg 209 years later.

Obeisance has been made to Royall Tyler, born at Faneuil Hall, a Boston suburb, in 1757, who became Chief Justice of the Vermont Supreme Court. Before that, in 1787, after having seen only one play, *The School for Scandal,* Tyler wrote *The Contrast* in three weeks, the first American comedy and, if performed with conviction, still amusing. Regional and university theaters have done their homework. New York, still indisputably the cultural and communications capital, has seen some, shuddered at most and welcomed a few shreds.

Contemporary professionals have delved into history. There was the drummed-up, chopped-off Alan Jay Lerner-Leonard Bernstein musical collaboration on the 19th century White House, *1600 Pennsylvania Avenue,* based on a preachy, questionably historic premise and financially the most spectacular of all Bicentennial disasters. There was the astonishingly creative, emphatically off-beat *Pacific Overtures,* the John Weidman-Stephen Sondheim-Hugh Wheeler-Harold Prince celebration of Admiral Perry's 1853 voyage to Japan. It stretched the boundaries of our musical stage, but the public never stretched the walls of the Winter Garden Theater in New York.

Ray Aranha, who had gained respect through *My Sister, My Sister,* may have been influenced by Fawn Browdie's recent biography to write of Thomas Jefferson and his assumed black mistress in *The Estate,* one of the few markedly Bicentennial black offerings. Jefferson's own Charlottesville saw the second summer of its professional Heritage Theater with a new play about him, *That Man Jefferson* by David Clapp and William Martin, as well as an 1819 revival with music added, *She Would Be a Soldier.*

Historian Richard Lee Marks's imagination was struck by Benjamin Franklin's Tory scion, William, coming up with an emotional *Bastard Son.* Despite endless efforts over the generations, Washington himself always came out a too-good-to-be-dramatic hero and ours is not an heroic time. Actor Anthony Holland and William M. Hoffman wrote *Cornbury—The Queen's Governor,* a comedy about Edward Hyde Cornbury, governor of New York and New Jersey from 1702 to 1708, who made all his public appearances dressed as a woman because "I represent Her Majesty the Queen."

Theodore Roosevelt went from San Juan Hill to the White House in a scattered California salute called *Teddy* by Jon Palmer. History was searched with fresh, perhaps too impressionable eyes. The American history plays of Anderson, Sherwood and Kingsley were largely ignored.

There were revivals of the not-yet-classics of such comparatively recent writers as O'Neill, Kelly, Barry, Wilder, Williams, Miller, Inge, Hellman, Albee, Kaufman and Hart, Hecht and MacArthur, Lawrence and Lee. Such appeared the most viable risks for Bicentennial retrospection.

There were the one-performer "plays," once a highly popular device for economical touring, which Hal Holbrook had kicked off again with his *Mark Twain Tonight!* James Whitmore went from Will Rogers to Harry S. Truman. TV's success with *The Adams Chronicles* gave heart to revivals of William Gibson's *American Primitive,* exchanges of John and Abigail letters.

Benjamin Franklin returned Howard Da Silva to his *1776* role for a radio series and William Peterson for further performances of his *A Profile of Benjamin Franklin*. Manned by all the Bicentennial names, *1776* had scores of productions, though, mysteriously, heavyweight producers thought it "too soon" for a big-name revival.

Eugenia Rawls continued her touring as the influential 19th century actress, Fanny Kemble, whose letters from Georgia swerved her native Britain from all-out Confederacy support. Julie Harris became Emily Dickinson in *The Belle of Amherst* and will probably act her off and on when nothing else interests her. Eileen Heckart became Mrs. Roosevelt in *Eleanor*, which gave that great lady 17 years after her death what she always so conspicuously had lacked in life, a sense of humor. Mrs. R. was too serious for one-liners.

Theaters tried matching old plays to their decor, *London Assurance* reopening Albany's Cahoes Opera House as it had originally in 1874. *Very Good Eddie*, the Jerome Kern hit of 1915, settled into New York's Booth Theater, which opened in 1913. From *The Boss*, Edward Shelton's documentary-like shocker of 1911, to *Clarence*, the Booth Tarkington role which made Alfred Lunt a star eight years later, the World War I period was tapped for disappointments. What price glory now?

The most ambitious Bicentennial series has been that introduced by Washington's Kennedy Center with a welcome financial boost from Xerox. Actually this generous aid from non-theatrical commerce was a somewhat misleading advantage, for the initial $400,000 would not suffice to produce the ten announced productions. What it was intended to do was to prime the box office pump. With the anticipated success of the series's first production, *The Skin of Our Teeth*, its income would go toward launching its successors. As it fell out, the staging by José Quintero and the cast headed by gum-chewing Elizabeth Ashley proved wholly inadequate to the late Thornton Wilder's comedy, and its move to New York predictably failed.

Percy MacKaye's *The Scarecrow*, admired by the literati of 1911, which never had been a success, did no better 64 years later. Jason Robards was to have come next in William Gillette's 1894 *Too Much Johnson*, but his filming for *All the President's Men* forced him to bow out. Substitution of *Summer Brave*, William Inge's "preferred" subsequent version of his successful *Picnic*, did well in Washington but its choice of plunging into New York instead of touring nipped that one. Then came *Rip Van Winkle*, staged by Joshua Logan and the University of Tennessee at Knoxville with no gleam of why Joseph Jefferson had acted it for near on 40 years.

Three comparatively recent works followed, *Sweet Bird of Youth*, which would win Irene Worth a Tony for her brilliant performance, *The Royal Family*, which netted Ellis Rabb another Tony for his direction, and *Long Day's Journey Into Night*, a heedless disaster brought on by too much haste in the staging and comparisons with almost concurrent versions from the Potomac to the Pacific. Still to come at this June 1976 writing is *The Magnificent Yankee*, with history-minded Whitmore as Justice Oliver Wendell Holmes; and, possibly, one of several commissioned but still unfinished new Bicentennial plays.

Thus, even with birthday-minded productions elsewhere, as noted in Ella A.

Malin's Directory, our dramatic essays into the past have not been inspiriting.

Aside from theater's ever-shifting fashions, what has gone wrong? Perhaps two dependent factors.

Firstly, we as a nation are blatently disinterested in our past. Studies over a 25-year period show that we are increasingly ignorant of our national history, indeed proud to be so. "Relevance!" is the cry. To suggest the relationship of past to present strains TV-addicted attention spans.

Secondly, when we do attempt to perform plays of the past, that relevance disease proves communicable. We do not trust them. They must be yucked up, made either cutesy or camp.

Basically, nothing fades faster than theatrical fashions. Those who discovered Robert Lowell's *Old Glory* plays of only ten years ago lately have used the words "dismaying" or "banal." Lorraine Hansberry's *A Raisin in the Sun* survives as the musical *Raisin,* but the original is dubbed "irrelevant." Not surprisingly, black theater Bicentennial observations have, so far, been barely audible. And whatever happened to Jack Richardson, Jack Gelber and Ronald Ribman? Fashion is perishable.

Thus, that combination of what is expected to be a disinterested audience and direction distrustful of the plays has hardly done justice to this season of lookings back.

Our theater's history is barely considered by those who are of it. As Benjamin Franklin wrote the young painter, Charles Willson Peale, "The Arts have always travelled westward and there is no doubt of their flourishing hereafter on our side of the Atlantic . . . To America, one schoolmaster is worth a dozen poets and the invention of a machine or the improvement of an implement is of more importance than a masterpiece of Raphael . . . Nothing is good or beautiful but in the measure that is useful . . . Poetry, painting, music (and the stage as their embodiment) are all necessary and proper gratifications of a refined state of society but objectionable at an earlier period since their cultivation would make a taste for their enjoyment precede its means."

Franklin's "refined state of society" did not live in the New England of rocky soil and harsh consciences but in the South, Maryland, Virginia and South Carolina, where the rich soil and the waterways created a leisured planter class which had the time and means to look home to England for amenities. So when the Hallams, vanguard of English performers who continue to our own day, looked for audiences, they found them in Annapolis, Williamsburg or Charleston and they brought with them English plays, Shakespeare and their contemporary 18th century. This has been, continues to be, the root of our English-speaking theater. It is part of this tradition that the nation's two official "state theaters" are in the South, Virginia and Florida.

By 1876 the railways were booming and in the decade they covered 50,000 miles. Noted players had travelled by flatboats and wagons to appear with resident companies; now whole companies would ride the rails, bringing their own scenery with them.

In New York such companies as Wallack's, Daly's and Palmer's became independent of stars, but subsequent national stars would develop from them.

Also developing was a naturalistic style of performing. While rural settings yielded to urban themes, there was also strong interest in the new West while the nation observed its Centennial, the Sierra country and the Mormon persuasion. New York had its German, French and Yiddish companies, but such non-English-speaking stars as Modjeska, Bernhardt and Duse toured the rails from the theater's capital.

A hundred years later that is changing, dramatized on April 18, 1976, when, for the first time, New York's prime commercial theater salute went to a non-New York achievement, a Tony to Washington's Arena Stage. The newly-formed American Theater Critics Association picked Arena, founded in 1950, as a leader in the national movement, which now finds more actors working outside New York than in it, and playwrights making livings, albeit tenuous, without benefit of New York productions. The number of like theaters, however much they vary in quality, recalls Franklin's observation that the arts travel westward. The year's spate of exhibits about the performing arts, from the Kennedy Center and Folger Library to Yonkers's Hudson River Museum and points west, traces Ben's theory in vivid practise.

Nor is the regional quality to be scorned. People forget that this is a huge country and that the regional strains form the whole. In Texas, Margo Jones turned up playwrights who didn't have a chance for New York productions—Williams, Inge, Lawrence and Lee.

From Arena came a Pulitzer, *The Great White Hope* and from the Dallas Theater Center may come a Pulitzer for the 1976–77 season with Preston Jones's Texas trilogy, *The Last Meeting of the Knights of the White Magnolia, Lu Ann Hampton Laverty Oberlander* and *The Oldest Living Graduate.* Never have full New York acting companies visited and triumphed in the Soviet Union, but both Arena Stage and San Francisco's ACT—American Conservatory Theater—have done so. Seattle was chosen by George Abbott for his effort to turn *Twelfth Night* into *Music Is,* not an unprecedented tryout but one bound to lead others to more workable tryout conditions.

New York remains the dream stage for performers, but now "Who's Who in the Cast" refers to the existence of 30 to 40 regional theaters as background for one company. At the world Shakespeare Congress an international audience listened to a knowledgeable theater man from Oregon trace how B. Iden Payne's 50-odd active years of Shakespearean direction influenced our nation's stages. But Joseph Papp, of the New York Shakespeare Festival, and Robert Brustein, of Yale Drama School, pointedly ignored their platform colleague. Angus Bowmer 41 years earlier had founded the Oregon Shakespeare Festival, which neither ever has visited, though some of their players started there. East has much to learn of Franklin's burgeoning West and the rare ideal of a cultural democracy.

Equally meaningful in our 200th year is Congressional authorization of $200 million for fiscal 1977 to be split equally between the Endowments for the Arts and Humanities, with promise of 27 million more the following year. Also passed was an extra $15 million under a challenge grant program which allows government funds to be used to aid financially troubled institutions if matching funds are available on a three-to-one ratio.

For a nation which consistently has ignored the arts (excepting the relief-oriented WPA art projects of the 1930s) and tossed aside at its start the emoluments of kings, dukes and princes for the arts, this turnabout within a decade is breathtaking. The House vote of 279 to 59 this spring showed that the hard-core opposition had been whittled down from the usually 110 to 120 votes. Begun under President Johnson, increased by Nixon and again by Ford, this has been a revolution in political thinking.

Another area easily forgotten in toting up the Bicentennial year is the American College Theater Festival, which finds some 350 college and university theaters participating in 13 regional gatherings which, in sum, are more important than the springtime fortnight which brings "representative" productions and tyro players to the Kennedy Center.

Under a whole battalion of allied participants pulled together by Michael Kanin—the Dramatists' Guild, the American Playwrights Theater, the William Morris Agency, the David Library of the American Revolution, the Samuel French publishing house, the Irene Ryan Foundation, TV producer Norman Lear, the McDonald Corporation and Amoco—this encourages the writing and production of new plays, an area that's been going through the professional economic roof. What began, through the persistence of actress Peggy Wood, as a showcase for college theater, has evolved into a complex means of providing what the professional theater can ill risk, new plays. These can be prepared without union conditions, rehearsed on real stages with actual settings and props for long rehearsal periods. This season the colleges produced 44 new playwrights. In time, experienced playwrights will find a way to use such conditions.

Whatever comes of this, the public is learning that the colleges and universities have theaters far better equipped and more adaptable to new forms than those of the straitened commercial theater. The professionals become "guest artists" in scores of such places. Most of the tens of thousands of theater students never will earn a living in theater, whatever happens with private or public subsidies. But they will become more sophisticated, alert audiences and demanding supporters of the regional theaters. They will be the taste-makers of our future theater. Some have been working in the dinner theater sector, whose audiences are not the usual theatergoers but who, exposed to the better such places, "move up" to "real" theater. It's an easily overlooked but strong branch of today's professional theater.

A final area of Bicentennial production is outdoor drama, begun after Paul Green wearied of New York following his Pulitzer-winning *In Abraham's Bosom*. His *The Lost Colony* has completed its 38th summer at Manteo, N. C., near the site of the Wright Brothers' first flight and where, in 1587, the events of the play occurred.

In theater minds, outdoor drama ranks with pageants, a theatrical form to be avoided as the plague. But they have an appeal, especially in a history-conscious time. They always are based on some regional fact or legend, if possible performed on the spot, a fusion of drama, music, dance and spectacle. Summer 1976 found 54 of these operating under the guidance of the Institute of Outdoor Drama, at Chapel Hill, N. C., home of the Carolina Players, for which Green wrote the first play he ever saw. Green has remained a champion in this field, with nine productions scattered across last summer's map.

Kermit Hunter, who followed Green, had ten such works playing last summer. From Florida to Alaska, these offer a range of themes performed by paid or volunteer actors. Mostly they are drawn from the colleges and are not up to professional standards, but they expose hundreds of thousands to their first "round" actors and employ some who will become professionals. Andy Griffith played Sir Walter Raleigh for seven years in *The Lost Colony,* now directed by Joe Layton. Not so many years ago you probably would not have noticed in its cast a girl named Louise Fletcher. She won this year's top Oscar for her Nurse Ratchett in *One Flew Over the Cuckoo's Nest.*

So, although at the halfway point the Bicentennial has not been theatrically dazzling, it has been reflecting fresh, unmistakable vitality beneath the surface.

A DIRECTORY OF PROFESSIONAL REGIONAL THEATER

Compiled by Ella A. Malin

Professional 1975–76 programs and repertory productions by leading resident companies around the United States, plus selected Canadian programs and major Shakespeare festivals including that of Stratford, Ontario (Canada), are grouped in alphabetical order of their locations and listed in date order from May, 1975 to June, 1976. This list does not include Broadway, off-Broadway or touring New York shows (unless the local campany took some special part), summer theaters, single productions by commercial producers or college or other non-professional productions. The directory was compiled by Ella A. Malin for *The Best Plays of 1975–76* from information provided by the resident producing organizations at Miss Malin's request. First productions of full cast and credits, as available. Figures in parentheses following title give number of performances and date given is opening date, included whenever a record of these facts was obtainable from the producing managements.

Augmented reports on other than regional theater production in Los Angeles by Rick Talcove and Washington, D.C. by David Richards are included under those cities' headings in this listing. A section on U.S. dinner theater by Francine L. Trevens appears at the end of this Directory.

Summary

This Directory lists 453 productions of 368 plays (including one-acters, workshop and plays-in-progress productions) presented by 46 groups in 79 theaters in 44 cities (39 in the United States and 5 in Canada) during the 1975–76 season. Of these, 217 were American plays in 181 full productions and 36 workshop productions. 62 were world premieres, 13 were American or North American continental premieres, one was a professional premiere and 34 were workshop premieres. In addition, 19 groups presented 34 children's theater productions of 34 plays, plus Bicentennial revues of Americana in story, poetry and song; improvisational story theater and participation programs, at their theaters and on tours. Other groups presented their regular repertory at special matinees for junior and senior high school students.

Frequency of production of individual scripts was as follows:

 1   play received 6 productions (*The Last Meeting of the Knights of the White Magnolia*)
 2   plays received 5 productions (*Kennedy's Children, Our Town*)
 8   plays received 4 productions (*The Collected Works of Billy The Kid, Equus, Of Mice and Men, A Midsummer Night's Dream, Much Ado About Nothing, A Streetcar Named Desire, Scapino, The Winter's Tale*)
16   plays received 3 productions (*Ah, Wilderness!, Arms and the Man, Black Comedy, Born Yesterday, The Crucible, The Devil's Disciple, General Gorgeous, On the Harmfulness of Tobacco, King Lear, Long Day's Journey Into Night, The Little Foxes, Measure for Measure, Once In a Lifetime, Private Lives, Relatively Speaking, The Two Gentlemen of Verona*)
40   plays received 2 productions
302   plays received 1 production

Listed below are the playwrights who received the greatest number of productions. The first figure is the number of productions; the second figure (in parentheses) is the number of plays produced, including one-acters.

Shakespeare	39 (22)	Peter Shaffer	7	(2)
Williams	13 (10)	Wilder	6	(2)
O'Neill	12 (7)	Brecht	5	(5)
Shaw	10 (6)	Molière	5	(4)
Coward	9 (7)	Cohan	5	(3)
Chekhov	9 (6)	Robert Patrick	5	(1)
Arthur Miller	7 (4)	Ray Aranha	4	(4)
Moss Hart	7 (3)	Ayckbourn	4	(4)
George S. Kaufman	7 (3)	Ibsen	4	(4)
Preston Jones	7 (2)	Horovitz	4	(3)

Hellman	4	(2)	Kanin	3	(1)
Ondaatje	4	(1)	Michael McClure	3	(1)
Steinbeck	4	(1)	Joanna Glass	2	(3)
Beckett	3	(3)	Christie	2	(2)
Orton	3	(3)	Eliot	2	(2)
Albee	3	(2)	Feydeau	2	(2)
Bond	3	(2)	Genet	2	(2)
George Kelly	3	(2)	Gurney	2	(2)
MacArthur	3	(2)	Kalcheim	2	(2)
Odets	3	(2)	Mrozek	2	(2)
Pinter	3	(2)	Neil Simon	2	(2)
Stoppard	3	(2)			

ABINGDON, VA.

Barter Theater: Main Stage

(Founder, Robert Porterfield; artistic director-manager, Rex Partington; designers: scenery, Bennet Averyt, James Franklin; lighting, Richard Marsters, Michael Dalzell, Don Coleman; costumes, Sigrid Insull, Carr Garnett)

THE BEAUX' STRATAGEM (24). By George Farquhar. June 3, 1975. Director, George Black. With Gwyllum Evans, Robert Browning, Tina Cartmell, Steve Novelli, George C. Hosmer, Margaret Lunsford.

THE MALE ANIMAL (24). By James Thurber and Elliott Nugent. June 24, 1975. Director, Charles Maryan. With Holly Cameron, George C. Hosmer, Mary Carney, Eric Conger, Gwyllum Evans, Katherine Manning.

BROADWAY (24). By Philip Dunning and George Abbott. July 15, 1975. Director, Charles Maryan. With Gwyllum Evans, Robert Rutland, Tina Cartmell, Holly Cameron, Mary Carney, David Darlow.

THE DIARY OF ANNE FRANK (8). By Frances Goodrich and Albert Hackett; based on the book *Anne Frank: Diary of a Young Girl.* August 5, 1975. Director, Owen Phillips. With Mary Carney, Pete Edens, Katharine Manning, George C. Hosmer, Peggity Price.

THE DEVIL'S DISCIPLE (8). By George Bernard Shaw. August 12, 1975. Director, Kenneth Frankel. With John Spencer, Rex Partington, Tina Cartmell, Linde Hayen, Mary Carney, Gale McNeeley, Gwyllum Evans.

LIGHT UP THE SKY (24). By Moss Hart. August 19, 1975. Director, Owen Phillips. With Holly Cameron, Robert Rutland, David Darlow, Gloria Maddox.

BIOGRAPHY (24). By S.N. Behrman. September 9, 1975. Director, John Going. With Cleo Hollady, Gale McNeeley, Gwyllum Evans, George C. Hosmer, Eric Conger, Joseph Costa, Mary Carney, Margaret Lunsford.

SLEUTH (24). By Anthony Shaffer. September 30, 1975. Director, Kenneth Frankel. With Gwyllum Evans, George C. Hosmer, Stanley Rushton, Robin Mayfield, Liam McNulty.

THE GLASS MENAGERIE (36). By Tennessee Williams. April 6, 1976. Director, Owen Phillips. With Virginia Mattis, Dan Deitch, Sharon Morrison, John Christopher Jones.

YOU CAN'T TAKE IT WITH YOU (20). By George S. Kaufman and Moss Hart. May 4, 1976. Director, Charles Maryan. With Cleo Hollady, Peggity Price, Paul Meacham, Harry Ellerbe, Holly Cameron, Gale McNeeley.

Barter Theater: Children's Theater—Barter Playhouse

THE AMERICAN EXPERIMENT (55). Written and directed by Peggity Price, with Margaret Lunsford and the Apprentice Ensemble. July 2, 1975. Schools tour, September 23, 1975.

Barter Theater: Intern Program—Barter Playhouse

Intern Company: Candace Sofia Carnichelli, Stanley Flood, Sarah Hofman, Wayne Eliot Knight, Ellen Painter, Bob R. Patterson, Jocelyne M. Pierrel, Alicia Quintano, Carol N. Rogers, Tyson Stephenson.

TWO ON AN ISLAND (25). By Elmer Rice. July 4, 1975. Director-designer, Owen Phillips.

LA RONDE (11). By Arthur Schnitzler. August 8, 1975. Director-designer, Eric Davis.

SUBREAL (10). By Daffy Nathanson. September 5, 1975 (world premiere). Director, Gloria Maddox; designer, Daffy Nathanson.
Mama ....Candace Sofia Carnicelli

Morey	Stanley Flood
Crystal	Sarah Hofman
Papa	Wayne Eliot Knight
Mohave	Ellen Painter
Red	Bob Patterson
Jackie	Jocelyne M. Pierrel
Mayor Mickey	Alicia Quintano
Litening	Carol N. Rogers
Stranger	Tyson Stephenson

Note: Members of the Barter Intern Company were selected by auditions around the country to participate in a two-year training/performance program leading to the formation of a resident company. They perform at the Barter Playhouse and on tours throughout the state.

Barter Theater: Guest Production

AN ECCENTRIC MIME SHOW with Avner Eisenberg. August 4, 1975.

Barter Theater Tidewater Season: Chrysler Museum Theater, Norfolk

YOU CAN'T TAKE IT WITH YOU (36). By George S. Kaufman and Moss Hart. January 29, 1976. With Cleo Holladay, Peggity Price, George Salerno, Harry Ellerbe, Holly Cameron, Gale McNeeley, Mary Carney.

THE DIARY OF ANNE FRANK (28). By Frances Goodrich and Albert Hackett; based on *Anne Frank: Diary of a Young Girl*. February 9, 1976. Director, Owen Phillips. With Cleo Hollady, Mary Carny, Pete Edens, Paul Collins.

TEN NIGHTS IN A BARROOM (18). By William W. Pratt; adapted by Fred Carmichael. March 11, 1976. Director, John Olon-Scrymgeour. With the Barter Theater Company.

BIOGRAPHY (14). By S. N. Behrman. April 1, 1976. Director, John Going. With Cleo Holladay, Gwyllum Evans, Gale McNeeley.

ASHLAND, ORE.

Oregon Shakespearean Festival: Elizabethan Theater (outdoors)

(Founder, Angus L. Bowmer; producing director, Jerry Turner; general manager, William W. Patton. Designers: scenery, Richard L. Hay; lighting, Steven A. Maze; costumes, Jeannie Davidson)

ALL'S WELL THAT ENDS WELL (32). By William Shakespeare. June 20, 1975. Director, Jon Jory. With Randi Douglas, Judd Parkin, Todd Oleson, le Clanche du Rand, Philip L. Jones, James Edmondson, Jeff Brooks, Christine Healy, Carmi Boushey.

HENRY VI, Part 1 (31). By William Shakespeare. June 21, 1975. Director, Will Huddleston. With Peter Silbert, Todd Oleson, James Edmondson, Jeff Brooks, William Moreing,

Barry Mulholland, Carmi Boushey, Randi Douglas.

ROMEO AND JULIET (31). By William Shakespeare. June 22, 1975. Director, James Edmondson. With Mark D. Murphey, Christine Healy, Randi Douglas, Denis Arndt, Eric Booth Miller, Michael Kevin Moore, Margaret Rubin, David L. Boushey, JoAnn Johnson Patton, Larry R. Ballard.

Oregon Shakespearean Festival: Angus Bowmer Theater (indoors)

LONG DAY'S JOURNEY INTO NIGHT (32). By Eugene O'Neill. June 21, 1975. Director, Jerry Turner. With Michael Kevin Moore, Jean Smart, Denis Arndt, William M. Hurt, Katherine James.

THE WINTER'S TALE (31). William Shakespeare. June 22, 1975. Director, Audrey Stanley. With James Edmondson, le Clanche du Rand, Brad O'Neil, Todd Reichenbach, Randi

Douglas, Philip L. Jones, Michael Horton, Carmi Boushey.

CHARLEY'S AUNT (30). By Brandon Thomas. June 24, 1975. Director, Pat Patton. With Mark D. Murphey, Judd Parkin, Peter Silbert, Christine Healy, Adrienne Alexander, Shirley Patton, Joseph De Salvio, Michael Kevin Moore.

Oregon Shakespearean Festival Stage II: Angus Bowmer Theater

(Designers: scenery, Richard L. Hay; lighting, Thomas White; costumes, Jeannie Davidson)

THE DEVIL'S DISCIPLE (15). By George Bernard Shaw. February 13, 1976. Director, Michael Leibert. With Joseph De Salvio, Christine Healy, Barry Mulholland, Denis Arndt, Ruth Cox, Brian Thompson.

BRAND (14). By Henrik Ibsen; adapted and translated by Jerry Turner. February 14, 1976 (matinee). Director, Jerry Turner. With Denis Arndt, Christine Healy, Virginia M. Bingham, Kathleen Worley.

THE TAVERN (15). By George M. Cohan. February 14, 1976 (evening). Director, Pat Patton. With Ron Woods, Larry R. Ballard, Kathleen Worley, Christine Healy, William Moreing, Will Huddleston, David Williams.

THE COMEDY OF ERRORS (14). By William Shakespeare. February 15, 1976. Director, Will Huddleston. With Cal Winn, Brian Mulholland, Barry Mulholland, Allen Nause, Joseph De Salvio, Virginia Bingham, Roberta Levitow, Ruth Cox.

BALTIMORE

Center Stage

(Artistic director, Jacques Cartier; managing director, Peter W. Culman.)

TARTUFFE (32). By Molière; English verse translation by Richard Wilbur. December 9, 1975. Director, Jacques Cartier; scenery, David Jenkins; lighting, Roger Morgan; costumes, Nancy Potts. With Henry Thomas, George Ede, Jane House, Vivienne Shub.

BUSY BEE GOOD FOOD ALL NIGHT DELICIOUS and BORDERS (32). By Charles Eastman. January 13, 1976 (world premiere). Directors, *Busy Bee* Jacques Cartier, *Borders* Charles Eastman; scenery and costumes, Kert Lundell; lighting, Roger Morgan.
Borders
Dot ....Ruth Gilbert
Larry ....Davis Hall
Arnold ....George Ede
Busy Bee Good Food All Night Delicious
Colona ....Helen Hanft
Winona ....Trinity Thompson
Roy ....Peter Vogt
    Time: The recent past. Place: A beach bar and grill on the Southern California coast. One intermission.

DREAM ON MONKEY MOUNTAIN (32). By Derek Walcott. February 17, 1976. Direc-

tor, Albert Laveau; scenery, Eugene Lee; lighting, Roger Morgan; choreographer, Carol La Chapelle; musical director, Andrew Beddeau. With Obba Babatunde, Anthony Chisholm, Charles Grant-Greene, Sam Singleton, David Pendleton, Clayton Corbin, Mame Calloway, Sullivan Walker.

OLD TIMES (32). By Harold Pinter. March 23, 1976. Director, Stan Wojewodski Jr.; scenery, Peter Harvey; lighting, Ian Calderon; costumes, Elizabeth P. Palmer. With Patricia Gage, George Taylor, Lois Markle.

THE CHERRY ORCHARD (32). By Anton Chekhov. April 27, 1976. Director, Jacques Cartier; scenery and costumes, John Jensen; lighting, Gilbert V. Hemsley Jr. With Patricia Gage, Henry Thomas, George Morfogen, Patricia Pearcy, Tana Hicken, Anita Keal, Paul C. Thomas.

THE REAL INSPECTOR HOUND by Tom Stoppard and BLACK COMEDY by Peter Shaffer (32). June 1, 1976. Director, Stan Wojewodski Jr.; scenery, Peter Harvey; lighting, Ian Calderon; costumes, Liz Covey. With

Christine Baranski, Lee Corbet, Paddy Croft, Patricia Gage, Charles O. Lynch, Andrew Rohrer, Henry Thomas, Paul C. Thomas, Dan Szelag, John Wylie.

Note: During the 1975-76 season, The Young People's Theater of Center Stage, a professional touring company, produced three plays for elementary and high schools in Maryland's 23 counties, and for junior high schools in Baltimore City. *Take Me to My Planet* by Mary Koisch, the musical adventure of a 21st Century space child, was directed by Stan Wojewodski Jr, with Susan Greenhill, Kila Kitu, Kaeren Peregrin, Daniel Szelag; *The Primary English Class* by Israel Horowitz, directed by Stan Wojewodski Jr., with Jay Ginsberg, Walter Hicklin, Michael Jeter; *The Clowns' Corner Concert* by Ray Aranha, directed by Jeffrey O. Rodman, with Larry Riley, Thelma Carter, Amandina Lihamba, Edward Hambleton.

BERKELEY, CALIF.

Berkeley Repertory Theater

(Producing director, Michael Leibert)

MUCH ADO ABOUT NOTHING (21). By William Shakespeare. June 13, 1975. Director, Michael Addison; scenery and costumes, John Freimann; lighting, Joan Liepman. With Holly Barron, Joe Spano, Terry Wills, Linda Lee Johnson, Paul Laramore.

HAMLET (21). By William Shakespeare. July 11, 1975. Director, Douglas Johnson; scenery, John Freimann; lighting, Matthew Cohen; costumes, Diana Smith. With Joe Spano, Linda Lee Johnson, Karen Ingenthron, Michael Renner, Rick Casorla, Terry Wills.

THE MERCHANT OF VENICE (21). By William Shakespeare. August 8, 1975. Director, Michael Leibert; scenery and costumes, John Freimann; lighting, Joan Liepman. With Robert Haswell, Anne Swift, Terry Wills, Sally Livingston, Paul Laramore.

SEVEN KEYS TO BALDPATE (32). By George M. Cohan; based on the novel by Earl Derr Biggers. September 19, 1975. Director, Douglas Johnson; scenery and costumes, Lesley Skannal; lighting, Joan Liepman. With Anne Swift, Michael Leibert, Terry Wills, Dale Elliott, Sally Livingston, Rick Casorla.

THE ICEMAN COMETH (32). By Eugene O'Neill. October 31, 1975. Director, Michael Leibert; scenery, Jeff Whitman; lighting, Matthew Cohen; costumes, Diana Smith. With Terry Mills, Joe Spano, Robert Haswell, Robert Hirschfeld, Linda Lee Johnson, Anne Swift, Holly Baron.

ARSENIC AND OLD LACE (32). By Joseph Kesselring. December 12, 1975. Director, Michael Addison; scenery, Ron Pratt and Gene Angell; costumes, Lesley Skannal; lighting, Joan Liepman. With Holly Barron, Karen Ingenthron, Anne Swift, Paul Laramore.

CAT ON A HOT TIN ROOF (32). By Tennessee Williams. January 30, 1976. Director, Douglas Johnson; scenery, Ron Pratt; lighting, Joan Liepman; costumes, Diana Smith. With Holly Barron, Joe Spano, Karen Ingenthron, Robert Hirschfeld.

OF MICE AND MEN (32). By John Steinbeck. March 12, 1976. Director, Michael Leibert; scenery, Jeff Whitman; lighting, Joan Liepman; costumes, Lesley Skannal. With Richard Marion, Terry Wills, Robert Haswell, John Oldham, Rick Casorla, Linda Lee Johnson.

YANKEE DOODLE (32). Book and Lyrics by Douglas Johnson; music by John Aschenbrenner. April 23, 1975. Director, Douglas Johnson; scenery and costumes, Lesley Skannal; lighting, Matthew Cohen. With Anne Swift, Joe Spano, Shelly Lipkin, Sheldon Feldner, Karen Ingenthron, Paul Laramore, Holly Barron.

BUFFALO

Studio Arena Theater

(Executive producer, Neal Du Brock)

BUTLEY (29). By Simon Gray. October 10, 1975. Director, Richard Barr; scenery and costumes, Frank J. Boros; lighting, David Zierk. With Tony Tanner, Katherine Bruce, Peter Burnell, Nancy Cushman, Bill Herndon, Andrea Stonorov, Bill VandeSande.

SCAPINO! (36). By Frank Dunlop and Jim Dale, adapted from Molière's *Les Fourberies de Scapin*. November 7, 1975. Director, Grover Dale; scenery and costumes, Frank J. Boros; lighting, David Zierk. With John Christopher Jones, John Abajian, Julia Barr, Denny Dillon, Mordecai Lawner, Tom Mardirosian, Albert Sanders, James Seymour.

A DOLL'S HOUSE (36). By Henrik Ibsen. December 12, 1975. Director, Stephen Porter; scenery and lighting, David F. Segal; costumes, Clifford Capone. With Betsy Palmer, James Cahill, Don Gantry, Bernie McInerney, Patricia O'Connell.

EQUUS (36). By Peter Shaffer. January 16, 1976. Director, Paul Giovanni; scenery and masks, Robert F. Van Nutt; lighting, Robby Monk; costumes, Clifford Capone; mime, Richard Clairmont. With Jeremiah Sullivan, Jonathan Howard Jones, Laurinda Barrett, Carol Mayo Jenkins, Jim Oyster, Peggy Whitton, Ben Fuhrman.

THE MAGIC SHOW (37). Book by Bob Randall; songs by Stephen Schwartz; magic by Doug Henning. February 20, 1976. Director, Jay Fox; scenery, Studio Arena Theater Scene Shop; lighting, Herb Vogler; costumes, Randy Barcelo; musical director, Peter Larson; dance arrangements, David Spangler. Original director-choreographer, Grover Dale. With Joseph Abaldo, Richard Balestrino, Serhij Bohdan, Gwendolyn Coleman, Connie Day, W. P. Drémak, Anthony Innèo, Rose Anna Mineo, John-Ann Washington, Rick Wessler.

A LITTLE NIGHT MUSIC (35). Book by Hugh Wheeler, suggested by a film by Ingmar Bergman; music and lyrics by Stephen Sondheim. March 26, 1976. Director-choreographer, Tony Tanner; scenery, Robert D. Soule; lighting, Robby Monk; costumes, Clifford Capone; musical director, Dorothy Opalach. With Rosemary Prinz, William Chapman, Paula Lawrence.

Studio Arena Theater: Guest Production

REPLIKA (28). Conceived and directed by Józef Szajna. April 30, 1976 (American premiere). Music by Boguslaw Schaffer. With Ewa Kozlowska, Irena Jun, Stanislaw Brudny, Antoni Pszoniak, Józef Wieczorek. A wordless odyssey through the holocaust, depicting the indomitable spirit of man, tempered by the inhumanity directed against him by himself. Performed without an intermission.

BURLINGTON, VT.

Champlain Shakespeare Festival: Royall Tyler Theater, University of Vermont

(Producer-director, Edward J. Feidner)

OUR TOWN (19). By Thornton Wilder. July 9, 1975. Director, Edward J. Feidner; scenery, W. M. Schenk; lighting, Charles Touers; costumes, Polly Smith. With Armin Shimerman, Robert Ousley, Rita Litton, Charles Touers, Jeffrey DeMunn, Susan Selig, Susan Donlop.

MUCH ADO ABOUT NOTHING (16). By William Shakespeare. July 16, 1975. Director, John Milligan; scenery, W. M. Schenk; lighting, Keith Gaylord, Charles Touers; costumes, Polly Smith; choreography, Ruthmary O'Brien. With Rita Litton, Dennis Lipscomb, Robert Ousley, Marcus Smythe, Margaret Klenck, Gerard E. Moses.

TIMON OF ATHENS (9). By William Shakespeare. August 6, 1975. Director, Edward J. Feidner; scenery, W. M. Schenk; lighting, Ed Tracy, Charles Touers; costumes, Polly Smith. With Gerard E. Moses, John Milligan, Marcus Smythe, Tom Carlisle, Robert Ousley, Jeffrey DeMunn, Dennis Lipscomb.

CHARLOTTESVILLE, VA.

Heritage Repertory Company: Culbreth Theater—University of Virginia

(Artistic Director, George Black; producing director, David W. Weiss; director of theater, Roger Boyle)

UNDER THE GASLIGHT (13). By Augustin Daly. June 26, 1975. Director, George Black. With Robert M. Hefley, Sally Drayer, Katherine Mary Brown, Lisa Sloan, Lee Ewing.

THE CRUCIBLE (13). By Arthur Miller. July 1, 1975. Director, Edward Stern. With David Cupp, Katherine Mary Brown, Lee Ewing, Robert M. Hefley, Nancy Boykin, Lisa Sloan.

FASHION (12). By Anna Cora Mowatt. July 4, 1975. Director, Edward Stern. With Sally Drayer, Joan Stapleton, Peter Moore, Jerry Bradley, David Cupp.

AH, WILDERNESS! (13). By Eugene O'Neill. July 8, 1975. Director, George Black. With David Cupp, Katherine Mary Brown, Peter McGehee, Robert M. Hefley, Joan Stapleton.

Designers: scenery, William C. Molyneux; lighting, James St. Germain; costumes, Lois Garren. Production Stage Manager, Bronson Platt.

CHICAGO

Goodman Theater Center: Goodman Theater—Main Stage

(Artistic director, William Woodman; managing director, John Economos)

OUR TOWN (35). By Thornton Wilder. October 3, 1975. Director, George Keathley; scenery, Joseph Nieminski; lighting, Gilbert V. Hemsley Jr.; costumes, James Edmund Brady. With Tony Mockus, George Womack, Avril Gentles, Jane Groves, David-James Carroll, Harriet Hall.

BENITO CERENO (35). By Robert Lowell; based on the novella, *The Piazza Tales* by Herman Melville. November 14, 1975. Director, Michael Montel; scenery, David Jenkins; lighting, Gilbert V. Hemsley Jr.; costumes, James Edmund Brady. With Tony Mockus, Gus Kaikkonen, Robert Guillaume, Paul Butler, Thomas A. Stewart, Lenard Norris.

MOURNING BECOMES ELECTRA (35). By Eugene O'Neill. January 2, 1976. Director, William Woodman; scenery, John Jensen; lighting, F. Mitchell Dana; costumes, James Edmund Brady. With Rosemary Murphy, Laura Esterman, Ben Masters, Robert Murch, Thomas A. Stewart, Tony Mockus.

THE LAST MEETING OF THE KNIGHTS OF THE WHITE MAGNOLIA (35). By Preston Jones. February 13, 1976. Director, Harold Stone; scenery, Joseph Nieminski;

lighting, F. Mitchell Dana; costumes, John David Ridge. With John Wardwell, Gordon Oas-Heim, Douglas Fisher, Jack Wallace, W. H. Macy, Brad O'Hare.

OUR FATHER'S FAILING (35). By Israel Horovitz. March 26, 1976 (world premiere). Director, John Dillon; scenery, Stuart Wurtzel; lighting, Arden Fingerhut; costumes, John David Ridge.

Sam ....Dominic Chianese
Pa ....Joseph Leon
Alfred ....Lawrence Pressman
Emily ....Lanna Saunders
  The play alternates between the porch and the backyard of the insane asylum and the living room of the Wakefield house in late fall. Act I: The asylum. Act II, Scene 1: The house. Scene 2: The asylum. Act III, Scene 1: The house. Scene 2: The house.

THE DEVIL'S DISCIPLE (35). By George Bernard Shaw. May 7, 1976. Director, William Woodman; scenery, James E. Maronek; lighting, Patricia Collins; costumes, Virgil C. Johnson. With Robert Murch, Allison Giglio, Kenneth Welsh, Pat Fraser, Wesley Ann Pfenning; Don Marston, Brian Murray.

Goodman Theater Center: Stage Two—Ruth Page Auditorium

AMERICAN BUFFALO (20). By David Mamet. October 23, 1975 (world premiere). Director, Gregory Mosher; scenery, Michael Merritt; lighting, Robert Christen; assistant director, Kathleen Hume.

Donny Dubrow..............J. J. Johnston
Walter Cole ....Bernard Erhard
Bobby................. William H. Macy

THREE PLAYS OF THE YUAN DYNASTY (10). Adapted and directed by June Pyskacek; translated by Liu Jung-en; music, Gerald W. Holbrook. December 4, 1975. Scenery, Rick Paul; lighting, Robert Christen; costumes, Uta Olson. With Dan Ziskie, Keith

Szarabayka, Felicity LaFortune, Michael Tezla, Glenn Kovacevich, Marge Kotlisky.

CHICAGO by Sam Shepard, directed by Dennis Zacek; and THE LOCAL STIGMATIC by Heathcote Williams, directed by Gary Houston (10). January 29, 1976. Scenery, Paul K. Basten; lighting, Robert Christen, costumes, Marsha Kowal. With Jim Jacobs, Mark Nutter, Arlene Schulfer, Sara Asher, Warren Leming, Jeanette Goldberg, Dan Ziskie, Leonard Kraft.

STATUES and THE BRIDGE AT BELHARBOUR (10). By Janet L. Neipris. April 22,

DISTINGUISHED PERFORMANCES

ENSEMBLES: *Above,* Barry Nelson, Ken Howard, Estelle Parsons, Carole Shelley with (on floor) Richard Benjamin and Paula Prentiss in *The Norman Conquests; below,* Sam Levene, Eva Le Gallienne, Joseph Maher, Mary Layne, Rosemary Harris and Mary Louise Wilson in *The Royal Family.*

John Wood as Henry Carr in *Travesties*

Irene Worth as Princess Kosmonopolis in *Sweet Bird of Youth* (FAR RIGHT)

Katharine Hepburn Mrs. Basil in *A Matter Gravity* (FAR LEFT)

George C. Scott as Wil Loman in *Death of Salesman*

Ron Leibman as one of many characters in *Rich & Famous*

Julie Harris as Emily Dickinson in *The Belle of Amherst* (FAR RIGHT)

Vanessa Redgrave Ellida in *The Lady Fro the Sea* (FAR LEFT)

Mako as Reciter in *Paci ic Overtures*

Raul Julia as Mack the Knife in *Threepenny Opera*

Linda Hopkins as Bessie Smith in *Me and Bessie* (FAR RIGHT)

Ian Richardson as Henry Higgins (FAR LEFT) and George Rose as Alfred P. Doolittle in *My Fair Lady*

Nicol Williamson as Henry VIII in *Rex*

Sam Waterston as Hamlet in *Hamlet* (FAR RIGHT)

Dorian Harewood as Carlyle in *Streamers* (FAR LEFT)

Shirley Knight as Carla in *Kennedy's Children*

IN DRAMA, A VERY GOOD YEAR: David Rabe's prizewinning *Streamers* (*left, on opposite page*), with Peter Evans, Mark Metcalf (who replaced Paul Rudd), Terry Alexander, Dolph Sweet and Kenneth McMillan; Lanford Wilson's *Serenading Louie* at Circle Repertory Company (*above*), with Trish Hawkins, Michael Storm, Edward J. Moore and Tanya Berezin; and Milan Stitt's *The Runner Stumbles* (*below*), with Nancy Donohue and Stephen Joyce

BRITISH COMEDIES

Above, John Wood and John Bott in Tom Stoppard's *Travesties; left,* Ian Trigger and Jean Marsh in *Habeas Corpus* by Alan Bennett, both plays imported from London.

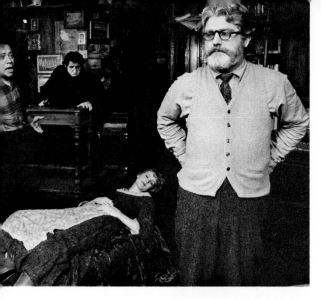

KNOCK TWICE: *Left,* Jules Feiffer's *Knock Knock* with Daniel Seltzer, Judd Hirsch, Nancy Snyder and Neil Flanagan in the original Circle Repertory production; *below,* the same scene restaged with a new Broadway cast of John Heffernan, Lynn Redgrave, Leonard Frey and Charles Durning

AMERICAN COMEDIES

Below left, Kathy Bates, Jane Galloway and Susan Merson in *Vanities* by Jack Heifner; *below right,* Diane Keaton, Richard Libertini and Sol Frieder in *The Primary English Class* by Israel Horovitz

N.Y. SHAKESPEARE
PUBLIC THEATER

Joseph Papp's downtown season included David Freeman's *Jesse and the Bandit Queen* with Barry Primus and Dixie Carter (*above*), who replaced Kevin O'Connor and Pamela Payton-Wright; Thomas Babe's *Rebel Women* (*left*) with Kathryn Walker and David Dukes as General Sherman; and Ntozake Shange's *For Colored Girls Who Have Considered Suicide/ When the Rainbow is Enuf* (*below*) with the author, Rise Collins, Paula Moss, Janet League, Aku Kadago, Laurie Carlos and Trazana Beverly

KENNEDY'S CHILDREN —*Left, from top,* Don Parker, Shirley Knight, Douglas Travis, Michael Sacks, Barbara Montgomery and Kaiulani Lee in the play by Robert Patrick

THE POISON TREE—*Below,* Cleavon Little, Northern J. Calloway (*at top*) and Dick Anthony Williams in prison drama by Ronald Ribman

REPLIKA—*Above,* a holocaust scene as presented by Joseph Szajna's Studio Theater, a Polish pantomime troupe

PACIFIC OVERTURES—*Above,* Boris Aronson's sketch of one of his Tony and Maharam Award-winning scene designs; *below,* Soon-Teck Oh, Yuki Shimoda, Alvin Ing, Conrad Yama, Isao Sato and Freddy Mao in a scene from the John Weidman-Stephen Sondheim-Hugh Wheeler-Harold Prince show

THREEPENNY OPERA

Above, in foreground, Elizabeth Wilson and C. K. Alexander as Mr. and Mrs. Peachum; *right,* Ellen Greene as Jenny Diver and Raul Julia as Mack the Knife in Joseph Papp's revival of the Brecht-Weill musical at the Vivian Beaumont

Patricia Zipprodt's sketches for her *Chicago* costume designs are pictured on these pages; *above,* the chorus of the Ebb-Kander-Fosse musical; *below, left to right,* costumes for Gwen Verdon, Jerry Orbach and Chita Rivera (a photo synopsis of *Chicago* appears elsewhere in this volume)

Cecil Beaton's *My Fair Lady* designs were recreated for the 1976 revival, as pictured above in the Embassy Ball scene

THE ROBBER BRIDEGROOM—*Above,* Kevin Kline and Patti LuPone in a scene from the Uhry-Waldman musical. SO LONG, 174th STREET—*Below,* Robert Morse and friends in the Stein-Daniels show directed by Burt Shevelove

TUSCALOOSA'S CALLING ME . . . BUT I'M NOT GOING —*Above,* Patti Perkins, Renny Temple and Len Gochman in the off-Broadway musical revue

REVIVALS

Right, Michael Moriarty and Jason Robards in American Bicentennial Theater production of *Long Day's Journey Into Night at the* Brooklyn Academy of Music

Below left, Ben Gazzara and Colleen Dewhurst in Edward Albee's *Who's Afraid of Virginia Woolf?* under the author's direction; *below right,* Roy Poole and Meryl Streep in Tennessee Williams's *27 Wagons Full of Cotton,* produced on the Broadway schedule of the Phoenix Theater

Above, Ron Randell, Lynn Redgrave, Philip Bosco, Ruth Gordon, Milo O'Shea and Edward Herrmann in *Mrs. Warren's Profession* produced by Joseph Papp at Lincoln Center

Left, Maureen Stapleton in Circle in the Square's *The Glass Menagerie*

Below, Kim Hunter and William Roe-Rick in the Roundabout's production of *The Cherry Orchard*

1976. Director, Gregory Mosher; scenery, Brian Laczko; lighting, Robert Christen; costumes, Marsha Kowal. With Judith Ivey, Mike Genovese.

Goodman Theater Center: Stage Two—Victory Gardens Theater II

DANDELION WINE (10). By Ray Bradbury; arranged and adapted by Peter John Bailey. March 18, 1976 (world premiere). Director, William Woodman; scenery, Michael Merritt; lighting, Robert Christen; costumes, Maggie Bodwell; sound, David Rice; assistant director, Kevin O'Brien.

Douglas Spaulding .... Scott Stevens
Tom Spaulding .... Scott Larsson
John Huff .... Tom McDonald
Father; Leo Auffman;
    Bill Forrester .... Danny Goldring
Grandfather; Mr. Sanderson;
    Mr. Triden .... Don Marston
Mother; Lena Auffman;
    Nurse; Lavinia Nebbs .... Cordis Fejer
Helen Bentley .... Jane MacIver
Colonel Freeleigh; Jonas .... Nesbitt Blaisdell
Helen Loomis; Great Grandma . Fern Persons
    Time: Summer 1928. Place: Green Town, Ill. One intermission. This production was a revision and re-staging of the play tried out in the Phoenix Theater's Side Show by William Woodman.

Goodman School of Drama: Children's Theater—Goodman Theater

(Dean, Charles McGaw; associate dean, Rea Warg)

TOM SAWYER (33). Book and lyrics by Sarah Marie Schlesinger; music by Michael Dansicker; adapted from Mark Twain's The Adventures of Tom Sawyer. October 18, 1975. Director, Ned Schmidtke; scenery, Eric Fielding; lighting, Dale Kovarik; costumes, Sandi Kabins; choreographer, Diane Parker. With Michael Riney, Anne Atkins, Carol Lang, Stuart Smith, Randy Snyder.

THE WIZARD OF OZ (36). By Adele Thane; music and lyrics by Brian Alan Lasser; adapted from the story by L. Frank Baum. December 6, 1975. Director, Dean Button; scenery, Gary Cartwright; lighting, Marc A. Warshell; costumes, Kaye Nottbusch; music director, Brian Alan Lasser; choreographer, Dawn Mora. With Nora Marie Cole, Jo Anne Gellman, Mary Beth Cobleigh, Tom Branthaven, Glenn Markgraf, Stanley Winiarski, Jim Shankman.

COYOTE AND HIS BROTHERS (31). By Lin Wright; adapted from Anna Moore Shaw's Tales of the Pima Indians. January 31, 1976. Director, Eleanor Logan; scenery, Eric Fielding; lighting, Curtis M. Jacobson; costumes, Julie Jackson. With Frank Archibeque, Nancy Mellon, Patrick Waddell, James Ragona.

YANKEE DOODLE (41). By Aurand Harris; music by Mort Stine. March 20, 1976. Director, Russell Chesson; scenery, Dean Taucher; lighting, G. E. Naselius; costumes, Judy Mackowsky; music director, Errol Pearlman; choreographer, Estelle Spector. With John Durkin and a Male and Female Chorus.

Note: The Goodman Drama School also presented the Goodman Studio, from November 6, 1975–May 9, 1976, Productions were: Speak of the Devil by Tom H. Sand and Herbert Hecht, director, Estelle Spector; Camino Real by Tennessee Williams, director, Joseph Slowik; Tobacco Road by Jack Kirkland; director, Libby Appel; Macbeth by William Shakespeare, director, Jack Jones; When You Comin' Back, Red Ryder? by Mark Medoff, director, Anthony Petito; Ah, Wilderness! by Eugene O'Neill, director, David Avcollie.

CINCINNATI

Playhouse in the Park

(Producing director, Michael Murray; general manager, Robert W. Tolan)

DEATH OF A SALESMAN (32). By Arthur Miller. October 21, 1975. Director, Michael Murray; scenery and lighting, Neil Peter Jampolis; costumes, Annie Peacock Warner. With Sam Gray, Paul Vincent, Richard Kline, Dorothy Stinnette.

RELATIVELY SPEAKING (32). By Alan Ayckbourn. November 25, 1975. Director, John Going; scenery, Eric Head; lighting, Mark Kruger; costumes, Annie Peacock Warner. With Leah Chandler, Jo Henderson, Douglas Jones, Robert Nichols.

THE LITTLE FOXES (32). By Lillian Hellman. January 13, 1976. Director, Israel Hicks; scenery and lighting, Neil Peter Jampolis; costumes, Annie Peacock Warner. With Jan Farrand, Louis Edmonds, Jo Henderson, Bryan Hull, Robert Baines, Beatrice Winde.

WHAT THE BUTLER SAW (32). By Joe Orton. February 17, 1976. Director, Michael Bawtree; scenery and lighting, Neil Peter Jampolis, Annie Peacock Warner. With Linda Alper, Philip Anglim, I. M. Hobson, Eric House, Jeanette Landis, Ronald Steelman.

THE CONTRAST (32). By Royall Tyler. March 23, 1976. Director, Michael Murray; scenery, John Lee Beatty; lighting, Mark Kruger; costumes, Elizabeth Covey. With Phillip Anglim, Jim Broaddus, Lisa Hemphill, I. M. Hobson, Tom Mardirosian, Fred McCarren, Monica Merryman, Lynn Milgrim, Pamela Rohs, Claudia Zahn.

WHERE'S CHARLEY? (32). Book by George Abbott, music and lyrics by Frank Loesser; based on Brandon Thomas' *Charley's Aunt*. May 4, 1976. Director, Michael Murray; scenery and lighting, Neil Peter Jampolis; costumes, Annie Peacock Warner; musical director, Fred Goldrich; musical staging, Nora Peterson. With Lee Roy Reams, Dan Diggles, Sally Mitchell, Marti Rolph, I. M. Hobson, Adrienne Angel, Keith Mackey.

CLEVELAND

The Cleveland Play House: Euclid—77th Street Theater

(Managing Director, Richard Oberlin)

IN CELEBRATION (22). By David Storey. October 1, 1975. Director, Larry Tarrant; scenery, Richard Gould; lighting, Richard Coumbs; costumes, Harriet Cone. With Paul Lee, Evie McElroy, June Gibbons, Daniel Desmond, Jonathan Bolt, Victor Caroli, Richard Halverson.

BINGO (27). By Edward Bond. October 31, 1975 (American premiere). Director, Jonathan Bolt; scenery, Richard Gould; lighting, Richard Coumbs; costumes, Joe Dale Lunday.
Shakespeare . . . . Robert Allman
Judith . . . . Jo Farwell
Old Man . . . . Richard Halverson
Young Woman . . . . Sharon Bicknell
Old Woman . . . . June Gibbons
William Combe . . . . J. D. Sutton
Son . . . . Dale Place
Joan . . . . Lizbeth Mackay
Jerome . . . . James Richards
Wally . . . . Daniel Desmond
Ben Jonson . . . . Jonathan Farwell

RELATIVELY SPEAKING (31). By Alan Ayckbourn. December 5, 1975. Director, Evie McElroy; scenery, Richard Gould; lighting, Russell Lowe; costumes, Joe Dale Lunday. With James Richards, Lizbeth Mackay, Richard Halverson, June Gibbons.

THE DARK AT THE TOP OF THE STAIRS (23). By William Inge. January 23, 1976. Director, Larry Tarrant; scenery, Timothy Zupancic; lighting, Richard Coumbs; costumes, Joe Dale Lunday. With Lizbeth Mackay, Kenneth Albers, Christina Moore, Sharon Bicknell, Allen Leatherman, Evie McElroy.

THE LAST MEETING OF THE KNIGHTS OF THE WHITE MAGNOLIA (22). By Preston Jones. February 27, 1976. Director, Larry Tarrant; scenery, Barbara Leatherman; lighting, R. O. Wulff, Tim Zupancic; costumes, Joe Dale Lunday. With Ray Walston, Richard Oberlin, Vaughn McBride, Allen Leatherman, Mark Gardner.

SCAPINO! (23). By Jim Dale and Frank Dunlop; adapted from Molière's *Les Fourberies de Scapin*. April 2, 1976. Director, Paul Lee; scenery, Timothy Zupancic; lighting, Richard Coumbs; costumes, Richard Gould. With William Rhys, Robert Snook, Richard Halverson, Dale Place, Dee Hoty.

The Cleveland Play House: Drury Theater

FIRST MONDAY IN OCTOBER (21). By Robert E. Lee and Jerome Lawrence. October 17, 1975 (world premiere). Director, Jerome Lawrence; scenery, Richard Gould; lighting, Richard Coumbs; costumes, Estelle Painter.
Justice Daniel Snow . . . . Melvyn Douglas
Ruth Loomis . . . . Jean Arthur
Chief Justice Jefferson
  Crawford . . . . George Brengel
Mason Woods . . . . Dennis Romer
Burton Schmertz . . . . Allen Leatherman
University President;
  Photographer . . . . Ralph Neeley
Justice Josiah Clewis . . . . . Spencer McIntyre
Justice Harold Webb . . . . Robert Snook

Justice Stanley Moorehead; Senate Chairman; Marshal........John Buck Jr. Night Watchman........Andrew Lichtenberg Other Justices: Howard Renensland Jr., Eugene Hare, Ben Letter, Earl Keyes. Senators: Andrew Lichtenberg, Howard Renensland Jr., Frederic Serino. Others: David Meyer, George Simms, Dee Hoty.
Time: Soon. Place: Backstage at the Supreme Court of the United States. The people and events of this play are entirely fictional. One intermission.

CAESAR AND CLEOPATRA (23). By George Bernard Shaw. November 21, 1975. Director, Paul Lee; scenery and lighting, Robert Steinberg; costumes, Diane Dalton and Play House Design Associates. With Clayton Corzatte, Yolande Bavan, Margaret Hilton, Ben Evett, Allen Leatherman.

DR. JEKYLL AND MR. HYDE (22). By Paul Lee, new dramatization based on the novel by Robert Louis Stevenson. December 26, 1975 (world premiere). Director, Paul Lee; scenery, Richard Gould; lighting, Richard Coumbs; costumes, Estelle Painter.
Henry Jekyll..............Jonathan Farwell
Dr. Lanyon..................Robert Snook
Mrs. Lanyon..................Jo Farwell
Celia.........................Leslie Rapp
Utterson...................Robert Allman
Guest......................Ralph Neeley
Hackett ....Andrew Lichtenberg
Anita.......................Marji Dodrill
Richard Enfield................Dale Place
May.......................Carol Schultz

Joan; Katie....................Lee Karnes
Annie; Rosie...................Dee Hoty
News Vendor..............Frederic Serino
Poole.............. Howard Renensland Jr.
Emmie.................Bonnie Sosnowsky
Edward..................Daniel Desmond
Barman ....John Buck Jr.
Ensemble: John Buck Jr., Spencer McIntyre, J. D. Sutton, Frederic Serino, Andrew Lichtenberg, George Simms, Tedd Rubinstein, Ellen Renensland, Paul Lee
Time: 1870s. Place: London. Act I, Scene 1: A street. Scene 2: The Lanyon house. Scene 3: A street. Scene 4: Utterson's office. Scene 5: The Lanyon house. Scene 6: Dr. Jekyll's study. Scene 7: St. Peter's Church. Scene 8: Dr. Jekyll's study. Act II, Scene 1: Utterson's office. Scene 2: Dr. Jekyll's study. Scene 3: The Lanyon house. Scene 4: A sleazy bar. Scene 5: Dr. Jekyll's study.

GET-RICH-QUICK WALLINGFORD (22). By George M. Cohan. February 13, 1976. Director, Paul Lee; scenery, Richard Gould; lighting, Russell Lowe; costumes, Estelle Painter. With Daniel Desmond, Dale Place, Dee Hoty, Leslie Rapp, Richard Halverson, June Gibbons.

OF MICE AND MEN (15). By John Steinbeck. March 19, 1976. Director, Evie McElroy; scenery, Richard Gould; lighting, Richard Coumbs; costumes, Harriet Cone. With Daniel Desmond, Kenneth Albers, Robert Allman, Jonathan Farwell, Frederic Serino, Lizbeth Mackay.

The Cleveland Play House: Brooks Theater

THE PRAGUE SPRING (26). Book and lyrics by Lee Kalcheim; music by Joseph G. Raposo; conceived and directed by J. Ranelli. October 24, 1975. Scenery and lighting, Robert Steinberg; costumes, Estelle Painter. With Yolande Bavan, David Berman, Norm Berman, Joel Brooks, Mike Dantuono, Richard Oberlin.

ABIGAIL ADAMS: THE SECOND FIRST LADY (17). Written and performed by Edith Owen. November 28, 1975. Directors,

Edith Owen and Evie McElroy; lighting, John Volpe; costumes, Estelle Painter.

A PROFILE OF BENJAMIN FRANKLIN (5). Compiled and edited by William Paterson; researched by Cora Paterson. February 4, 1976. Lighting, John Volpe.

THE WORLD OF CARL SANDBURG (18). By Norman Corwin. April 9, 1976. Director, Jonathan Farwell; scenery, Richard Gould; lighting, John Volpe; costumes, Estelle Painter. With John Buck Jr., Evie McElroy, Dana Hart.

DALLAS

Dallas Theater Center: Kalita Humphreys Theater

(Managing director, Paul Baker)

THE AMOROUS FLEA (33). Book by Jerry Devine; music and lyrics by Bruce Montgomery; based on Molière's School For

Wives. June 3, 1975. Director, Ken Latimer; scenery, Yoichi Aoki; lighting, Robert Duffy; costumes, Diana Devereaux; musical director, Miriam Guten. With John Henson, Cindy McHugh, Richard F. Ward.

PROMENADE, ALL! (33). By David V. Robison. July 15, 1975. Directors, Randy Moore and Judith Davis; scenery, John Henson; lighting, Robyn Flatt; costumes, Kathleen Latimer. With Mary Sue Jones, Ken Latimer, Matt Tracy, John Stevens.

COUNT DRACULA (16). By Ted Tiller; based on Bram Stoker's novel. September 4, 1975. Director, Judith Davis; scenery, John Henson and Robert Duffy; lighting, Robert Duffy; costumes, Sarah Converse. With John Henson, Paul Callihan, Norma Moore, Randy Moore, Rebecca Logan, Bryant J. Reynolds.

SATURDAY, SUNDAY, MONDAY (33). By Eduardo de Filippo; English adaptation, Keith Waterhouse and Willis Hall. October 7, 1975. Director, David Healy; scenery, Mary Sue Jones; lighting, Allen Hibbard; costumes, Randolf Pearson. With Mary Sue Jones, Preston Jones, Barnett Shaw, Judith Davis, Randy Moore.

MANNY (41). Music by Randolph Tallman and Steven Mackenroth; words by Glenn Allen Smith. November 18, 1975 (world premiere). Director and choreographer, Dolores Ferraro; scenery and lighting, Sam Nance; costumes, Gina Taulane; arranger and conductor, D. Michael Patterson.

Cast: Woman in Black Dress—Norma Moore; Lust, Banner Carrier, Cousin, Lady —Sally Kushner; Pride, Buddy, Fellowship of Four, Treasure, Gentleman—Robert A. Smith; Avarice, Banner Carrier, Fellowship of Four, Lady—Carolyn R. Ward; Gluttony, Man on Crutches, Fellowship of Four, Man in White Robe, Gentleman—Cliff Samuelson; Wrath, Ancient Man, Buddy, Kindred, Gentleman— Jay Trimble; Envy, Nurse, Banner Carrier, Fellowship of Four, Lady—Rebecca Logan; Manny—Randolph Tallman; Guy Pushing Broom—John Henson; Girl Holding Small Bouquet; Girl Holding Large Bouquet—Gloria Hebert.

Band: Bill Brown, George Patterson, Ron Floreno, D. Michael Patterson, Pam Nagle. One intermission.

A PLACE ON THE MAGDALENA FLATS (33). By Preston Jones. January 13, 1976 (world premiere). Director, Ken Latimer; scenery, Yoichi Aoki; lighting, Randy Moore; costumes, Susan A. Haynie.
Carl Grey .... Drexel H. Riley
Charlene Grey .... Synthia Rogers
Frank Grey .... Keith Dixon
George Sandoval .... Randy Bonifay
Mary Helen
    Kilgore ...... Martha Robinson Goodman

Bud Kilgore .... Tim Green
Booger .... Fritz Lennon
Wanda .... Shelley McClure
Patsy Jo Boatright .... Judith Davis
Time: 1956. Place: The Magdalena Flats area of Southwestern New Mexico. Act I, Scene 1: The kitchen of the Carl Grey ranch house, late afternoon. Scene 2: The Bud Kilgore ranch, about three hours later. Scene 3: The Grey kitchen, later that same night. Scene 4: The Grey kitchen, about noon the next day. Act II, Scene 1: The Busy Bee Cafe in Magdalena, two days later. Scene 2: The Grey kitchen, that same day. Scene 3: A spot on the ranch not far from the water canyon tank, one week later. Scene 4: The Grey kitchen, about 7 the next morning. Act III, Scene 1: The Grey kitchen, two days later, Scene 2: The Busy Bee Cafe, three months later. Scene 3: The water canyon tank area, later that same day. Scene 4: The Grey kitchen, two days later.

MUCH ADO ABOUT NOTHING (45). By William Shakespeare. February 24, 1976. Director, Robin Lovejoy; scenery, John Henson; lighting, Allen Hibbard; costumes, Kathleen Latimer. With Randy Moore, Rebecca Logan, Ken Latimer, Matt Tracy, Nick Dalley, Judy Bridges, Randolph Tallman.

STILLSONG (33). By Sallie Laurie. April 20, 1976 (world premiere). Director, Paul Baker; scenery, Virgil Beavers; lighting, Randy Moore; costumes, Gina Taulane; piano compositions and sound design, Pam Nagle.
Grandfather Morgan
    Thompson .... Ryland Merkey
Samuel Thompson .... Matt Tracy
Katrinka Thompson .... Jacque Thomas
Sal Thompson .... Denise Drennen,
                            Carolyn Pines
John Thompson .... Ken Keiffer,
            Quinn Mathews, Philip Schenkler
Jill Thompson .... Kristy Flatt, Lisa Kramer
Pete Ashworth .... Ted Bowlin
Maddie Thompson Ashworth .. Judith Davis
Caroline Ashworth .... Robyn Flatt
Tom Ashworth .... William George
Chris Ashworth .... Matthew Broussard,
                            Sheff Chastain
Jean Thompson Hemphill ...... Sally Netzel
Ben Thompson .... John Henson
Electra Thompson
    Sommers .... Lynn Trammell
Sue Carter .... Juanamaria X. Parres
Herb Carter .... Roger Richards
Ellen Sommers Patterson .. Libby Blackwell
Margaret Ashworth .... Mona Pursley
Fred Bryant .... Keith Dixon
Thelma Bryant .... Rebecca Ramsey
Dr. Stafford .... Paul Buboltz

Place: The attic, front porch, parlor, bedroom and yard of the Thompson farmhouse in Bedford County, Virginia. Act I, Scene 1: May 1, 1960, 3 a.m. Scene 2: The same day, 8 a.m. Act II, Scene 1: The same day, 10 a.m. Scene 2: The same day, 7 p.m.

Dallas Theater Center: Down Center Stage

A MARVELOUS WAR (12). By Charles Beachley III. October 30, 1975 (world premiere). Director, Rebecca Ramsey; scenery, Gerald Jines; lighting, Linda Blase; costumes, Susan A. Haynie.
Mohammed ....Fred Moore
Sir Henry Gilbey ....Matt Tracy
Lt. John Reeve ....Paul Buboltz
Eleanor Gilbey ....Sallie Laurie
William Gilbey ....Nick Wollner
Regina Reeve ....Jaye Z. Restivo
  Time: August 27, 1896. Place: The library of the Gilbey home in Zanzibar.

STANDOFF AT BEAVER AND PINE (12). By Sally Netzel. December 4, 1975 (world premiere). Director, Mary Lou Hoyle; scenery and costumes, Robert Duffy; lighting, Matt Tracy.
Matthew Schultz ....Fritz Lennon
Gertrude Schultz ....Mona Pursley
Ethel Bureen ....Cheryl Denson
Dan Cowls ....Roger Richards
Patricia Meshena ....Ruth Cantrell
Jerald Kozinski ....William George
Miriam Gajewski ....Cynthia Smith
  Time: September 7, 1975. Place: The living room of the Schultz home in a small town in Wisconsin. One intermission.

CANZADA AND THE BOYS (12). By Sam Havens. January 29, 1976 (world premiere). Director, John Logan; scenery, Sallie Laurie; lighting, Robin Crews; costumes, Denise Drennen.
Canzada ....Lynn Trammell
Shel ....Allen Hibbard
Brudge ....Paul Buboltz

Dougie ....Tom C. Smith
P.J. ....Bryant J. Reynolds
  Place: The den at the rear of Canzada's home in a small city on the Gulf Coast. Act I, Scene 1: A late afternoon in autumn. Scene 2: The next morning. Act II, Scene 1: The same evening around 8 p.m. Scene 2: That evening around 10:30. Scene 3: Dawn the next day. Scene 4: Late afternoon the same day.

FACES OF U.S. (12). Written by the Dallas Theater Center Mime Troupe. March 4, 1976 (world premiere). Directors, Robyn Flatt and John Stevens; scenery and visual effects, Linda Blase; lighting, Suzanne Chiles; costumes, Pamela Jensen and Cheryl Denson; sound, Paul Callihan. With Paul Buboltz, Paul Callihan, Ruth Cantrell, Jane Farris, Robyn Flatt, William George, Martha Goodman, Beverly Renquist, Robert A. Smith, John Stevens. Voices: Fred Moore and Karyl Kesmodel.
  Act I. Beginnings—Seek the Seeds of Liberty! Act II. Dixie!; Tumbleweeds. Act III. Concrete and Steel; The Entertainers.

MIRROR UNDER THE EAGLE (12). By Philip C. Lewis. April 8, 1976 (world premiere). Directors, John Stevens and Steve Lovett; scenery, Steve Wallace; lighting, Mac Smotherman and Robert Duffy; costumes, Randolf Pearson. With Cheryl Denson, Robert Duffy, Tommy G. Hendrick, Mary Rohde, Mac Smotherman, Celeste Varricchio. This production toured throughout Texas prior to its presentation at Down Center Stage.

Dallas Theater Center: Magic Turtle Children's Theater

(Producer, Ken Latimer)

LADY LIBERTY: CELEBRATION '76 (8). October 18, 1975. Directors, Robyn Flatt and John Stevens; scenery, Peter Lynch and Randy Bonifay; lighting, Mac Smotherman, costumes, Cheryl Denson and Pam Jensen; sound, Paul Callihan and Steve Lovett. Act I, written and performed by Tommy Cantu, Denise Drennen, Bill George, Karyl Kesmodel, Steve Lovett, Fred Moore, Beverly Renquist. Act II, written by Robyn Flatt and John Stevens; words by Sally Netzel; performed by the Dallas Theater Center Mime Troupe.
POCAHONTAS (8). By Aurand Harris. December 13, 1975. Director, John Figlmiller;

scenery, Randy Bonifay; lighting, Bob Bovard; costumes, Jesse Y. Ramos. With Tom C. Smith, Riho Mitachi, Marc Calloway.

THE ADVENTURES OF BRER RABBIT (8). Book and lyrics by Pat Hale; music by Paul Spong. February 7, 1976. Director, Jesse Y. Ramos; scenery, Robert Bovard; lighting, Paul R. Bassett; costumes, Linda Blase. With James Myers, John Nichols, Shannon Wilson, Marc Calloway, Gail Henderson.

ROAD TO YONDER: THE BOYHOOD ADVENTURES OF ABE LINCOLN (8). By Pamela Jensen; based on an idea by Louise

Mosley. April 3, 1976 (world premiere). Director, Louise Mosley; scenery, Yoichi Aoki; lighting, Warren Deckert; costumes, Gloria Hebert; composer, Carolyn Pines; choreographer, Sally Kushner.

Magic Turtle ....Cliff Samuelson
Mr. Lincoln ....Tom C. Smith
Nancy Hanks Lincoln ......Joslyn Anderson
Tom Lincoln ....Wayne Lambert
Mr. Sparrow ....Ron Larson

Mrs. Sparrow ....Christenia Alden
Dennis Hanks ....Michael Krueger
Sarah Lincoln ....Sandy Moore
Abe Lincoln ....Robert Putnam
Mr. Riney, the schoolmaster ..Rodger Wilson
Ned ....Fred Moore
Square Dancers, Friends, School Children: Riho Mitachi, M. Randall Russell, Shau-Di Wang, Karon Cogdill, Sally Kushner.

Note: Dallas Theater Center is affiliated with the graduate program of Trinity University. Its resident professional company is augmented by journeymen and apprentices who work from three to four years in a comprehensive professional career program.

HARTFORD, CONN.

Hartford Stage Company

(Producing director, Paul R. Weidner; managing director, Jessica L. Andrews)

AWAKE AND SING (44). By Clifford Odets. September 19, 1975. Director, Irene Lewis; scenery, Santo Loquasto; lighting, Ian Calderon; costumes, Linda Fisher. With Elaine Bromka, Frances Chaney, Jerry Jarrett, Will Lee, Richard Lieberman, Paul Marin, Larry Ross, Marco St. John.

ALL OVER (44). By Edward Albee. October 31, 1975. Director, Paul Weidner; scenery, Marjorie Kellogg; lighting, David Chapman; costumes, Claire Ferraris. With Myra Carter, Humphrey Davis, Anne Shropshire, Anne Lynn, Pirie MacDonald, David O. Petersen, Margaret Thompson.

OH COWARD! (44). Devised and directed by Roderick Cook; words and music by Noel Coward. December 12, 1975. Scenery, Hugh Landwehr; lighting, Arden Fingerhut; costumes, Caley Summers. With Roderick Cook, Dalton Cathey, Kimberly Gaisford.

THE ESTATE (44). By Ray Aranha. January 23, 1976 (world premiere). Director, Paul Weidner; scenery, Marjorie Kellogg; lighting, Arden Fingerhut; costumes, Claire Ferraris.
Garth ....Geddeth Smith
Will ....Jeffrey B. McLaughlin
Benjamin Banneker ....Ray Aranha
Minta Banneker Black ....Gertrude Blanks

Thomas Jefferson ....Josef Sommer
Sally Hemings ....Seret Scott
Martha "Patsy" Jefferson ....Jennifer Jestin
John Walker ....Ted Graeber
Elizabeth Walker ....Anne Lynn
Cal ....William Jay
Tom ....Mel Johnson Jr.
Abigail Adams ....Anne Shropshire
Time: Late 18th century. Place: The farm of Benjamin Banneker, Baltimore County, Maryland, and Thomas Jefferson's estate, Monticello, Virginia. Act I, Scene 1: Early fall, dawn. Scene 2: Late fall, evening. Act II: The same evening. Act III, Scene 1: The same evening. Scene 2: Winter, evening.

DREAM ON MONKEY MOUNTAIN (44). By Derek Walcott. March 19, 1976. Director, Charles Turner; choreographer, Kelvin Rotardier; scenery, Hugh Landwehr; lighting, David Chapman; costumes, Caley Summers. With Al Freeman Jr., David Downing, William Jay, Mel Johnson Jr., Leroy Lessane, Count Stovall, Rosanna Carter, Bette Carole.

BORN YESTERDAY (60). By Garson Kanin. April 30, 1976. Director, Irene Lewis; scenery, Hugh Landwehr; lighting, Peter Hunt; costumes, Claire Ferraris. With Joseph Mascolo, Anita Morris, Edmond Genest, Macon McCalman, Alan Gifford, Lois Holmes.

Note: The Hartford Stage Company Touring Theater presented productions of *Squeeze Play* by Slawomir Mrozek; *Way Back When* by Ray Aranha; *Workman! Whoever You Are* based on *Working* by Studs Terkel and devised by the touring company and Oriole O'Neill, throughout Southern New England during the 1975-76 season. The plays, directed by Irene Lewis and designed by Hugh Landwehr, were performed by Samuel Barton, Cynthia Crumlish, Jeffrey Horowitz and Neil Napolitan.

HOUSTON

Alley Theater: Large Stage

(Producer-director, Nina Vance. Designers: scenery, William Trotman, John Kenny, Michael Olich; lighting, Jonathan Duff, Matthew Grant; costumes, Barbara C. Cox, Michael Olich)

INDIANS (36). By Arthur Kopit. October 23, 1975. Director, Beth Sanford. With Dale Helward, Tony Russel, Rutherford Cravens, Mark Murphey, David Wurst, Dwight Schultz.

THE FRONT PAGE (44). By Ben Hecht and Charles MacArthur. December 4, 1975. Director, Robert E. Leonard. With Tony Russel, Lyle Talbot, Ginger Bongle, Leta Bonynge, Concetta Tomei, Daniel Therriault.

THE LAST MEETING OF THE KNIGHTS OF THE WHITE MAGNOLIA (44). By Preston Jones. January 22, 1976. Director,

Robert E. Leonard. With Lyle Talbot, David Wurst, Philip Davidson, William Hardy, Dale Helward.

JUNO AND THE PAYCOCK (36). By Sean O'Casey. March 11, 1976. Director, Beth Sanford. With Bettye Fitzpatrick, Leslie Yeo, Cristine Rose, Mark Murphey, Dermot McNamara.

THE SHOW-OFF (44). By George Kelly. April 22, 1976. Director, Robert E. Leonard. With Dwight Schultz, Robert Symonds, Jeanne Bates, Cristine Rose, Lillian Evans, Carl Davis.

Alley Theater: Arena Stage

THE COCKTAIL PARTY (13). By T. S. Eliot. November 19, 1975. Director, Nina Vance. With Cristine Rose, Brenda Forbes, Roderick Cook, Briain Petchey, Charmion King, David Raschey.

SCENES FROM AMERICAN LIFE (13). By A. R. Gurney Jr. January 13, 1976. Di-

rector, William Trotman. With members of the Company and Interns.

TINY ALICE (13). By Edward Albee. February 25, 1976. Director, Nina Vance. With Dwight Schultz, Bella Jarrett, Robert Symonds, John Gardiner, William Trotman.

Alley Theater: Lunchtime Theater—Arena Lobby

PURGATORY (12) by William Butler Yeats, with Robert Symonds, Daniel Therriault, Haskell Fitz-Simons; and ON THE HARMFUL-

NESS OF TOBACCO (12) by Anton Chekhov, with Robert Symonds. May 4, 1976.

Note: *Scenes From American Life* was presented free in support of Alley Theater's Intern Program, an on-the-job training program for actors, technicians and designers. TREAT (Traveling Repertory Ensemble of Alley Theater), a new community outreach program, presented a three-month pilot tour in Houston and seven other Texas communities. Members of the regular resident company, Mimi Carr, Cristine Rose, Haskell Fitz-Simons, Rodger McDonald, and the tour manager Paul La Prise, presented a Bicentennial tribute of American writings and songs, *You and U.S.*, directed by William Trotman.

INDIANAPOLIS

Indiana Repertory Theater: Main Stage

(Artistic director, Edward Stern; producing director, Benjamin Mordecai)

THAT CHAMPIONSHIP SEASON (22). By Jason Miller. October 16, 1975. Director, Edward Stern; scenery and lighting, Raymond C. Recht; costumes, Sherry Mordecai. With Robert Elliott, John Grassilli, Robert Scogin, John C. Capodice, Alfred Hinckley.

ARMS AND THE MAN (22). By George Bernard Shaw. November 13, 1975. Director,

Vincent Dowling; scenery, John Ezell; lighting, Michael Watson; costumes, Susan Tsu. With Linda Atkinson, Dee Victor, Priscilla Lindsay, Jack Donner, Donald Ewer, Steven Ryan, Robert Elliott.

LONG DAY'S JOURNEY INTO NIGHT (22). By Eugene O'Neill. December 11, 1975. Director, Thomas Gruenewald; scenery, John

Lee Beatty; lighting, Michael Watson; costumes, Barbara Medlicott. With Edward Binns, Elizabeth Franz, Steven Ryan, T. Richard Mason, Priscilla Lindsay.

THE ENVOI MESSAGES (22). By Louis Phillips. January 15, 1976 (world premiere). Director, Edward Stern; scenery and lighting, Raymond C. Recht; costumes, Linda Fisher.
Blythe Donner.............Brenda Currin
Winthrop Hall;
  Phantom Gordon.......Maxwell Glanville
1st Apache;
  Moon Monroe..........Henry Kaimu Bal
2nd Apache; Chess Shire...Robert Machray
Hawk Woman;
  Speech-Maker...........Delia Hattendorf
1st Cannibal; Chauffeur Jeffrey V. Thompson
2nd Cannibal..............Chenault Lillard
Elizabeth Donner...........Loretta Yoder
Mattie Trueridge.......... Rosanna Carter
Albert Donner;
  Chief Dancing Fox.........Robert Scogin
Mark Ballanger; Announcer..Bernard Kates
Mrs. Horace Desmond.......Linda Selman
Officer Milton; Referee......Lou Malandra

XT-N-R4; Private Mason....Barry Cullison
Man With A Rope...........Jack L. Davis
  Crowd: Duncan Larsen, Robert Machray, Loretta Yoder. Incidental piano music, John Muir.
  Time: 1934. Place: A small Midwestern community. Two intermissions.

THE REAL INSPECTOR HOUND by Tom Stoppard and BLACK COMEDY by Peter Shaffer (22). February 12, 1976. Director, Edward Stern; scenery, Bill Stabile; lighting, Jody Boese; costumes, James Edmund Brady. With John Abajian, John Guerrasio, Carol Gustafson, Delia Hattendorf, Bernard Kates, Robert Machray, Gun-Marie Nilsson, Robert Scogin, Edward Stevlingson.

THE TAVERN (22). By George M. Cohan. March 11, 1976. Director, John Going; scenery and costumes, William Schroder; lighting, Michael Watson. With Bernard Kates, Jeremiah Sullivan, Edward Stevlingson, Carol Gustafson, Robin Pearson Rose, Robert Scogin.

Indiana Repertory Company: 2d Stage

THE CARETAKER (10). By Harold Pinter. November 12, 1975. Director, Edward Stern; scenery, Keith Brumley; lighting, Timothy K. Joyce; costumes, Thomas W. Schmunk. With John Grassilli, Robert Scogin, Bernard Kates.

THE SEA HORSE (12). By Edward J. Moore. January 7, 1976. Director, Bernard Kates; scenery, Keith Brumley; lighting, Carl Roetter; costumes, Florence L. Rutherford. With Susan Riskin, Steven Ryan.

THE OLD JEW by Murray Schisgal, directed by Jack L. Davis; ON THE HARMFULNESS OF TOBACCO by Anton Chekhov, English version by Eric Bentley and THE MAN WITH THE FLOWER IN HIS MOUTH by Luigi Pirandello, translated by William Murray, directed by Edward Stern (12). April 7, 1976. Scenery, Keith Brumley; lighting, Allen Cornell; costumes, Florence L. Rutherford. With Robert Scogin, Bernard Kates, Shelley Joyce.

Note: In addition to the regular season, Indiana Repertory Theater also presented *Musical Mirage Express '76,* with members of the company, which played 38 performances, and toured *Women and Those Other People,* excerpts from Mark Twain, James Thurber, Jules Feiffer and William Shakespeare, with Gun-Marie Nilsson and John Abajian.

KANSAS CITY, MO.

Missouri Repertory Theater: University of Missouri

(Director, Patricia McIlrath)

DEAR LIAR (6). By Jerome Kilty; adapted from the correspondence of George Bernard Shaw and Mrs. Patrick Campbell. June 5, 1975. Director, Patricia McIlrath; scenery, John Ezell; lighting, Joseph Appelt; costumes, Anne Thaxter-Watson. With Liza Cole, Vincent Dowling.

I AM BLACK (6). Compiled, arranged and performed by Ray Aranha. June 6, 1975.

BORN YESTERDAY (17). By Garson Kanin. June 26, 1975. Director, Robin Humphrey; scenery, James Hart Stearns; lighting, Curt Ostermann; costumes, Judith Dolan. With Al Christy, Susan Borneman, Steve Ryan, Henry Strozier, Ronetta Wallman.

THE CHERRY ORCHARD (16). By Anton Chekhov; adapted and directed by Vincent Dowling. July 3, 1975. Scenery, John Ezell;

lighting, Joseph Appelt; costumes, Vincent Scassellati. With Meg Myles, Walter Rhodes, Eberle Thomas, Liza Cole, Maria Frumkin, Lynn Cohen, Al Christy, John Maddison.

MUCH ADO ABOUT NOTHING (17). By William Shakespeare. July 10, 1975. Director, James Assad; scenery, Michael J. O'Kane; lighting, Joseph Appelt; costumes, Judith Dolan. With Steve Ryan, John Q. Bruce Jr., Michael LaGue, Walter Rhodes, Lynn Cohen, Nina Furst, Robert Elliott.

THE LAST MEETING OF THE KNIGHTS OF THE WHITE MAGNOLIA (14). By Preston Jones. July 17, 1975. Director, Thomas Gruenewald; scenery, J. Morton Walker; lighting, Joseph Appelt; costumes, Barbara E. Medlicott. With Henry Strozier, Leslie Robinson, Al Christy, Richard C. Brown, Eberle Thomas, Robert Elliott, Von H. Washington.

A STREETCAR NAMED DESIRE (14). By Tennessee Williams. July 31, 1975. Director, Francis J. Cullinan; scenery, John Ezell; lighting, Curt Ostermann; costumes, Vincent Scassellati. With Steve Ryan, Meg Myles, Richard C. Brown, Marla Frumkin.

IN THE WELL OF THE HOUSE (13). By Charles C. Mark. August 7, 1975 (world premiere). Director, Tunc Yalman; scenery, Frederic James; lighting, Joseph Appelt; costumes, Judith Dolan; sound, David D. Richardson; original music, Gerald Kemner, James Rothwell.
Speaker of the House . . . . . Bramwell Fletcher
Rep. Clarence Henry . . . . Henry Strozier
Lester Green . . . . Steve Scearcy
Thelma . . . . Gloria P. Terrell

Bushy . . . . Ted McKim
Spook . . . . Sam R. McCorvey
Rep. Richard S. (Pearly)
  Gates . . . . Von H. Washington
Rep. Dixie Grogan . . . . Walter Rhodes
Rep. Katherine Eaton . . . . Harriet Levitt
Star . . . . John Cothran Jr.
Princess Atursa . . . . Harri Etta Martin
  Act I, Scene 1: The offices of Rep. Richard Gates and Rep. Clarence Henry. Washington, D.C., the 1960s (the action is simultaneous in the two offices). Scene 2: Gates's office. Scene 3: Henry's office. Scene 4: The Well of the House of Representatives. Scene 5: Henry's office. Scene 6: The pulpit of Gates's church in Harlem. Scene 7: A public telephone booth. Act II, Scene 1: A meeting of the Democratic caucus, one month later. Scene 2: The two offices (the action is simultaneous). Scene 3: Henry's office. Scene 4: Gates's office. Scene 5: Several days later in the members' lounge of the House. Scene 6: Gates's office, a few weeks later.

THE RAINMAKER (14). By N. Richard Nash. February 5, 1976. Director, James Assad; scenery, G. Philippe de Rosier; lighting, Joseph Appelt; costumes, Vincent Scassellati. With Jeannine Hutchings, Robert Elliott, Art Ellison, Ron Durbian, Michael LaGue, John Q. Bruce Jr., Walter W. Atamaniuk.

THE MORGAN YARD (14). Written and directed by Kevin O'Morrison. February 6, 1976. Scenery, Max A. Beatty; lighting, Joseph Appelt; costumes, Vincent Scassellati. With Michael LaGue, John Q. Bruce Jr., Walter W. Atamaniuk, Ronetta Wallman, Susan Borneman. Robert Elliott.

Note: Missouri Vanguard Theater, the touring unit of Missouri Repertory Theater, presents major productions and children's programs to outlying towns and communities throughout the state. In October 1975, Born Yesterday and A Streetcar Named Desire, summer season productions, toured cities in Missouri, Kansas, Nebraska, and Oklahoma. The Rainmaker and The Morgan Yard, on completing their resident runs, toured in March and April, 1976. The spring schools programs included Adaptation by Elaine May, directed by David Dannenbaum and designed by Joseph Appelt; and The Disenchanted Forest, a puppet show by Robert Evans adapted from Joella Brown's version of The Frog Prince. It was staged and performed by Jeannine Hutchings and Walter Atamaniuk, designed by Joseph Blackwood, with puppets by Baker S. Smith.

LAKEWOOD, OHIO

The Great Lakes Shakespeare Festival: Lakewood Civic Auditorium

(Producer-director, Lawrence Carra)

AS YOU LIKE IT (19). By William Shakespeare. July 3, 1975. Director, Lawrence Carra; scenery Warner Blake; lighting Frederic Youens; costumes, Michael Olich.

THE MISER (18). By Molière. July 10, 1975. Director, Jean Gascon; scenery, Warner Blake; lighting, Frederic Youens; costumes, Michael Olich.

OUR TOWN (18). By Thornton Wilder. July 24, 1975. Director, Lawrence Carra; scenery, Wynn P. Thomas; lighting, Frederic Youens; costumes, Michael Olich.

THE FROGS (12). By Burt Shevelove, freely adapted from Aristophanes; music and lyrics by Stephen Sondheim. August 7, 1975. Director-stager, Lawrence Carra; scenery, Warner Blake; lighting Frederic Youens; costumes, Jacqueline Raschke Lehane; music director, Stuart W. Raleigh. (This production of *The Frogs* has a revised script for non-swimming-pool theaters and includes the following new musical numbers: "Evoe!" by Sondheim/Dio-

nysians; "Fear No More" by Sondheim/Shake-speare.)

THE WINTER'S TALE (9). By William Shakespeare. August 21, 1975. Director, Ted Danielewski; scenery, Warner Blake; lighting, Frederic Youens; costumes, Michael Olich.

Acting Company: Robert Allman, Michael R. Boyle, Gregory Lehane, Keith Mackey, Tom Mardirosian, Erika Petersen, James Selby, Billie Anita Stewart, Edward Stevling-son, John Straub, Patrick Watkins, David Williams, Susan Willis, Kate Young.

LOS ANGELES

Center Theater Group: Ahmanson Theater

(Managing Director, Robert Fryer)

THE NORMAN CONQUESTS: TABLE MANNERS (17). October 10, 1975; LIVING TOGETHER (23), October 13, 1975; ROUND AND ROUND THE GARDEN (18), October 29, 1974. By Alan Ayckbourn. American Premiere. Director, Eric Thompson; scenery and lighting, Robert Randolph; costumes, Noel Taylor.

Norman .... Richard Benjamin
Annie .... Paula Prentiss
Tom .... Ken Howard
Sarah .... Estelle Parsons
Reg .... Barry Nelson
Ruth .... Carole Shelley

THE NIGHT OF THE IGUANA (51). By Tennessee Williams. December 19, 1975. Director, Joseph Hardy; scenery and lighting, H. R. Poindexter; costumes, Noel Taylor. With Richard Chamberlain, Dorothy McGuire, Raymond Massey, Eleanor Parker, Allyn Ann McLerie.

SAME TIME, NEXT YEAR (51). By Bernard Slade. February 6, 1976. Director, Gene Saks; scenery, William Ritman; lighting, Tharon Musser; costumes, Jane Greenwood. With Joyce Van Patten, Conrad Janis.

CALIFORNIA SUITE (51). By Neil Simon. April 23, 1976 (world premiere). Director, Gene Saks; scenery, William Ritman; lighting, Tharon Musser; costumes, Jane Greenwood.
Visitor From New York
Hannah Warren .... Tammy Grimes
William Warren .... George Grizzard
Time: About 1 p.m. on a sunny, warm day in late fall.
Visitor From Philadelphia
Marvin Michaels .... Jack Weston
Bunny .... Leslie Easterbrook
Millie Michaels .... Barbara Barrie
Time: 11 a.m., mid-December.
Visitors From London
Sidney Nichols .... George Grizzard
Diana Nichols ....Tammy Grimes
Time: Scene 1, about 5 p.m., early April. Scene 2, about 3 a.m.
Visitors From Chicago
Mort Hollender .... Jack Weston
Beth Hollender .... Barbara Barrie
Stu Franklyn .... George Gizzard
Gert Franklyn .... Tammy Grimes
Time 4 p.m. Sunday afternoon, July 4.

LOS ANGELES

Center Theater Group: Mark Taper Forum

(Artistic director, Gordon Davidson; associate director, Edward Parone; director of Forum/ Laboratory, Robert Greenwald; director of Improvisational Theater Project, John Dennis)

ONCE IN A LIFETIME (54). By Moss Hart and George S. Kaufman. July 17, 1975. Director, Edward Parone; scenery, Jim Newton, lighting, Tharon Musser; costumes, Pete Mene-

fee. With Dennis Dugan, Marcia Rodd, Charles Thomas Murphy, Jayne Meadows Allen, Sharon Ullrick, Harold Gould, Dody Goodman, Richard Lenz, Arnold Soboloff.

In repertory:
TOO MUCH JOHNSÓN (52) by William Gillette, adapted by Burt Shevelove, September 25, 1975; and THE SHADOW BOX (34), by Michael Cristofer, October 30, 1975 (world premiere). Director, Gordon Davidson; scenery, Robert Zentis; lighting, H. R. Poindexter; costumes, Ron Rasmussen.

Too Much Johnson with Laurence Luckinbill, Rose Gregorio, David Huffman, Cynthia Harris, Marge Redmond, Tom Rosqui, Simon Oakland.

Shadow Box
Interviewer .... Tom Rosqui
Joe .... Simon Oakland
Steve .... Brad Rearden
Maggie .... Marge Redmond
Brian .... Laurence Luckinbill
Mark .... David Huffman
Beverly .... Cynthia Harris
Felicity .... Mary Carver
Agnes .... Rose Gregorio

THE DUCHESS OF MALFI (72). By John Webster. January 22, 1976. Director, Howard Sackler; scenery, Paul Sylbert; lighting, John Gleason; costumes, Dorothy Jeakins. With Eileen Atkins, Robin Gammell, Olivia Cole, Philip Larson, Byron Jennings, Henry Hoffman, G. Wood, Byron Webster, Sally Kemp.

In repertory (scenery, Sally Jacobs; lighting, F. Mitchell Dana; costumes, Julie Weiss):
AND WHERE SHE STOPS NOBODY KNOWS (22). By Oliver Hailey. April 1, 1976 (world premiere). Director, Gordon Davidson; choreographer, Marge Champion. With Eileen Brennan, Lou Gossett. One intermission.
ASHES (16). By David Rudkin. April 3, 1976 (matinee) (American premiere). Director, Edward Parone.
Colin .... Michael Cristofer
Anne .... Tyne Daly
Man .... James Ray
Woman .... Andra Akers/Janet Johnson
One intermission.
CROSS COUNTRY (17). By Susan Miller. April 3, 1976 (evening) (world premiere). Director, Vickie Rue.
Perry .... Francis Lee McCain
Louis .... Robin Strasser
Avra .... Sharon Ullrick
Dan .... Ron Rifkin
No intermission.
THREE SISTERS (36). By Anton Chekhov; new translation by Michael Heim. May 6, 1976. Director, Edward Parone. With Tyne Daly, Laurie Kennedy, Barra Grant, Michael Cristofer/Marc Alaimo, Berry Kroeger, Lou Gossett/Warren Hammack, Ron Rifkin, Frances Lee McCain, David Ogden Stiers.

Center Theater Group: Mark Taper Forum—Forum/Laboratory

THE GREAT POTATO FAMINE (3). By Daniel Wray and Brendan Noel Ward. August 29, 1975. Director, Richard M. Johnson; designers, Ron Rudolph and Louise Hayter; music composed and recorded by Steven Wells and Ray Doyle. With Blanche Bronte, Judy Chaikin, Maryellen Clemons, Duncan Gamble, Sindy Hawke, Kay Howell, Drew Lovenstein, John Megna, Tony Papenfuss, E. A. Sirianni, David Stifel, Steven Wells, Terry Wolf.

DIAMONDS IN THE ROUGH (1). Conceived by Jeremy Blahnik, David Copelin and Vickie Rue. September 14, 1975. With Herb Foster, Barra Grant, Henry Hoffman, Mark Jenkins, Julie Payne, Carolyn Reed, Robin Strasser, Sharon Ullrick, Rick Vartorella.

OEDIPUS AT COLONUS (3). By Sophocles. October 9, 1975. Director, Sally Jacobs; designers, Julie Weills, Ron Rudolph, Steven Wells. With Andrew Cole, Joe Hudgins, Philip Larson, Ralph Lev Mailer, Julie Payne, John Roddick, Gene Rosen, Benjamin Stewart, Kate Woodville.

ELECTRA (3). By Robert Montgomery. January 22, 1976. Director, Joseph Chaikin; dramaturg, Mira Rafalowicz; designers, Gwen Fabricant, Arden Fingerhut. With Shami Chaikin, Tina Shepard, Paul Zimet.

TO SEE THE ELEPHANT (3). By Elizabeth Clark. January 24, 1976. Director, Liebe Gray; designers, Ellyn Gersh, Durinda Wood, Susie Helfond; music, Cris Williamson. With Terri Carson, E. Marcy Dicterow, Carol-Lynn Fillet, Janet Johnson, Frances Lee McCain, Belita Moreno, Shirley Slater, Sharon Ullrick, Cris Williamson, Carrie Zivetz.

THE COMMON GARDEN VARIETY (3). By Jane Chambers. March 4, 1976. Director, Gwen Arner; designers, Robert Zentis, Durinda Wood. With Anne Gee Byrd, Mary Jackson, Marc McClure, Anne O'Donnell, Betsy Slade.

JACK STREET (3). Written and directed by Joan Tewkesbury. April 15, 1976. Designers, Erik Brenmark, Louise Hayter, Pamela Cooper; musical director, Tony Berg. Music by Tony Berg, Albert Greenberg, Melissa Murphy, Ted Neeley, Allan Nichols. With Paul Ainsley, Tony Berg, Ed Buck, Hannah Dean, Bob DoQui, Tom Eden, Scott Glenn, Mariette Hartley, Joan Hotchkis, Lee Jones-DeBroux, Johnny Ray McGhee, John Megna,

Melissa Murphy, Ted Neeley, Craig Richard Nelson, Julie Newmar, Paul Potash, Cristina Raines, Rod Rimmer, Susan Tyrrell, Herve Villechaise, Joe Zaloom.

UPROOTED (3). By Humberto Robles-

Arena; English adaptation by Severo Perez. June 3, 1976. Director, Margarita Galban; designers, Estela Scarlata, Jason Shubb. With Linda Dangcil, Ronald Joseph Godines, Rafael Lopez, Julio Medina, Drew Michaels, Karmin Murcelo, Carmen Zapata.

Note: Mark Taper Forum continued its Improvisational Theater Project for young theatergoers under director John Dennis and supervising producer Ditta Oliker, December 30, 1975–January 4, 1976 and May 10-14, 1976.

The Season Elsewhere in Los Angeles

By Rick Talcove

Theater critic of the Van Nuys, Calif. *Valley News*

If you want to be optimistic about local theater in Los Angeles during 1975–76, you could say the season was mediocre. On the other hand, if you simply wanted to be honest, disappointing wouldn't be too far from the truth. It's generally agreed that local stagecraft in Los Angeles is on the verge of something, but what that illusive "something" is simply can't be defined as yet.

Probably the most anticipated event was the opening of the Westwood Playhouse, a comfortable 500-seat theater right across the street from UCLA. Here, theater purists insisted, was the house that was going to compete with the Mark Taper Forum. It never happened. A theater needs time to find its roots, but the Westwood took ten months and nearly that many productions to confound both itself and the theatrical community. The opening attraction, an all-star revival of *The Little Foxes* (with Lee Grant, Carroll O'Connor, Burgess Meredith, Harris Hulin, etc.) was a respectable, yet off-center, production that seemed virtually lifeless. It was followed by a feuding Shelley Winters in *Cages,* a futile *Opening of a Door* (a re-write of *Kind Lady* with Cathleen Nesbitt in an abbreviated run), a fragmented *Rodgers & Hart* (with a stunning Constance Towers), and decent productions of *P.S. Your Cat is Dead* (featuring Keir Dullea and Jeff Druce) and *The Heiress* (with a promising local debut by Marsha Mason). The Westwood also worked in a benefit run for Tao House of O'Neill's *Hughie* with Jason Robards and Jack Dodson in their original roles. The theater ended its first year with *Anything . . . Anything,* a new comedy that collapsed in rehearsals. Obviously artistic director Margy Newman needs some advice . . . fast.

On other fronts, two groups made promising beginnings. The Globe Playhouse hosted the Shakespeare Society of America that began, typically, with a superb revival of *Cyrano de Bergerac* with a towering performance by DeVeren Bookwalter in Anthony Burgess's lilting new translation. The Globe then embarked on an ambitious project of staging all of Shakespeare's plays within the next two years. Early reports are mixed, though Bookwalter displayed a good *Hamlet* and *Richard III.* A group of actors called The Colony began producing out of the Studio Theater Playhouse and offered superior productions of *The Sign in Sidney Brustein's Window, The Royal Hunt of the Sun* and Truman Capote's straight play version of *The Grass Harp.*

Of the new scripts, two bitter comedies attracted some attention and managed decent runs. Brian Taggert's *When Last I Saw the Lemmings* displayed an alternately sardonic and dramatic touch in its examination of a welcome-home party that goes off-balance. In the interests of reporting I must also cite my own play *Ping-Pong,* offering a view of divorce as seen by a battling couple, their current romantic interests, and the couple's son—all trapped on Christmas Eve in a snowbound cabin. The play alternated its humor of situation with conflicts of emotion.

Two new musicals also made debuts in Los Angeles: David Merrick's production of *The Baker's Wife,* from Pagnol's film, with Topol in his American debut; and Patricia Morison and Janet Blair as Virginia Woodhull, an early feminist, and her sister in *Winner Take All.* Both shows needed further work at press time, so it's not known what their ultimate destiny will be. Finally, the theaters along Melrose Avenue had the sensible idea of forming "Theater Row" to let the theatergoers know of some of this community's better small theaters. A day of open-house activities did much to stimulate interest in the ever-growing local stage scene in Los Angeles.

The following is a selection of the most noteworthy Los Angeles productions of the year. The list does not include the numerous touring shows nor the Center Theater Group productions at the Ahmanson and the Mark Taper Forum (see the Regional Theater listing above). A plus sign (+) with the performance number indicates the show was still running on June 1, 1976.

WHEN LAST I SAW THE LEMMINGS (41). By Brian Taggert. January 23, 1976 (world premiere). Director, Michael Shawn; scenery, James Eric and Carrie Humble; lighting, John M. Wright. At the Matrix Theater.

Jesus .... Karl Ellis
Constance .... Lois Walden
Vera .... Patricia Blore
Phil .... Eddy Carroll
Harrison .... Ray Stewart
Clea .... Sheila Stephenson
Oliver .... Robert Redding
One intermission.

PING-PONG (33). By Rick Talcove. February 28, 1976 (world premiere). Director, Patricia Kane; scenery, Russ Butler; costumes, Mary Taylor; lighting, John Banichi and Kevin O'Sullivan. At the Onion Company.

John Morgan .... Henry Darrow
Rene Kelton .... Patricia Kane
Phyllis Morgan .... Jodean Russo
Elliot Gruen .... John Williams
Larry Morgan .... Cliff Wilson
One intermission.

THE BAKER'S WIFE (23+). Musical with book by Joseph Stein; music and lyrics by Stephen Schwartz; based on *La Femme du Boulanger* by Marcel Pagnol and Jean Giono. May 11, 1976 (world premiere). Director, Joseph Hardy; choreographer, Dan Siretta; scenery, Jo Mielziner; costumes, Theoni V. Aldredge; lighting, Jennifer Tipton. Produced by David Merrick at the Dorothy Chandler Pavilion.

Aimable .... Chaim Topol
Genevieve .... Carole Demas
Dominique .... Kurt Peterson
Le Marquis .... Keene Curtis
Antoine .... Gordon Connell
Barnaby .... Pierre Epstein
Therese .... Portia Nelson
Priest .... David Rounds
One intermission.

SMALL CRAFT WARNINGS (32). By Tennessee Williams. June 1, 1975. Director, John Allison; scenery, Jack De Govia; lighting, Cole Roberts. With Helena Carroll, Cherry Davis, Judson Morgan, Maxwell Gail, Jack Riley, Gary Rethmeier, Robert Gray, and Frederick Downs. At the Callboard Theater.

THE MISER (16). By Molière; translated by John Wood. September 4, 1975. Director, Joseph Ruskin; scenery, Joseph McArdle; costumes, Jacki Harmon; lighting, Flora Plumb. With John Harding, Don Vilotti, Dennis Robertson, Diana Hale, Elizabeth Herbert, David Bulasky. At Theater 40.

LOUISVILLE, KY.

Actors' Theater of Louisville: Pamela Brown Auditorium

(Producing director, Jon Jory)

TEN LITTLE INDIANS (31). By Agatha Christie, December 11, 1975. Director, Adale O'Brien; scenery, Paul Owen; lighting, Geoffrey T. Cunningham; costumes, Kurt Wilhelm. With Jean De Baer, Eric Booth, Michael Gross, John Hancock.

OEDIPUS THE KING (26). By Sophocles. January 15, 1976. Director, Jon Jory; scenery, Paul Owen; lighting, Geoffrey T. Cunningham; costumes, Kurt Wilhelm. With Michael Gross, Adale O'Brien, John Hancock, Ray Fry, Michael Kevin.

SCAPINO! (29). By Frank Dunlop and Jim Dale, adapted from Molière's *Les Fourberies de Scapin*. February 12, 1976. Director, Christopher Murney; scenery, Anne A. Gibson; lighting, Geoffrey T. Cunningham; costumes, Kurt Wilhelm. With Peter Silbert, Leo Burmester, Ray Fry, Lee Anne Fahey.

THE LAST MEETING OF THE KNIGHTS OF THE WHITE MAGNOLIA (27). By Preston Jones. March 11, 1976. Director, Jon Jory; scenery and lighting, Paul Owen; costumes, Kurt Wilhelm. With Victor Jory, Peter Silbert, Michael Gross, Barry Corbin, John H. Fields, Michael Kevin.

THE SUNSHINE BOYS (28). By Neil Simon. April 8, 1976. Director, Clifford Ammon; scenery, Paul Owen; lighting, Vincent Faust; costumes, Kurt Wilhelm. With Ray Fry, Jim Baker, William Cain, Don Johnson.

Actors' Theater of Louisville: Victor Jory Theater

SCOTT AND ZELDA (18). By Paul Hunter. November 12, 1975 (world premiere). Director, Elizabeth Ives; scenery and costumes, Kurt Wilhelm; lighting, Geoffrey T. Cunningham.

F. Scott Fitzgerald . . . . Michael Gross
Zelda Sayre Fitzgerald . . . . . . Lauren Levian

Act I is in three major scenes and occurs in various parts of the U. S. and Europe between 1918 and 1930. Act II is in two major scenes, occuring between 1930 and 1948.

MEASURE FOR MEASURE (18). By Charles Marowitz, adapted from the play by William Shakespeare. February 11, 1976 (American premiere). Director, Charles Kerr; scenery and lighting, Paul Owen; costumes, Kurt Wilhelm.

Duke . . . . Michael Kevin
Escalus . . . . Earle Edgerton

Angelo . . . . John Hancock
Bishop . . . . Bob Burrus
Provost . . . . John Meadows
Claudio . . . . Eric Booth
Lucio . . . . Michael Thompson
Isabella . . . . Sara Atkins

THE SEA HORSE (18). By Edward J. Moore. March 10, 1976. Director, Charles Kerr; scenery, Paul Owen; lighting, Geoffrey T. Cunningham; costumes, Kurt Wilhelm. With Adale O'Brien, Robert Forster.

DEAR LIAR (18). By Jerome Kilty; adapted from the correspondence of George Bernard Shaw and Mrs. Patrick Campbell. May 6, 1976. Director, Ray Fry; scenery, Paul Owen; lighting, Geoffrey T. Cunningham; costumes, Kurt Wilhelm. With Adale O'Brien, William Cain.

Actors' Theater of Louisville: Guest Production

A MIDSUMMER NIGHT'S DREAM (11). By William Shakespeare. September 10, 1975.

Director, Allen Cook. Montana Repertory Theater production.

Note: ATL presented two Christmas specials: *A Christmas Memory* by Truman Capote, read by Adale O'Brien, and *A Child's Christmas In Wales* by Dylan Thomas, read by Michael Kevin, on December 15, 1975. Another special event was a 5-performance presentation, beginning January 19, 1976, of a troupe of 11 high school students selected by audition, in a Bicentennial production of American songs, poems, folklore and prose, assembled and directed by Carolyn Bezenek with costumes by Kurt Wilhelm. ATL's production of *Arms And The Man* by George Bernard Shaw began a statewide tour on April 6, 1976. Added to the original cast were Katharine Houghton as Louka, Ken Jenkins as Bluntschli and Vaughn McBride as The Officer.

MADISON, N.J.

New Jersey Shakespeare Festival: Drew University

(Artistic director, Paul Barry; designers: scenery, David M. Glenn; lighting; Gary C. Porto; costumes, Gay Beale Smith and Dean H. Reiter)

HENRY IV, Part 1 (19). By William Shakespeare. June 24, 1975. Director, Paul Barry. With Edward Rudney, Ron Mangravite, Clarence Felder, Richard Graham, David Howard, Tarina Lewis, Alan Jordan.

JOHN BROWN'S BODY (17). By Stephen Vincent Benet. June 28, 1975. Director, Paul Barry. With Lloyd Kay, Y. Yve York, Edward Rudney, Alan Jordan, J. C. Hoyt, Susanne Marley.

HENRY IV, Part 2 (15). By William Shakespeare. July 4, 1975. Director, Paul Barry. With Clarence Felder, Ron Mangravite, Edward Rudney, Eric Tavaris, William Preston.

THE TWO GENTLEMEN OF VERONA (15). By William Shakespeare. July 25, 1975. Director, Paul Barry. With Eric Tavaris. Susanne Marley, Alan Jordan, Y. Yve York, Tarina Lewis, Richard Graham.

THAT CHAMPIONSHIP SEASON (18). By Jason Miller. August 13, 1975. Director, Paul Barry. With David Howard, Eric Tavaris, Clarence Felder, Ronald Steelman, J. C. Hoyt.

In repertory:
UNCLE VANYA (21). By Anton Chekhov. October 5, 1975. Director, Davey Marlin-Jones. With Humbert Allen Astredo, Ellen Barry, J. C. Hoyt, Richard Graham, Tarina Lewis, William Preston, Margery Shaw.
SWEET BIRD OF YOUTH (21). By Tennessee Williams. October 7, 1975. Director, Paul Barry. With Daryn Kent, Dale Robinette.
THE LADY'S NOT FOR BURNING (21). By Christopher Fry. October 28, 1975. Director, Paul Barry. With Margery Shaw, Paul Barry, Naomi Riseman, Ronald Steelman, William Preston, Kathy Dyas.

Note: New Jersey Shakespeare Festival's Intern Program presented two workshop productions in August 1975, 3 performances each. They were *Moonchildren* by Michael Weller, directed by Ted Gargiulo; and *The Madwoman of Chaillot* by Jean Giraudoux, directed by Tom Borsay.

MILWAUKEE

Milwaukee Repertory Theater Company: Todd Wehr Theater

(Artistic director, Nagle Jackson; managing director, Sara O'Connor)

KING LEAR (44). By William Shakespeare. September 12, 1975. Director, Nagle Jackson; scenery and lighting, Christopher M. Idoine; costumes, Elizabeth Covey. With Richard Risso, Daniel Davis, William McKereghan, Glenn Close, Rose Herron, Penelope Reed, Daniel Mooney, Stephen Stout, Durward McDonald.

DEMOCRACY (44). By Romulus Linney; based on novels by Henry Adams and the administration of Ulysses S. Grant. October 24, 1975. Director, John Olon-Scrymgeour; scenery and lighting, R. H. Graham; costumes, Elizabeth Covey; musical director, Edmund Assaly. With Durward McDonald, Jill Heavenrich, Daniel Mooney, Penelope Reed, Jose-

phine Nichols, Robert Lanchester, Peggy Cowles, William McKereghan, Ruth Schudson.

THE SCHOOL FOR WIVES (44). By Molière; English verse translation by Richard Wilbur. December 5, 1975. Director, Nagle Jackson; scenery and lighting, Christopher M. Idoine; costumes, Elizabeth Covey. With Jeffrey Tambour, Leslie Geraci, Stephen Stout, James Pickering, Robert Ingham.

THE VISIONS OF SIMONE MACHARD (44). By Bertolt Brecht and Lion Feuchtwanger; translated by Carl Richard Mueller. January 23, 1976 (American premiere). Director, Nagle Jackson; scenery and lighting, Christopher M. Idoine; costumes, Elizabeth Covey.

Robert Prieux .... Robert Dawson
Maurice Prieux .... Daniel Mooney
Georges .... James Pickering
Père Gustave .... William McKereghan
Simone Machard; Joan of Arc .. Mary Wright
Henri Soupeau; Constable .... Jeffrey Tambor
Colonel .... Robert Ingham
Marie Soupeau; Isabeau .Sirin Devrim Trainer
Sergeant .... Stephen Stout
Mayor Philippe Chavez;
   Charles VII .... Robert Lanchester
Angel .... Tom Blair
Monsieur Machard .... Michael Weller
Madame Machard .... Penelope Reed
Policeman; Engineer ..... Daniel Hargarten
Woman With Baby .... Rose Herron
Therese .... Leslie Geraci
German Captain; Refugee ...John Mansfield
German Orderly; Refugee .... Jim Buske
German Soldier; Engineer;
   Refugee .... Binky Goncharoff
Capt. Honore Fetain;
   Duke of Burbundy ....Durward McDonald
Gray Ladies; Refugees .... Joyce Kinonen,
                 Marilyn Meissner
Time: June 14-22, 1940. Place: The French
village of Saint-Martin. One intermission.

NEVER A SNUG HARBOR (44). By David
Ulysses Clarke. March 12, 1976 (world pre-
miere). Director, John Dillon; scenery and
lighting, R. H. Graham; costumes, Ellen M.
Kozak.
Will Brent .... Tom Blair
Gwilym Williams .... Stephen Stout
Teddy Brent .... Robert Lanchester
Simon Brent .... Robert Ingham
Mary Burns Brent .... Ruth Schudson
Charlie Brent .... Jim Buske
Joe Brent .... James Pickering
Ellen Brent Fitzgerald .... Rose Herron
Jack Fitzgerald .... Durward McDonald
   Place: The Brent home at 17 Fieldstone
Street in Upper Bangor, North Wales. Act I:
January 1, 1900, late afternoon. Act II, Scene
1: Two days later, early afternoon. Scene 2:
That evening. Act III, Scene 1: May, 1902,
late afternoon. Scene 2: January, 1903, night.
Scene 3: The next night.

MY SISTER, MY SISTER (44). By Ray
Aranha. April 23, 1976. Director, Paul Weid-
ner; scenery and lighting, Christopher M.
Idoine; costumes, Ellen M. Kozak. With Seret
Scott, Jessie Saunders, Beatrice Winde, Ray
Aranha, John Mansfield.

Milwaukee Repertory Theater Company: Court Street Theater

OUT AT SEA by Slawomir Mrozek, directed
by William McKereghan; and OUT by Penel-
ope Reed, compiled and directed by Robert
Lanchester from his work in progress on Cus-
ter (16). January 2, 1976. Scenery, James
Wolk; lighting, Frances Aronson; costumes,
Ellen M. Kozak. With Tom Blair, Jim Buske,
John Mansfield, Durward McDonald, Daniel
Mooney, Penelope Reed, Michael Wellert.

FANSHEN (10). By David Hare; from the
book by William Hinton. March 18, 1976
(American premiere). Director, Barry Boys;
scenery, Johniené Papandreas; lighting, Chris-
topher M. Idoine; costumes, Ellen M. Kozak,
Holly Olsen, Susan Perkins.
   Cast: Shen Ching Ho, Kuo-Te-Yu, Chou
Har, Hu Hsueh, Chen's Husband, Lai-Tzu,
Wen-Te—Montgomery Davis; Cheng-K'uan,

Wen Chi-yung, T'ao Yuan, Secretary Lieu—
Robert Dawson; Chung Lai's wife, Hsien-ai,
Chi-Yun—Leslie Geraci; Tui-Chin, Secretary
Ch'en, Ting Fu—Binky Goncharoff; T'ien-
Ming, Hou-Pau-Pei—John Mansfield; Wang
Yu-Lai, Yuan Lung—William McKereghan;
Fa-Liang, Shen Chi-Mei, Magistrate Li—Dan-
iel Mooney; Hu Hsueh-Chen, Hsien-e, Old
Lady Wang—Penelope Reed; Man-Hsi, Chung-
Wang, Chang Chu'er, Huan Ch'ao—Michael
Wellert.
   One intermission.

HAPPY DAYS (10). By Samuel Beckett.
April 15, 1976. Director, Montgomery Davis;
scenery, Valerie Kuehn; lighting, Charles Got-
wald; costumes, Joanne Karaska. With Penelope Reed, Robert Dawson.

Note: This Milwaukee Repertory production of *Democracy*, first produced in 1974 by the
Virginia Museum Theater, is considered by Romulus Linney the final and definitive version,
to be published by Dramatists Play Service. Prior to its presentation at the Todd Wehr
Theater, *The School For Wives* gave 24 performances from October to November 1975 in
Iowa, Minnesota, North Dakota, South Dakota and Wisconsin.

MINNEAPOLIS

The Guthrie Theater Company: Guthrie Theater

   (Artistic director, Michael Langham; managing director, Donald Schoenbaum. Designers:
scenery, Jack Barkla, John Jensen, Robert Ellsworth, Desmond Heeley; lighting, Duane Schuller; cosumes, Lewis Brown, Nancy Potts, Jack Edwards, Robert Ellsworth, Desmond Heeley)

ARSENIC AND OLD LACE (50). By Joseph Kesselring. June 2, 1975. Director, Thomas Gruenewald. With Barbara Bryne, Virginia Payne, Ken Ruta, Karen Landry, Maury Cooper, Jim Baker, Peter Michael Goetz, Nicholas Kepros.

THE CARETAKER (19). By Harold Pinter. June 4, 1975. Director, Stephen Kanee. With Mark Lamos, Eric Christmas, Jeff Chandler.

A STREETCAR NAMED DESIRE (44). By Tennessee Williams. June 18, 1975. Director, Ken Ruta. With Patricia Conolly, Richard Council, Karen Landry, Peter Michael Goetz.

LOOT (24). By Joe Orton. August 6, 1975. Director, Tom Moore. With Eric Christmas, Cara Duff-MacCormick, Mark Lamos, Richard Council, Ken Ruta, Oliver Cliff, Michael Hendricks.

MOTHER COURAGE AND HER CHILDREN (32). By Bertolt Brecht; American version by Robert Hellman; music by Paul Dessau. August 20, 1975. Director, Eugene Lion. With Barbara Bryne, Marcy Mattox, Jim

Baker, Maury Cooper, Peter Michael Goetz, Nicholas Kepros.

UNDER MILK WOOD (23). By Dylan Thomas. October 8, 1975. Director, Kenneth Welsh. With members of the Company.

PRIVATE LIVES (45). By Noel Coward. October 22, 1975. Director, Michael Langham. With Patricia Conolly, Michael Allinson/ Ken Ruta, Mark Lamos, Cara Duff-MacCormick, Virginia Payne, Richard Burton Brown.

A CHRISTMAS CAROL (20). By Charles Dickens; adapted by Barbara Nosanow; music, Hiram Titus. December 10, 1975. With King Donovan, Nicholas Kepros, Barbara Bryne, Jim Baker, Fran Bennett, Jeff Chandler, Oliver Cliff, Cara Duff-MacCormick, Peter Michael Goetz, Mark Lamos.

MEASURE FOR MEASURE (37). By William Shakespeare. February 4, 1976. Director, Michael Langham. With Nicholas Kepros, Mark Lamos, Ken Ruta, Barbara Bryne, Patricia Conolly, Karen Landry.

The Guthrie Theater Company: Guthrie Two

THE COLLECTED WORKS OF BILLY THE KID (10). By Michael Ondaatje. January 14, 1976. Director, Eugene Lion; designer, Richard Hoover. With the Guthrie Two Company.

THE FUTURE PIT (28). By Menzies McKillop. February 5, 1976 (world premiere). Director, David Feldshuh; scenery, Richard Hoover; lighting, Jeff Bartlett; costumes, F. Maurice Palinski; composer, Mark Bloom; choreographers, Cathy Grasiorowicz and Susan Reiner; projections, Lynn Ball, Julia Jenkins.
Cast: Girl, Young Woman, Monk—Anita Grumish; Wife, Teacher—Rosemary Hartup; Young Man, Janitor, Monk, Boy, Soldier— J. Patrick Martin; Girl, White Figure, Elderly Woman, Sybil—Barbara Morin; Girl, Teacher, Doorkeeper, Rebel Boss—Irene O'Brien; Director of Education, Classics Master, Doorkeeper—John Pielmeier; Teacher—Kent Rizley; Headmaster, Donald—T. J. Skinner; Janitor, Sailor, Soldier, Sir Hector McNamara— Bruce W. Somerville.
One intermission.

Triple Feature: Waterman; Glutt; Cold (20). March 17, 1976 (world premieres).
WATERMAN by Frank B. Ford. Director, Jim Wallace; scenery and costumes, William Daniel File; lighting, Eric Goldscheider; sound, Brad Morison.

Waterman . . . . Bruce W. Somerville
Figmo; Maj. Kim . . . . J. Patrick Martin
Junior . . . . John Pielmeier
Zwardowski; Mother . . . . Ken Rizley
Good; Jesus Christ . . . . T. J. Skinner
Evelyn Waterman . . . . Anita Grumish
Grease . . . . Rosemary Hartup
GLUTT by Gladden Schrock. Director, Stephen Kanee; scenery and costumes, William G. Marshall; lighting and sound, Bob Jorissen.
Glutt . . . . T. J. Skinner
Attendant . . . . Bruce W. Somerville
Woman . . . . Rosemary Hartup
COLD by Michael Casale. Director, Emily Mann; scenery and costumes, Maurice Palinski; lighting, Bob Jorissen; composer, Michael Victor.
MM . . . . Irene O'Brien
Marilyn . . . . Anita Grumish
Norma Jean . . . . Barbara Morin
Old Russian Woman . . . . . . Rosemary Hartup
Man . . . . Bruce W. Somerville
G. I. . . . . Kent Rizley
Butler . . . . J. Patrick Martin
Kid . . . . John Pielmeier

HELLO AND GOODBYE (28). By Athol Fugard. April 21, 1976. Director, Mark Lamos; scenery and costumes, Frank Rahn; lighting, Jeff Bartlett. With Kent Rizley, Rosemary Hartup.

OPEN SHUT (28). By Robert Hellman. May

26, 1976 (world premiere). Director, Eugene Lion; scenery and costumes, Maurice Palinski; lighting, Karlis Ozols; choreographer, Jo Lechay.

Herman .... Clyde Lund
Sybilena .... Barbara Morin
Herbert ... . Bert Rosario
One intermission.

Note: Guthrie Two also offered frequent events at 10:30 p.m., sometimes featuring actors from the main stage company, visiting performers in dance, films, variety acts, plays and concert. Among these was a production of *Pilk's Madhouse* by Henry Pilk, compiled and edited by Ken Campbell. Chris Langham directed; scenery and costumes were by Robert Ellsworth; lighting by Jeff Bartlett. The cast included Erik Brogger, Karen Landry, Michael Laskin, Bert Rosario, Bill Schoppert, Sheriden Thomas. Guthrie continued its community outreach program. In conjunction with the Minnesota Department of Corrections, Drew Birns instituted voice, movement and improvisational theater workshops which culminated in the presentation of two one-act plays in the fall of 1975 for an invited public audience. The second project, under the direction of David Felshuh, with a mobile touring company, provided two shows, one for children, one for adults during the 1975–1976 season.

NEW HAVEN

Long Wharf Theater

(Artistic Director, Arvin Brown, executive director, M. Edgar Rosenblum)

ARTICHOKE (28). By Joanna Glass. October 17, 1975 (world premiere). Director, Arvin Brown; scenery, David Jenkins; lighting, Ronald Wallace; costumes, Bill Walker.
Jake .... Louis Beachner
Archie .... James Greene
Margaret .... Colleen Dewhurst
Grampa .... Emery Battis
Walter .... Rex Robbins
Lily Agnes .... Ellin Ruskin
Gibson McFarland .... Brian Murray
    Place: Two neighboring farm houses on the Saskatchewan prairie. One intermission.

THE SHOW-OFF (28). By George Kelly. November 21, 1975. Director, Peter Levin; scenery, Kenneth Foy; lighting, Jamie Gallagher; costumes, Linda Fisher. With William Atherton, Jan Miner, Susan Sharkey, Emery Battis.

WHAT EVERY WOMAN KNOWS (28). By J. M. Barrie. December 26, 1975. Director, Kenneth Frankel; scenery, Steven Rubin; lighting, Judy Rasmuson; costumes, Jania Szatanski. With Joyce Ebert, Christopher Lloyd, Mildred Dunnock, Blair Brown, William Swetland.

STREAMERS (28). David Rabe. January 30, 1976 (world premiere). Director, Mike Nichols; scenery, Tony Walton; lighting, Ronald Wallace; costumes, Bill Walker.
Martin .... Michael-Raymond O'Keefe
Richie .... Peter Evans
Carlyle .... Joe Fields
Billy .... John Heard
Roger .... Herbert Jefferson Jr.
Sgt. Rooney .... Kenneth McMillan
Sgt. Cokes .... Dolph Sweet
M.P. Officer .... Stephen Mendillo
Hinson .... Ron Siebert

Clark .... Michael Kell
    Time: 1965. Place: An Army barracks in Virginia. One intermission.

ON THE OUTSIDE by Thomas Murphy and Noel O'Donoghue and ON THE INSIDE by Thomas Murphy (28). March 5, 1976 (American premiere). Director, Arvin Brown; scenery, David Jenkins; lighting, Ronald Wallace; costumes, Jania Szatanski.
On the Outside:
Kathleen .... Suzanne Lederer
Anne .... Swoosie Kurtz
Joe .... Jarlath Conroy
Frank .... Stephen McHattie
Drunk .... James Greene
Mickey .... Lance Davis
Bouncer .... Michael Houlihan
On the Inside
Miss Darcy .... Linda McGuire
Angela .... Ellin Ruskin
Collins .... Don Gantry
Mrs. Collins .... Elizabeth Parrish
Kieran .... Sean Griffin
Malachy .... Frank Converse
Margaret .... Dorothy Lyman
Sean .... John Roddick
Willie .... James Hummert
Bridie .... Bara-Cristin Hansen
    Time: A Sunday night in the 1950s. Place: A rural Irish dance hall. One intermission.

THE HOUSE OF MIRTH (28). By Clyde Fitch; new adaptation by John Tillinger. April 9, 1976. Director, Waris Hussein; scenery, Majorie Kellogg; lighting, Judy Rasmuson; costumes, Bill Walker. With Fran Brill, George Hearn, Mary Fogarty, Ben Kapen, William Swetland, Elizabeth Parrish, James Greene, Joyce Ebert, Fiddle Viracola, Paul Rosson.

DAARLIN' JUNO (28). Book by Joseph Stein; music and lyrics by Marc Blitzstein; based on *Juno and the Paycock* by Sean O'-Casey; adapted by Richard Maltby Jr. and Geraldine Fitzgerald; additional lyrics by Richard Maltby Jr. May 14, 1976. Director, Arvin Brown; scenery, David Jenkins; lighting, Ronald Wallace; costumes, Bill Walker; music arranged, adapted and directed by Thomas Fay. With Geraldine Fitzgerald, Milo O'Shea, Emery Battis, Suzanne Lederer, Sean Griffin, Joyce Ebert.

Long Wharf Theater: Monday Night Specials

DOOLEY'S BAR (7). Excerpts from Finley Peter Dunne's *Mr. Dooley* columns, adapted and presented by Emery Battis. November 24, 1975.

SONGS OF THE STREETS (2). Music and stories, selected and performed by Geraldine Fitzgerald. February 9, 1976.

DEVILS AND DIAMONDS (5). Theater and song, presented and performed by Stephanie Cotsirilos. March 29, 1976.

Long Wharf Theater: Young People's Theater

(Artistic director, Terrence Sherman)

MARCH TO A DIFFERENT DRUMMER (12). Written and directed by Carl Schurr. October 25, 1975.

SCIENCE FANTASY THRILLER, PART II (8). Written and directed by Terrence Sherman. January 10, 1976.

SCRAPBOOK: AN IMPROVISATIONAL REVUE (19). Written and directed by Terrence Sherman, based on material developed by the company. March 13, 1976.

The Company: Glenn Barrett, Suzanne Carns, Jack Hoffman, Barbara MacKenzie, Michaelin Sisti. Designers: Wilton Duckworth, Wayne Durst, Betty Jo Durst, Karen Kinsella, Jania Szatanski.

Note: Long Wharf Theater continued its New Plays Readings on Monday nights. Presented with members of the professional company and guests from February-June, 1976, were: *When the Old Man Died* by Keith Aldridge; *Arthur* by Jim Peck; *Children of the Sun* by Maxim Gorky (first English translation); *Dance for Me, Simeon* by Joseph Maher; *Blues in North America* by James Harvey; *I Can See It in His Eyes* by John Tobias; *A Voice and Nothing More* by James Child.

Yale Repertory Theater

(Artistic director, Robert Brustein; associate director, Alvin Epstein)

A MIDSUMMER NIGHT'S DREAM (24). By William Shakespeare. October 3, 1975. Director, Alvin Epstein; scenery, Tony Straiges; lighting, William B. Warfel; costumes, Zack Brown; music, Henry Purcell, adapted by Otto-Werner Mueller; music director and conductor, Gary Fagin; choreographer, Carmen de Lavallade. With Philip Kerr, Carmen de Lavallade, Randall Duk Kim, Christine Estabrook, Stephen Rowe, Victor Garber, Paula Wagner.

DON JUAN (25). By Kenneth Cavander; based on Molière's play. October 31, 1975. Director, Robert Brustein; scenery, Michael Yeargan; lighting, Stephen R. Woody; costumes, Tony Straiges and Jeffrey Higginbottom. With Philip Kerr, Eugene Troobnick, Paula Wagner, Frederic Warriner, James Brick, Carmen de Lavallade.

DYNAMITE TONITE! (23). By Arnold Weinstein; music by William Bolcom. November 14, 1975. Directors, Alvin Epstein and Walt Jones; musical director, Gary Fagin; scenery, Heidi Ettinger; lighting, Lewis A. Folden; costumes, Suzanne Palmer. With Joel Polis, Eugene Troobnick, Alvin Epstein, Charles Levin, Paul Schierhorn, Linda Lavin, Andrew Davis, Kenneth Ryan, Stephen Rowe, Jeremy Geidt.

WALK THE DOG, WILLIE (24). By Robert Auletta. January 16, 1976 (world premiere). Director, Walt Jones; scenery and costumes, Michael H. Yeargan; lighting, Donald Bondy Lowy; music and sound, Carol Lees.

Jennifer	Christine Estabrook
Bijou Billins	Tom Hill
Mr. Browfield	Eugene Troobnick
Rose Billins	Norma Brustein
Ronnie Billins	Charles Levin

Lou Ann Bilcott ....Lynn Oliver
Willie ....Kenneth Ryan
One intermission.

BINGO: SCENES OF MONEY AND
DEATH (23). By Edward Bond. January 30,
1976. Director, Ron Daniels; scenery, David
Lloyd Gropman; lighting, Steve Pollock; cos-
tumes, Annette Beck. With Alvin Epstein,
Philip Kerr, Tom Hill, Linda Atkinson, Alma
Cuervo.

GENERAL GORGEOUS (24). By Michael
McClure. February 27, 1976. Director, Lawrence Kornfeld; scenery, Ursula Belden; lighting, Lloyd S. Riford III; costumes, Jeanne

Button; special effects, William B. Warfel;
music composed and directed by Paul Schierhorn. With Dan Hamilton, John Paul, Lynn
Oliver, Marcell Rosenblatt, Christine Estabrook, Charles Levin, Carmen de Lavallade,
Alma Cuervo, Eugene Troobnick, Norma
Brustein.

TROILUS AND CRESSIDA (24). By Wil-
liam Shakespeare. April 2, 1976. Director, Al-
vin Epstein; scenery, Tony Straiges; lighting,
Paul Gallo; costumes, Michael Yeargan. With
Dan Hamilton, Laurie Heineman, Jeremy
Geidt, Avram Hellerman, Anne Gerety, Barry
Primus, Robert Brustein.

Yale Repertory Theater: Guest Production

AN EVENING WITH SAMUEL BECKETT
(4). March 24, 1976. Compiled, directed and

performed by Patrick Magee.

Note: Yale Repertory Theater and School of Drama sponsor Yale Cabaret, Experimental
Theater, studio projects (including Playwright's workshops and Sunday Series of new play
readings) with students, faculty and members of the professional company; as well as a Student Repertory subscription series, all of which are open to the public. *Lady With the Alli-
gator* by Peter Blanc, *Uncommon Women and Others* by Wendy Wasserstein; *Efforts and
Study Habits* by Mark Buckholtz; *Attempt At Conversation* by Edward Gold were presented
at a New Plays Festival, December 10-13, 1975. Productions in the School of Drama Repertory included *The Visit* by Friedrich Duerrenmatt, directed by Robert Lewis; *The Duchess
of Malfi* by John Webster; *Narrow Road to the Deep North* by Edward Bond; *The Family
Reunion* by T. S. Eliot, directed by Robert Lewis; *Three Sisters* by Anton Chekhov, directed
by Walt Jones (November 1975 through May, 1976). The Sunday Series gave one reading each
of *Trade-Offs* by Lonnie Carter; *From the Memoirs of Pontius Pilate* by Eric Bentley and
Manfly by Sam Shepard during the 1975-1976 season.

PRINCETON, N.J.

McCarter Theater Company: McCarter Theater

(Producing director, Michael Kahn)

A GRAVE UNDERTAKING (14). By Lloyd
Gold. October 9, 1975. Director, Michael
Kahn; scenery, Paul Zalon; lighting, John
McLain; costumes, Lawrence Casey. With
Richard Dix, Chris Sarandon, Pat Hingle, Wil-
liam Larsen, Deborah Offner.

THE ROYAL FAMILY (14). By George S.
Kaufman and Edna Ferber. October 30, 1975.
Director, Ellis Rabb; scenery, Oliver Smith;
lighting, John Gleason; costumes, Ann Roth.
With Rosemary Harris, Eva Le Gallienne,
George Grizzard, Sam Levene, Joseph Maher,
Rosetta LeNoire, Eleanor Phelps.

SECTION NINE (14). By Philip Magdalany.
November 20, 1975 (American premiere). Director, Michael Kahn; scenery, Kert Lundell;
lighting, John McLain; costumes, Jeanne Button.

Adriane Mackenzie ....Conard Fowkes
Vivien 532 ....Elaine Kerr
Jasper 906 ....Richard Lenz
Marlon 845 ....Jerry Lanning
Fenwick 747 ....Drew Snyder
Winifred 601 ....Carol Morely
Sen. Sinclair Caldwell ....William Larsen
Gen. Enfield Muster ....Barton Heyman
Somerset Swayze, M. D. ....Richard Dix
Ubell Untermeyer ....David Rounds
Attendant ....Henry Glassman
Bearded Man. ....Michael Houlihan
Man With Blond Hair ....Joseph Jamrog
Man With Dark Glasses ......Dennis Papara
Place: Washington D. C. One intermission.

THE HEIRESS (14). By Ruth and Augustus
Goetz; based on *Washington Square* by Henry
James. February 12, 1976. Director, Michael
Kahn; scenery, David Jenkins; lighting, L. B.
Achziger; costumes, Jane Greenwood. With

Maria Tucci, Jack Gwillim, Richard Backus, Kate Wilkinson.

AWAKE AND SING (14). By Clifford Odets. March 4, 1976. Director, Kenneth Frankel; scenery, Marjorie Kellogg; lighting, John McLain; costumes, Jeanne Button. With Morris Carnovsky, Joan Lorring, Steven Gilborn; Richard Gere, Martin Rudy.

THE WINTER'S TALE (14). By William Shakespeare. March 25, 1976. Director, Michael Kahn; associate director, Larry Carpenter; scenery, John Conklin; lighting, John McLain; costumes, Jane Greenwood; music, Lee Hoiby. With Maria Tucci, Philip Kerr, Ian Trigger, Richard Dix, Bette Henritze, Richard Backus, Curt Dawson, Josef Sommer, William Larsen.

PROVIDENCE, R.I.

Trinity Square Repertory Company: Lederer Theater—Upstairs

(Producer-director, Adrian Hall)

CATHEDRAL OF ICE (31). By James Schevill. October 14, 1975 (world premiere). Director, Adrian Hall; scenery, Eugene Lee; lighting, Mark Rippe; costumes, Franne Lee and Betsey Potter; music and additional lyrics, Richard Cumming; dances, Brian R. Jones; props, Sandra Nathanson.

Cast: Beverly Andreozzi, Robert Colonna, William Damkoehler, Timothy Donahue, Peter Gerety, Bradford Gott-Lin, Ed Hall, Richard Jenkins, David C. Jones, Melanie Jones, Richard Kneeland, Howard London, George Martin, Derek Meader, Barbara Meek, Julie Miterko, Nancy Nichols, Barbara Orson, William Radka, Bonnie Sacks, William Sadler, Cynthia Strickland, Daniel Von Bargen.

TWO GENTLMEN OF VERONA (46). By John Guare and Mel Shapiro; lyrics by John Guare; music by Galt MacDermot; adapted from the play by William Shakespeare. December 30, 1975. Director-choreographer, Word Baker; scenery, Eugene Lee; lighting, Mark Rippe; costumes, James Berton Harris; musical director, Richard Cumming; additional music and lyrics by Robert Black, William Damkoehler, Vern Graham, Richard Cumming and Queen Elizabeth I. With Robert Black, William Damkoehler, Melanie Jones,

Cynthia Strickland, Richard Jenkins, Rose Weaver.

BASTARD SON (27). By Richard Lee Marks. February 17, 1976 (world premiere). Director, Vincent Dowling; scenery, Eugene Lee; lighting, Mark Rippe; costumes, James Berton Harris.

William Franklin . . . . Robert Black
Benjamin Franklin . . . . William Cain
William Temple Franklin . . . . John Chase
General Sir. Henry Clinton . . . George Martin
General Moses Hazen . . . William Damkoehler
Captain Charles Asgill . . . . . . Derek Meader

Others: Citizen, rebel, Lippincott, British Captain, Vergennes—Ed Hall; Citizen, English Lord, Rebel, Reverend Woodhull, Loyalist, British Captain—Peter Gerety; Citizen, Mrs. Edwards, Loyalist, Lady Asgill—Barbara Orson; Citizen, Serving Girl, Loyalist, Rebel—Mina Manente; Servant, Continental Soldier—Bradford Gott-Lin; English Lord, Jack Huddy, British Captain, British Soldier—Richard Jenkins; Lord Bute, Citizen, Rebel, Loyalist British Captain—Daniel Von Bargen; Elizabeth Downes, Sarah Russell—Margo Skinner; Citizen, Constable Loyalist, Drummer—William Sadler; Citizen, British Soldier, Philip White—Timothy Donahue.

Trinity Square Repertory Company: Lederer Theater—Downstairs

ANOTHER PART OF THE FOREST (34). By Lillian Hellman. November 1, 1975. Director, Adrian Hall; scenery, Robert D. Soule; lighting, John Custer; costumes, James Berton Harris. With Zina Jasper, Marguerite Lenert, Richard Kneeland, Richard Kavanaugh, Mina Manente.

THE LITTLE FOXES (54). By Lillian Hellman. December 2, 1975. Director, Adrian Hall; scenery, Robert D. Soule; lighting, John Custer; costumes, James Berton Harris. With Zina Jasper, Richard Kavanaugh, Richard

Kneeland, Mina Manente, Marguerite Lenert, William B. Cain.

EUSTACE CHISHOLM AND THE WORKS (33). By Adrian Hall and Richard Cumming; adapted from the novel by James Purdy. April 6, 1976 (world premiere). Director, Adrian Hall; scenery, Eugene Lee; lighting, Mark Rippe; costumes, Betsey Potter; props, Sandra Nathanson.

Cast: Richard Kavanaugh, Peter Gerety, William Damkoehler, Margo Skinner, Daniel

Von Bargen, Cynthia Strickland, Richard Kneeland, Barbara Meek.

Time: October, 1933 through the summer of the following year. Place: Chicago, USA.

Part I: *The Sun At Noon.* Part II: *Under Earth's Deepest Stream.* Epilogue: *After The Terrible Events Of The Summer.* One intermission.

RICHMOND, VA.

The Repertory Company of the Virginia Museum Theater

(Artistic director, Keith Fowler; managing director, Ken Letner)

GUYS AND DOLLS (21). Book by Jo Swerling and Abe Burrows; music and lyrics by Frank Loesser; based on a story and characters by Damon Runyon. October 22, 1975. Director, Keith Fowler; scenery, Richard Norgard; lighting, Michael Watson; costumes, Frederick N. Brown; musical director, William Stancil; choreographer, Nat Horne. With Roger Rathburn, Jim Cyrus, Marie Goodman Hunter, Maureen O'Kelley; Nico Boccio, Walter Rhodes.

SHERLOCK HOLMES IN SCANDAL IN BOHEMIA (20). Written and directed by Ken Letner; based on the stories of Arthur Conan Doyle. November 13, 1975. Scenery, Robert Franklin; lighting, James D. Bloch; costumes, Frederick N. Brown. With John Wylie, Barbara Redmond, Walter Rhodes, William Pitts.

THE MEMBER OF THE WEDDING (21). By Carson McCullers. December 4, 1975. Director, Tom Markus; scenery, Richard Norgard; lighting, James D. Bloch; costumes, Frederick N. Brown. With Marie Goodman Hunter, Prudence Wright Holms, Christopher Owen Ayres.

THE CRUCIBLE (21). By Arthur Miller. January 8, 1976. Director, James Kirkland; scenery, Richard Norgard; lighting, Michael Watson; costumes, Frederick N. Brown. With Walter Rhodes, Marjorie Lerstrom, Dottie

Dee, Sarah Brooke, Shelia O. Spurlock, K. Lype O'Dell, Ken Letner.

CHILDREN (2). By A. R. Gurney Jr.; suggested by a story by John Cheever. January 29, 1976 (American premiere). Director, Keith Fowler; scenery, Tony Straiges; lighting, Michael Watson; costumes, Frederick N. Brown.
Barbara .... Lynda Myles
Randy .... Dennis Howard
Mother .... Carmen Mathews
Jane .... Heather MacRae
    Time: Saturday, July 4th, 1970. Place: An island off the coast of Massachusetts.

THE EMPEROR JONES (21). By Eugene O'Neill. February 19, 1976. Director, Ken Letner; scenery, Don Pasco and Richard Norgard; lighting, Michael Watson; costumes, Don Pasco and Frederick N. Brown. With Earle Hyman, Jim Cyrus, Marie Goodman Hunter, Carl Blackwell Lester, Millledge Mosley.

THE CONTRAST (2). By Royall Tyler; adapted by Ken Letner and William Stancil. March 11, 1976. Director, James Kirkland; scenery, Richard Norgard; lighting, James D. Bloch; costumes, Frederick N. Brown; music, additional material and musical director, William Stancil. With Alan Brooks, Sarah Brooke, Dottie Dee, Maury Erickson, Ken Letner, Maureen O'Kelley, William Pitts, David Pichette, Eloise Zeigler.

ROCHESTER, MICH.

Oakland University Professional Theater Program: Meadow Brook Theater

(Artistic director, Terence Kilburn; managing director, David Robert Kanter; resident costume coordinator, Mary Lynn Bonnell)

A MIDSUMMER NIGHT'S DREAM (29). By William Shakespeare. October 9, 1975. Director, Terence Kilburn; scenery, Peter Hicks; lighting, Larry Reed. With Curtis J. Armstrong, Evelyn Baron, Cheryl Giannini, Robert Grossman, William Halliday, Susanne Peters, Eric Tavaris, Fred Thompson.

WITNESS FOR THE PROSECUTION (29). By Agatha Christie. November 6, 1975. Director, Terence Kilburn; scenery, Peter Hicks;

lighting, Robert Neu. With James Corrigan, Cheryl Giannini, William Halliday, Donald C. Moore, Elisabeth Orion.

ARMS AND THE MAN (29). By George Bernard Shaw. December 4, 1975. Director, Terence Kilburn; scenery, Nancy Thompson; lighting, Jeffrey Schissler. With Cheryl Giannini, Robert Grossman, Mae Marmy, Donald C. Moore, Susanne Peters, David Schurmann, Eric Tavaris, Richard Riehle.

THE LITTLE FOXES (29). By Lillian Hellman. January 1, 1976. Director, Charles Nolte; scenery, Lance Brockman; lighting, Jean Montgomery. With Nancy Coleman, John Hallow, Polly Holliday, William LeMassena, Joseph Warren.

RELATIVELY SPEAKING (29). By Alan Ayckbourn. January 29, 1976. Director, Terence Kilburn; scenery, Peter Hicks; lighting, Larry Reed. With Donald Ewer, Cheryl Giannini, Elisabeth Orion, Steven Sutherland.

UNDER MILK WOOD (29). By Dylan Thomas. February 26, 1976. Director, Michael Montel; scenery, Larry A. Reed; lighting, Robert Neu. With Mary Benson, Peter Brandon, Donald Ewer, Cheryl Giannini, Marianne

Muellerleile, Elisabeth Orion, Steven Sutherland, Fred Thompson.

BORN YESTERDAY (29). By Garson Kanin. March 25, 1976. Director, Anthony Mockus; scenery, Thomas A. Aston; lighting, Fred Fonner. With Peter Brandon, Marie Wallace, Guy Stockwell.

YANKEE INGENUITY (29). Book and lyrics by Richard Bimonte; music by Jim Wise; based on Anna Cora Mowatt's *Fashion*. April 22, 1976. Director, Terence Kilburn; scenery, Peter Hicks; lighting, Larry A. Reed; music director, Richard Sharp; choreographer, Don Price. With Stephen Berger, Cheryl Giannini, Marianne Muellerleile, Michele Mullen, Phillip Piro, Max Showalter.

Note: *Born Yesterday* toured Michigan during the Spring 1976 season.

ST. LOUIS

Loretto-Hilton Repertory Theater

(Managing director, David Frank; consulting director, Davey Marlin-Jones)

A MIDSUMMER NIGHT'S DREAM (27). By William Shakespeare. October 24, 1975. Director, David Frank. With Christine Wiedemann, James Anthony, Henry Strozier, Margaret Winn, Wil Love, Robert Spencer, Arthur A. Rosenberg, Valery Daemke.

DESIRE UNDER THE ELMS (27). By Eugene O'Neill. November 28, 1975. Director, Davey Marlin-Jones. With Robert Darnell, Margaret Winn, J. C. Hoyt, Joneal Joplin, Arthur A. Rosenberg.

TOM JONES (27). By Henry Fielding; adapted and directed by Larry Arrick; songs and music written and directed by Barbara Damashek; lyrics by Barbara Damashek and Larry Arrick. January 2, 1976. With Scott Robertson, Margaret Winn, Christine Wiedemann, Wil Love, Robert Darnell, Brendan Burke.

A MEMORY OF TWO MONDAYS by Arthur Miller and BRANDY STATION (world premiere) by Davey Marlin-Jones (27). February 6, 1976. Director, Davey Marlin-Jones. *A Memory of Two Mondays* with Margaret Winn, Arthur A. Rosenberg, Robert Darnell, Wil Love.

Brandy Station

Wolverton Wain	Henry Strozier
Cabel Seifer	Robert Darnell
Amos Herrod	Arthur A. Rosenberg
Art Fry	Bob Ari
Cletus Addington	Bill Nunnery
Vernon Hitchcock	Kevin Pawley
Peyton Capeless	Joneal Joplin
Gabriel Lenz	Robert Spencer
Avra	Valery Daemke
Lucy	Margaret Winn

Time: early October, 1863. Place: Culpepper, Va. and in the memory and imagination of Capt. Wolverton Wain. One intermission.

ONCE IN A LIFETIME (27). By George S. Kaufman and Moss Hart. March 5, 1976. Director, Jack O'Brien. With Robert Spencer, Valery Daemke, Wil Love, Margaret Winn, Christine Wiedemann, J. C. Hoyt, Robert Darnell, Arthur A. Rosenberg, Brendan Burke, Henry Strozier.

Designers: scenery, John Kavelin, Grady Larkins; lighting, Peter E. Sargent, Glenn Dunn, Stephen Ross; costumes, John C. Sullivan, Bill Walker, Mary Strieff.

Note: During their first national tour for the 1975-76 season, Bert Houle and Sophie Wibaux with Vic Grayson and Keith Brzozowski presented an evening of mime March 31-April 3, 1976 at their home theater, the Loretto-Hilton. The Young People's Theater of the Loretto-Hilton Repertory Theater toured 60 schools in Missouri with a Story Theater production baesd on American heritage and folklore. The YPT Company consisted of James Anthony, John Cothran Jr., Ruth Priwer, Stephen Walker, Addie Walsh, Rebecca Uphouse.

SAN FRANCISCO

American Conservatory Theater: Geary Theater

(General director, William Ball)

TINY ALICE (15). By Edward Albee. October 4, 1975. Director, William Ball; associate director, Eugene Barcone; scenery, Ralph Funicello; lighting, F. Mitchell Dana; costumes, Robert Morgan. With Hope Alexander-Willis, Sydney Walker, Earl Boen, Nicholas Cortland, Anthony S. Teague.

THE MATCHMAKER (31). By Thornton Wilder. October 7, 1975. Director, Laird Williamson; associate director, James Haire; scenery, Richard Seger; lighting, F. Mitchell Dana; costumes, Robert Fletcher. With Elizabeth Huddle, William Paterson, James R. Winker, Daniel Zippi, Deborah May.

DESIRE UNDER THE ELMS (23). By Eugene O'Neill. October 21, 1975. Director, Allen Fletcher; associate director, David Hammond; scenery, Robert Blackman, lighting, Dirk Epperson; costumes, Cathy Edwards. Ray Reinhardt, Rick Hamilton, Daniel Kern, Megan Cole, Raye Birk.

GENERAL GORGEOUS (23). By Michael McClure. November 25, 1975 (world premiere). Director, Edward Hastings; associate director, Sabin Epstein; scenery, Ralph Funicello; lighting, F. Mitchell Dana; costumes, Robert Morgan; music, Bruce Bitkoff, Fae McNally; sound, Bartholomeo Rago.

Pink Mutation

One	Franchelle Stewart Dorn
Pink Mutation Two	Francine Tackler
Blue Mutant	Stephen Schnetzer
Gen. Gorgeous	Nicholas Cortland
Angela	Deborah May
Pam	Barbara Dirickson
Roar	Charles Hallahan
Mouse Woman	Joy Carlin
John Paul	Rick Hamilton
Lilah	Hope Alexander-Willis

THE MERRY WIVES OF WINDSOR (25). By William Shakespeare. December 16, 1975. Director, Jon Jory; associate director, Eugene Barcone; scenery, Robert Blackman; lighting, F. Mitchell Dana; costumes, Dorothy Jenkins. With Ray Reinhardt, Fredi Olster, Megan Cole, Janice Garcia, Marrian Walters, Earl Boen, Anthony S. Teague.

THIS IS (AN ENTERTAINMENT) (21). By Tennessee Williams. January 20, 1976 (world premiere). Director, Allen Fletcher; associate director, James Haire; scenery, John Jensen; lighting, F. Mitchell Dana; costumes, Robert Morgan; music, Conrad Susa; sound,

Bartholomeo Rago.

Elderly Princepessa	Marrian Walters
Ancient Dandy;	
Voice of the Secretary	Sydney Walker
Hotel Manager	Ronald Boussom
Assistant Manager;	
Voice of a Newscaster	Ross Graham
Footman; Guerrilla	J. Steven White
Doorman; Interpreter; Voice over	
Loudspeaker; Guerrilla	Michael Keys-Hall
Baronessa; Secretary	Candace Barrett
Kewpie	Nathan Haas
Children	Amy Terris, Edward Lampe
Nanny	Hope Alexander-Willis
Countess	Elizabeth Huddle
Count	Ray Reinhardt
Chauffeur;	
Gen. Capricorn	Nicholas Cortland
Mitzi; Grande-Dame;	
Lady in Waiting	Francine Tacker
Fritzi; Grande-Dame;	
Lady in Waiting	Barbara Dirickson
Barber; Colonel	Rick Hamilton
Manicurist; Elderly Lady	Sandra Shotwell
Bootblack	Tyrone Clinton
Lawyer	James R. Winker
Doctor	Eric Boen
Duchess	Franchelle Stewart Dorn
Titled Poet	Laird Williamson
Cardinal	Joseph Bird
Brother	Al White
Mother	Anne Lawder

Bellboys and Maids: Karen Bebb, Bruce Geller, James Gray, Ken Krider, Emily Patt, Rebecca Soladay, Chris Valentine.

Place: The Grande Hotel Splendide, a lakeside resort in the capitol city of a small monarchy between Western and mid-Eastern Europe. One intermission .

EQUUS (70). By Peter Shaffer. February 10, 1976. Director, William Ball; associate director, Eugene Barcone; original scenery by John Napier, adapted by Robert Blackman; lighting, F. Mitchell Dana; costumes, Robert Morgan. With Peter Donat, Daniel Zippi/ Harry Hamlin, Fredi Olster/Hope Alexander-Willis, Michael Keys-Hall, Charles Hallahan/ Earl Boen, Megan Cole/Anne Lawder, Janice Garcia.

PEER GYNT (24). By Henrik Ibsen; translated and directed by Allen Fletcher. March 9, 1976. Associate director, David Hammond; scenery, Ralph Funicello; lighting, Dirk Epperson; costumes, Robert Blackman. With Daniel Davis, Joy Carlin, Anne Lawder, Hope Alexander-Willis.

THE TAMING OF THE SHREW (15). By William Shakespeare. March 30, 1976. Director, William Ball; associate director, Eugene Barcone; scenery, Ralph Funicello; lighting, F. Mitchell Dana; costumes, Robert Fletcher. With Anthony S. Teague, Fredi Olster, Sandra Shotwell, William Paterson.

American Conservatory Theater: Geary Theater—Guest Production

SCAPINO (48). By Frank Dunlop and Jim Dale; adapted from Moliere's *Les Fourberies de Scapin.* July 22, 1975. Director, Frank Dunlop; scenery and costumes, Carl Toms; lighting, F. Mitchell Dana; music, Jim Dale. With Jim Dale, Gavin Reed, Ian Trigger; Sarah Jane Atkins, Raye Birk, J. Frank Lucas (members of the ACT company).

American Conservatory Theater: Marines' Memorial Theater—Guest Productions

EL GRANDE DE COCA-COLA (29). By Ron House, John Neville-Andrews, Alan Shearman, Diz White, Sally Willis; from an idea by Ron House and Diz White. January 30, 1976. Scenery, Michael Garrett. With Ron House, James Howard Laurence, Jonathan Gardner, Diz White, Janet McGrath.

KENNEDY'S CHILDREN (32). By Robert Patrick. March 3, 1976. Director, Clive Donner; scenery and costumes, Santo Loquasto; lighting, Martin Aronstein. With Shirley Knight, K. C. Kelly, Kaiulani Lee, Bobo Lewis, Don Parker, Michael Sacks.

American Conservatory Theater: Marines' Memorial Theater--Special Production

AMERICA MORE OR LESS (20). By Imamu Amiri Baraka, Frank Chin, Leslie Silko; conception, continuity and lyrics by Arnold Weinstein: music by Tony Greco. April 21, 1976 (world premiere). Directors, Lee D. Sankowich and John Henry Doyle; designer, Ronald Chase; lighting, Dirk Epperson; stage movement, Raymond Sawyer; musical director, Tony Greco. With Bianca, Frank Chin, Michael Cavanaugh, Ben W. Dun, III, Garry Goodrow, Tony Greco, O-Lan Johnson-Shepard, Rodney Kageyama, Donna LaBrie, Anna Mathias, Don McAlister, John Salazar, Bobby Joe Woodward.

American Conservatory Theater: Playroom Studio—Plays in Progress

WHAT DO THE JEWS DO ON CHRISTMAS? and PLANETS APART (14). By Jonathan Licht. November 21, 1975. Director, Paul Blake; scenery and lighting, Michael Garrett; costumes, Cathy Edwards; sound, J. S. McKie Jr.
What Do the Jews Do on Christmas?
Adam 1 ....Peter Schuck
Adam 2 ....Traber Burns
Deborah Stone ....Jane Bolton
Joseph Stone ....Lawrence Hecht
Judith Stone ....Gina Franz
Mailman; Billy ....J. Steven White
Lee Frankel; the Whale ......Kraig Cassity
Rabbi; Harold Adams ....Harry R. Hamlin
Townsperson; Teacher ....Barta Lee Heiner
Caroline Marshall ......Susan E. Pellegrino
Townsperson; Ethel Burke ..Caroline Smith
Planets Apart (words and music by Jonathan Licht; musical director, Jon Lind): *Faraway*
Dennis ....Kraig Cassity
Carlo ....Harry R. Hamlin
Rachel ....Susan E. Pellegrino
Eddie ....Peter Schuck

Guenivere ....Caroline Smith
Planets Apart: Lunchtime Blues
Jacob Riskin ....Traber Burns
Robert Marco ....Lawrence Hecht
Barbara Marco ....Susan E. Pellegrino
Eileen ....Jane Bolton
  Guests: Kraig Cassity, Harry R. Hamlin, Peter Schuck, Caroline Smith, J. Steven White.
Planets Apart: Loving
Marta ....Gina Franz
Ray ....J. Steven White

ANIMALS ARE PASSING FROM OUR LIVES (16). By Robert Eisele. December 20, 1975. Director, Laird Williamson; scenery, Michael Garrett; lighting, Kendall D. Tieck; costumes, Barbara Affonso; sound, Gamble Wetherby.
Irene ....Deborah May
Michael ....Gregory Gillbergh
Anna ....Lou Ann Graham
Jessie ....Stephen Schnetzer
Papa ....Charles Hallahan
Tulip ....Rodney Kageyama

Juna ....Christie S. Mellor
Gabrielle ....Joy Camp
  Act I: Twilight. Act II: Dawn.

THE HUNTER GRACCHUS (19). By John
Robinson. February 4, 1976. Director, Joy
Carlin; scenery, Kendall D. Tieck; lighting
and sound, J. S. McKie Jr.; costumes, Cathy
Edwards; music composed and performed,
Bruce Bitkoff.
Gracchus ....Lawrence Hecht
Gilga ....Rick Hamilton
Erma ....Francine Tacker
Hazel ....Mary Lou Stewart
Mother ....Anne Lawder
Father ....Bruce Gerhard
  Chorus: Franchelle Stewart Dorn, Gregory
Itzin, Sandra Shotwell.

THE GIRL WITH A SENSE OF FAIR
PLAY (15). By Carole Braverman. March
27, 1976. Director, Edward Hastings; scenery
and lighting, G. W. Bolton; costumes, Kim
Dennis; sound, J. S. McKie Jr.

Bess ....Marrian Walters
Trina ....Hope Alexander-Willis
Royce ....Candace Barrett
Paul ....Nathan Haas
Dave ....Joseph Bird
Mrs. Fishbein ....Barta Lee Heiner
Jeanette ....Caroline Smith
Hare Krishna Devotee ....Wayne Alexander
  Time: Summer of 1972. Place: A New
York Jewish kitchen.

PLAY-PLAY (16). By Joe Landon; music
by Joe Landon and Jerry Frankel. May 5,
1976. Director, Paul Blake; scenery and lighting, G. W. Bolton; costumes, Barbara Affonso; combat sequence, J. Steven White;
musical director-orchestrator, Jerry Frankel;
additional lyrics, Paul Blake.
John ....E. Lamont Johnson
Dave ....Gregory Itzin
Jane ....Franchelle Stewart Dorn
Nancy ....Francine Tacker
Ted ....Charles Coffey

Note: On May 23, 1976, ACT began a 4-week tour to the U.S.S.R. in Moscow at the Moscow
Art Theater, followed by appearances at the Palace of Culture of Lensoviet in Leningrad and
at the State Dramatic Theater of Latvia de Upit in Riga. Plays presented were *The Matchmaker* and *Desire Under the Elms,* from the 1975-1976 repertory.

SARASOTA, FLA.

Asolo State Theater Company: Ringling Museum's Court Playhouse

(Artistic director, Robert Strane; managing director, Howard J. Millman; executive director,
Richard G. Fallon; resident designers: scenery, Rick Pike; lighting, Martin Petlock; costumes,
Catherine King, Flozanne John)

TARTUFFE (20). By Molière; English version by Eberle Thomas and Robert Strane.
June 25, 1975. Director, Robert Strane; lighting, Martin Petlock and Dan Gwin.

THERE'S ONE IN EVERY MARRIAGE
(12). By Georges Feydeau; translated and
adapted by Suzanne Grossmann and Paxton
Whitehead. July 8, 1975. Director, Howard J.
Millman.

KING LEAR (15). By William Shakespeare.
July 25, 1975. Director, William Woodman.

THE NEW YORK IDEA (26). By Langdon
Mitchell. February 19, 1976. Director, John
Ulmer; scenery, Holmes Easley; music ar-
ranged and played by Florence Mosser; Sara-
sota Boy's Choir under direction of Julie
Rohr.

HOGAN'S GOAT (20). By William Alfred.
February 27, 1976. Director, William Woodman; scenery, Joseph Nieminski.

GOING APE (24). By Nick Hall. March 5,
1976 (world premiere). Director, Janet Mc-
Call; scenery, Bennet Averyt. With Pamela
Lewis, Dennis Michaels, Kelly Fitzpatrick,
Isa Thomas, Bradford Wallace.
  Time: Now. Place: The study of a large
house. Act I: Mid-morning. Act II: Thirty
minutes later.

BOY MEETS GIRL (34). By Bella and
Samuel Spewack. April 2, 1976. Director,
Howard J. Millman; scenery, Jim Chestnutt.

A STREETCAR NAMED DESIRE (22). By
Tennessee Williams. April 9, 1976. Director,
Neal Kenyon; scenery, Peter Harvey.

THE QUIBBLETOWN RECRUITS (25). By
Eberle Thomas. May 7, 1976 (world premiere). Director, Robert Strane; scenery,
John Scheffler; dance, musical numbers, special staging, Jim Hoskins; editorial supervision of text and additional dialogue, Barbara
Redmond; sound, Bert Taylor.

Col. Philip Brazen ....David S. Howard
Capt. Frost ....Stephen Van Benschoten
Capt. Richard Plume ....Steven Ryan
Sgt. Lucius Kite ....Bradford Wallace
Jack Worthy ....Dennis Michaels
Chester Shelnutt ....Robert Stallworth
Ralph Rumph ......Frederic Winslow Oram
Rose Loughlin ....Janice Clark
Cpl. Ned Whisk ....Steven J. Rankin
Melinda Watson ....Martha J. Brown
Lucy ....Beth Lincks
Alexandra Balance ....Bette Oliver
Lt. Gov. Edward Balance ....Ken Costigan
Silvia Balance ....Pamela Lewis
Peggy ....Cathy S. Chappell
Maj. Laurence Higgins ....Kelly Fitzpatrick
Lt. Helmut Schnapps ....James Hillgartner
Justice Archibald Sharp ......David Kwiat
Mally Prince ....Donna Pelc
Cpl. Harbuck ....John Gray
Capt. William Balance ....Clark Niederjohn
Cpl. Fletcher ....Jim Crisp Jr.
  Men and women of Quibbletown, British
and patriot Soldiers: Stephen Joseph, Rom-
ulus E. Zamora, Nora Chester, Patricia Oet-
ken, Bill Herman, John Gray, Jim Crisp Jr.,
Peter Ivanov, Deborah Unger. King George

and the Washing Tones Band: Steven J. Ran-
kin, Clark Niederjohn, Fred Davis, Peter
Ivanov, Stephen Joseph, John Gray.
  Time: June 1777. Place: In and around
Quibbletown, N.J. Act I, Scene 1: Col.
Brazen's office, Monday morning. Scene 2:
Tavern porch and street, that afternoon.
Scene 3: The Balance residence, the same.
Scene 4: Melinda's garden, the same. Act
II, Scene 1: Col. Brazen's office, Tuesday
evening. Scene 2: Melinda's garden, the
same. Scene 3: The Balance residence, the
same, around midnight. Act III, Scene 1:
Tavern porch and street, Wednesday morn-
ing. Scene 2: A wooded area overlooking the
Rebel camp, just before dawn, Thursday.
Scene 3: The same, just after dawn. Scene 4:
The Balance residence, Thursday evening.

  Acting Company: (summer 1975 and win-
ter-spring, 1976): Martha J. Brown, Burton
Clarke, Ken Costigan, Kelly Fitzpatrick, Max
Gulack, James Hillgartner, David S. Howard,
Stephen Johnson, Henson Keys, William
Leach, Philip LeStrange, Robert Murch,
Bette Oliver, Barbara Reid, Barbara Rue,
Steven Ryan, Isa Thomas, Bradford Wallace.

Asolo State Theater: Children's Theater

TROLLS AND BRIDGES (20). By Sandie
Hastie and Jon Caulkins. August 1, 1975.
Director, Sandie Hastie; scenery, Sam Bager-
ella; lighting, Dan Gwin; costumes, Joy
Grozinger. With Janice Clark, Stephen
Joseph, David Kwiat, Clark Niederjohn, Don-
na Pelc, Bob Stallworth. The play is an inter-

national collage of eight folk tales—Uncle
Bouki Rents a Horse (Haiti), Jean Labadie's
Dog (Canada), How Wihio Trapped the Sun
(American Indian), The Three Hunters
(France), Why Cats Always Wash After Eat-
ing (Holland)—and several troll stories of
various origins.

Asolo State Theater: Special Production

THE PATRIOTS (8). By Sidney Kingsley.
October 24, 1975. Director, Robert Strane;
scenery, Rick Pike; lighting, Martin Petlock;
costumes, Catherine King. With Robert
Murch, Philip LeStrange, Ralph Clanton,

Catherine Rao, Bradford Wallace, Stephen
Johnson, Barbara Reid McIntyre, Martha J.
Brown, Bette Oliver. Performed in Sarasota,
Daytona, Tampa, and produced on public
television.

Note: Asolo State Theater's Conservatory of Acting provides an MFA program for actors
and theater technicians. They constitute the Associate Company, performing in Asolo productions, understudying the professional company and producing/performing in Theater for
Young People.

SEATTLE

A Contemporary Theater

  (Artistic director, Gregory A. Falls; general manager, Andrew M. Witt. Designers: scenery,
Bill Forrester and Jerry Williams; lighting, Al Nelson and Phil Schermer; costumes, Donna
Eskew and Sally Richardson).

SLEUTH (18). By Anthony Shaffer. June 19,
1975. Director, James Higgins. With Don
Ewer, Henry Hoffman, Frank Ewbanks, Alex
Sinclair, Ralf Blair.

THE RESISTIBLE RISE OF ARTURO UI

(18). By Bertolt Brecht; adapted by George
Tabori. July 10, 1975. Director, Gregory A.
Falls. With John Horn, Richard Blackburn,
Henry Hoffman, Donald Ewer, Dean Gard-
ner, Kurt Garfield, Jane Bray.

WHEN YOU COMIN' BACK, RED RYDER? (17). By Mark Medoff. July 31, 1975. Director, M. Burke Walker. With Dean Gardner, Mada Stockley, Ben Tone, Edwin Bordo, Tanny McDonald, Tobias Andersen, John Aylward, Patricia Murray.

QUIET CARAVANS (17). By Barry Dinerman. August 21, 1975 (world premiere). Director, Gregory A. Falls.

Bella .... Sylvia Gassell
Louis .... Ben Tone
Mrs. Mirsch .... Marjorie Nelson
Sergeant Farkas .... John Renforth
Mickey .... Susan Ludlow

Place: A boarding house along the Boardwalk of Atlantic City. Act I is in 3 scenes; Act II, in 2 scenes.

OF MICE AND MEN (17). By John Steinbeck. September 11, 1975. Director, Robert Loper. With Clayton Corzatte, Frederick Coffin, Robert Donley, Vern Taylor, William C. Witter, Joseph Edward Meek, Gail Hebert.

OH COWARD! (33). By Roderick Cook, devised from the words and music of Noel Coward. October 2, 1975. Director, Jack Sydow. With Brian Avery, Eve Roberts, G. Wood.

Note: A Contemporary Theater sponsors a resident company of eight actors, known as The Young Act Company which performs on tour for schools, as well as for adult audiences. Their productions included *Absurd Musical Revue for Children* and *The Christmas Show,* directed by Gregory A. Falls; *Fire!* by John Roc, directed by Eileen MacRae Murphy. A Contemtemporary Theater also presented several specials, including *Contact: Fred Coffin* with Frederick Coffin: *We Three* with Leon Bibb, Gail Nelson, Stan Keen and *See the Players* with Kimberley Ross and Mark Buchan. These were presented between September 1975 and April 1976.

Seattle Repertory Theater: Main Stage

(Artistic director, Duncan Ross; producing director, Peter Donnelly; assistant artistic director, Arne Yaslove; resident costume designer, Lewis D. Pampino)

CYRANO DE BERGERAC (34). By Edmond Rostand. October 22, 1975. Director, Duncan Ross; scenery, Eldon Elder; lighting Steven A. Maze. With James Cahill, Lee Corbet, Katherine Ferrand, Paul C. Thomas, Max Wright.

JUMPERS (28). By Tom Stoppard. November 19, 1975. Director, Duncan Ross; scenery, John Lee Beatty; lighting, Steven A. Maze. With Max Wright, Marilyn Meyers, John Newton, Paul C. Thomas, Jerome Collamore, Zoaunne Le Roy.

SEVEN KEYS TO BALDPATE (28). By George M. Cohan; adapted from the novel by Earl Derr Biggers. December 17, 1975. Director, Arne Zaslove; scenery, Jerry Williams; lighting, Phil Schermer; film sequences, Karl Krogstad. With James Staley, Katherine Bruce, James Carruthers, Frances Peter, Katherine Ferrand, Paul C. Thomas.

THE LAST MEETING OF THE KNIGHTS OF THE WHITE MAGNOLIA (28). By Preston Jones. January 14, 1976. Director, Harold Scott; scenery, Robert Dahlstrom; lighting, Richard Devin. With Robert Donley, Joseph Regalbuto, Henry Butler, Andy Backer, John Wylie.

THE MADWOMAN OF CHAILLOT (28). By Jean Giraudox. February 11, 1976. Director, Duncan Ross; scenery, Eldon Elder; lighting, Richard Devin. With Jeannie Carson, John Gilbert, Ted D'Arms, Alan Zampese, Margaret Hilton, Marjorie Nelson, Dorothy Chace, Gardner Hayes.

PRIVATE LIVES (32). By Noel Coward. March 10, 1976. Director, Duncan Ross; scenery, Robert Dahlstrom; lighting, Richard Devin. With Farley Granger, Margaret Hall, Gil Rogers, Sharon Spelman, Lucy Russ.

Seattle Repertory Theater: Second Stage

BENITO CERENO (18). By Robert Lowell, based on Herman Melville's novella, *The Piazza Tales.* February 24, 1976. Director, Arne Zaslove; scenery, Michael Mayer; lighting, Cynthia Hawkins. With Gary Reineke, John Peter Benson, David Connell, Nick Lewis Jones, Rafic Bey.

ENTERTAINING MR. SLOANE (18). By Joe Orton. March 16, 1976. Director, Clayton

Corzatte; scenery, Charles Kading; lighting, Cynthia J. Hawkins. With Michael Christensen, Marjorie Nelson, Paul C. Thomas, Ed Kemp.

MADE FOR TV—A REAL TIME EVENT (14). Created by the Acting Company. April 6, 1976. Director, Arne Zaslove; scenery, Charles Kading; lighting and audio-visual effects, Jim McKie; costumes, Donna Eskew;

video, Brandon Wilson; music, John Enger-
man. With John Aylward, Katherine Ferrand,
Dean Melang, Michael Christensen, Marjorie
Nelson, Gerald Burgess, Maureen Hawkins,
Jean Marie Kinney, Demetra Pittman, William
Rongstad, Alvin Lee Sanders and Phil Shallet.

KENNEDY'S CHILDREN (17). By Robert
Patrick. April 27, 1976. Director, Duncan Ross;
scenery, Michael Mayer; costumes, Lewis D.
Rampino and Donna Eskew; lighting, Cynthia

J. Hawkins. With Katherine Ferrand, Jean
Marie Kinney, Madeleine Le Roux, Dean Melang, William Rongstad, Michael Christensen.

THE COLLECTED WORKS OF BILLY
THE KID (18). By Michael Ondaatje. May
18, 1976. Director, Arne Zaslove; scenery and
lighting, Phil Schermer; costumes, Donna
Eskew. With John Aylward, William Rongstad, Katherine Ferrand, Dean Melang, Demetra Pittman.

Note: During the 1975-76 season, Seattle Repertory Theater also presented Jessica Tandy and
Hume Cronyn in *The Many Faces of Love* for 8 performances, December 2-7, 1975 and a
one-performance concert by Bobby Short. Tours included 30 performances of *The History
Show—Believe It or Not* at local area schools; 39 performances of Rep'n Rap by Clayton
Corzatte and Susan Ludlow, presenting their adaptations of *The Diary of Adam and Eve, A
Village Wooing* and *Life, Love and Other Laughing Matters* at libraries and recreation cen-
ters, and at the Alaska Festival in Anchorage, during the summer months; and 39 performances
of the Main Stage production of *Seven Keys to Baldpate* in 11 cities in five states (Washington, Oregon, Idaho, Nevada, Utah) from January 10, 1976.

STAMFORD, CONN.

Hartman Theater Company

(Producing directors, Del and Margot Tenney; managing director, Daniel B. Miller)

THE GOVERNMENT INSPECTOR (24). By
Nikolai Gogol; English version by Edward O.
Marsh and Jeremy Brooks. November 5, 1975.
Director, Byron Ringland; scenery, Peter Har-
vey; lighting, John McLain; costumes, Dona
Granata. With George S. Irving, Josef Som-
mer, David MacNeill, Bernard Frawley, Sloane
Shelton, Eren Ozker, Austin Pendleton.

THE HOSTAGE (26). By Brendan Behan.
December 2, 1975. Director, John Beary; scen-
ery, John Wright Stevens; lighting, John Mc-
Lain; costumes, Rachel Kurland. With Ber-
nard Frawley, Sasha von Scherler, Robert
Donley, Eren Ozker, William Bogert.

THE RUNNER STUMBLES (26). By Milan
Stitt. December 30, 1975 (world premiere.)
Director, Austin Pendleton; scenery, Robert
Verberkmoes; lighting, Cheryl Thacker; cos-
tumes, James Berton Harris.
Guard .... Morrie Piersol
Father Rivard .... Stephen Joyce
Erna Prindle .... Katina Commings
Toby Felker .... James Noble
Sister Rita .... Nancy Donohue
Mrs. Shandig .... Sloane Shelton
Prosecutor .... William Bogert
Monsignor Nicholson ...... Bernard Frawley
Louise .... Eren Ozker
   Time: April, 1911. Place: A cell and a
courtroom in Solon, Michigan. Two intermis-
sions.

TOM JONES (35). By Henry Fielding;

adapted and directed by Larry Arrick; songs
and music written and directed by Barbara
Damashek; lyrics by Barbara Damashek and
Larry Arrick. January 27, 1976. Scenery, Akita
Yoshimura; lighting, Roger Meeker; costumes,
Rachel Kurland. With Jill Eikenberry, James
Naughton, James Noble, Margot Tenney.

JOAN OF LORRAINE (26). By Maxwell
Anderson. March 2, 1976. Director, Alan
Arkin; scenery, Robert Verberkmoes; lighting,
Roger Meeker; costumes, Rachel Kurland.
With Barbara Dana, John Horn, Adam
Arkin, Roy Brocksmith, Michael Granger,
Alex Rocco.

PORTRAIT OF A MADONNA; 27 WAG-
ONS FULL OF COTTON; I RISE IN
FLAME, CRIED THE PHOENIX (26). By
Tennessee Williams. March 30, 1976. Director,
Del Tenney; scenery, Robert Verberkmoes;
lighting, Roger Meeker; costumes, Rachel
Kurland. With Margot Tenney, Louis Turenne,
Peter Gatto, Greg Kolb, Sandy Martin, Dennis
Cooney.

CATCH-22 (26). By Joseph Heller. April 27,
1976. Director, Larry Arrick; scenery, Akita
Yoshimura; lighting, Roger Meeker; costumes,
J. D. Ferrara. With Robert Balaban, George
Martin, T. Richard Mason, Ed Rice, Louis
Turenne, David Ackroyd, Betty Gordon.

STAG AT BAY (6). By Charles MacArthur
and Nunnally Johnson. May 27, 1976 (profes-

sional premiere). Director, Stephen Rothman; scenery and lighting, Roger Meeker; costumes, Rachel Kurland; sound, Charles Pistone.

Albert; Narration	Alan Brooks
Dwight Stanford	William Leach
Miss Casey; Helga	Judith Light
Rodney; Mulrooney;	
Narration	Henson Keys
Gainsborough; Narration	John Ulmer
Bart Starling	Alfred Drake
Maj. Lionel Upshaw	Dick Shawn
Mrs. Welsh	Heidi Mefford
Mildred Baldwin	Joy Smith
Penelope Hunter	Anne Scurria

Miriam	Marilyn Hase
Velma Richardson	Joan Friedman
Frances Hilton	Rosalyn Farinella
Mrs. Grant	Jillian Lindig
Jennifer	Barbara Dana

Act I: Time, spring 1939; place, the private office of Dwight Stanford's theatrical agency in the penhouse of an office building in New York. Act II: Time, the next day; place, the green room of St. Cecilia's School for Girls. Act III: Time, afternoon, a week or so later; place, the living room of a faculty cottage on the school grounds.

STRATFORD, CONN.

American Shakespeare Company

(Artistic director, Michael Kahn; managing director, William Stewart. Designers: scenery, David Jenkins and John Conklin; lighting, Ken Billington; costumes, Jane Greenwood and Lawrence Casey)

KING LEAR (33). By William Shakespeare. June 21, 1975. Director, Anthony Page. With Morris Carnovsky, Michael Houlihan, Maria Tucci, Jane White, Michele Shay, Lee Richardson, William Larsen, Jack Ryland, John Glover.

OUR TOWN (32). By Thornton Wilder. June 22, 1975. Director, Michael Kahn. With Fred Gwynne, William Larsen, Eileen Heck-

art, Lee Richardson, Geraldine Fitzgerald, Richard Backus, Kate Mulgrew.

THE WINTER'S TALE (15). By William Shakespeare. July 30, 1975. Director, Michael Kahn. With Donald Madden, Maria Tucci, Briain Petchey, Wyman Pendleton, William Larsen, Bette Henritze, Gregg Almquist, Richard Backus, Laurinda Barrett.

American Shakespeare Theater: Outback—New Playwright Series

THE LADY IN THE OBLONG BOX (3). By Alexander Panas. July 3, 1975 (world premiere). Director, Larry Carpenter; scenery, John Gisondi; lighting, Fred Mills; costumes, John Arnone; sound, Frank Esposito

Edgar Allen Poe	Greg Almquist
Helen Tarkington	Julia MacKenzie
Junior McFinney	Richard Dix

Tessie	Sally Backus
Lulu	Francesca Poston
Maj. Armstrong	Marshall Shnider
Junious Brutus Booth	Powers Boothe
Inspector Sterne	E. E. Norris
Father Roderick	Robert Beseda
Nicholas Montressor	David Suehsdorf

SYRACUSE

Syracuse Stage

(Artistic director, Arthur Storch; general manager, Karl Gevecker)

MORNING'S AT SEVEN (27). By Paul Osborn. October 24, 1975. Director, Arthur Storch. With Robert Allen, Grace Carney, Elizabeth Council, Ernest Graves, Lois Holmes, Mary Loane, Don Lochner, Brooks Morton, Peggy Winslow.

NO EXIT by Jean-Paul Sartre and THE MAN WITH THE FLOWER IN HIS MOUTH by Luigi Pirandello (27). November 21, 1975. Director, John Dillon. With Minnie Gordon Gaster, David Kagen, Rich-

ard Lynd, William Metzo, Gerard E. Moses, Joan Welles.

THE BEAR; ON THE HARMFULNESS OF TOBACCO; THE MARRIAGE PROPOSAL (27). By Anton Chekhov. December 19, 1975. Director, Gene Lesser. With C. K. Alexander, Peter Bosche, David Cromwell, Richard Greene, Lynn Milgrim, Peggy Pope.

BLITHE SPIRIT (27). By Noel Coward. January 16, 1976. Director, John Going.

With Avril Gentles, Virginia Kiser, Kathleen O'Meara Noone, George Taylor.

DYNAMO (27). By Eugene O'Neill. February 13, 1976. Director, Arthur Storch. With William Carden, Ruth Fenster, Edward Holmes, John Kellogg, Lisa Pelikan, Lenka Petersen.

A FLEA IN HER EAR (27). By Georges Feydeau. March 12, 1976. Director, Philip Minor. With Lori Burgess, David Darlow, James Gallery, Dale Hodges, Nicholas Hormann, Morris Lafon, Frolic Taylor, James Tripp.

Designers: scenery, David Chapman, John Doepp, Eric Head, Scott Johnson; lighting, James Stephens, William Schroeder, Lee Watson; costumes, Nancy Adzima, James Edmund Brady, Jerry Pannozzo, Judy Rasmuson.

WALTHAM, MASS.

Brandeis University: Spingold Theater

(Chairman, Theater Arts Department, Martin Halpern)

THE TIME OF YOUR LIFE (9). By William Saroyan. October 8, 1975. Director, James H. Clay; scenery, David Potts; lighting, Delmadean Bryant; costumes, Amy Kaplow. With Terrence Beasor, Ken Baltin, Elena Nierman.

SPARED (5). Written and directed by Israel Horovitz. November 15, 1975 (American premiere). With Lenny Baker. Act I, *Misfires from the Canon*, collected and uncollected verse read by Israel Horovitz, and introduction to Act II, *Spared*.

CAMINO REAL (10). By Tennessee Williams. December 3, 1975. Director, Charles Werner Moore; scenery, Diana Greenwood; lighting, John A. Olbrych Jr.; costumes, Wendy Pierson. With Carl Whidden, Terrence Beasor, Andrew Traines, Ken Baltin, Maya Mork.

THE CRADLE WILL ROCK by Marc Blitzstein and A DICK SHAWN CONCERT OF

BANANAS AND DRUMS (9). March 3, 1976. Directed by Howard Bay; scenery, Steven C. Berkowitz; lighting, Michael-john Zolli; costumes, Anna Belle Kaufman; musical director, Michael Kluger; dances, Anne Tolbert. With Terrence Beasor, Charles Werner Moore, Annette Miller, David A. Lewis, Dick Shawn, Ken Baltin.

THE TENANTS (9). By Martin Halpern; based on the novel by Bernard Malamud. May 12, 1976 (world premiere). Director, Ted Kazanoff; scenery, John A. Olbrych Jr.; lighting, David Potts; costumes, Delmadean Brant.

Harry Lesser .... Andrew Traines
Irving Levenspiel .... Terrence Beasor
Willie Spearmint .... Gustave Johnson
Irene Bell .... Donna Charron
Mary Kettlesmith .... Loretta Devine
Sam Clemence .... Kerry Ruff
    Place: a nearly abandoned tenement on the East Side of New York City. Act I: Winter. Act II: Spring.

Brandeis University: Laurie Theater

THE CHALK GARDEN (5). By Enid Bagnold. October 22, 1975. Director, Nancy Alexander; scenery, James J. Moran; lighting, Steven C. Berkowitz; costumes, Michael-john Zolli. With Donna Charron, Randall Forsythe, Sarah R. Pearson, Edith Agnew.

THE MAIDS (5). By Jean Genet; translated by Bernard Frechtman; additional translation by Chris Wheatley. November 19, 1975. Director, Stephen Drewes; scenery, Anna

Belle Kaufman; lighting, Michael-john Zolli; costumes, Mary McCluskey. With Donna Charron, Mary Clifford, Jennifer McLogan.

HAY FEVER (5). By Noel Coward. March 24, 1976. Director, Stephen Drewes; scenery, Daniel Veaner; lighting, Harry Feiner; costumes, Amanda Klein. With Lisa Kaufman, Michal Guido, Donna Charron, Ted Kazanoff.

Brandeis University: Playwrights Festival '76—Laurie Theater

THE SEPTEMBER MOVEMENT (5). By Jonathan Bloch. May 5, 1976 (world premiere). Director, Nancy Alexander; scenery,

Christine Kaseta; lighting, James J. Moran; costumes, Steven C. Berkowitz.
Tom .... David A. Lewis

Alan .... Aalan Kobritz
Fred .... Michael Angelo Castellana
Cage .... Scott Richards

Time: Labor Day, early afternoon. Place: A house in the suburbs of Boston. One intermission.

Brandeis University: Playwrights Festival '76—Merrick Theater

(Festival directors: Ken Baltin, Sean Hartley, David Krentzman; designers: scenery, Harry Feiner; lighting, Daniel Veaner; costumes, Frances Blau; April 30-May 9, 1976; world premieres)

KNOW IT ALL by Daniel Lyon, directed by David Krentzman; MUSEUM PIECE by David Sweeney, directed by Sean Hartley (4).
Know It All
Marsha .... Mary Clifford
Alain .... Robert Stachel
Corrine .... Sharon Asro
Time: Saturday afternoon, summer. Place: Alain and Marsha's living room and Marsha's desk at the library.
Museum Piece
Andy .... Randolph Forsythe
Ambrose .... David Krentzman
Eugene .... Michael Kluger
Mary .... Edith Agnew
Sharon .... Lisa Kaufman
Place: The Martha Hammond Museum.

CORNER, 28TH AND BANK by Linda Segal, directed by Sean Hartley; DECATHLON by Sean Hartley, directed by Ken Baltin (5).
Corner, 28th and Bank
Trummel .... Randolph Forsythe
Sport .... Annette Miller
Mac .... Michael Kluger
DeFusco .... Rob Weiss
Time: 8 o'clock on a Saturday morning.

Place: A city street corner.
Decathlon
Nick .... Bill Borenstein
Hank .... Spencer Cherashore
Eddy; Lary .... David A. Duddy
Marie; Jessie; Mother; Penelope .. Kat Krone
Gabriel .... Chris Wheatley
Charles .... Carl Whidden
Louis; Stranger .... Frederick Zollo
Place: Nick's Room; Gabriel's Room; Niven's Bar; elsewhere about town.

FRIENDS INDEED! (5). By David Cohen, directed by Ken Baltin.
Scott .... David A. Duddy
Cassie .... Jennifer McLogan
McGillicuddy .... Michael Guido
Bernice .... Sarah R. Pearson
Helen .... Edith Agnew
Ginny .... Laura Bennett
Ralph .... Gregg Bedol
Place: Ralph's secluded ski lodge in New Hampshire. Act I, Scene 1: Friday afternoon. Scene 2: The following morning. Act II, Scene 1: A few minutes later. Scene 2: Immediately following.

WASHINGTON, D.C.

Arena Stage: Kreeger Theater

(Producing director, Zelda Fichandler; associate producer, George Touliatos; executive director, Thomas C. Fichandler)

LONG DAY'S JOURNEY INTO NIGHT (47). By Eugene O'Neill. October 17, 1975. Director, Martin Fried; scenery, Karl Eigsti; lighting, William Mintzer; costumes Gwynne Clark. With James Broderick, Leora Dana, Stanley Anderson, Mark Metcalf, Halo Wines.

THE TOT FAMILY (47). By Istvan Orkeny. January 21, 1976 (American premiere). Director, Edward Payson Call; scenery, John Lee Beatty; lighting, Hugh Lester; costumes, Marjorie Slaiman; music, Robert Dennis
Mailman .... Gary Bayer
Mariska Tot .... Regina David
Anna Tot .... Le Clanche Du Rand
Lajos Tot .... Robert Prosky
Cesspool Cleaner .... Bob Harper
Lorincke .... Mark Hammer

Mrs. Geza Gizi .... Leslie Cass
Elegant Major;
    Professor Cipriani ...... Stanley Anderson
Orderly .... Eric Weitz
Major .... MacIntyre Dixon
Father Tomaji .... Howland Chamberlin
Dr. Eggenberger .... Jason Alexander/
                        Norman Martin
Cipriani's Assistant .... Michael Mertz
    The Band: David Garrison, Bob Harper, Michael Mertz, Gene S. Minkow, David Schaeffer.
Time: World War II. Place: A small mountain village in Hungary.

HEARTBREAK HOUSE (40). By George Bernard Shaw. February 11, 1976. Director, John Pasquin; scenery, Santo Loquasto;

lighting, William Mintzer; costumes, Marjorie Slaiman. With Dianne Wiest, Robert Pastene, Barbara Caruso, Carolyn Coates, Max Wright, Jack Ryland, Howard Witt.

DANDELION WINE (47). By Ray Bradbury; adapted by Peter John Bailey. April 14, 1976. Director, Martin Fried; scenery, Karl Eigsti; lighting, William Mintzer; costumes, Marjorie Slaiman. With Norman Martin, Alexander Metcalf, Michael Miller, Michael Joyce Miller, Bill Moor, Joan Pape, Vance Sorrells, Barbara Tarbuck, James Tolkan, Eleanor D. Wilson.

Arena Stage: Guest production—Kreeger Theater

CHARLES   DICKENS   (9).   Compiled, adapted and performed by Emlyn Williams, from stories and novels by Charles Dickens. December 26, 1975.

Arena Stage: Arena Theater

AN ENEMY OF THE PEOPLE (40). By Henrik Ibsen; English version by John Patrick Vincent; new acting version by Zelda Fichandler. October 29, 1975. Director, Zelda Fichandler; scenery, Grady Larkins; lighting, Hugh Lester; costumes, Marjorie Slaiman. With Robert Prosky, Leslie Cass, Dianne Wiest, Mark Hammer, David Leary, Howard Witt.

ONCE IN A LIFETIME (40). By Moss Hart and George S. Kaufman. December 10, 1975. Director, Tom Moore; scenery, Karl Eigsti; lighting, Allen Hughes. With Edward Herrmann, Joan Pape, Gary Bayer, Robert Prosky, Bella Jarrett.

WAITING FOR GODOT (40). By Samuel Beckett. March 24, 1976. Director, Gene Lesser; scenery, Ming Cho Lee; lighting, Hugh Lester; costumes, Marjorie Slaiman. With Howard Witt, Max Wright, Michael Mertz, Mark Hammer, Liam Clark/Eric Weitz.

In repertory (scenery, Karl Eigsti; lighting, Hugh Lester; costumes, Marjorie Slaiman):

DEATH OF A SALESMAN (15). By Arthur Miller. May 2, 1976. Director, Zelda Fichandler. With Robert Prosky, Dorothea Hammond, Bruce Weitz, Stanley Anderson, Howard Witt, Mark Hammer.
THE FRONT PAGE (17). By Ben Hecht and Charles MacArthur. May 7, 1976. Director, Edward Payson Call. With Gary Bayer, Halo Wines, Howard Witt, Eric Weitz.
OUR TOWN (15). By Thornton Wilder. May 23, 1976. Director, Alan Schneider. With Robert Prosky, Leslie Cass, Jane Groves, Howard Witt, Gary Bayer, Dianne Wiest, Terrence Currier.

Arena Stage: In The Process—Old Vat Room Cabaret Theater

CABRONA (7). By Cynthia Buchanan. January 13, 1976 (workshop premiere).
Verity Massey ....Sudie Bond
Pratt Massey ....Ned Beatty
Opal Massey ....Lily Tomlin
Marcus Roper ....Lane Smith
Jessie Lee ....Conchata Ferrell
   Time: 1976. Place: Punkin Junction, Arizona. One intermission.

WHAT THE BABE SAID and TOTAL RECALL (7). By Martin Halpern. March 2, 1976 (workshop premieres). Director, David Chambers.
What the Babe Said
Sal ....Robert Prosky
Buck ....Gary Bayer
   Place: The manager's office of the visiting team clubhouse, in a major league baseball stadium.
Total Recall
Wilfred Porter ....Stanley Anderson
Eleanor Manning ....Halo Wines

Place: A one-room studio apartment in New York's West Village.

MADMEN (7). By Steven Stosny. March 16, 1976 (workshop premiere). Director, Douglas C. Wager.
Mott ....Robert Stattel
Lu ....Regina David
1st man ....Jay Allison
2d man ....Gary Bayer
Woman ....Kathleen Lindsey
Psychiatrist ....Bob Harper
   Time: The present. Place: The solarium of a poorly funded state mental hospital. Act I: Early evening. Act II: A few minutes later. Act III: A half hour later.

BUSY DYIN' (7). By Sheila Quillen Hofstetter. March 30, 1976 (workshop premiere). Director, Norman Gevanthor.
Rima ....Marilyn McIntyre
Junior ....David Garrison
Ray ....Terrence Currier

Benny........................Bob Leslie   Detroit, Michigan. Act I, Scene 1: 5:30 a.m.,
Hazel........................Leslie Cass   Friday. Scene 2: 5:30 p.m., same day. Act
Susie.. .... Pat Karpen   II, Scene 1: 9 a.m., Saturday. Scene 2, 5:30
    Time: September of the early 1960s. Place: p.m., Saturday. Scene 3: 5:30 a.m., Monday.

Note: *Living Stage*, a professional improvisational theater, directed by Robert Alexander, provided workshops and performances in its seventh season as part of the Arena Stage program, for children, young people, the deaf and the physically handicapped, as well as in penal institutions.

The Season Elsewhere in Washington

By David Richards

Drama Critic of the Washington *Star*

Arena Stage, which once nurtured *The Great White Hope* to full muscularity and then saw it stride off to New York with nary a backward glance (or a penny in royalties), finally got something in return from Broadway this season—the first Tony award ever given to a regional theater. The recognition, which came 26 years and 211 productions after Zelda Fichandler first hatched the idea of a resident theater company here, was not so much repayment for the Arena-bred shows that found their way into the commercial marketplace (among them *Indians, Moonchildren* and *Raisin*). Rather, the award cited Arena for the wealth and diversity of the fare it has lavished on Washington over the years.

Indeed, the 1975-76 season was once again dominated by Arena and to a lesser degree by its richer competitor up the river, the Kennedy Center. While the Center, along with much of the country as a whole, was caught up in the fervor of Bicentennial revivalism, Arena went with another of its characteristically balanced seasons—plays both native and foreign, new and old, the only criterion being that they relate somehow to present-day concerns. Arena's *Long Day's Journey Into Night* (with Leora Dana, James Broderick, Stanley Anderson and Mark Metcalf) was far outweighed on the marquee by the Center's subsequent production (with Zoe Caldwell, Jason Robards, Michael Moriarty and Kevin Conway). But for capturing the longstanding aches and agonies of the Tyrone family, Arena's was definitely the one to see.

With *The Tot Family* by Hungary's Istvan Orkeny, Mrs. Fichandler found a wonderfully macabre comedy about a peasant family that goes to any and all lengths to please their son's commanding officer on the illusory hope that he will remember the favors when he returns to the trenches. It was madly staged and played to suggest a mechanical toy village that had been overwound and had dislocated a few springs essential to its smooth functioning. Arena's concurrent productions of *Waiting for Godot* and *Dandelion Wine* also demonstrated the kind of counter-programming that makes this place such a vital institution. While in the Arena proper, Beckett's tramps played out their waiting games in a desiccated universe about to exhale a last, dusty gasp, next door in the Kreeger Ray Bradbury's characters were awakening to the lush greenness of the slow summer of 1928. Both plays dealt with the nature of time and the ways we perceive its passage, but in such diametrically opposed fashions that no one could accuse Mrs. Fichandler of taking sides—only provoking thought.

Tom Moore staged a zany Art Deco version of *Once in a Lifetime,* complete with a quartet of crooning Al Jolsons, while for the season's end three American classics were brought back in repertory—*The Front Page, Death of a Salesman* and an *Our Town* that was a bit too overproduced for my tastes. Meanwhile, in a third theatrical space, the underground Old Vat room, a stage was erected for plays "in the process"—no critics, please; just actors, playwrights and audiences reacting jointly to new "voices" that have caught Mrs. Fichandler's ear. The amount of activity was staggering, no less than its almost consistent quality.

Although there exists no spoken rivalry between Arena and the Center, the latter's decision to mount a *Long Day's Journey* in the same season did make for a fascinating contrast in theatrical approaches. The Center continued to rely on big, established names, although under the auspices of the American Bicentennial Theater it began producing, not merely booking, its star-laden fare. Backed by a $400,000 grant from the Xerox Corporation, the Center announced a season of ten representative American plays, chosen in collaboration with a panel of literary lights, and the commissioning of six new works by major playwrights. As of June, the ABT had delivered eight revivals, not always those announced.

The ABT had some deserved triumphs with *Sweet Bird of Youth* and *The Royal Family.* Lower on the ladder, but satisfying for the most part, were *Summer Brave* and *The Skin of Our Teeth.* But *The Scarecrow,* an appallingly saccharine *Rip Van Winkle* (rewritten and staged by Joshua Logan) and *The Heiress* were projects of the "why bother?" variety. *Long Day's Journey* was "what happened?" bewilderment.

The Center's indisputable coup was its mounting of *A Texas Trilogy,* which Roger Stevens and Robert Whitehead produced independently of the ABT. The three plays (*Lu Ann Hampton Laverty Oberlander, The Last Meeting of the Knights of the White Magnolia* and *The Oldest Living Graduate*) revealed Dallas actor Preston Jones as a major playwriting talent, reaffirmed Alan Schneider as a director of uncommon strength, and marked Diane Ladd as an actress of power and versatility. Interrelated but not interdependent, the plays examined lives up and down the social scale in a fictional West Texas hamlet, and while Jones was seemingly more comfortable with its lower class denizens (the redneck lodge members, the town lush, a gallant divorcee) as opposed to its parvenue, the trilogy was nonetheless a stunning achievement.

Elsewhere, there was less excitement, although the Folger's production of *Medal of Honor Rag*—the actual case history of a black Vietnam war hero who couldn't adjust back home and was ultimately gunned down in a grocery store robbery—packed a real wallop, reinforced by the fact that the Capitol Building, its dome awash in light, is only three short blocks from the Folger.

After its long-running *Your Arm's Too Short to Box With God,* an evening of gospel songs, Ford's Theater fell into a biographical rut with plays about Dr. Martin Luther King Jr. (*I Had a Dream*) and Eleanor Roosevelt (*Eleanor*), both of which had a lot in common with the talking historical exhibits at Disneyland. The American Theater, lit once again under new management, went all season without a fully satisfying production, while the Olney Theater-Hugh Leonard alliance, now seven plays old, fell below par with a trio of one-acts entitled *Irishmen.*

The experimental theaters, which have always had a hard time in this least experimental of cities, made an effort to pool their meager resources in order to get a little attention. But attention was not forthcoming. The D.C. Black Repertory Company also suffered its problems, cash being the foremost, and had a limited season of only two productions. Black audiences seemed more willing to go to the National, which was back in the pre-Broadway tryout business with *Bubbling Brown Sugar,* an all-black *Guys and Dolls, A Matter of Gravity* and that musical about the town's best address, *1600 Pennsylvania Avenue.*

The big crowds mostly flocked to the Center, however, now the most popular tourist attraction here after the Smithsonian Institution. Arena, meanwhile, persisted in bringing home the laurels.

American Theater

DAMN EVERYTHING BUT THE CIRCUS (24). One-man show compiled from the works of e. e. cummings. June 2, 1975. Director, Henry Kaplan; scenery, Michael Molly; lighting, Barry Steinman and Alice O'Leary. With William Mooney.

THE DUNGEON (6). By W. Randolph Galvin. July 7, 1975. Director, W. Randolph Galvin; scenery, W. Randolph Galvin; lighting, Alice O'Leary. With Brad Armacost, Roger Wooden, Paula Barga.

PINOCCHIO (45). Life-size marionette show designed and created by B. Clark and Charles Budrow. July 21, 1975. Music, Arnold Miller. With puppeteers Charles Budrow, Douglas Feltch, Victoria Budrow, Mary Tom, Eileen Brindza, Dave Brindza, John Armijo, Connie Feast.

NO PLACE TO BE SOMEBODY (79). By Charles Gordone. August 12, 1975. Director, G. Tito Shaw; scenery, Conrad Penrod; lighting, John Retsek. With Terry Alexander, Roger Hill, Lee Roy Giles, Yolande Bryant, Roxanne Reese, Douglas Stark, Robert Burgos.

ROTUNDA (30). Musical by Gloria Broide, Robin Leroy Ellis and Joseph Leonardo; music by Robin Leroy Ellis; lyrics by Gloria Broide and Robin Leroy Ellis. November 18, 1975 (world premiere). Director, Joseph Leonardo; scenery, Richard Ferrer; lighting, Jeffrey Schissler; costumes, Neil Bierbower; musical director, John Burr.

Senator James McVale	Robert Brooks
J.D. Carter	Patrick Quinn
Herbert Baldwin	Jack Sevier
Joe Gomez	Edmond Dante
Florence Gomez	Patrick Kilgarriff
Bernie Martin	William W. Sean
Ms. Fish	Edie Behr
Sandy Johnson	Christine Campbell
Cylde Barton	Don Bradford
Beverly McVale	Sally-Jane Heit
Kathleen Harrison	Laura Waterbury
Senator J. Hammond Peel	Charles Antalosky
Representative Berkley	Joseph Eubanks
Cheri Bennet	Kirsten Sonstegard
James McVale Jr.	Gary Brubach

Time: The present. Place: Washington, D.C. and the campaign trail. A satire of political doings on Capitol Hill in the course of which Senator James McVale acquires integrity. One intermission.

Musical numbers: Act I—"We the People

of America," "We Need a Man Who's Not for Sale," "On the Hill," "All in the Public Interest," "Means I Love You," "Until the Next Time," "Don't Mess with the Press," "We Are the Washington Press Corps," "The Old Soft Sell," "You Gotta Go Along to Get Along," "That Busy, Busy Man," "He's a Man of the People." Act II—"Here We Are Out Again," "Just to Secure You Success," "Sometimes in the Still of the Night," "I Belong to Me," "I'll Never Run Again," "I Knew a Man," "Your Devoted Public Servant," "Round and Round."

GODSPELL (17). Musical conceived by John-Michael Tebelak; music and lyrics by Stephen Schwartz. January 12, 1976. Directors, Peter Jurasik and Marley Sims; scenery,

Joe Lazarus; costumes, Debbie Thompson. With David Kousser, Alphanzo Harrison, Maureen McNamara, David Morgan, Lee Carlin.

THE SQUARE ROOT OF SOUL (15). One-man recital of black poetry with connective dialogue by Adolph Caesar. February 4, 1976. Director, Dean Irby; lighting, Sati Jamal. With Adolph Caesar.

MIDNIGHT SPECIAL (23). By Clifford Mason. March 2, 1976. Director, Cliff Goodwin; scenery, David Chapman; lighting, Stephen Harty. With Thomas Anderson, Don Blakely, Stanley Greene, Ben Prestbury, Ed Heath, Sarallen, Margo Barnett.

D.C. Black Repertory Company

SWING LOW, SWEET STEAMBOAT (20). By Ron Daniels. Nov. 12, 1975 (world premiere). Director, Motojicho; scenery, Jaye Stewart and Theetta Bell; lighting, James Hooks; costumes, Victoria Payton.

Siheave	Kene Holliday
Buster Collins	Jaye Stewart
Scatmammy Morgan	Carol Maillard
Buddy Williams	Luzern
Clink West	Robert Hatcher
Nan Walker	Darrell O. D. Winstead
Snags	Lyn Dyson
Beatrice Bufford	Janifer Baker Holliday
Elenor Whiteside	Gloria Hill
John Goode	Chester Sims
Minnie Goode	Lumengo
Wilda Walker	Lynn Whitfield
Charles Walker	Ed DeShae
Willie Joe Jackson	Edward Mays

Time: The present. Place: A New Orleans pier and a middle-class living room. A group of derelicts and a stuffy middle-class family are inadvertently brought together for a funeral. One intermission.

A DAY, A LIFE, A PEOPLE (35). Musical by Bernice Reagon. December 17, 1975 (world premiere). Director, Bernice Reagon; scenery, Motojicho; lighting, Marvin Watkins; costumes, Motojicho. With Ayodele Akinwole, Terri Dobson, Evelyn Harris, Janifer Baker Holliday, Lumengo, Rosie Lee Hooks, Pat Johnson, Carol Maillard, Louise Robinson, Sadiqa, Jimmye Claire, Lyn Dyson, Mike Hodge, Leslie Howard, Chester Sims, Jaye Stewart, Ronald Stevens, LeTari.

Time: The present. Place: A black urban community. The daily rituals of a black community at home, at the office and at play, as depicted through chanted dialogue and song fragments. One intermission.

Folger Theater Group

THE COLLECTED WORKS OF BILLY THE KID (37). By Michael Ondaatje. October 10, 1975. Director, Louis Scheeder; scenery, David Chapman; lighting, Hugh Lester; costumes, Randy Barcelo. With Allan Carlsen, Guy Boyd, Mark Robinson, Sandy Faison, Albert Malafronte, Anne Stone, Brad Sullivan, Richard Greene.

THE COMEDY OF ERRORS (53). By William Shakespeare. November 28, 1975. Director, Jonathan Alper; scenery, Stuart Wurtzel; lighting, Arden Fingerhut; costumes, Bob Wojewodski; music, William Penn. With Mike Champagne, Deborah Darr, Kathleen Doyle, Paul Milikin, Peter Riegert, Marshall Lee Shnider, Donald Warfield.

MEDAL OF HONOR RAG (44). By Tom Cole. January 23, 1976. Director, David Chambers; scenery, Raymond C. Recht; lighting, Betsy Toth; costumes, Deborah Walther. With David Clennon, Howard E. Rollins Jr., David M. Levine.

HENRY V (44). By William Shakespeare. March 19, 1975. Director, Louis Scheeder; scenery, David Chapman; lighting, Betsy Toth; costumes, David Chapman and Carol Oditz; music, William Penn. With Richard Kline, Patrick Beatey, Mike Champagne, David Cromwell, Clement Fowler, Charles Morey, Antonino Pandolfo, Terrance O'Quinn.

ALL'S WELL THAT ENDS WELL (21+).
By William Shakespeare. May 14, 1976. Director, Jonathan Alper; scenery, Raymond C. Recht; lighting, Arden Fingerhut; costumes, Bob Wojewodski; music, William Penn. With Albert Corbin, Mark Winkworth, Clement Fowler, Michael Houlihan, David Cromwell, Etain O'Malley, Mary Carney, Carla Meyer.

Ford's Theater

ARE YOU NOW OR HAVE YOU EVER BEEN? (40). By Eric Bentley. September 22, 1975. Director, William Devane; scenery, Barry Robison; lighting, Robert Bye. With David Spielberg, John Lehne, Allan Miller, Charles Weldon, Beeson Carroll.

YOUR ARM'S TOO SHORT TO BOX WITH GOD (168). Musical conceived by Vinnette Carroll; music and lyrics by Alex Bradford. November 4, 1975 (American premiere). Director, Vinnette Carroll; scenery and costumes, William Schroder; lighting, Gilbert Hemsley Jr.; choreography, Talley Beatty; orchestrations, Billy Taylor. With Lamar Alford, Salome Bey, Alex Bradford, Sharon Brooks, Maryce Carter, Billy Dorsey, Thomas Jefferson Fouse Jr., Cardell Hall, Delores Hall, William Hardy Jr., Jan Hazell, Aisha Khabeera, Michelle Murray, Stanley Perryman, Zola Shaw, Alwin Taylor.

A gospel celebration of the passion of Jesus. One intermission.

Musical numbers: Act I—"Stranger in Town," "Do You Know Jesus, He's a Wonder," "Just a Little Bit of Jesus Goes a Long Way," "Hail the Saviour Prince of Peace," "Alone," "There Are Days I'd Like to Be," "Be Careful Whom You Kiss," "Your Arm's Too Short to Box With God," "Give Us Barabbas," "Why Did I Do It," "See How They Done My Lord," "Somebody Here Don't Believe in Jesus," "What Have I Done to Thee," "The Hour of Darkness," "Were You There," "Can't No Grave Hold My Body Down." Act II—"Didn't I Tell You," "When the Power Comes," "Following Jesus," "I Love You So Much," "On That Day," "How Can I Make It," "Everybody Has His Own Way," "I Know He'll Look Out For Me," "The Band."

I HAVE A DREAM (24). By Josh Greenfeld. April 6, 1976 (world premiere). Director, Robert Greenwald; scenery, Donald Harris; lighting, Martin Aronstein; costumes, Terrence Tam Soon.
Dr. Martin Luther King Jr .... Billy Dee Williams
The Woman; The Actress.. ...Judyann Elder
The Woman; The Singer....Marion Ramsey
Singing accompaniment.....Merria A. Ross
Time: Act I, December 1955-August 1963; Act II, September 1963-April 1968. Place: Various cities and towns in America. The life and civil rights career of Dr. Martin Luther King Jr., using many of King's actual speeches. One intermission.

ELEANOR (33+). By Arlene Stadd. May 3, 1976 (world premiere). Director, Michael Kahn; scenery, Ed Wittstein; lighting, John McLain; costumes, Jane Greenwood.
Eleanor Roosevelt........ .. ...Eileen Heckart
Time: 1934, 1941-62. Place: The White House and Hyde Park. A one-woman show about Eleanor Roosevelt from her days as First Lady to her death.

John F. Kennedy Center: Eisenhower Theater

THE SCARECROW (24). By Percy MacKaye. August 10, 1975. Director, Austin Pendleton; scenery, John Conklin; costumes, Carrie F. Robbins; lighting, John Gleason; incidental music, Arthur B. Rubenstein. With William Atherton, Barbara Baxley, Leonard Frey, King Donovan, Ralph Byers, Susan Sharkey. An American Bicentennial Theater production, produced by Roger L. Stevens and Richmond Crinkley for the Kennedy Center and presented in conjunction with the Xerox Corporation.

RIP VAN WINKLE (30). Adapted by Joshua Logan and Ralph Allen from Washington Irving's story and plays by John Kerr, Charles Burke and Dion Boucicault. January 29, 1976. Director, Johsua Logan; scenery, Robert Cothran; costumes, Marianne Custer; lighting, David F. Segal; traditional airs adapted by Trude Rittmann. With Anthony Quayle, Annie McGreevey, Bernerd Engle, Jay Doyle, Deborah Fezelle, Michael Petro. An American Bicentennial Theater production, produced for the Kennedy Center by Roger L. Stevens and Richmond Crinkley and presented in conjunction with the Xerox Corporation and the Clarence Brown Company of the University of Tennessee.

THE AMERICAN COLLEGE THEATER FESTIVAL. Eighth annual two-week festival of representative college productions, selected from across the country. April 5-18, 1976. Held in the Eisenhower Theater and George Washington University's Marvin Theater. Produced by the Kennedy Center in conjunction with the Alliance for Arts Education, the American Theater Association and Amoco Oil Company.
CONPERSONAS (3). By Paul Stephen Lim. April 7, 1976. Director, David Cook; scenery, Gregory Hill; lighting, Cathy Corum; costumes, Chez Haehl. Produced by the University of Kansas, Lawrence. Winner of the ACTF playwriting competition.

Miles Zeigler .... Paul Hough
Jesse Jugenheimer .... Peter Miner
Rhoda Abrams ....'.. Victoria Stevens
Shelagh Abrams .... Nancy Flagg
Mark Zeigler .... Paul Hough

Time: Thanksgiving Day. Place: Miles Zeigler's Upper East Side apartment in New York. A Jesuit priest tries to uncover the reason for his twin brother's suicide and finds himself drawn into a similar life and death. One intermission.

The festival also included: THE LIBERTY DANCE OF HENRY SPARROW (3). By Edward F. Emmanuel, California State University, Fresno; winner of the David Library Award. THE BRASS MEDALLION (3). By Ajamu, Howard University; runner-up in the ACTF playwriting competition. THE ME NOBODY KNOWS (3). University of Detroit/Marygrove College. AH, WILDERNESS! (3). University of Evansville, Evansville, Ill. HAIR (3). Indiana University/Purdue University. MOBY DICK REHEARSED (3). Temple University.

In repertory—A Texas Trilogy, three full-length plays by Preston Jones; director, Alan Schneider; scenery and lighting, Ben Edwards; costumes, Jane Greenwood; produced for the Kennedy Center by Robert Whitehead and Roger L. Stevens:

LU ANN HAMPTON LAVERTY OBERLANDER (17+). April 29, 1976.
Claudine Hampton .... Kate Wilkinson

Lu Ann Hampton .... Diane Ladd
Billy Bob Wortman .... James Staley
Skip Hampton .... Graham Beckel
Dale Laverty .... Everett McGill
Red Grover .... Patrick Hines
Rufe Phelps .... Walter Flanagan
Olin Potts .... Thomas Toner
Corky Oberlander .... Baxter Harris
Milo Crawford .... Josh Mostel
Charmaine .... Kristin Griffith

Time: 1953, 1963, 1973. Place: The Hampton home and Red Grover's bar in Bradleyville, Texas. Twenty years in the life of a small-town Texas girl who never manages to get out. Two intermissions.

THE LAST MEETING OF THE KNIGHTS OF THE WHITE MAGNOLIA (17+). April 30, 1976.

Ramsey Eyes .... John Marriott
Rufe Phelps .... Walter Flanagan
Olin Potts .... Thomas Toner
Red Grover .... Patrick Hines
L.D. Alexander .... Henderson Forsythe
Colonel J.C. Kinkaid .... Fred Gwynne
Skip Hampton .... Graham Beckel
Lonnie Roy McNeil .... Paul O'Keefe
Milo Crawford .... Josh Mostel

Time: 1962. Place: The meeting room in the dilapidated Cattleman's Hotel in Bradleyville. The members of a waning lodge, not unlike the Ku Klux Klan, gather for what turns out to be the collapse of their sorry brotherhood. One intermission.

THE OLDEST LIVING GRADUATE (16+). May 1, 1976.

Martha Ann Sickenger ...... Kristin Griffith
Maureen Kinkaid .... Patricia Roe
Colonel J.C. Kinkaid .... Fred Gwynne
Mike Tremaine .... Ralph Roberts
Floyd Kinkaid .... Lee Richardson
Clarence Sickenger .... Henderson Forsythe
Maj. Leroy Ketchum .... William Le Massena
Cadet Whopper Turnbill .... Paul O'Keefe
Claudine Hampton .... Kate Wilkinson

Time: Summer of 1962. Place: The den of Floyd Kinkaid's ranch-style home on the outskirts of Bradleyville. New Texas (the country club set) and Old Texas (crusty Colonel Kinkaid) clash over a real estate development scheme. One intermission.

Note: Other American Bicentennial Theater productions were: *The Skin of Our Teeth* (32). By Thornton Wilder. July 9, 1975; *Summer Brave* (32). By William Inge. September 7, 1975; *Sweet Bird of Youth* (37). By Tennessee Williams. October 9, 1975; *The Royal Family* (39). By Edna Ferber and George S. Kaufman. November 12, 1975; *Long Day's Journey Into Night* (43). By Eugene O'Neill. December 19, 1975; and *The Heiress* (44). By Ruth and Augustus Goetz. February 27, 1976. They were all picked up for New York engagements after their Washington runs.

Note: The John F. Kennedy, Center Opera House season included pre-Broadway productions of *Treemonisha, A Musical Jubilee, Pacific Overtures* and *Rex,* and touring productions of *Jesus Christ Superstar, Hello, Dolly!* and *Mark Twain Tonight.*

National Theater

SABRINA FAIR (16). By Samuel Taylor. September 30, 1975. Director, Harold J. Kennedy; scenery, John Pitt. With Arlene Francis, Robert Horton, Katharine Houghton, Sam Levene, Russell Nype, Maureen O'Sullivan.

THE DEVIL'S DISCIPLE (16). By George Bernard Shaw. October 15, 1975. Directors, Paxton Whitehead and Tony Van Bridge; scenery, Maurice Strike; lighting, Donald Acaster; costumes, Hilary Corbett. With Paul Hecht, Elizabeth Shepherd, Neil Vipond, Paxton Whitehead and members of Canada's Shaw Festival. Presented by The Canadian Department of External Affairs in cooperation with The Canada Council Touring Office as part of the Kennedy Center's Canadian Festival.

IT'S SHOWDOWN TIME (16). By Don Evans. April 20, 1976. Director, Shauneille Perry; scenery, C. Richard Mills; lighting, George Greczylo; costumes, Kadiatou. With Charles Brown, Lynn Whitfield, Gloria Edwards, Clebert Ford, Harrison Avery. Presented by the D.C. Black Repertory Company in association with Woodie King Jr. and George Schiffer.

GUYS AND DOLLS (23+). Musical by Jo Swerling and Abe Burrows; music and lyrics by Frank Loesser. May 5, 1976. Director, Billy Wilson; scenery, Tom H. John; costumes, Bernard Johnson; lighting, Thomas Skelton; musical supervision and additional arrangements, Danny Holgate; choreographer, Billy Wilson; entire production supervised by Abe Burrows. With Norma Donaldson, Robert Guillaume, Ernestine Jackson, James Randolph, Edye Byrde, Kenneth Page, Christophe Pierre, Emett Wallace.

Note: The National season also included pre-Broadway tryouts of *Bubbling Brown Sugar, A Matter of Gravity* and *1600 Pennsylvania Avenue*, and touring productions of *Purlie* and *What the Wine-Sellers Buy*.

Olney Theater

THE GOOD DOCTOR (21). By Neil Simon. June 3, 1975. Director, Leo Brady; scenery and lighting, James D. Waring; costumes, Wallace G. Lane Jr. With Keith Charles, Ruby Holbrook, Davis Hall, Kathleen O'Meara Noone, Peter Vogt.

THE SHOW-OFF (21). By George Kelly. June 24, 1975. Director, James D. Waring; scenery and lighting, James D. Waring; costumes, Wallace G. Lane Jr. With Jan Miner, Wil Love, Pat Karpen, Kathleen O'Meara Noone, Peter Vogt, Charles White, Michael Haney.

THE UNEXPECTED GUEST (21). By Agatha Christie. July 15, 1975. Director, Leo Brady; scenery and lighting, James D. Waring; costumes, Meg Patterson and Jo-Ellen LaRue. With Kathleen O'Meara Noone, Mel Boudrot, Anne Chodoff, Eleanor Phelps, Paul Collins, Peter Vogt, Michael Haney.

IRISHMEN (21). Three one-act plays by Hugh Leonard. August 5, 1975 (world premiere). Director, James D. Waring; scenery and lighting, James D. Waring; costumes, Marguerite Mayo.

A Time of Wolves and Tigers
Jumbo Beamish .... Terrence Currier
Nothing Personal
Pat Nagle .... Jarlath Conroy
Philip Agnew .... John Wylie
Betty Hand .... Pauline Flanagan
The Last of the Last of the Mohicans
Dominick Studley .... Terrence Currier
Finbar Reidy .... John Wylie
Grace Lamb .... Judith Reagan
Ita Studley .... Pauline Flanagan
Seamus Lamb .... Jarlath Conroy
    Time: Around midnight. Place: The living rooms of three neighboring houses in a suburban Dublin development. Leonard looks at the foibles of his countrymen—their fondness for drink and self-deception, their proclivity for telling dangerously tall tales and their penchant for philandering. One intermission.

THE GLASS MENAGERIE (21). By Tennessee Williams. August 26, 1975. Director, James D. Waring; scenery and lighting, James D. Waring; costumes, Joan Thiel; musical score, Emerson Meyers. With Jan Miner, Stephen Joyce, Pat Karpen, Peter Vogt.

Wolf Trap Farm Park

KISMET (5). Musical by Charles Lederer and Luther Davis; music and lyrics by Robert Wright and George Forrest. July 17, 1975. Director, Gene Lesser; scenery, John

Conklin; lighting, Duane Schuler; choreo-
raphy and musical staging, Ethel Martin.
With John Reardon, Jane A. Johnston, Richard Bauer, Ethel Martin, Mark Hammer and
members of the Wolf Trap Company.

WATERFORD, CONN.

Eugene O'Neill Theater Center: National Playwrights Conference

(President, George C. White; artistic director, Lloyd Richards, assistant artistic director, Nancy Quinn; designers, Peter Larkin, Fred Voelpel, Arden Fingerhut. All programs new works in progress)

Barn Theater (Indoors)

DEAD AND NEVER CALLED ME MOTHER (2). By Robert Lord. July 23, 1975. Director, Hal Scott; dramaturgs, Arthur Ballet and Martin Esslin.

Sarah ....Jill André
Sean ....Ben Masters
John ....Joel Brooks
Alice ....Meryl Streep
Albert ....Jay Garner
Paul ....Andy Backer
The acts of the play take place on two consecutive Saturdays in summer. One intermission.

JESSE AND THE BANDIT QUEEN (2). By David Freeman. July 25, 1975. Director, James Hammerstein; dramaturg, Marlis Thiersch; piano played by Steven Crist.

Jesse ....Bryan Clark
Belle ....Jill Eikenberry
No intermission.

Barn El (Indoors)

MARCO POLO (2). By Jonathan Levy. July 26, 1975. Director, Lynne Meadow; dramaturg, Edith Oliver; music, Michael Posnick.

Harlequin ....Joe Grifasi
Nicolo Polo ....Jay Garner
Maffeo Polo ....Kevin O'Connor
Marco Polo ....Ben Masters
Musician ....Michael Posnick
Prop Man ....Louis Giambalvo
Counsellors ....Dan Hedaya, David Berman
Yellow Lama ....Ed Zang
Achmed ....Christopher Lloyd
Kogatin ....Meryl Streep
Kublai Khan ....Andy Backer
A fantasy for children in two Acts and a Harlequinade. No intermission. Place: The city of Venice, the court of Kublai Khan at Cambalu', the province of Yang Chow, and everywhere in between.

WIN WITH WHEELER (2). By Lee Kalcheim. August 2, 1975. Director, James Hammerstein; dramaturgs, Edith Oliver and Marlis Thiersch.

Sam Duffy ....Bryan Clark
P. J. Whittlsie ....Ben Masters
Mason Sternwell ....Andy Backer
Kathy Meyer ....Louise Heath
Reese Mandel ....Joel Brooks
Sarah ....Peggy Pope
Bellboy; Sy ....Edward Zang
Harvey; TV Announcer ......Dan Hedaya
Mrs. Wheeler ....Eleanor Ellsworth
Jack Davis ....Kevin O'Connor
Locker Room Sportscaster;
Coach ....Joe Grifasi
No intermission.

Amphitheater (Outdoors)

THE SPELLING BEE (2). By Marsha Sheiness. July 17, 1975. Director, Harold Scott; dramaturgs, Martin Esslin and Edith Oliver.

Freddie Stans ....Ed Zang
Steven Roberts ....Joel Brooks
Maggie Roberts ....Peggy Pope
Nina Gold ....Meryl Streep
Bart Powell ....Ben Masters
Thelma Powell ....Jill André
Ralph Pikes ....Robert Christian
Arlene Pikes, Ralph's Mother. Veronica Redd
One intermission.

DEBTS (2). By Dan Owens. July 29, 1975. Director, Harold Scott; dramaturg, Edith Oliver.

Felix Lane ....Robert Christian
Johnson Lee ....Bill Cobbs
Sandra Lane ....Veronica Redd
Bianca Lane ....Louise Heath
Aunt Lil ....Jessie Saunders

CRACKS (2). By Martin Sherman. July 31, 1975. Director, Tony Giordano; dramaturg, Arthur Ballet.

Rick ....Ben Masters

Sammy .... Joe Grifasi
Nadine .... Rosemary De Angelis
Jade .... Meryl Streep
Clay .... Ed Zang
Gideon .... Christopher Lloyd
Maggie .... Jill André
Roberta .... Louis Giambalvo
Irene .... Jill Eikenberry

THE BROWNSVILLE RAID (2). By
Charles Fuller. August 5, 1975. Director,
Harold Scott; dramaturg, Edith Oliver.
Pvt. James W. Newton ....Charles Holmond
Sgt. Mingo Saunders .... Earle Hyman
Pvt. John Holliman .... Bill Cobbs
Pvt. Dorsey Willis .... Brent Jennings
Pvt. Rueben Collins .... Bill Jay
Cpl. Clifford I. Adair ..... Robert Christian
Cpl. Boyd Conjers .... Lee Roy Giles
Pvt. Richard Johnson .... Ray Aranha
Dolly Saunders .... Jessie Saunders
Captain .... J. T. Walsh
Orderly .... Andre Mtumi
Mayor Combs; Maj. Blockson;
Gen. Garlin .... Gil Rogers

Instant Theater (Outdoors)

THE PRIMARY ENGLISH CLASS (2). By
Israel Horovitz. July 16, 1975. Director,
James Hammerstein; dramaturgs, Arthur Bal-
let and Martin Esslin.
Mr. La Patumiera .... Bryan Clark
Mr. La Poubelle .... Dan Hedaya
Translator .... Kevin O'Connor
Mr. Mulleimer .... Andy Backer
Mrs. Pong .... Lori Chinn
Yoko Kuzukago .... Kitty Chen
Debbie Wastba .... Jill Eikenberry
No intermission.

HOLLINRAKE'S GAMBIT (2). By Lance
Lee. July 21, 1975. Director, Lynne Meadow;
dramaturgs, Martin Esslin and Marlis
Thiersch.
John Hollinrake .... Bryan Clark
Faith Hollinrake .... Jill Eikenberry
Peter Finch .... Kevin O'Connor
Martin Capon .... Robert Christian
Jack .... Edward Seamon
Mildred Henslowe .... Peggy Pope
1st Lady .... Veronica Redd
2d Lady .... Marlis Thiersch

Theodore Roosevelt .... Jay Garner
Emmett Scott .... Count Stovall
The Raiders: Norm Johnson Jr., Louisa
Anderson, Samuel Harris, Tom Costello.
Drums: Scott Richards.
Act I: August 13 and 14, 1906, Browns-
ville, Texas. Act II: Several weeks later. Act
III: Two weeks later.

ISADORA DUNCAN SLEEPS WITH THE
RUSSIAN NAVY (2). By Jeff Wanshel.
August 8, 1975. Director, James Hammer-
stein; dramaturgs, Arthur Ballet and Marlis
Thiersch.
Author .... Robert Christian
Producer .... Ed Zang
Isadora Duncan .... Meryl Streep
Lenin .... Andy Backer
Chorus (representing about 100 charac-
ters): Joel Brooks, Jean Campbell, Bryan
Clark, Jill Eikenberry, Ben Masters, Peggy
Pope.
Place: Hollywood.

3d Lady .... Phyllis Kaye
Sheriff Lou Wilson .... Dan Hedaya
Officer Chuck Angerson ..Louis Giambalvo
Time: Now. Place: Hollinrake's house and
garden along the Mendocino Coast in
Northern California. Scene 1: Afternoon.
Scene 2: That night. Scene 3: The following
afternoon.

LAMENT: FOR CHOO-CHOO (2). By Neil
Yarema. August 7, 1975. Director, Tony Gi-
ordano; dramaturgs, Arthur Ballet and Mar-
lis Thiersch.
Monk .... Dan Hedaya
Little Joe .... Joe Grifasi
Arnie Brown .... Kevin O'Connor
Wop .... Christopher Lloyd
Old Man .... Tom Costello
Larry Snyder .... Andy Backer
Charlie Keller .... Charles Stavola
Georgie .... Louis Giambalvo
Lou Cerafice .... Ed Setrakian
Woman .... Marlis Thiersch
Child .... Peter Thorn
Elaine .... Jill André

WEST SPRINGFIELD, MASS.

Stage/West

(Managing director, Stephen E. Hays; resident director, Rae Allen; resident costume designer, Sigrid Insull)

AH, WILDERNESS (22). By Eugene O'Neill.
November 15, 1975. Director, Rae Allen;
scenery, Lawrence King; lighting, Ron Wallace. With Robert Pastene, Elizabeth Parrish, Graham Beckel, Tom Crawley, Nancy
Snyder.

THE TEMPEST (22). By William Shakespeare. December 13, 1975. Director, Edward Berkeley; scenery, Charles G. Stockton; lighting, Judy Rasmuson. With John Milligan, Lillah McCarthy, Yusef Bulos, Franklyn Seales, Michael Miller, Graham Beckel.

THE BALCONY (22). By Jean Genet. January 10, 1976. Director, Rae Allen; scenery, Eugene Warner; lighting, Ron Wallace. With Barbara Tarbuck, Gwyllum Evans, Patricia Cray, Michael Miller.

THE COUNTRY GIRL (22). By Clifford Odets. February 7, 1976. Director, Martin Fried; scenery, Marc B. Weiss; lighting, Jamie

Gallagher. With John Ryan, Michael Miller, Barbara Tarbuck.

DESIGN FOR LIVING (22). By Noel Coward. March 27, 1976. Director, John Milligan; scenery, Fredda Slavin; lighting, Judy Rasmuson. With Patricià Cray, James Secrest, Tom Crawley.

SERENADING LOUIE (22). By Lanford Wilson. April 3, 1975. Director, Rae Allen; scenery, Fredda Slavin; lighting, Jamie Gallagher. With David Gale, Patricia Cray, Janis Young, James Secrest.

Note: Stage/West sent *Hugo The Clown* on a three-week tour of schools in the area. The production, directed by Marjory Sigley, with Phillip Littell, Nancy Sellin, Christopher Romilly, Leslie Leonelli, played 30 performances, beginning March 29, 1976.

CANADA

HALIFAX, NOVA SCOTIA

Neptune Theater Company

(Artistic director, John Wood)

DUTCH UNCLE (24). By Simon Gray. June 16, 1975. Director, John Wood; designer, Jack Simon; lighting, Robert C. Reinholdt. With Jack Medley, Florence Paterson, Brian McKay, Zoe Alexander, David Hemblen, Gordon Clapp.

MY FAT FRIEND (24). By Charles Laurence. July 14, 1975. Director, David Brown; designer, Fred Allen; lighting, Robert C. Reinholdt. With Jack Medley, Zoe Alexander, Brian McKay, David Hemblen.

THE COLLECTED WORKS OF BILLY THE KID (24). By Michael Ondaatje. November 3, 1975. Director, John Wood; designer, John Ferguson; music, Alan Laing. With Neil Munro, Patricia Collins, David Renton, Robert A. Elliott, Carole Galloway.

MISALLIANCE (24). By George Bernard Shaw. December 1, 1975. Director, John Wood; designer, Susan Benson; lighting, Michael Whitfield. With Peter Hutt, Patricia Collins, Jack Medley, Eric Donkin.

BRECHT ON BRECHT (16). By George Tabori. January 12, 1976. Director, David Renton; designer, Susan LePage; lighting, Robert A. Elliott; musical director, Monique Gusset. With Gordon Clapp, Denise Fergusson, Monique Gusset, David Hemblen, Joan Orenstein.

JOHN AND THE MISSUS (24). By Gordon Pinsent. February 2, 1976 (world premiere). Director, Donald Davis; designers, Susan Benson and Michael Whitfield; music composed and performed by Kenzie MacNeil.

Sid Peddigrew ......Douglas Chamberlain
Holly Picard; Mrs. Sheppard ....Gail Clapp
Ted Pratt; Tom Noble Jr. ....Gordon Clapp
Faith ....Brenda Devine
Mr. Burridge;
  Raymond Burgess ....David Hemblen
Jimmy Ludlow ....Peter Hutt
Tom Ivany; Frank ....Larry Lamb
Rev. Wood; Alf Sheppard Raymond Landry
Fred Budgell ....Frank Maraden
Matt ....Frank Moore
Mrs. Crummy; Mrs. Noble ..Joan Orenstein
The Missus ....Florence Paterson
John Munn ....Gordon Pinsent
Tom Noble ....David Renton
Nish ....Chuck Robinson
Fudge ....Dennis Thatcher
Mrs. Burridge;
  Margaret Burgess ....Faith Ward
  Townspeople: Douglas Augustus Grant, Maggie Grice, Bob Martyn, Meredith Pugsley, Amy Newman.
  Time: 1975. Place: A mining community, Newfoundland. One intermission.

THE TORCHBEARERS (24). By George Kelly. March 1, 1976. Director, John Wood;

designer, Robert Doyle; lighting, Donald Acaster. With Douglas Chamberlain, David Hemblen, David Renton, Gordon Clapp, Patricia Collins, Joan Orenstein.

THE GLASS MENAGERIE (16). By Ten-

nessee Williams. March 29, 1976. Director, John Wood; designers, Jack Simon, Susan LePage; lighting, Robert A. Elliott; music, Alan Laing. With Rita Howell, R. H. Thomson, Carole Galloway, Neil Munro.

MONTREAL

Centaur Theater Company: Centaur 2: Main Stage

(Artistic director, Maurice Podbrey)

ONE CRACK OUT (33). By David French. October 2, 1975. Director, Maurice Podbrey; designer, Felix Mirbt; lighting, Harry Frehner. With Arnie Achtman, Griffith Brewer, Doris Cowan, Michael Fernandes, Peggy Mahon, Alain Montpetit, Jim Morris, Robert O'Ree, Michael Reynolds.

THE BARBER OF SEVILLE: OR THE FUTILE PRECAUTION (33). By Beaumarchais; translated by David Calderisi. November 13, 1975. Director, David Calderisi; designer, Real Quellette; lighting, Vladimir Svetlovsky; music composed and performed by Pierre Voyer. With Arnie Achtman, Griffith Brewer, Michael Fernandes, Joan Karasevich, Budd Knapp, Robert O'Ree, August Schellenberg.

A STREETCAR NAMED DESIRE (33). By Tennessee Williams. January 1, 1976. Director, Neil Vipond; scenery, Ed Fisher; lighting, Trevor Parsons; costumes, Neil Vipond. With Elizabeth Shepherd, Nick Mancuso, Janet Barkhouse, Richard Donat.

KENNEDY'S CHILDREN (33). By Robert Patrick. February 12, 1976. Director, Eric Steiner; scenery and costumes, Shawn Kerwin; lighting, Harry Frehner. With Janet Barkhouse, Neil Vipond, Michael Fernandes, Garry Chipps, Patricia Phillips, Elizabeth Sheperd.

THE DIVINE SARAH (33). By Jacques Beyderwellen. March 25, 1976. Director, Louis-Georges Carrier; designer, Francois Barbeau. With Denise Pelletier.

Centaur Theater Company: Centaur 1: Small Stage

CANADIAN GOTHIC and AMERICAN MODERN (33). By Joanna M. Glass. November 27, 1976. Director, William Davis; designer, Barbara Matis; lighting, Trevor Parsons. With Mary Pirie, Maurice Podbrey, Aileen Taylor Smith, Gordon Tootoosis, Jim Whelan.

ON THE JOB (33). By David Fennario. January 29, 1976. Director, David Calderisi; scenery, Felix Mirbt; lighting, Tim Williamson; costumes, Diane Johnston. With Grif-

fith Brewer, Alex Bruhanski, Edmond Grignon, Terry Haig.

I.W.A.—THE NEWFOUNDLAND LOGGERS' STRIKE OF 1959 (18). By Rick Salutin, as created by the Mummers Troupe of Newfoundland; music by Ron Hynes. March 11, 1976. Director, Christopher Brookes; designer, Frank Lapointe. With Rick Boland, Donna Butt, Ron Hynes, Ray Landry, Rhonda Payne, Wayne McNiven, Jeff Pitcher.

Montreal Theater Lab

(Director, Alexander Hausvater)

THE ROGUES' TRIAL (20). By Ariano Suassuma. June 14, 1975. Director, Alexander Hausvater.

CRIME AND PUNISHMENT (20). By Dostoyevsky; adapted and directed by Alexander Hausvater. November 5, 1975 (world premiere). Scenery and costumes, Danielle Ross; lighting, Philip Cheveldayoff.
Cast: Dunya; Nastassia; Woman—Judith Elizabeth; Raskolnikov—A. J. Henderson;

Razumkhin; Nicolay; Priest—Peter MacNeill; Mme. Raskolnikov; Street Walker; Aliona; Foot—Elizabeth Mudry; Luzhin; Ilya Petrovich; Customer; Marmeladon; Dimitri; Old Man—Wendell Smith; Sonia; Arm—Colleen Wagner Porfiry; Cab driver—Jack Wetherall.
One intermission.

FULL CIRCLE (20). By Erich Maria Remarque; adapted by Peter Stone. April 7, 1976. Director, Alexander Hausvater.

LOVERS OF VIOREN (20). By Marguerite Duras. May 16, 1976. Director, Alexander Hausvater.

The Company: Louis de Bianco, Judith Elizabeth, A. J. Henderson, Peter McNeil,

Elizabeth Mudry, Tom Rack, Vlasta Vrana, Colleen Wagner, Jack Weatherall; and David Burke, Terry Donald, Gordon Smith, Wendell Smith. Designers, Charles Van Vliet, Danielle Ross.

STRATFORD, ONT.

Stratford Festival: Festival Theater

(Artistic Director, Robin Phillips; director Festival/Stage, William Hutt; founder, Tom Patterson)

SAINT JOAN (36). By George Bernard Shaw. June 9, 1975. Director, William Hutt; designer, Maxine Graham; lighting, Gil Wechsler. With Pat Galloway, Stephen Macht, Leslie Yeo, William Needles, Max Helpmann.

TWELFTH NIGHT (35). By William Shakespeare. June 10, 1975. Director, David Jones; designer, Susan Benson; lighting, Gil Wechsler. With Kathleen Widdoes, Marti Maradan, Denise Fergusson, Leslie Yeo, Brian Bedford, Stephen Macht.

MEASURE FOR MEASURE (21). By William Shakespeare. June 11, 1975. Director, Robin Phillips; designer, Daphne Dare; lighting, Gil Wechsler. With William Hutt, Brian Bedford, Stephen Macht, Martha Henry, Kathleen Widdoes.

TRUMPETS AND DRUMS (17). By Bertolt Brecht; translated by Kyra Diets and Alan Brown. July 29, 1975 (North American premiere). Director, Robin Phillips; designer, Daphne Dare; lighting, Gil Wechsler.

Capt. William Plume ...... Gordon Pinsent
Capt. .... William Hutt
Sgt. Kite .... Tom Kneebone
Balance .... Leslie Yeo
Victoria .... Jackie Burroughs

Worthy .... Nicholas Pennell
Simpkins .... Richard Curnock
Melinda Moorhill .... Diane Grant
Lucy .... Linda Huffman
Lady Prude .... Denise Fergusson
Rose .... Pat Bentley-Fisher
Bullock .... Graeme Campbell
Thomas Appletree .... Lewis Gordon
Costar Pearmain .... Michael Liscinsky
Mike .... Marc Connors
Bridwell .... Mervyn Blake
Broadshoulders .... Daniel Buccos
William .... Stephen Russell
Mrs. Cobb; Innkeeper's Wife.. Sheena Larkin
Maggie .... Jan Kudelka
Molly .... Barbara Budd
Court Attendant .... Rod Beattie
Servant .... Keith Batten
Father of Five .... Martin Donlevy
Collier .... Larry Lamb
    Soldiers, Townspeople, Prisoners, etc.: Michael Fletcher, Richard Partington, Bob Baker, Paul Batten, Geoffrey Bowens, Don Hunkin, Peter Hutt, Robert More, Robin Nunn, Jack Roberts, Georgina Spelvin, John Sweeney, Robert Vigod, Ian Wallace. Trumpeter: James Spragg. Drummer: Gregory Law.
    Time: During the American War of Independence. Place: Shrewsbury, England. Two intermissions.

Stratford Festival: Avon Theater

THE COMEDY OF ERRORS (42). By William Shakespeare. June 10, 1975. Directors, Robin Phillips, David Toguri; designer, Jeffrey Sisco; lighting, Gil Wechsler, Nicholas Pennell, Barry MacGregor, Bernard Hopkins, Richard Whelan, Jackie Burroughs, Gale Garnett.

THE TWO GENTLEMEN OF VERONA (40). By William Shakespeare. June 11, 1975. Directors, Robin Phillips, David Toguri; designer, Molly Harris Campbell; lighting, Gil

Wechsler. With Stephen Russell, Nicholas Pennell, Bernard Hopkins, Eric Donkin, Mia Anderson, Gale Garnett, Douglas Chamberlain, Jackie Burroughs.

THE CRUCIBLE (14). By Arthur Miller. July 28, 1975. Director, John Wood; designer, Susan Benson; lighting, Gil Wechsler. With Stephen Macht, Martha Henry, Marti Maradan, Gale Garnett, Douglas Rain, Odetta, Sheila Haney.

Stratford Festival: Third Stage Theater

(Designers: scenery, John Fergusson, Gayle Tribick, Molly Harris Campbell; lighting, Michael J. Whitfield, Robert Scales)

LE MAGICIEN, music and libretto by Jean Vallerand, director, Pat Galloway; and THE FOOL by Harry Somers, libretto by Michael Fram, director, Jan Rubes (6). July 30, 1975. Musical director-conductor, Raffi Armenian.

ARIADNE AUF NAXOS (5). By Richard Strauss; libretto by Hugo von Hofmannsthal. July 31, 1975. Director, Jan Rubes; musical director-conductor, Raffi Armenian.

Opera Company: Robert Calvert, Barbara Carter, D. Glyn Evans, Mary Lou Fallis, Giulio Kukurugya, Gary Relyea, Brian Roberts, Roxolona Roslak, Jeannette Zarou.

FELLOWSHIP (11). By Michael Tait. August 7, 1975 (world premiere). Director, Bernard Hopkins.

Anna Windgate	Doris Petrie
Sally Geary	Elva Mai Hoover
Peter Solant	Jack Wetherall
Gerald Teale	Guy Bannerman
Monica Pierce	Lynne Griffin
May Saunders	Nan Stewart
Ruth George	Dena Saxer

Agnes Pierce	Patricia Hamilton
Harold Geary	Neil Vipond
Rev. Alexander Cranford	John Innes
Hugo Pierce	Robert Benson

Two intermissions.

OSCAR REMEMBERED (13). Compiled and performed by Maxim Mazumdar. August 16, 1975. Director, William Hutt. A portrait of Oscar Wilde as seen by Lord Alfred Douglas.

KENNEDY'S CHILDREN (9). By Robert Patrick. August 25, 1975. Director, Bill Glassco. With Andrew V. Arway, Gary Bayer, Brenda Donohue, Denise Fergusson, Richard Monette, Dena Saxer.

THE IMPORTANCE OF BEING EARNEST (9). By Oscar Wilde. September 29, 1975. Director, Robin Phillips. With Richard Monette, Nicholas Pennell, William Hutt, Pat Galloway, Marti Maraden, Meg Hogarth, Tom Kneebone.

VANCOUVER

Playhouse Theater Center of British Columbia: Queen Elizabeth Theater— Main Stage Company

(Artistic director, Christopher Newton)

EQUUS (16). By Peter Shaffer. November 10, 1975. Director, Peter Dews; designer, Cameron Porteous; lighting, Graham Cook. With Christopher Newton, Tom Wood, Al Kozlik, Irene Hogan, Donna Haley, Heather MacDonald, Norman Browning.

THE SPECKLED BAND (16). By Sir Arthur Conan Doyle. December 15, 1975. Director, Alan Dossor; designer, Cameron Porteous; lighting, Jeffrey Dallas. With Richard Fowler, Michael Ball, Diana Belshaw, Norman Browning.

MACBETH (16). By William Shakespeare. January 19, 1976. Director, Christopher Newton; designer, Cameron Porteous; lighting, Graham Cook. With Kenneth Welsh, Patricia Gage, Michael Ball, Terence Kelly, Donna Haley.

LEONCE AND LENA (16). By Georg Buechner. March 1, 1976. Director-designer, Livui Ciulei; lighting, Jeffrey Dallas. With

Ivar Brogger, Heather MacDonald, Kenneth Welsh, Donna Haley, Tom Wood.

CAMILLE (16). By Robert David MacDonald. April 5, 1976 (North American premiere). Director, Christopher Newton; designer, Cameron Porteous; lighting, Jeffrey Dallas.

de Varville	Michael Ball
Alexandre	Ivar Brogger
Atalante	Valerie Bromfield
Armand	Norman Browning
Alfredo	Doug Cameron
Germont; Man	Andrew Czaplejewski
Doctor	Alex Diakun
Croupier	Alan Gray
Marguerite	Donna Haley
Prudence	Irene Hogan
Gaston	Terence Kelly
Duke	Al Kozlik
Cupidon	Glen MacDonald
Marie	Heather MacDonald
Olympe	Kate McDonald
Duval; Valet	Derek Ralston
Violetta	Gayle Roberts
Auctioneer	Tom Wood

Prologue. Act I: The auction; resurrection; the supper party; the examination; recrimination. Act II: Pastoral variations; the gaming table; death.

Playhouse Theater Center of British Columbia New Company: New Stage

KENNEDY'S CHILDREN (11). By Robert Patrick. October 14, 1975. Director, Arif Hasnain. With the New Company.

DEAR JANET ROSENBERG, DEAR MR. KOONING by Stanley Eveling, director, Derek Ralston; and WHY HANNA'S SKIRT WON'T STAY DOWN by Tom Eyen, director, Bob Baker (11). November 18, 1975. With Heather Brechin, LeRoy Schulz, Diana Belshaw, Allan Stratton.

THE KOMAGATA MARU INCIDENT (11). By Sharon Pollock. January 20, 1976 (world premiere). Director, Larry Lillo.
Woman .... Diana Belshaw

Evy .... Heather Brechin
Sophie .... Nicola Cavendish
Hopkinson .... Richard Fowler
Georg .... LeRoy Schulz
T.S. .... Allan Stratton

BACK TO BEULAH (11). By W. O. Mitchell. March 9, 1976. Director, Bob Baker. With the New Company and Kate McDonald.

The New Company: Diana Belshaw, Heather Brechin, Nicola Cavendish, Richard Fowler, LeRoy Schulz, Allan Stratton. Designers: Scenery and costumes, Jack Simon; lighting, Gary Clarke.

Note: Playhouse Theater Center's Theater-in-Education Company toured British Columbia in the fall of 1975 with *Clown,* a presentational documentary; *Planit* and *Hellas,* participation programs. The New Company toured in the Spring of 1976 with *Suddenly at Home, Kennedy's Children,* and *The Komagata Maru Incident.*

WINNIPEG

Manitoba Theater Center: Main Stage

(Artistic director, Len Cariou)

CYRANO DE BERGERAC (26). By Edmond Rostand; translated and adapted by Anthony Burgess. October 17, 1975. Director, Jean Gascon; scenery and costumes, Mark Negin; lighting, Robert R. Scales. With Len Cariou, Susan Kapilow, Robin Ward, Roland Hewgill, Claude Dorge.

THE PRICE (26). By Arthur Miller. November 21, 1975. Director, Robert Bilheimer; scenery and lighting, Raymond C. Recht; costumes, Taras Korol. With Robert Benson, Angela Wood, Milton Selzer, Roland Hewgill.

EQUUS (26). By Peter Shaffer. January 9, 1976. Director, Edward Gilbert; scenery and costumes, Peter Wingate; lighting, Gil Wechsler. With Len Cariou, Ian Deakin, Patricia Hamilton, Robin Ward, Zoe Alexander.

COMPANY (26). Book by George Furth;

music and lyrics by Stephen Sondheim. February 13, 1976. Director-stager, Dean Regan; scenery and costumes, Lawrence Schafer; lighting, Bill Williams; musical director-conductor, Victor Davies. With Brian McKay, Evelyne Anderson, Marilyn Boyle, Janis Dunning, Cliff Gardner, Patricia Hamilton.

OF MICE AND MEN (26). By John Steinbeck. March 19, 1976. Director, Len Cariou; scenery and costumes, James R. Bakkom; lighting, Robert R. Scales. With Erik Fredricksen, John-Peter Linton, Martin Doyle, Janis Nickleson.

PRIVATE LIVES (26). By Noel Coward. April 23, 1976. Director, Frances Hyland; scenery and costumes, Peter Wingate; lighting, Bill Williams. With Zoe Alexander, David Calderisi, Clare Coulter, Robin Ward, Doreen Brownstone.

Manitoba Theater Center: Warehouse Theater

THE COLLECTED WORKS OF BILLY THE KID (16). By Michael Ondaatje. November 25, 1975. Director, Arif Hasnain; scenery and costumes, Doug McLean; lighting, Bill Williams; music, Des McAnuff. With Peter Jobin, Des McAnuff, Patricia Hamil-

ton, Claude Bede, Trudy Cameron, Guy Bannerman, Larry Davis.

BEYOND WORDS (8). Devised by the Canadian Mime Theater Company. January 23, 1976. With Adrian Pecknold, Harro Maskow,

Robin Patterson, Paulette Hallich, Larry Lefevbre.

ENDGAME (16). By Samuel Beckett. February 24, 1976. Director, Robert Bilheimer; scenery and costumes, Doug McLean; lighting, Bill Williams. With Roland Hewgill, David Calderisi, Christopher Britton, Doreen Brownstone.

CREEPS (16). By David Freeman. March 30, 1976. Director, Robert Bilheimer; scenery and costumes, Doug McLean; lighting, Bill Williams. With Guy Bannerman, Jay Brazeau, Christopher Britton, Fran Gebhard, Joseph Horvath, Brian Richardson, Aaron Schwartz.

Manitoba Theater Center: Theater for Children

A CHRISTMAS CAROL (14). A story Theater adaptation by David Ball and David Feldshuh. December 22, 1975. Director, Robert Bilheimer; scenery and costumes, Doug McLean; lighting, Bill Williams. With David Calderisi, Jay Brazeau, Doreen Brownstone, Christopher Britton, Alexe Duncan, Duffy Glass, David Gillies, Susan Kapilow.

RED NOSES (40). Created by the Canadian Mime Theater Company. January 19, 1976. Director, Adrian Pecknold. With Harro Maskow, Paulette Hallich, Larry Fefevbre, Adrian Pecknold.

DINNER THEATER

In 1976, a Poker Game

By Francine L. Trevens

Playwright and co-founder of Readers and Playwright's theater, Springfield, Mass.

The dinner-theater scene in 1975-76 has been less like the clinking of cash registers and more like a poker game than in the past. Many theaters (including Oklahoma's Lincoln Plaza Playhouse and Addison, Texas's Windmill Dinner Theater) played their final hand, folded, and left the table. Some opted for the lower stakes of the non-Equity gamble. It might look bleak, except that so many new hands have opened. The Equity total dropped from 70 last year to 60 this year, but there are still several hundred non-Equity theaters providing regular or intermittent dinner-theater fare, including Mama Gail's Theater-Restaurant in New York City, where Equity companies frequently book in their shows, as the T. Schreiber Studio did for two plays at the end of the season.

Among the most striking and glamorous of the new players in the dinner-theater game is Glen Cove, Long Island's Northstage which premiered in April after several months' delay with a lavishly costumed *Funny Girl* complete with a 15-piece orchestra. What makes these producers believe they can succeed where Sardi's Dinner Theater, also on Long Island, and the Parkway Casino in Tuckahoe, N.Y. both closed this year? Perhaps since Northgate's people previously helped others start dinner theaters they feel they have the expertise. Other new theaters throughout the country share their enthusiasm.

Jay Devlin, a dinner-theater headliner for some years now, is confident of dinner theater's future, "if the unions and management can come to closer terms." He feels their disagreements have caused many theaters to turn non-Equity, a trend most obvious this year.

Devlin also believes the most successful operations have owners like Dow Sherwood of Tiffany's Attic and Waldo's Astoria in Kansas City, Mo.—a gentleman with marvelous elan who always greets his patrons personally and treats his actors like persons. This actor also credits Ruth, Sam and Janis Belkin of Connecticut's Coachlight Dinner Theater in this regard.

Imogene Coca is another dinner-theater enthusiast, who gives economy and convenience as the chief reasons "dinner theaters are multiplying. The things I've seen in dinner theater I'd say are pretty good. I've yet to see a show in dinner theater that was awful. I've seen some Broadway that was awful!"

Sarah Churchill launched her short story *The Boy Who Made Magic* into a stage version and portrayed one of the major roles. Outstanding in this fairy-tale-style musical was the singable score and lilting lyrics of Andy Badale, Frank Stanton and Murray Semos—a team to watch for future wonders.

Dinner theaters report their most successful shows this season were musicals and Broadway-style comedies interesting to the over-30 generation (*Hello, Dolly!, Zorba, Six Rms Riv Vu, Forty Carats, etc.*) Revues and variety shows were drawing less well.

While some dinner theaters report premieres do poor business, many indicate these original productions do the *best* business. The Windmill chain of Texas and environs scored best with *Ginger in the Morning*. Pheasant Run Playhouse in Illinois's biggest hit was *The Nearlyweds*. And the Firehouse Dinner Theater, Omaha, Neb. revived last year's premiere *Red Dawg* to make it their most successful show of the year.

Marvin Poons, executive secretary of the American Dinner Theater Institute, notifies us that over 15,000 people attend ADTI theaters nightly, contributing to gross receipts of $20 million annually.

No one denies dinner theater is a gamble, as are all entertainment enterprises. The gamble seems to be paying off for many actors, most audiences and administrators. As Poons put it, "Although dinner-theater growth has suffered a serious setback, dinner theaters have established a definite place in the American theater scene, and we expect next year will again be a period of expansion."

The players may change, but the game goes on. Major 1975-76 premiere productions were the following:

GINGER IN THE MORNING (5 weeks) by Mark Miller. December 2, 1975. Directed by Marjorie Lord; scenery and lighting, Tony Neighbors. With Davia Sacks, Mark Miller, Greg Callahan, Corinne Michaels, Richard Maggi, Ron Scott, Al Evans. Windmill Theater, Dallas, Tex. and Country Dinner Playhouse, Denver, Colo.

THE BOY WHO MADE MAGIC (7 weeks) dramatized by James Liggat from a short story by Sarah Churchill; music by Andy Badale; lyrics by Frank Stanton and Murray Semos. February 25, 1976. Directed by Carl Schurr; scenery, Robert Troll; lighting, Paul Pavis; costumes, Christianne Sachanen; musical direction, John Franceschina; choreography, Carol Haught. With Sarah Churchill, Alan Sharp, Kathleen Conry, Karen Dwyer, Jack Sevier, Joel Kramer, Helen Masloff. Hayloft Dinner Theather, Manassas, Va.

THE FIFTH CUP (2) by Gershon Kingsley and Norman Simon: April 12, 1976. Musical direction, Gershon Kingsley; choreography, Crandall Diehl; costumes, Janis Belkin. With Theodore Bikel, Dennis Arlen, Fran Dorsey, Mickey Gunnersen, Leah Malamud, Paul Merrill, Lloyd Sannes. Coachlight Dinner Theater, East Windsor, Conn.

THE HONEYMOON CAPER (3 weeks) by James Lockhart. May 13, 1975. Directed by Ed Aldridge; scenery, Greg Etcheson; lighting, Mark Fasset; costumes, Katy Koutts. With Betty Endrizzi, Roger Howell, Bonnie Hellman, Debra Savage. Allenberry Playhouse, Boiling Springs, Pa.

THE HOT LINE (5 weeks) by George Gipe. January 6, 1976. Directed by Robert Minford; scenery, Tony Mendez; lighting, Judy Hashagen; costumes, Jay Scott. With Casey Craig, Richard Zavaglia. Limestone Valley Dinner Theater, Cockeysville, Md.

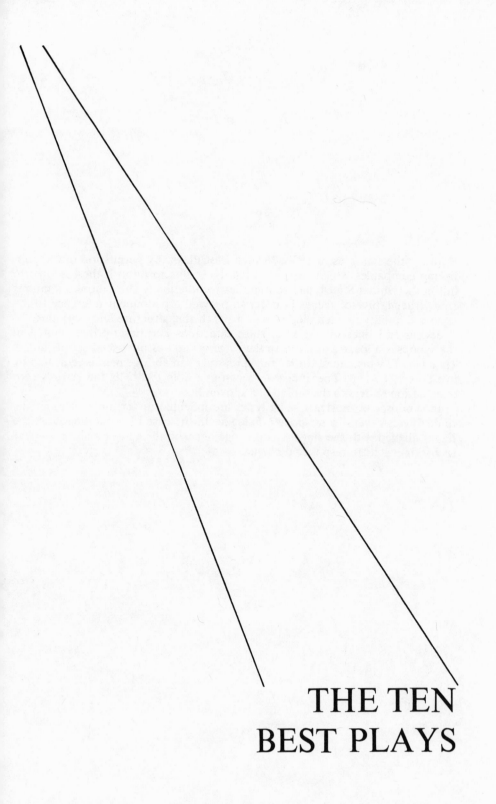

THE TEN
BEST PLAYS

Here are the synopses of 1975-76's ten Best Plays. By permission of the publishing companies which own the exclusive rights to publish these scripts in full in the United States, our continuities include many substantial quotations from crucial/pivotal scenes in order to provide a permanent reference to the style and quality of each play as well as its theme, structure and story line.

Scenes and lines of dialogue, stage directions and descriptions quoted in the synopses appear *exactly* as in the stage version or published scripts unless (in a very few instances, for technical reasons) an abridgement is indicated by five dots (. . . . .). The appearance of three dots (. . .) is the script's own punctuation to denote the timing of a spoken line.

In synopses of musicals, song lyrics are indented under the singer's name, to distinguish them from spoken dialogue. In the case of a one-line lyric, the line is aligned with the singer's name together with the stage direction (*sings*) to distinguish it from spoken dialogue.

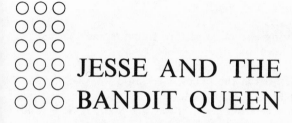

JESSE AND THE BANDIT QUEEN

A Play in Two Acts

BY DAVID FREEMAN

Cast and credits appear on page 364

DAVID FREEMAN was born in Cleveland in 1941 and after completing his education has pursued a writing career through many phases as a journalist, publicist, author, screen writer and playwright. His collection of stories about New York City, U.S. Grant in the City, *was published by Viking Press in 1971. His play productions have included* Captain Smight's Return *at the Theater Company of Boston,* Frank Buck Can't Make It *off off Broadway at WPA Theater and a series of his works at Island Repertory Theater on Martha's Vineyard.* Jesse and the Bandit Queen *is his first professional New York stage production.*

Time: Just after the Civil War till the early 1880s

Place: Missouri, Kansas and the Indian Territories

ACT I

SYNOPSIS: The stage is divided into platformed areas and set with a desk, a piano, a rocking chair and two coat trees which are to hold the symbolic articles of costuming. The backdrop is a high sky over a lonely place on the prairie. Hanging above the setting is a large picture frame, somewhat askew, seeming to frame a part of the outdoors.

Belle (*"about 30 . . . . . an attractive woman, but a little hard; a woman who was kicked around a bit"*) sits at the piano, wearing a long velour cape and playing "Bright Morning Stars." Jesse, a few years older, wearing hat, leather jacket and chaps, sits across from her in a rocking chair. Jesse is holding a copy of *The Police Gazette* and contemplating his stomach.

Jesse calls offstage to his wife Zee that he will straighten the picture, remarking to the audience, "Why anybody who lives out in the country needs a picture of the country is beyond me. You could just look out the window." But Jesse remains seated as the lights dim on him and come up on Belle. Belle tells the audience that she's always expected the worst of people and seldom been disappointed, starting at 11 years old with her history teacher, who couldn't keep his hands to himself.

BELLE (*to the audience*): . . . . . I had a horse that I loved more than any man. A mare, a brown and white mare. I called her Venus and she was better to me that I ever was to her. I was never proud of what happened to my babies, and when Pearl run off, and Little Ed come at me like that, I just got on Venus and rode away. I wore my lavender dress draped in black fringe and with a plume in my hat and a riding crop at my wrist, dangling . . . there.
　　Rises and pulls a gun out of her cape.
Except for the gun I always tucked into the folds of my skirt, I was one first-class lady.
　　The lights fade on Belle and come back up on Jesse still in his rocker.
JESSE: Fat now, yes fat. But oh once. All right Zee, I'm doing it now.
　　Rising, removing his hat, and walking to the picture frame, about to straighten it.
Could spend the rest of my life straightening up this house. Why anybody who lives out in the country needs a picture of the country is beyond me.
　　Belle as Bobby Ford points a gun at Jesse's back. He hears the gun being cocked and turns to face Belle.
Little Bobby Ford. It'll have to be a bullet in the back son, and there'll be no praise for you. No glory, no honor for little Bobby Ford.
　　Jesse turns back toward the picture, presenting his back to Belle. She moves quickly toward Jesse, dropping the gun to her side. Jesse spins back around as the lights change sharply. He has become Belle's son Ed, threatening her with a knife.
BELLE (*as herself*): Eddie. Don't. My little baby. My only son, I'm so sorry. You have to go away now. You have to forget about all of that. Eddie, you mind your mama and put that down.
　　Jesse hands Belle the knife as she hands him the gun.

Both Belle and Jesse have become aware of danger threatening them just before the moment of their deaths. But time slips backward as Belle steps downstage into a pool of light to address the audience.

BELLE: It ain't fair. It ain't true and it ain't fair. Never with Ed. Never. With a lot of them, oh Lord, a lot of them, but never with my own baby.
Putting her knife into her scabbard.
I might of made a mess with my babies, but at least I tried with Jesse. Just like my babies though, couldn't live with him, and couldn't live without him. I gave my name to everybody only nobody wanted it except Mr. Richard Fox of *The Police Gazette* and he just made up a lot of garbage. I guess I added to the confusion but at least it was something. It was more fun being written up in them magazines than never being wrote up at all.
The lights go out on Belle and come up on Jesse, still at the picture. Belle crosses behind the piano, removes her cape and bodice and hangs them on her coat tree.
JESSE (*addressing the audience*): Sixteen years of making history and little Bobby Ford was the best they could do. All them Pinkerton men with their squads and staffs and long guns and little Bobby Ford was the winner . . . . .

Jesse doesn't believe the story about the governor paying Ford $10,000 to kill him (he tells the audience), he thinks Ford probably wanted to get his hands on Zee, Jesse's wife. When he was Ford's age, Jesse remembers, he couldn't keep his hands off Belle (who puts on her shawl and sits at the piano).

The lights dim on Jesse and come up on Belle who is now 17, in the private quarters of her father's inn in Carthage, Mo., struggling with a Mozart sonata. Jesse comes up to Belle wearing his hat (which he takes off when she speaks to him) and carrying his boots. Jesse jokes with Belle about her piano playing, which is rather good.

Belle has been watching the road for Jesse's companion and cousin, Cole Younger, whom she rather favors. Jesse competes with the piano for Belle's attention by trying to play it, at first pounding on the keys and finding out from Belle where middle C is located, sharing the stool as she teaches him, putting his arm around her, earning a resounding slap from Belle but blocking her way as she tries to leave the room.

Jesse is on his way to Kansas to join Capt. William C. Quantrill, he tells Belle. The lights change and Jesse is older, in his early 30s, putting on his boots—"high ones, hand tooled and with silver heels"—remembering how it was to ride with Quantrill: "The fighting was maybe over for the rest of them, but me and Billy, we kept up our own war, and to hell with the army."

Belle puts on Jesse's hat and assumes the character of Quantrill, a messianic fanatic haranguing Jesse (again as a mere youth) about the cause lost in the South but to be still pursued in the West: "We will be as gods to the people. You will have a pair of riding boots, of marching boots, and they will make you a man of mine."

Belle, as Quantrill, observes that Jesse is "So very pretty with your pouty little mouth" that he'd be useful as a decoy for Yankee soldiers. Wearing Belle's shawl and armed with a knife, Jesse entices Belle (playing a Union soldier) into the shadows and stabs her to death. Both fall to the ground.

The lights change. Jesse and Belle, now in their early 20s, lie relaxed, chatting.

JESSE: That's what Quantrill and me and the others done all over Missouri. He was dead at 28. But we did it. We surely did it. No matter what anybody said though, I never took to perfume.

BELLE: The hell you didn't. Dresses was the part you liked the best. You keep playing soldier boy, you won't even live as long as Billy.

JESSE: I only did it because I was good at it and I loved the surprise on their faces.

BELLE: If I'd known you liked dresses back when you come through Carthage, I'd have given you a couple.

JESSE: I got what I wanted back in Carthage.

BELLE: I didn't know you was going off to fight a war in a dress. Did you and Billy ever argue over who got to wear it? (*She laughs.*)

JESSE: Me and Billy was fighting a war. You was off parading around with my cousin Cole not caring about anything.

BELLE (*sitting up*): I was so hot to get out of Carthage and that goddamned hotel, I'd have gone off with any dog that asked.

JESSE: So you went with Cole. Figures. You could have waited for me.

BELLE: And I'd still be waiting. I didn't do nothing but sit around that place all day and play the piano. When my father found out I had Cole's baby, he tried to kill me. You should have come to me then, Jesse. You should have come.

JESSE: I had a mission. Me and Billy was going to change the whole country around. When we won I was going to get Montana for my own.
Lays back, arms extended, holding the knife straight up.
Billy was going to make me king of Montana.

BELLE (*taking the knife, laughing*): Instead, he made you Queen of the Night.

Jesse remembers how Quantrill made a soldier of him, teaching him to ride and kill, "spouting the Bible while he was burning the church. Quoting Shakespeare and raping the school teacher." Jesse believed that wiping out a whole town was justified because even the little girls would grow up to be Union-lovers some day.

BELLE: You think because you went around waving that black flag and saluting each other that made you an army.

JESSE: We was an army because we won.

BELLE: You was the only one who ever believed that soldier crap Quantrill dished out. At least all the others knew what they were: bunch of thug outlaws. Nothing more.

JESSE: Only cause we lost. We split up. Little groups. Billy got killed. Now I got every federal soldier in the country chasing me.

BELLE: So you come running to me.
> *Sits left of Jesse and speaks softly to him.*

They'll kill you. All you got to do is stay here in the Indian nations and they can't touch you.

JESSE: You ain't turning me into one of your Indians following you around in some goddamned feather suit.
> *Jesse rises. Belle then rises, crosses to her coat tree, picks up her bodice and puts it on.*

You know I took a bullet in my gut back there. A bullet. That's when you should have come to me.

BELLE: Since when was I supposed to keep track of you and crazy Billy?

JESSE: Zeralda managed. There was a bullet in my gut and Zee was there cooking tea and fixing me up.

BELLE: So you married her. All over a cup of tea.

JESSE: I married her because she was there when I needed her. You was with your Indians and your goddamn baby. While you was being thrown out of the Carthage Academy, I was graduating from the William Quantrill Military College.
> *Picking up his hat.*

I have to go, Belle.

BELLE: Yeah, college of murder, arson, horse stealing and all around hell-raising.

JESSE: Horse stealing? Every *Police Gazette* I read's got: Belle Starr the biggest horse thief in the country.
> *Putting on his hat.*

I am a soldier.

BELLE (*throwing Jesse the blanket*): You're a soldier cause everywhere you go there's a war.

JESSE: At least I'm no thief. I never been arrested for nothing and I never will be. I'm going to earn a living.

Jesse moves upstage, taking the blanket, as Belle comes down to tell the audience about her various trials, including one before the noted hanging judge, Judge Parker. Jesse takes on the character of Judge Parker and warns Belle that though no woman has ever been hanged west of the Pecos, horse stealing is a hanging offense and there is always a first time. Belle argues that Venus is her own horse, not stolen property. She manages to seduce the judge, so that the point becomes moot.

The lights change, and Belle and Jesse, now in their late 20s, are sitting on the blanket as though before a campfire. Belle notices a tattoo on Jesse's chest reading "Enter Here" and wonders what it's supposed to be. Jesse replies: "To confuse the vulgar while I live—and baffle God when I die."

Belle admits that Jesse is as good at loving as he is at robbing banks. Jesse is jealous of Belle's succession of Indian husbands, but he can't marry Belle because he already has a wife.

BELLE: I never asked you. And I never will. You could never change your name.

JESSE: Belle, that ain't how it works.

BELLE: It is with me. I changed my name the first time. After that, the men change. (*Laying back.*) Jesse Starr. How do you like it?

JESSE: I ain't changing my name.

BELLE: That's right. And that's why I ain't marrying you. I marry you and you'd have to go shooting at yourself. That's your custom, ain't it, find my men and try to blow their heads off.

JESSE (*removinig his holster*): Cole? You only married him to spite me.

BELLE: And every time you took a shot at him, even after we wasn't together no more, I knew that was just Jesse saying, "Hello Belle, don't forget me."

JESSE (*removing his belt and touching her breast with it*): Hello Belle, don't forget me.

BELLE: What makes you think I remember? So busy all the time trying to be famous.

JESSE: You could be famous as me if you wasn't so busy littering babies all over the place. What did you name this one?

BELLE: Not Jesse, I'll tell you that.

JESSE: Yeah, Little Cloud or Big Duck or Feather Brain. Or—

BELLE: His name's Ed. Ed Starr.

JESSE: (*sitting up, taking off his hat*): Pearl and Ed. I could never take you with me. We'd ride into town looking for the bank and you'd turn it into a nursery.

BELLE: Like a little boy robbing a piggy bank.

JESSE: Piggy bank! Hell woman, I invented the American bank robbery. You know what that means? Before me nobody ever thought of it.

> *Belle sits up and removes her boots. Jesse pulls his gun out of his pants.*

St. Valentine's Day, 1866, Clay County Missouri, I invented robbing banks. Me and Frank and Cole after we sobered him up, come riding into the town of Liberty at nine in the morning shooting and hollering and scaring the shit out of everybody. I applied Quantrill's military techniques to robbing banks. We even brought the flag.

> *Jesse holds his gun up like a flag. Belle takes it from him.*

Billy taught me, make enough noise and you can have all you want so long as you take it quick. We took it quick all right, fifteen thousand in gold, a pile of non-negotiable bonds, and a few hundred in cash.

> *Removing his boots.*

We got drunk on the cash, wiped our behinds with the bonds, and sold the gold to a peddler named Prominent Abromovitz in San Antone. And that's how bank robbing was invented.

They killed people in that robbery, in order to follow Billy Quantrill's dictum, "Kill a couple on Monday, and the rest'll cooperate on Tuesday."

Belle is sick of hearing about Quantrill. She has her own memories of wearing hand-tooled boots ("Boots make the difference") and her husband Jim Starr's clothing in order to fool and scare an Indian who had been stealing gold.

Belle puts Jesse's belt around his neck like a bridle and climbs onto his shoulders to ride him, forcing him to play the part of her beloved horse Venus. Then Belle dismounts and turns Jesse into Blue Duck, her Indian lover: "You clean her hooves with a green stick and you comb her mane . . . . . You clean her good and stroke her fine and then you can stroke me."

Belle lies down under the blanket and Jesse reaches for her, but she kicks him away. Jesse moves away to his coat tree, taking his boots, shirt and belt, while Belle talks to the audience: "Six Indian lovers I had, each one prettier than the last; two were hanged, two died in prison, one got his head blowed off and the other just ran away. More Indians than I could count. All my Cherokees, and everywhere I went there was my lovely brown braves behind me. I was in all them magazines and *The Police Gazette* had Jesse's picture in every saloon and barbershop in the country. He was everywhere and I was in the Indian nations. Mr. Richard Fox said so right there in *The Police Gazette,* but still he never come to me."

After a change of lights, Jesse assumes the character of Richard Fox of *The Police Gazette,* interviewing Belle at his desk. He is a legend-builder, making larger-than-life-sized heroes out of common Western clay like Jesse James and Belle—or Bella Starr, as he means to call her, in *The Bandit Queen* by Richard Fox. Belle objects to having her name changed, and she is contemptuous of Fox's imaginings about herself and about Jesse: "Hah! He's a thug. Your giant Jesse gets so confused from guns and dresses, that half the time he don't know who he is and he don't love nobody but himself."

Fox explains the *Gazette's* rules for gun play: "One: Always fight fair. Two: Look a man square in the eye before you shoot him. Three: Never shoot a small person . . . . . It doesn't matter what you do, only what I say you do."

Belle perceives that Fox has invented a heroic Jesse James, but she means to invent Belle Starr herself. Fox prepares to write down the details Belle is going to give him.

JESSE (*as Fox*): We had you running the Long Branch Saloon in Kansas City.

BELLE (*sitting on the stool*): Oh yeah. I rode into Kansas every Tuesday on my brown and white mare.

JESSE (*taking notes throughout*): Venus.

BELLE (*putting on her boots*): I wore buckskin breeches and a ten gallon hat and I shot up the streets and robbed the banks before breakfast. I spent the money on lavender velvet dresses—

Draping the bodice over her shoulders.

—and in the evenings I became Rosa McComus— (*Seductively.*) —the spitfire of the plains, queen of the dance hall.

JESSE: Great stuff. How about lovers?

BELLE: Yeah. Sure. There was Jack Spaniard, Jim French, Sam Starr, Jim July and my own sweet Cherokee, the Blue Duck.

JESSE (*looking up from the manuscript*): Blue Duck? What'd you call him, Duckie?

BELLE: I called him boy. I took them two at a time, and I kept one on the shelf till I wanted him.

Fox wants to know something about Belle's "sweet mop haired children" Pearl and Eddie, but Belle doesn't want their names in the paper. Fox means to push the "female Jesse James" angle, though Belle assures him Jesse is nothing but "a trigger-happy lunatic." Nevertheless Fox has decided to call his next story "Bella Starr the Bandit Queen, or the Female Jesse James."

The lights change. Belle gives Jesse back his gun, holster and hat, and Jesse sits in the rocker reading *The Police Gazette,* a family man talking to his wife Zee (played by Belle with a ribbon in her hair). Zee wants Jesse to take a look at the baby, who may have the croup. Jesse doesn't want to look at the baby, and he hates being called by his alias "Mr. Howard" because he's proud of the name he's made for himself and not afraid to be called by it. Zee fears for Jesse's safety, though, and makes him promise not to rob any more banks.

Zee reports that Bobby Ford has been by again. Jesse knows what he came for and that he's not getting any. Jesse sends Zee out to make pancakes and, at her urging, gets up to straighten the picture. Before he can do so, Zee complains that she doesn't feel well. Her complaints turn Jesse away from her, toward the audience.

Putting on his vest, holster and boots, Jesse explains to the audience that he never intended to become a bank robber, he was like a ball being bounced from one event to another. He knows it will probably end badly, but before it does "I'll surely make this country bleed."

Jesse gathers up his shaving things, sits, and Belle joins him, now as herself. She proceeds to lather Jesse and sharpen the razor preparatory to shaving him. Now that every banker in the country is looking for Jesse, Belle suggests, why not change his style and rob a train? Jesse thinks that is "a first class A number one idea."

Belle flourishes the razor, cuts a lock of hair and suggests that she cut all Jesse's hair off.

BELLE: It'd be good for you. Nobody'd recognize you.

JESSE: I wouldn't even recognize me.

BELLE (*flicking the cut hairs in front of his eyes*): Nothing new about that.

JESSE: (*grabbing Belle's wrist*): I know who I am, Belle. It's other people including you who have trouble figuring it out.

    Drops Belle's arm and points to The Police Gazette.

Why do you keep telling this guy this junk?

BELLE (*looking over his shoulder*): Let me see.

JESSE: Listen to this crap. (*Reads.*) "Jesse and Bella. Jezabel. Mated by history. Riding the wild pampas together, the burning dust of the desert in their lungs. Bang went the guns, pop goes the heart of America."

BELLE: I love it. Wish they would get my name right, though.

Belle tries to grab the magazine, but Jesse pulls it away.

JESSE: It matters what they say in these things about me. I can't let this Fox junk be the record of me.

Jesse has decided to take charge of his own life and legend and write a book himself about himself. Belle tells him, "Jesse you are such a fool, that you are supposed to be some kind of hero is God's joke."

Belle proceeds to shave Jesse; then they start playing with the razor, as though to cut each other. Jesse kisses Belle, smearing lather on her face. Belle grabs his hair and puts the blade to Jesse's throat.

BELLE: What would you say if, if I . . . was to slide this right into your throat. You probably wouldn't be saying much.

JESSE: I'll do some sliding in.

He grabs her legs and makes a few small humping motions against her. Belle quickly brings the razor close to Jesse's eyes. He slowly leans back.

BELLE: How about you do that while I slit open your eyes. Then Jesse love, you can flow into me all you want. And all your blood, if you have any, can wash down my face. Think it'll spurt? Or just drip?

By now, Jesse is leaning all the way back, supporting himself with his arms on the floor.

JESSE: What's that razor do for you, make you me? Make you Jesse James? That what it does for you? Good. Now we'll both be Jesse. And do twice as many trains.

He makes a small motion to sit up, but Belle holds the razor right next to his eyes, keeping him down.

BELLE: No. More what I had in mind is slicing off chunks of you and putting them on me.

Making large motions with the razor which come very close to Jesse's ears and nose.

I might hack off an ear and stick it on, or maybe your nose. That way I can be either one of us or both. I'll use you for spare parts.

She holds the razor very still and right next to his face.

JESSE: Yeah, or maybe I'll use you for something.

He grabs Belle's thighs and begins to sit up slowly, defying Belle and the razor. She persists, keeping the razor close to his eyes.

Cause that's what you really want, ain't it? Well, I'll make you a deal. You can have it on temporary loan. Whenever I feel like giving it to you.

Belle pulls the razor back as though to come at him with it. Jesse grabs her wrist and squeezes it. Belle drops the razor. He rises,

*carrying her down center and laying her down on her back. He
puts on his hat as Belle, still on her back, tries to escape.*

BELLE: Jesse, Jesse, I'll slit your throat. I will. I really, really will. I'll kill
you. I really, really will. I'll kill you—

JESSE: Ride 'em.

*Belle tries to kick Jesse but he catches her feet and flips her over
on her stomach. She becomes Venus and starts to crawl. Jesse
grabs her by the waist, pulling her back to him, and mounts her.*

Ride, Venus. Ride . . . I am the real Jesse. The only one. Only I am Jesse—

BELLE: Starr. Jesse Starr. The only Jesse Starr.

*Jesse waves his hat in the air; they are silhouetted against the back-
drop as the lights fade out. Curtain.*

ACT II

Belle is at the piano playing the Mozart sonata and Jesse is sitting in the
rocking chair laboring at an old-fashioned typewriter. Then he picks up *The
Police Gazette* and reads aloud from it.

JESSE (*reading*): "The masked outlaws had spread themselves along the
line of the train. 'Well Frank, everything seems to be working all right,' Jesse
remarked. 'I was right sorry we had to shoot Jack Farley,' said Frank."

He throws down the magazine and talks to the audience.

Je-sus! If that don't beat all. There's people reading that crap and thinking I
go around talking like that.

Belle stops playing and sits quietly at the piano.

No wonder the whole damn world's confused about who I am and what I
done. Oh, we done plenty of trains all right. But there wasn't much in the way
of polite conversation going on while we was at it. Trains are a pain in the ass.
Always moving, not like banks which just sit right there where they're supposed to, waiting for you. Robbing trains is done one of two ways: dumb and
bloody or smart and bloody. Dumb and bloody is when you and a bunch of
drunks see a train coming and you ride down onto the tracks shooting at it.
The train just keeps coming, and the passengers fire back at you like you was
a herd of buffaloes, which you are. The blood is yours. The smart way is you
bribe somebody to tell you which train is worth bothering with and then you
buy a ticket for a dollar, and get on when it's stopped.

Jesse puts on his vest and coat while telling the audience how he and Belle
would get on the train carrying a valise like any other couple. Belle would
create a disturbance, attracting everyone's attention, and when they turned
around there was Jesse covering them with his Colt. After Jesse and Belle
became famous and their faces known they couldn't use this modus operandi
any more.

Belle takes up a carpetbag and Jesse holsters his gun. They have just robbed a train, and Belle dumps wallets out of the carpetbag and counts money while Jesse writes in his manuscript.

Jesse is angry with Belle for making up stories about him and telling them to Richard Fox of *The Police Gazette,* hopelessly confusing his identity and the facts of his life. His manuscript is his only hope for eventually restoring the truth.

Belle divides the money, but Jesse refuses to accept his share. Jesse has decided he's tired of running around and being shot at by Pinkertons. He's going home.

Belle takes off her shawl and comes forward to tell the audience about the year she spent in federal prison in Detroit, for horse stealing. When she got out, she met an actor named Scarvey McCargo and worked up a Wild West act. With Jesse as McCargo, Belle acts out a simplistically romanticized stage coach robbery, with lines like "Traveller, your luck has run out. This is the end of the journey for you if you don't follow my instructions . . . . . Sir, guns are the words of the West, and I'm doing the talking." In the skit, Belle reveals to her victim that she is the one and only Jesse James. The victim— played by Jesse as Scarvey McCargo—is much impressed but suddenly tries to wrestle the gun away from the outlaw.

> *Jesse (as Scarvey) crawls toward the gun, which is next to Belle's foot.*

BELLE: . . . . . You have, sir, an excess of earthly riches and there are homesteaders and little people who have not at all. I am here to set that aright.

> *Belle stomps her foot, supposedly on Jesse's hand. He falls back down, cringing in mock pain.*

Now. Stand and deliver.

> *He starts to rise. She pushes him back down with a kick that is much more real than anything else in the Wild West show. She picks up the gun and points it at him. This is not what Scarvey has rehearsed, and it surprises him.*

(*As Jesse, realistically, intensely.*) I am the real Jesse James. The others, all the others, are not me. Only I am Jesse, golden Jesse. Hunt for me, pursue me, chase me across my prairie and I will find you. I am your one true hero and you will love me more when I am dead because this country's greatest fear is not for its heroes, but of them.

> *Belle rises, speaking to the audience. Jesse gets on his knees, waving his wallet at her, trying to get her back into the Wild West show.*

They were afraid of me while I lived and they will surely build a tower to me when I die.

McCargo finally fired Belle, but not before they had been on a long and successful tour with the show. Belle made so much money, she hired a groom for Venus and named him Jesse.

The lights change. Jesse, as himself, is at his desk working on his book, determined to set down all the facts appropriately embellished with sonorous phrases. Belle enters as Zee, with the ribbon in her hair, and complains about the *Gazette's* stories calling Belle "The female Jesse James." Zee is a bit jealous of Belle's notoriety, but Jesse soothes Zee: "That guy just makes that stuff up. I only met her once or twice. Back when she was with Cole."

Jesse placates Zee with promises of a trip to South America, where they can live like royalty on the money he will acquire in his next robbery, which unfortunately must be postponed for a year or so until his notoriety cools down somewhat. Jesse dismisses Zee and returns to his memoirs. He is beginning to understand his power to make the facts of his life serve his reputation: "If reputation: "If Richard Fox can say whatever he wants, so can I. I'm going to put in how I only stole from the rich and give to the poor when they needed it. How the railroads were the robbers stealing the land from homesteaders and how I set it right, how I was a man of the people and how they loved me. Sure. Why the hell not?"

The lights change, and Jesse is again with Belle, both as themselves. Jesse is planning his death scene for his memoirs—not dying in bed with the undignified ministrations of doctors, but "Big, and taking plenty with me . . . . . I will ride through the bullets and they will not touch me. I will ride into history and no man's gun can stop me. Northfield. I am in Northfield. Billy's military techniques can't save us. They are too smart in Northfield. They are waiting. The long rifles of the farmers—all those blonde haired Swedes from Minnesota—they cover us in bullets. I have never been so far north. Frank is shot, Cole is shot. I can see my men falling but still I ride. There is a glow around me, a white light that no bullet can enter. Only I can escape. It is my fate. And my glory."

Jesse imagines it another way, as a showdown gunfight in the street against three or more enemies. Jesse shoots them down but is ringed by riflemen. Jesse laughs and picks off the riflemen, but their bullets cut him down and his blood flows in the street as he falls.

Jesse almost believes that imagining and writing down a death will make it come to pass. Maybe he will invent Belle's death too, killing her himself and making her part of his legend.

       The lights fade to evening.

JESSE: Now, every last blood letting drop of it. My life and my death, straight and true and permanent.

       Belle steps into the scene as Bob Ford. She has taken off her bodice and carries Jesse's gun at her hip. Bobby is about 17. He's oily and ingratiating and doesn't fool Jesse for a moment.

BELLE (*as Ford*): Evening Mr. Howard.

       Jesse spins around to see her, instinctively reaching for a gun which he is not wearing. When he realizes it's Bobby, he relaxes.

JESSE: Hello Bobby. Do me a favor.

BELLE: Yes sir.

JESSE: Save the Mr. Howard crap for my wife. You just call me by name.

Bobby thanks Jesse for the gun Jesse gave him—Bobby hasn't fired it yet, no reason to. Bobby has paid his usual respects to Zee, Jesse observes, and Zee has asked Bobby to straighten the picture. Jesse takes the gun from Bobby while Bobby works on the picture frame. Jesse sights the gun at Bobby's back. Bobby, seeing the gun when he turns around, is frightened and tries to soften Jesse with fawning praise. Jesse finally lowers the gun and orders Bobby away from the picture: "It's my job to straighten it and I'll take care of it."

Belle, as Bobby Ford, turns away from the picture and becomes herself talking to the audience about her children and Jesse's. Jesse had two, a boy and a girl, and so did Belle—Pearl and Ed: "They got in trouble them two and I ain't proud of it. It was the living away from everything and me being away so much of the time. It ain't natural what happened, but my kids ain't the first that ever done it. Probably won't be the last."

The lights change suddenly and Jesse enters as Ed, Belle's son, "16 and capable of anything." Belle asks about Pearl's whereabouts, then berates Ed for his behavior.

BELLE: She is your sister. Your sister! It'll kill you. That will strike you down dead if you do that with your own sister. That is a sin against God.

JESSE (*as Ed, looking at her defiantly*): When you going?

BELLE: I'm taking her with me. Away from you. Do you understand?

Jesse starts to leave. Belle pulls him back, slapping his face and then hitting him again and again. He falls to the floor.

Do you? Do you? You do that with your own sister and I will take you out behind the barn and cut it off with a butcher knife. You understand? Do you?

Pulling him up to his knees.

I will take a knife to you and slice it off and feed it to the pigs.

Belle is horrified at what she has just said to her son. She pulls him to her trying ot comfort him. With her son's head pulled to her breast, she sinks to her knees. The embrace turns from a maternal one to a sexual one. Neither is certain of what is happening. It is neither a seduction nor a rape, but a moment that they can neither understand nor control. Belle clings to him as they fall to the floor.

Let go of me. You let go of me. Eddie.

They lie there entwined in each other's arms. They are still for a moment, both frightened by what has happened.

JESSE: Mama, I'm sorry. I'm so sorry.

BELLE: Oh, Eddie, my little Eddie.

They pull away from each other.

You have to go away now.

Jesse moves away as Belle, upset by what has happened, pulls herself together and tells the audience that Pearl and Ed went away while she went looking for her "Jesse Starr." She played piano and worked as a dealer in a dance hall, and she was at the piano playing Mozart when Jesse turned up.

Jesse moves forward carrying his boots, with gun and holster slung over his shoulder, echoing their first meeting 17 years before. The governor has made a speech about Jesse, calling him "A menace to the community of free peace-loving people," and Jesse needs a place to hide for the time being. He sits at the piano and shows Belle that he has learned to pick out a few bars of "Bright Morning Stars."

Belle finds that Jesse has done another bank job without her, and she is angry—she wishes Jesse would take her on permanently as a partner. Jesse grabs Belle but she pulls his gun out of the holster and points it at him. Jesse moves away.

BELLE: You'll have to get at it first.

JESSE: I been there. I know where to find it.

BELLE: Whyn't you just come riding in here and shoot me? Ain't that your military techniques?

> *Jesse takes a step toward Belle. She stomps her foot on the key-board and extends the gun further, stopping him.*

Lock up your daughters, hide your wives, here comes Jesse James the bandit queen.

> *Jesse reaches for the gun but before he can grab it she lets the bar-rel drop and swing free. He takes it and aims it at her.*

JESSE: Bang.

BELLE: Banged by Jesse James.

JESSE: It ain't the first time.

BELLE: And as usual it didn't take long.

Jesse asks about Belle's life; she is doing well in the dance hall and not currently tied to any man. Jesse tells her both his wife and his mother (both of whom happen to be named Zeralda) send their love to Belle, whose feelings about Jesse's wife, at least, are anything but loving. Jesse tries to caress Belle's breast but is rebuffed: "I'll never understand why it is men make such an un-ending fuss over an inch or two of flesh . . . . . Jesse, it's like this piano. The decoration is fine, but it ain't got nothing to do with the music it makes."

Apparently Belle hasn't heard the news about Jesse's mother, and Jesse brings her up to date. Yankee soldiers, looking for Jesse and Frank, threw a bomb in the window of his mother's house and blew her arm off. His mother survived, and Jesse and his friends took measures: "Army post in St. Joe. Before we burned the place, we rounded up all the officers. Sawed their arms off."

BELLE: My gentle Jesse.

JESSE: I ain't your Jesse.

BELLE: You ain't even your own Jesse.

> *They kiss.*

JESSE: Goodbye Belle.

BELLE: What's that supposed to mean?

JESSE: I come to say goodbye.

BELLE: You come to hide. You got in trouble and you come to hide in my skirts.

JESSE: That ain't what I do in your skirts.

BELLE: You don't do nothing with my skirts but wear them.

> *Jesse pulls away from her.*

JESSE: I'm going down to South America with Zee and the kids. Rio.

BELLE: Stay here till you get tired of me, then run away with your wife. It ain't going to work. I don't want you and you couldn't spend that much time with her. (*Imitates.*) "Jesse . . . do this . . . do that."

JESSE: Zee's okay. She's regular and permanent.

BELLE: What do you think we are?

JESSE: We're permanent okay, permanent crazy.

BELLE: You get on that boat and you'll die there.

JESSE: There's worse places to die.

Belle reminds Jesse about his intention to fulfill his legend with a glorious gunfighting death. Belle puts it to Jesse: at 34, he's getting too old and fat to keep on living a legend. It's time he decided to come with Belle to the Indian nations "and be who you are" or go back to Zee and the legend and get himself killed.

The thought of living like a Cherokee disgusts Jesse. Belle in her turn accuses Jesse of not knowing the difference between the two Zeraldas. Jesse threatens to write in his manuscript about Belle and Ed and/or Pearl and Ed, and Belle insists that none of this is true. She doesn't care what else Jesse writes about her as long as he doesn't write that.

Belle warns Jesse that he's going to get his head blown off like Billy Quantrill. And if Jesse gets killed, Belle tells him, then she will become Jesse. Belle takes off her cape and puts on Jesse's jacket and chaps, insisting "Only I am Jesse." Jesse in his turn puts on Belle's cape.

BELLE: I don't need you, Jesse. Because I am Jesse. The best you ever been was when you was being me.

JESSE (*picking up Belle's shawl from the piano and draping it around his neck*): Me being you is me being better at it than you, Belle. It's always you and me in the end. Ain't it?

> *Belle puts on Jesse's hat. They face each other from opposite sides of the platform.*

BELLE (*as Jesse*): Hello, Belle.

JESSE (*as Belle*): Hello, Jesse. Jesse, Jesse Starr.

Belle becomes Jesse at home, with Zee asking him to straighten the picture. Belle goes toward the picture, while Jesse picks up his gun and explains to the audience that Robert Ford shot him in through the window, in the back, with the pearl-handled gun Jesse had given him. Ford went on to stardom in a Wild West show, reenacting Jesse's murder. They buried Jesse unceremoniously, with his boots on and without a coffin, wood being scarce on the prairie.

JESSE (*addressing the audience, as Belle*): I know. I was there. Nobody knew me, but I was there. He is timeless, he will never die. A hero and a legend and he will never die. Only he did.

> *He cocks the gun and becomes Bobby Ford, pointing the gun at Belle's back.*

BELLE (*turns to Jesse when she hears the click*): There'll be no praise for you. No glory, no honor for little Bobby Ford.

> *She turns back to the picture, presenting her back to Jesse. He fires the gun, and runs toward Belle as she jumps off the platform, pulling out her knife. Jesse has become Belle again, being threatened by her son Eddie. They face each other from opposite sides of the platform.*

JESSE: Eddie. Don't. No. You have to go away now. You have to forget about all of that. Eddie you mind your mama and you put that down.

> *They step onto the platform. Belle stabs Jesse and they collapse onto the platform. The lights brighten, revealing Belle and Jesse as themselves, relaxing on the platform.*

BELLE: Jesse, when I wasn't pretending to be the desperado of the stage coaches, I wore a crisp white blouse and me and Venus and little Jesse, we took in the races, the circus and the county fair. Except for the gun I always tucked into the folds of my skirt, I was one first class lady.

JESSE: Fat now, yes fat. But once, oh once.

> *They kiss. As they separate, we hear "Bright Morning Stars" fading in. Jesse slowly crawls up the platform, stopping beneath the picture frame. He has become Venus and Belle mounts him. The picture is similar to the end of Act I, except now Belle has mounted Jesse. The weapons have been left next to each other on the platform.*

BELLE: Come Venus. Up girl. My pretty girl. Oh, my sweet girl. To ride you, to touch you, my hands on your mane.

JESSE: (*rising to his knees*): Jesse Starr, Jesse Starr.

> *They are silhouetted against the backdrop.*

BELLE: The only Jesse Starr.

> *Belle waves Jesse's hat in the air as the lights fade out. Curtain.*

PACIFIC OVERTURES

A Musical in Two Acts

BOOK BY JOHN WEIDMAN

MUSIC AND LYRICS BY STEPHEN SONDHEIM

ADDITIONAL MATERIAL BY HUGH WHEELER

Cast and credits appear on pages 339-340

JOHN WEIDMAN (book) was born in New York City in 1946, the son of the distinguished novelist and dramatist Jerome Weidman. He was educated in public schools when his family moved to Westport, Conn. and then back in New York at Collegiate School, graduating in 1964. He went on to Harvard where he wrote for the university's humor magazine Lampoon, *graduated in 1968 and continued to contribute to the* National Lampoon, *which was founded in 1970 as an offshoot of the undergraduate publication.*

Weidman continued his studies at Yale Law School, from which he graduated in 1974. His father expected that he would pursue a career in either law or politics and "never pushed me toward or away from writing." Pacific Overtures *is the first work of any size that Weidman ever set out to write.*

121

STEPHEN SONDHEIM (music, lyrics) was born March 22, 1930 in New York City. The Oscar Hammerstein IIs were family friends, and it was under Hammerstein's influence and guidance that young Sondheim became interested in the theater and was induced to write a musical for his school (George School, a Friends school in Bucks County, Pa.). At Williams College he won the Hutchinson Prize for musical composition. After graduating B.A. he studied theory and composition with Milton Babbitt. He wrote scripts for the Topper *TV series and incidental music for the Broadway productions of* Girls of Summer *(1956) and* Invitation to a March *(1961).*

It was as a lyricist that he first commanded major attention, however. He'd written a show called Saturday Night *which never made it to Broadway, but Arthur Laurents remembered it, liked the lyrics and took steps to bring Sondheim into collaboration on the great* West Side Story *(1957) as its lyricist. Sondheim wrote both the music and the lyrics for* A Funny Thing Happened on the Way to the Forum *(1962) and* Anyone Can Whistle *(1964), as well as his three straight Best Plays and Critics Award winners produced and directed by Harold Prince:* Company *(1970),* Follies *(1971) and* A Little Night Music *(1973). He and his shows have won numerous Tony Awards, and he has walked away with almost every recent poll that has a "best lyricist" or "best composer" category. This year's* Pacific Overtures *makes it four straight Best Plays and Critics Awards for Sondheim as composer-lyricist of a Harold Prince show.*

Other major Sondheim credits include the lyrics for Gypsy *(1959) and* Do I Hear a Waltz? *(1965) and additional lyrics for the 1974 revival of* Candide, *still another Sondheim-Prince winner of the Critics Award. His other recent works have included incidental music for the play* Twigs, *the script for the movie* The Last of Sheila, *the score for the movie* Stavisky *and the music and lyrics for Burt Shevelove's adaptation of Aristophanes's* The Frogs, *performed in the Yale University swimming pool.*

Sondheim is president of the Dramatists Guild, the professional association of playwrights, composers, lyricists and librettists. He lives in New York City.

*HUGH WHEELER (additional material) was born in London March 19, 1916, the son of a civil servant. He was educated at the Clayesmore School and the University of London, graduating in 1936. During World War II he served in the U.S. Army medical corps, and he became a naturalized American citizen in 1942. He soon established and maintained a wide reputation as a mystery writer under the pseudonyms Patrick Quentin and Q. Patrick. Four of his novels—*Black Widow, Man in the Net, The Green-Eyed Monster *and* The Man With Two Wives—*have been made into motion pictures, and he wrote the screen plays for* Something for Everyone *and* Travels With My Aunt.

Wheeler didn't begin his playwriting career until the Broadway production of Big Fish, Little Fish *March 15, 1961 for 101 performances, a Best Play of its season. His next was* Look: We've Come Through *(1965), followed by an adaptation of Shirley Jackson's* We Have Always Lived in the Castle *(1966).*

He was the co-author of two musical hits of the 1973 Broadway season as co-adapter with Joseph Stein of Irene, *as well as of the Best Play and Critics Award-winning* A Little Night Music. *The following season, the revival of* Candide *with book revised by Wheeler also captured the Critics Award, which he now wins for the third time along with his third Best Play citation as a* Pacific Overtures *collaborator. Wheeler makes his home on a farm in Monterey, Mass.*

Time: Act I—July, 1853. Act II—From then on

Place: Japan

ACT I

Scene 1

SYNOPSIS: Three Japanese musicians take their places on a platform at the left of the stage. Briefly there is the sound of their shamisen and song; then a drum beats loudly and wooden blocks are struck and resound sharply.

The lights go to black. When they come up again, a Reciter is seated in front of the show curtain.

RECITER: Nippon. The Floating Kingdom. An island empire which for centuries has lived in perfect peace, undisturbed by intruders from across the sea. There was a time when foreigners were welcome here, but they took advantage of our friendship. Two hundred and fifty years ago we drove them out—by sacred decree of the great Shogun Tokugawa—and ordered them never again to set foot on our ancestral soil. From then on until this day, in the month of July, 1853, there has been nothing to threaten the serene and changeless cycle of our days.

> *A stagehand runs the show curtain across the stage, revealing the members of the company.*

RECITER (*sings "The Advantages of Floating in the Middle of the Sea"*):
In the middle of the world we float,
In the middle of the sea.
The realities remain remote
In the middle of the sea.
Kings are burning somewhere,
Wheels are turning somewhere,
Trains are being run,
Wars are being won,
Things are being done
Somewhere out there, not here.
Here we paint screens.
Yes . . . the arrangement of the screens:

We sit inside the screens
And contemplate the view
That's painted on the screens
More beautiful than true.
Beyond the screens
That glide aside
Are further screens
That open wide
With scenes of screens like the ones that glide.
And no one presses in,
And no one glances out,
And kings are burning somewhere,
    ALL:
Not here!

As the hurricanes have come, they've passed
In the middle of the sea.
The advantages are made to last
In the middle of the sea.
Gods are crumbling somewhere,
Machines are rumbling somewhere,
Ways are being found,
Watches being wound,
Prophets being crowned
Somewhere out there, not here.
Here we plant rice . . . . .

The Reciter and the company continue in song, describing "The arrangement of the rice," how it is planted and distributed. The Reciter then describes his society's protocol of reverence and respect—"The arrangement of the bows"—in the hierarchy of Emperor (personified by a tiny puppet), Shogun and feudal lords.

The song finished, the Reciter, alone on stage, admits that there are sometimes disturbances, or rumors of disturbances. Two bearers come onto the stage with a cage in which is imprisoned a Japanese in Western clothing. A curtain drops revealing the Shogun's court. The Shogun's mother is present, together with various councillors, but the Shogun is absent.

The first councillor, Lord Abe, questions the others about this strangely-dressed person. The prisoner is a fisherman named Manjiro who was shipwrecked in a storm six years before and rescued by Americans who took him home to Massachusetts with them and introduced him to Western ways.

SECOND COUNCILLOR: But why has he come back? Does he not know that he has violated our laws twice—first when he left Japan, and then when he returned. Each crime is punishable by death. (*To Manjiro.*) Why have you come back?

(CLOCKWISE) ISAO SATO, MAKO, SOON-TECK OH, CONRAD YAMA,
FREDDY MAO, YUKI SHIMODA, SAB SHIMONO AND (CENTER)
HARUKI FUJIMOTO IN "PACIFIC OVERTURES"

RECITER (*as Manjiro*): There were rumors in America, my lord. Rumors which I thought my countrymen should hear.

SECOND COUNCILLOR: What did the rumors say?

RECITER (*as Manjiro*): That America would send an expedition to Japan.

ABE (*carefully*): And are these rumors true?

RECITER (*as Manjiro*): They are, my lord. As I made my way back home I stopped in Okinawa. In the harbor there were four black ships, Western warships, fitted out with giant cannon, manned by sailors, armed with weapons such as you have never seen. Americans, my lord, and their ships are coming here!

THIRD COUNCILLOR: It is obvious. The man is a traitor, sent here by the Westerners to spy on us.

The Reciter (as Manjiro) denies this and warns the others they should prepare to deal with the Americans' arrival. Abe sends away the cage with its prisoner and wonders who will deal with the intruders.

A young samurai, Kayama Yesaemon, enters with his wife, Tamate. They are stopped by two other samurai, who inform Kayama he's wanted by the

Shogun's council. Kayama obeys, prostrating himself before Abe, who appoints the bewildered young samurai Prefect of Police for the city of Uraga.

RECITER: A haiku:
A gift unearned
And unexpected
Often has a hidden price.

ABE: And so, when the Americans arrive, you will take a boat to their ships and you will order them to return immediately from whence they came. Is that understood?

KAYAMA: I ... my lord ... in a boat, my lord ... ordering ...?

ABE: You will inform them of the sacred decree. You will terrify them with the fate that awaits all foreign devils who dare to set foot on our holy soil. Kayama Yesaemon, may the Gods of our fathers make you equal to this awesome task.

Scene 2

The court vanishes and Kayama's small house appears. The young samurai discusses Abe's orders with his wife. No doubt Kayama has received this appointment because if the barbarians in their ships refused to leave it would be too great a national shame for a more important person to be disobeyed. If Kayama fails, he and Tamate will recover their honor on the point of his own blade.

A warning bell rings—the Americans have indeed arrived. Two Observers enter and sing "There Is No Other Way," as Tamate dances.

FIRST OBSERVER (*sings*):
..... The leaf shakes, the wings rise.
The song stops, the bird flies.
The storm approaches.

SECOND OBSERVER (*sings*): I will have supper waiting.

FIRST OBSERVER:
The song stops, the bird flies.
The mind stirs, the heart replies,
"There is no other way."

SECOND OBSERVER (*sings*):
I will prepare for your return.
I shall expect you then at evening.
The bells sound again. Tamate pauses before Kayama. He hesitates, then turns quickly on his heel and exits.

FIRST OBSERVER:
The word stops, the heart dies.
The wind counts the lost goodbyes.

SECOND OBSERVER:
There is no other way.

There is no other way.
> *Tamate takes a sheathed knife from the household shrine, kneels, pulls the knife halfway out, looks up sharply as the bells sound once more.*

Scene 3

A huge bell is lowered, and a fisherman runs in and rings it in alarm. He sings the opening verses of "Four Black Dragons"—he was standing on the beach this July morning, and suddenly the American ships, which he took to be "Four black dragons! Spitting fire!", broke through the mist. The fisherman is sounding the alarm for the end of the world.

Others are panicking too. A merchant and his family are fleeing with a load of lacquer boxes, fearful that the oncoming barbarians mean to kill everybody. A thief and various townspeople appear, creating a melee and singing of the "Four Black Dragons." The thief tries to steal one of the boxes in the confusion, but a samurai catches him and lops off his hand.

COMPANY (*sing*):
And the sun darkened
And the sea bubbled,
And the earth trembled,
And the sky cracked,
And I thought it was the end
Of the world!

FISHERMAN (*sings*):
I had seen
Dragons before
Never so many,
Never like these,
And I thought it was the end
Of the world!

> *Behind the frozen townspeople, the U.S.S. Powhatan appears and begins moving ominously downstage. The townspeople panic and run off in all directions.*

RECITER (*sings*): And it was.

Scene 4

The Powhatan and its sailors are extravagantly stylized, the ship to suggest something of the dragon the Japanese insist on believing it is, and the American sailors as ferocious monsters. *"A sudden spot reveals Commodore Matthew Calbraith Perry, isolated in some conspicuous position on the deck. He is a lion-like figure of terror from a child's dream, complete with flowing white mane."*

The Reciter exclaims, "Surely he is the King of the Demons come to strike us blind and to devour our children! In this darkest hour, who will save Japan?"

The Reciter's question is answered by the arrival of Kayama in a small guard boat. At first the sailors don't notice him. When they do, they aim weapons at him and make threatening sounds, but brave Kayama stands his ground.

KAYAMA: Sir, I have orders. You must go away. There is a sacred decree. No foreigner can come to our land.

SECOND OFFICER: What are you?

KAYAMA: I am Prefect of Police for the city of Uraga and I demand that you—

SECOND OFFICER (*breaking in*): You . . . policeman?

KAYAMA: Yes, the Prefect of—

SECOND OFFICER: You think officers of great Commodore Payry speak with policeman? (*Scary guffaw.*) HA-HA!

KAYAMA: But I am the representative of the Shogun. I have the authority—

SECOND OFFICER: Americans speak only to great men. Send great man. You hear? Policeman! Ha!

The ship's officers order Kayama away, laughing at him, much to Kayama's humiliation. Kayama goes ashore and reports to the councillors the Americans' failure to obey him and his consequent shame. The councillors are terrified when Kayama suggests they might have to deal with the barbarians themselves. They jump at Kayama's suggestion that they send the condemned fisherman, Manjiro, to parley with the Americans.

The councillors dress Manjiro in a handsome robe to make the Americans believe he is a "great man" and send him off with Kayama. Manjiro knows Americans, and he adopts a domineering attitude and orders the ship's officers to attend him in a haughty tone. The ship's officers hesitate at first but then obey, calling Manjiro "sir" and explaining Commodore "Payry's" mission: "We bring greetings and friendly letter from our great President Millyard Fillmore."

Manjiro demands that they hand over the letter and depart. The officers explain that it can be handed only to the Emperor "Or, if against religion, to Shogun." They suggest an elaborate ceremony ashore in six days' time, when the Commodore will hand the Shogun the President's letter. Kayama reminds them that this would violate Japan's sacred decree.

MANJIRO: You do not land here. No barbarian sets foot on shore here. You go and you tell that to your Payry. Go, I say. Go tell your Payry! All landing—forbidden. Go."

The officers hesitate.

On the double!

The officers scurry off to confer with Perry.

How'm I doing?

KAYAMA: They seem to be impressed.

MANJIRO: Americans are easy. They shout. You shout louder.

Their conference wtih Perry concluded, the officers come striding back to the rail.

SECOND OFFICER: You want hear great Commodore Payry's reply to you?

MANJIRO: I will listen.

SECOND OFFICER: Commodore Payry say: Much honored by visit of Japanese lord. Sends warm greetings.

MANJIRO: I accept his greetings.

SECOND OFFICER: Commodore Payry say: Not to worry. All Japanese customs will be respected in all possible ways.

MANJIRO (*to Kayama*): Didn't I tell you.

SECOND OFFICER: Commodore Payry also say: If big arrangement not made to greet him on land, he turn all cannon on Uraga and blast it off face of earth!!

> *There is a roar of laughter from the Americans, as Kayama and Manjiro fall back into their boat, terrified.*

Scene 5

The Reciter becomes the Shogun in his chamber with his wife, mother, sumo wrestlers, priests and other attendants. His wife plays the koto and sings while his physician brews tea. The Shogun eats rice, drinks sake and tries to ignore the problem which has entered his life in the form of the American ships riding at anchor in the harbor below.

The Shogun's mother insists that her son should pay attention to the crisis.

MOTHER (*sings "Chrysanthemum Tea"*):
It's the Day of the Rat, my lord.
There are four days remaining,
And I see you're entertaining,
But we should have a chat, my lord.
To begin, if I may, my lord,
I've no wish to remind you
But you'll notice just behind you
There are ships in the bay,
They've been sitting there all day
With a letter to convey
And they haven't gone away
And there's every indication
That they're planning to stay, my lord . . .

> *He looks behind him; the ships glow faintly; he stares, transfixed. He looks at her in alarm; she gestures to the physician to bring the tea.*

Have some tea, my lord,
Come chrysanthemum tea.
It's an herb that's superb
For disturbances at sea.

> *The Shogun makes a face at the taste.*

Is the Shogun feeling better?
Good! Now what about this letter?
Is it wise to delay, my lord?
With the days disappearing,
Might we benefit from hearing
What the soothsayers say, my lord? . . .

The soothsayers call the omens excellent and predict victory. The Shogun takes up his opium pipe as a new day dawns—perhaps it is the pipe that gives him difficulty in focusing his eyes. His mother is still advising him in song to act and pressing more chrysanthemum tea upon him. The priests give their opinion: Japanese soil is sacred and inviolable, so the ships must be merely an illusion.

On the third day the Shogun's mother is still plying him with tea and pressing him to act. The Shogun, growing weaker, agrees to let the samurai, the sumo wrestlers and others pray for a wind to blow the ships away.

On the fourth day the ships are still there. As the mother is prodding him with advice, the Shogun keels over. The physician pronounces him dead, but there is still a whisper of life left in him, enough to hear his mother explain her policy.

MOTHER (*sings*):
 . . . . . When the ships came our way
 On that first disturbing day
 And I gave consideration
 To this letter they convey,
 I decided if there weren't
 Any Shogun to receive it,
 It would act as a deterrent
 Since they'd have no place to leave it,
 And they might go away, my lord . . .
 Do you see what I say, my lord?
  The physician offers tea to the Shogun, who pushes it away as he
  realizes what it is; his mother nods.
 In the tea, my lord,
 The chrysanthemum tea—
 An informal variation
 On the normal recipe.
 Though I know my plan had merit,
 It's been slow in execution.
 If there's one thing you inherit,
 It's your father's constitution,
 And you're taking so long, my lord . . .
  As he sinks.
 Do you thing I was wrong, my lord? . . .
  He tries to say something.
 No, you must let me speak:
 When the Shogun is weak,
 Then the tea must be strong, my lord . . .
  He falls back.
 My lord?
  He dies. The physician sings with the mother.
 The blossom falls on the mountain.

The mountain falls on the blossom.
All things—
> *She checks the body.*
—fall.
> *The ships glow again; the mother looks at them, smiles and fans;*
> *the sumo wrestlers and the physician and the wife clear the stage.*

Scene 6

Kayama and Manjiro are kneeling before Abe and the two councillors, with a samurai standing guard and a sumo wrestler honing a sword in hopes that he'll be called upon to express the lords' displeasure at the failure of the mission. But Kayama has a plan. What if they welcomed the Americans to the very small cove at Kanagawa, which could be covered with tatami mats. A special treaty house could be built. After the Americans' departure, "We destroy the house and burn the mats and, my lord, neither the decree nor our honor will have been betrayed. The Americans will have come and gone, without setting foot on our sacred soil."

Abe is delighted with Kayama's plan and appoints him Governor so that he can receive the deputation of Western barbarians. Abe also grants Kayama's request to revoke Manjiro's death sentence and attach him to Kayama's service.

When the court departs, Manjiro expresses his gratitude for Kayama's friendship and comments "This is America . . . . . It is not the Americans who are barbarians. It is us! If you could have seen what I have seen in America . . . . ."

The two set off for Kayama's house, exchanging verses to the music of "Poems."

KAYAMA (*sings*):
> Rain glistening
> On the silver birch,
> Like my lady's tears.
> Your turn.

MANJIRO:
> Rain gathering,
> Winding into streams,
> Like the roads to Boston.
> Your turn . . . . .

KAYAMA:
> Moon,
> I love her like the moon,
> Making jewels of the grass
> Where my lady walks,
> My lady wife.

MANJIRO:
    Moon.
    I love her like the moon
    Washing yesterday away,
    As my lady does,
    America . . . . .

Kayama continues singing to the wife he loves, while Manjiro sings to America. They exchange poem after poem as they go.

BOTH (*sing*):
    Leaves,
    I love her like the leaves,
    Changing green to pink to gold,
    And the change is everything.
    Sun,
    I see her like the sun
    In the center of a pool,
    Sending ripples to the shore,
    Till my journey's end.
        Kayama's house appears.

After finishing the song, Kayama enters his house and approaches Tamate, who is still kneeling at the shrine and doesn't move when Kayama appears. He put his hand on her shoulder; her body falls into his arms, the front of her robes bloodsoaked and a short sword still in her hand. The Reciter sobs, but Kayama woodenly wipes his hands and makes his exit with Manjiro, who doesn't notice his friend's distress and is explaining: "These Americans may be tough and impolite, but they are the most amazing people. You'll see. Their coming here is the best thing that ever happened to Japan."

The two exit, passing *"a garish, middle-aged madam"* entering.

Scene 7

The madam is followed by four girls, whom she is hurrying toward Kanagawa to welcome the American sailors. The madam sings "Welcome to Kanagawa."

GIRLS (*sing*):
    I hear they're covered all with hair, like some disease.
MADAM: Sh!
GIRL (*sings*): Except their knees.
MADAM: Sh! (*To the audience; sings.*)
    The arrival of these giants
    Out of the blue,
    Bringing panic to my clients,
    Alters my view.

With so many of them fleeing,
Conferring, decreeing,
I find myself agreeing
With the ancient haiku:
RECITER:
The nest-building bird,
Seeing the tree without twigs,
Looks for new forests.
MADAM: Exactly.
A forest of bamboo poles, carried on by stagehands, forms on stage.
Yo-ho Americans!
GIRLS: Yo-ho! Americans!
MADAM (*sings*): Welcome to Kanagawa.
GIRLS (*sing*): Welcome to Kanagawa!
MADAM (*sings*): No . . . (*Delicately.*) Welcome to Kanagawa.
GIRLS (*sing*): Oh . . . (*Imitating.*) Welcome to Kanagawa.
MADAM: So . . .
As the girls continue singing softly.
With all my flowers disappearing
In alarm,
I've been reduced to commandeering
From the farm. (*Shrugs.*)
But with appropriate veneering,
Even green wood has its charm . . . . .

Continuing the song "Welcome to Kanagawa," the madam hands out fans carrying instructions in the form of erotic drawings of special pleasures which she hopes will please the American sailors, despite the girls' inexperience. The madam sends the girls off to provide their special welcome to Kanagawa.

Scene 8

American officers are arranging for an exchange of gifts. Their offerings are collected into a huge pile which includes arms of all kinds, spirits, lithographs, potatoes, various U.S. history books and a complete list of United States Post Offices. In contrast, a tea table with a few *"exquisitely wrapped packages"* destined as gifts from the Japanese to the Americans seems pitifully small— and the American sailors haven't yet brought ashore "six hundred yards of telegraph cable, the fire engine and the working locomotive." The two groups carry off their presents.

Scene 9

A samurai, now an old man, ruefully recalls how they tried to trick the Americans by placing 5,000 horsemen behind screenes with the hooves showing, hoping the enemy would think the force was several times as numerous as it was. The Americans only laughed and called from their ships: "What kind of army hides behind a parlor curtain!"

Scene 10

RECITER: From the personal journal of Commodore Matthew Calbraith Perry. 14 July, 1853. As I supervise the final preparations for this afternoon's historic landing at Kanagawa, I am moved to hope the Japanese will voluntarily accept the reasonable and pacific overtures embodied in our friendly letter. Should I hope in vain, however, should these backward, semi-barbarous people be reluctant to forsake their policy of isolation, then I stand prepared to introduce them into the community of civilized nations by whatever means are necessary. It is my understanding that this preposterous empire has been closed to foreigners for over two hundred and fifty years, and I for one feel that that has been more than long enough!

> *The treaty house at Kanagawa is assembled onstage. Festive kites are lowered from the flies, a tree is rolled on—the stage is set for the Americans' arrival. Lord Abe, the Second Councillor, Kayama and several samurai emerge from the house.*

SECOND COUNCILLOR: They are late. It is an insult.

ABE: Where is the warrior?

KAYAMA: Here, my lord!

> *Kayama slides back a panel in the base of the house, revealing a samurai hidden under the floorboards.*

ABE: He understands the signal?

KAYAMA: Yes, my lord. If the Westerners should draw their weapons, I will knock twice and he will come up through the floor and cut them down.

SECOND COUNCILLOR: Pity the Americans if they should draw their guns.

The sound of an American march is heard. Perry and two officers enter, escorted by ranks of enlisted men and a marching band. As Perry and his officers disappear into the treaty house with the Japanese plenipotentiaries, the Reciter comments: "No one knows what was said behind the shutters of the treaty house. The Shogun's councillors kept their story secret, and though the Westerners had their own official version—I would not believe a word of it. What a shame there is no authentic Japanese account of what took place on that historic day."

An old man enters, carrying an attache case. He begins his song, "Someone in a Tree," informing the Reciter that there *was* a witness, himself as a ten-year-old boy who climbed a nearby tree and watched the proceedings through the window. The tree is gone and the old man's youth is gone; he could no longer climb now, but, as he explains to the Reciter naively, "I was younger then," and proudly, "I was part of the event."

A boy enters and acts out the old man's memory, climbing a tree and peering into the treaty house.

BOY (*sings*):
>   I see men and matting.
>   Some are old, some chatting.

OLD MAN (*sings*): If it happened, I was there!

BOTH (*sing*): I saw/see everything!

OLD MAN (*sings*): I was someone in a tree.

BOY (*sings*): Tell him what I see!

OLD MAN (*sings*): Some of them have gold on their coats.

BOY (*correcting him*):
>   One of them has gold.
>   He was younger then.

OLD MAN (*sings*): Someone crawls around, passing notes—

BOY (*sings*): Someone very old—

OLD MAN (*to the Reciter, sings*): He was only ten.

BOY (*sings*): And there's someone in a tree—

OLD MAN (*sings*): —Or the day is incomplete.

BOTH:
>   Without someone in a tree,
>   Nothing happened here.

OLD MAN (*sings*): I am hiding in a tree.

BOY (*sings*): I'm a fragment of the day.

BOTH:
>   If I weren't, who's to say
>   Things would happen here the way
>   That they happened here?

OLD MAN (*sings*): I was there then.

BOY:
>   I am here still.
>   It's the fragment, not the day.

OLD MAN (*sings*): It's the pebble, not the stream.

BOTH:
>   It's the ripple, not the sea,
>   Not the building but the beam,
>   Not the garden but the stone,
>   Not the treaty house,
>   Someone in a tree . . . . .

The warrior opens his panel in the treaty house and insists he was here that day too; he couldn't see anything, being under the floor (he sings as the song continues), but he could hear everything. Sometimes the Americans and Japanese shouted at each other and argued. They read lists; they discussed laws. While the warrior was listening, the old man was watching them through the night as they signed papers by candle light. The warrior, the old man and the boy agree: "Not the garden but the stone/Only cups of tea/And history/ And someone in a tree."

The three exit as the Reciter takes up the narrative.

RECITER: Whatever happened behind the shutters of the treaty house, Kayama Yesaemon's plan was a success. The letter was delivered. The Americans were satisfied. And they left.

> *The American officers emerge from the house, followed by Abe and his retainers. Bows are exchanged, then the officers lead the American enlisted men away.*

ABE (*to his retainers*): Quickly there, nothing must remain!

> *The treaty house is dismantled and the stage is cleared.*

RECITER: We tore down the house, rolled up the mats, taking great care that the contaminated side should not touch the ground. Once again, all was as it had been. The barbarian threat had forever been removed. Ha!

Scene 11

> *Suddenly the lion-like figure of Commodore Perry leaps out on-stage and performs a strutting, leaping dance of triumph. Curtain.*

ACT II

Scene 1

The Reciter enters and a musician plays the shamisen as a stagehand runs a curtain across the stage revealing the throne room of the Imperial court at Kyoto—"the palace of the living god." Abe and his entourage bow low to the puppet-Emperor whose legs and arms are moved by a priest pulling the strings.

The priest, speaking for the Emperor, rewards the servants who have so faithfully prevented the barbarians from setting foot on the sacred soil of Japan. Abe is made Shogun—the real ruler of the country. Kayama is confirmed as Governor of Uraga. Manjiro is pardoned and raised to the rank of samurai. Manjiro is profoundly stirred by his elegant robing ceremony and prostrates himself in deeply grateful obeisance to the Emperor.

No sooner is Abe made Shogun than the Emperor's spokesmen register complaints about various problems and shortages. Abe makes good his exit, backing from the august presence, and commenting, "Goodbye America, come back in two hundred fifty years!" The court disappears behind the curtain.

Scene 2

There is the sound of an American marching band. An American admiral enters carrying a plaque and documents.

AMERICAN ADMIRAL (*sings "Please Hello" to Abe*):
Please hello, America back,
Commodore Perry send hello.
Also comes memorial plaque
President Fillmore wish bestow.

Emperor read our letter? If no,
Commodore Perry very sad.
Emperor like our letter? If so,
Commodore Perry very merry,
President Fillmore still more glad.

Last time we visit, too short.
This time we visit for slow.
Last time we come, come with warships,
Now with more ships—
Say hello!
This time request use of port,
Port for commercial intention,
Harbor with ample dimension.

ABE (*sings*): But you can't—

AMERICAN ADMIRAL:
Only one
Little port
For a freighter.

ABE (*sings*): But you can't—

AMERICAN ADMIRAL:
Just for fun,
Be a sport.

ABE (*sings*): Maybe later—

AMERICAN ADMIRAL:
But we bring many recent invention:
Kerosene
And cement
And a grain
Elevator.
A machine
You can rent
Called a "train"—

ABE (*sings*): —Maybe later—

AMERICAN ADMIRAL:
—Also cannon to shoot
Big loud salute,
Like so:
>   *An explosion offstage. Light flashes. Abe cowers in fear, accepts the document.*

Say hello!
>   *Explosion. Abe takes the pen and signs.*

As the song continues, the American admiral gives Abe the pen as a souvenir, well satisfied to have the signed agreement.

A British admiral appears and sings his own "hello" song in the Gilbert-and-Sullivan manner befitting an emissary from Queen Victoria:

BRITISH ADMIRAL (*sings*):
.... Her letters do contain a few proposals to your Emperor
Which if, of course, he won't endorse, will put her in a temper, or,
More happily, should he agree, will serve to keep her placid, or
At least till I am followed by a permanent ambassador.

The British admiral has brought gifts, and papers to sign guaranteeing a treaty port, and a man-of-war firing a salvo offstage to emphasize his request. Again, a frightened Abe signs.

A Dutch admiral enters dressed as a Weber-and-Fields comic, waving documents, demanding two ports and firing his ship's guns. But now the American and British admirals want more—and a Russian admiral arrives, bored and rather detached but carefully explaining the meaning of his Czar's claim of "extraterritoriality," and in his turn firing his guns. And now the French admiral—"*a dandy, disgustingly gay and charming*"—comes on to sing his own greeting.

FRENCH ADMIRAL (*sings*):
.... Would you like to know ze word
From Napoleon ze Third?
        Shoves a bundle of papers at Abe.
It's *détente! Oui, détente!* ....
Zat's zee only thing we want!
Leave ze grain, leave ze train,
Put champagne among your imports!
Tell each man zat Japan
Can't be bothered giving him ports
While she's in a tizzy,
Dizzy wiz ze
Mutual *détente!*

The sound of the explosion from the French guns is the loudest of all. The song continues: everyone sings at once, including Abe, who pleads with the admirals to wait for a year because Japan has suffered catastrophes like drought and famine and its situation is uncertain at present. The number ends with the Europeans arguing over trade rights and threatening each other, as though Japan belonged to them.

Scene 3

At the Imperial court, the puppet Emperor seems to have aged and grown somewhat larger. The Reciter explains that the Emperor lives such a sheltered life that ordinarily he wouldn't be told about the barbarians and Abe's inability to keep them out. For some reason, though—the Reciter isn't sure why—this time the Emperor (manipulated again by a priest) is being informed by means of an enigmatic story told him by a storyteller brought by the Lords of the South, ostensibly as a mere entertainment.

The Emperor grants the storyteller permission to tell him "The Tale of the Courageous King," who goes hunting tigers on the river bank near Seoul. While his beaters went out, the king relaxed, drinking tea with his Lord High Protector and noticing how even the butterflies seemed obedient to his royal wishes.

Suddenly there was the sound of tearing brush, signaling the approach of a beast and causing the Lord Protector to draw his sword.

STORYTELLER: . . . . . The bamboo trees were thrust aside and there appeared—no tiger, but a man! Then two men, three, then more than one could count. Bearded men wtih pale white skin, waving swords and spears. "We are emissaries from the King of France, come to open up Korea, come to civilize the savages!" When he heard that, the Lord Protector cast aside his sword and fled. The King was left alone. Oh, what will become of him, abandoned by his treacherous protector? Surely, the savages from across the sea will cut him down! But look . . . how superbly he stands his ground! Look how his sword leaps from its scabbard! One Frenchman—gored in the stomach! Another! See how the head flies from the body! And another! Another! And now, hear the shouts, hear the roars of defiance as the King's faithful beaters rush to his side. All join in the fray as the screams of the dying Frenchmen echo and re-echo down the forest ravine. Oh yes, here was a great victory—for in an hour not a single barbarian was left alive, as once again the butterflies returned to float and shimmer over the wildflowers, dyed crimson by the blood of foreigners. And then, just as the young King sheathed his sword, into the glade strode a magnificent tiger. "Your majesty," the tiger said, "you are the king of your domain, and I the king of mine. But from the forest I have watched you fight these Western beasts, and surely you, and you alone, deserve to wear the royal crown." So saying, he kow-towed and led the hunters in a shout: "All hail the King. All hail our Courageous King!"

The storyteller bows as the nobles turn to face the Emperor and quietly applaud.

RECITER: An intriguing performance. But one wonders what message the Lords of the South intended to convey. For, unlike the Korean King, the Emperor cannot take up arms and drive the Westerners away. That is the Shogun's duty. Unless, of course, the Shogun—failing in his duty—were forced to step aside.

He smiles in mock surprise at his apparent insight.

Scene 4

Dressed in traditional costume, Kayama and Manjiro kneel by small Japanese tables on either side of the stage. Manjiro is arranging the objects of the tea ceremony. Kayama is writing to him on a scroll with a brush, telling Manjiro that there are now 200 Westerners in Uraga. Kayama takes a box from beneath his table, out of which he takes a bowler hat. His song—"A Bowler Hat"—together with narration by the Reciter is a series of letters to Manjiro describing changes over the years caused by the Western presence.

KAYAMA (*sings*):
> It's called a bowler hat.
> I have no wife.
> The swallow flying through the sky
> Is not as swift as I
> Am, flying through my life.
> You pour the milk before the tea.
> The Dutch ambassador is no fool.
> I must remember that.

> *Stagehands enter and replace Kayama's writing brush with a steel pen. They add a line or two to his face. Manjiro is similarly aged, but everything else about him remains unchanged. The Reciter continues with Kayama's letter.*

RECITER: Three years ago we set aside one district of the town for Westerners, and yet we are still unable to provide them with residences which they consider suitable. For this I humbly ask your indulgence.

KAYAMA (*sings*):
> I wear a bowler hat.
> They send me wine.
> The house is far too grand.
> I've bought a new umbrella stand
> Today I visited the church beside the shrine.
> I'm learning English from a book.
> Most exciting.
> It's called a bowler hat.

Stage hands touch Manjiro's and Kayama's hair with gray, give Kayama a Western table. Kayama is having trouble controlling the foreign merchants (he writes to Manjiro), but he now has a pocket watch and a wife. Even as Manjiro is performing the tea ceremony, the stagehands replace Kayama's tea things with 19th century ones.

Kayama has had to take away the samurai's swords when they enter his city to prevent friction with the foreigners. After eight years, Kayama is still trying to ignore the rowdy behavior of the Western sailors, but admires the Western gentleman-diplomats. He has left his wife and no longer wears a bowler. The Reciter continues reading Kayama's letter, while Manjiro dresses himself in the ceremonial costume for sword practise.

RECITER: My lord, here in Uraga we have reached an understanding with the Westerners. Of course I wish them gone, but I shall try to turn their presence into an advantage rather than a burden. Last week I joined them in a fox hunt.

> *Kayama puts glasses on.*

KAYAMA (*sings*):
> They call them spectacles.
> I drink much wine.

I take imported pills.
I have a house up in the hills
I've hired British architects to redesign.
One must accommodate the times
As one lives them.
One must remember that.

RECITER: Your humble servant, Kayama Yesaemon.

A stagehand runs on with a gray tailcoat and holds it out to Kayama.

KAYAMA (*sings*): It's called a cutaway . . .

Exits, followed by the stagehand; a beat, then Manjiro exits, completely dressed.

Scene 5

The invention of the ricksha is enacted. Jonathan Goble had visited Japan as a marine on a Perry ship. When he returned home he devised a vehicle which "Turns in a very little space. Great advantage in the crowded streets of Yokohama." After testing it in Chicago, Goble brought it to Japan.

The Reciter as Goble, wearing a Stetson, demonstrates his vehicle's biggest asset to a Japanese merchant: "The motor's self-contained, requires very little maintenance—and can be very easily replaced." Goble and the merchant are seated in the ricksha, being drawn along by the "motor," an old man who is replaced by another and another and another as each wears out. The Merchant is impressed and agrees to become a partner in the manufacture of rickshas.

RECITER (*as Goble*): We gonna turn these beauties out dirt cheap, and sell 'em all across Japan. Why, before you know it—

A fifth old man enters as the Reciter steps down.

—why before you know it— (*To the audience, dropping Goble's persona.*)
—before you know it, every city in our country will be overrun by rickshas. Invented, manufactured, marketed by Westerners—

He looks at the line of old men, then hurls away his Stetson hat.

—but pulled by Japanese.

The old men collapse.

Scene 6

Manjiro is practising swordsmanship under the tutelage of an older samurai in the ritual of kenjutsu. The older man's beautiful daughter brings in the tea things and goes out to her garden to pick flowers while the men continue fencing. Stagehands place a small, low wall upstage and three British sailors enter on the far side of the wall. Wooden blocks are beaten, and the actors reverse position, as the stagehands move the wall so that the sailors are now downstage.

The sailors speculate that this "lovely piece of work" may be "one of those geisha girls," not understanding that she is in fact a samurai's daughter. They approach her tentatively, tip their hats and ask for flowers, which she gives them.

The sailors sing to the girl of their longings and loneliness in this faraway place after the long, long voyage.

> THIRD SAILOR (*sings "Pretty Lady"*):
> Pretty lady in the pretty garden, can't you stay?
> Pretty lady, we got leave and we got paid today.
> Pretty lady with a flower,
> Give a lonely sailor 'alf an hour.
> Pretty lady, can you understand a word I say?

The three sailors continue the song in unison. Their plea becomes more specific.

> FIRST SAILOR (*sings*):
> Pretty lady, how about it?
> Don't you know how long I been without it?
> Pretty lady in the garden, what you say?
> Can't you stay? . . . Hey, wait, don't go yet.
> Pretty lady with the pretty bow,
> Please don't go, it's early.
> Won't you walk me through your pretty garden?
> ALL SAILORS:
> Pretty lady, look, I'm on my knees,
> Pretty please.

The sailors offer the girl money, and their gestures frighten her. She calls in alarm for her father, who turns, sees the situation and cuts the Third Sailor down before he can explain himself and slashes the First Sailor as he makes his escape with the Second Sailor. The stage is cleared.

Scene 7

The palanquins of Abe and Kayama, with bearers and a samurai body-guard, meet on the road from Edo to Kyoto to discuss the murder of the English sailor. An indemnity has been paid, the Emperor will apologize to Queen Victoria and the killer has been reprimanded but not punished because he is something of a hero among the Lords of the South, who have adopted a new slogan: "Restore the Emperor and expel the barbarians."

Abe bitterly condemns this aggressive policy: their swords would be useless against Western weapons, Western ships: "We must appease the Westerners until we have learned the secrets of their power and success. Then, when we have become their equals. Then, perhaps. Then, if we are sure the time is right—"

Four assassins enter and kill Abe in his palanquin before they in their turn are felled by the samurai bodyguard. A fifth assassin comes on, kills the samurai and reveals himself to Kayama as Manjiro.

To Manjiro, all who befriend and consort with Westerners and adopt Western ways are the mortal enemies of Japan—Kayama included. Instead of killing Kayama outright, Manjiro offers his former friend the chance to die the death of a samurai, in combat. Kayama accepts, draws his sword. Kayama and Manjiro fight, and Kayama is killed.

Two Lords of the South enter carrying the Emperor, now a much larger puppet. They thank Manjiro for eliminating the Shogun and giving them the opportunity now to attack the Westerners and drive them out.

The Lords of the South pick up the strings to work the Emperor-puppet, when a voice emerges from it, declaring, "In the name of the Emperor—enough!"

>*Long pause as they stare at the puppet. Magically, real hands emerge from the sleeves, break off the puppet sticks and toss them away. Then the hands strip away the mask, revealing the face of the Reciter. As he continues speaking, stagehands enter and remove layer upon layer of his Imperial robes.*

RECITER (*as Emperor*): The day when others speak for me is past. From now on, my word shall be law. And mine alone. I am the Emperor Meiji. Rise—and listen! No more will we draw sword, one Japanese against another. Those who have committed murder in my name have been misguided. In the future they will be restrained along with those who have encouraged them. Rise!

Lords of the South and others kneeling onstage rise and listen as the Emperor outlines the future: they will put aside archaic trappings like the samurai's sword and build a modern nation with a modern army and navy: "We will open up Formosa, Korea, Manchuria and China. We will do for the rest of Asia what America has done for us!"

Taking the cue from the Reciter as Emperor, the company sings "Next," whose lyrics describe the rapid process of Westernization that is to come. The company exits.

RECITER (*as Emperor*): The day will come when the Western powers will be forced to acknowledge us as their undisputed equals.

>*The entire stage begins to fill with contemporary Japanese figures, everything from women in pantsuits to teenagers in leather jackets.*

COMPANY (*sings*):
Tower tumbles,
Tower rises—
Next!

RECITER (*as Emperor*): All of this will be achieved—sooner than you think!

COMPANY (*sings*):
Tower crumbles,
Man revises.
Motor rumbles,
Civilizes.
More surprises—
Next!

Learn the lesson
From the master.
Add the sugar,
Spread the plaster.
Do it nicer,
Do it faster—
Next!

RECITER (*who has stripped off his Emperor's uniform and stands in plain black pants and t-shirt*):
The practical bird,
Having no tree of its own,
Borrows another's.

COMPANY (*sings*):
. . . . . Streams are drying,
Mix a potion.
Streams are dying,
Try the ocean—
Brilliant notion—
Next!

Never mind a small disaster.
Who's the stronger, who's the faster?
Let the pupil show the master—
Next!
Next!

A VOICE: There are 223 Japan Airlines ticket offices in 153 cities throughout the world.

COMPANY (*sings*): Next!

ANOTHER VOICE: There are eight Toyota dealerships in the city of Detroit, and Seiko watch is the third best selling watch in Switzerland.

COMPANY (*sings*): Next!

THIRD VOICE: Fifty-seven percent of the Bicentennial souvenirs sold in Washington, D.C. in 1975 were made in Japan.

COMPANY (*sings*): Next!

FOURTH VOICE: This year Japan will export sixteen million kilograms monosodium glutamate, and four hundred thousand tons of polyvinyl chloride resin.

COMPANY (*sings*): Next!

FIFTH VOICE: From the Ministry of Health: By 1978 some of the beaches on the Inland Sea will be reopened for public bathing.

COMPANY (*sings*): Next! . . . . .

SIXTH VOICE: 1975 Weather Bureau statistics report 162 days on which the air quality in Tokyo was acceptable.

COMPANY (*sings*): Next! . . . . .

> *There is a frenzied dance, suddenly interrupted by the Reciter.*

RECITER: Nippon. The floating kingdom.

> *Wood blocks usher on the traditionally dressed figures of Kayama and Tamate, who pass silently through the company.*

There was a time when foreigners were not welcome here. But that was long ago. A hundred and twenty years. (*Pause.*) Welcome to Japan.

COMPANY (*sings*):

Next! Next!
Brilliant notions,
Still improving—
Next! Next!
Make the motions,
Keep it moving—
Next!
Next!
Next!

> *Blackout. Curtain.*

CHICAGO

A Musical in Two Acts

BOOK BY FRED EBB AND BOB FOSSE

MUSIC BY JOHN KANDER

LYRICS BY FRED EBB

BASED ON THE PLAY BY MAURINE DALLAS WATKINS

Cast and credits appear on pages 318-319

FRED EBB (book, lyrics) is a New Yorker born April 8, 1932 and educated at New York University and Columbia. He wrote both book and lyrics for the Phoenix Theater production of Morning Sun *(1963) and has contributed lyrics to such revues as* Put It in Writing *and* From A to Z *and sketches to the TV show* That Was the Week That Was. *His collaboration with John Kander began with the songs "My Coloring Book" and "I Don't Care Much" (a Bar-*

bra Streisand hit). It has continued through the Broadway shows Flora, the Red Menace *(1965),* Cabaret *(1966, a Best Play and the Tony and Critics Award winner as best musical),* The Happy Time *and* Zorba *(1968),* 70 Girls, 70 *(1971) and now* Chicago, *Ebb's and Kander's second Best Play (and for the last two named shows Ebb also co-authored the books). The Kander-Ebb collaboration has also brought forth a number of leading night club and concert acts including those of Liza Minnelli, Kaye Ballard, Chita Rivera, Juliette Prowse and Carol Channing.*

BOB FOSSE (book) is a native Chicagoan, born there June 23, 1927. His Broadway career as a choreographer began with The Pajama Game *in 1954. In his next show,* Damn Yankees *(1955) Fosse also staged the musical numbers and continued in this double capacity with* Bells Are Ringing *(1956, co-staging the musical numbers with Jerome Robbins) and* New Girl in Town *(1957) and was responsible for the musical staging of* How to Succeed in Business Without Really Trying *in 1961. In 1959 he took on full directorial as well as choreographic duties for* Redhead *and continued in these capacities for* Little Me *(1962, co-director with Cy Feuer)* Sweet Charity *(1966),* Pippin *(1972) and now* Chicago. *His only author's credits have been for the conception of* Sweet Charity *and the co-authorship of the book of the present show.*

Fosse pulled off a show-business equivalent of the hat trick in 1973, becoming the first director in history to win an Oscar (for the movie version of Cabaret*), a Tony (for* Pippin*) and an Emmy (for the TV special* Liza With a Z*) in a single season. He is the recipient of seven Tonys in all and was nominated this season for an Academy Award for his film* Lenny.

JOHN KANDER (music) was born in Kansas City, Mo., March 18, 1927. He received his B.A. at Oberlin in 1951 and his M.A. at Columbia in 1953. His early theatrical experience included conducting stock productions and doing the dance arrangements for Gypsy *and* Irma La Douce. *His first Broadway show as composer was* A Family Affair *(1962, with book and lyrics by James and William Goldman), and later that year he wrote the incidental music for the Broadway comedy* Never Too Late.

Kander's collaboration with Fred Ebb began and flourished as outlined in Ebb's biographical sketch above, through their five previous Broadway musicals including their Best Play and Tony and Critics Award-winning Cabaret *and its movie version which collected eight Academy Awards, to their second Best Play* Chicago *in 1975–76. Other recent Kander-Ebb collaborations were Liza Minnelli's Emmy Award-winning TV special* Liza With a Z, *Frank Sinatra's* Ole Blue Eyes Is Back, *the new material for the Barbra Streisand–James Caan movie* Funny Lady *and the music including the title song for the movie short* Norman Rockwell.

Our method of representing Chicago *in these pages differs from that of the other Best Plays. The musical appears here in a series of photographs with synopsis and examples of the script and lyrics, recording the overall "look" of its visually expressive concept and characters, as well as its story structure and style.*

The photographs of Chicago *depict scenes as produced by Robert Fryer and James Cresson and directed and choreographed by Bob Fosse, as of the opening June 3, 1975 at the Forty-Sixth Street Theater, with scenery by Tony Walton, costumes by Patricia Zipprodt and lighting by Jules Fisher.*

Our special thanks are tendered to the producers and their press representatives, Cheryl Sue Dolby, Sandra Manley and Harriett Trachtenberg, for making available these selections from Martha Swope's excellent photographs of the show.

1. Velma (Chita Rivera, *above*) begins "a story of murder, greed, corruption, violence, exploitation, adultery and treachery—all those things we all hold near and dear to our hearts" with the song "All That Jazz."

Come on, babe
Why don't we paint the town?
And all that jazz

I'm gonna rouge my knees
And roll my stockings down
And all that jazz

Start the car
I know a whoopee spot
Where the gin is cold
But the piano's hot

It's just a noisy hall
Where there's a nightly brawl
And all that jazz! . . .

2. Velma is one of six Merry Murderesses (*above*) in the Cook County Jail. They've murdered their lovers in crimes of passion and insist in song, "He Had It Coming." Facing trials, they hope to be defended by Billy Flynn (Jerry Orbach, *right*). His fee is $5,000 per case, no exceptions. But it's his boast: "If Jesus Christ had lived in Chicago today—and if he had five thousand dollars—things would have turned out differently." Billy sings:

I don't care about expensive things
Cashmere coats, diamond rings
Don't mean a thing
All I care about is love. . . .

Not physical love, Billy explains, love of legal procedure.

3. Roxie Hart (Gwen Verdon, *right* and *below*) joins the Murderesses in jail after shooting her disappointing lover in a drunken rage. Her poor husband promises Billy $5,000 to defend Roxie, even if it means auctioning her clothes as souvenirs of "the hottest little jazz slayer since Velma Kelly." Billy coaches Roxie in a sob story (*right*): convent, runaway marriage, foolish affair and then "We both reached for the gun."

4. Roxie tells her rehearsed story to the reporters, who race to their phones— and soon headlines are screaming "Roxie Rocks Chicago!" Roxie muses: "If this Flynn guy gets me off, and with all this publicity, I could get into vaude-ville." She sings "Roxie":

The name on everybody's lips
Is gonna be Roxie
The lady rakin' in the chips
Is gonna be Roxie

I'm gonna be a celebrity
That means somebody everyone knows
They're gonna recognize my eyes
My hair, my teeth, my boobs, my nose

From just some dumb mechanic's wife
I'm gonna be Roxie
Who says that murder's not an art?

And who in case she doesn't hang
Can say she started with a bang?
Roxie Hart!

5. Roxie hogs the limelight, crowding even Velma out. Velma asks Roxie to team up, but Roxie, a hot news item on her own, refuses. Then along comes a triple murderess who steals even Billy's attention. Now Roxie teams up with Velma (*right*) in the duet "My Own Best Friend":

... And trusting to luck
That's only for fools
I play in a game
Where I make the rules
And rule number one
From here to the end
Is I am my own best friend.

6. Roxie faints. When the others crowd around her (*above*), she lifts her head and reassures them, "Oh, don't worry about me. It's just that I'm going to have a baby." Reporters react in a hubbub, as Billy calls for "the best doctor in Chicago" and Velma comments, "Shit."

VELMA (*sings*): And all that jazz! (*Flashbulbs pop. Everyone is talking to Roxie at once. She is loving it, as the curtain falls.*)

ACT II

7. Roxie's self-effacing husband Amos (Barney Martin, *right*) is persuaded by Billy to sue for divorce because Roxie's supposedly pregnant. Amos, putty in everyone's hands, sings:

Mister Cellophane
Should have been my name
Mister Cellophane
'Cause you can look right
    through me
Walk right by me
And never know I'm there
Never even know I'm there.

8. Billy sketches the forthcoming courtroom scene for Roxie: she'll be knitting on the witness stand, and she and Amos will reconcile in front of the pitying jury. Roxie resents being ordered around by Billy. She thinks she's big enough now to manage alone. She fires him, though he warns her, "In a couple of weeks nobody'll even know who you are."

One of the Murderesses is hanged, the first woman to be executed in Cook County in 47 years. Frightened, Roxie runs back to Billy, ready to obey him in everything. Billy prepares for his big courtroom performance by assuming his "Clarence Darrow look" (*below*), rumpling his clothes and telling Roxie, "It's all a circus, kid. A three-ring circus. These trials—the whole world—all show business. But kid, you're working with a star, the biggest." He's prepared to "razzle dazzle" the court.

9. In court, after using Amos to soften the jury's heart, Billy questions Roxie (*above*) about events leading up to the killing. Because she'd quarreled with her beloved husband, she drifted into an affair with one Fred Casely. She soon tried to end it, but Fred persisted.

BILLY (*super dramatic*): Roxie Hart, the State has accused you of the murder of Fred Casely. Are you guilty or not guilty?

ROXIE: Not guilty! Not guilty! Oh, I killed him—yes—but I'm not a criminal! (*Billy hands Roxie a handkerchief.*)

On the fateful night, Fred forced his way into Roxie's bedroom. "I love my husband," she protested. Fred replied, "I'll kill you before I'll see you have another man's child! And then, Roxie testifies, "We both reached for the gun. But I got it first."

BILLY: Then, it was his life or yours?

ROXIE (*goes to jury, pats her stomach*): And not just mine! And I closed my eyes and shot. . . .

BILLY: In defense of your life? . . .

ROXIE: To save my husband's innocent unborn child!

COMPANY (*sing*): Razzle dazzle . . . and they'll make you a star.

10. Hearing about Roxie's charade of innocence in a radio report, the jail Matron (Mary McCarty, *left*) and Velma sing about "Class":

Whatever happened to fair
  dealing?
And pure ethics
And nice manners?
Why is it everyone now
  is a pain in the ass?
Whatever happened to
  class?

11. Meanwhile, the jury finds Roxie not guilty—but once again another murder steals the press's attention before Roxie can capitalize on her notoriety. Even Billy is through with her, exiting with his fan dancers. Only Amos remains loyal, but Roxie brushes him off, telling him there's no baby coming. She ponders life "Nowadays" in song: ". . . There's men, everywhere/Jazz, everywhere/Booze, everywhere . . . Grand, isn't it?/Great, isn't it?/Swell, isn't it?/Fun, isn't it?"

The scene changes as a night club M.C. announces a new act: "Not one little lady, but two! You've read about them in the papers and now here they are—a double header! Chicago's own killer-dillers—those two scintillating sinners—Roxie Hart and Velma Kelly!" (*below*).

12. At the end of their act, Roxie and Velma are handed bouquets (*above*), take their bows and address the audience, giving thanks for "your faith and your belief in our innocence" and for helping "see us through our terrible ordeal." The orchestra strikes up "The Battle Hymn of the Republic."

VELMA: You know, a lot of people have lost faith in America.

ROXIE: And for what America stands for.

VELMA: But we are the living examples of what a wonderful country this is. (*They hug and pose.*)

ROXIE: So we'd just like to say thank you and God bless you.

VELMA & ROXIE: God bless you. Thank you and God bless you . . . God be with you. God walk with you always. God bless you. God bless you. (*Music up. They stand, bowing, throwing roses to the audience, waving and smiling as the curtain falls.*)

TRAVESTIES

A Play in Two Acts

BY TOM STOPPARD

Cast and credits appear on pages 330-331

TOM STOPPARD was born in 1937 in Zlin, Czechoslovakia, where his family name was Straussler. When he was 18 months old his father, a physician, moved the family to Singapore, and from that time on Stoppard was brought up within the English-speaking culture. During World War II the doctor sent his wife and son to India for safety, and the boy attended an American school in Darjeeling. His father was killed in Singapore by the invading Japanese.

After the war Stoppard, age 9, and his mother (remarried to an English major) moved to England, where Stoppard attended school until age 17 and then entered upon a writing career, first as a journalist and then as a free-lance whose credits include several TV and radio plays. His first stage play, A Walk on the Water, was first produced on BBC-TV in 1963 and reached the stage in Hamburg and Vienna in 1964; then, under the title Enter a Free Man, it was done in London in 1968 and off off Broadway at Theater at St. Clements last season. Other Stoppard TV offerings have included The Engagement and a recent adaptation of Three Men in a Boat, and he is the author of the novel Lord Malquist and Mr. Moon.

The first Stoppard play to appear on the New York stage was Rosencrantz and Guildenstern Are Dead. It began as a one-act verse burlesque written in Berlin on a Ford Foundation grant in 1964, titled more simply Rosencrantz and Guildenstern. The full-length version was produced by the Oxford Theater group at the 1966 Edinburgh Festival before moving on to London and then to Broadway Oct. 16, 1967 for a year's run, a Best Plays citation and the Drama Critics and Tony Awards for the best play of the season.

Stoppard's The Real Inspector Hound *was produced in London in 1969, and his* After Magritte *appeared there the following year. Combined on a single program, these two short plays were produced April 23, 1972 for 465 performances, followed by a national U.S. tour under the auspices of Kennedy Center. His* Albert's Bridge, *a version of a Prix Italia-winning drama, was produced in London in 1971. A year later his* Jumpers *appeared at the National Theater and, in the words of the critic Ossia Trilling, "introduced, unless I'm much mistaken, full frontal nudity for the first time on this august stage in the shape of the shapely Diana Rigg."* Jumpers *was produced in Washington in February, 1974 by Kennedy Center and in April 1974 was brought to Broadway for a short run of 48 performances and a Best Play citation.*

Stoppard's playwriting career continued with a new English version of Lorca's The House of Bernarda Alba, *staged in Greenwich, England. His new work* Travesties *was produced by the Royal Shakespeare Company June 10, 1974 for 39 performances in repertory and crossed the Atlantic to Broadway on October 30, 1975, with John Wood continuing in the leading role he created in London, winning for its author his third Best Play citation.*

Stoppard's plays are small in number so far but much produced. His 7 productions placed him fourth in frequency of American regional theater stagings last season, bested only by Shakespeare (44), Shaw (10) and Noel Coward (9) and well in front of his nearest American competition, Lanford Wilson (6) and Neil Simon (5). The playwright resides near London with his wife and child, a son.

Time: Zurich, 1917

Place: A section of the Public Library and the drawing room of Henry Carr's apartment

ACT 1

SYNOPSIS: The opening scene, a kind of prologue, takes place in the Zurich Public Library. Gwendolen (*"Henry Carr's younger sister; young and attractive but also a personality to be reckoned with"*) is seated with James Joyce (*"aged 36; he wears a jacket and trousers from two different suits"*) poring over books and papers. Also seated in the library, writing, are Lenin, aged 47, and Tristan Tzara (*"the Dadaist of that name. He was a short, dark-haired, very boyish-looking young man, and charming—his word. He wears a monocle"*).

Tzara cuts up the page he has been writing with a pair of scissors, puts the pieces into a hat, tosses them out and reads the random result.

TZARA: Eel ate enormous appetzara
        key dairy chef's hat he'lllearn comparah!

Ill raced alas whispers kill later nut east,
noon avuncular ill day Clara!

CECILY (*entering; young, attractive, to be reckoned with*): Sssssssh!
　　　　*Her admonition is to the Library in general. She enters from one
　　　　wing, not through the door, and crosses the stage, leaving by the
　　　　opposite wing, moving quite quickly, like someone who is busy.
　　　　No one takes any notice.*
JOYCE (*dictating to Gwen*): Deshill holles eamus . . .
GWEN (*writing*): Deshill holles eamus . . .
JOYCE: Thrice.
GWEN: Uh-hum.
JOYCE: Send us bright one, light one, Horhorn, quickening and wombfruit.
GWEN: Send us bright one, light one, Horhorn, quickening and wombfruit.
JOYCE: Thrice.
GWEN: Uh-hum.
JOYCE: Hoopsa, boyaboy, hoopsa!

And so it goes, with Lenin and his wife Nadya adding to the verbal confusion by conversing in Russian. Meanwhile, Cecily comes back in, takes a folder from Lenin just as Gwen takes one from Joyce. Putting them down and taking them up again, the women manage to confuse and exchange the folders, each leaving with the wrong one: Gwen with Lenin's, Cecily with Joyce's.

The Lenins discuss the revolution which has taken place in St. Petersburg and the Tsar's imminent abdication, while Joyce reads aloud gibberish from scraps of paper he finds in his pockets. Lenin drops one of his papers. Joyce picks it up, peruses it, finds that it's some sort of economic notation about the U.S.A., hands it back to Lenin.

Lenin follows his wife out. Cecily sees Joyce out. He is singing "Galway Bay" as he exits.

A garrulous, somewhat muddled old man enters as the scene changes to the drawing room of Henry Carr's apartment. The old man is Henry Carr at an advanced age, mulling over his memories; the apartment is that of Henry Carr as young man in the British Consular Service in Zurich during World War I. Old Carr goes on and on, shuttling back and forth among his memories ("constant digression being the saving grace of senile reminiscence"), pretending that he was well acquainted with fellow-sojourners in Zurich who later became famous: Joyce and Lenin in particular. It is certain that there really was a Henry Carr and that he knew Joyce slightly (he acted in a play Joyce put on, became involved in a lawsuit against him and is mentioned by name in *Ulysses*). It's obvious, however, that this boastful old man's recollections are more wish-fulfilling than truthful.

OLD CARR: . . . . . My memoirs, is it then? Life and times, friend of the famous. Memories of James Joyce. James Joyce As I knew Him. The James Joyce I Knew. Through the Courts with James Joyce . . . What was he like, James Joyce, I am often asked. It is true that I knew him well at the height of his powers, his genius in full flood in the making of *Ulysses,* before publication and fame turned him into a public monument for pilgrim cameras more often than not in a velvet smoking jacket of an unknown color, photography being in those days a black and white affair, but probably real blue if not empirical purple and sniffing a bunch of sultry violets that positively defy development, don't go on, do it on my head, caviar for the general public, now then—*Memories of James Joyce* . . . It's coming. To those of us who knew him, Joyce's genius was never in doubt. To be in his presence was to be aware of an amazing intellect bent on shaping itself into the permanent form of its own monument—the book the world now knows as *Ulysses!* Though at that time we were still calling it (I hope memory serves) by its original title, Elasticated Bloomers . . . . . Further recollections of a Consular Official in Whitest Switzerland. The Ups and Downs of Consular Life in Zurich During the Great War: A Sketch. 'Twas in the bustling metropolis of swiftly gliding trams and greystone banking houses, of cosmopolitan restaurants on the great stone banks of the swiftly-gliding snot-green (mucus mutandis) Limmat River, of jewelled escapements and refugees of all kinds, e.g. Lenin, there's a point . . . Lenin As I Knew Him. The Lenin I Knew. Halfway to the Finland Station with V.I. Lenin: A Sketch. I well remember the first time I met Lenin, or as he was known on his library ticket, Vladimir Ilyich Ulyanov. To be in his presence was to be aware of a complex personality . . . . . Ulyanov, Mrs. Ulyanov, Zinoviev and a police spy. And now they want to know what was he like? What was he like, Lenin, I am often asked.

He makes an effort.

To those of use who knew him Lenin's greatness was never in doubt.

He gives up again.

So why didn't you put a pound on him, you'd be a millionaire, like that chap who bet sixpence against the Titanic. No. Truth of the matter, who'd have thought big oaks from a corner room at number 14 Spiegelgasse? . . . . . number 14 the house of the narrow cobbler himself, Kammerer his name, Lenin his tenant—and across the way at number One, the Meierei Bar, crucible of anti-art, cradle of Dada !!! . . . . . historical halfway house between Futurism and Surrealism, twixt Marinetti and André Breton, 'tween the before-the-war-to-end-all-wars years and between-the-wars years—*Dada!*—down with reason, logic, causality, coherence, tradition, proportion, sense and consequence, my art belongs to Dada 'cos Dada 'e treats me so—well then, *Memories of Dada by a Consular Friend of the Famous in Old Zurich: A Sketch* . . . . . Carr of the Consulate!—first name Henry, that much is beyond dispute, I'm mentioned in the books. For the rest, I'd be willing to enter into discussion but not if you don't mind correspondence, into matters of detail and chronology— I stand open to correction on all points, except for my height which can't be far off, and the success of my performance, which I remember clearly, in the demanding role of Ernest (not Ernest, the other one)—*that,* and the sense of sheer relief at arriving in a state of rest, namely Switzerland, the still center of the wheel of war. That's really the thing—

Carr is now a young man in his drawing room in 1917. Ideally the actor should simply take off e.g. a hat and dressing gown—no wig or beard, no makeup—Carr's age has been in his voice. As his youthful self, Carr dresses in a most elegant way and is especially interested in the cut of his trousers; he has the figure for it.

CARR (*continuing, as a young man*): —the first thing to grasp about Switzerland is that there is no war here. Even when there is war *everywhere else,* there is no war in Switzerland.

Carr's manservant, Bennett (*"quite a weighty presence"*), enters with a tea tray set for two. Carr remarks on Switzerland's "reassuring air of permanence" in contrast to the rest of the world. Carr himself is a veteran of the trenches, he reminds Bennett, where "Bliss it was to see the dawn! To be alive was heaven!" In the next breath Carr instructs Bennett as to his sartorial selections for that day. (*"This scene—and most of the play—is under the erratic control of Old Carr's memory, which is not notably reliable, and also of his various prejudices and delusions. One result is that the story—like a toy train perhaps—occasionally jumps the rails and has to be restarted at the point where it goes wild . . . . . The effect of these time-slips is not meant to be bewildering, and it should be made clear what is happening."*)

Carr tells Bennett he was at his tailor's when he heard the news about the start of war, "talking to the head cutter at Drewitt and Madge in a houndstooth check slightly flared behind the knee, quite unusual. Old Drewitt, or Madge, came in and told me. Never trusted the Hun, I remarked. Boche, he replied, and I, at that time unfamiliar with the appellation, turned on my heel and walked into Trimmett and Punch where I ordered a complete suit of Harris knickerbockers with hacking vents. By the time they were ready, I was in France. Great days! Dawn breaking over no-man's-land. Dewdrops glistening on the poppies in the early morning sun—All quiet on the Western Front . . . Tickety boo, tickety boo, tickety boo."

Bennett informs his master that a Tristan Tzara recently called and left his card. He also tells Carr the latest news about the class warfare of the Russian revolution, about which Carr observes, "I don't wish to appear wise after the event, but anyone with half an acquaintance with Russian society could see that the day was not far off before the exploited class, disillusioned by the neglect of its interests, alarmed by the falling value of the ruble, and above all goaded beyond endurance by the insolent rapacity of its servants, should turn upon those butlers, footmen, cooks, valets . . . . ."

Bennett advises Carr that Lenin may be a man to reckon with and Kerensky is the man to watch. All at once, visitors are arriving: Bennett announces Tzara, then Gwendolen, then James Joyce. They find themselves exchanging pleasantries in the form of limericks. Gwen introduces Joyce to her brother, Carr.

GWEN: He's a poor writer—
JOYCE: —Aha!
   A fine writer who writes caviar
   for the general, hence poor—
TZARA: Wants to touch you for sure.

JOYCE: I'm addressing my friend, Mr. . . .
CARR (*gulp*):   . . . Carr.
GWEN: Mr. Tzara writes poetry and sculpts
    with quite unexpected results.
    I'm told he recites
    and on Saturday nights
    does all kinds of things for adults.
JOYCE: I really don't think Mr. Carr
    is interested much in da-dah—
TZARA: We say it like Dah-da.
JOYCE (*to Carr*): The fact is I'm rather
    hard up.
CARR: Yes, I'm told that you are.
    If it's money you want, I'm afraid . . .
GWEN: Oh, Henry!—he's mounting a play,
    and Mr. Joyce thought
    your official support . . .
CARR: Ah!
JOYCE: . . . and a couple of pounds till I'm paid.
CARR: I don't see why not. For my part,
    H.M.G. is considered pro-art.
TZARA: Consider me anti.
GWEN: Consider your auntie?
JOYCE: A pound would do for a start.
CARR: The Boche put on culture a-plenty
    for Swiss, what's the word?
JOYCE: Cognoscenti.
CARR: It's worth fifty tanks
JOYCE: Or twenty-five francs
CARR: Now . . . British culture . . .
JOYCE: . . . I'll take twenty.
TZARA (*scornful*): Culture and reason!
JOYCE: Fifteen.
TZARA: They give us the mincing machine!
GWEN: That's awf'ly profound.
JOYCE: Could you lend me a pound?
TZARA: All literature is obscene!

The manic verbalizing finally runs down. Tzara and Gwen exit, leaving Joyce behind, still producing limericks. Finally Joyce moves out and Tzara comes back—a different Tzara behaving, as does Carr, as though he were a character in *The Importance of Being Earnest.* They touch lightly on the war and its causes and then move like butterflies onto the subject of art. Tzara and the Dadaists are redefining the meaning of art to include poems created by drawing words out of a hat. Carr denies that this can be considered art: "An artist is someone who is gifted in some way that enables him to do something more or less well which can only be done badly or not at all by someone who is not thus gifted. If there is any point in using language at all it is that a word is taken to stand for a particular fact or idea and not for other facts or ideas. I might claim to be able to fly . . . Lo, I say, I am flying. But you are not propelling yourself about while suspended in the air, someone may point out. Ah no, I reply, that is no longer considered the proper concern of people who can fly. In fact, it is frowned upon. Nowadays, a flyer never leaves the ground and wouldn't know how. I see, says my somewhat baffled interlocutor, so when you say you can *fly* you are using the word in a purely private sense. I see I have made myself clear, I say. Then, says this chap in some relief, you cannot actually *fly* after all? On the contrary, I say, I have just told you I can. Don't you see my dear Tristan you are simply asking me to accept that the word Art means whatever you wish it to mean; but I do not accept it."

Tzara points out that all the catchwords of patriotism are also made to mean whatever is wished. Tzara argues for "anti-art"; more and more heatedly Carr replies that it is "the loss of nerve and failure of talent." Carr is finally infuriated by the Rumanian's neutralism and iconoclasm. Their anger suddenly becomes a chant which in turn becomes a memory of the trenches voiced by Carr: ". . . . . the courage, the comradeship, the warmth, the cold, the mud, the stench—fear—folly—Christ Jesu!, but for this blessed leg!—I never thought to be picked out, plucked out, blessed by the blood of a blighty wound—oh *heaven!*—released into folds of snow-white feather beds, pacific civilian heaven!, the mystical swissticality of it, the entente cordiality of it!, the Jesus Christ I'm out of it!—into the valley of the invalided—Carr of the Consulate!"

Time slips backward to Tzara's entrance. Tzara comes in again and greets Carr, talking of cucumber sandwiches, a pretty "librarianness" named Cecily and an obscure Irish writer named Joyce. Tzara tells Carr he has come to meet Gwendolen and propose to her. Carr isn't sure that he'll give his brotherly permission for Gwendolyn to marry Tzara, especially as there seems to be some mystery about Tzara's first name: Tristan in society, Jack on his library card.

Tzara explains this apparent contradiction: he happened to meet Lenin one day at the Cafe Zum Adler when Lenin was lashing the Dadaists. Tzara tells Carr: "Well, as a Dadaist myself I am the natural enemy of bourgeois art and the natural ally of the political left, but the odd thing about revolution is that the further left you go politically the more bourgeois they like their art. Fortunately at the Zum Adler my name meant nothing to Lenin, but a few days later I met him at the library and he introduced me to Cecily. 'Tzara!' said she. 'Not the Dadaist, I hope!' 'My younger brother, Tristan,' I replied. 'Most unfortunate. Terrible blow to the family.' When I filled up my application form, for some reason the first name I thought of was Jack."

The fact that Cecily knows Lenin and is working with him interests Carr. But soon he and Tzara have locked horns again, quarreling over the meaning of art and the role of the artist, with Carr resenting the artist's considering himself especially blessed and exalted. Tzara defends the artist heatedly as "the priest-guardian of the magic that conjured the intelligence out of the appetites" of primitive man. Later on, he admits, "Art created patrons and was corrupted." His last thought on the subject is: "Without art man was a coffee-mill: but *with* art, man—is a coffee-mill! That is the message of Dada. —dada dada dada dada dada dada dada dada dada dada dada dada . . ."

This diatribe is interrupted by another time slippage back to the entry of Gwendolen with Joyce. Gwen introduces Joyce to the two others again, and again Joyce informs Carr that the loan of a couple of pounds would be very convenient, but that isn't what he's come about.

JOYCE: . . . . . By the fortune of war, Zurich has become the theatrical center of Europe. Here culture is a continuation of war by other means—Italian opera against French painting—German music against Russian ballet—but nothing from England. Night after night, actors totter about the raked stages of this Alpine renaissance, speaking in every tongue but one—the tongue of Shakespeare—of Sheridan—of Wilde . . . The English Players intend to mount a repertory of masterpieces that will show the Swiss who leads the world in dramatic art.

CARR: Gilbert and Sullivan—by God!

GWEN: And also Mr. Joyce's own play *Exiles* which so far, unfortunately—

JOYCE: That's quite by the way—

CARR: *Patience!*

JOYCE: Exactly. First things first.

CARR: *Trial by Jury! Pirates of Penzance!*

JOYCE: We intend to begin with that quintessential English jewel, *The Importance of Being Earnest.*

CARR (*pause*): I don't know it. But I've heard of it and I don't like it. It is a play written by an Irish— (*Glances at Gwendolen*) Gomorrahist—Now look here, Janice, I may as well tell you. His Majesty's Government—

JOYCE: I have come to ask you to play the leading role.

CARR: What?

JOYCE: We would be honored and grateful.

CARR: What on earth makes you think I am qualified to play the leading role in *The Importance of Being Earnest?*

GWEN: It was my suggestion. Henry. You were a wonderful Goneril at Eton.

CARR: Yes. I know, but—

JOYCE: We are short of a good actor to play the lead—he's an articulate and wittty English gentleman—

CARR: Ernest?

JOYCE: Not Ernest—the other one.

It isn't the character's wit but his wardrobe (two complete changes including a gaily striped blazer and cream flannel trousers) that begins to persuade Carr to play Algernon. Carr retires with Joyce to read the play and at the same time lends him two pounds.

Tzara comes forward and offers Gwen a love poem: Shakespeare's 18th sonnet cut in pieces and mixed up in a hat (Gwen knows the poem by heart and recites it). Tzara declares his admiration for Gwen, who admits she feels an "irresistible fascination" for him in return, not least because Tzara edits a magazine "of all that is newest and best in literature." Gwen happens to be carrying the folder she acquired in the opening scene, which she thinks is Joyce's work but actually is Lenin's. Gwen gives the folder to Tzara and then kisses him as Joyce enters.

Joyce admonishes Tzara "Your monocle is in the wrong eye," picks up his hat and exits—only to return almost at once, covered in the pieces of paper of Shakespeare's 18th sonnet (apparently Tzara was using Joyce's hat as the receptacle for his "poem").

JOYCE: What is the meaning of this?

TZARA: It has no meaning. It is without meaning as Nature is. It is Dada.

JOYCE: Give further examples of Dada.

TZARA: The Zoological Gardens after closing time. The logical gardenia. The bankrupt gambler. The successful gambler. The Eggboard, a sport or pastime for the top ten thousand in which the players, covered from head to foot in eggyolk, leave the field of play.

JOYCE: Are you the inventor of this sport or pastime?

TZARA: I am not.

JOYCE: What is the name of the inventor?

TZARA: Arp.

Arp is himself an ambivalent person (Tzara tells Joyce) whose first name is Hans or Jean; who was born either French or German in Alsace. Under Joyce's stiffly formal questioning, Tzara gives an account of how Arp, Hugo Ball, Marcel Janco and others founded the international cabaret where Dadist works of performing and plastic art are displayed in Zurich.

Joyce amuses himself by conjuring a carnation, a handkerchief, flags, etc. from his hat, while Tzara goes on: "Tristan Tzara discovered the word Dada by accident in a Larousse Dictionary. It has been said, and he does not deny, that a paper-knife was inserted at random into the book. In French *dada* is a child's word for a hobbyhorse."

When Tzara goes on to say that "making poetry should be as natural as making water," Joyce's sarcastic reply infuriates him.

TZARA: By God, you supercilious streak of Irish puke! You four-eyed, bog-ignorant, potato-eating ponce! Your art has failed. You've turned literature into a religion and it's as dead as all the rest, it's an overripe corpse and you're cutting fancy figures at the wake. It's too late for geniuses! Now we need vandals and desecrators, simple-minded demolition men to smash centuries of baroque subtlety, to bring down the temple, and thus finally, to reconcile the shame and the necessity of being an artist! Dada! *Dada! Dada!*

He starts to smash whatever crockery is to hand; which done, he strikes a satisfied pose. Joyce has not moved.

JOYCE: You are an over-excited little man, with a need for self-expression far beyond the scope of your natural gifts. This is not discreditable. Neither does it make you an artist. An artist is a magician put among men to gratify—capriciously—their urge for immortality. The temples are built and brought down around him, continuously and contiguously, from Troy to the fields of Flanders. If there is any meaning in any of it, it is in what survives as art; yes even in the celebration of tyrants, yes even in the celebration of nonentities. What now of the Trojan War if it had been passed over by the artist's touch? Dust. A forgotten expedition prompted by Greek merchants looking for new markets. A minor redistribution of broken pots. But it is we who stand enriched, by a tale of heroes, of a golden apple, a wooden horse, a face that launched a thousand ships—and above all, of Ulysses, the wanderer, the most human, the most complete of all heroes—husband, father, son, lover, farmer, soldier, pacifist, politician, inventor and adventurer . . . It is a theme so overwhelming that I am almost afraid to treat it. And yet I with my Dublin Odyssey will double that immortality, yes by God *there's* a corpse that will dance for some time yet and *leave the world precisely as it finds it*—and if you hope to shame it into the grave with your fashionable magic, I would strongly advise you to try and acquire some genius and if possible some subtlety before the season is quite over. Top o' the morning, Mr. Tzara!
> *With which Joyce produces a rabbit out of his hat, puts the hat on his head, and leaves, holding the rabbit.*

Carr's voice is heard offstage reading from *The Importance of Being Earnest,* as Tzara exits. When Carr enters it is as Old Carr, muttering over his memories of the play: he paid for his own trousers and helped fill the house and then fell into a lawsuit with Joyce over who owed who a few francs. The result was what Old Carr calls "a travesty of justice," as the court awarded Joyce his 25 francs claim and 60 francs more for costs.

OLD CARR: . . . . . Well, it was a long time ago. He left Zurich after the war, went to Paris, stayed twenty years and turned up here again in December 1940. Another war . . . But he was a sick man then, perforated ulcer, and in January he was dead . . . buried one cold snowy day in the Fluntern Cemetery up the hill. I dreamed about him, dreamed I had him in the witness box, a masterly cross-examination, case practically won, admitted it all, the whole thing, the trousers, everything, and I *flung* at him—"And what did you do in the Great War?" "I wrote *Ulysses,*" he said. "What did you do?" Bloody nerve.
Blackout. Curtain.

ACT II

In the library, Cecily's desk is prominent downstage, backed by several rows of bookcases. The entrance door is upstage center. The set is not really lit, the houselights are still up and some members of the audience have yet to take their seats as Cecily takes a position in front of the desk and, with the words "To resume," lectures on the origins of Marxism, the late 19th century struggles of the Russian people to better their condition (during which Lenin's older brother Alexander was arrested and hanged), Lenin's early life and his espousal of Marxist philosophy, his arrival in Switzerland with his wife at the beginning of the war. The stage is now lit and the houselights dark as Cecily tells how Lenin settled in Zurich because of the size of that ctiy's library.

> *Joyce is now passing among the bookshelves; and also Carr, now monocled and wearing blazer, cream flannels, boater . . . and holding a large pair of scissors which he snips speculatively as he passes between the bookcases. Joyce and Carr pass out of view.*

CECILY: Every morning at nine o'clock when the library opened, Lenin would arrive.

Lenin arrives, saying "Good morning" in Russian.

He would work till the lunch hour, when the library closed, and then return and work until six, except on Thursdays when we remained closed. He was working on his book on imperialism.

Lenin is at work among books and papers.

On January 22nd, 1917, at the Zurich People's House Lenin told an audience of young people, "We of the older generation may not live to see the decisive battles of the coming revolution." We all believed that that was so. But one day hardly more than a month later, a Polish comrade, Bronsky, ran into the Ulyanov house with the news that there was a revolution in Russia . . .

Nadya enters as she did in the opening scene and converses with Lenin in Russian about the Tsar's overthrow, as Cecily translates for the audience. Lenin is burning to get to Russia, but it is clear to Cecily that the British and French will try to prevent him from leaving Switzerland and will have him watched.

The Lenins leave the library, as Carr enters. *"Carr has come to the library as a 'spy,' and his manner betrays this."* Carr hands Cecily Tristan Tzara's calling card, so that Cecily takes him for "Jack" Tzara's "younger brother."

CARR: . . . . . My brother Jack is a booby, and if you want to know why he is a booby, I will tell you why he is a booby. He told me that you were rather pretty, whereas you are at a glance the prettiest girl in the whole world. Have you got any books here one can borrow?

CECILY: I don't think you ought to talk to me like that during library hours. However, as the reference section is about to close for lunch I will overlook it. Intellectual curiosity is not so common that one can afford to discourage it. What kind of books were you wanting?

CARR: Any kind at all.

CECILY: Is there no limit to the scope of your interests?

CARR: It is rather that I wish to increase it. An overly methodical education has left me to fend as best I can with some small knowledge of the aardvark, a mastery of the abacus and a facility for abstract art. An aardvark, by the way, is a sort of African pig found mainly—

CECILY: I know only too well what an aardvark is, Mr. Tzara. To be frank, you strike a sympathetic chord in me.

CARR: Politically, I haven't really gotten beyond anarchism.

CECILY: I see. Your elder brother, meanwhile—

CARR: Bolshevism. And you, I suppose?

CECILY: Zimmervaldism!

CARR: Oh, Cecily, will you not make it your mission to reform me? We can begin over lunch. It will give me an appetite. Nothing gives me an appetite so much as renouncing my beliefs over a glass of hock.

CECILY: I'm afraid I am too busy to reform you today. I must spend the lunch hour preparing references for Lenin.

CARR: Some faithful governess seeking fresh pastures?

CECILY: Far from it. I refer to Vladimir Ilyich who with my little help is writing his book on *Imperialism, the Highest Stage of Capitalism*.

Cecily reveals to Carr that Lenin is planning to go to Russia in disguise, but is being watched. She tells Carr (who she thinks is Tzara) that the British Consul in Zurich has been receiving cryptic telegrams like "Drive 'em Wilde" and "Break a Leg" which must have something to do with the surveillance of Lenin. Not at all, Carr explains: the Consul is appearing in an amateur play production, and these are telegrams of encouragement.

Cecily reveals that while in rehearsal the Consul has left his affairs in the hands of a manservant of radical sympathies who has turned all the Consular correspondence over to "Jack" Tzara. Cecily, with her strong socialist convictions, disapproves of manservants, and she gradually draws Carr into a heated argument about the function of art in modern society. Angrily, Carr uses Gilbert and Sullivan titles as epithets to hurl at Cecily.

All at once there is a time slip, and the scene goes back to Cecily's comment about intellectual curiosity. She can't go to lunch with Carr today, she tells him, because she's translating a Lenin article about French and German socialist recidivism. (*"She hands Carr the folder which came into her possession in the opening scene. It is identical to the one given by Gwen to Tzara."*) Cecily thinks it is Lenin's but it is in fact Joyce's.

Cecily criticizes the "imperialist war" and Ramsay MacDonald's "revisionism" in English socialist leadership. Cecily views Marx as a beacon pointing the way to the future, while Carr views him as merely the victim of a historical accident.

CARR: . . . . . By bad luck he encountered the capitalist system at its most deceptive period. The industrial revolution had crowded the people into slums and enslaved them in factories, but it had not yet begun to bring them the benefits of an industrialized society. Marx looked about him and saw that the system depended on a wretched army of wage slaves. He drew the lesson that the wealth of the capitalist was the counterpart to the poverty of the worker and had in fact been stolen from the worker in the form of unpaid labor. He thought that was how the whole thing worked. That false assumption was itself added to a false premise. This premise was that people were a sensational kind of material object and would behave predictably in a material world. Marx predicted that they would behave according to their class. But they didn't. Deprived, self-interested, bitter or greedy as the case may be, they showed streaks of superior intelligence, superior strength, superior morality . . . Legislation, unions, share capital, consumer power—in all kinds of ways and for all kinds of reasons, the classes moved closer together instead of further apart. The critical moment never came. It receded. The tide must have turned at about the time when *Das Kapital* after eighteen years of hard labor was finally coming off the press, a moving reminder, Cecily, of the folly of authorship. How sweet you look suddenly—pink as a rose.

CECILY: That's because I'm about to puke into your nancy straw hat, you *prig!*—you swanking canting fop, you bourgeois intellectual humbugger, you— to vote, to buy or not buy, allowed this and allowed that?—*do you think it's about winning concessions?*—Socialism is about *ownership*—the natural right *artist!* Do you think that's what socialism is about?—being allowed to strike, of the people to the common ownership of their country and its resources, the *land,* and what is *under* the land and what *grows* on the land, and all the profits and the benefits! . . . . .

Cecily continues to cite earnestly the benefits of Marxism and the policies of Lenin to bring about revolution. But Carr is not paying much attention. He is thinking about her body, and seductive lights and music come up, mirroring his thoughts. Carr throws off this thought (and the lights and music cease) just as there is another time slippage and the scene returns again to Cecily's "intellectual curiosity" comment.

CECILY: . . . . . What kind of books were you wanting?

CARR: Books? What books? What do you mean, Cecily, by books? I have read Mr. Lenin's article and I don't need to read any more. I have come to tell you that you seem to me to be the visible personification of absolute perfection.

CECILY: In body or mind?

CARR: In every way.

CECILY: Oh, Tristan!

CARR: You will love me back and tell me all your secrets, won't you?

CECILY: You silly boy! Of course! I have waited for you for months.

CARR (*amazed*): For months?

CECILY: Ever since Jack told me he had a younger brother who was a decadent nihilist it has been my girlish dream to reform you and to love you.

CARR: Oh, Cecily!

> *Her embrace drags him down out of sight behind her desk. He resurfaces momentarily—*

But, my dear Cecily, you don't mean that you couldn't love me if—
—and is dragged down again.

Lenin's wife Nadya enters and addresses the audience on the subject of Lenin's several bold, impractical and eventually discarded plans to get to Russia. Tristan Tzara enters, then Lenin, clean-shaven and wearing a wig. Lenin recites his latest scheme to cross England and Holland in disguise, and Carr listens intently from his place of concealment.

Cecily reveals herself and tells Tzara that his "brother Jack" is here. When Tzara sees Carr, he is furious at Carr's impersonation. Cecily runs offstage weeping at the "brothers'" quarrel, followed by Carr.

Nadya explains to the audience that the England-Holland plan was never realized (but Carr does not hear this, being offstage). When she mentions a meeting of Russian emigres to devise means of getting Lenin back to Russia, Old Carr comes in and takes up where Nadya leaves off: ". . . . . Here's the picture: middle of March: Lenin and I in Zurich. I'd got pretty close to him, had a stroke of luck with a certain little lady and I'd got a pretty good idea of his plans, in fact I might have stopped the whole Bolshevik thing in its tracks, but—here's the point. *I was uncertain.* What was the right thing? And then there were my feelings for Cecily. And don't forget, *he wasn't Lenin then! I mean who was he?* as it were. So there I was, the lives of millions of people hanging on which way I'd move, or whether I'd move at all, another man might have cracked. . . . ."

Old Carr exits. Nadya and Lenin (who has taken off his wig) outline a developing plan to cross Germany in a sealed train.

Young Carr comes back and joins Tzara—and it is now obvious that the scene has changed away from the library. Carr and Tzara carry on a cafe conversation about the political situation. Tzara comments: "To a Dadaist history comes out of a hat too."

Lenin and Nadya exit to board their sealed train to cross Germany to Russia, just as Carr makes up his mind that liberal democracy must have its chance in Russia, and therefore Lenin must be stopped. Carr follows Tzara offstage as the train noise becomes very loud.

Lenin reappears, bearded and bald as in his most famous photos. Alone onstage, he harangues a Russian crowd on the subject of freedom of expression: everyone is free to write as he chooses but will be expelled from the party if he writes against it. Lenin expostulates: "Are you free in relation to your bourgeois publisher, Mr. Writer? And in relation to your bourgeois public which demands that you provide it with pornography? The freedom of the bourgeois writer, artist or actor is simply disguised dependence on the moneybag, on corruption, on prostitution. Socialist literature and art will be free because the idea of socialism and sympathy with the working people, instead of greed and careerism, will bring ever new forces to its ranks. It will be free because it will serve not some satiated heroine, not the bored upper ten thousand suffering from fatty degeneration, but the millions and tens of millions of working people, the flower of the country, its strength and its future."

Nadya explains that though Lenin made few statements about art he liked circus clowns and the theater, where *Camille* made him cry. Lenin observes that Tolstoy sensed his people's discontent and caught a glimpse of the future. As for later artistic trends, he says, "Expressionism, futurism, cubism . . . I don't understand them and I get no pleasure from them."

Lenin disliked Mayakovsky, admired Pushkin and felt very close to Gorky both as a man and an artist. At times Lenin felt that Gorky was wasting himself and neglecting his talent on "the whining of rotting intellectuals" about such matters as the arrest of a few artists and others "to prevent plots which threaten the lives of tens of thousands of workers and peasants."

Nadya recalls some of her husband's other preferences in theater and in music.

> *The "Appassionata" Sonata of Beethoven is quietly introduced.*

NADYA: . . . . . I remember him one evening at a friend's house in Moscow, listening to a Beethoven sonata . . .

LENIN: I don't know of anything greater than the "Appassionata." Amazing, superhuman music. It always makes me feel, perhaps naively, it makes me feel proud of the miracles that human beings can perform. But I can't listen to music often. It affects my nerves, makes me want to say nice stupid things and pat the heads of those people who while living in this vile hell can create such beauty. Nowadays we can't pat heads or we'll get our hands bitten off. We've got to *hit* heads, hit them without mercy, though ideally we're against doing violence to people . . . Hm, one's duty is infernally hard . . .

> *The light goes out on him. He leaves. The music continues.*

NADYA: Once when Vladimir was in prison—in St. Petersburg—he wrote to me and asked that at certain times of day I should go and stand on a particular square of pavement on the Shpalernaya. When the prisoners were taken out for exercise it was possible through one of the windows in the corridor to catch a momentary glimpse of this spot. I went for several days and stood a long while on the pavement there. But he never saw me. Something went wrong. I forget what.

> *The "Appassionata" swells in the dark to cover the set change to Henry Carr's room. Gwen is seated. There are tea things on the table. The "Appassionata" degenerates absurdly into "Mr. Gallagher and Mr. Shean." Bennett enters, followed by Cecily.*
>
> *The rhyme-scheme of the song is fairly evident. The verses are of ten lines each, the first line being a non-rhyming primer.*

BENNETT: Miss Carruthers . . .

CECILY: . . . Cecily Carruthers . . .

GWEN: Cecily Carruthers! What a pretty name!
  According to the Consul
  'Round the fashionable fonts you'll
  often hear the Cecily's declaimed.

CECILY: Oh dear Miss Carr, oh dear Miss Carr,
  please remain exactly where you are

I beg you don't get up—
GWEN (*to Bennett*): I think we'll need another cup—
  Pray sit down, Miss Carruthers . . .
CECILY: . . . So kind of you, Miss Carr.
      Exit Bennett.
GWEN: Miss Carruthers, oh Miss Carruthers . . .
  I hope that you will call me Gwendolen,
  I feel I've known you long
  And I'm never ever wrong—
  Something tells me that we're going to be great friends.
CECILY (*upper class*): Oh, Gwendolen! Oh, Gwendolen!
  It sounds ez pretty *ez* a mendolen!
  I hope that you'll feel free
  to call me Cecily . . .
GWEN: Absolutely, Cecily . . .
CECILY: . . . Then that's settled Gwendolen . . . . .

Continuing in the same cadence, Cecily reminds Gwen that they have met
before—at the library. Cecily has called (she tells Gwen) because two books
Joyce is using are overdue on Gwen's ticket. Bennett enters, and there is the
business of pouring and sipping tea while the ladies continue their rhythmical
conversation.

GWEN: Oh Cecily, Oh Cecily . . .
  Aren't you the girl who has that Russian friend?
  I pass him every day
  by Economic A to K—
CECILY (*sadly*): It's never going to be the same again.
  Oh, Gwendolen, Oh Gwendolen!
  He left this afternoon on the three-ten.
  I've just come from the train.
  But we'll hear from him again . . .
GWEN (*insincerely*): Absolutely, Cecily . . .
CECILY: . . . *Positively,* Gwendolen!
      Exit Bennett.
CECILY: Oh Gwendolen, Oh Gwendolen . . .
  The library is going to seem so sad.
  Apart from Mr. Tzara
  all the Bolsheviki are a-
  board that special choo-choo bound for Petrograd.
GWEN: Excuse me Cecily, dear Cecily . . .
  This Mr. Tzara, does he spell it with a T?
  T-Z-A-R-A
  A Bolshevik, you say?
CECILY: Absolutely, Gwendolen . . .
GWEN: . . . You surprise me, Cecily . . . . .

Gwen and Cecily (stil in cadence) misunderstand each other on the subjects of Tristan and "Jack" Tzara, because of Carr's impersonation. They can't agree on the two "brothers' " views on politics or art. This leads them into a quarrel, and Cecily, now icily cool toward Gwen, prepares to depart.

Carr enters and his impersonation is exposed at once: he is not Tristan Tzara, as Cecily believes, but Gwen's brother Henry, of the British Consulate. The real Tristan Tzara enters carrying a folder, and *his* pretension to be his own "brother" Jack is instantly stripped away. The two women are once again in sympathy with each other as mutual victims of the hoax.

Before leaving, Gwen and Cecily want to know what Carr and Tzara thought of the material in the folders they were given to read, the one supposed to be by Joyce but actually by Lenin, the other supposed to be by Lenin but actually by Joyce. The men try weakly to pretend they liked what they read but are forced to confess they found it "rubbish!" and "bilge!" The women's scorn softens only for a moment when Carr professes his love for Cecily, but they finally decide "Our intellectual differences are an insuperable barrier." They exit.

Carr lets Tzara know he knows Bennett has been showing Tzara the Consulate correspondence. Bennett announces to his master the good and bad reviews of *Earnest* in the local papers. Carr already resents the fact that Joyce came to the dressing room after the show and handed him ten francs payment for his performance, as though it were a tip.

Joyce enters and demands of Carr 25 francs which he says is due for the tickets given to Carr to sell. Carr argues that he spent 350 francs of his own money on his costume and owes Joyce nothing, daring him to sue. Carr calls Joyce "a swindler and a cad!" Tzara hands Joyce back "his" folder with the scathing comment, "As an arrangement of words it is graceless without being random; as a narrative it lacks charm or even vulgarity; as an experience it is like sharing a cell with a fanatic in search of a mania."

Gwen and Cecily enter. Joyce is scanning the manuscript.

JOYCE: Who gave you this manuscript to read?

GWEN: I did!

JOYCE: Miss Carr, did I or did I not give you to type a chapter in which Mr. Bloom's adventures correspond to the Homeric episode of the Oxen of the Sun?

GWEN: Yes, you did! And it was wonderful!

JOYCE: Then why do you return to me an ill-tempered thesis purporting to prove, amongst other things, that Ramsay MacDonald is a bourgeois lickspittle gentleman's gentleman?

GWEN: Aaaah.

TZARA: Ohhhh.

CECILY: Oops!

CARR: Aaah!

JOYCE (*thunders*): Miss Carr, where is the missing chapter???

CARR: Excuse me—did you say Bloom?

JOYCE: I did.

CARR: And is it a chapter, inordinate in length and erratic in style, remotely connected with midwifery?

JOYCE: It is a chapter which by a miracle of compression, uses the gamut of English literature from Chaucer to Carlyle to describe events taking place in a lying-in hospital in Dublin.

CARR (*holding out the folder*): It is obviously the same work.

The mixup is discovered and the folders exchanged to cries of joy and reconciliation: "Cecily! Gwendolen! Henry! Tristan!" Everyone begins to dance with everyone else. Carr and Cecily drift offstage as the others continue dancing; then they come back on as Old Carr and Old Cecily as the others dance offstage.

OLD CECILY: No, no, no, no, it's pathetic though there was a court case, I admit, and your trousers came into it, I don't deny, but you never got close to Vladimir Ilyich, and I don't remember the other one. I do remember Joyce, yes you are quite right and he was Irish with glasses but that was the year after—1918—and the train had long gone from the station! I waved a red hanky and cried long live the revolution as the carriage took him away in his bowler hat and yes, I said yes when you asked me, but he was the leader of millions by the time you did your Algernon . . .

OLD CARR: Algernon—that was him.

OLD CECILY: I said that was the year after—

OLD CARR: After what?

OLD CECILY: You never even saw Lenin.

OLD CARR: Yes I did. Saw him in the cafes. I knew them all. Part of the job.

OLD CECILY (*small pause*): And you were never the Consul.

OLD CARR: Never said I was.

OLD CECILY: Yes you did.

OLD CARR: Should we have a cup of tea?

OLD CECILY: The Consul was Percy somebody.

OLD CARR: Bennett.

OLD CECILY: What?

OLD CARR (*testily*): I said the Consul's name was Bennett!

OLD CECILY: Oh yes . . . Bennett . . . (*Pause.*) That's another thing—

OLD CARR: *Are we going to have a cup of tea or not?*

OLD CECILY: And I never helped him write *Imperialism, the Highest Stage of Capitalism.* That was the year before, too. 1916.

OLD CARR: Oh, Cecily. I wish I'd known then that you'd turn out to be a pedant! (*Getting angry.*) Wasn't this—Didn't do that—1916—1917—*What of it? I* was here. They were here. They went on. I went on. We all went on.

OLD CECILY: No, we didn't. We stayed. Sophia married that artist. I married you. You played Algernon. They all went on.

Most of the fading light is on Carr now.

OLD CARR: Great days . . . Zurich during the war. Refugees, spies, exiles, painters, poets, writers, radicals of all kinds. I knew them all. Used to argue far into the night . . . at the Odeon, the Terrasse . . . I learned three things in Zurich during the war. I wrote them down. Firstly, you're either a revolutionary or you're not, and if you're not you might as well be an artist as anything else. Secondly, if you can't be an artist, you might as well be a revolutionary . . . I forget the third thing.

    Blackout. Curtain.

THE NORMAN CONQUESTS

Three Interlocking Plays, Each in Two Acts:
TABLE MANNERS, LIVING TOGETHER and
ROUND AND ROUND THE GARDEN

BY ALAN AYCKBOURN

Cast and credits appear on page 335

ALAN AYCKBOURN was born in London in 1939. He was educated at Haileybury and went straight into the theater after leaving school, working as an actor and stage manager in Edinburgh, Worthing, Leatherhead, Oxford and Stoke-on-Trent. He joined Stephen Joseph's company at Scarborough as an actor and there began writing plays, achieving his first West End production with Mr. Whatnot at the Arts Theater in 1964. While connected with the BBC in Leeds as a radio and drama producer, he wrote his second West End production, the highly successful Relatively Speaking at the Duke of York's Theater in 1967. His short play Countdown was part of a program about marriage at the Comedy Theater in 1969.

The first Ayckbourn play to reach Broadway was How the Other Half Loves, produced in the West End in 1970 with Robert Morley and on Broadway at the Royale in 1971 with Phil Silvers for 73 performances. His Time and Time Again played 229 performances at the Comedy Theater in 1972-73, and it was followed by his Absurd Person Singular which opened in London in July, 1973 and on Broadway in October, 1974 and was still running in both places at the time of the opening of The Norman Conquests in London in 1974 and on Broadway in 1975, its author's first Best Play.

Ayckbourn's newest play, Absent Friends, was produced in London this season. Currently, he serves as Director of Productions at the Library Theater in Scarborough, where he lives.

The Norman Conquests *is a portmanteau title for three full-length plays:* Table Manners, Living Together *and* Round and Round the Garden. *They have exactly the same set of characters, but we would have to call them a continuum—if that word can be stretched a little—rather than a trilogy, because they take place within the same time frame of a single weekend. Literally and figuratively, they are separate rooms of the same house: in the first play we see what was going on that weekend in the dining room, in the second play in the living and in the third play the terrace. It's an identical time period, however, and the plays couldn't be staged in a long three-play performance because much of the activity in them overlaps in time.*

Presented in rotating repertory, The Norman Conquests *is designed like a revolving door to be entered at any segment. We've chosen* Table Manners *to be fully synopsized in these pages, but it's the full concept of* The Norman Conquests *which we designate a Best Play in this volume. In order to represent it, we've inserted a few clearly-identified excerpts from* Living Together *and* Round and Round the Garden *at the places where they would occur if the plays were going on simultaneously.*

Time: A weekend in July

Place: An English country house

TABLE MANNERS

ACT I

Scene 1: Saturday, 6 p.m.

SYNOPSIS: The sun streams through the window of the country house dining room, *"large and high ceilinged and like the rest of this Victorian vicarage-type building badly needs redecorating."* The room is furnished with a table, some chairs, a sideboard at left and a window seat. The dining room may be entered through the garden (up right) as well as through the door to the rest of the house (up left).

Annie, an attractive young woman who hides her looks under a bushel of *"baggy sweater, jeans and raffia slippers,"* enters with a vase for some roses on the sideboard. Shortly afterward, Annie's sister-in-law Sarah enters. *"She wears a light summer coat and dress. She is breathless."* Sarah has just arrived for the weekend with her husband, Annie's brother Reg, who drove too fast as usual.

The women embrace, and Sarah declares her joy at being here for the weekend—though Reg is an estate agent, Sarah's own house is small and feels confining.

SARAH: . . . . . You're so lucky, Annie, you have no idea. Just to see a tree once in a while and the birds . . . I really miss it. Now then, how are you, let's look. Oh, Annie, darling, you look just the same. Your hair . . .

ANNIE (*self-consciously smoothing her tangle*): I know . . . I haven't brushed it today. I washed it, though, this morning.

SARAH: What's the good of washing it if you don't brush it? It's like a gorse bush.

ANNIE: Well, nobody sees it. The postman, the milkman, couple of cows and Mother.

SARAH: And Tom.

ANNIE: Oh, yes. Tom.

SARAH: You mustn't forget Tom. And how's Mother?

ANNIE: No better, no worse. She hasn't felt like getting up, not for weeks . . .

SARAH: Well, you should make her. She needs to.

Sarah and Reg have come to take care of the old lady for a weekend, to give Annie a little holiday. Annie is going away for the weekend—not to Hastings, where she wanted to go (there was no room), but to East Grinstead, because it sounded interesting. Sarah is doubtful: "I've never heard of anybody having a holiday in East Grinstead."

If the care and medication of the old lady are complicated, Sarah comments, "Reg can cope with them. He's going to do most of the running up and downstairs anyway. I mean, this is a holiday for me too. She's his mother. He can do something for her for a change." Inertia, Sarah observes, is her husband Reg's outstanding characteristic: "There are times I think he's sleep walking . . . . . heaven knows how he runs a business."

Annie has prepared a cold supper for Reg and Sarah and left it on the kichen table. Sarah inquires about Annie's friend Tom. Annie seems indifferent to him. Tom is a veterinarian who happens to be present in the house at this moment, attending to their cat, which has a sore paw. Sarah remembers Tom as being a bit ponderous. Annie agrees.

ANNIE: . . . . . He just comes around when he's bored, that's all.

SARAH: A man doesn't spend as much time as Tom does round here without having a very good reason. Believe you me. You don't have to be psychic to know what that is.

ANNIE: Well, if it's that he's never asked for it and even if he did he wouldn't get it. So I don't know why he bothers.

SARAH: Annie! You're getting dreadfully coarse.

ANNIE: Oh, you're just a prude.

SARAH: No, I'm not a prude. No, I've never been called that. You can't call me a prude. That's not fair, Annie, I mean, I don't care for smutty talk or dirty jokes. I just don't find them funny. Or particularly tasteful. But that isn't being a prude. That's normal decent behavior which is something quite different.

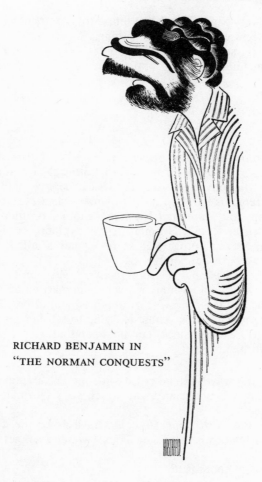

RICHARD BENJAMIN IN
"THE NORMAN CONQUESTS"

ANNIE: Yes.

SARAH: I won't have the television set on at all these days.

ANNIE: Anyway, all that happens is that Tom comes round here like he has done for years. I feed him. He sits and broods. Sometimes we talk. That's all.

SARAH: Talk about what?

ANNIE: Oh, super exciting things like does the kitchen ceiling need another coat and distemper and hardpad and foot and mouth and swine vescular disease. Then I pot Mother and retire to bed—alone—itching.

SARAH: Oh.

ANNIE: And count sick sheep crashing headlong into the gate. Look, for all I know he may be passionately in love with me. He may be flashing out all sorts of secret signals which I just haven't noticed. But he's never even put a hand on my knee. (*Reflecting.*) God forbid.

SARAH: But you're fond of him?

ANNIE: He's—very kind. Yes, I like him a lot. I sometimes miss him when he's not here. I suppose that means something.

SARAH: Yes. You see, I was rather hoping—I know it's wicked of me—I was rather hoping that you were both planning to go off for this weekend together.

ANNIE: Oh. No.

SARAH: You're not, are you?

ANNIE (*uneasy*): No. Not at All.

Sarah insists on believing that Annie is going off with Tom for the weekend (and Sarah is rather proud of herself for tolerating this arrangement). Annie sees that nothing will convince Sarah otherwise except perhaps a confession of the truth. Annie reminds Sarah of last Christmas, when everybody was sick or out of town except for Annie and Norman (another brother-in-law, married to Annie's older sister Ruth). Norman, Annie explains, is "just the opposite to Tom. Norman doesn't bother wtih secret signals at all. It was just wham, thump and there we both were on the rug."

This news shakes Sarah, but she soon recovers. She is not fond of Norman's wife Ruth but "I would not wish my worst enemy married to a man like that." Sarah is glad that Annie's fling with Norman is behind her. It takes Sarah a long time to comprehend what Annie is trying to tell her: Annie is going off on her weekend to East Grinstead, not alone, and not with Tom, but with her brother-in-law Norman.

ANNIE: . . . . . the way Norman put it—it sounded simple. Just a weekend.

SARAH: Norman will put it any way which suits Norman. Did you think of Ruth? And Tom?

ANNIE: Oh, to hell with Tom. He could have asked me if he'd wanted to but he didn't. If I wait to be asked by Tom, I won't even get on an old folks' outing.

SARAH: Well, what about Ruth?

ANNIE: That's up to Norman. He wrote to me and then he phoned and asked me and I suddenly thought, well yes . . . I think, actually if I'm being really truthful and, knowing Norman, I didn't think it would ever happen.

SARAH: You were certain enough about it to get Reg and I down. We've had all the trouble of having to take the children to their grandparents so that we wouldn't have to bring them down here because we knew they would disturb Mother. I've had all the trouble of delegating responsibility for the "Bring and Buy Sale" which I'm sure will be a disaster because I'm the only one among them with any sort of organizing ability. And Reg has had to cancel his golf.

ANNIE: I'm sorry. I've been feeling sick all morning. I'm sorry.

SARAH: Yes, well I'm sure we all are.

ANNIE: Well . . .

     She moves to the door.

SARAH: Where are you going?

ANNIE: I don't know. I was just—I don't know.

SARAH: I think it's just as well we are here. You quite obviously need a rest. Now, I want you to sit down here and leave everything to me.

ANNIE: No, it's all right I—

SARAH: And let's get this quite clear to start with. You are not going anywhere. Not while I'm in this house.

ANNIE: What about my weekend?

SARAH: You can have your weekend here. Reg and I will cope. That's what we came down for. You can rest. You can certainly forget the idea of going anywhere with Norman. That's final. You're staying here.

ANNIE: Yes. I rather thought I would be.

Tom (*"a pensive, thoughtful man . . . . . casually dressed in weekend country clothes*) comes in. His greeting amounts to the single expression "Ah." In a few words, mostly of one syllable, Tom informs them that the cat is up a tree with its septic paw and won't come down. Sarah quickly informs Tom that Annie isn't going away after all and invites Tom to dinner, which Sarah and Reg will organize and produce.

Sarah learns from Tom that Norman is actually on the premises—in the garden, talking to Reg. Sarah hurries out, en route to the garden and her entrance into a scene in another of the *Norman Conquests,* excerpted immediately below.

Excerpt from ROUND AND ROUND THE GARDEN

Act I, Scene 1

In the garden, Norman (*"bearded, a rather aimless sort of beard"*), wearing a woolly hat and a disreputable macintosh, is chatting with Reg, who is nattily turned out in cap and sports jacket. There are two suitcases on the ground beside Reg and one beside Norman. Sarah enters.

SARAH: Reg—oh. (*She sees Norman.*) Hallo, Norman.

NORMAN: Hallo, Sarah. How's Sarah?

SARAH: Very well, Norman. Surprised to hear you were here.

NORMAN: Yes. Well, I was passing.

SARAH: That's nice.

NORMAN: Yes. Thought I'd look in on the old home.

SARAH: Naturally.

NORMAN (*uneasy at her manner*): Well, I must be off.
        He gathers himself together and picks up his suitcase, preparing to leave.

SARAH: Are you taking those in, Reg?

REG: Oh, yes. Yes—
        He starts to move in with one suitcase.

SARAH: I've just been talking to Annie.

NORMAN (*freezing in his tracks, warily*): Have you?

SARAH: Yes. Oh, Reg, rather good news. She's decided she doesn't want to go away, after all.

REG: She doesn't?

NORMAN: Eh?

SARAH: No. Isn't that nice?

REG: Well, we needn't have bothered to come then.

SARAH: I think it's just as well we did.

REG (*going in*): All this racing about and we didn't need to come at all.

Reg goes inside.

SARAH (*following him*): It gets difficult for her, coping entirely on her own . . .

Turning back and smiling brilliantly at Norman.

Bye, bye Norman. I expect you'll want to hurry along to East Grinstead.

Sarah goes inside. Norman stands speechless with fury. He puts down his suitcase and paces up and down in silence for a second.

NORMAN (*exploding with a fierce yell and kicking his suitcase frenziedly*): Damned—stupid—interfering—rotten—bitch!

Reg comes out to fetch the bag he's left behind.

REG: Are you dashing off immediately or can you stay for a bit?

NORMAN: I'm staying. You bet your sweet life I'm staying.

He snatches up his suitcase and strides angrily into the house. Reg, a little bewildered, follows him.

TABLE MANNERS (*continued*)

Act I: Scene 1 (continued)

In the dining room, following Sarah's exit, Tom tries awkwardly to make conversation with Annie, who seems indifferent to his comments about her need for a rest. She is taking out knives and forks to set the table, while Tom helps himself to a stale biscuit from a tin.

Annie provokes Tom into talking about her planned weekend.

TOM: . . . . . It did occur to me that you might have liked someone to come along with you . . .

ANNIE: It did?

TOM: And then I thought, well, probably not.

ANNIE: Why? What on earth made you think I wanted to go off and sit in some dreary hotel room on my own?

TOM: Yes, it did seem rather odd, I must say.

ANNIE: How long have you known me?

TOM: Oh—years . . .

ANNIE: Years. And in all that time have I ever even hinted that I'd like to go off on my own?

TOM: Not as far as I know.

ANNIE (*angrily*): Then why the hell should I suddenly decide to do it now?

TOM: Well, I don't know. Simmer down.

ANNIE: Why didn't you say—Annie, will you be all right on your own? Would you like company? Someone to come along too? Someone to talk to? Why didn't you think of saying it? Just once?

TOM: Oh, come on . . .

ANNIE: Or was the whole prospect just too awful?

TOM: No—

ANNIE: Well, then?

TOM: You should have said something. You should have asked me along. I'd've come. You should've asked me.

ANNIE (*weakly*): Oh, dear God. Yes, I'd have had to have done.

TOM: Don't blame me.

ANNIE: I'm not blaming you. Oh—nun's knickers!

Annie stamps out, and Tom helps himself to another biscuit as Reg comes in, prepared to greet his sister Annie warmly but finding only Tom. Reg is chuckling at the memory of his earlier chat with Norman in the garden, and he confides to Tom that he likes Norman, no matter what, even though Sarah doesn't want Norman in the house. In a joking fashion, Reg advises Tom to marry Annie, but Tom doesn't take Reg seriously.

Tom is concerned because he's noticed the two women are "All on edge," for no apparent reason. They seem startled by some mysterious agency; Reg guesses that maybe it's Norman's presence that's upsetting them. Reg talks on, whether or not Tom is listening.

REG: . . . . . Better go and see Mother in a minute. Sarah's up there at the moment. I'll wait till she comes down. Two of them, too much of a good thing. I'll put it off as long as I can. Mother always says the same thing. What did you go and marry her for? Biggest mistake of your life. You'll live to regret it. Trouble is, I can never think of a convincing answer. (*He laughs.*) She's probably right. I mean, there are compensations. Children—sometimes. Even Sarah—sometimes. But when I sit here in this house and listen to the quiet, you know, I wonder why I left. I had my own room here, you know. All my books, my own desk, a shelf for my hobbies. I'd sit up there in my school holidays . . . happy as a sandboy. I'd make these balsa wood airplanes. Dozens of them. Very satisfying. Mind you, they never flew. Soon as I launched them—crack—nose dive—firewood. But it didn't really matter. It was a hell of a bore winding them up, anyway. I built one for the kids the other day. They didn't really take to it. Where's the guns, dad? Where are the bombs, then? (*He shakes his head.*) Oh, well, what do you expect?

Tom is still thinking about his own problems and has come to the conclusion that he let Annie down by not offering to go away with her. Reg is beginning to get hungry and tries a stale biscuit, as Sarah enters. Sarah is worried that Annie and Norman are alone together in the living room, and she sends

Reg in to see what they're up to, on a pretext of fetching something.

Tom is still blaming himself for ruining Annie's weekend. After a short interval, Reg comes back carrying a waste paper basket—the pretext of his errand—and reporting that, yes, Norman and Annie are in the living room together. Sarah sends Tom off to the living room with orders to declare himself to Norman on the subject of Annie, once and for all.

Sarah informs Reg about Norman and Annie's weekend plans, and Reg is much amused. Sarah complains that Reg doesn't take enough responsibility for his younger sister or even for his own children, leaving Sarah to bear the whole burden: "You sit in that room, which I spend my whole life trying to keep tidy, fiddling with airplanes and bits of cardboard and now you can't even be bothered with your own sister—"

Reg's reaction to his wife's accusations is first to try to induce her to leave off, and finally telling her plainly to shut up. Hysterical and infuriated, Sarah throws the biscuit canister at Reg, scattering its contents all over the room. Sarah sits and sobs while Reg starts picking up the biscuits, as Annie enters, takes in the scene and calmly goes to get a dustpan. The quarrel between Reg and Sarah sputters as Tom comes in and out, and as Annie returns to help sweep up the biscuits.

Under Sarah's questioning, Annie reports that Tom and Norman don't seem to have any major differences to sort out, and that Norman is getting drunk. Annie has reconciled herself to the fact that she's not going away for the weekend with Norman; and she's rather pleased that she's the object of two men's attention.

Reg and Annie reminisce about their childhood, as Sarah goes in and out getting lunch ready. For a moment they can hear Norman singing drunkenly in the living room. Tom comes in with a bottle of home carrot brew he's managed to save from Norman's depredations. Reg samples it and finds it's not bad on the tongue but hits bottom very hard.

Annie and Sarah announce that lunch is ready, which causes Reg to remark that "The great caterpillar hunt is on." They decide not to call Norman in to join them."

REG: What I always say about your salads, Annie, is that I may not enjoy eating but I learn an awful lot about insect biology. My appreciation of the anatomy of an earwig has increased enormously . . .

SARAH: Could we keep off this subject, please?

TOM: Wine, Sarah?

SARAH: What is it?

TOM: Wine. Home-made.

SARAH: Oh well, just a little. Thank you.

    They sit and eat in silence.

REG: Could you pass the centipede sauce please.

    Annie giggles. Sarah glares.

(*Raising his glass.*) Well, here's to us.

SARAH: I think it would be fitting to drink to Annie and Tom.

PAULA PRENTISS, CAROLE SHELLEY AND ESTELLE PARSONS
IN "THE NORMAN CONQUESTS"

TOM: Really? Why is that?

ANNIE: Because we're here.

TOM: Oh, I see. I thought there was a special reason.

SARAH: That's rather up to you, isn't it, Tom?

TOM: Um?

REG: Cheers, anyway.

SARAH: Good health, Tom, Annie.

> *Sarah drinks, puts down her glass. Her stomach explodes. She lets out a gasp. Tom and Annie half rise.*

ANNIE: Sarah!

TOM: All right?

> *He begins to bang her back rather heartily.*

SARAH (*regaining her breath*): Yes—it took me by surprise.

ANNIE: Yes, it tends to do that.

SARAH (*not enjoying Tom's attentions*): That will do Tom, thank you. That will do.

REG: It'll kill off any beetles you've swallowed.

SARAH: Will you stop making remarks like that.

REG (*raising his knife by way of apology*): Sorry . . . sorry.

SARAH: For goodness sake. For once in this family, let's try and have a civilized meal.

> *They eat in silence. From a distance Norman is heard singing in the living room. They hear this, catch each other's eyes and then, under Sarah's withering gaze, continue to eat. As Norman's singing becomes louder and more boisterous, Annie, Tom and Reg become helpless with stifled laughter. Curtain.*

Excerpt from LIVING TOGETHER

Act I, Scene 2: Saturday, 8 p.m.

That night in the living room, Norman (who passed out earlier in the day but is somewhat irritably sobered up and back on his feet now) is talking to his wife Ruth on the telephone, while Reg is trying to organize Sarah, Tom and Annie into playing a new board game he has invented. It's a game of cops vs. robbers, with the board representing the district of a city.

On the phone, Norman calls Ruth a "selfish bitch," as Reg doggedly continues to explain his game to his skeptical listeners.

REG: . . . . . The police cars can see up to twenty spaces ahead of them and up to four spaces each side. They can't see behind them and they can't see round corners.

SARAH: Why can't they see behind them?

REG: Because they can't, that's why.

TOM: Motto: don't drive behind a police car.

NORMAN (*on the phone, loudly for a second*): Love? What do you know about love . . . ? (*With an apologetic look at the others, continuing in a lower tone.*) Have you ever felt love for a single human being in your life?

REG: The police also have the Chief Superintendant.

> *Holding him up.*

This chap . . . He can see up to three spaces ahead of him him and three spaces round a corner . . .

TOM: Useful chap in a crisis.

SARAH: Oh, this is absurd.

REG: What's absurd?

SARAH: How can you have a man see three spaces ahead and three round the corner?

REG: Because he's got a very long neck. I don't know, it's a game, woman.

SARAH: It's not even realistic.

REG: What's that got to do with it?

SARAH: It's not much of a game if it's not even realistic.

REG: What are you talking about? Realistic? (*Leaping up.*) What about chess? That's not realistic, is it? What's wrong with chess?

SARAH: Oh well, chess . . .

REG: In chess, you've got horses jumping sideways. That's not realistic, is it? Have you ever seen a horse jumping sideways?

SARAH: Yes, all right . . .

REG (*leaping about*): Like this. Jumping like this. That's very realistic, I must say.

SARAH: You've made your point.

ANNIE: Reg . . .

REG: And bishops walking diagonally. (*Demonstrating again.*) You ever seen a bishop walking like this? Well, have you? I'm asking you, have you ever seen a flaming bishop walking like this?

SARAH: Reg, will you please sit down and get on with it.

REG (*sitting triumphantly*): Well then.

NORMAN: Don't you hang up on me—Ruth! Ruth!

He jangles the receiver up and down.

Hallo? Hallo? What? Who's this? Mother . . . what are you doing on the line, get off.

SARAH: Who's he talking to?

NORMAN: Ruth! Hallo . . . Mother, will you please get off this line?

ANNIE: Oh, my God. He jiggled the receiver . . .

NORMAN: Mother!

ANNIE: He rang the extension bell in Mother's bedroom.

NORMAN (*into the phone*): Look—would you shut up, both of you, for a minute and let me get a word in . . . Mother, if you don't hang up, I'll come and sort you out personally.

ANNIE (*moving to Norman*): Norman . . .

NORMAN (*into phone*): What did you say? (*To Annie.*) Go away.

ANNIE: Norman—please . . .

NORMAN: All right, Mother, I've warned you . . . I'll come up and wrap it round your neck . . .

Norman bangs the receiver down on the table and strides out.

All thought of the game is abandoned by everyone except Reg. Annie and Sarah go out after Norman, to try to prevent him from carrying out his threat to the old lady upstairs. Tom goes to the phone, where he can hear the ruckus through the still-open extension upstairs. Norman's wife Ruth too is still on her end of the phone, and Tom is talking to her as Annie comes back. Annie speaks sharply to Tom, accusing him of standing apart while others cope with the family crisis, calling him "useless." Tom puts down the receiver.

TOM: Now look here, I wish you'd stop going on at me like this. You're damned lucky to have me around, you know.

ANNIE: Oh really?

TOM: Yes, really. Every time anything goes wrong, you seem to take it out on me. First of all, it's your holiday, then it's Norman . . . well, it's just not on, it really isn't.

ANNIE: Um?

REG: Won't somebody play with me, please . . .

TOM: The next time you're planning holidays for two, if you want me along, perhaps you'd be good enough to be polite enough to ask me.

ANNIE: You've got a hell of a nerve.

TOM: And anyway, if you want to be seen with me, you better smarten yourself up a bit. You're a mess, you know. You look like something that's fallen off a Post van.

ANNIE: I beg your pardon?

Norman returns.

NORMAN (*crossing straight to phone*): That's settled that.

ANNIE: Norman . . .

NORMAN (*into phone*): Ruth? Hallo? . . . She's hung up. Would you believe it, she's hung up on me.

TOM (*to Annie*): I'm going home, I'm fed up. Just count yourself lucky I don't belt you one and give you rabies.

Tom strides out. Sarah enters with her blue bed jacket now in two halves.

SARAH: Look what you've done. Look what you've done to my bed jacket.

NORMAN (*collapsing*): Nobody loves me. Nobody loves me any more.

ANNIE: Norman . . .

SARAH: Look at this. Will somebody look at this?

REG: Won't anybody play with me? Please . . .

Curtain.

TABLE MANNERS (*continued*)

Scene 2: Sunday, 9 a.m.

In the dining room the next morning, Sarah brings in a tray of breakfast things and tries to ignore Norman standing there in pyjamas and bare feet.

Sarah goes out and Annie comes in with another tray, also ignoring Norman though he tries to engage her in small talk about the weather and how everybody slept.

Reg comes in, cheerful until he sees Norman, whom he also tries to ignore as he sits at the table with the others. Each fixes a breakfast to his or her own taste as Norman plays games of tricking his silent companions into speaking to him. Norman launches into a monologue, pretending to read their minds and tell them what they're thinking of him: "He came down here to seduce his wife's own sister." Norman notes that the sister was perfectly willing to leave Tom behind and come away with him, and he continues to defend himself in monologue: "And what is little Annie thinking, I wonder? Maybe furtively admiring my pyjamas, who knows? Pyjamas that could have been hers. With all that they contain. These nearly were mine. Or maybe she is thinking . . . Phew, that was a close shave. I could have shacked up in some dreadful hotel with this man—at this very moment . . . what a lucky escape for me. Thank heavens, I am back here at home amidst my talkative family exchanging witty breakfast banter. Knowing my two-legged faithful companion and friend, Tom the rambling vet, is even now planning to propose to me in 1997 just as soon as he's cured our cat . . . . ."

Norman's banter drives Annie from the room, as he yells at her "I didn't even book the hotel. I knew you wouldn't come. You didn't have the guts."

Sarah runs out to comfort Annie, and Norman continues his monologue, addressing himself to Reg, his only remaining audience, who's too busy eating to interrupt. Nobody has considered his feelings, Norman complains. ". . . . . What about my wife? Don't you think I'd take Ruth away, just the same? If she'd come. But she won't. She has no need of me at all, that woman, except as an emotional punch bag . . . I tell you, if you gave Ruth a rose, she'd peel all the petals off to make sure there weren't any greenfly. And when she'd done that, she'd turn round and say, do you call that a rose? Look at it, it's all in bits. That's Ruth. If she came in now, she wouldn't notice me. She'd probably hang her coat on me . . . It's not fair, Reg. Look, I'll tell you. A man with my type of temperament should really be ideally square jawed, broad shouldered, have blue twinkling eyes, a chuckle in his voice and a spring in his stride. He should get through three women a day without even ruffling his hair. That's what I'm like inside. That's my appetite. That's me. I'm a three a day man. There's enough of me in here to give. Not just sex, I'm talking about everything. The trouble is, I was born in the wrong damn body. A gigolo trapped in a haystack . . . . ."

Reg mutters a not unfriendly comment, as Sarah comes in and out of the dining room just long enough to announce the arrival on the premises of Norman's wife, Ruth—Reg's and Annie's sister.

Ruth enters, peering shortsightedly and finally seeing her husband Norman. Ruth is crisply tailored and coiffed; she is crisp and businesslike in every way except that she refuses to admit that she can see almost nothing without her glasses, which she seldom wears.

Reg makes his escape from the dining room, but Ruth thinks he's still there and talks to him until Norman informs her Reg has left the room. Ruth tells Norman she decided to join him here, not because of Norman's weird phone call, but because Sarah later phoned and advised her that she ought to be here.

Ruth sits at the table and gropes for breakfast materials as Norman complains that Ruth has removed all the warmth from their marriage and regards it merely as a legal contract. Ruth pours hot water on her cereal, takes a deep breath and tries to consider the subject rationally and calmly.

RUTH: I have a great deal of work I should be doing at home. I have given that up. I have come down here because I was asked to come. I did not want to come. I want to stay as short a time as possible. Is that clear?

NORMAN: Oh, yes. Got to get back to your work.

RUTH: Yes, I do. I have two full reports that have to be in tomorrow. If they are not in, I shall probably be fired. If I'm fired, we will have no money to pay the mortgage, no money for three quarters of the gas and electricity bills . . .

NORMAN: All right, I'm a kept man. A married ponce.

RUTH: I don't mind keeping you. Not in the least. But I cannot continually chase after you all over the countryside. I just cannot spare the time, I'm sorry. As it is, you've held my career back about ten years. You interrupt me at meetings with embarrassing phone calls . . .

NORMAN: To tell you I love you, that's all. Is that wrong?

RUTH: You're continually bursting into my office when I'm seeing clients . . .

NORMAN: My God, is it wrong to love your wife?

RUTH: You behave abominably when I bring business friends home to dinner . . .

NORMAN (snarling): What do they know about love?

RUTH: You have even been known to scrawl obscenities over my business papers.

NORMAN: All right, all right. I love you. I'm sorry.

RUTH: Yes, I love you, too, Norman, but please leave me alone.

NORMAN: All right. In future, I'll whisper it quietly from Brazil. Would that suit you?

RUTH: All I'm saying is, please try and see my point of view. Try and consider me.

NORMAN: I feel trapped. I'm a captive husband. That's what I am. (He sinks his head in his hands.)

Ruth changes the subject, inquiring sharply what Norman has been doing that so upset Sarah. Norman tells Ruth frankly he'd planned to go off with another woman this weekend. Norman has to stand up to tell her this, and his doing so makes Ruth nervous because she can't see him (she declares it's not vanity that keeps her from wearing her glasses, it's the fact that they press on her sinuses and make her sneeze—and besides, she can't see anything with them, anyway).

Norman confesses further that it was Ruth's younger sister Annie he'd planned to carry off for a weekend in East Grinstead. Ruth's immediate reaction is to burst out laughing, which angers Norman. Ruth is still seized with laughter when Annie enters with a tray.

NORMAN (to Ruth): Why won't you believe me? We were going away— together . . . Annie, you tell her, you tell her . . . You'd have lost me forever, do you know that?

ANNIE: Oh, Norman . . .

RUTH (drying her eyes): I'm sorry—it's just East Grinstead . . .
    She starts laughing again.

NORMAN: All right, go on, laugh. We're in love.

> *Norman strides across to Annie, seizes her and her tray rather awk-*
> *wardly and clasps her to him.*

Don't you care? We're in love.

> *Sarah comes in with a second tray. She stops in the doorway.*

ANNIE: (*struggling, muffled as she is clasped to Norman's bosom*): Norman, don't . . .

NORMAN: We're in love . . .

> *Ruth continues to laugh. Sarah, surveying the scene, looks on hor-*
> *rified. Curtain.*

Excerpt from ROUND AND ROUND THE GARDEN

Act II, Scene 1: Sunday, 11 a.m.

Alone with Ruth in the garden later the same morning, both sitting in folding chairs, Tom awkwardly seeks her advice. He decided to try bullying Annie the evening before, he tells Ruth, but now in the cold light of day he fears it may have been the wrong move.

RUTH: Well. Some women do respond awfully well to that sort of treatment. They enjoy tremendously being told they look a mess—and they actually thrill to the threat of physical violence. I've never met one that does, mind you, but they probably do exist. In books. By men. But then, there are probably some women who enjoy being thrown into canals. One just doesn't bump into them every day—not even in this family.

TOM: You reckon I might possibly have been on the wrong track?

RUTH: I'd have thought so.

TOM: Oh, well. For once he was wrong.

RUTH: Who was wrong?

TOM: Norman.

RUTH: Norman? Did Norman tell you to do that?

TOM: He suggested I do something of the sort.

RUTH: Insult her and threaten to beat her up?

TOM: Yes. He's generally right. About women, anyway. He's got a good instinct, has Norman. Has a way with women. I shouldn't really be saying this, should I?

RUTH (*after looking at Tom for a while incredulously*): Tom.

TOM: Um?

RUTH: At the risk of pouring bad advice on bad, I think perhaps I ought to point you in the right direction . . .

TOM: Do. Yes, do. Any advice . . .

RUTH: Firstly, there are fallacies in Norman's well-known universal theory of womanhood with which, as it happens as his wife, I am familiar. He claims that women can be divided into two groups—the ones you stroke and the ones you swipe. There has been some research done on this and it's been discovered quite recently that they are actually a little more complex.

TOM: Yes, yes. It follows . . .

RUTH: Good. They enjoy flattery no less than a man does. Though if you are flattering a woman it pays to be a little more subtle. You don't have to bother with men, they believe any compliment automatically . . .

TOM: Oh, come on. Hardly, hardly . . .

RUTH: Well, we won't argue that. All I'm saying is, Tom, you're an intelligent man, you're not unattractive . . .

TOM: Oh well, thank you very much.

RUTH: And you obviously feel a lot of things that you don't show—necessarily. Which is marvelous in a crisis but a bit disheartening in times of peace.

TOM: How do you mean?

RUTH: I think you have to give a little. Give, Tom, do you see?

TOM: Ah.

Talking to Tom is very frustrating to Ruth, but she perseveres.

RUTH (*studying him*): I think your brain works all right. I think what must happen is, it receives a message from outside—but once that message gets inside your head, it must be like an unfiled internal memo in a vast civil service department. It gets shunted from desk to desk with nobody willing to take responsibility for it. Let's try some simple reactions, shall we? I hate you, Tom. Do you hear? I hate you.

TOM: Um?

RUTH: Oh well, try again. I love you, Tom. I love you . . .

TOM (*laughing nervously*): I don't quite get this—a game, is it?

RUTH: No, Tom, it is not a game. It's an attempt to communicate.

TOM: Ah.

Ruth's mention of love has finally sunk in—perhaps too deeply. Tom notices how well Ruth looks without her glasses. Ruth fails to notice how much of an impression she's made on Tom, and she persists.

RUTH: I have a desire to put on my glasses and take off my clothes and dance naked on the grass for you, Tom. I'd put on my glasses not in order to improve the shape of my face, but in order to see your reaction, if any. And as I whirled faster and faster—the sun glinting on my lenses—flashing messages of passion and desire, I would hurl you to the ground, rip off your clothes and we would roll over and over making mad, torrid, steaming love together. How does that grab you, Tom?

TOM (*after a moment*): Good Lord. (*He laughs.*) Have to be careful where you rolled on this grass.

RUTH: Oh.

She sits exhausted, head in hands.

TOM (*watching her anxiously*): Ruth? Are you all right? Fairly hot this sun. Nearly overhead. Perhaps you ought to have a lie down . . .

RUTH: I'm sorry. I'm exhausted. I've done my best. I'm sorry.

TOM (*rising and flapping round her*): Can I get you an aspirin?

    Ruth lies back with her eyes closed. Tom moves about anxiously.
Look, I had no idea you felt like this. I honestly had no idea.

RUTH: Like what?

TOM: Like that. With me.

RUTH (*through gritted teeth*): I have never hidden my feelings towards you,
Tom.

TOM: I just thought of us as friends. Nothing more or less. I had no idea . . .

RUTH: What are you talking about, Tom?

TOM: I feel terrible about this. Absolutely terrible. This has complicated
things no end. I mean, it looks as if the ball's in my court rather. Yes, you've
bowled me a googly there.

RUTH: What the hell is a googly?

TOM: If a woman, unexpectedly, suddenly tells you she loves you, where do
you go from there?

RUTH: Are we talking theoretically?

TOM: If you like.

RUTH: Well, it's rather up to you then, isn't it? Firstly, you have to ask
yourself, do I love her?

TOM: Well, I haven't had much time to think. I mean, love's a bit strong.
Anyway, there's somebody else.

RUTH: What are you talking about?

TOM: Well, there's Norman. I've got to think of Norman's feelings.

RUTH: Norman? Don't be so damned ridiculous. As far as Norman's concerned, this is some passing romantic pipe-dream. So stop using Norman as
an excuse for your own inadequacy. If you don't grab quickly, somebody else
will sooner or later. Someone with a little more determination than Norman
ever had.

TOM: Well. I'm sorry. That's all I can say. I had no idea. Does Norman
know, do you think?

RUTH: What?

TOM: About me.

RUTH: Of course he knows.

TOM: Oh, that explains it. That's why he's been a bit odd towards me.
Slightly strained, you know. Oh well.

    Pause.
You're looking very nice, by the way. Lovely. Very nice indeed. Very well
turned out.

RUTH: I think you're a raving lunatic.

TOM (*modestly*): Well, I go a bit over the moon, sometimes. You don't
need to worry.

RUTH: I'm terrified to be left alone in the same county. . . .

TABLE MANNERS (*continued*)

ACT II

Scene 1: Sunday, 8 p.m.

Annie is putting knives and forks away in the sideboard, when Norman tiptoes in and tries to woo her in whispers, so that the others can't hear. Annie rejects him firmly, which leads Norman to believe that something has changed Annie from her usual "innocent and pure and fragile" self. Annie replies, "You do talk rubbish. No one can spend five years looking after that cantankerous woman upstairs and remain innocent and pure. And after lugging her in and out of bed single-handed, day in day out, I'm the last person in this world you'd call fragile. I mean, look at me, Norman, do I look even remotely fragile?"

Annie is tired of being used as a battle ground by Norman and Ruth. She picks up a vase and bangs it down to express her anger; then, when Tom enters, she stalks coldly out.

Tom tries rather ineffectually to threaten Norman with a punch in the nose if he continues his advances to Annie. Sarah interrupts the scene, and Tom gives up and exits.

Sarah tries to be polite to Norman in spite of her dislike of him. She begs him not to disrupt the evening; she has very sensitive nerves which won't stand much more strain.

NORMAN: Yes. Your trouble is you're over-emotional.
SARAH: Very possibly.
NORMAN: You're like me.
SARAH: Are you sure I am?
NORMAN: We feel. We've got nerve-endings sticking out of our heads. We've no cynicism or skepticism to act as shock absorbers. Everything that is, that happens, becomes part of us. We're probably a new race. Had you thought of that? Born too early.
SARAH: All I'm saying is, if there's too much noise, I get these headaches.
NORMAN: We're not understood. None of that lot out there understand us. They're all bogged down in their own little lives.
SARAH: Yes . . .
NORMAN: Self-obsessed. Annie, Tom, Ruth—even Reg. Don't worry, Sarah.
SARAH: What?
NORMAN: This evening's going to be all right.
SARAH: Is it?
NORMAN: We'll both go flat out together to make it a success.
SARAH: Oh, yes?
NORMAN: For God's sake, this is a family. We should care. If we don't care, brothers, sisters, husbands, wives . . . if we can't finally join hands, what hope is there for anybody? Make it a banquet, Sarah my love, make it a banquet.

SARAH: There's nothing in the larder.

NORMAN: Improvise. We can improvise . . . . .

Norman pulls silver and linen from the sideboard, as Sarah is beginning to believe they can really improvise a festive family party. Norman goes upstairs to find some sort of appropriate costume, as Sarah continues setting the table. Reg joins Sarah. He's not optimistic about the chances for a happy evening with this ill-assorted family group. He's worried about the state of his wife's nerves and tries to soothe her. Reg is assigned to collecting chairs. Annie comes in to tell them, "Well, I've scraped together what there is. It should just about feed us all. Opened every tin we had and poured them into a saucepan. Made a sort of gluey stew. Then there's the salad we can finish . . ."

Age has taken its toll of the dining room chairs, and now there aren't enough to seat them all. Reg goes into the living room to scavenge one from there. Annie notices that Sarah has put on the best place mats and is told that this evening is to be a special, happy family party. Reg comes back with a chair and goes for another as Ruth enters. Sarah goes out to see to the food. Alone with Annie, Ruth tells her of that morning's conversation with Tom in the garden.

RUTH: It was rather unfortunate. Believe it or not, I was attempting unsuccessfully to give him lessons on how to woo you. Tom being Tom assumed I was giving him lessons on how to woo me. I managed to load him all right but I pointed him in the wrong direction. It was silly of me to interfere, I'm sorry. Serves me right. I'll leave it to Sarah in future. I mean, I don't know, you may not even care for the man. You've never really said one way or the other. We've always assumed you and Tom, Tom and you. Presumably you wouldn't have him round here at all if you didn't. You do like him, don't you?

ANNIE: Yes. I'm very fond of him.

RUTH: I think he's in love with you. As far as one can fathom. It's just he's so—well, one could be nice and say deep. Except if you say someone's deep, it more or less implies there's something at the bottom. I'm not so sure with Tom.

ANNIE: Oh, you'd be surprised.

RUTH: All he needs is a shove. Somebody needs to do it. Anybody. Except Norman, that is. Whose sole advice to Tom was to throw punches at you.

ANNIE: Norman told him to do that?

RUTH: It's Norman's answer to female psychology. He's very subtle. Have you noticed? Well, you probably have. You nearly fell for it.

ANNIE: I'm sorry. I never for a minute intended to take Norman away from you or anything.

RUTH: Forget it. You couldn't possibly take Norman away from me. That assumes I own him in the first place. I've never done that. I always feel with Norman that I have him on loan from somewhere. Like one of his library books. I'll get a card one day informing me he's overdue and there's a fine to pay on him. Oh, I should have gone back to town this afternoon. I'm going to have to phone the office tomorrow and plead illness. Again. Of all the working days lost in this country over the year, half are due to strikes and illness and the other half to people chasing after Norman.

Reg comes in with a chair, followed by Sarah with a bottle of home-made wine, as Ruth goes out. Reg goes out to call the others in for dinner. Tom comes in and Sarah asks him to open the wine. Sarah goes out to get the salad, giving Tom a chance to tell Annie that he's confronted Norman and warned him off. Annie reminds Tom that they've all promised to make this a happy family evening, with no friction.

Sarah comes back with a tray of plates on which the leftover salad is evenly but very sparsely divided. Reg and Ruth drift in, and Sarah has great difficulty getting the family seated properly, shifting everyone around again and again. Norman comes in dressed in an old-fashioned, ill-fitting suit he found upstairs. He insists on sitting between Reg and Tom (the tallest of the group, who has drawn a low, baby-sized chair), so Sarah gives up trying to arrange any kind of appropriate seating.

Trying to lighten things up, Reg tells a joke, but it falls flat. Norman insists on admiring the salad. He tries to make small talk but is silenced by Ruth. They stack the salad plates. Annie goes out to get the stew, helped by Reg. Norman pours the wine. Ruth is nervous, spoiling for a fight. Sarah is icily calm.

Tom starts telling a joke about some missionaries in Africa, but soon no one is paying any attention to him because Annie and Reg have returned and are serving the stew from a saucepan into soup plates. Tom doggedly moves ahead with his story while the others comment on the peculiar individuality of the stew (which may contain canned pears along with other ingredients). There is barely enough to cover the bottoms of the plates all around.

Sarah comments that this dinner, whatever its shortcomings, at least represents a respite from her usual chores at home, taking care of husband and children. This remark triggers Ruth's attack on Sarah for using her children as an excuse both for self-pity and self-congratulation: "You're always making out they're some dreadful burden. Like a penance. You never seem to enjoy them . . . . . I simply cannot bear this blind pig-headed assumption that you're a totally unfulfilled second-class woman until you've had children." Sarah defends herself, and a family quarrel is on.

RUTH: By all means have your children. I'm not asking you to deny yourself, as you put it. All I'm saying is, for God's sake don't stand about looking martyred once you've had them. And don't look down your nose at the rest of us.

SARAH: I'm not prepared to get into another argument over this, Ruth. You don't know what you're talking about. You never will.

RUTH: She is so dogmatic. Reg, I feel sorry for you. How do you live with a woman like this who's so pig-headed? She just will not listen.

SARAH: Listen . . .

RUTH: She will not listen to a single word.

SARAH: Will you listen to me for a minute? If I feel sorry for anyone, it's Norman.

NORMAN: A blow for the rational man.

SARAH: Have you ever consulted him? Of course you haven't. You've just gone selfishly ahead with your own career . . .

RUTH: While you're busy manufacturing lots more little Reggies and Sarahs. What a wonderful contribution that is.

SARAH: Oh well, if we're going to get personal.

RUTH: If that isn't selfishness and conceit of the worst sort, I don't know what is.

    Banging down her spoon angrily.

And this is absolutely revolting, I don't know how anyone can eat it.

    Ruth pushes her bowl angrily from her. It knocks Reg's wine glass
    and spills the contents over his trousers.

REG (*jumping up angrily*): Oh, for crying out loud.

Sarah turns on Reg and warns him not to lose his temper over a little thing like stained trousers. Norman blames Ruth and her attitude for the whole thing, challenging her with "You've got as much feeling as a dried-up tea bag." Tom, thinking Norman is addressing Annie and calling her names, lands a sneak punch that topples Norman out of his chair.

Ruth stalks from the room angrily. Tom follows her in embarrassment when he learns that he was mistaken, that Norman wasn't calling Annie "an old tea bag." Annie follows Tom, leaving Sarah shaking in a state of near-shock and Norman furious with righteous indignation. Suddenly Norman and Sarah seem to have something in common: they are both misunderstood by the others. Sarah grabs Norman and clings to him as the curtain falls.

Scene 2: Monday, 8 a.m.

The next morning, Annie enters the dining room with a tray of breakfast materials, closely followed by Sarah, who plans an early start. Annie goes to the living room to tell Reg that breakfast is ready. Sarah fixes herself some breakfast. Norman comes in and prepares to do the same. Sarah confesses that she has "never been through such a shattering weekend in my life," and Norman attempts to comfort her, inquiring after her children, making much of Sarah's motherhood. Norman urges her to treat herself to a holiday, let Reg take care of the children for once.

SARAH: I wouldn't want to go on my own. What fun is it on your own?
    Pause.

NORMAN: I'll take you if you like.

SARAH: I beg your pardon?

NORMAN: I said I'll take you.

SARAH: On holiday?

NORMAN: If you'd like to go.

SARAH: You must think I was born yesterday.
NORMAN: I would.
SARAH: You really have got a nerve.

Norman suggests that Bournemoth might be just the place: "Think about it. It would be above board. I'd book us a nice hotel. Breakfast in bed—separate breakfast. Separate beds. Separate rooms. Can't you imagine it? . . . . ."

Sarah is just beginning to imagine it, when Reg enters in search of breakfast. Sarah reminds Reg that she wants to get home early to clean the house in time for the cleaning woman's visit the next day. Reg is preoccupied with hunger. Not liking what he sees on the table, he goes out to make some fresh toast. The instant they are alone Norman pats Sarah's hand.

SARAH: Were you just thinking about my health?
NORMAN: When?
SARAH: When you mentioned about this holiday? Did you want to take me away just for my health?
NORMAN: Well, that came into it. There might be any number of reasons. I'm easy. (*He smiles.*)
SARAH: So long as I know. (*She smiles.*)

Ruth enters, interrupting, telling Norman she's ready to leave. She will have her breakfast later. She says good morning to Sarah, who isn't speaking to her after last night's quarrel and doesn't reply. Ruth goes out.

Sarah's goodbye to Norman is wistful, friendly, inviting. Norman assures Sarah he could make her happy, then he goes out, following his wife Ruth into the living room for the scene excerpted immediately below.

Excerpt from LIVING TOGETHER

Act II, Scene 2

Norman joins his wife in the living room, from which Tom and Annie have just exited in the direction of breakfast. Norman compliments Ruth on her looks and tries to coax her to take the whole day off and stay home with him. Norman suggests that Ruth phone her office and pretend to be ill, as Norman has already done with the library where he works. Norman kisses her to show her he means business.

NORMAN: Do I make you happy at all?
RUTH: Well . . .
NORMAN: Say you're happy.
RUTH: Why? Is it important?
NORMAN: Yes. I want you to be happy. I want everyone to be happy. I want to make everyone happy. It's my mission in life . . .
RUTH: Yes all right, Norman. Well, let's not worry about other people too

much, just concentrate on making me happy, will you? The other people will
have to try to be happy without you, won't they?

NORMAN: But you are happy?

RUTH: Yes. I'm fairly happy.

NORMAN: And you might possibly—feel ill—if you drove very fast all the
way home and—somebody made you a cup of tea and—made the bed and—
ran you a bath and—put in the bath salts and—

RUTH: Yes. I might.

NORMAN: How are you feeling?

RUTH: Dreadful.

NORMAN (*with a great cry of joy*): Ha—ha!

   He grabs her and whirls her around . . . . .

TABLE MANNERS (*continued*)

Act II, Scene 2 (continued)

Meanwhile, in the dining room, Reg has returned, giving up trying to make
more toast. He is joined by Tom and Annie. Annie goes to heat up the tea
for Tom, who is busy apologizing to Sarah for disrupting her evening. Sarah
accepts Tom's apology and reminds him they expect him to "look after Annie
for us."

Annie comes back with the tea and then exits with Reg and Sarah to see
them off in the scene excerpted immediately below.

Excerpt from LIVING TOGETHER

Act II, Scene 2

In the living room, Sarah glances out the window and sees that Norman is
trying to push his car to get it started. Annie says her goodbyes and then exits
to return to the dining room to keep Tom company.

As he gathers up his suitcases, Reg notices how very cheerful Sarah seems
to be this morning. In her turn, Sarah wonders out loud what Bournemouth
might be like this time of year.

REG: What made you suddenly think of Bournemouth?

SARAH: It just occurred to me.

REG: You don't want to go to Bournemouth, do you?

SARAH: Not now . . .

REG: I thought we were going home.

SARAH: Not now. Sometime. I think I'd rather fancy it. Next year—perhaps.

REG: All right. I'll take you. If it'll make you happy.

SARAH: No, you don't need to bother. I could go on my own easily.

REG: On your own?

SARAH: Leave you in peace for a bit. Just for the weekend. Be rather nice
to get away. For a weekend . . .

Sarah goes out.

REG: Don't know why you want to go to Bournemouth. Why Bournemouth? Why not make it Brighton? Or Worthing? Or Reigate, for that matter?
Or East Grinst—

He pauses. An awful thought.

Oh, my God. Sarah! Wait for me, love. Sarah . . .

*Reg hurries out with his cases. Curtain. End of LIVING TO-
GETHER.*

TABLE MANNERS (*continued*)

Act II, Scene 2 (continued)

Meanwhile, in the dining room Tom has amused himself in Annie's absence by playing a kind of solitaire with the breakfast things. When Annie
comes back into the dining room, she apologizes to Tom for behaving badly
this weekend. She tells Tom how lonely she feels sometimes, overburdened
with the monotony of taking care of her mother and the house. Tom won't
take the hint. He goes only so far as telling Annie, "It's all right. We all get
lonely. If you're lonely again and I'm not here, why don't you give me a ring?"

Annie tells Tom she will have to sell this house eventually and move
away—perhaps far away.

TOM: Wouldn't see much of me.

ANNIE: No.

TOM: Well, if you do sell it, make sure you give me first refusal, won't you?
(*He gets up.*) Well, I'd better go and see to my horse.

ANNIE: Yes. Go and see to your horse.

*Annie turns the sideplate in front of her upside down on the table.
She bangs on it deliberately with a spoon. A regular sort of rhythm
which, although not fast, grows in intensity until the plate breaks.*

TOM (*watching her curiously*): What on earth are you doing?

ANNIE: Breaking things. Breaking things for breakfast.

TOM (*laughs awkwardly*): Careful of splinters.

Norman rushes in in coat and hat.

NORMAN: Disaster! We cannot start it.

TOM: Oh goodness. Want a hand?

NORMAN: Need one of these ex-boxers to give it a shove.

TOM: Right. My pleasure. Probably see you later, Annie.

ANNIE: Yes.

*Tom goes. Norman is about to follow. He notices Annie and the
plate.*

NORMAN: What are you doing? Don't tell me, you've finally run out of food.
I told you, you'd get round to eating the plates eventually. Now the nicest

way to eat a plate—is spread it with a thin layer of jam and then pour custard all over the—

> *Annie flies at Norman and clings onto him.*

ANNIE: Oh, Norman . . .

NORMAN: Only you want to make sure it's thick custard.

ANNIE (*muffled*): I want—

NORMAN: Eh?

ANNIE: I want . . .

NORMAN: I can't hear you. What?

ANNIE (*a wail*): I want to go to East Grinstead.

NORMAN (*soothing her*): All right. Fine. I'll take you. I'll take you.

ANNIE (*tearfully*): Will you?

NORMAN: Just say the word. Come now, don't cry. I'll make you happy. Don't worry. I'll make you happy.

> *He hugs her to him. Annie clings on. Norman smiles happily. Curtain. End of TABLE MANNERS.*

Excerpt from ROUND AND ROUND THE GARDEN

Act II, Scene 2: Monday, 9 a.m.

Tom has gotten Norman and Ruth's car started, and they are off, with Norman driving, at about the same time as Reg and Sarah make their departure. Alone with Annie in the garden, Tom finally suggests marriage, but Annie tells him he'll have to wait "at least until I've had a chance to—go away somewhere."

There is a loud crash in the distance as of automobiles colliding, and soon all the others return. Norman has run his car into Reg and Sarah's. No one is hurt but both vehicles are badly damaged.

Reg goes into the house to phone for help, while Tom goes to the cars to fetch back the luggage.

NORMAN: Definitely my mistake.

> *Silence. Norman stands regarding the three women who are now seated. They look at him.*

Well. Back again.

ANNIE: Oh, Norman . . .

RUTH: If I didn't know you better, I'd say you did all that deliberately.

NORMAN: Me? Why should I want to do that?

SARAH: Huh.

NORMAN: Give me one good reason why I'd do a thing like that?

RUTH: Offhand, I can think of three.

> *Pause.*

NORMAN: Ah. (*Brightening.*) Well, since we're all here, we ought to make the most of it, eh? What do you say?

Norman smiles round at the women in turn. Ruth gets up and without another word, goes.

(*After her.*) Ruth . . .

He turns to Annie but she too has risen and is going.

Annie . . .

He turns to Sarah. She likewise rises and leaves.

Sarah!

Norman is left alone, bewildered, then genuinely hurt and indignant.

(*Shouting after them.*) I only wanted to make you happy.

Curtain. End of ROUND AND ROUND THE GARDEN.

KNOCK KNOCK

A Comedy in Three Acts

BY JULES FEIFFER

Cast and credits appear on pages 344 and 368-369

JULES FEIFFER was born in New York City Jan. 26, 1929. He studied at the Art Students League and Pratt Institute and he served in the Army 1951–53. In 1956 he became contributing cartoonist for the Village Voice. *His reputation as a humorist and social commentator in drawings and words rose steadily and internationally. He has been a regular contributor to the London* Observer *and* Sunday Telegraph *and* Playboy *and* The New Republic. *His cartoons are syndicated in more than 100 newspapers around the world.*

Feiffer's broad range of activity includes the movies, where he won an Academy Award for the animated cartoon Munro *in 1961 and wrote the screen plays for* Carnal Knowledge *and* Little Murders. *He is the author of 11 books of cartoons, a memoir* The Great Comic Book Heros, *a book of drawings of the Chicago conspiracy trial* (Pictures at a Prosecution), *two novels* (Harry, the Rat With Women *and the new* Ackroyd), *as well as many stories, one of which,* Passionella, *was adapted by Jerry Bock and Sheldon Harnick into one act of the three-part musical* The Apple Tree, *a Best Play of 1966–67.*

The early 1960s saw productions of Feiffer's first works for the theater: the revue The Explainers *staged by Chicago's Second City troupe and the one-acter* Crawling Arnold *produced in Spoleto, Italy and in London. His first full-length play,* Little Murders, *was produced on Broadway in April 1967, lasted only 7 performances, but reappeared in January 1969 in an off-Broadway revival that ran for 400 performances and won Obie and Outer Circle Awards. In a Royal Shakespeare Company production, the London critics voted it the best foreign play of the season. Another Feiffer play,* God Bless, *was produced in London in 1968 and had its American premiere in a Yale University production. That same year his short dialogue* The Unexpurgated Memoirs of Bernard Mergendeiler *was produced off Broadway as part of the* Collision Course *program.*

In 1969, Feiffer's The White House Murder Case *was produced off Broadway for 119 performances and won its author his first Best Play citation, was a strong contender in the Critics Circle balloting for best American play and won the Outer Circle Award for best off-Broadway play. That same year Feiffer contributed to Kenneth Tynan's hit Broadway revue* Oh! Calcutta! *His second Best Play,* Knock Knock, *was produced off Broadway by Circle Repertory Company this season before moving uptown for a Broadway run.*

Time: The present

Place: A small house in the woods

ACT I

SYNOPSIS: The one room which serves for everything except a bedroom in this small, unpainted log house in the woods is *"cramped, containing the worldly goods of two lifetimes, Cohn's and Abe's. Books and periodicals litter every surface, including the floor."* The furnishings, or in many cases obstacles, include a couple of old TV sets and an old radio-phonograph console; a multipurpose oak table; a tattered screen covered with photos of the famous, dividing the room into dining and sitting areas; an iron range; shelves of supplies; a large steamer trunk next to the fireplace; an open ironing board; Cohn's violin and music stand and his old rocker; Abe's typewriter and shabby overstuffed chair. Curtained doorways lead to the bedrooms at right and a door with a small window leads to the outside up left, with scrofulous vegetation visible through two windows at center.

Cohn—*"overweight and 50"*—is at the stove cooking, while Abe—*"underweight and 50"*—is sitting in his chair, spoiling for an argument. Cohn holds up two fingers to prove a point about Abe's vision, and Abe claims he is holding up five fingers (though only two are extended), launching them into a wrangle.

COHN: I was holding up two . . . (*Holds up two fingers.*) . . . and you said I was holding up five! (*Holds up five fingers.*)
ABE: You *are* holding up five.
          Cohn quickly puts down his hand.

COHN: What's the use?

ABE: Cohn, I'll tell you something—you're rigid. I'm flexible.

COHN: Mindless.

ABE: You only believe in what's in front of your nose. That's not mindless?

COHN: I don't make things up.

ABE (*points to curtained doorway*): What's that?

COHN: Don't bother me.

> *Abe continues to point.*

It's my bedroom.

> *Goes back to his cooking.*

Pest!

ABE: I don't see any bedroom.

COHN: You know it's my bedroom!

ABE: I beg your pardon. All I see is a curtain.

> *Cohn goes and pulls back the curtain.*

Ah hah! A bedroom!

> *Abe rises, crosses to the doorway and pulls the curtain back into place.*

A curtain.

> *Pulls the curtain back and forth.*

A bedroom. A curtain. A bedroom. A curtain. A bedroom. Is it still a bedroom when you don't see it?

COHN: It's always a bedroom!

ABE: So for you it's always a bedroom and for me it's always five fingers.

In revenge, Cohn ladles himself all the stew and invites Abe to sup on what's left, an imaginary meal consisting of nothing. Cohn then offers Abe a plate of uncooked spaghetti. Finally Cohn takes pity on Abe (who knows nothing whatever about cooking) and dumps the spaghetti into a pot of water. But Abe has not softened his position at all. He reminds Cohn of the difference between winning an argument and being right (which also gave Abe problems with his ex-wife).

Cohn challenges Abe to find the moral in a parable about a handsome maid and an enchanted frog who turned into a prince in the night—"And that's the way she explained it to her parents when they walked in on the two of them." Abe accuses Cohn of tainting a fairy tale with cynicism; Cohn jibes at Abe about being gullible enough to believe the frog story, which logically must be either a deliberate lie or a hallucination, in either case distressing. Abe argues: "Because her mind can conjure with change—with ugliness turning into beauty—you call that hallucinating? And what *you* see—only beauty turning into ugliness—you call that reality? I beg your pardon, Cohn, you're living in a stacked deck. You give me a choice, I prefer frogs into princes over princes into frogs."

They continue wrangling. Cohn claims that they can't even be sure who they are, let alone who they may have been in past lives. Abe maintains that anything—anything—is possible.

COHN: And it's possible that if I rub this lamp a genie will come out?

ABE: All I'm saying is we don't know, do we?

    Cohn rubs the lamp.

COHN: Now we know.

ABE: I beg your pardon, we know about one lamp. We don't know about all lamps. Also we don't know that a genie *didn't* come out. We don't know that there isn't a genie in this room this very moment. And that he isn't saying "Master, I am the genie of the lamp and I have three wishes to grant you and anything you wish will come true." Maybe he's there and maybe we've been taught how not to see genies in our time. Or hear them. Or take advantage when they offer us three wishes. That's all I'm saying. That it could be us, not him.

COHN: Who?

ABE: The genie.

COHN: Abe, if I had three wishes you know what would be my first wish? That instead of you to talk to, to drive me crazy for another twenty years, I had somebody with a brain I could talk to! That's what I wish!

    A sudden explosion engulfs Abe. Light and music effect. The smoke clears, and sitting in his place is a bearded wise man in robes. He holds a clipboard and a pen.

WISEMAN: Name?!

COHN (*shaken*): Cohn.

WISEMAN (*checks the clipboard*): That's right—Cohn. Occupation?

COHN: Musician.

WISEMAN (*smiles*): Musician. Where are you a musician, Cohn?

COHN: At the present I am unemployed.

The genie continues questioning Cohn in this patronizing manner, reflecting on the level of Cohn's intelligence. Cohn is beginning to wonder what has happened to his friend Abe who has apparently disappeared into thin air. Cohn identifies Abe to the genie as a mutual-fund stockbroker, wealthy and retired. Wiseman runs Cohn around in argumentative circles, discussing whether it's Abe's chair he's sitting in, whether this house is Cohn's and Abe's or Wiseman's, even which of them is Cohn and which Wiseman. There is a knock on the door, but Wiseman ignores it.

WISEMAN: . . . . . I'm going to bed.

    Wiseman rises and disappears behind the curtained doorway leading into Cohn's bedroom.

—A terrible day. I want to leave a call for 7.

    Cohn crosses to the doorway.

If you don't have 7 in stock, make it 9.

    Another knock. Cohn turns to the door.

COHN: Who—who's there?

JOAN (*offstage*): Joan.

COHN: Joan who?

JOAN (*sings*): Joan know why there's no sun up in the sky, stormy weather.
    Cohn growls and grabs the poker from the fireplace.
COHN: Enough's enough! (*To Joan.*) Did you hear? Enough is enough!
WISEMAN: Will you kids quiet it down in there?
COHN (*whirls toward bedroom*): Wiseman!!
    Advances on bedroom with poker.
I warn you I'm armed!!

Cohn goes behind the curtain and soon there are the sounds of a scuffle,
during which Wiseman calmly enters, crosses, takes a carrot from the refrigerator and returns to the bedroom.
    Cohn exits from the bedroom with his clothes in tatters. He takes a shotgun
from the trunk and returns to the bedroom, where a shot is heard, soon followed by the reappearance of Cohn dragging Wiseman's body.
    The knocking at the door starts again, as Cohn stuffs Wiseman into the
trunk. Wiseman's feet stick out, but Cohn covers them with a rug. Outside,
Joan is talking to a pair of voices urging her to go inside. Joan knocks again.

JOAN: Knock knock.
COHN (*reloads shotgun*): Who's there?
JOAN: Joan.
COHN (*getting ready*): Joan who?
JOAN: Joan of Arc.
    *Cohn whips open the door and blasts away. A loud clang. Cohn
    recoils in horror, drops the gun and backs off. In walks a vision of
    loveliness wearing a suit of armor. The breastplate has a big black
    dent in it. Joan glares at Cohn, crosses herself and starts talking to
    her body?*
Are you all right?
FIRST VOICE: I'm all right—a little shaky.
SECOND VOICE: I'm upset but I'm all right.
COHN (*gasping*): Who are you?
FIRST VOICE: That's some greeting.
SECOND VOICE: You got any more surprises like that?
COHN: Who are they?
JOAN (*taps the dent in her armor*): My voices.

Cohn throws the shotgun into the bedroom out of sight and tries to confront
Joan rationally. Joan pities Cohn for his lack of understanding of the meaning
of life, its holiness for example, and she informs him that he is to come away
with her to see some Emperor for whom she is a messenger, explaining: "The
sky is missing! We must find the Emperor to give him the wonderful news that
the sky is missing and that mankind's path to heaven is at last unblocked and
unimpeded, and that God calls on His Highness, the Emperor, to build a
thousand space ships and put on them two of every kind and blast off for
heaven. Before the holocaust."

Cohn reviews this information, mulling it over. He suggests to Joan that it might be cruel to abandon the majority of the human race to some kind of holocaust. Joan replies: "I, too, thought it was cruel but my voices tell me that people will never know it's a holocaust. They'll adapt themselves. Many may even find happiness."

Cohn answers Joan with his own kind of logical statement: there is no Emperor, no God, no Joan of Arc, no Voices. Cohn will concede only the existence of Cohn. This girl is like his friend Abe—she makes up fairy tales: "Abe . . . . . *He'd* go with you to see the Emperor. Not that he'd believe. He wouldn't believe. But just in case . . . . . He has no convictions! *No convictions!* I much prefer someone crazy like you who thinks she's Joan of Arc."

Cohn has to stay here to take care of Abe, even though just at the moment he doesn't know where Abe is. Cohn tells Joan about the wishes, about wishing that Abe would stop bothering him, after which Abe vanished. Joan suggests that Cohn try wishing Abe back again. Cohn doesn't believe it would do any good. He is a realist, but his realism looks very like sadness and despair to Joan. Joan understands—she used to be like that herself, once. She also used to be Cinderella (she tells Cohn) before she became Joan of Arc.

JOAN: . . . . . After the ball, I thought the Prince loved me and I dreamed— well, no matter what I dreamed—he came looking for me, door to door, with a glass slipper. Like a salesman! . . . Can you imagine my shame? That he, my true love, would only know me by trying a shoe on my foot! I walked barefoot on rocks, soaked my feet in brine, anything to fail such a test. But it was never to be made. One door away from ours the Prince was suddenly called to war and I was left with a broken heart and a size nine foot. So I became a nun. A very poor nun. Night after night, visions of Our Lord came to see me bearing a glass slipper. So I fled the nunnery and travelled the land as a migrant fruit- picker. I married and begat five Portuguese children. My husband was a sot and beat me. When my children grew of age, they beat me. So I threw myself off a bridge, into the river. I landed on my feet and, to my considerable sur- prise, saw that I was standing on the water. I walked on the water for miles trying to decipher the meaning of my fate. Half-mad with the complexities of it all, I tried again to drown myself; this time by standing on my head and ducking it under the water. But the further under I ducked, the more the water level receded, until finally the river ran dry. I knew that it was a sign! I fell to my knees and prayed God for His forgiveness and that I should prove myself worthy of being His servant. And on the fortieth day my voices came and told me who I was and what I must do. And now, praise God, I am Joan and I am here!

COHN (*stares at her; after a long silence*): I really miss Abe.

Joan urges Cohn to wish Abe back, and finally Cohn does. There is an effect of lights and music, but apparently no Abe. To Cohn's horror, Joan looks into the trunk and tells him that Abe is here in the trunk—but dead.

Cohn thinks it is still Wiseman in the trunk. He looks at the body, sees it is Abe and falls over in a dead faint.

The shotgun comes flying out through the curtains and lands on the floor, as Joan works on Cohn until he regains his senses. Joan offers to bring Abe back to life, if Cohn will promise to come with her to see the Emperor. Cohn agrees to believe she is Joan of Arc and to follow her if she can do that.

Abe's legs twitch, then he gets up, punches a key on his typewriter and looks around for something to eat. Cohn embraces his friend and welcomes him back from the dead, though Abe isn't conscious of having taken any such journey. Abe notices Joan and wonders who she can be.

ABE: Intrigue is going on here. This is my house. I beg your pardon, Miss. It's not personal. The house is in my name. But can I ever invite guests? Who was my last guest? Fifteen years ago. I'll show you the guest book. Look— here's the guest book. Blank, see? Hundreds of pages—wait, here's the guest— no, it reminds me—not even a real guest—a Jehovah's Witness. Came in out of the blue. We had coffee, a pleasant chat about religion. Cohn, here, throws a fit. Facts are facts, Cohn. It's nothing personal, miss. Cohn and I don't entertain. He agreed and I agreed. When we entertain we differ. It ends up in a fight. So we agreed to live and let live and not entertain. I didn't make up the rule. Now he breaks it. Is this a way to run a household? Anarchy? I beg your pardon, Cohn, I thought we'd agreed—anarchy is for outside.

COHN (*to Joan*): Is that a mouth? I love that mouth! (*Beaming at him.*) Abe, not five minutes ago you know what you were?

ABE: What?

COHN: You weren't! That's what you were. You were *not!* You were dead! You were dead! You were dead! (*Smile slowly fades.*) You weren't dead. (*Turns to Joan.*) He wasn't dead.

JOAN: He was dead.

Cohn reverts to his rationalistic position and insists that Abe merely fainted. Abe claims he never fainted and there was no hiatus—he didn't see Joan come in because Cohn had smuggled her in long before, and he still wonders who she is with all that armor. Cohn wavers—perhaps Abe was dead—but Abe scoffs at the idea.

> *Joan crosses to Abe. He backs away. She takes his hand and stares into his eyes.*

JOAN: I am Joan of Arc.

ABE: It's possible. You could be anybody. I won't fight over it.

COHN: He doesn't believe you.

ABE: It doesn't matter what I believe, it's what you believe.

COHN: She believes you were dead!

ABE (*to Cohn*): That's her privilege.

JOAN: You *were* dead.

ABE (*to Joan*): As far as you were concerned. You never saw me, I never saw you. In that sense I was dead.

JOAN: I brought you back to life.

ABE: In a physical way? Well, who knows? It's been a long time. But I do feel a certain arousal—

Cohn tries to make Abe see that Joan is telling him the truth. Cohn's belief astonishes Abe. Cohn explains that he and Joan have a mission to go see the Emperor. Cohn prepares to depart. This astonishes Abe even more: "It's—it's a miracle! To change Cohn—to make him move an inch, not to mention he goes outside is nothing less than a miracle. Who are you?" Joan tells him again, and when Abe says "It's possible" this time he means it.

Abe refuses to go with them; he'll stay home, even if he risks starvation. Joan opens the door and Cohn goes out, remarking "It's not so bad!"

FIRST VOICE: Joan—

JOAN (*freezes*): Yes.

ABE: What's that?

SECOND VOICE: You can't leave.

ABE: Who said that?

JOAN: But my mission—

FIRST VOICE: Your mission is to take two of every kind.

ABE (*looks around*): Who said that?

JOAN: I know.

FIRST VOICE: That includes schleppes.

ABE (*still looking*): Who said that?

FIRST VOICE: You need one more.

> Abe walks around looking for the voices. Joan moves away from the door, back into the room. Cohn appears in the doorway.

COHN: Well?

> Nobody moves. Curtain.

ACT II

A month later, the room has been straightened up but seems even smaller now that a cot for Cohn has been set up in the corner near the bedrooms. Obviously, Joan has taken over Cohn's sleeping quarters.

Cohn is sitting at the oak table, praying. Abe comes out of his bedroom, punches a key at the typewriter and, obviously uncomfortable in Cohn's presence, goes back to his bedroom without a word.

Cohn addresses God, wondering how long he and Joan will have to wait for Abe. Joan comes in and tells Cohn how proud she is of his conversion, for which she gives credit to God Himself, though Cohn credits Joan and her tangible proof.

Cohn offers Joan a plate of delicious antipasto which he has prepared for her, along with a veal loaf. Cohn is looking forward to an end to hunger everywhere, when they all go to heaven.

Abe comes in and tries to avoid the others as he pours himself a cup of coffee and exits with the comment "Abe's my name. Invisibility's my game." Joan and Cohn are having great difficulty creating an opportunity to talk to Abe. Abe soon comes back and goes to the refrigerator for milk. This time Joan stands in his way, crowding him.

> *Abe retreats even further into the refrigerator, until more of him is in than out.*

JOAN: May I say something, Abe?

> *A long wait.*

I'd like to speak to you.

> *Joan does not move. Abe does not move. Finally he sneezes. Instinctively Joan puts a hand on his shoulder.*

Abe—

> *Abe reacts as if he's been shot. His head jerks up against the roof of the fridge with a resounding clunk. Stunned, his entire body, or what we see of it, sags. If we can see his head, it now lies on the the first shelf. Joan drags him out, closes the door and half carries him to his chair.*

ABE: I never felt better.

JOAN: Abe, why won't you speak to me? (*Abe doesn't answer.*) I've been here for weeks and we haven't exchanged a dozen words.

ABE: A dozen eggs?

JOAN: A dozen words.

ABE: What do you want to exchange a dozen words for? Are they dirty? How do I know you even bought them here?

JOAN: You confuse me, Abe.

ABE: Confusme. That's a Chinese philosopher.

JOAN: That's Confucius.

ABE: Confucius is a color.

JOAN: That's fuchsia.

ABE: Fuchsia is what you say when there's a bad smell.

JOAN: That's phew.

ABE: Phew is a body of water in Norway.

JOAN: That's fjord.

ABE: Fjord is a car.

JOAN: That's Ford.

ABE: Ford is the number after three.

JOAN: That's four.

ABE: What's four?

JOAN: A number!

ABE: Absolutely right. I was so cold I was number. (*Rises.*) It's a pleasure finally talking to you.

> *He staggers on the run into his room.*

Joan appeals to Cohn for help, reminding him that God depends on him. Cohn goes over to attend to the cooking, while Joan consults her Voices. She wants encouragement, but the Voices are very critical of her recent behavior: eating too much, never going out, apparently losing her faith. Joan protests that she'd rather try to move a mountain than try to move Abe, but the Voices insist that her trial is here.

As the Voices are criticizing Joan, a rock crashes through the window and lands at her feet. Cohn and Abe come running, fearful that it might be a bomb. Joan picks it up; it's only a rock with a message written on it: "You will meet new challenges which can be turned into opportunities. Beware of January, February and March."

There's a knock on the door—it's an aged, stooped messenger with another rock warning Joan to beware of April, May and June. Another rock falls out of the refrigerator warning of the other six months. "That's it as far as I am concerned," says Abe, exiting on the run to his bedroom.

Cohn thinks they should make a break for it. He could drug Abe's soup, and once they got him outside he would stick with them. Or they could try to fool Abe, pretending that they were off on some glamorous summons to a golden future.

JOAN: You actually want me to lie!

COHN: It's no bed of roses out there. In me, you're fortunate to find a man of imagination, but out there, you tell them you're Joan of Arc, I guarantee it's no laugh riot.

JOAN: They will believe me.

COHN: *What?* Two bricklayers? Two carpenters? Two truck drivers? Two taxi drivers? Two advertising agency executives? Joan. Joan, what am I going to do with you? It's a whirlpool you're walking into. Not even you can walk on whirlpools. It takes fiddling. A story here. A little piece of business there. You maneuver. You manipulate. Push comes to shove, a wheel, a deal, we got ourselves an army. Trust me.

JOAN: I trust God.

COHN: No argument. No argument. He gives policy, I carry it out. Where's the contradiction?

JOAN: I trust my Voices.

COHN: Voices always have to be right? Believe me, Joan, I've worked this out.

JOAN: Believe you? I can scarcely believe my senses!

COHN: Voices talk, they don't listen. They're Voices. What do they know? Two of every kind. Abe and me? Never! Not in a million years! Even superficially—Glutton. Gourmet. If they could see they'd know.

Joan has difficulty seeing how Cohn has faith and yet can still question. Cohn replies that he doesn't question. He believes in Joan, he believes in her cause, he believes that the sky is missing, but he observes: "You want to know who's two of the same kind, not Abe and me, *you* and me!" Cohn suggests that they leave together, travelling light without Abe. He opens the door to emphasize his point. *"A soldier in combat dress, wearing a gas mask and carrying an automatic rifle, stands in the doorway. Cohn, still staring at Joan, does not see him. Cohn holds his hand out, beckoning to the great outdoors. His hand brushes against the soldier's gas mask. Cohn turns, very slowly, to see what he's touching, sees and slams shut the door."*

Suddenly there are sirens and searchlights and a voice commanding them to send out the girl. Abe crawls into the room, keeping low. Joan offers to go out. Cohn won't let her go, but Abe shouts to the besiegers, "You can have her!" Outdoors, the police voices admit that they want the girl in order to kill her, to burn her at the stake. Cohn won't hear of this; he gets his shotgun while Abe leaps into the trunk, pulling the cover down over him, and Joan tries to unlock the door to go outside. Cohn fires a blast through the window. At once the outside forces wave a white flag through the broken glass.

> POLICE VOICE: Don't shoot. I'm coming in to parley.
>> *The door opens. Joan leaps back. In walks Wiseman, in robes as before, but with a gold star pinned to his chest. He crosses to the table, sits, puts on a green eyeshade and begins shuffling a deck of cards. Cohn backs off in horror.*
>
> WISEMAN: To make it interesting we play for the girl. (*Looks at them.*) Who plays?
>> *Stares at Cohn who backs into the trunk. Abe lifts the lid and peers out at Wiseman. He climbs out of the trunk as Cohn climbs in and pulls shut the lid. Abe crosses to Wiseman and sits.*
>
> ABE: We play for peace and quiet.
>
> WISEMAN: I win I get the girl, you win you get peace and quiet.
>> *He deals the cards. They study their hands. As each discards, he calls out his card.*

Fifty-five.

> ABE: Seventy-one.
> WISEMAN: King.
> ABE: Einstein.
> WISEMAN: Queen.
> ABE: Garbo.
> WISEMAN: Jack.
> ABE: Daniels.
> WISEMAN: One.
> ABE: Meatball.

They continue in this fashion until Abe shouts "Bunko!" after Wiseman's "Banco!" Abe has won the game—whatever it is—and Wiseman, growling, makes his exit. Joan admires Abe's skill at cards. Abe challenges Joan to another kind of game: Abe will give her the answer and she must guess the question.

ABE: Chicken teriyaki.

> *Joan looks at him nonplussed.*

You don't know? The question is: Who is the oldest living kamikaze pilot? Here's another: 9-W. (*Joan doesn't respond.*) Now you give me the question.

JOAN: I wasn't listening.

ABE: The answer is 9-W. What's the question?

JOAN: I don't know.

ABE: The question is: Do you spell your name with a "V," Herr Wagner? You ready for another?

> *Joan reaches out to him.*

JOAN: Abe—

> *Abe pulls away. A pause.*

ABE: All right, here's another. The answer is: From birth I was taught to believe, where there's a will there's a way. But nobody wrote me into his will, so I had to make my own way. Still, I had hope. Some day I would find the right situation. In the meantime I piled up money. For when I found the right situation. Also I married. A mistake, but bearable. It didn't take too much of either of our time. Whenever we exchanged understanding stares, I found out later it was a misunderstanding. So I wondered: Is this all? I couldn't accept yes for an answer, so I left my wife and I started looking. She sent Cohn to bring me back. Instead, he talked me into looking where he wanted to look instead of where I wanted. Finally, we split up. I went on looking. High and low, inside and out, until I got so depressed I couldn't hold my head up. So not being able to hold my head up I saw straight in front of me for the first time. And looking right in my face was the answer. In life you don't look too high and you don't look too low, you look straight down the middle. The answer lies in the middle. In the middle there's always room for hope and not too much room for disappointment. So the lesson of life is to settle. So I came to the woods. To settle. I found this house, I knocked on the door and Cohn opened it. He had settled the year before me. It's not terrific. But also it's not painful. I don't hurt anybody. It's an across-the-board settlement. I don't love it, I don't hate it. That's the answer, what's the question?

JOAN: The question is: if you want to believe in something, can't you come up with anything better than that?

> *They continue to stare at each other.*

ABE: I beg your pardon.

> *Rises, looks at typewriter, punches a key, looks at paper, pulls it out and crumples it.*

I'll put it this way. I'll start. How far I get is another question.

JOAN (*slowly realizing*): You'll go? You'll come?

ABE (*smiles*): I'll accompany.

> *Backs off into his doorway where he lingers for a moment, then disappears.*

JOAN: You'll accompany! You'll accompany! Cohn! (*Looks for him.*) Abe will accompany!

> *Cohn lifts the lid of the trunk an inch or two and peers out.*

Abe will accompany! He'll accompany!

Joan goes through the curtain to help Abe get ready for departure. Cohn doubts that Abe will really go with them and fears Abe will slow them down if he does. But despite Cohn's doubts, Abe finally comes out of the bedroom muffled up in winter clothes and carrying a huge suitcase. Joan follows him.

ABE: What a sensational day for a trip!

JOAN: Onward to the Emperor.

FIRST VOICE: Onward to the Emperor!

SECOND VOICE: Onward to the Emperor!

> *Abe and Joan move to the door. Joan throws open the door. Cohn disappears into the trunk and slams shut the lid. Abe and Joan stand watching.*

COHN (*raises the lid a half inch*): You know what you can do with those buttinsky, wiseacre voices of yours? I *wish* you never heard of them! You know what I *wish*—I *wish* you never heard of Joan of Arc!

> *Slams shut the lid. Light and music effect.*

JOAN (*puts on bandana cap, grabs broom, starts sweeping; turns to Abe*): Abe, what are you all bundled up for?

> *Starts unwrapping him.*

You're not going out in this weather. After dark? In the night air? Without your dinner? Cohn, can you imagine? Honestly! You two!

> *She continues to unbundle the stunned Abe. Cohn stands up in the trunk and looks on. Curtain.*

ACT III

Five months later, the house is in even more disarray, with Joan's tarnished armor hanging on the clothes tree. Abe's typewriter has been removed from the room. Abe enters and bumps into the armor—which is in the way—as Joan comes out from behind steaming pots on the kitchen counter. *"She wears an old fashioned flowered dress and a frilly apron. Her complexion is pale and waxen."*

Joan burns her hand on a pot cover and screams, as Cohn enters. She is having great difficulty cooking but resents Cohn's offers of help.

JOAN: The trick is to get the roast and the beans and the cauliflower and the potatoes all done at the same—I think it's ready.

> *Opens the oven door. Thick black smoke spurts out darking Joan's face and sending her into a fit of coughing. She grabs a dish towel and covers her face. Staggering around, she backs into the stove and knocks the pots off.*

COHN (*alarmed*): Careful!

> *Joan manages to escape the downpour of boiling water and vegetables. In her jumping about she sends the spice shelf flying. In her*

attempt to regain her balance she flails out and grabs hold of the bottom shelf of the dish cabinet. The shelf gives way and all the dishes descend on her. Joan disappears from view under a pile of debris. Cohn leans forward tensely. Abe leans back, contemptuous.

ABE: Typical.

Cohn starts toward the kitchen.

JOAN (*out of sight*): Everyone stay out of here.

Cohn keeps coming. He gets to the kitchen. Joan screams.

Stay out! I had a little accident. No one's hurt. (*Snarls to Cohn.*) Everything's under control.

COHN (*advances a step*): Let me—

JOAN (*screams*): *I don't need help!*

Rises from the floor, her hair in disarray, her blouse ripped, but with a blackened roast pig on a platter, an apple in its mouth. She marches proudly to the dining table and slams down the platter.

No vegetables tonight. (*Glares at Cohn.*) All right?

COHN: Fine.

JOAN (*glares at Abe*): All right?

ABE: I had vegetables yesterday.

Cohn carves the pig as Joan starts cleaning up the kitchen mess, making a racket. Abe complains about the food. In the kitchen, Joan cuts her finger. She makes light of it but faints, and Cohn carries her to the couch. Cohn rushes around collecting first aid equipment.

Abe accuses Joan of faking: "I only get fooled once. A stranger cries 'Heaven!' You take a look. It's only polite, what could it hurt? If it turns out heaven, so much the better. If not, what's to lose? . . . . ."

The bleeding has stopped, and while Joan is still unconscious Cohn offers to fix Abe something palatable like a nice omelet. Abe declines the offer; somehow he's lost interest in food.

Joan wakes. Cohn offers to clean up the kitchen for her, but she won't accept this as a gesture of friendship; she believes that both Abe and Cohn hate her. She is useless (she insists) and a bore. She offers to leave but has nowhere to go.

Now it's Cohn's turn to accuse Joan: "If you knew where to go you'd be out of here like a shot." Joan denies this; she wouldn't go even if she could. Cohn assures Joan he just wants her to be happy. He doesn't notice that when Joan gets up she faints once more. This time it's Abe who reaches her first, feels her pulse and declares "She's dead. You really did it this time."

Cohn works frantically to revive Joan, then becomes angry at her and throws her onto the couch when she doesn't respond. Cohn shouts at her lifeless body: "Faints! Faints! Faints! You could clock it on the hour. As if she has anything really wrong with her; don't tell me! Hysterical reaction. Getting even. Childish! Childish! What did I do? What was my crime! Why all this torture? If I'm a criminal, get it over, put me on trial!"

Immediately, Cohn gets his wish: Wiseman enters in judge's robes and holds mock court with Abe prosecuting Cohn on a charge of being a bore. On the subject of Joan of Arc, Cohn maintains she isn't really Joan and she isn't really dead. An argument develops between Abe and Cohn about who owns the house and who found it originally. Cohn declares, "I felt sorry for you. That's my weakness. Softness of heart. I took you in. I felt sorry for her, I took her in. So tell me, where's the gratitude? Him twenty years, her six months, I'm still waiting. I won't hold my breath. I'm guilty all right, guilty of being an innocent set loose in a world full of thieves. Cutthroats. Ingrates. That's my crime. Never again."

The "judge," Wiseman, declares Cohn "guilty of being innocent" and falls asleep. Abe and Cohn resume arguing, this time over which one was taken in by Joan. Cohn claims he was only trying to please a pretty girl by pretending to believe her saintly masquerade. Abe accuses Cohn of wishing her out of her miraculous identity and thereby killing her.

COHN: Killed her? Killed her? What are you saying? What a thing to say. I loved her! I believed in her! Killed her? Before her, I'd kill myself.
Rushes over to Joan and picks her up in his arms.
The one person in this world who gave me anything! You gave me joy, I gave you doubt! You gave me hope, I gave you despondency! You gave me a second chance! And what did I do with it? What I did with my whole life! I killed! I'm a killer! I should be killed. Locked up till I learn my lesson! I can't learn! I never learned! Never! Never! Never! Don't deny it, Abe, you're a saint! A saint! How could you put up with it?
Embraces Abe.
A man's best friend!
Whips out a pistol.
Kill me! Shoot me!
Abe shoots—and misses. He blows a big hole in the back wall. Sunlight pours in. Cohn and Abe squint in the sudden light. Joan is bathed in light. She sits up slowly, rubbing her eyes. Cohn does not see her.
(*To Abe.*) Idiot! Numbskull! Can't you do anything right?
Grabs pistol from Abe and turns it on himself.
JOAN: Cohn!
Joan's cry causes Cohn's hand to jerk at the moment of fire. A great hole is blown in the side wall. Sunlight pours in. Cohn whirls on Joan, drops the gun and falls to his knees beside her. He covers his face with his hands and weeps, Joan strokes his head.
COHN: A miracle! An angel from heaven!
JOAN: No, it's only me.
COHN: Say you forgive me.
JOAN: For what?
COHN (*angry*): *Never mind for what! Say it!* (*In self-reproach.*) I did it again! (*Starts banging his head.*) Dog! Vermin! Pestilence!

Joan tells Cohn she must leave. She asks Abe's forgiveness for causing him anger and disappointment, but Abe insists that she never penetrated his objectivity.

Cohn begs Joan to let him hear her Voices before she goes. In trying to detain her he struggles with her, and once more she collapses; Cohn has done it again. Cohn begs her to wake up and go tree, he'll detain her no more. Abe again believes that Joan is dead. Joan comes to her senses, rises out of Cohn's arms and floats above his head. She is enjoying a happy anticipation of heaven—she can get there easily, without a rocket ship because, she says, she is now dead. Cohn denies that Joan is dead, but Abe insists that she is and orders Cohn to stop arguing and show a little respect.

In the meantime, Joan is summing up her earthly experience, thinking out loud: "I am going far but I have come far. I have been several people, seen terrible things, had my heart broken and then spliced, have been shot at . . . . . have escaped, have been trapped, have escaped, have found God and lost him, found hope, lost it, grown weak, grown ill, passed out, recovered, walked on water, performed miracles, died and floated up to the ceiling. And out of these myriad experiences I have learned all that I know and this is the sum of it: I have learned that however prosperous you should get out of the house, however satisfied you should be dissatisfied, however disillusioned you need hope, however hopeless you need patience, however impatient you need dignity, however dignified you need to relax, however relaxed you need rage, however enraged you need love, however loved you need a sense of proportion, however dispassionate you need passion, however possessive you need friends, however many friends you need privacy, however private you need to eat, however well-fed you need books, however well-read you need trials, however tried you need truth and with truth goes trust and with trust goes certainty and with certainty goes calm and with calm goes cool and with cool goes collected but not so cool and collected you can't be hot and bothered . . . . ."

Joan continues in this vein until she comes to her last will and testament, in which she bequeaths Abe her armor "in the hope of inspiring strong resolve and the courage to find a conviction" and her Voices to Cohn "because he needs all the help he can get."

The Voices begin quarreling over whether to go or stay. Wiseman wakes up, bangs his gavel, grabs Joan's armor and runs off with it through the hole in the wall, with Abe in hot pursuit. Cohn becomes involved in the Voices' quarrel, and they push him around, stumbling. Abe comes back dressed in Joan's armor and brandishing her sword.

ABE: Onward!
    Sword high, he stalks out of sight.
COHN (*runs to hole in wall*): Abe! It's pouring! You'll catch your death of cold! Viral pneumonia! A stroke!
    Suddenly stumbles toward hole.
SECOND VOICE: Quit shoving!

Cohn, struggling to stay erect, loses the struggle and tumbles backward through the hole, disappearing from view.

FIRST VOICE: Now you did it!

SECOND VOICE: Who did it?"

FIRST VOICE: I didn't.

SECOND VOICE: No. You're the innocent one around here.

Cohn rises into view, blinking in the strong sunlight.

COHN: It's not as bad as it looks. (*Holds out a hand.*) It's only a drizzle.

FIRST VOICE: It's getting better.

SECOND VOICE: By whose evidence?

FIRST VOICE: The evidence of my senses.

SECOND VOICE: Your senses should have their head examined.

COHN: Shut up. Follow me.

Cohn walks off. Lights fade on Joan frozen in space, apparently heaven-bound. Curtain.

STREAMERS

A Play in Two Acts

BY DAVID RABE

Cast and credits appear on pages 379-380

DAVID RABE was born March 10, 1940 in Dubuque, Iowa, the son of a school teacher. He was educated at Loras Academy and Loras College, both in Dubuque, graduating B.A. in 1962 and gong east to get his M.A. in theater at Villanova. He was drafted and served in the Army from January 1965 to January 1967 as a Specialist 4th Class, the final 11 months in Vietnam.

Rabe describes his pre-playwriting career as "formerly egg carrier, bellhop, parking lot attendant, teacher" and meanwhile he studied writing with Ray-mond Roseliep, Dick Duprey and George Herman and in 1967 and 1968 at Villanova (under a program partly supported by the Rockefeller Foundation) he wrote the first drafts of two plays about the Vietnam War: The Basic Train-ing of Pavlo Hummel *and* Sticks and Bones. *He went from Villanova to the New Haven* Register, *where he won an Associated Press award for feature writing; then, in 1971, he went back to Villanova to teach in the graduate theater department.*

Joseph Papp gave Rabe his professional stage debut with the New York Shakespeare Festival Public Theater production of Pavlo Hummel *May 20, 1971 for 363 performances, winning its author a citation as "most promising playwright" in* Variety's *poll of drama critics and in the Drama Desk voting, plus an Obie Award and the Hull-Warriner Award voted by the Dramatists Guild Council as the season's best play on a controversial subject. While* Pavlo Hummel *was still running, on November 7, 1971, the Public Theater produced Rabe's* Sticks and Bones *(which had been staged at Villanova in 1969) for 121 performances, then moved it to Broadway for another 245 performances, winning the Tony Award for best play, a special Critics Circle citation as the close runner-up to* That Championship Season *in their annual voting and our citation as a Best Play of its season.*

The New York Shakespeare Festival has produced all of Rabe's subsequent work, which has included The Orphan *(an adaptation of the Oresteia as an American drama) March 30, 1973 for 53 performances,* Boom Boom Room *at Lincoln Center November 8, 1973 for 37 performances,* Burning *as a work in progress April 13, 1974,* In the Boom Boom Room *(a revision) November 20, 1974 for 31 performances and now* Streamers, *Rabe's second Best Play and first outright winner of the Critics Award for best American play.*

Rabe is now a member of the Dramatists Guild Council. He is married and lives in Pennsylvania where he teaches and serves as playwright in residence at Villanova.

The following synopsis of Streamers *was prepared by Jeff Sweet.*

Time: 1965

Place: An army barracks in Virginia

ACT I

SYNOPSIS: *"It is evening in an army barracks cadre room. There are three bunks. Wall lockers surround the area."* The lights rise on two young *"slightly built"* enlistees—Richie and Martin. Martin was attempting suicide by cutting his wrist when Richie happened on him and stopped him. With a towel wrapped around the wrist, Martin explains that he hates the army so much he had the impulse to get out any way he can. Richie hates the army too. Neither were drafted; both enlisted.

They are interrupted by the appearance of Carlyle, *"a large black man"* who is looking for the black man he heard is bunking in this room. Richie tells him the person he is looking for is Roger, that Roger isn't here, and that he should check back later. Martin makes a move to display his wrist to Carlyle. "Martin, Jesus!" cries Richie. Carlyle doesn't understand; confused and angry at his confusion, he starts toward them. Billy, another young white enlistee, enters at this point, asking, "Hey, what's goin' on?" "Nothin', man. Not a thing," says Carlyle, purposely knocking over a chair as he leaves.

Martin tells Billy of his cut wrist. Billy asks if there's anything he can do to help, but Richie tells Billy he has everything under control and hustles out the door with Martin. Billy follows them out.

A moment later, Roger, *"a tall, well-built black in khakis,"* enters and starts doing pushups. He finishes and moves to his bunk as Billy returns. Roger tells him he is itching to get "outa this goddamn typin' terrors outfit and into some kinda real army; or else out and free." They discuss their alcoholic sergeant, Rooney, who has just gotten orders to Vietnam where he will be a demolition expert.

Billy tells Roger that as a kid during the Korean War, he used to discuss with his friends whether, given the choice, he'd "rather fight in a war where it was freezin' cold or one where there was awful snakes." Now it seems likely that he and Roger will be following their sergeant to a war neither was particularly aware of before getting into the army. Billy finds it hard to conceive of the idea of other people shooting at him, trying to kill him. Roger asks him which he finally decided he preferred—the snakes or the snow, saying, " 'Cause it looks like it is going to be the snakes." Billy says the snow, and Roger jokes that maybe he should tell the army this. "Maybe they get one goin' special just for you up in Alaska. You can go to the Klondike. Fightin' some snowmen."

Richie returns and undresses at his locker, in a good mood as he believes his talk with Martin has done the would-be suicide some good. Richie playfully suggests to Billy that they go to the movies together, promising, "I'll get myself very clean." The homosexual overtones in Richie's banter obviously irritate Billy. Cheerfully, Richie heads for the showers.

Roger and Billy speculate on whether Richie is really gay. Billy is certain he is. Roger says he thinks he is just joking around, or why would he have a pin-up of a naked woman in his locker? The conversation ends with Billy stepping out to get buckets, mops and wax so that he and Roger can clean the floor.

Alone, Roger looks at the pin-up in Richie's locker. Carlyle returns and, though they have never met before, the two black men instantly fall into street jive. Carlyle asks if that locker with a picture of a white woman is Roger's. No, Roger replies, "This here the locker of a faggot." " 'Course it is; I see that; any damn body know that," says Carlyle, giving Roger a drink from his bottle. Carlyle complains that from what he has been able to see, he and Roger are two of only a handful of blacks on the base.

ROGER: It ain't so bad around here. We do all right.

CARLYLE: How about the white guys? They give you any sweat? What's the situation? No jive. I like to know what is goin' on within the situation before that situation get a chance to be closin' in on me.

ROGER: Man, I'm tellin' you, it ain't bad. They're just pale, most of 'em, you know. They can't help it; how they gonna help it? Some of 'em got a little bit a soul, couple real good boys around this way. Get 'em little bit of coppertone, they be straight, man.

CARLYLE: How about the NCO's? We got any brother NCO watchin' out for us or they all white, like I goddam well KNOW all the officers are. Fuckin' officers always white, man; fuckin' snow cones and bars everywhere you look.

ROGER: First sergeant's a black man.

CARLYLE: All right; good news. Hey, hey, you wanna go over the club with me, or maybe downtown? I got wheels. Let's be free. Let's be free.

Roger says he wants to stick around and clean the room up some, but maybe some other time. Carlyle continues to list his grievances. He has recently come back from a leave and is aching at having had to return from the freedom of the streets to the army. Just before the leave he had finished basic training, which he loathed. If life on this base is going to be anything like basic, he warns, "I'm gonna be bustin' some head . . . . . 'cause I ain't gonna be able to endure it, man, not that kinda crap, understand?" The idea of going to Vietnam doesn't appeal to him either. "It ain't our war, brother," he insists, yet everybody seems to be ready to follow orders to go and be blown up there. For the moment he intends to go out and get away from the thought. Roger again declines to join him, and Carlyle heads for the door.

> *And as he is moving he is extending his right hand out palm up and when he speaks now, it is an imperative, demanding from Roger the appropriate response.*

CARLYLE: Baby! Gimme! Gimme!

ROGER (*nearly leaping to reach the extended hand and slap the up-turned palm*): Go'wan home! Go'wan home.

CARLYLE: You gonna hear from me. (*Exits.*)

ROGER: I can . . . and do . . . believe . . . that.

Richie, who has entered in time to see Carlyle leave, begins to dress as Billy returns with the gear for cleaning the floor. As Billy and Roger begin the chores, Richie again needles Billy by making gay-tinged jokes.

ROGER: They got to put me in with the weirdo's—why is that, huh? How come the army hate me, do this shit to me—*know* what to do. (*Whimsical until here, then suddenly loud, angered, violent.*) Now you guys put socks in your mouths, right now—get shut up—or I am gonna beat you to death with each other. Roger got work to do. To be doin' it!

RICHIE: Roger, I think you're so innocent, sometimes. Honestly, being queer isn't such a terrible thing. Is it, Billy?

BILLY: Go fuck yourself.

RICHIE: Well, I can give it a try. Can I think of you as I do?

BILLY: You sonofabitch! You mealy-mouthed little son of a bitch! That's it! IT! Now I am gonna level with you, are you gonna listen? You gonna hear what I say, Rich; and not what you think I'm sayin'?

> *Richie turns away, tisking, a flip of his head.*

NO! Don't get cute; don't turn away cute. I wanna say somethin' straight out to you and I want you to hear it!

RICHIE: I'm all ears, goddamit! For what, however, I do not know, except some boring evasion.

BILLY: At least wait the hell till you hear me!

RICHIE (*in irritation*): Okay, okay! What?

BILLY: Now this is level, Rich; this is straight talk. (*He is quiet, intense, seeking the exactly appropriate words of explanation.*) No b.s. No tricks. What you do on the side, that's your business and I don't care about it. But if you don't cut the cute shit with me, I'm gonna turn you off. Completely.

You ain't gonna get a good mornin' outa me, you understand, because it's gettin' bad around here. I mean, I know how you think—how you keep lookin' out and seein' yourself and that's what I'm tryin' to tell you, because that's all that's happenin', Rich. That's all there is to it when you look out at me and think there's some kind of approval or whatever you see in my eyes— you're just seein' yourself. And I'm talkin' the simple quiet truth to you, Rich, I swear I am.

Billy goes back to mopping as, in a somewhat apologetic tone, Richie explains he has been privileged all of his life, used to having whatever he wanted. Roger asks Richie if he has really done "that fag stuff." Richie claims that he has, and knows all about it, but Roger doubts that Richie is a "screamin' goddam faggot" like the ones Roger knew back in his old city neighborhood.

ROGER: . . . . . Oh, oh, that ole neighborhood put me into all kindsa crap . . . . . like this once, I'm swingin' on up the street after school, and outa this phone booth comes this man with a goddamed knife stickin' outa his gut. So he sees me and starts tryin' to pull his motherfuckin' coat out over the handle, like he's worried about how he looks, man. "I didn't know this was gonna happen," he says. And then he falls over. He was just all of a sudden dead, man; just all of a sudden dead. You ever seen anything like that, Billy? Any crap like that?
BILLY: You really seen that?
ROGER: Richie's a big city boy.
RICHIE: Oh no; never anything like that.
ROGER: "Momma, help me," I am screamin'. "Jesus, momma help me." Little fella, he don't know how to act, he sees somethin' like that.

They begin to wonder how long it will take before they are sent to Vietnam, or "Disneyland," as the men on base ironically refer to it. Roger isn't clear about his attitude towards the war or America. He feels patriotic twinges when he hears the national anthem at a ball game, but he also recognizes the pain being black in America has put him through. Billy tells Roger he thinks the intervention in Vietnam is necessary, comparing Ho Chi Minh to Hitler and citing the domino theory.

Richie chips in horror stories about Viet Cong tortures—about stakes in the ground covered with elephant dung which, if stepped on, cause horribly infected wounds, and about caves booby-trapped with snakes tied to the ceiling which, in thier fury, bite the faces of American troops pursuing the Cong.

Roger is skeptical of Richie's stories, but Billy reacts viscerally. He insists that if the Cong really do that, then they deserve to be wiped out, only he'd just as soon not be one of the people sent over to do the job. He leaves the room.

Richie tells Roger he is surprised that Roger and Billy take the Army as seriously as they do. Roger says that it's a fact of their existence that they are in the Army, so it's only sensible they take it seriously. Richie tells Roger he envies the closeness of his and Billy's friendship. "I never had that kind of friend ever," Richie says. "Not even when I was little."

ROGER (*after a slight pause*): You ain't really into that stuff, are you, Richie? (*It is a question that is a statement.*)

RICHIE: What is that, Roger?

ROGER: That fag stuff, man. You know. You ain't really into it, are you? You maybe messed in it a little is all, am I right?

RICHIE: I'm very weak, Roger. And by that I simply mean that if I have an impulse to do something, I don't know how to deny myself. If I feel like doing something, I just do it. I . . . will . . . admit to sometimes wishin' I . . . was a little more like you . . . and Billy, even, but not to any severe extent. It's like you're across the room, you see; and it's just a distance I don't . . . finally . . . see the point in walking.

ROGER: But that's such a bad scene, Rich. You don't want that. Nobody wants that. Nobody wants to be a punk. Not nobody. You wanna know what I think it is? You just got in with the wrong bunch? Am I right? You just got in with a bad bunch, that can happen. And that's what I think happened to you. I bet you never had a chance to really run with the boys before. I mean, regular normal guys like Billy and me. How'd you come in the army, huh, Richie? You get drafted?

RICHIE: No.

ROGER: That's my point, see.

RICHIE: I just went to a party about four years ago. I was very young and I went to a party with this friend who was a little older and it was going on— at the party—so I did it.

ROGER: And then you come in the army to get away from it, right? Huh?

RICHIE: I don't know.

ROGER: Sure.

RICHIE: I don't know, Roger.

ROGER: Sure; sure; and now you're gettin' a chance to run with the boys for a little; you'll get yourself straightened around. I know it for a fact; I know that thing.

> *From off there is the sudden loud bellowing sound of Sgt. Rooney's voice.*

ROONEY: THERE AIN'T BEEN NO SOLDIERS IN THIS CAMP BUT ME. I BEEN THE ONLY ONE—I BEEN THE ONLY ME!

> *And Billy comes dashing into the room.*

Sgt. Rooney staggers into the room with an old friend named Cokes. They are both very drunk. As they pass around their bottle, Rooney tells them that Sgt. Cokes has recently returned from Vietnam. The proof is in his boots— Cokes has canvas-topped boots designed for jungle wear. A man "don't have no boots like that unless he been to the war!" says Rooney. "Which is where I'm goin', and all you slap-happy motherfuckers, too."

Rooney and Cokes reminisce about the old days when they were in the 101st Airborne Division together. They whoop and holler around the barracks. They mime jumping out of a plane, shouting "Geronimo!" and then pretending to descend in parachutes. "Beautiful feeling . . ." says Rooney.

COKES: Remember that one guy. O'Flannigan—he was this one guy—O'Flannigan—we was testing new chutes where you could just pull a lever by your ribs here when you hit the ground . . . see . . . and the chute would come off you, because it was just after a whole bunch a guys had been dragged to death in an unexpected and terrible wind at Fort Bragg. So they wanted you to be able to release the chute when you hit if there was a bad wind when you hit. So O'Flannigan was this kinda joker who had the goddam sense of humor of a clown and nerves I tell you of steel and he says he's gonna release the lever mid-air, then reach up, grab the lines, and float on down, hanging. So I seen him pull the lever at 500 feet and he reaches up to two fistfuls of air, the chute's twenty feet above him and he went into the ground like a knife.
BILLY: Geezus . . .
ROONEY: Didn't get to sing the song, I bet.
COKES: No way.
RICHIE: What song?
COKES: . . . . . He went right by me. We met eyes sort of. He was lookin' real puzzled. He looks at me. Then he looks up in the air at the chute, then down at the ground.
ROONEY: Did he sing it?
COKES: He didn't sing it. He started goin' like this.
> And Cokes begins to reach upward with his hands and try to step upward with his legs. He is like a man trying to climb rapidly and frantically a ladder that isn't there. It is a pantomime of the falling man.

Like he was gonna climb right up the air.

More grisly reminiscences follow. Rooney describes how Cokes blew up "47 chinky Chinese gooks" in Korea and won the silver star. Then Cokes describes the time he chucked a grenade into a spider hole, "which is a hole in the ground with a lid over it," and sat on the lid as the enemy sniper trapped inside tried in vain to get out before the explosion. "Bouncin' and yellin' under the lid. I could hear him. Feel him. I just sat there."

ROONEY: He was probably singin' it.
COKES: I think so.
ROONEY: You think we should let 'em hear it?
BILLY: We're good boys. We're good ole boys.
COKES: I don't care who hears it, I just wanna be singin' it.
ROONEY: You listen up; you just be listenin' up; 'cause if you hear it right you can maybe stop bein' shitsacks. This is what a man sings, he's goin' down through the air, his chute don't open.

COKES AND ROONEY (*singing; after a little roughness getting going, they sing it pretty well; to the tune of "Beautiful Dreamer"*):
>Beautiful streamer
>Open for me.
>The sky is above me,
>But no canopy.

BILLY (*murmuring*): I don't believe it.

COKES AND ROONEY (*sing*):
>Counted ten thousand
>Pulled on the cord.
>My chute didn't open,
>I shouted "Dear Lord."
>
>Beautiful streamer
>This looks like the end.
>The earth is below me,
>My body won't bend.
>
>Just like a mother
>Watching o'er me.
>Beautiful streamer,
>Ohhhh, open for me.

ROGER: Unfuckin' believable.

ROONEY: Ain't that a beauty.
>*And Sgt. Cokes topples over sideways, falling flat.*

The others rush to his aid. Cokes regains consciousness, and during the ensuing conversation it comes out that he was sent back from Vietnam because the Army suspects his fainting spells are symptoms of leukemia and they want to run tests. Cokes insists that his falling down has nothing to do with leukemia. Chronic drunkenness yes, leukemia no. Rooney assures him that soon the two of them will be doing demolition duty together in Nam. The two sergeants decide it's light-out time and stagger out of the room, flicking the switch as they go.

Their visit leaves Roger, Richie and Billy sad. They get into their beds, say goodnight, and it is quiet for a moment. Then Billy tells Roger about Frankie, a tough friend he used to have. He and Frankie used to go to bars and allow gays to buy them drinks. When it was time to leave the bar and the gays would invite them back to their places, Billy and Frankie would turn on them and "call 'em fag and queer and jazz like that and tell 'em to fuck off." One night, however, Frankie decided to actually be picked up. Before long, as Billy tells it, Frankie had dropped his girlfriend and was "hooked . . . . . my boy Frankie, my main man, and he was a fag." Roger tells Richie that he should think about Billy's story.

Carlyle, drunk, enters crawling on his hands and knees, imitating the sounds of gunfire and artillery. Roger, Richie and Billy rise and watch him. Carlyle explains he's only putting to use a skill he learned in basic training. He returns to the subject of Vietnam. He is certain that because they have special jobs, the other three will not be sent over. "You got jobs they probably ain't ever gonna ship you out, you got so important jobs. I got no job. They don't even wanna give me a job. I know it. They are gonna kill me. They are gonna send me over there to get killed, goddamit. *Whatsamatter with all you people?"*

Roger tells him that the truth is they will probably all end up in the war, and that the best thing Carlyle could do now would be to cool it and go to sleep. Carlyle asks if he can sleep on the floor, and Roger says OK, giving him a blanket to sleep on. Billy contributes a blanket, too. As Carlyle begins to slip into sleep, he mumbles, "How come I gotta be there?" Roger gets into bed, but Richie goes over to cover Carlyle with a blanket.

> *Richie is straightening up now, from having covered Carlyle.*
> BILLY: Richie . . . Richie, how come you gotta keep doin' that stuff? (*Silence.*) How come?
> > *Silence. Richie does not move, though he had started to just before Billy first spoke; it is as if Billy's voice froze him.*
> ROGER: He dunno, man. Do you? You dunno, do you, Richie?
> RICHIE: No.

Recalling in his sleep the happy days of his leave, Carlyle murmurs, "It . . . was . . . so pretty . . . !" Richie says, "No," again and the lights fade as taps is played. *Curtain.*

ACT II

Scene 1

In late afternoon, Roger and Billy are in khakis. Billy tells Roger that in his home town in Wisconsin he got a reputation for being "a busybody," and for seeing "complications" in the life around him that others apparently couldn't see. In the midst of all that normalcy, he was aware that people could become unglued. He recalls the instance of a neighbor who one day attacked cars on the street with a pair of axes. "An' we all knew why he did it, sorta." For awhile, Billy confides, he wanted to be a priest, so that he could be in a position to help people in that kind of pain. Roger replies that nobody is a stranger to that kind of pain.

Changing the subject, Roger tells Billy he should put in more time at basketball. Billy says he'd be more interested in spending off-duty hours in a job helping out at a local bar. Roger joshes him into owning up that his interest in working at the bar is rooted in a good-looking waitress-dancer there. Billy has a very romantic turn of mind, and he talks about getting to know her and having wonderful heart-to-heart conversations with her. If sex were to happen, fine. If not, OK, it would still be good.

The two remember how they became friends—Roger simply approached and started talking. Roger tells him that he tried talking to a number of others, but that Billy was the first to respond in a friendly way. The first white, that is.

Roger and Billy have tentatively planned to go out for some fun that night. Roger suggests they do some pushups and take showers first, and then they'll be eager to roll. Billy is feeling a bit under the weather, but, with Roger's urging, is soon doing pushups next to him. Richie enters while they are at it. He tells them they're not doing it right. "You're so far apart and you're both humping at the same time. And all that counting. It's so unromantic." As Richie stands at his locker about to apply some cologne, Billy testily picks up the basketball and knocks the bottle out of his hand. Billy and Roger leave the room to hit the showers.

For the hell of it, Richie takes a shot at doing pushups. He changes his mind halfway through the first one. Carlyle enters, looking for Roger. "I am not his keeper, you know," Richie tells Carlyle. Carlyle realizes he made a fool of himself in front of everyone the other night, crawling on the floor, etc., and he wants to redeem himself and show them all "the real Carlyle."

Richie informs Carlyle that someone told the authorities about Martin's attempted suicide, and they are sending Martin home. Carlyle assures Richie that it wasn't he who told. Richie begins to warm to Carlyle's presence.

RICHIE (*Rising, walking toward Carlyle and the door, cigarette pack in hand*): You want a cigarette? Or don't you smoke? Or do you have to go right away? (*Closing the door.*) There's a chill sometimes coming down the hall. I don't know from where. (*Walking back to the bed.*) And I think I've got the start of a little cold. Did you want the cigarette?

Silence, and then Carlyle starts toward Richie.

CARLYLE: You know what I bet. I been lookin' at you real close. It just a way I got about me. And I bet if I was to hang my boy out in front of you, my big boy, man, you'd start wantin' to touch him. Be beggin' and talkin' sweet to ole Carlyle. Am I right or wrong? (*Silence.*) What do you say?

RICHIE: Pardon?

CARLYLE: You heard me. Ohhh, I am so restless I don't even understand it. My big black boy, is what I was talkin' about. My thing, man. My rope, man; my joint, Jim. HEY RICHIE! How long you been a punk? Can you hear me? Am I clear? Do I talk funny?

Carlyle's manner disturbs Richie and he backs off, but Carlyle presses the issue. Doesn't Richie want to be friends and share innermost thoughts and feelings? "I don't think that's what you want," Richie replies. Sure it is, says Carlyle, and he starts complaining again about being in ". . . . . that goddam transient company. It like they think I ain't got no notion what a home is—no nose for no home—like I ain't never had no home. I had a home. IT LIKE THEY THINK THERE AIN'T NO PLACE IN THIS MOTHER ARMY BUT K.P." He has been on K.P. nonstop since arriving on the base. He asks Richie when he last pulled K.P. Richie explains that he and Roger and Billy have special jobs so are exempt from that kind of duty.

Carlyle taunts Richie by pretending that Richie made advances to him the other night while Carlyle was sleeping on the floor—or perhaps he just dreamed it, or perhaps they both did. Carlyle calls Richie an "ugly queer, a punk," and at the same time makes physical insinuations meant to interest him. But Richie merely departs for the showers. Carlyle takes out a bottle and, lying on Richie's bed, tells himself a "fag joke" and laughs at it.

Billy returns and Carlyle leaps to his feet. Carlyle tells Billy that he expects to take Vietnam in stride because he grew up dodging bullets. The black man's problem, he continues, is that he has, "Too much feelin'. He too close to everything. He is, man; too close to his blood, to his body. It ain't that he don't have no good mind, but he BELIEVE in his body."

Then abruptly Carlyle asks Billy if Richie is the only "punk" in this room. Billy dodges the question by asking Carlyle if he's gotten his orders yet. Carlyle isn't about to be sidetracked, however, and asks if there's a three-way gay scene going on in this room. If so, Carlyle wants to get in on the action. Billy denies vigorously that any such thing is happening, or that Richie is a practising homosexual. Richie comes back into the room and voices his opinion of Carlyle.

RICHIE: He's one of them who hasn't come down far out of the trees yet, Billy; believe me.

CARLYLE: You got rudeness in your voice, Richie—you got meanness I can hear about ole Carlyle. You tellin' me I oughta leave, is that what you think you're doin'? You don't want me here?

RICHIE: You come to see Roger who isn't here, right? Man like you must have important matters to take care of all over the quad; I can't imagine a man like you not having extremely important things to do all over the world, as a matter of fact; Carlyle—

CARLYLE (on his feet, moving for the door): Ohhhh, listen, don't mind all the shit I say. I just talk bad is all I do, I don't do bad. I got to have friends just like anybody else. I'm just bored and restless, that all; takin' it out on you two. I mean, I know Richie here ain't really no punk, not really, I was just talkin', just jivin' and entertainin' my own self. Don't take me serious, not ever. I get on out and see you all later. You be cool, hear? Man don't do the jivin', he the one gettin' jived. That what my little brother Henry tell me and tell me. (He exits.)

BILLY: I am . . . (Slowly, thoughtfully) gonna have to move myself outa here, Roger decides to adopt that sonofabitch.

RICHIE: He's an animal.

BILLY: Yeh, and on top a that, he's a rotten person.

This rare shared moment between Billy and Richie evaporates when Richie asks whether, in his story about Frankie, Billy was really talking about himself. Billy reacts hostilely, calling Richie "sick."

Roger enters fresh from a shower and ready to go. He tells them he has just encountered Carlyle who asked to have his apologies conveyed once again. This doesn't mollify Billy and Richie, who tell Roger that Carlyle frightens them. Roger assures them that Carlyle is basically all right and invites them to join him and Carlyle for an excursion to the city. The lure which finally makes Billy say yes is a promised visit to a whorehouse. Carlyle reappears and Roger tells him that Billy will be joining them. Carlyle is pleased, saying, "We all goin' to be friends!" "What about me, Carlyle?" Richie asks. *"And Carlyle laughs and laughs and laughs. Blackout."*

Scene 2

Later that night, Carlyle, Billy and Roger have returned from their excursion. They and Richie have been drinking beer and talking for awhile as the lights come up. Richie is in the middle of telling them about a dream he'd had about his father. He doesn't remember much of the dream, but he remembers his father, who apparently was an alcoholic, a gambler and something less than a family man. Richie especially remembers coincidentally encountering his father in the process of walking out on his wife and son. The man ordered his six-year-old son not to cry, pushed him out of the way and disappeared with his suitcases.

Carlyle tells them he was illegitimate. His mother would point out his father to him. One day, the man came up to Carlyle. " 'Boy,' he said, 'I ain't your daddy. I ain't. Your momma's crazy.' 'Don't you be callin' my momma crazy, Daddy,' I tole him. Poor ole thing didn't know what to do."

Richie returns to the subject of his father, remembers seeing a TV documentary about bums and being reminded of his father by a bum dancing in the background of one shot.

Carlyle and Richie appear to be making friends. They exchange innuendos which irritate Billy, who feels that Richie is carrying his effeminate poses too far. Angrily, Billy boasts that the three of them have just visited a whorehouse on the wrong side of the tracks that evening and suggests that Richie do the same—"Or don't they have faggot whorehouses?"

Richie starts playing footsie with Carlyle and suggests that the other two go outside and leave them alone. After all, Carlyle, Roger and Billy all went out and had their fun tonight, so why shouldn't he? The idea appeals to Carlyle, but Roger refuses to leave. He intends to hit the sack and he advises Billy to do the same and to ignore whatever might happen between Carlyle and Richie. Billy is outraged at the idea of Roger's telling him that they should allow Carlyle and Richie to have homosexual relations while he and Roger are in the same room. Carlyle thinks their presence might be a little "weird," but he's game.

The situation gets more and more tense. Richie suggests to Carlyle that they go outside, but Carlyle is adamant about not being run out of the room. Billy gets progressively more hysterical. This is not to happen in *his* room.

Roger tells Carlyle he's behaving like an animal, but Carlyle ignores him. Roger decides to go out of the room and wait till Richie and Carlyle are finished and advises Billy to do the same, but Billy insists on staying. He will not be driven out of his room. Roger exits and Carlyle is about to lower his trousers and get on with it, but Billy disrupts by turning on a light Carlyle has just turned off. Carlyle *"flashes open a switchblade."*

CARLYLE: I SAY! CAN'T YOU LET PEOPLE BE?
>   *Billy throws his shoe at him.*

Goddam you, boy! I'm gonna cut your ass—just to show you how it feel . . . and cuttin' can happen—this knife true.

RICHIE: Carlyle, now c'mon.

CARLYLE: Shut up, Pussy.

RICHIE: Don't hurt him, for crissake.

CARLYLE: Goddam man throw a shoe at me, he don't walk around clean in the world thinkin' he can throw another. He get some shit come back at him.
>   *He has been moving toward Billy who has feinted to move toward the door to break free, but has been stopped by a quick move on Carlyle's part. Carlyle forces Billy down to Richie's bed.*

No, no. No, no. Put you hand out there. Put it out. (*Slight pause.*) DO THE THING I'M TELLIN'!
>   *And Billy does.*

That's it. That's good. See? See?
>   *And he slits the palm of Billy's hand. . .*

BILLY: Motherfucker.
>   *He slits it again.*

RICHIE: Oh, my god, what are you—

CARLYLE (*backing away*): That you blood. The blood inside, you don't ever see it—there—take a look how easy it come out—and enough of it come out, you in the middle of the worst goddam trouble you ever gonna see. And know I'm the man can deal that kinda trouble, easy as I smile. And I smile . . . easy. Yeah. Bastard ruin my mood, Richie. He ruin my mood. Fightin' and lovin' real different in the feelin's I have. I see blood come outta somebody like that it don't make me feel good—hurt me—hurt on somebody I thought was my friend. But I ain't supposed to see. One dumb nigger. No mind, he thinks, no heart, no feelings a gentleness. You see how that ain't true, Richie. Goddam man threw a shoe at me, a lotta people woulda cut his heart out. I gotta make him know he throw shit, he get shit. But I don't hurt him bad, you see what I mean?

BILLY: Jesus H. . . . Christ . . . ! Do you know what I'm doin'? Do you know what I'm standin' up here doin'?
>   *And he is stepping forward now, a straight-edged razor in his hand.*

I'm a twenty-four-year-old goddam college graduate—intellectual goddam scholar-type and I got a razor in my hand, and I'm thinkin' about comin' up behind one black human being and I'm thinkin' nigger-this and nigger-that—and I wanna cut his throat. THAT IS RIDICULOUS. I NEVER FACED ANYBODY IN MY LIFE WITH ANYTHING TO KILL THEM. YOU UNDERSTAND ME? I DON'T HAVE A GODDAM THING ON THE LINE HERE!
>   *As Roger comes back.*

Look at me, Roger, look at me. I got a razor in my hand, I got a cut palm, I don't know how it happened. Jesus Christ, I got sweat all over me when I think what I was near to doin'. I swear it, I mean, do I think I need a reputation as a killer, a bad man with a knife. BULL SHIT, I NEED SHIT. I GOT SWEAT ALL OVER ME. I GOT THE MILE RECORD IN MY HOME TOWN. I did 4:42 in high school and that's the goddamn record in Windsor country. I don't need approval from either one of the pair of you. You wanna be a goddam swish—a goddam faggot-queer—GO! Suckin' cocks and takin' it in the ass, the thing of which you dream—GO. AND YOU— (*To Carlyle now.*) You wanna be a bad-assed animal, man, get on it—go—but I wash my hands—and I am not human as you are. It put it down, I put you down, you gay little piece of shit-cake—SHIT-CAKE—and you—you— (*To Carlyle, very near him.*)—you are your own goddam fault, SAMBO! SAM-BO!
> *And the knife flashes up in Carlyle's hand into Billy's stomach, and Billy yells.*

Ahhhhhhhhhh.
> *And pushes at the hand.*

RICHIE: Well, fuck you, Billy.
BILLY: Get away, get away.
RICHIE: You're so messed up.
ROGER: Man, what is the matter with you?
CARLYLE: Don't nobody talk that weird shit to me, you understand?
ROGER: You jive, man. That all you do, jive.
RICHIE(*hearing Billy hit the locker*): Billy! Oh, Billy!
BILLY: Ahhhhhh! Ahhhhhhh!
RICHIE: I think he stabbed him. I think Carlyle stabbed Billy, Roger.
BILLY: SHUT UP! IT'S JUST A CUT, IT'S JUST A CUT. HE CUT MY HAND, HE CUT GUT. It took the wind outta me, scared me, that's all.

Roger is concerned about Billy, who insists he's all right but sinks to the floor. Carlyle is babbling, Richie accusing. Roger tries to help Billy.

ROGER: Get up, okay. Get up on the bed.
BILLY: I am on the bed.
ROGER: What?
RICHIE: No, Billy, no, you're not.
BILLY: Shut up!
RICHIE: You're on the floor.
BILLY: I'm on the bed. I'm on the bed. (*Looking around.*) What?
ROGER: Let me see what he did.
> *Billy's hands are all over the wound. He resists Roger's hands.*

Billy, let me see where he got you. . . . . . .
BILLY (*pushing Roger away*): NOOOOOO, you nigger!
ROGER (*whirling on Carlyle*): What did you do?
CARLYLE: Shut up.
ROGER: What did you do, nigger, you slit him or stick him? (*Whirling back.*) Billy, let me see.

BILLY: Noooooo! Shit, shit, shit.

RICHIE: Oh my God, my God, ohhhh, ohhhh, ohhhh.

> *He is on his bed, on his knees, bouncing.*

CARLYLE: FUCK IT, FUCK IT, I STUCK HIM. I TURNED IT. This mother army break my heart, I can't be out there where it pretty, don't wanna live! Wash me clean, shit-face!

RICHIE: Ohhhh, ohhhhh, ohhhhhhhhhhhh. Carlyle stabbed Billy, oh, ohhhh, I never saw such a thing in my life. Ohhhhhh. Don't die, Billy. Don't die.

ROGER (*to Richie*): Shut up and go find somebody to help. Richie, go!

RICHIE: Who? I'll go, I'll go.

> *Getting off the bed.*

ROGER: I don't know, JESUS CHRIST! DO IT!

RICHIE: O.K. O.K. Billy, don't die. Don't die.

ROGER: The Sarge, or C.Q.

BILLY (*suddenly doubling over, vomits blood as Richie is gone*): Ohhhhhhhhhh. (*Coughing.*) Blood, blood.

ROGER: Be still, be still.

BILLY (*pulling at a blanket beside him, to cover himself*): I wan to stand up. I'm—

> *Making no move to stand, only to cover himself.*

Vomiting blood. What does that mean?

ROGER: I don't know.

BILLY: Yes, yes, I want to stand up. Give me a blanket, blanket.

ROGER: RIICCHHHIIIEEEE!

> *As Billy is furiously pulling at the blanket.*

No, no.

> *Then leaping up to run for help.*

Wait on, be tight, be cool . . .

BILLY: Cover me. Cover me.

> *Struggling with the blanket, he pulls it over him until he is com-*
> *pletely covered.*

CARLYLE: I'm sorry, man. I'm sorry.

> *He rises from the footlocker and crosses to where Billy is lying.*
> *Placing the knife down on Roger's footlocker, he lifts the blanket*
> *from Billy's face.*

BILLY: I don't want to talk to you right now, Carlyle, all right? (*Silence.*) Where's Roger? Do you know where he is? (*Silence.*) Don't . . . stab me anymore, Carlyle, okay? I was dead wrong doin' what I did. I know that now. Carlyle, promise me you won't stab me anymore. I couldn't take it . . . okay? I'm cold . . . my blood . . . is . . .

> *And Sgt. Rooney is standing in the doorway.*

ROONEY: Cokes? Cokesie. (*Seeing Carlyle.*) What's this? What's this goin' on here?

> *As Carlyle whirls, poised with the knife.*

Whoooaaa . . . now. Whoooaaaaa . . . You got a knife there. What's with the knife? Who are you soldier? I mean . . . I'm just askin' . . .

> *Richie rushes in.*

RICHIE: Ohhhhh, Sergeant, Sergeant, I've been looking for you everywhere
—where have you been? Carlyle stabbed Billy, he stabbed him.

ROONEY: What?

RICHIE: Carlyle stabbed Billy.

ROONEY: Who's Carlyle?

RICHIE: He's Carlyle.

As Carlyle seems about to advance.

Carlyle, don't hurt anybody more!

ROONEY: WHAT'S GOIN' ON HERE?

RICHIE: Carlyle, don't—don't—

ROONEY: WAIT! (*Pointing to Carlyle.*) NOW, WAIT! You watch your
step, you understand?

Raising the bottle he has in his hand as if it were a weapon.

You see what I got. You watch your step—motherfucker— Relax, I mean,
we can straighten all this out—we—

Carlyle swipes at Rooney with his knife.

RICHIE: Carlyle!

Richie runs from the room.

ROONEY: I'm just askin' what's goin' on, that's all I'm doin'. No need to get
all—

As Carlyle swipes again and Rooney steps back.

MOTHERFUCKER! GODDAMIT, I'LL CUT YOU GOOD—I'LL—

*And he slams the bottle against the frame of the bed in order to
shatter it into a weapon, and he yells.*

Ahhhhhgggggggghhhhhh! Ohhhhhhhh! I hurt myself, I cut myself.

Dropping everything, his hand bleeding, fingers tense.

I cut myself—my hand—wait a minute—wait—

As Carlyle stabs him.

I hurt my hand, goddamit—I HURT MY HAND! WHAT ARE YOU
DOING? I HURT MY HAND! WAIT, WAIT! WHAT ARE YOU DOING?

*Carlyle stabs again and the sergeant waves, then kicks, Carlyle
grabbing the foot, knocking the sergeant back and down, falling
then in a wildness upon him.*

No fair, no fair!

*Carlyle stabs and stabs and begins to sob. He rises and collapses
on Billy's bed. Roger enters and stops, seeing the sergeant and then
seeing Billy. There are sirens outside. Carlyle now rises, looking at
Roger, pointing at him with the knife.*

CARLYLE: You don't tell nobody on me you saw me do this, I let you go,
okay? Ohhhh, how'm I gonna get back to the world now, I got all this mess
to—

ROGER: What happened?

As Carlyle moves toward the door...

Where are you going? I don't understand. I don't— That you did this! That
you did this!

CARLYLE: YOU SHUT UP! I don't know what you talkin' all that weird
shit to me—don't you go talkin' all that weird shit.

ROGER: Noooooooooo!

CARLYLE: I'm Carlyle, man. You know me. You know me.

> *He is gone, fleeing out the door. Roger, alone, moves to bend over Billy.*

BILLY: Carlyle, no, ohh, Christ, I'll die. I will, I'll die. Don't stab me anymore. Don't make me die. I'll get my dog after you. I'LL GET MY DOG AFTER YOU!

ROGER: Oh, Billy; oh, man, oh, man. GODDAMIT, BILLY.

A Military Police lieutenant enters and immediately assumes Roger is responsible for the carnage. A second M.P., Pfc. Hinson, enters with Richie, who tries to explain that Roger is innocent. The lieutenant tells him to keep quiet.

Another M.P., Pfc. Clark, enters with Carlyle. Carlyle tries to float a story that he was attacked by practical jokers who poured chicken blood on him. Nobody buys it. Roger and Richie tell something approaching the true story. Carlyle gets indignant. "This is my house, sir. This is my goddam house." He orders the M.P.s to remove the handcuffs and give him a bus ticket home. "I am quittin' this jive-time army," he says.

Hinson and Clark drag him away, then come back and remove Billy's and Rooney's bodies. The lieutenant gives Roger and Richie forms to fill out and orders them to come to his office the next day. "Two perfectly trained and primed, strong pieces of U.S. Army property got cut to shit up here. We are going to find out how and why," he says. And he leaves.

Roger and Richie are alone. Roger takes out the mop and begins to clean up the blood, as a shocked Richie watches.

RICHIE: That's Billy's blood, Roger. His blood.

ROGER: Is it? (*He mops.*)

RICHIE: I feel awful.

ROGER: How come you made me waste all that time talkin' shit to you, Richie? All my time, talkin' shit, and all the time you was a faggot, man; you really was. You shoulda just tole ol' Roger. He don't care. All you got to do is tell me.

RICHIE: I been telling you. I did.

ROGER: Jive, man, jive.

RICHIE: No!

ROGER: You did bullshit all over us! ALL OVER US!

RICHIE: I just wanted to hold his hand, Billy's hand, to talk to him, go to the movies hand in hand like he would with a girl or I would with someone back home.

ROGER: But he didn't wanna; *he* didn't wanna.

RICHIE: He did.

ROGER: No, man.

RICHIE: He did.

ROGER: No, man.

RICHIE: He did. He did. It's not my fault.

ROGER: You know what you oughta do and do it quick. You grow you a mustache, man. You get a little beard. You get some hair around your mouth, make it look like what you think it is. You do that!

They have not noticed Cokes who stands in the doorway.

Cokes enters, drunk as usual. He has lost Rooney, he tells them. They were playing hide-and-seek and he guesses that Rooney has hid too well this time. Roger tells him that they don't know where he is, at the same time telling Richie not to contradict him, to let the matter rest for the moment.

Cokes tells them of the riotous day he and Rooney have had, during the course of which they were involved in four slapstick-like accidents and inadvertently emerged clean. Then they came back to play hide-and-seek, and here he is.

Richie begins to cry. Cokes asks why, and Roger says, "He's cryin' 'cause he's a queer." Surprisingly, Cokes reacts sympathetically. Knowing that he is dying of leukemia has made him take a second look at a lot of things, and he's come to the conclusion that being queer isn't so bad. It isn't as bad as having leukemia, for instance.

Cokes begins to wonder about things he might have done differently; maybe he would have freed the sniper he trapped in the spider hole with the grenade. He remembers again sitting on the lid and the man underneath desperately trying to get out, and in his memory the incident takes on the characteristics of a silent film comedy.

Cokes asks if he can sleep in their room tonight, as he isn't in shape to walk. Roger and Richie tell him it's OK.

> *Slight pause.*

COKES: I mean, he was like Charlie Chaplin. And then he blew up.

ROGER: Sergeant. Maybe you was Charlie Chaplin, too.

COKES: No. No. (*Pause.*) No. I don't know who I was. 'Night.

ROGER: You think he was singin' it?

COKES: What?

ROGER: You think he was singin' it?

COKES: Oh, yeah. Oh, yeah; he was singin' it.

> *Slight pause. Cokes, sitting on the footlocker, begins to sing a makeshift languge imitating Korean to the tune of "Beautiful Dreamer/Beautiful Streamer." . . . . . The lights go to dark. Curtain.*

SERENADING LOUIE

A Play in Two Acts

BY LANFORD WILSON

Cast and credits appear on pages 368-370

LANFORD WILSON was born in Lebanon, Mo., April 13, 1937 and was raised in Ozark, Mo. He was educated at San Diego State College and the University of Chicago, where he started writing plays. Arriving in New York in 1963, he gravitated to the Caffe Cino, one of the first of the off-off-Broadway situations, and made his New York playwriting debut with the one-acter So Long at the Fair, *followed by* Home Free *and* The Madness of Lady Bright, *which latter work claims an OOB long-run record of 250 performances. In 1965 his first full-length play,* Balm in Gilead, *was produced at the Cafe La Mama and directed by Marshall W. Mason, who has figured importantly in Wilson's later career. That same year the prolific author's* Ludlow Fair *and* This Is the Rill Speaking *were presented at Caffe Cino.*

During the mid-1960s, Wilson's plays began to receive productions in the professional segment, both in New York and abroad. His off-Broadway debut took place with the appearance of Home Free *on a New Playwrights Series program for 23 performances at the Cherry Lane Theater in February, 1965.* Ludlow Fair *and* The Madness of Lady Bright *appeared off Broadway and in London in 1966.* The Rimers of Eldritch *(a development of* This Is the Rill Speaking) *won its author a Vernon Rice Award off Broadway in 1967. In 1968 his* Wandering *was part of the off-Broadway program* Collision Course, *and he tried out an untitled new work with Al Carmines at Judson Poets' Theater.*

In 1969, Wilson moved uptown to Broadway with the short-lived but favorably remembered The Gingham Dog, *following its production a year earlier at the Washington, D.C. Theater Club. His only other Broadway production to date was the almost equally short-lived but even more favorably received (in subsequent productions)* Lemon Sky *in 1970. The following year he wrote the libretto for composer Lee Hoiby's opera version of Tennessee Williams's* Summer and Smoke, *which premiered in St. Paul, Minn. and was presented by New York City Opera in 1972. He also collaborated with Williams on the film script* The Migrants *which was produced by CBS and won an Emmy nomination and a Christopher Award.*

In 1970, Wilson joined Marshall W. Mason's off-off-Broadway Circle Theater (now Circle Repertory Company) as its playwright-in-residence. His plays produced by this group have included Sextet (Yes) *in 1971 and* The Great Nebula in Orion *(named by Stanley Richards as one of the best short plays of the year),* Ikke, Ikke, Nye, Nye Nye *and* The Family Continues *during the 1972 season. They were directed by Mason, as was* The Hot l Baltimore *in its OOB premiere at the Circle January 27, 1973. It moved to an off-Broadway theater March 22, 1973, set a new off-Broadway long-run record for an American play of 1,166 performances, was named a Best Play of its season, won the Critics (best American play), Obie and Outer Circle awards and was adapted into a TV series.*

In 1975 Wilson's The Mound Builders *was produced at the Circle under Mason's direction, won an Obie and was filmed for the Theater in America series on WNET-TV. This season, the well-established group has crossed the ill-defined boundary between OOB and the professional "off-Broadway" area, so that its productions now qualify for Best Play selection on their own. Two of the Circle's 1975–76 offerings directed by Mason are cited as Best Plays in this volume: Wilson's new* Serenading Louie *(written between* Lemon Sky *and* The Hot l Baltimore *and rewritten for this production) and Jules Feiffer's* Knock Knock.

Wilson has been the recipient of Rockefeller, Guggenheim and Yale fellowships. He is a bachelor and lives in Sag Harbor, N.Y.

Time: The present

Place: A suburban home, north of Chicago

ACT I: FRIDAY AFTERNOON AND EVENING AT THE END OF OCTOBER

Scene 1

SYNOPSIS: A spacious living room with fireplace, furnished with sofa, chairs, desk, etc., with stairs leading off right to the floor above, occupies most of the area center and right. At left downstage is the bar, dining room and door leading off left to the kitchen. Upstage from it there is a large foyer with the front door at left and doors leading to a hall closet and a downstairs bedroom. This single setting represents the homes of both the couples in the play, as though such residences are so alike and furnished so similarly as to make scene changes redundant.

Mary and Carl are at home, Carl helping Mary into her dress. Mary is rushing out to a birthday-and-bridge party for a woman friend who had to schedule it on the weekend because she has a job. Their friend Gabby, who is married to Alex, is going to this party too. "Gabby scares me," Mary tells Carl, because some unknown man is following her around: "Oldish, very distinguished she thought. Very unlike a rapist."

Mary grabs for purse and wrapped present, meanwhile issuing instructions for picking up their daughter Ellen at ballet school and turning on the chicken pot pie.

CARL (*frowning, reluctantly*): I'd like to—
   Halts, looking to her. She to him. All movement and sound arrested for a count of 15; then a rapid, overlapping exchange.
MARY: What, doll?
CARL: Talk, you know.
MARY: I know—we will. Nothing's wrong is there?
CARL: No, no.
MARY: With that Atlanta business?
CARL: No, no.
MARY (*still lightly*): What is it?
CARL (*also lightly*): No, no, it's nothing.
MARY: We're running all over, we're never home together, I know—
CARL: —It's nothing, Mary, I get—edgy—it'll pass.
MARY (*maneuvering him to the sofa*): I know, baby. It'll pass.

They sit on the sofa and discuss a shadow puppet which is part of the decor, speculating on its probable religious function in the thousand-year-old civilization that produced it. Carl cheers up a bit, remembering the obligatory Sunday School of his youth, learning the psalms by heart and occasionally performing the birthday ritual of dropping a number of pennies into the collection box (an empty Quaker Oats box) equal to the number of years old on the given birthday.

CARL: That was an Event—kids came from the other classrooms to watch. Everything was an Event then. The smallest thing that happened was an Event.
MARY: Of course.
CARL: And we don't have those anymore. Why is that? What's happened?
   He slides from his mood, back closer to his first one.
MARY (*quizzically*): What?
CARL: I don't know. That wars, and deaths, birthdays, Easter, even Christ-

mas. Nothing gets to me like that now. (*A slight pause.*) Things go by and nothing reaches us does it? Nothing's an Event any more.

MARY: Ummm.

CARL (*more or less coming out of it for her benefit*): You've got to go.

MARY: Oh, I know.

Mary becomes as efficient as before, issuing instructions. She suggests that they go out together tomorrow, Saturday, just the two of them for supper and a movie. Carl agrees: it's a date. Mary rushes off to her women's lunch. "*Carl's smile fades, he looks down to the floor with a worried look. After a count of ten he looks up to the audience with a sense of urgency—the buzzer sounds in the kitchen offstage. Carl turns his head to the sound. Blackout.*

Scene 2

It's the same set but now represents Gabby and Alex's house. Gabby is asleep in the chair and awakes as Alex comes in the front door. She is the first to say hello, making small talk about the day she's had and the evening before with Carl and Mary. Gabby is the type who runs through a series of thoughts and comments, leaving many unfinished and hanging in air. Alex puts his coat in the closet, brings his briefcase to the living room and sits without saying a word in reply to Gabby's non-stop monologue.

GABBY: . . . . . Like a drink? What kind of day?
    A pause.
I was in town and going to stop by or call and then just got too tired. Allison wanted to call it a day too; she's really— Oh, I don't want to say anything, I suppose we all are; but she really is, more and more . . . ? You know I went back to bed and slept till almost ten thirty. I thought pot wasn't supposed to give you a hangover. Maybe I'm just getting something. You slept terribly; perspiring all . . . I think I enjoyed last night, you seemed to. Carl's fun isn't he? Of course Mary's great. I kept thinking that my head was going to—leave my—you know with pot I've decided that it changes the focus of my eyes. I see things at a distance more clearly. Or something. I don't know, it's very funny.

Gabby goes into the kitchen as Alex fetches some cigarettes and then sits down to study the papers in his briefcase. Offstage, Gabby is still talking about the roast, about how she loves autumn and Thanksgiving. She drifts back into the room and gazes out of the window. She proposes they have an old-fashioned "Holloween," with a jack-o-lantern; she tries to get Alex to talk to her, but he's reluctant to begin conversation, feigns preoccupation with his papers. Finally Gabby asks him, "It isn't going to be one of those 'silent' nights, is it? (*Rather all in one breath.*) Working all night silently and then going to work and calling me five times to talk about nothing as though you hadn't been silent? I don't much like those nights, but I rather enjoy the phone calls or aren't we supposed to talk about it? (*Beat.*) Would that impede your spontaneity?"

Alex just shakes his head without answering. When he finally does make a remark as he disappears into the hall, she misses it. He's on his way to lie down but changes his mind when Gabby tells him dinner's nearly ready. He takes refuge in his papers again, as Gabby complains that "when you're home you spend every waking hour asleep."

The absolute non-communication continues. But Alex seems to listen when Gabby asks him, "Do we know a man with white hair? We don't know many older people, do we? A very—well not quite distinguished looking man but nearly. I think he's—following me."

Gabby's pursuer followed her to the supermarket and the florist but didn't seem to want to approach any closer. Alex is a lawyer who sometimes handles sensitive cases. There's nothing threatening at the present time, but Gabby nevertheless feels jumpy and insecure.

Alex doesn't spare her so much as a word of reassurance, and Gabby wonders out loud: is there someone else, some other woman in Alex's life putting him in these moods? Alex tells her no, now quite irritated but still taciturn. Gabby tells him, "I was with Mary yesterday. For some reason she decided to be confiding. I don't know why me. I suppose she thought— Poor Mary. She's having an affair. Did you know that? I don't know if you know him. He's very good looking. We saw them on the street, they have three kids— girls too. His wife's very attractive, I couldn't imagine. Apparently they're in love. Of course they both have the children. It just makes me nervous. I wish she hadn't told me. (*Alex stares at her. A pause.*) Did you know anything about it?"

Alex considered it possible, that's all. Gabby continues talking, telling Alex that Carl and Mary sold their cabin on the lake, which they hadn't used in a long time. She tells him that a friend's sister is dying of cancer; still Alex doesn't respond.

GABBY (*looks down, then up to him again; not smiling; pleading*): Alex? (*More urgently.*) Alex? (*After a second.*) I don't want to . . .
      Smiles, looks down, out the window. Hand to her face. She begins to cry. Alex without looking at her puts his work aside, stubs out the cigarette and gets up, walking briskly to the closet. Gabby frantically wipes her cheeks, running after him.
I'm sorry, honey, I can't imagine! Alex? It's just—I'm sorry, Alex— Come on.
      He has taken his coat from the closet, puts it on on his way to the the front door.
Alex, where—Baby, I don't know what's wrong— (*Laughing.*) I think it must be—Baby, please don't go! Alex!
      Alex slams the door on her last word and the lights black out with the sound.

Scene 3

After an interval of blackness, the lights come up again. The TV has a football game on (but not the sound). Alex is holding a large newspaper clipping,
while Carl enters from the kitchen with a tray of cheese and bologna. The clipping is about an old Army buddy of Carl's. Carl turns off the TV (it's a replay
of an old game) and asks Alex about what he's doing these days. He suspects
Alex has some interesting news and wants to hear about it. Alex tells him to
wait till Monday.

CARL: Tell me.

ALEX: Better not, right now. Wait till it's official.

CARL: No, better tell me now, I have to be in Cincinnati Monday, I have to
see some people about an office building.

ALEX: Carl, you're going to be the youngest dead millionaire I know—

CARL: —Have you ever heard me say I liked it? Running around like this,
I don't go more than I have to—it's not my money, it's the bank's money, the
investors' money.

Alex bites into a sandwich and hurts an ailing tooth. Everything seems to
be falling apart around Alex. Last week he was conducting hearings before
14 TV cameras and tearing his opponent to pieces, when his fountain pen
started leaking down the front of his shirt.

ALEX: . . . . . Oh, Jesus, Carl, I keep feeling my real life will begin any day
now. This can't be it. This is just temporary. A dry run. I have a whole agenda
of tabled activities. I've got two temporary fillings I've had for a year and a
half. They're wearing away a little bit every day. I can feel it with my tongue.
My mother keeps calling me collect to tell me to write her more often. I have
my girl send her clippings. She writes me to get a haircut; you look too thin;
I bet you eat nothing but sandwiches. Everything is tabled until next meeting.

CARL: Waiting for some day when the taxes go down and you get the mortgage paid off.

ALEX: I have to discuss this appointment, this total upheaval, with Gabby;
I've known for a week and a half.

CARL: That's the Monday thing? Appointment with whom?

ALEX: Did I say that? Forget I said it.

CARL: I'm going to figure it out and I'm going to kick your ass.

ALEX: Trouble is, the other day I had a flash of objectivity and made the
mistake of asking myself what I wanted to do with my life. You're better off
to go at it blind. You take it all in and it all begins to look . . .

CARL: And it all falls apart, I know the feeling.

ALEX: Never do that: ask what it's all about. (*To the audience.*) Never do
that.

Alex tells Carl that on his 34th birthday, thinking it all over, he decided
maybe he wasn't going to be President, or change the world. On the other

hand, he doesn't want to spend his life just burning leaves to make his lawn look neater, as the other fellows on his block seem to be doing. He envies an old law school friend who chucked it all and is growing strawberries in Ibitza.

Carl agrees with Alex that "Life is a ballbreaker," with 20 per cent of the population leaning on some kind of drug because they can't bear reality. When Carl was younger he thought work would be fun. Building and developing sounded like worthy occupations. "I didn't know it'd take business managers and advisers and accountants and lawyers and investors and every time you wanted to do something as simple as plant a tree you couldn't get ahold of the landscaper's accountant's secretary. I didn't know you had to get ahead, I thought you could just lope along . . . . . In the beginning it was fun, hell, it was a ballgame, but people aren't prepared if you just want to play fair. It amazes me. The whole country's profiteering and pickpocketing each other, it's a daisy chain . . . . . It strains all our faculties keeping all the lies straight and juggling all the rationalizations and pretending we don't notice everyone struggling with it and you tell me you're not contented with your lot—Jesus Christ, Alex, it's a lousy lot—nobody's content with it . . . . ."

Carl guesses that since Alex has been investigating a Transportation and City Funding scandal, the Monday secret is that Alex is going to be named head of that municipal department. No, it's bigger than that, Alex tells Carl. Carl wonders why Alex hasn't told Gabby if it's that important. Alex explains that he can't talk to Gabby; their conversation degenerates into "long analytical examinations of the day's minutiae" of appointments, homecoming times, etc.

"I'm apparently no good for her at all," Alex confides to Carl, telling of how Gabby will wake him up gently after he's gone to sleep, turning him off with the very effort she's making to turn him on: "Apparently never notices the effect of a thing she does. Every time I do turn on to her she tells me she's deliberately turned off to see if I'll come around—so I come around and she starts that 'Oh, I know you so well' routine. So she's playing little secret intrigues with me. It's ridiculous; I don't enjoy it. Being raped. Every night. By my own wife. What kind of married life is that?"

Alex believes that the women of his generation are more preoccupied with sex than the men. They should have gotten their illusions about it out of their systems early, but they didn't, and so now "They think that's the only way they can make their husbands happy. Gabby could make me most happy by going home to mother for a month. I understand. I finally understand why men have children when they don't really want them, can't afford them, don't want them—they think maybe something two feet long and that big around stuffed up there for a couple of months day and night will finally satisfy them and they can get some sleep."

Carl is so entertained by Alex's diatribe that he turns to the audience and points out his friend's ability as a talker. Alex in his turn tells the audience that Carl is a former football hero.

They go back to speculating about the behavior of women; then all at once Carl has an intuition about Alex's Monday secret. Alex is going to be appointed by the governor to fill the term in Washington of their Representative, who died before taking office. Carl can't see why Gabby wouldn't go along with it. Alex doesn't want to talk about that side of it, though he admits he's considering accepting the appointment. In the outside world, Gabby seems to be all right—she and Alex appear to be an ideal couple, but the minute they're alone together Gabby changes, turns herself into the kind of sex object that turns him off instead of the kind that turns him on.

Carl feels that Alex and Gabby have a simple problem of differing sexual tastes. Alex apologizes to Carl for harping on his own married life, commenting sarcastically that "Your married life is on such solid rock, so idyllic." Carl tells Alex he hasn't been feeling well lately, he's been having headaches, and he doesn't feel like being cross-examined about his marriage.

ALEX: Hells bells and goddam, Carl, you *know* she's cheating on you don't you?

CARL: —You son of a bitch!—

A pause.

ALEX: Don't you?

CARL (*pause; sits; loses air; finally*): Does everybody know?

ALEX: I don't think so. Gabby told me.

CARL: She isn't a whore. I think she really loves him. It isn't like that.

ALEX: Did she tell you?

CARL: No, she doesn't know I know. I don't imagine. I saw them once. Well, I knew before that. I mean, it's something you know. There uh—"There needs no ghost" you know? "Come from the grave . . ."

ALEX: Yeah, yeah, I know, got it.

CARL: He has a family too. Three girls.

ALEX: You know who he is?

CARL: Oh, sure—no, skip it. This isn't any good. It's no big deal. It's a comedy—it's farce; it's not to be serious about.

ALEX: But you know who he is?

CARL: Yes. He's my CPA. (*To audience.*) See? (*To Alex.*) His firm does the accounts for my office. Now, no more. I don't think about it. It's all the same to me.

ALEX: Mary is a pretty fast pacer, Carl, you've got to keep ahead of her— hell, you know that. You used to be ahead of things.

Carl feels like everybody else, detached from it all and looking at life from a distance. He and Mary have been married nine years, and he'll just wait until this affair burns out. Carl doesn't seem to be able to get involved with things that are happening. He's not even interested in Alex's career as he sees it develop on the TV news. Carl "can't galvanize any concern" over anything these days. He reminds Alex—and the audience, too—of an incident years ago when a little girl fell into a mine shaft and everyone in the world stayed glued to their radios, concerned about the fate of this one child. "I remember she died before they could reach her, but that wasn't why I—I didn't tell it to be sad. I just think of that time as a time when people were involved."

Carl wonders whether they haven't become too civilized; whether the pagans weren't right believing it necessary to have a public sacrifice from time to time, a sacrifice of self or of something very dear. Perhaps Mary feels a deep need to expose their marriage to the danger of this affair—"But then probably I just want to think that because I don't like believing that she loves someone else more than she does—but I can't so . . ."

But when all's said and done, Carl concludes, deep down inside he really doesn't care—can't care—and envies anyone who can.

Carl even knows that his wife and her lover make love in the afternoon: "We never did that; not even before we got married." Under Carl's questioning, Alex says yes, he and Gabby sometimes make love in the afternoon, but when they go out afterwards he feels castrated: "Sometimes I get really mad at her for having robbed me of something. It's like I'm 'safe' now."

Alex tells Carl he's lucky to have it the way he has.

ALEX: You'll never have that delicious feeling of being in service.

CARL: You know, I don't agree with any of your—I always feel very proud—

ALEX: Hell, you don't know how good you've got it. Mary plays around with your accountant and you stay—

CARL: Come on—

ALEX: —home, crocheting a goddam afghan or something.

CARL (an enormous desperate cry; crying, flooding): ALEX. ALEX. I do! I do. I try to understand and see what's going on and I see it all go by sometimes like a movie. And I'm *not* involved and a lot of the time, a lot of the time Mary is the same, so I try to understand why she needs this or how it happened and because I rattle on about—it I think it doesn't move me any more than anything else—Alex why does she have to do it?

Alex, taken completely off stride, is trying to answer, which is not possible.

WHAT'S SHE TRYING TO DO? I DON'T KNOW WHAT TO SAY. I DON'T KNOW HOW TO FEEL, ALEX. I DON'T KNOW HOW TO FEEL; I WANT IT BACK—LIKE IT WAS. It was good then.

Flooding. Alex over can mumble "What, Carl, what?"

IT WAS GOOD THEN, GODDAMIT, WHEN I WAS OVER THERE, OVERSEAS, AND WE WROTE LETTERS TO EACH OTHER, IT WAS GOOD THEN, IT WAS GOOD THEN. IT WAS GOOD. IT WAS.

Blackout. Simultaneously the bedroom door opens and Gabby in a nightgown, clutching a pillow to her side, is standing silhouetted in the doorway. The TV is showing a test pattern.

GABBY (worried): Alex? are you in here? Alex?

ALEX: (if we could see him we'd see he is lying on the sofa, staring; we can only hear his voice in the dark): Yes.

GABBY: Were you asleep?

ALEX (bored, unsympathetic, but polite): No, that's all right.

GABBY (*the beginning of a deeply felt plea*): Honey . . . ?

ALEX: Oh, God.

GABBY: What's wrong?

ALEX: When you get into that tone of voice and say honey like that I know we're up for the night.

GABBY: No, we aren't . . . I . . .

> *Pause.*

ALEX: What, Gabby?

> *Pause. He turns the TV off.*

What, I'm sorry.

GABBY: Nothing. What can I say? . . . Nothing . . .

ALEX: I said I'm sorry.

GABBY (*very tired, turning into the bedroom*): No, nothing.

> *Alex has crossed and is now standing silhouetted, looking into the the bedroom.*

ALEX (*rather listlessly, but with an attempt at sympathy*): Gabby?

> *A pause.*

Gabby, baby, I'm sorry, what?

> *A pause.*

Gabby?

> *He goes into the bedroom, shutting the door after him. Curtain.*

ACT II: A WEEK LATER, SATURDAY NIGHT AND SUNDAY MORNING

On a Saturday night at Carl and Mary's, Mary and Alex are chuckling over a memory of bringing spiked oranges to a football game at which Carl was their star quarterback.

Carl enters, returning from having taken the baby sitter home (they've all been to the movies). He is wearing his coat—it's cold out. He is *"rather troubled, not in their tempo"* as they try to sing the old college drinking songs, and he keeps his coat on.

Mary decides they all need one more strong drink to toast the new Congressman (though Alex hasn't accepted the appointment yet, and Carl would probably prefer that the guests go home soon). Alex and Mary remember how beautiful the Northwestern campus was. Gabby didn't go to college with the others, she went to Stevens and doesn't know how Northwestern used to look.

Carl picks up a plastic mask of a bull and shows them all how he looked when he and his daughter Ellen went out trick-or-treating on Halloween. Mary passes around the nightcaps, and they all decide to sing "The Whiffenpoof Song":

> ". . . . . We will serenade our Louie
> While life and song shall last,
> Then we'll pass and be forgotten with the rest . . . . ."

Gentlemen, songsters all are we,
Damned from here to eternity,
God have mercy on such as we,
Baa . . . Baa . . . Baa . . ."
Soon Alex is reminiscing about Carl in college.

ALEX: You should have seen this nut at school. I'll bet they were sorry they ever let him in. Nobody needs a quarterback that bad. I mean he was a legend—
CARL: —No, I—
ALEX: —He was, he was a legend. Like Paul Bunyan or something. He used to live way the hell out in the boondocks. Out of town about a mile from—
MARY: —Two miles—
ALEX: —Way the hell out, halfway to Skokie—
CARL: It kept me in shape . . . . .

Carl used to jog into town in sweatpants, refusing offers of a ride. "I mean he was a character!" Alex exclaims, remembering how Carl used to string his laundry on a line across their room.

ALEX (to Mary): Well, I don't have to tell you what it was like.
MARY: It was different, though. I only dated him a couple of times before he decided the Army needed him. It was incredible. I didn't know what to think. He used to come to me with shoe polish on his cuffs, smelling like a bootblack—and he'd always had a couple of drinks to steel his nerve. When we moved back up to Evanston he was out of the service—we were ancient compared to the other kids.
GABBY: And he was still on the team?
MARY: Not then, lord no. Business School. Carl thought he should have a couple of years. He was the returning Star and I was the returning Homecoming Queen. All very lauded over, though they couldn't see allowing us to live in the fraternity house.
GABBY: With his wife, I guess not.
MARY: Not wife—
ALEX: Concubine—
MARY: —Paramour. That was the whole problem. Total scandal. Local girl makes out. Dash the dreams. And of course Mom, who's more conservative than—well, you know—was ready to disinherit me.
GABBY: Oh, God, no. All that Wedgewood
Carl crosses to bar and pours another drink.
MARY: Exactly, almost an ultimatum—the carpets or Carl. No, the wife came afterwards. Everyone was greatly relieved.
Mary includes the audience; not quite an aside.
This is when people still pretended to be moral, you understand. (*Back to*

Gabby.) They celebrated for days. I should say nights. We really had a neat little house.

CARL: It was cozy. It was cozy.

MARY: Small, but with drain pipes that made disconcerting digestive noises night and day and a fireplace you could have built a closet in. But not a fire, of course.

GABBY: Unfortunately.

MARY (*hugging Carl; more to the audience*): And we did not "have" to get married.

CARL: Not at all, not at all. Ellen was two years yet.

MARY: I just held out as long as I could.

CARL: Yeah? Yeah? I thought you just finally saw the light. It was something else. I mean living with this chick. I'd never seen anything so clean. Not just the house, but I used to come home, walk in the door and the place smelled of—not perfume—but powder—nothing smells that clean. Used to blow my mind.

MARY: It was— (*To the audience.*) —very special. Carl was thinner, firmer then. Hard as a wall. And agile, for his weight, and eager. We made love after he had studied till midnight. And then—sleeping so close and warm, we used to wake up just as it got light out—

CARL (*gently*): Summertime; summer term.

MARY: —and go at it all over again. I'd fall back asleep, sort of coast out in a kind of dizzy exhaustion, falling asleep curled up against his chest with his sweaty-wet face at my ear, murmuring, "Marry me, Mary, marry me, Mary, marry me . . ." (*Distantly musing.*) I don't actually think . . . that I loved him then. But I love him then now.

Alex turns the conversation back to Carl as a football player. They asked him to coach, but he didn't have time, concentrating on his studies and then supporting his wife first with a little travel agency and then expanding into other businesses.

Gabby isn't happy at the thought of moving to Washington, with its city crowds. Gabby hates crowds. She disliked being caught in a student demonstration when she and Alex were trying to get to the movies the other evening—though Alex seemed almost to want to participate in the students' action. If they are going to Washington, Gabby feels, she should have more convictions. Mary feels just the other way—perhaps withdrawal is the best response to modern life. Mary tells them she is gradually losing patience with everyone around her and tolerance for their preferences in even such small matters as whether or not they drink coffee black. She doesn't understand the younger generation: "So bright and so damn dull all at once."

Alex finally admits, yes, of course he'd like to join the younger generation, he'd like to be seventeen again. Mary goes to get more drinks, though Carl has had more than enough and Gabby doesn't really want another.

The subject of prayer comes up, and Carl reveals that "Now I lay me down to sleep" is part of his nightly ritual. Trying to keep up with the conversation

THE BEST PLAYS OF 1975–1976

but lagging behind nevertheless, Carl tells Alex that seventeen isn't the right age to be.

Gabby notes how late it is—1:30 a.m.—and she and Alex start going through the motions of leaving, putting on coats, making last-minute comments, noticing how cold it is outside (and Carl has still not taken off his topcoat with the collar turned up). Finally, after Gabby sings a quick verse of "God Rest Ye Merry, Gentlemen" to remind them all that Christmas is just around the corner, Mary closes the door on the departing guests.

> *Carl pours the last drink from the pitcher into his glass. Mary collects the glasses and the pitcher.*

MARY: Poisonous movie, didn't you think?

CARL: Pretty bad.

> *Mary exits into the kitchen with the tray. Carl, alone on stage, looks out to the audience.*

(*To the audience, worried, briefly*): Yes, it's . . . very difficult.

MARY (*re-entering*): I'll check on Ellie. You'll be up? Well, don't bother, I'll be right down.

CARL: Check.

MARY: Don't you think you can take your coat off? They've gone.

CARL: Huh? No, I didn't . . .

MARY: I'm kidding.

> *Kisses him on the cheek, turns out one lamp.*

Goodnight, love; don't drink any more.

CARL: No, no.

> *Mary exits. Carl, after a moment, looks out to the audience.*

I'm not what you'd call particularly religious. I wouldn't want to misrepresent myself. Like everyone else who sits up for the Late Late Show—I jump up to turn off the Sermonette before the Rabbi from the Cicero precinct can tell me I'm not saved. I've only been terribly religious—passionately religious once . . . . .

Carl was 14, he tells the audience, and his mother was facing an operation. Carl made a deal with God that he would give up his bad habits if God would spare his mother's life. When his mother recovered quickly, Carl was sure it was as a result of his prayers.

CARL: . . . . . It's very odd. About prayer. I don't just quit, because I've thirty-some years invested in it. When the sky suddenly splits wide open one day and angels sing—you look up and say—thank God, I kept up my praying. (*A beat; not too seriously, but down.*) But I don't think—a paradox here—I don't think I ever quite forgave Mom for causing me to make a solemn promise I wasn't strong enough to keep.

Carl exits into the kitchen with his glass. A key turns in the front door, and now this is Alex and Gabby's house. The two are returning home from the party at Carl and Mary's. Gabby is exhausted. She falls onto the sofa.

GABBY: I feel terrible. God, I hated that movie.

ALEX: All right. Enough. I've heard enough about that movie. I guess it wasn't a very good idea.

GABBY: Wonderful idea. Lousy movie. Will you think less of me if I don't bathe?

ALEX (*trying to get onto the soft with Gabby*): No, I might have to sleep on the sofa.

GABBY (*escaping*): Be my guest. Carl was really belting them down at dinner, wasn't he?

ALEX: Yes, well, he does that you know.

GABBY (*crossing around sofa, taking dress off*): Are you coming to sleep? You must be dropping.

ALEX: I'm not all that tired, actually.

GABBY: There's a switch.

ALEX: If I turn in early you aren't obliged to go to bed too.

GABBY: If I didn't want to I wouldn't.

She sits on the back of the sofa.

You want to tuck me in?

ALEX: Yeah, I'll be in.

She slips her arms around his neck and kisses him. Alex groans.

GABBY (*crossing around sofa and retrieving her shoes*): Don't get tense, I'm too tired!

ALEX: Tense? What the—what are you talking about?

GABBY (*crossing to bedroom*): OK, darling. If I fall asleep, I love you.

Gabby exits into the bedroom. Alex rises, crosses to the bedroom door and stands outside talking to her clownishly, in an assumed German accent. But Gabby doesn't respond in kind—she's tired, she wants to go to sleep, and finally Alex closes the door and turns back into the living room. He switches on the radio, lights his pipe. He dials a number on the phone, listens, looks at his watch, puts the phone back in the cradle. He finally sits in the nearly darkened room.

Carl comes back from the kitchen, as though both homes were superimposed upon each other in the single proscenium frame. He is still wearing the coat; he takes it off and puts it in the closet, at the same time taking out a rifle. He cleans ashtrays, turns out the outside light and goes into the dining room and sits.

There is a sound, Gabby comes in from the bedroom, walking in her sleep. Alex wakes her gently, reassures her, and she kisses him before returning to the bedroom. Alex shuts the bedroom door again, *"wiping his mouth with the back of his hand, unconsciously."* Alex dials the phone number again, as Carl comes into the living room, sits on the end of the sofa and tells the audience that he is staying up watching the Late Late Show because his trick knee is giving him pain. The thought of Mary gives him pain too: "It's all got to break!"

ALEX (*re the phone*) : God damn.

CARL: Who you calling?

ALEX: A girl.

CARL: Age?

ALEX: Seventeen.

CARL: Relationship?

ALEX: I'm not sure.

CARL: You've had her?

ALEX: No. I take her places.

CARL: The ball game, the movies, the museum, the zoo.

ALEX: The botanical gardens once.

CARL: She studies botany.

ALEX: At University of Chicago.

CARL: And you're in love with her.

ALEX: Something like that.

CARL: Where is she?

ALEX: I was just wondering.

CARL (*glances at his watch*) : It's nearly two.

ALEX: Yeah, I know. Well.

> *He hangs up the phone.*

CARL: No, no, no, this has got to break wide open.

Alex confides to Carl and to the audience that he may be in love with this teen ager, Debbie, but he's not sure; he's not even sure what love is. Carl thinks the relationship "sick" and Alex tries to explain: "It's like I was never young. I must have been purblind and deaf. I didn't see things. We drank and had fun and sang, but I didn't *see* things. This girl knows things I don't even know yet. She knows how to leave herself alone. She has no allegiance, no priorities—everything is valuable to her—equally. As it comes."

Carl addresses the audience, changing the subject and explaining that he'd badly wanted a son. When Ellen was born he was disappointed at first, but not any more. Ellen brought Mary and Carl closer together. Having another child wouldn't do the same thing again. Carl finds it amusing that his CPA, Donald, has had only daughters, no sons.

Mary comes down from Ellen's room. She wonders about the possibilities of a new career for Alex: "If he's not political he'll be eaten alive and if he is political, then I've no interest in him."

CARL (*as Mary starts to go*) : You know I had to make a lot of quick phone call confirmations and I knocked them off this afternoon in about ten minutes flat.

MARY: Good.

CARL (*gets the poker*) : And without even skipping a beat I called Donald and asked him how about knocking it off with my wife.

> *Freeze. Long pause. Alex dials a number, looks at his watch.*

MARY: And what did he say?

CARL: I wasn't even sure I could call him; I didn't actually know I was going to until I hung up.

MARY: Whatever gave you the idea there was anything to knock off?

CARL: No, we won't do that—

MARY: Won't do what?

CARL: Pretend. We won't pretend. Of course I'd know. I've known for months. Every Wednesday.

Mary tries to pretend she visits her mother on Wednesdays, but Carl has been watching the Chicago apartment Wednesday afternoons and knows they meet there. Carl didn't say anything about it to Mary until now because he couldn't bring himself to, and he hoped the affair would end. Beating up Donald—who's only about half Carl's size—and/or Mary wouldn't make Carl feel any better (and he puts the poker away).

MARY: Oh, God, Carl, couldn't I have seen him because—

CARL: No, I don't like "seen," that's too easy, say "screwed," say—

MARY: All right, then, just because I enjoyed it? Without dragging romance through it? Because I dug him?

CARL: OK, it was hot stuff—better than—

MARY: —My responsibility to you hasn't altered in the least degree.

CARL: Yeah, yeah, and Ellen, I know, I know, I know, and with all this great guilt we should be even closer now; hell, I guess I should thank him, huh? No, just call it off. That's it. It's over. From now. Finis. And that's all. That's all I have to say.

>   *A long pause.*

Mary?

MARY: I couldn't do that, Carl.

>   *Carl sits with his head in his hands. Mary has moved to the desk and is seated there, sitting forward, her eyes on Carl.*

Carl?

CARL (*without looking up*): I'm here.

MARY: Well, say something.

ALEX: Jesus God, you add it all up and I don't understand!

>   *Rises and sits on edge of desk.*

The farthest star is several billion light years away on the edge of the universe—beyond which is nothing—Einstein tells us. Not even cold, empty space—nothing. Tricky . . . . .

Alex continues philosophizing, mostly to the audience, about problems of earth and its people: starvation, investment, invention. Gabby comes in through the front door, obviously upset, and takes off her coat. Alex continues his monologue, reflecting upon the savage monster that lurks inside every human being and is capable of breaking out at any moment.

ALEX: . . . . . In the middle of culminating a particularly successful business deal; or relaxing on the beach in the clean salt air; you still feel it way down deep in your nature somewhere; "well, tonight, God help me, I may just run completely amuck with a meat cleaver."

> *He finishes in a position, an arm over his head or some such—an arrested position—turns his head to see Gabby.*

GABBY (*evenly*): Who's Debbie Watkins?

> *A pause. Alex's gesture remains arrested.*

ALEX: I don't know.

> *Now we can see Gabby is about to break.*

GABBY: I think if you'd have said almost anything else I'd have thought it was a lie.

> *A long pause.*

ALEX: Your—mysterious—man caught up with you.

GABBY: Umm. Her father.

> *Long silence, controls herself.*

I was shown what I was told was a rather unflattering photograph of her.

ALEX: A girl. Student. She goes to University of Chicago.

GABBY: Well, I wish we could bring her out here so I could tear the bitch—!

Alex swears he's never touched the girl. Gabby is infuriated at the thought of her husband chasing around after a teen ager. It gives Gabby some satisfaction to inform Alex that the girl's father has sent her away to her mother in Hawaii, so the affair is over for the time being—though Gabby wonders whether there mayn't be someone else too in Alex's life. When Alex moves toward her, Gabby warns him not to touch her. She wonders in what way Alex gets satisfaction from the relationship, at the same time she is kicking herself for not guessing what was going on: "I thought when the sex started slacking off and constant attention waned we had reached a marvellously settled plateau. I felt married. Jesus! ....."

All at once Mary breaks into the conversation, speaking to Alex about degrees of love and devotion. Carl breaks in, addressing Mary.

CARL: You didn't think of Ellen or me or—?

MARY: Don't ask questions; I'll only answer—my defenses are always down when they should be up and up when they should be down. Do I love Carl? I ache for him, I worry, I pray I won't hurt him; I'll spend my life trying to convince him that I do rather than hurt him, isn't that enough?

CARL: You love me?

MARY: Yes.

CARL: I love you.

MARY: I know you do, Carl.

CARL (*quite loud; finished*): All of my life!

MARY (*now she must go to him but holding back as much as possible*): I know, darling.

CARL: All my life! Since I was a kid. (*In desperation.*) I was a hero in school and all I wanted, Mary. Everything! Nothing meant anything, nothing was of value to me! In myself! A home, any accomplishment, achievement, position! Any value! Morality! Respect! Nothing was of value if I couldn't lay it at a woman's feet some day as a sacrifice! A pledge! The value of everything was in what it meant to you! It was never a game!

MARY (*crying*): I know, I know.

CARL: Don't answer me! Help me. Marry me, Mary! Take—take—take from me. If you can't let me give then . . . what is there . . .

Mary tries to comfort Carl, who slowly pulls himself together. He invites Mary into the bedroom, and Mary tries to respond with a semblance of warmth and playfulness. Carl takes her in his arms and carries her into the bedroom.

When they have gone, Alex confesses to Gabby that he's been the victim of his own fantasy about a perfect woman and a perfect love. He's almost sacrificed their marriage to this fantasy, but now he has had enough of it and suggests to Gabby that it's not too late ". . . . . if we take this opportunity to go to Washington and start fresh. I don't want us to stay out here in this wilderness. And we'll try to help the kids—and the people who need it. I think we could do something. Gabby? Can we do that? Finally?"

This is no time to decide such a thing, Gabby tells him, and then the phone rings. Alex answers it. The caller is Carl. From Alex's end of the conversation, it seems that Carl is very drunk, planning a trip with Mary and calling to say goodbye.

Gabby finally decides that Washington is probably right for Alex, but it isn't what she wants out of life: ". . . . . I want a home and children and love . . . . . and I don't want to help anyone. I'd—in the first place—never be able to convince myself I wasn't helping someone to make myself feel noble and I'd feel better making myself feel noble honestly. I can't live like that."

Gabby exits into the bedroom. Carl comes into the hall to phone Alex. His white undershirt is stained with blood. We now hear Carl's half of the phone conversation that has just taken place.

CARL (*enormously jovial, into the phone*): Al? Alex? Hey, meathead! This you? Hell, I didn't recognize your voice!

This is all very rapid and almost without pause to listen.

Baby, I tell you, I am the prize hamburger! Well, what do you think? Listen, we talked it over, we sat down like two human beings for a change and—well, of course! Hell, she didn't feel anything about that guy—man, I mean the guy's half my size!! What could she— (*Laughing.*) Yeah, yeah, yeah, right, right, right—Hell he must know himself 'cause Mary can't fake it! Alex it's great! Now listen—

Holds the phone away for a second, gasping for breath, a look of intense pain on his face. The happy look is forced back as he speaks again.

Now, listen, you're going to understand this—you know that place up at the lake? Well, we're going to drive up there the three of us tonight. And—no, we're leaving right now, buddy—I just wanted to . . . (*Breaking down, but he keeps trying.*) . . . tell you and thank you for listening to all my—I know! What it must have been! Yeah! (*The laughter becomes blubbering—almost incoherent, still trying to speak jovially.*) Alex, Alex, she's got hold of my elbow, boy. We're leaving right this minute. I just wanted you to know so you wouldn't worry. All right, boy? Huh? (*Breaking down completely.*) Listen you take care of yourself, you hear? Old buddy? Huh? Old buddy? Alex, she's pulling me to the door . . . you know her! OK buddy, OK now—hell, I'm so happy, Alex, you take care of yourself, you hear? You hear that? I'm O.K. I'm O.K. You be good, buddy!

> *Still nodding, crying, Carl manages to hang up the phone. A clang as the phone hits the cradle. Carl takes the rifle and exits upstairs to Ellen's room.*

ALEX: Gabby, did you tell me that Carl and Mary had sold—?

> *Stands frozen.*

Oh, God!

> *Grabbing up his coat.*

Oh, God! Oh, God!

> *Exits. Gabby re-enters and goes to the closet, getting her coat. Alex breaks through the front window.*

(*Yelling.*) Carl? Carl? Ellen?

> *Gabby exits.*

Mary?

> *Gunshot. Gunshot. Curtain.*

REBEL WOMEN

A Play in Three Acts

BY **THOMAS BABE**

Cast and credits appear on pages 364, 366

THOMAS BABE was born March 13, 1941 in Buffalo, N.Y. and went to high school in Rochester prior to Harvard, where he received his B.A. in 1963. He went on to Yale Law School, graduating in 1972, but he'd already been bitten by the playwriting bug, having won the first Phyllis Anderson Award at Harvard in 1963 for his script The Pageant of Awkward Shadows. *His second play was* Kid Champion *with which Babe made his professional playwriting debut last season in a 48-performance off-Broadway production by Joseph Papp at the Public Theater, where his new* Rebel Women, *his first Best Play, was produced in the final month of the 1975–76 season.*

Another Babe script, Mojo Candy, *was given a production by Yale Summer Cabaret in 1975. He is also the author of poems published in English magazines. With Timothy S. Mayer, he founded and ran the Summer Players at Agassiz Theater, Cambridge, Mass. from 1966 to 1968. He lives in New Haven, was married and is now divorced, with one daughter.*

Time: December 5-6, 1864

Place: The summer home of the Law family in Vidalia, Ga.

ACT I: LATE AFTERNOON

SYNOPSIS: The large living room is very sparsely furnished. It is elegantly shaped but now rather barren, with doors giving off to a hallway backed by a staircase upstage and with french windows lining the wall at left. The back of the house is reached through an alcove at right.

The noisy activity of advancing soldiery and fleeing civilians is heard and very occasionally glimpsed through the windows. It is tea time, with the mistress of the house, 57-year-old Mrs. Mary E. Law, presiding. Her daughter Mary Law Robarts, 27 years old and four months pregnant, Katherine King, a pretty 19-year-old neighbor, and the black serving woman Tussie are sorting out various belongings they've brought with them from Atlanta in trunks.

MRS. LAW: We simply will not concern ourselves with this Sherman.

TUSSIE: Amen.

KATE: They're all frightful little boys, but I do think they'll be of use to us, in some way, I don't know how.

Explosion.

KATE: Now that's not more than a mile off. See, I told you, I told you!

MRS. LAW: What cannot be helped must be endured.

MARY ROBARTS: They burned his church, too, did you hear? My husband's church. The blue-bellied sons of bitches.

MRS. LAW: Mary, I must ask you . . .

KATE: Well, I think I'd do anything for a taste of their company.

MARY: Who?

KATE: Men.

MARY: You are a foolish thing, Kate King. Is there anybody in the world, I wonder, who doesn't know that? Three days ago these Lincolnite soldiers under Sherman arrived in Roswell, oh, you remember what a tiny, peaceful place that Roswell was. Five hundred women, old, young, black, white, comely, pitted and scarred, working peacefully in the two big mills, spinning cotton for uniforms and bedclothes and bandages. Well, Sherman arrested every one of them and after peaceful Roswell was pillaged and burned to the ground before their eyes, the women were loaded, five hundred of them, into railway freight cars and shipped North, declared criminal traitors. Some died outright, naturally; some suffered nervous collapses and will never recover. Others just fell quiet and stared at each other hopelessly as the dusty, turd-strewn cars travelled North over a hard roadbed lambasted by shells. I know all about that. I dreamed about it last night, riding with them. When I think about it, I am so shaking with rage I can hardly be still a moment.

Kate calms Mary and warns her to think of her unborn child. The sight of three Union soldiers approaching, seen through the window, gives Mary a chill. The soldiers, dirty and coarse but very young, enter the room unceremoniously and warn the four women: "We can burn down your goddam house and everything in it if you don't respond to our lawful summons, did you know that?"

The soldiers pretend to be interested in firearms and silver (Mrs. Law coldly declares there are none). They call Mrs. Law "an old rebel whore," and she informs them icily that there is a limit to their right to impose on civilians. These men know no law or rights, however, except their orders from Gen. Sherman to make examples of anyone who resists them. If the women cooperate, the soldiers will post a notice placing the house under Federal protection. Mrs. Law believes this is just a ruse to gain their confidence.

The soldiers admit all they're looking for is wine. The women refuse to supply it and the soldiers exit, deliberately smashing a vase on their way out. Mary Robarts felt calmer in their presence than she'd expected, even enjoying parts of the experience. Mary fears that her husband, Rev. Robarts, who has gone on an errand to deliver some mules, will be shot forthwith by the soldiers if they encounter him. As for women, Mary believes, "When they find us, we shall be toyed with and they will ask us politely for that they don't really want, then take outright what is never mentioned."

Mrs. Law recalls her dead husband, Mary's father: "We were so close for so long that we rather became one another." Another explosion causes Kate to start prattling about a happy pre-war time she remembers.

The sound of boots thumping on the porch signals the arrival of Maj. Robert Steele Strong (*"28, adjutant to Sherman"*) and Samuel Sutler (*"in his 30s, doctor of philosophy and merchant, handsome and outlandishly dressed"*). Maj. Strong informs Mrs. Law: "Your house has been commandeered by the Army of the West, William T. Sherman commander, for purposes of temporary headquarters and hospital for said army. You will be compensated for such viands and other supplies as we may have occasion to use."

Mrs. Law orders Tussie to remove the tea things. Strong tells the ladies their sleeping quarters will be considered inviolate, but they're confined to the house for the time being.

Sutler offers his services to the ladies. Kate is attracted to this handsome peddler-philosopher, but Mrs. Law is wary of his apparent friendliness. Mary is downright insulting, which doesn't seem to faze him. The women are curious about what kind of man Sherman is, and Sutler obliges them with information: "As God is my witness, William Tecumseh Sherman is the remarkable man that this remarkable sectional upheaval has elevated."

Sutler explains Sherman's march-to-the-sea strategy of occupation and plunder: "You see privates dressed in ball-gowns on every flank. But it's

O.K. . . . . . they're not forcing white women, no sir. Those broad-backed Johnnies are coupling with Negresses in the dark round every campfire. . . . ."

Sherman's men have committed no atrocities, Sutler informs the ladies. He is interrupted by a commotion of troops. Gen. Sherman strides into the room accompanied by several aides including Strong and Lt. Henry Hitchcock (*"20, staff assistant, a good old boy"*). Soldiers set up Sherman's brass-bound folding field desk down left.

MRS. LAW: Excuse me. (*She is ignored.*) Excuse me.

SHERMAN (*slightly annoyed*): What is it?

MRS. LAW: Shall we be expected to do anything for you?

SHERMAN: Do anything?

MRS. LAW: Will there be any demands?

SHERMAN: Does anybody have any idea what this woman is talking about or why she should be standing there, molesting me?

STRONG: This is her house.

SHERMAN: Well, it is a nice house, one of the nicer ones I've seen. I hope it comes to no harm.

    Pause, notices all the women for the first time.

Go on now. No one will hurt you.

MRS. LAW: I must say that your decency becomes you.

SHERMAN: Is that so?

MARY: Well, I am nearly bored to tears with being terrified of this man, this beast here. How do you do, General? My name is Mary Law Robarts.

SHERMAN: How do you do, Mrs. Robarts?

MARY: This is Katherine King.

SHERMAN: How do you do, Miss King?

MARY: And she is also pleased to meet you, and the Major, and everybody, but she, like the rest of us, is constrained to hate you.

SHERMAN: That's the color of things, Mrs. Robarts. No one is sorrier than myself.

MARY: I don't think so.

MRS. LAW: Mary, if you would be so good, dear.

MARY: This man is obviously a hypocrite. He exhibits a false piety about the way in which he happens to earn his living.

MRS. LAW: Mary, the General's philosophy is essentially alien and you will only demean yourself by making yourself available to him.

Sherman indicates that he understands their hostility, their difficulty in perceiving that his actions are for the best in the long run. Mary startles him by quoting a letter of his decrying all hypocritical claims to righteousness and humaneness by either South or North. Sherman repeats to her his succinct "War is hell" statement. Sherman tries to break off the conversation, but Mary persists in defining him as a sort of rapist without passion. Sherman defends himself; "You make war and I must break the will to make that war. Therefore, I purposefully demoralize every man, woman and child in this bloody land. Your crops will vanish, your animals, your houses, every last shred of sustenance until it is so excruciating to continue to make war that you will stop, you will cease altogether."

Sherman admits, however, that he has no passion for war, nor malice toward his enemy. He admires the South's courage. Mary comments "He means to hurt us, quite deeply," and Sherman, angry, orders Strong to remove the women from his presence. All depart except Kate, who stays by her trunk.

Sherman calls for his whiskey and issues orders for his generals in the field to send representatives for a meeting. Hitchcock goes to carry them out, as Sutler addresses Kate on the subject of the Ten Commandments: "I'm a businessman and a certain amount of my work, alas, is stealing. I do indeed covet my neighbor's ass, if not his man-servant; that's my ambition. Killing, I think, for strictly policy reasons, should be limited. As for the worship of false gods, revering mothers and fathers, adultery—filling, all of it, to get the number up to ten."

Kate admires Sutler's worldly cynicism. He's making an easy conquest of her—though she insists that she must be won, and won with dignity.

Across the room, Sherman angrily decries the introduction of a bill in Congress designed to inhibit his scorched-earth policy. Strong is sure the bill won't pass. Along with his other accomplishments, Sherman is a consummate politician.

Strong compliments his commander, assuring him that he's widely admired —perhaps even in the South—and loved by his soldiers. Sherman is uncomfortable with this kind of hero-worship. His father died when he was six years old and he was brought up by a stepfather; to Sherman, soldiering is "the best thing on earth." To Strong, it is just the opposite: "I know I'm going to run in the other direction as soon as Lee surrenders, and that's my word."

Sherman invites Strong to join him in a whiskey. He expounds on the subject of Gen. Grant: "You know Strong, Grant runs in a narrower compass than me. I'm smarter than he is by a damn sight, we both know that: I see into things. But what I see very often frightens me, and he doesn't give a good God damn. I am a brilliant tactician, but he is certain, even when he's wrong, and I admire him for that. He just goes on."

Sherman tells Strong he was once a lawyer, untrained, in Tennessee, a state that "needed lawyers more than law." Sherman didn't go to Harvard like Strong (Sherman is a West Pointer) but he loves Shakespeare. Strong confides to Sherman his own past history: his father shot himself when Strong was 8 years old, and Strong was brought up by his mother.

Sherman hears Mary coming down the stairs in the hall. Sherman and Strong pretend to be busy, to avoid contact with Mary's "demoralizing" and "morbid" opinions. Mary has come to collect Kate, who is happily asleep beside her trunk, with Sutler watching her. Mary wakes Kate and warns her: "It is not quite seemly for us to spend too much time among these types of men. Mother and I have withdrawn to an apartment above where we feel certain we won't be bothered. You must join us. We must barricade the door."

Grudgingly, Kate agrees to go with Mary, but not before saying goodnight to Sutler, "the doctor" of philosophy. Sutler tries to speak to Mary in a friendly manner, but Mary resents the very presence of the enemy in the house. She accuses Sherman of being drunk, and Sherman counters by calling her "churlish."

Kate apologizes to Sutler for Mary's rudeness. Mary asks Strong for his assistance in removing Kate from the room, but Sherman orders Strong not to comply. Sherman feels that they are all too vulnerable to women's manipulation, himself particularly, who has found himself easily manipulated by his wife.

SHERMAN: My wife once wanted me to leave California because she was not happy there and missed her parents. She is a plain woman, by her own admission, but that is of more concern to her than to me. Yet that day she said to me: "You deserve something better," she said, "a smart splendid woman you can shape to your ends. I am nothing. Let me go." I was entirely and properly moved by what she said, and her confessions of plainness especially touched me. As a consequence, we left. I lost a good business chance, we returned to nothing, we were not measurably better. I mention this anecdote apropos of the way in which my natural feelings have been played upon in the past and as a warning that I have since resolved never to be so pliable again.

MARY: So your wife is plain, Sherman, but thinks you ought to have some smart, splendid woman to shape to your purposes?

SHERMAN: That was incidental to what I was saying.

MARY: It is everything, you demented toad, you butcher, well you can't have us, you barker!

SHERMAN: I don't think I want anything, but to finish up and go home.

Mrs. Law enters.

MRS. LAW: Excuse me. Mary, there is a gentleman here who says that your husband, the Reverend Mr. Robarts, has been captured and detained by Federal soldiers. I don't know on what grounds. I can't quite make it out.

MARY: Poor Freddy!

MRS. LAW: Apparently they believe that the Reverend Mr. Robarts is a guerrilla or a bushwacker, or alternately, that because such guerrillas and bushwackers exist, ordinary people are to be rounded up as hostages, and when one of them is killed from ambush, then one of us will be executed in cold blood. Do I have that policy correctly, General, is that how your order reads?

SHERMAN: In substance.

MRS. LAW: I thought that was how you meant it. In any event, there's nothing we can do about it at the moment. They won't shoot Mr. Robarts tonight, otherwise they wouldn't have allowed for him to send for his Bible and communion set, don't you think? We shouldn't worry too much until tomorrow, for I believe he will be tried before a proper military court and released according to the older and fairer rules of war.

Leading her daughter off, out of room, Kate and Tussie following.

It will be so awful if he is killed, I know that, but we must see what will be decided for us. You shouldn't cry so much for him yet. You shouldn't cry so much for yourself. (*Surprised.*) Are you crying for yourself?

Women start to exit, freeze, as lights fade. Curtain.

ACT II: EVENING OF THE SAME DAY

Lt. Hitchcock and soldiers sing the verses of "Hitchcock's Lament," a song whose burden is expressed in the last three lines of its chorus: ". . . . . But one night more/Without a whore/And we'll die of starvation."

At 9 p.m., the room is occupied by soldiers and Hitchcock is sitting having his hair cut. Strong is talking to a Southern civilian who has come to beg for food; neither man enjoys his role. After the civilian leaves, Strong expresses compassion for the starving enemy population. Hitchcock thinks they're just putting on an act of suffering. This angers Strong, and he sends Hitchcock away.

Mary enters, sits on the sofa and asks to see Sherman, but the General is away on an errand. Mary discusses the military situation with Strong, who warns her that she shouldn't try to know too much about it. Mary tells Strong about her brother Charles, "likely the best man who ever lived," a Harvard law student like Strong, killed six months ago. Strong knew and liked him and expresses his regrets.

Mary asks for Strong's advice as to how to move Sherman to save her husband. She tries to enlist Strong's sympathy by counting him one of the "legion of decent people" in the North who will have to help the South after the war is over.

MARY: . . . . . We will need an underground of people in the North who are feelingly engaged with us: people of the classical stripe, passionate, rooted, who lack all this unprincipled ambition and cold method, method about everything, getting everything done, getting it all cleared up in time for dinner and amusements, that part of the day, methodical procreational activities. We shall need every well-placed man who knows that some people, some schemes, some ways of living are better, there is no other word for it, are better than any others, just as you know. It is really foolish to pretend you don't understand me, Major. Sherman, whom you worship, will gobble you up for lunch one day and explain the thing as necessity. I'm warning you.

STRONG (*hurt, bewildered, defensive*): I don't worship the General. I admire his abilities.

MARY: You love him like a father. Well, don't be ashamed of it. If I were in your place, I would love him too, but I would use my position, you can be sure: I would play him a little before me.

STRONG: It would be unbecoming for me to advance your cause.

MARY: Is it unbecoming for people of the classical stripe to be heroic a little, as God means them to be?

STRONG: Your husband, Mrs. Robarts—I must tell you—may be the instrument by which the life of one or more of my comrades in arms will be saved from the savage, cowardly ambushes of your people, these passionate people who have lived by making other men slaves. Do you understand?

MARY: That's Sherman talk, all that brazen swing of the scythe of what must be and canting explanation. I was speaking of love. What does it take to make you see love and hate, too, how you hate us, how you hate me, how you all do, every last one of you, blood-hate. And how you love us, too.

Mary sends Strong to get her a glass of claret from the cupboard and of course he obeys her. Strong advises her that no one can approach Sherman, but Mary is determined to try.

Sherman enters, harsh and brisk in manner, sending Strong off on an immediate duty. Before Mary can begin a conversation, Mrs. Law and Kate come in. Mrs. Law is indignant because two soldiers came into her room and took the sword which her grandfather carried against the British. Sherman calls for Strong, who enters with Hitchcock. Sherman wants the room cleared of the women at once, even if it means an injury to one of them. Mrs. Law is so insistent, however, that Sherman finally orders, "Find the bloody goddam sword and give it back to Mrs. Law."

Mrs. Law collapses into a chair, suffering a seizure. Sherman calls for the Army surgeon and decides that with all the distractions he can't stay here any longer, he'll move to division headquarters.

Mary begs Sherman on her knees to spare her husband, but Sherman refuses to interfere in this "administrative detail." Mary proceeds to have hysterics, which Sherman is certain are a calculated measure. Finally Sherman begs her to stop—which she does—and eases her into a rocker. Strong comes in with Sutler, who helps Kate and Tussie get Mrs. Law to her feet and maneuver her upstairs.

Strong informs Sherman his horse is ready, and Sherman orders him to pour a whiskey, then sends Strong away. Sherman unburdens himself to Mary about an unhappy incident that caused him to resign his commission and almost to take his own life: he was facing a superior Confederate force, "it was like the shadow of death itself." He asked for reinforcements but the peril of his situation was not believed by the press or Congress, to his utter humiliation.

Sherman remembers other failures in his career outside the military, which he now realizes is his only life. He cannot bear the seeming haphazard mob rule which is civilian life. Sherman wanders on: "It was Bull Run, that set the cap on it. You have never seen human bodies, the bodies of men, so badly defiled, all that flesh filled with capacities, and it became swill, raw swill, in every shape, mangled, and the horses without mounts ran on, blood flowing from their nostrils, except the ones that were hitched to the shattered caissons, and they lay on the ground, gnawing at their sides. 'Thou art beautiful o my love, comely as Jerusalem, terrible as an army with banners.' The Song of Solomon. 'Stay me with flagons, comfort me with apples, for I am sick of love.' Or the conflict. Or I was then. Grant's right when he has to be a sot;

I never could. (*Pause.*) Yes, I have been melancholic, but that is a thing of the past. Now I have found my station. I never was really insane."

Mary observes that perhaps they've both been kept down in life. Sherman's emotional near-catastrophe came about, he thinks, partly because he felt utterly alone, "as no man has ever been since Cain."

Sherman is succumbing to Mary's charms, but he's afraid that if he lets himself go she will take advantage of him in some way.

MARY: . . . . . I conclude I must do something for your sake and for my own, but I don't know what. What can I do for you, you bloody Sherman, that will matter? Will you take my prayers, and my sorrows?

SHERMAN: Well, I must warn you that I cannot and will not interfere with subordinates in this matter of your husband and I must say that I feel aggrieved that it should be between us, or between any people, like that sharp point of pain. That's hard and I'm sorry, but I do not like to be beholden, which is what you attempt to make me.

MARY: I am wishing to hope to want to love you with compassionate passion, you bloody man. Is that so hard?

SHERMAN: Why?

MARY: I have no idea in the world. I am raw with fretting and it's a deal since I sat down to a decent table. I am angry, too. So there! This way is as good as any.

SHERMAN: You are obtuse, Mrs. Robarts. If not your husband, then what, as you are, is it that you want from me?

MARY (*defeated*): I don't know. If you would set my husband free, that would do for now, that would suffice.

SHERMAN: I don't know. I don't think so. (*Pause.*) Well, I know what I want. (*With great effort.*) I want to put my hand on your head, to touch your hair. Would that be acceptable?

MARY (*frustrated*): That would be acceptable.

> Sherman crosses and puts his hand on her head. At first, it is a a grave, monumental act; then his hand begins to move on her head, slowly, feeling the texture of her hair, and interlaces his fingers with her hair. He has averted his eyes, and Mary, who has been still through this, now extends her hand, and they lock fingers. Mary suddenly jumps up, moves away, and then towards him, and kisses him. They mutually embrace. Tussie has been singing a lullaby offstage. Then, suddenly, Mary pulls away.

Oh, no, Uncle Billy, I think not, not now, at this moment.

> Sherman stands looking at her, awkwardly.

I must go upstairs, do you understand me?

SHERMAN: I am going to follow you, if that would not too heavily indebt us, do you understand me?

MARY: I wish you would come along, certainly.

> She goes to the doors, opens them, steps into the hall, and turns

to look at him once more. She then continues upstairs. He crosses
to desk, but just as he gets there he stops suddenly.
SHERMAN (*self-pleased*): Great God in heaven, I am ACCEPTABLE!
He follows her.

The soldiers who've been guarding Sherman disappear as Kate enters calling for Sutler to follow her, which he does. Kate wonders what's going to happen to her now. Sutler reassures her that it will be pleasant: "It will not hurt. Well, yes, perhaps it will, a little at first. I have no first-hand knowledge of these things and I must say I don't care. Sometimes, I'm told, it is absolutely nothing. Sometimes it takes away the whole taste, so I'm told. These things have been borne, Katherine, so many thousands have borne them before. I am a careful and tender trader, Katherine, and I can regulate your pain to benefit. I am interested that you experience some degree of pleasure yourself, as is befitting, I will not steal you blind!"

They start to embrace, but are interrupted by a knock on the door. They exit, as Strong enters the room looking for Sherman. Hitchcock comes in; both officers have been drinking and are soured with the taste of war. Hitchcock has already lost his brother and his oldest friend, who insisted one night that Hitchcock sleep on the side closest to the enemy and then was killed in his sleep by a bullet someone had fired into the air.

HITCHCOCK: . . . . . They're gonna shoot that reverend who's husband of the crazy woman.
STRONG: They won't.
HITCHCOCK: I heard. He's accused a spy.
STRONG: In the name of God, who set this up? Sherman? Did Sherman order the execution?
HITCHCOCK: Nobody ordered it. It's by the book.
STRONG: I have never been so sorry. The General must be told.
HITCHCOCK: Hey, Major, I wanna lie straight by you, tonight. I'm gonna show you something, I am.
STRONG (*surprised, touched*): Why do you want to?
HITCHCOCK: I'm horny, man, hell is just as bright as that. I want some ease.
STRONG: Well, so do I, so do I. But I've got to extricate myself from this God-awful obligation to care so much about these people: the woman, all the women, Sherman, even you, Henry.
HITCHCOCK: Well, I'm sure it's a serious problem but there's not a hell of a lot to do about it now, so come on, Major, or we'll be the only heroes awake tonight, outside the pickets, and I wouldn't put no money out there, hell no. Now come on, Major. It's okay. Everything's okay.
They exit. Curtain.

ACT III: DAWN, THE FOLLOWING DAY

Sutler is curled on the floor, fully dressed, with Kate sitting beside him sing-ing softly. The door opens and Kate pulls a shawl over herself pretending to be asleep. Mrs. Law comes in and sees the sleepers. She pours a pitcher of water over Sutler to wake him and then exits.

Kate tells Sutler she means to follow him wherever he goes. She loves him and intends to pursue him. Kate finally makes Sutler admit that he loves her too, but he is reluctant to make her a part of his peculiar existence as a travel-ling merchant who satisfies people's need to buy some trifling object when they can't have what they really want, as a sort of substitute.

Sutler digresses, telling Kate how Sherman once had a 10-year-old son who died of typhoid and left an unfillable hole in his father's heart. Sutler then begins to ask himself why he can't have Kate if he wants her. He needs time to think out their situation, and Kate exits.

Strong comes in looking for Sherman. The Major and Sutler dislike each other, and their meeting is full of hostility. Sutler goes out as Hitchcock comes in, advising Strong not to push the peddler too far.

HITCHCOCK: We been crazy, and killin', and concupiscent, and he knows it, the drummer, and I know it, and you sure as hell know it, and 50,000 men, they know it, and the General, he first of all knows it and he knows we all know it, 50,000 strong, but, you know, Major, the General doesn't even want to know he knows it, let alone we know it neither: shit, we better wake up every morning, virginal, you just ask Uncle Bill. (*Pause.*) This here's a real virginal morning, ain't it?

STRONG: It's another day, lieutenant.

HITCHCOCK: Yeah, I can see that. I suppose back in Boston you're very highly regarded, Major: they probably have high hopes for you. But still I don't think you know piss-all about life.

STRONG: What life? This one? This bloody one? The next?

HITCHCOCK: The last one, Major, the last horseshitting one, yesterday.

Sherman enters and goes to his desk. He motions for Hitchcock to leave the room and then addresses himself to the Major.

SHERMAN: Strong, at your convenience, would you pass the word to Oster-haus that General Sherman would be greatly pleased if he, Osterhaus, did not butcher that bloody God-bothering Reverend Robarts but instead returned the same undeserving God-bothering reverend bastard to his natural bed and board. Would you do that?

STRONG: They're going to shoot him today.

SHERMAN: Really? Then would you do that immediately? Would you tell Osterhaus that it would please me to have this done, it would ease my own predicament, but that I am not ordering him and if the prayerful reverend is fated ineluctably to be extirpated, then that is how it must be. Only it is my pleasure he not be, nothing more?

STRONG: Yessir.

Strong exits as Tussie comes in with the coffee tray, followed by Mary. Mary gives Sherman what she considers a compliment by calling him "the most American specimen I ever saw" and deciding that he'll probably be President some day, after the war is over. Sherman, on edge, insists on his identity as a soldier and warns Mary to stop talking politics. Sherman admits "I am in personal debt to you for a kindness," and Mary comments, "It is a good thing we did not fall fast in love."

Sherman informs Mary that he has given orders to save her husband from the firing squad and advises her never to tell him of their intimacy (she believes she must). He tells her he never wants to hear from her again. Mary wonders if Sherman is ashamed of their romantic adventure. He denies this vigorously.

SHERMAN: There is much to regret, Mrs. Robarts, but not my knowing you. We were fairly served; we matched well.

MARY: Well, say we leave it then that I traded myself for my husband's life. All that makes more sense to me, and you have a peddler's sense of propriety after all. Really! I have to be paid with something, since this is harlotry, but I don't care about that. I must have something from you, your good estimation, an afterthought. You must give me more than a poke; you must think well of me.

SHERMAN: You have my good estimation.

MARY: Oh? (*Coolly.*) I am inclined to believe that when this is over and you are done stringing us up, in a few months, I will end up very coarse. I will be a terrible hard bitch, unconquerable.

SHERMAN: Good for you, then, because I am a notorious son of that same hard species. We'll grind it all up, you and I, and it has been, may I say, momentous.

MARY: It has been exciting and rotten and I feel quite empty.

Disentangling herself after a brief embrace.

Well, you've got to march, Sherman, so march, and I don't wish you well, I really don't: I had to try to cut you down a little. It took up the night at least.

SHERMAN: Quite so.

Pause.

They're coming now. It would be better all around if you went to your rooms. I dislike to say goodbye and goodbye again.

MARY (*with firm love*): Very well. Goodbye. (*Pause.*) And goodbye again.

Mary exits as Strong reappears with soldiers. Strong tries to call Sherman's attention to the dispatches which arrived during the night, calling them "things," and his unmilitary manner greatly annoys the General. Strong attempts to outface Sherman with sarcasm, but this only makes Sherman angrier, and he warns Strong to watch his step. Strong imprudently speaks his mind: "I have concluded that we—this army—are irrevocably in the wrong, morally and God-foreknowingly in the wrong in how we have concluded this malignant rooting out and rooting up of this land and these people. And I must forbid myself from having any further part of it, and you sir, you must forbid yourself from having any further part of it."

Sherman cries "I AM IT!" and places Strong under arrest for insubordination. Hitchcock takes Strong's sword and they both exit.

Mary, Kate and Mrs. Law come back into the room, as Sutler enters with a bottle of Napoleon brandy found buried with a cache of liquor which the soldiers have consumed during the night. Mary calls Sutler a son of a bitch for taking property that doesn't belong to him. Kate leaps to Sutler's defense.

Mrs. Law thanks Sherman for returning her grandfather's sword. Sherman orders the brandy bottle returned to its rightful owners, over Sutler's protest.

"That is all there is," declares Sherman and leads his troops off. Sutler throws back a parting "Next year, Kate. Be constant," and Kate declares to the other women that she loves him. All is now silent as the four women stand alone in the living room. Mary observes that she'll probably stay in Georgia instead of moving North or to England. Mrs. Law expects that her end will come soon. Kate dreams of a summer in Europe at the best hotels accompanied by beautiful children and a rich husband.

Three Union soldiers enter with smouldering torches, and the women brace themselves for the burning of their house. The soldiers haven't come to burn, however, but to inform the ladies that the Rev. Robarts has been released and is on his way home. And three horses and a mule have graciously been left to them by Sherman.

The soldiers leave, and Mrs. Law expresses her determination to save the house if she can. She tells Mary and Kate "You have both had a spell of being fantastic" and advises them to make ready some food and brandy for the Rev. Robarts's imminent return.

After Mrs. Law exits, Mary tells Kate that the war will probably be over by Tuesday and encourages her to dream on about Europe.

MARY: I think I'll go out for a minute, walk around. I need to leave this house.

KATE: I don't think you should.

MARY: Here's something you can do. Set out some bread, if there is any, and a pitcher of coffee for Mr. Robarts. Just set it out and say I left it for him. I'll just be a moment.

KATE: Do you think so?

MARY: And the brandy. He is fond of the smallest amount, he genuinely is. Would you?

     Pause.

I want to say just a few more things about this. Excuse me.

     Exits.

KATE: Well, I'm not just going to wait here, Mary Robarts. I've had a taste of it too. You can take one of those horses if you want to, go ahead, though I think it is usually unwise for a woman expecting a child to be rushing here and there, but take it if you want and ride to Eden or New Place Station or Hopewell or beyond or wherever, but I think—O *merde!*

TUSSIE: It's like Fanny dreamed it in her visions. Hubert and William James and Nate all gone along with the soldiers, singing like fools, and Dan Josiah got so little humility he got him some crutches and a sling for his arm and a bandage for his head and he stood him by the road lookin' pretend hurt and he's never been sick a day in his life, let alone kilt and so some man give him a hand up on a wagon. And Rhody and Abram, they just vanished from the earth. And Stella won't manage it through; and Andrew Dirt is so mad he run the other way to join Lee, he don't know where, totin' his old flintlock, even though I said, "You're black and you're carrying a gun and that means, Andrew Dirt, you're dead." So there's Gramma Cealy and Maggie and Adline, though she's simple-minded, and me. Miss Kate, we're gonna be free. How about that? Ain't that wonderful, to be free?

KATE: I don't know, and truth to tell, I don't care. You just see what we've got for the Reverend to eat and set out some strong waters—there's a bottle over the kitchen cupboard, set it out, and mind, none for you. I . . . I don't care where you went, Mary Robarts, I don't. But I know where I shall take a horse or two.

> *Exits.*

TUSSIE (*alone*): She needn't said that to me. I never took anything that wasn't offered, not me. But that's not my concern, what she knows or doesn't know. (*Pause.*) It's bein' freed, that's my concern. My won't that be nice? Oh, yes, yes, sweet Jesus, won't that be something?

> *Closes doors, exits. Blackout. Curtain.*

THE RUNNER STUMBLES

A Play in Two Acts

BY MILAN STITT

Cast and credits appear on pages 252-253

MILAN STITT was born in Detroit in 1941. He studied with Kenneth Rowe at the University of Michigan, where he won two Avery Hopwood Playwriting Awards, and with John Gassner at the Yale School of Drama, where in 1965 he wrote the first of many drafts of The Runner Stumbles. *The development of this script continued in a Boston University Playwrights Workshop production at the Berkshire Theater Festival (1971), an off-off-Broadway staging at the Manhattan Theater Club (1974) and this season's regional theater production at the Hartman Theater in Stamford, Conn. which was brought to Broadway May 18, 1976 as its author's professional playwriting debut and first Best Play.*

Stitt is the founder and director of an off-off-Broadway group, Triad Playwrights Company, which helps writers develop new plays. He produces and teaches playwriting there, and his own one-character play Edie's Home *was staged by Triad this season and taped for broadcast by WBAI.*

Stitt lives in New York City.

Time: April 1911

Place: A cell and courtroom in Solon, Michigan

ACT I

The Cell

SYNOPSIS: A guard leads Father Rivard (a priest in the vigor of early middle age) from his "arraignment" to his "cell" on a stage that is almost bare. Only a few simple props are used to suggest changes of scenes, several of which take place in Father Rivard's mind.

Father Rivard hears the sound of children singing in a nearby school, reminding him of the Catholic school in the parish he once headed. The woman who cooks for the prisoners—Erna Prindle—enters with some mince meat muffins made especially for Father Rivard. Erna persuades the guard to leave them alone in the cell so that she can tell Rivard she hasn't been to confession in more than four years. She's happily married, with three children, but her husband isn't a Catholic.

RIVARD: I remember.

ERNA: You do? But it's wrong.

RIVARD: Marriage, if you're happy, if it does that, Erna, how can it be wrong?

ERNA: If you look out your window, Father, you can see Holy Rosary Church up on the hill. I can see it from my kitchen. If you're troubled or scared, you can just stand and look at it. It's a comfort, a real comfort.

GUARD (*as he enters*): You better get moving, Erna. His lawyer just came and is talking with the sheriff. Then he'll be coming back here.

ERNA: But I didn't ask him. Everyone says you did it, Father, but they don't know you the way I did. If you plead guilty to murder, it's what they call a technicality. That still wouldn't mean you did it. You'd just have a better chance.

RIVARD: What chance?

GUARD: Come on, Erna.

     Lawyer enters.

ERNA: If you say you're guilty, no matter what the jury thinks, they can only sentence you to life. They can't hang you.

RIVARD: Do you think I'm guilty, Erna? That I could kill Sister Rita?

ERNA (*uncertain*): No.

Erna exits, followed by the guard, as the court-appointed defense counsel, Toby Felker, introduces himself to the prisoner, his client. The lawyer is an earnest young man who has a reputation for never winning a case, but he's the only lawyer available in the area. He met Rivard once before, at a Grange meeting in Leland. He'll take the case if Rivard accepts him, though he'd rather be out fishing.

RIVARD: As long as you believe I'm innocent.

FELKER: But that means a trial. And I'd have to know, well, a lot. What did happen that last day?

Silence.

The day of the fire. Four and a half years ago. You both disappeared the same night. Everyone figured—but you tell me, what did happen?

RIVARD: I don't know. I know nothing happened. It couldn't have. I'm not a violent man.

FELKER: All right. All right. We could start at the beginning. Say, when she arrived.

A nun—Sister Rita—enters.

RIVARD: I couldn't live through it again.

FELKER: Rivard.

Silence.

RIVARD: All right. I can do it. I can remember every detail if I want. Then we'll know. I'm strong enough. She came here in the spring. About this time of year. There were lilacs.

Sister Rita steps closer. She is carrying a bunch of lilacs and a rattan suitcase. She is warm, having walked up the steep hill on which Holy Rosary and its adjacent buildings sleep. Now at the top she stops and looks back at the valley's toylike town.

The Hill

The scene shifts into Rivard's memory of his first meeting with Sister Rita. She finds the place beautiful, a wilderness of trees (she grew up in nearly treeless Detroit). She has noticed the absence of birds. Rivard, who has walked part way down the hill to meet her, informs her that they are in the midst of a serious drought. Rivard warns her that the winters can be very bleak and suggests she keep busy to avoid homesickness and other feelings of regret for renouncing the outside world. Sister Rita reassures him: "I believe everything I've done is part of me. I had to be a child then to be a nun now. I've kept a diary. Since I was old enough to write, really. When I look through it now, I see that most of the worries I had at fifteen, I have today. The present is little more than a mirror of the past. I am a person who is a nun, not a nun who used to be a person."

Rivard changes the subject abruptly, telling Sister Rita that his housekeeper, Mrs. Shandig, can be called upon for help, since the other two nuns on duty here—Sisters Mary Martha and Immaculata—haven't been feeling well lately. Sister Rita fears she may have annoyed Rivard by speaking too plainly and personally, but such is not the case. Rivard explains that his seeming awkwardness probably arises from lack of practise in conversation. The other sisters seldom communicate with him.

SISTER RITA: I think conversation is as essential as air. If people don't talk with each other, what good is anything?

RIVARD: You know, when I first came to Solon I too made a completely terrible start.

SISTER RITA: I don't feel I've made a completely terrible start.

RIVARD: No. No, you haven't. I didn't mean that. But when I came to Solon, I was the first priest appointed to Holy Rosary in nine years. The Bishop didn't even know if the church would still be here. But you know how eager Bishop Ginter is to expand, which is why I think he sent me here. And also I needed a quiet parish to work on my book. It's called "Augustinian Order (colon) An Examination and Extension." And surprisingly enough, what with starting the school, convincing the men to build the convent, converting one of them in the process, and . . . well, the book is coming along. Not as fast as I'd hoped because . . . At any rate, when I arrived here, no one met me. I asked the blacksmith for directions. Maurice Prindle, the blacksmith, is rather a practical joker and he sent me to that little church down there. And when I saw the sign "Solon Evangelical Methodist," I thought—

The Cell

A comment by Felker, the lawyer, brings Rivard's thoughts and the scene back to the jail cell. Rivard describes how the memory of Sister Rita haunted him after he had left Solon and buried himself in Detroit, working hard on an assembly line trying to forget her. Rivard says, "The only time I actually approached happiness was during those last few months in Detroit. No one knew my name. No one expected anything of me."

Felker has a hunch that Rivard is innocent. Rivard is certain that the nun was alive when he left Solon, and he only learned of her death when he was arrested in Detroit. He thinks perhaps Maurice Prindle may be able to testify that she was alive when he left.

Back Porch and the Kitchen

The scene shifts to Solon and the Holy Rosary, where the children can be heard laughing in school offstage as Sister Rita enters Mrs. Shandig's kitchen and invites her to join the class whenever she pleases; Mrs. Shandig, Father Rivard's housekeeper, is illiterate and Sister Rita will teach her to read.

At the moment, Mrs. Shandig's mind is on Father Rivard—he is working too hard on his book since Sister Rita arrived, Mrs. Shandig feels, and she can't offer to help him because she can't read. Sister Rita learns that Mrs. Shandig, who knows the Catholic mass by heart, is a convert brought into the church by Father Rivard. Mrs. Shandig had previously worked as cook in a rough lumber camp where her husband was the hunter who "brought me those bleeding animals." She hoped he wouldn't come back from his hunting trips, and one day he didn't—but she soon had to leave the camp because with her husband gone the men started "poking at me with their spoons."

MRS. SHANDIG: . . . . . I never saw a town until I saw Solon. I didn't. They told me down there that Father needed a housekeeper. I never knew there was Catholics before that. I didn't. Just God. I owe everything to Father, so I have to help as much as can be. I try to be the best Catholic I can for him, but it's harder. Me being only a convert.

SISTER RITA: They always told me that converts make the best Catholics. Did you know that? You can be proud of it. You made a choice. I never had a choice.

MRS. SHANDIG: Don't tell anyone I wasn't born Catholic. No one else knows.

SISTER RITA: Sometime you look through Father's Saints Book and count how many of the saints were converts. You'll see.

MRS. SHANDIG: I can't read yet. I just want to.

SISTER RITA (*handing her a student paper*): Keep this. Think about the shapes and I'll tell you their names later.

MRS. SHANDIG: I can't go to the school.

SISTER RITA: Suppose after supper, you come to the convent then.

MRS. SHANDIG: But the sisters—

SISTER RITA: We'll sit on the porch. They don't even have to know.

MRS. SHANDIG: I'll tell Father though. That's all right. I'm doing it for him.

The Court

The scene shifts to a courtroom where Father Rivard's trial is in progress. The prosecutor is questioning Monsignor, Bishop Ginter's secretary, about a visit to Father Rivard's cell—did Rivard make a confession? Monsignor tells the court no, Rivard is no longer a practising Catholic. Rivard's lawyer, Felker, objects to this reference to the defendant's religion.

Felker then confers with his client about another matter. Maurice Prindle did indeed run the errand for Rivard at the Holy Rosary after Rivard left, but Maurice saw no sign of Sister Rita and will swear to this under oath.

The Study

The scene shifts again in Rivard's memory to the rectory study where Mrs. Shandig is bringing him an egg nog. With all the things Rivard has on his mind—his book, fund-raising, other local problems—Mrs. Shandig wishes she could help him, if only to listen while he talks out his problems. This suggestion reminds Rivard that Sister Rita likes conversation and could discuss his book if he invited her to dinner some night.

MRS. SHANDIG: You'd be alone with a nun, Father.

RIVARD: Well, believe it or not, Mrs. Shandig, I am capable of remarkable propriety.

MRS. SHANDIG: I know that. Why Father, everyone thinks you are the finest person that ever they knew.

RIVARD: And well they should, shouldn't they?

MRS. SHANDIG: I think so.

RIVARD: I care about other people, don't I?

MRS. SHANDIG: Yes you do, Father.

RIVARD: Like Sister. With the other nuns ill, Sister has no one to eat with, and therefore—

MRS. SHANDIG: Father, you know nuns expect to be lonely.

RIVARD: No. No one expects that.

MRS. SHANDIG: Father, I don't like to see you like this. You should be happy here. What do I do wrong? I follow all the rules.

RIVARD: And they make us lonely. Why should the Church cause it? That's what I don't understand. Why do we cause it? Loneliness is not contagious, you know, yet people stand by and willingly watch others suffer as if they were afraid they'll catch it by intervening. It makes me wonder if we are naturally cruel. Something, here, inside makes us, unlike God, revel in misery.

MRS. SHANDIG: Those are beautiful words, Father. Are they from your book?

RIVARD: Yes. They shouldn't be. You are certainly right this time, Mrs. Shandig. But I can't figure out how I can be so wrong all the—

He is interrupted by the unannounced arrival of Sister Rita who—Rivard and Mrs. Shandig agree—should have sent a note first, to avoid encouraging the students to run up here whenever they feel like it. Sister Rita apologizes, but she is bubbling over with the enthusiasm of her errand: she has come to suggest that painting be added to the curriculum at the school. Rivard can't change the curriculum without consulting the Bishop, which he doesn't want to do—but he likes the idea very much. They discuss how they might acquire the paints and paper. Sister Rita offers to write the Bishop in Rivard's stead. Rivard says she must not write to the Bishop lest she end up in as much difficulty as he is in.

The Court

The scene changes to the courtroom, where the prosecutor is questioning the Bishop's secretary about Rivard's appointment to the Holy Rosary. The prosecutor suggests that Rivard was sent to this remote spot because he was a troublemaker. The secretary explains: "Father Rivard was incredibly energetic and popular with parishioners and therefore a bit of an aggravation to the senior priests wherever we put him. The Bishop thought by bringing him into the Bishopric he might personally be able to guide the young priest. But Father Rivard did not readily accede to such help. The Bishop had to request me to stop Father Rivard from entering his office without an appointment. He would burst in and no matter who was present bring up an obscure theological point, suggest his ideas for raising funds through games of chance as is done in certain eastern cities . . . And there was ultimately an incident of his usurping a responsibility that was distinctly the privilege of Bishop Ginter."

The Bishopric

Instructed to visit an ailing nun, Father Rivard found her apparently *in extremis* and administered last rites. This was the Bishop's prerogative—he was to visit her the following morning—and besides, the sick woman did not die after all. For this excess of zeal—or compassion—Father Rivard is posted to Solon for exclusion and self-reexamination.

The Study

Back in the study of the rectory, Sister Rita again urges Rivard to write to the Bishop for permission to add painting to the curriculum. She will pray for the success of his plea. In the meantime, Mrs. Shandig is beginning to learn to read.

The Cell

Back in the jail cell, Felker is questioning his client Rivard about why he permitted Sister Rita to move in with him, warning "The prosecutor can build his whole case on this. High enough to hang a noose."

Rivard explains that the other nuns were sick with consumption and could not be moved. At the same time, the doctor ordered Sister Rita out of the convent because "she couldn't live under the same roof with two consumptives." If Sister Rita was forced to move out, the school would have to be closed because Father Rivard couldn't handle all the classes by himself.

The Classroom

The scene shifts to the Holy Rosary classroom, where Sister Rita is begging Father Rivard to find some way, any way, to keep the school open.

SISTER RITA: . . . . . God knows everything we do is for the Church. He knows we do it for the sake of His children. They are responding, learning from me. They need me, Father. It could be months before there'd be another teaching assignment for me again. I don't think they believe I'm a very good teacher. They didn't really want to send me up here, but I have been good. Haven't I?

RIVARD: This is not a personal question. I built the school. I want it open.

SISTER RITA: What have I done wrong? Why do you want me to leave?

RIVARD: I didn't say I want you to leave. I'd rather you stayed.

SISTER RITA: . . . . . Tell me. Please. There are ways around this if you want. Why don't you? I thought you liked what I was doing here.

RIVARD: This is not a personal question. Why do you always insist upon making everything a personal question?

The Study

MRS. SHANDIG: The letter's here. From the Bishop, Father. He won't let Sister move in here.

Rivard opens the letter.

I'm certain of it. I don't know why you even asked him.

RIVARD (*reading letter*): Mrs. Shandig, he gave permission for you to live here.

MRS. SHANDIG: But I'm not a nun. I'm not. That makes all the difference.

Rivard finishes reading. Silence.

What did he tell you, Father?

RIVARD: He doesn't want me to close the school.

MRS. SHANDIG: But Sister. What does he say about Sister?

RIVARD: Nothing. He didn't mention her.

MRS. SHANDIG: No. He had to. He told you she can't live here, didn't he?

RIVARD (*reading*): "I am stunned to read that you considered suspending classes at the very time our Bishopric is enjoying the most rapid rate of expansion of any in America. Your fine record cannot but reassure me that you have already resolved your local administrative problem without further need of advice from me. I am certain you are finding staying in the village uncomfortable. but it will surely not be for long." The Bishop didn't answer me. It's Monsignor, that hypocrite.

MRS. SHANDIG: Father, what's wrong? You mustn't talk so.

RIVARD: You hear what he wants. He wants me to live in town. To leave four women defenseless on this hill.

MRS. SHANDIG: No. You can't live down there. Those men are vicious. They're vicious, Father. I go down every day. I know.

But Rivard can't let Sister Rita live down there either, and even Mrs. Shandig wouldn't want her to. Rivard is convinced that he must keep the school open, and the only way is to move Sister Rita into his rectory. He decides to do so, in spite of Mrs. Shandig's lamentations.

The Court

In the courtroom, the prosecutor is questioning one of Sister Rita's former pupils, Louise, who remembers the day the nun moved into the rectory—it seemed like a holiday.

The Dining Room

In the rectory dining room, Mrs. Shandig is setting the table when Sister Rita brings in some flowers to brighten her first dinner here. She and Rivard agree that a flower garden is needed at Holy Rosary. Mrs. Shandig exits disapprovingly, leaving the two diners alone.

Sister Rita tells Rivard of her aunt—not really her aunt, but a woman paid to take care of her, whose husband suffered a serious accident: "I had to sit by his bed then. I was so scared. I didn't know what was to become of me if he died. I watched a sparrow in the garden, and he made me laugh. My aunt heard me laughing. It made her so mad that she said terrible, cruel . . . that nobody loved me or would ever love me. She said no one would ever even talk with me after what I'd—I don't know exactly what happened. There were days then . . . well, they said the priest, Father Walling, could hear me when he came and made her unlock me. He took me away, to Guardian Angel Convent, and the good sisters watched over me."

Mrs. Shandig comes in, and Sister Rita tries to cheer her up by offering to share the housework in future. Mrs. Shandig tries to ignore the flowers Sister Rita has brought, but Father Rivard insists she bring a glass of water for them. Rivard begins to talk of his past and remembers a teen-aged crush on a merchant's daughter with blonde sausage curls (the girl thought Rivard's eyelashes "a marvel of the modern world"). Then Rivard talks of the present.

RIVARD: During the past winter here with these slow country people, the sisters both sick, it seemed as though—well, I weakened. I wondered if the Church were as perfect as I believed. Then you came, with your vitality, your joy in the Church, and all my enthusiasm returned. But now . . . people talking about you moving in here.

Rivard takes Sister Rita's hand.

It's like a cloud settling on us. Sometimes, sometimes I nearly despair there will ever be justice in people.

SISTER RITA (*putting other hand on Rivard's which holds hers*: We don't always see it, I know, but God is just. And we couldn't know God if justice weren't in us.

Rivard withdraws his hand as he realizes what has happened.

RIVARD: This, Sister, this now, is exactly why people think nuns and priests should not be alone together.

SISTER RITA: I don't know—

RIVARD: This kind of informal conversation encourages what I feared would —encourages a lack of discipline. (*Pause.*) We, we won't be able to take our meals together.

SISTER RITA: But Father, when we talk, everything seems all right.

RIVARD: What does that mean?

SISTER RITA: Like I'm a person. I am so weary of hearing Sister's rosary, Sister's book, Sister's this, Sister's that. Never just hers.

RIVARD: It is not for us to worry how we are feeling. We must be separate from the world. All that chaos.

SISTER RITA: God isn't separate. Not from the world. Not from the things people do and feel. He came to earth as a baby. He worked as a carpenter, drank wine, loved the children. We are like God. You can't make God into something else than what you already know. If you do, then you're making God into your image. And God made us in—

RIVARD (*angry*): Sister. (*Smiling.*) Oh, Sister, do you know, you sound very much like a Protestant?

The Court

The scene shifts to the courtroom, where the prosecutor is questioning the former pupil, Louise, about the Father Rivard–Sister Rita relationship after she moved into the rectory. Louise and a friend made up a fiction for their own amusement about the nun and the priest being in love. After her friend "dared me to ask Sister Rita why priests and nuns couldn't marry," the priest called Louise to his study to talk to her and try to set her curiosity at rest.

The Study

In the study, Rivard assures Louise that he wants to answer any questions she may have. Louise asks Rivard about love, and Rivard answers that a priest's kind of love is universal and addresses itself to general needs, not the specific needs of person-to-person romantic love.

Mrs. Shandig enters with two of her egg nogs and overhears Louise ask

Father Rivard what he'd do if someone told him they loved him. Rivard replies, "There are things, young lady, that are a sin even to think about, let alone say," and advises her to discipline her thoughts.

The Court

The scene shifts to the courtroom and the questioning, in which the prosecutor is trying to get Louise to testify about "telling details" of fact. The defense lawyer objects, and the prosecutor ceases his questioning of the witness.

The Study

Back to the study in Father Rivard's memory, the Bishop's secretary is paying Holy Rosary a surprise visit to look into the situation, following the extraordinary request in the recent letter. Father Rivard gives Monsignor the completed three chapters of his seven-chapter book to read while Rivard goes to fetch Sister Rita.

Mrs. Shandig's Kitchen Garden

In the kitchen garden, Mrs. Shandig is telling Sister Rita "I never wanted you to move in because of the rule, but I like having you at the rectory. I do." Rivard enters and tells the women he'd rather the visiting Monsignor wouldn't find out that Sister Rita has been living at the rectory. He asks them to keep the secret by all means "short of lying."

The Study

Father Rivard escorts Sister Rita to the study, where the secretary's comment about Rivard's book is "Pithy, Father. Far more than I expected."

Monsignor suggests to Sister Rita that it might be wise to close the school until the danger of catching consumption from the sick sisters is past. Sister Rita assures him there's no danger, as she doesn't sleep in the room with the invalids.

Monsignor asks Sister Rita where she *does* sleep, and she manages to change the subject. Monsignor persists in wanting to know the answer, and Rivard diverts him with talk about the book. But the Bishop's secretary is not to be put off so easily and comments: "You are all hiding something from me." Sister Rita tells him: "I sleep in the Convent, of course," saving the situation with a lie. Sister Rita exits with Monsignor, talking of paints for her children's class. When they have gone, Rivard throws his manuscript across the room and demands of himself, "What have I done?"

The Kitchen

In the kitchen, Mrs. Shandig tells Sister Rita she doesn't need reading lessons any more, and she doesn't intend to take a day off any more for the time being.

Father Rivard enters, ignoring Sister Rita.

RIVARD: Mrs. Shandig, I have to go over to Leland. I will not be back in time for dinner.

SISTER RITA: Father, I could wait up and cook you some—

RIVARD (*to Mrs. Shandig*): I am speaking at the Grange. I believe they will serve supper there.

SISTER RITA: Why are you pretending that I'm not here?

RIVARD: Because as far as I'm concerned you are not.

SISTER RITA: What do you mean?

MRS. SHANDIG: Father, would you excuse me, I have to feed the—

RIVARD: No. You stay. It was wrong of me to have Sister move in here. You were right, Mrs. Shandig. But I can't send Sister to Detroit now that she lied to Monsignor. They'd punish her so that—

SISTER RITA: But you were there. You could have corrected me, Father.

RIVARD: From now on, if you see me on the stairs, in the hall, anywhere, you will think the same. If it is ever necessary for me to speak to you, I will come to the school.

SISTER RITA: Father, I only lied to Monsignor so that you wouldn't—
Father Rivard exits.

The Parlor

In the parlor a month later, Father Rivard is still ignoring Sister Rita, much to her frustration. Mrs. Shandig enters and starts to peel apples while Father Rivard works at a harness. Irritated by the absence of any conversation, Sister Rita starts scissoring brown paper rather noisily, cutting out flower shapes for the school (there is such a drought that real flowers are scarce).

Sister Rita offers to resume Mrs. Shandig's reading lessons, but Mrs. Shandig doesn't feel she has the time. Mrs. Shandig's light burns late at night because she can hear Sister Rita walking up and down so she stays awake too, doing the mending.

SISTER RITA: I'm sorry. I didn't know you could hear me.
She waits for someone to speak.
I like to look at the few lights down in the valley, try to imagine why those three or four windows have a warm glow so late at night. Someone sick, a party, a student preparing for an exam, a baby being born. Do you ever do that?
Silence.
Then I look up at those trees behind the convent. Trees. They catch the stars, darken the ground. It's like you said, Father. I pray against the dark.
Silence.
Do you know what I mean, Mrs. Shandig? About praying.

MRS. SHANDIG: I don't know, Sister. You are a nun. I never know what to say about such things. I don't stand when I pray. I didn't think you are supposed to. Are you, Father? I'm sorry. You want to read, don't you?

SISTER RITA: It is not disrespectful if you want to pray, Mrs. Shandig. God gave us a brain after all, and I think he expects us to use it.

MRS. SHANDIG: Father, I wish Sister wouldn't talk personal like this. I don't understand things the way you do, Sister.
Silence.

SISTER RITA: Well, you talk personal with the other sisters. I hear you, Mrs. Shandig.

MRS. SHANDIG: Not blasphemy, Sister.

Father Rivard sends Mrs. Shandig out so that he can talk to Sister Rita. Rivard tells her they can't have this sort of conversation. Sister Rita argues that they haven't exchanged a word in a month, and Rivard says that's how he wants it. Sister Rita declares "I won't be ignored," and Rivard instructs her that the proper place for her to speak to him is in the Confessional.

Sister Rita complains that even the other two sisters fall silent when she approaches. She has the children for company, of course, but that isn't enough; she'd like to have dinner with Rivard as before and talk things out: "It couldn't be God's will that we go out of our way to be unhappy."

Rivard accuses her of wanting the Church to be humanly imperfect, but the Church (he tells her) is capable of demanding and smiling upon painful sacrifice. He instructs her to kneel when she prays, to remind herself of her humility.

SISTER RITA: Stop it. Stop. I can't stand this. I can't.
     Silence.
Have you ever been human? God is perfectly aware I respect and love Him, Father. And He knows I am human. Every breath I let out and every movement I make I try to make for Him. And if I felt closer to Him standing on my head when I pray, I would stand on my head.

RIVARD: Christ knelt.
     Sister Rita slaps Rivard. He slaps her.

SISTER RITA: How do I—I'm all alone. If there were just one thing about you that was human. I don't believe you have the same blood in your veins as I do. I don't believe it. Do you? Do you bleed when you're cut? There's nothing human about you.
     Father Rivard grabs paring knife, jabs hand, holds it so Sister Rita can see blood, then smears blood on Sister Rita's face.

RIVARD: Stay away from me.
     Mrs. Shandig, unaware of what has transpired, enters on the striking of the hour, carrying two rosaries. Sister Rita quickly hands her handkerchief to Father Rivard so Mrs. Shandig doesn't notice. Father Rivard wraps bleeding hand. Mrs. Shandig gives Father Rivard his rosary. They kneel, each facing a separate way.

RIVARD, SISTER RITA and MRS. SHANDIG (*crossing themselves*): In the name of the Father, the Son and the . . .
     Fast curtain.

ACT II

The Cell

It is night, but Rivard can't sleep and calls the guard for company. The guard informs him that Erna Prindle is to take the stand tomorrow. Her husband Maurice hates everything to do with Roman Catholicism. Rivard would like to see Erna, to warn her not to say anything that would incur her husband's wrath, but the guard won't permit Rivard to talk to her.

Erna's Parlor

Father Rivard remembers a visit he and Sister Rita paid to Erna when Erna's mother was sick. It was a routine act of priestly comfort, but Father Rivard brought Sister Rita along because after the knife wound and other events of the previous night, "I'm so confused that, I know I need help. I have to if I'm to be a good priest."

Erna's mother is going to die, and it is Rivard's job to tell her so and give her as much solace as he can. He tells the nun, "I decided that you should be here, that you would help me make a new start."

Erna enters. She is on the verge of tears but trying to believe that her mother isn't going to die. Sister Rita tells Erna a story about a hungry sparrow, trying to persuade her that God is watching and will continue to watch over her and her mother, whatever happens. Sister Rita is reaching out to Erna, offering sympathy, encouraging her to weep, but the priest sternly advocates self-control and the acceptance of God's will.

RIVARD: Your mother is in God's hands, isn't she? Don't cry, Erna.

ERNA: But I can't help it. When it starts, I just can't .

RIVARD: Pray for strength, say your rosary. "They who wait upon the Lord shall renew their strength. They shall mount up with wings as eagles, they shall run and not be weary . . ." See, if you try hard enough, you can resist the temptation to—

SISTER RITA: To be human? People have to cry, Father. Before you said that you—

RIVARD: Erna. Tears are personal destruction. Destruction of anything is an affront to God.

SISTER RITA: But Jesus wept. God was not affronted when His only begot—

RIVARD: Erna, you must accept all of God's world. Not just that which pleases you. Let me tell you a story of when I was a boy.

ERNA: Are you from Detroit too, Father?

RIVARD: No. I came from a large family, very large. There were so many of us, in fact, that in order to feel important I told strangers I was an only child. But a real problem hit me and my family. Diphtheria. In one winter I saw nine brothers and sisters buried. Also my father. After the first one, the baby, no amount of coaxing could get me to stop crying. Oh yes, I cried, Sister. I could not understand how God allowed such cruelty, those meaningless deaths. Why the baby? Papa? By Christmas I was the oldest brother. The house had been quarantined so I had to help. However, in the sick rooms, I just kept right on crying as if whoever I was serving was already dead. After a visit from me, mother would have to spend an hour in the sick room quieting the patient. Even though we were forbidden to leave the yard, I had to get away. I thought if I ran hard enough and fast enough the tears would dry in my eyes and I would stop crying. I asked God to give me the strength not to cry. He didn't hear me. I sat by the river. I thought it was so useless that it would make no difference if I just relaxed and slid down the steep bank and let myself drown.

ERNA: No, Father.

RIVARD: I thought how can God let things be so bad. After all we know everything is God. He even allows evil so that we can confront it. And then I understood. Even the bad, the ugly, the cruel is part of God. To deny it, any part of it, is to deny God. I understood the world is evil and that unless I confronted it with strength I could never see the face of God. If you persist in believing only in His goodness, then he casts you into everlasting—

    (*Silence.*)

I stopped crying. I returned home and worked hard, harder than even my mother. I went through the crisis nights with a sister and then a brother, and the doctor said I may have saved their lives. As soon as I stopped crying, I became useful to God. I have not cried since then.

Erna pulls herself together and goes to get coffee and the kind of muffins Father Rivard likes. Rivard rebukes Sister Rita for influencing Erna to cry, but the nun still believes her kind of sympathy was appropriate to the situation. Rivard orders her: "While you are in my charge, you will never question me again."

The Confessional

Sister Rita tries to confess to Father Rivard that she still can't understand what she did wrong that day at Erna's. Father Rivard finds that he can't maintain the proper "attitude of distance" from this penitent and walks away from the Confessional, leaving Sister Rita unshriven.

The Court

The prosecutor questions Erna about her faith; she is ostensibly a Methodist as her husband Maurice wishes, but she was born a Catholic and is surreptitiously teaching her children the rosary.

After her mother died (Erna testifies), Sister Rita told her it'd be all right to go to the Methodist socials because she was all alone and there were no Catholic young men in the community. She met and married Maurice, and she doesn't think this was wrong but is torn by the questioning.

Rivard interrupts the trial to stop the prosecutor from torturing Erna with his questions. The prosecutor asks that Rivard's unruly protest be placed in the record. Rivard is crying "I know I was wrong . . . . . Everything I did was for the Church" and is hauled out by the guard as the prosecutor rests his case.

Sister Rita's Garden

Sister Rita is in her garden, wearing a shawl, singing and tatting as Father Rivard approaches and tells her he is through with his book. Sister Rita goes to Traverse City for confession now—she managed to persuade Maurice to take her, without consulting Father Rivard. She means to continue helping Erna as much as she can.

SISTER RITA: I intend to waste even more time on Erna. I don't really care what you do or think.

RIVARD: Please, Don't talk like that.

SISTER RITA: I know what it's like for Erna day after day. Night after night. Those dreadful stripes on my bedroom wall. It's like a prison. I can't sleep. I can't breathe. I have to get out and walk in the hall up there.

RIVARD: The same wallpaper is all through the house. In my room too.
    Silence.
Let Erna go to the Methodist socials.

SISTER RITA: What do you mean, Father?

RIVARD: Let her go. Maybe you shouldn't say that I'm allowing it. Otherwise, everyone in the parish—

SISTER RITA: Thank you, Father. I'll tell her. Thank you.
    Putting her hand on his arm.
I can't even say how I feel. That you're helping Erna. That you finished your book. That maybe now you'll have time for— That we could— That you'll bring me that lilac bush from the valley you promised.
    They laugh.
I, I'd like to read your book.

RIVARD: I destroyed it.

SISTER RITA: What?

RIVARD: I'll never leave here. I burned it.

SISTER RITA: Why, Father?

RIVARD: Well. I thought I knew God. God, the Vengeful. The God of Job. That God, He was the one I set out to write about. Then you came, and I tried to fit into what I know the things you said, the things you— It wasn't possible. I don't know God now.

SISTER RITA: Father, your life work. To destroy it.

RIVARD: Sister, I am fit for nothing more than this small parish. If this. And I will have to fight to be worthy of this.

Sister Rita is appalled that she might have said something that caused Father Rivard to destroy his book. Rivard reassures her: it is part of God's order of deprivation. Sister Rita is not so sure.

The Cell

Back in the cell, Rivard's lawyer warns his client that he's never argued a case in court before or cross-examined witnesses and will need all the help he can get, instead of the type of outburst that could be harmful to his cause.

The lawyer accuses Rivard of lying to him. The lawyer, Felker, saw a light at the Holy Rosary the previous evening and went up there and found a note written by Rivard but never mailed. The note reads: "Bishop, I beg that you transfer Sister Rita. I know now I shall never leave this place. Sister does live in the rectory. I made her lie to the Monsignor for my own selfish reasons. Sister has a way about her, and it makes me think I am loving her. I know I must run from this temptation, and I do, but I grow weary. Very weary."

Rivard admits he wrote it the last day he spent on the hill, but he wants to forget all about it now. The lawyer advises him to change his plea to guilty in the second degree, to avoid the noose which is almost certainly awaiting Rivard. Rivard doesn't care whether he lives or dies, however, he only wants to keep his sanity. The lawyer opines: ". . . . . You're saner than the crazies up here. They drink and spit, plant and wait, sit and stare. After a while the pupils in their eyes seem to enlarge so that all they can see clearly are grave-stones, and two-headed calves, and the wounds of the horses which they them-selves back into unseen equipment. They are past care, so I argue their deeds and wills, travel to Leland to see lantern slides of European castles and wonder how men lost the ability to dream and accomplish. And I fish. Mainly I fish."

But Felker cares about Rivard now and wants to save him any way he can. Rivard refuses to change his plea, though Felker warns him he means to get to the bottom of events that last night, "the night of the fire." The lawyer knows that Mrs. Shandig is still alive and probably living in a deserted logging camp in the area. Possibly last night's light showing at Holy Rosary signifies that Mrs. Shandig has come back. Felker intends to find out.

Rectory Front Porch

The scene shifts back to the past in Rivard's memory. Alarm bells ring and Sister Rita runs in, clad in a street dress, because her nun's habit caught fire from the flying sparks. Father Rivard has hurt his leg fighting the fire down in the town, which has been saved. So has Holy Rosary, by means of a fire ditch dug at the last minute. The farm lands have borne the brunt of the flames.

RIVARD: Please. You shouldn't be out of your habit. When we're so tired, when we're so tired . . . you shouldn't be out of your habit. Go inside. Put it on.

SISTER RITA: It's only us. Everyone else is down there. I have this feeling. And it's us. I know it's only us. What is it? It's not knowing that hurts so much. If I could understand, if I could, then it would be all right again. I could do what is right. But I don't know. Please help.

RIVARD: The Bishop will help. I wrote him today. I asked that you be trans-ferred.

SISTER RITA: No, not that. I'll never know.

RIVARD: We don't want to.

SISTER RITA: I want to. All my life I'll wonder.

RIVARD: No. You'll forget. Go upstairs. Now.

SISTER RITA: How could I . . . how could I be so wrong?

RIVARD: Don't do this.

SISTER RITA: I felt this, and . . . I wish I'd die.

Rivard urges her to go to her room and pray for salvation for both of them. Sister Rita exits, leaving Rivard praying to God for strength.

Sister Rita's Room
Father Rivard enters the rectory and goes to Sister Rita's room, where the nun is sobbing because the fire ditch that saved the rectory destroyed her garden. The priest tries to comfort her.

> *Father Rivard holds Sister Rita until the sobbing subsides.*
RIVARD: At night I wonder how you are feeling, what you think, if you're happy, if you can sleep. Even when I pray, I wonder what you're doing. I look up through a window if it's recess or I listen for your steps in the hall. I can only concentrate if I pray about you. Almost to you.
> *He is about to kiss her.*
SISTER RITA: Please. Tell me what it is.
RIVARD: I have.
> *Silence.*
I love you.
> *They kiss.*
SISTER RITA: I never dared think—I thought who else would have me but the Church? But with you, I'm not nothing, am I?
RIVARD: No. You're not.
SISTER RITA: I'm just like everyone else.

She takes out her diary, which no one has ever seen, and shows it to Rivard. It contains drawings of various people, including Rivard, as well as text. Sister Rita leads Rivard to the window to show him where she stood so many nights looking down on the town: "See. We can be with all the other people now. We aren't so different after all, are we? Don't look at the Church. Look down there with the other families. We'll be like that too. We'll have our own children."

Father Rivard doesn't believe they can move down there and live like the other people. Sister Rita insists they can, she sensed it before she understood it—her recent diary entries prove that she sensed the growing conflict between the rules and her feelings, and that her feelings and not the rules were right.

Father Rivard pulls Sister Rita away from the window so that Mrs. Shandig, on her way up the hill, won't see them.

SISTER RITA: But we can tell her. Everyone.
RIVARD: No.
SISTER RITA: Why?
RIVARD (*moving to exit*): Because I, I—I'm their priest. She depends on me. They all do. I'm the only way they have of understanding.
SISTER RITA: People understand.
RIVARD: It's not how you think it is. Their homes have photographs of babies in coffins. Adolescents pour kerosene on kittens, and their fathers laugh

when they set the fire. Sometimes wives cannot cook breakfast. Their fingers are broken from their husbands' beatings. It's only because they think I'm different; it's only because they think I'm worthy that I can help them. I must be worthy.

SISTER RITA: I think you're worthy. Please. You said you loved me. I know you're too good, too precious to escape, desert me when—

RIVARD: I'm not, not what you think. I, I, I've destroyed all that. For the Church. There's nothing left for you. I can't be a husband. I can't be a father. There's nothing left but cruelty. That's all I know. That's all I worship. All I need. Not the resurrection, life. It's the nails. My salvation. Only the agony . . . . .

Sister Rita believes that things can be different now, but Father Rivard disagrees. She tries to calm him. He raises his arm to strike her again; she stops him, tells him the time is past for that. He grabs her by the shoulders and shakes her violently. He insists: "You can't know me. I'll destroy you. You can't know me. You'd hate me. I hate myself."

SISTER RITA: I don't hate you. God doesn't hate you.
RIVARD (*trying to exit*): Don't talk about God.
SISTER RITA (*holding him from exit*): We still have God.
RIVARD: I don't want God. I don't want you.
        Starting to choke Sister Rita.
I hate God. I hate God. I want to kill God. I always wanted to kill—
        Sister Rita falls on floor. For a moment of silence, she appears dead. Rivard slaps her on back. She coughs. He drags her to bench. He gets wet cloth, sits next to her, wiping her brow.

Mrs. Shandig enters in time to hear Sister Rita exclaim to Rivard, "We have to help each other. It's all we have now. We only have each other." Mrs. Shandig can hardly believe what she's hearing. Sister Rita insists that Rivard tell Mrs. Shandig of his love. Rivard denies that there's anything to tell and suggests that Sister Rita must leave now—he'll walk her to the train.

SISTER RITA (*suddenly embracing Rivard*): Don't leave me. I don't care if I go to hell.
MRS. SHANDIG (*pulling Sister Rita from Rivard*): Father, you hear her. (*About to hit Sister Rita.*) Don't touch him.
RIVARD (*catching Mrs. Shandig's hand*): Stop it. (*To Sister Rita.*) I won't hurt you any more. You can leave. But you must leave the right way, when your community tells you. Go back to your order.
SISTER RITA: I'm not a nun now. I'm nothing.
RIVARD: There's still a place for you. They need you.
MRS. SHANDIG: She's not a nun. She said so.
SISTER RITA: I haven't even said it to you.

RIVARD: Don't say anything. Don't think it. Honor your vows. It's the only way.

MRS. SHANDIG: She can't. What she said. Father . . .

RIVARD (*continuing through Mrs. Shandig's speech*): The rest is me. I cause it. God isn't cruel.

SISTER RITA (*crying, hitting Rivard*): No. No. No. There's nothing left.
> *As Father Rivard starts down the hill.*

(*Softly.*) But I never told you. You never heard the words. Let me tell you.

The Court

The spotlight remains on Mrs. Shandig as the scene changes to the courtroom, where the housekeeper testifies under Felker's questioning that Sister Rita screamed "I love you" after the disappearing Father Rivard, but he didn't hear. Sister Rita exits as the questioning continues. The only other person who came up the hill that night was Maurice, to plant a lilac bush arranged for previously by Father Rivard.

"Did Sister see Maurice?" Felker asks, but Mrs. Shandig ignores the question and instead tells how Sister Rita went to her garden, saw the lilac and "went all crazy," throwing herself onto the ground and rolling back and forth until she fell into the fire ditch.

MRS. SHANDIG: . . . . . She just lay there in the ditch shaking, like deep sobbing, staring up at me with dead eyes.

FELKER: I see. I see what you mean. Then what did you do?

MRS. SHANDIG: I prayed to St. Jude for strength and guidance. He answered my prayer, because I understood the lilac was a sign from Father. He paid Maurice to plant the lilac as a sign to me to bury her in the garden. She was too evil to put in the cemetery. I looked at her down there like a snake. She was laying there just like a dead snake. I know that look. When I was a girl I had a snake. My mother saw me playing with it. She took a hatchet and ran into the yard and chopped it all up. It kept wiggling after it was dead. All the pieces moved. I didn't know then that they kept moving until the sun set. She was wiggling down there and making noises, but it was near on to the moonrise, so I knew she was dead. I went to get the shovel. I scraped the dirt back into the fire ditch over her dead wiggling body. I was nearly finished when the dirt over her started to rise. The earth didn't want her body, but I hit the snake's head and shoveled the dirt faster on its face and then it was peaceful. The moon came up and Holy Rosary was silvery and white again, and the fire was far, far away.

FELKER (*addressing audience as court*): I move this case be dismissed on the grounds that the People's case can not support a verdict of guilty beyond a reasonable doubt.
> *Mrs. Shandig looks at Rivard. Guard crosses to her with his handcuffs clearly in sight. He touches her arms. She looks at him, confused. He leads her to exit. Prosecutor exits.*

Graveside
Felker and Rivard climb the hill to see where Sister Rita was buried.

FELKER: Mrs. Shandig killed herself at the jail. Banged her head against the wall till she died.

RIVARD: No, no. It will not stop.

FELKER (*reaching out to touch Rivard's shoulder*): I'm sorry. Sorry I called Shandig, and sorry I thought I was so damned clever. At least, you can have forgiveness in your church, can't you?

RIVARD: Not unless you know God. She gave me a chance. Will I never see the face of God?

FELKER: What are you planning you'll do, Rivard?

RIVARD: What are you going to do?

FELKER: Fish. Mainly I fish.

RIVARD: Mourn her. Mainly I'll mourn her.

> *Rivard reaches for a branch of lilac in bloom on the ground. Felker stands and steps slightly back, his head bowed. Sister Rita enters in street dress. Rivard kneels. At the moment he could see her face he looks up into her face. She stops for a moment and then continues up center. As the nun continues, Rivard begins to cry. Felker takes a step toward him. Blackout. Curtain.*

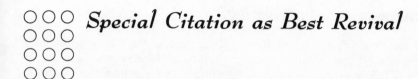

Special Citation as Best Revival

THREEPENNY OPERA

A Musical in Three Acts

BOOK AND LYRICS BY BERTOLT BRECHT

MUSIC BY KURT WEILL

NEW TRANSLATION BY RALPH MANHEIM
AND JOHN WILLETT

Cast and credits appear on pages 325-327

BERTOLT BRECHT (book, lyrics) and KURT WEILL (music), two of the most gifted dramatists of the international 20th century theater, have been the subjects of detailed biography and analysis far too voluminous even to summarize in this space. Brecht (1898-1956) and Weill (1900-1950) pursued largely separate careers in the German and American theaters. Their two major collaborations are landmarks of the musical stage, however: The Rise and Fall of the City of Mahagonny *(1927) and* Threepenny Opera *(Dreigroschenoper, 1927). The latter work, very loosely based on John Gay's 1728 play* The Beggar's Opera, *had its New York professional premiere on Broadway April 13, 1933 for 12 performances in a Gifford Cochran-Jerrold Krimsky adaptation. As* The Threepenny Opera *in a Marc Blitzstein adaptation it opened off Broadway in 1954 and ran for six years and 2,611 performances, second only to* The Fantasticks *as off Broadway's longest run ever.*

In its 1976 incarnation at the Vivian Beaumont under the aegis of Joseph Rapp, Threepenny Opera *had a new translation which pays homage of faith-*

fulness to the original, astringent Brecht-Weill verson. This new production fairly demanded our special attention and citation as the best of an exceptionally good 1975-76 revival season. It is synopsized in these pages in the same manner as the Best Plays.

RALPH MANHEIM (co-translator) was born in 1907 in New York City and graduated from Harvard with a B.A. in 1926. He is the author of more than 50 translations of books and plays including Tango *by Slawomir Mrozek,* Amphitryon *and* Polly *by Peter Hacks and* Arturo Ui, The Good Woman of Setzuan *and* Puntila *by Bertolt Brecht. With his collaborator John Willett, Manheim is co-editor of a nine-volume edition of Brecht's dramatic works, with five volumes now in print and the sixth in production. His many awards include P.E.N. prizes for his translations of Gunter Grass's* The Tin Drum *(1961) and Peter Handke's* A Sorrow Beyond Dreams *(1976) and a National Book Award for Celine's* From Castle to Castle *(1969). He is married, with two daughters.*

JOHN WILLETT (co-translator) was born in the Hempstead section of London in June 1917. He was educated at St. Edmund's School, Winchester College and Christ Church, Oxford, graduating M.A. He held major editorial positions on the Manchester Guardian *from 1948 to 1951 and* The Times Literary Supplement *from 1960 to 1973, and teaching posts at the California Institute of the Arts 1972-73 and Flinders University of South Australia 1975. In addition to his current assignment as co-editor of the Random House editions of Brecht with Ralph Manheim, Willett has published* The Theater of Bertolt Brecht, Brecht on Theater, Expressionism, *and* Brecht Poems 1913-1956. *In the theater he served as compiler-translator of* Never the Twain, The Rehabilitation of F 100 *and* Alive and Kicking, *and he collaborated with Val Cherry on the production conception of* Threepenny Opera *at the Adelaide Festival Playhouse in 1975. He is now working on a program of Brecht's poetry for the National Theater.*

Time: Queen Victoria's Coronation, rearranged in Brecht's imagination

Place: London

PROLOGUE

SYNOPSIS: At a fair in Soho, a company of beggars, thieves and whores is plying their trades. A ballad singer cranks his hurdy-gurdy and holds the attention of the crowd with "The Ballad of Mack the Knife."

BALLAD SINGER (*sings*):
    See the shark with teeth like razors.
    All can read his open face.
    And Macheath has got a knife, but
    Not in such an obvious place

    See the shark, how red his fins are
    As he slashes at his prey.
    Mack the Knife wears white kid gloves which
    Give the minimum away.

    By the Thames's turbid waters
    Men abruptly tumble down.
    Is it plague or is it cholera?
    Or a sign Macheath's in town? . . .

Others join the singer in subsequent verses conjecturing about the sudden disappearance of a wealthy merchant and his cash box and other recent strange occurrences.

BALLAD SINGER (*sings*):
    . . . . . And the ghastly fire in Soho
    Seven children at a go—
    In the crowd stands Mack the Knife, but
    He's not asked and doesn't know.

    And the child-bride in her nightie
    Whose assailant's still at large
    Violated in her slumbers—
    Mackie, how much did you charge? . . .

The song ends, the whores laugh, and a man detaches himself from the crowd, walks across the square and disappears—Mack the Knife.

ACT I

Scene 1

At Jonathan Peachum's headquarters for the beggars of London, Peachum is singing his cynical morning hymn about man's aberrant ways and God's inevitable judgement.

Peachum reflects on his business problems: human beings are capable of turning their emotions off completely, even in the face of suffering which once had the power to move them to pity.

PEACHUM: . . . . . Suppose, for instance, a man sees another man standing on the corner with a stump for an arm; the first time he sees him he may be shocked enough to give him tenpence, but the second time it will only be fivepence, and if he sees him a third time he'll hand him over to the police without batting an eyelash. It's the same with the spiritual approach.

> *A large sign saying "It is more blessed to give than to receive" is lowered from the grid.*

What good are the most beautiful, the most poignant sayings, painted on the most enticing signs, when they get expended so quickly? The Bible has four or five sayings that stir the human heart; but once they are expended, there's nothing for it but starvation. Take this one, for instance—"give and it shall be given unto you"—how threadbare it is after being exposed to perusal a mere three weeks. No, you have to keep on offering something new. So it's back to the good old Bible again, but how long can it go on providing?

A young man, Filch, enters Peachum's business establishment, Beggar's Friend, Ltd. and introduces himself. Filch gives Peachum a sample of his begging speech—abandoned by parents, down on his luck, etc. Peachum recognizes Filch as an intruder who dared to accost passers-by in "District 10" the day before, was beaten up by Peachum's own people and given their boss's business card.

Peachum explains that London is divided into fourteen begging districts, which no one may work without a license from Jonathan Jeremiah Peachum & Co. For such a license, Peachum will charge Filch a pound plus 50 per cent of his eventual take and another 20 per cent for his beggar's outfit. Filch agrees. Peachum calls his wife in to register Filch: Number 314, Baker Street District.

It's the firm's prerogative to decide what costume each of its beggars will wear. Peachum opens a curtain to display five hideous dummies representing basic types of human misery most likely to arouse pity and attract alms.

PEACHUM: . . . . . Outfit A: Victim of the traffic speed-up. The merry cripple, always cheerful—always carefree, emphasized by arm-stump . . .

> *He acts it out to the instrumental music of "Song of the Insufficiency of Human Endeavor."*

Outfit B: Victim of the Higher Strategy. The Tiresome Trembler, molests passers-by, operates by inspiring nausea—

> *He acts it out.*

Outfit C: Victim of modern Technology. The Pitiful Blind Man, the Cordon Bleu of Beggary.

> *He acts it out, staggering toward Filch. The moment he bumps into Filch, Filch cries out in horror. Peachum stops at once, looks at him with amazement.*

(*Suddenly roars.*) He's nauseated! He'll never be a beggar as long as he lives! He's only fit to be begged from! Very well, oufit D. . . . . (*To Filch.*) You get out of those clothes and put this on, but mind you, look after it!

FILCH: What about my things?

PEACHUM: Property of the firm. Outfit E: Young man who has seen better days or, if you'd rather, never thought it would come to this.

FILCH: Oh, you use them again? Why can't *I* do the better days act?

PEACHUM: Because nobody can make his own suffering sound convincing, my boy. If you have a bellyache and say so, it will only make people disgusted. Anyway, you're not here to ask questions. Just get into those clothes.

Filch goes behind a screen to change, while Peachum asks Mrs. Peachum about their daughter Polly's current attachment to a handsome captain. Mrs. Peachum likes the captain, who always wears kid gloves and asked mother and daughter to the Cuttlefish Hotel for a dance. Peachum muses: "White kid gloves and a cane with an ivory handle and spats and patent leather shoes and a charismatic personality and, ah yes, a scar . . ." He identifies Polly's captain as Mack the Knife.

Mrs. Peachum is appalled; she runs upstairs to Polly's bedroom and finds her daughter missing and the bed not slept in. The Peachums step forward to sing "No They Can't."

PEACHUM (*sings*):
. . . . . No, they *can't,* no they *can't*
See what's good for them and set their mind on it.
It's fun *they* want, it's fun *they* want
So they wind up on their arses in the shit.
BOTH (*sing*):
Then where's your moon over Soho?
What's come of your infernal "D'you feel my heart beating" line?
Where's the old "Wherever you go, I shall be with you, Honey?"
When you're flat in the shit mourning love's decline?

Scene 2

In an empty stable which doesn't belong to him, but which he's taking over with his henchman Matthew, Macheath is preparing to celebrate his wedding to Polly Peachum. Macheath's friends transform the bare stable into a banquet hall by bringing in sumptuous carpets and furniture which they've stolen for this great occasion. Polly sheds a tear at the thought of the rightful owners' loss.

MACHEATH (*sees Polly in tears*): Use your heads! For once I'm having a wedding, and how often does that happen? Shut up, Dreary! How often does it happen that I leave you to do something on your own? And when I do you make my wife unhappy right at the start.

NED: Dear Polly . . .

MACHEATH (*knocks Ned's hat off*): "Dear Polly!" I'll bash your head through your kidneys with your "Dear Polly," you squirt. Have you ever heard the like? "Dear Polly!" I suppose you've been to bed with her?

POLLY: Mack!

NED: I swear . . .

WALTER: Dear madam, if any items of furniture should be lacking, we'll be only too glad to go back and . . .

MACHEATH: A rosewood harpsichord and no chairs. (*He laughs.*) Speaking as a bride, what do you say to that?

POLLY: It could be worse.

MACHEATH: Two candelabra and a telescope and the wedding couple has to make their way through the horse manure.

POLLY: Something new, I'd say.

MACHEATH (*sharply*): Get the legs sawn off the harpsichord! Go on!

Four men obey, making a bench of the harpsichord, at the same time singing 'Wedding Song for the Less Well-Off'": ". . . . . It was over and they exchanged a kiss/He was thinking, 'Whose wedding dress was this?'/While his name was a thing she would have liked to know."

Polly is worried about what might happen if the authorities should raid this place looking for the stolen goods. Macheath kisses away her fears and asks for a song before they begin eating. Polly is the only one ready to oblige. Since she's about to become a married woman, it's all right now for her to sing the suggestive lyrics of a little ditty she once heard at a street fair in Soho, "For That's My Way": "If a woman's hips are ample/Then I want her in the hay/Skirt and stockings all a-rumple/For that's my way. . . . ."

Polly's audience thought she was "nice" singing the song. Macheath contradicts them sharply: "It's not nice, you idiot! It's art, and art isn't nice."

A friend runs in to warn them that Tiger Brown, the High Sheriff of London, is on his way in. Macheath seems unconcerned as Brown enters, commenting, "Does it have to be somebody else's stable? Why, this is breaking and entering again!" But Brown is obviously a friend of Macheath's and is introduced to Polly and friends (whom Brown recognizes as notorious crooks) as though he were just another wedding guest.

Macheath invites Brown to sit down and have a drink, telling the company that he and the Sheriff served in the Army together in India. By way of illustration of their friendship, Macheath and Brown sing "The Cannon Song."

MACHEATH (*sings*): John was all present and Jim was all there

BROWN (*sings*): And Georgie was up for promotion

MACHEATH (*sings*): Not that the army gave a bugger who they were

BROWN (*sings*): When confronting some heathen commotion.

BOTH (*sing*):
The troops live under
The cannon's thunder
From Sind to Cooch Behar.

BROWN (*sings*): Moving from place to place

MACHEATH (*sings*): When they come face to face
BROWN (*sings*): With men of a different color
MACHEATH (*sings*): With darker skins or duller
BOTH (*sing*): They quick as winking chop them into beefsteak tartare. . . . .
MACHEATH (*sings*): Johnnie is a write-off and Jimmy is dead
BROWN (*sings*): And Georgie was shot for looting
MACHEATH (*sings*): But young men's blood goes on being red
     Pause.
BROWN (*sings*): And the army still goes on ahead recruiting . . . . .
MACHEATH: Though life with its raging torrents has carried us boyhood friends far apart, although our professional interests are very different, some people would go so far as to say diametrically opposed, our friendship has come through unimpaired. Let that be a lesson to all of you. Castor and Pollux, Hector and Andromache and so on. Seldom have I, the humble bandit, well, you know what I mean, made even the smallest haul without giving him, my friend, a share, a sizeable share, Brown, as a gift and token of my unswerving loyalty.
    He takes Brown by the arm.
Well, Jackie, old man, I'm glad you've come, I call it real friendship.
BROWN: You know, Mack, that I can't refuse you anything. I really must be going, I've got so much on my mind; if the slightest thing should go wrong at the Queen's Coronation . . .
MACHEATH: See here, Jackie, my father-in-law is a rotten old stinker. If he tries to make trouble for me, is there anything on record against me at Scotland yard?
BROWN: There's nothing whatsoever on record against you at Scotland Yard.
MACHEATH: I knew it.
BROWN: I have seen to that. Goodnight.

Macheath sees Brown out. The others go upstage behind a hanging carpet to prepare a surprise. They sing "Wedding Song for the Less Well-Off" and when Macheath returns they lower the carpet revealing their surpise: a bed.
    The gang leaves. Macheath and Polly sing "Liebeslied": ". . . . . The platter off which you are eating your bread/Give it one brief look; fling it far/ For love will endure or not endure/Regardless of where we are."

Scene 3

At Peachum's establishment, Polly stands in her travelling clothes while her parents complain that she has thrown herself on the garbage heap. They wonder if she's really married. To convince them, Polly sings them the "Barbara Song" about the propriety of saying "No" politely to polite suitors.

POLLY (*sings*):
    . . . . . But then one day, and that day was blue

Came someone who didn't ask at all
And he went and hung his hat on the nail in my little attic
And what happened I can't quite recall.
And as he's got no money
And was not a nice chap
And his Sunday shirts, even, not like snow
And as he'd no idea of treating a girl with due respect
I could not tell him: No . . . . ."

The Peachums finally understand that their daughter is now firmly married to a notorious criminal. Peachum is unconsolable: "If I give away my daughter, the last prop of my old age, my house will cave in and my last dog will run off."

Beggars come in and complain about the equipment. Peachum gives one a new arm stump, fires another for eating and thus looking well-fed.

The beggars go out and the Peachums return to the subject of Polly's marriage. Polly argues that Macheath can support her: "He is not only a first-class burglar but a far-sighted and experienced stick-up man as well." Peachum argues for an immediate divorce, but Polly has an answer to that: she loves Macheath and will not consider it.

The Peachums decide their best move would be to turn Macheath in to the sheriff for hanging—that way, they'd get rid of him and at the same time collect 40 pounds reward. They've got to find him first, though. Mrs. Peachum remarks: "He's holed up with his tarts. . . . . Money rules the world. I'll go to Tunbridge right away and talk to the girls. Give us a couple of hours, and after that if he meets a single one of them he'll be handed over."

Polly and her parents sing the First Threepenny Finale, entitled "Concerning the Insecurity of the Human State." Man should have some rights, some happiness—the song goes—and try to be good, but in the present state of society it's impossible.

PEACHUM: (sings):
. . . . . Who wouldn't like an earthly paradise?
Yet our condition's such it can't arise.
Out of the question in our case.
Let's say your brother's close to you
But if there's not food enough for two
He'll kick you smartly in the face.
And so will all the human race.
But say your wife is close to you
And finds you're barely making do
She'll kick you smartly in the face.
And so will all the human race.
But say your son is close to you
And finds your pension's not come through

He'll kick you smartly in the face.
And so will all the human race.
POLLY & MRS. PEACHUM:
That's what you're all ignoring.
That's what's so bloody boring.
The world is poor, and man's a shit
And that is all there is to it.
PEACHUM:
Of course that's all there is to it
The world is poor, and man's a shit.
We should aim high instead of low
But in our present state this can't be so . . . . .
POLLY & MRS. PEACHUM:
Which means he has us in a trap:
The whole damn thing's a load of crap.
PEACHUM:
The world is poor, and man's a shit
And that is all there is to it.
ALL:
That's what you're all ignoring
That's what's so bloody boring.
That's why he's got us in a trap
And why it's all a load of crap.
  Curtain.

ACT II

Scene 4

In their stable, Polly warns her husband Macheath about her father's plan to destroy him.

POLLY: I've been to see Brown, my father went too, they decided to pull you in; my father made some terrible threats and Brown stood up for you, but then he weakened, and now he thinks too that you'd better bestir yourself and make yourself scarce for awhile, Mack. You must pack right away.

MACHEATH: Pack? Nonsense. Come here, Polly. You and I have got better things to do than pack.

POLLY: No, we mustn't now. I'm so frightened. All they talked about was hanging.

MACHEATH: I don't like it when you're moody, Polly. There's nothing on record against me at Scotland yard.

POLLY: Perhaps there wasn't yesterday, but today there's suddenly a terrible lot. You—I've brought the charges with me, I don't even know if I can get them straight, the list goes on and on. You've killed two shopkeepers, more than thirty burglaries, twenty-three holdups, and God knows how many acts of arson, attempted murder, forgery and perjury, all within eighteen months. You're a dreadful man. And in Winchester you seduced two sisters under the age of consent.

MACHEATH: They told me they were over twenty. What did Brown say?

He stands up slowly and goes whistling to the right.

POLLY: He caught up with me in the corridor and said there was nothing he could do for you now. Oh, Mack!

She throws herself on his neck.

Macheath is beginning to agree that perhaps the time has come for him to lie low for awhile. If he does, Polly will have to "run the business," supervise the gang of thieves. Macheath goes down the list, issuing instructions: keep an eye on Crook-finger Jake, fire Dreary Walter, give Jimmy II a raise, don't depend on Robert the Saw, and in all other respects just keep the gang operating and "You will go on sending the profits to Jack Poole's banking house in Manchester. Between you and me, it's only a matter of weeks before I go over to banking altogether. It's safer and it's more profitable."

Macheath orders Polly to dispose of the business in a couple of weeks by turning over the list of "employees" to Brown, who'll stow them safely in jail.

The selfsame gang, led by Matthew, enters; they want to prepare for an early start on Coronation day. Macheath explains that he can't join them and is turning matters over to Polly. Matthew has his doubts about being bossed by a woman, but Polly soon puts him in his place, thus winning the approval of the other gang members.

Macheath makes Polly promise to take care of herself and make up every day, just as though he were with her. Polly in her turn makes Macheath promise to be faithful and to leave the city immediately, without dallying with his other women. Macheath replies, "Oh, Polly, why should I go around drinking up the empties? I love only you." He promises to steal a horse and gallop away at twilight.

The lovers part, and Polly sings "Polly's Lied": "Nice while it lasted, and now it's all over/Tear out your heart, and goodbye my lover!/What use of grieving, when the mother that bore you/Knew it all before you?"

The Coronation bells peal forth. Mrs. Peachum comes forward with Low-Dive Jenny, offering her money to report Macheath to the nearest constable if he should show up. Mrs. Peachum believes he will, she tells Jenny, because of "sexual obsession."

MRS. PEACHUM (*sings "The Ballad of Sexual Obsession"*):
There goes a man. The gallows loom above him.
They'll get the quicklime mixed in which to shove him.
They'll put his neck just under where the noose is
And what's he thinking of, the idiot? Floozies.
They've all but hanged him, yet he can't ignore that call
Sexual obsession has him in its thrall. . . . .

Scene 5

In a Tunbridge whorehouse, the women are going about their chores of ironing clothes, etc. Crook-fingered Jake is looking at a newspaper and telling the whores that Macheath will certainly not put in his usual appearance this day.

Macheath instantly belies him by entering and calling for his coffee as usual, permitting no such annoyances as a police manhunt to interfere with his habits, especially "my Thursday." Macheath jokes with Jenny and the other girls about the warrant listing his many offenses.

Jenny sings about a dream she has—"Pirate Jenny," her song is called. She will keep on with her whore's drudgery, obliging the customers and polishing the glasses, until one day "A ship with eight sails and/Its fifty guns loaded" arrives in the harbor. The ship's guns will fire and devastate the town—all but the "tatty hotel" where Jenny lives. The sailors will come ashore, drag the whole population before Jenny for her merciless judgement, and then Jenny will sail away triumphantly in the ship.

Jenny slips away as Macheath tells the others of his early days of struggle, when he loved Jenny best of all. As Macheath sings his "Ballad of Immoral Earnings," Jenny gives a signal to Constable Smith outside.

MACHEATH: (*sings*):
    There was a time, now very far away
    When we set up together, I and she.
    I had the brains, and she supplied the breast.
    I did her right, and she supported me—
    A way of life then, if not quite the best.
    And when a client came I'd slide out of our bed
    And treat him nice, and go and have a drink instead
    And when he paid I'd address him: Sir,
    Come any time you feel you fancy her.
    That time's long past, but what I would not give
    To see that whorehouse where we used to live? . . . . .

Jenny appears with Constable Smith behind her. She sings her verse of the song—she has tender memories of Mack's rough treatment of her. The two sing together: when Jenny became pregnant, they dealt with it together and solved the problem.

The song finished, Smith lays a hand on Macheath's shoulder. Macheath jumps out of the window into the arms of other constables brought by Mrs. Peachum.

Scene 6

At the Old Bailey, six constables drag Macheath into a barred cage, while Tiger Brown looks on, weeping, protesting to his friend that it wasn't his fault.

Brown's daughter, Lucy, comes into the area. Macheath has been carrying on with Lucy Brown behind her father's back. Now he will have to play along with Lucy, hoping her father doesn't find out, until Polly can come up with the cash to get him out of here.

Macheath launches into the "Ballad of Gracious Living."

MACHEATH (*sings*):
Is this a life for one of my proud station?
I take it, I must frankly own, amiss.
From childhood up I heard with consternation:
One must live well to know what living is!

I've heard them praising single-minded spirits
Whose empty stomachs show they live for knowledge
In rat-infested shacks awash with ullage.
I'm all for culture, but there are some limits.
The simple life is fine for those it suits.
I don't find, for my part, that it attracts.
There's not a bird from here to Halifax
Would peck at such unappetizing fruits.
What use is freedom? In a world like this.
One must live well to know what living is. . . . .

Lucy approaches Macheath; she is in a jealous rage, having heard that Macheath is married to Polly. Macheath denies this and has just promised to marry Lucy when Polly enters, calling Macheath husband. Polly takes in the situation with Lucy, and soon the two are singing "Jealousy Duet," calling each other names and combining voices in a name-calling contest: "Mackie and I, see how we bill and coo/He's lost his taste for tawdry rendezvous/Your story's an invention/I will not pay attention/To damaged goods like you/Shit pot!"

The argument continues, as Lucy demonstrates to Polly that she's pregnant. Mrs. Peachum comes to take her daughter away. She drags Polly out.

MACHEATH: Lucy, you were magnificent. Of course I felt sorry for her. That's why I couldn't treat the slut as she deserved.

LUCY: It makes me so happy to hear you say that from the bottom of your heart. I love you so much I'd almost rather see you on the gallows than in the arms of another. Isn't that strange!

MACHEATH: Lucy, I should like to owe you my life.

LUCY: It's wonderful the way you say that. Say it again.

MACHEATH: Lucy, I should like to owe you my life.

LUCY: What can I do to help you, dearest?

> *Peachum's assistant comes forward as the music of "The Ballad of Mack the Knife" is heard.*

PEACHUM'S ASST. (*sings*): See the shark with teeth like razors

MACHEATH (*to Lucy*): Bring me my hat and cane.

> *Lucy comes back with his hat and cane.*

PEACHUM'S ASST. (*sings*): All can read his open face

MACHEATH: Lucy, the fruit of our love which you bear beneath your heart will hold us forever united.

> *Lucy goes out, opening the cell door.*

CONSTABLE SMITH: Let's have that cane.

PEACHUM'S ASST. (*sings*):

> And Macheath has got a knife, but
> Not in such an obvious place.
>
> > *After a brief chase, in which Smith pursues Macheath with a chair and a crow bar, Macheath jumps over the bars. Constables run after him.*

Brown enters and is delighted to see that Macheath has escaped. Peachum enters and claims his 40 pounds reward. But Peachum's prize has slipped through Brown's fingers. Peachum coldly reminds Brown of a supposed incident in 1400 B.C.: "On the death of the Egyptian King Ramses II, the police captain of Nineveh, or it may have been Cairo, committed some minor offense against the lower classes of the population. Even at that time the consequences were terrible. Historians still shudder at the cruel way the new Queen Semiramis treated her police captain. I only remember dimly, but there was some talk of snakes that she fed on his bosom."

Peachum thus makes Brown painfully aware of the possible consequences of his having let his friend Macheath escape. Brown calls for his constables and his sergeants.

Macheath and Jenny appear for the Second Threepenny Finale, "What Keeps Mankind Alive?"

MACHEATH (*sings*):

> You gentlemen who think you have a mission
> To purge us of the seven deadly sins
> Should first sort out the basic food position
> Then start your preaching: that's where it begins.
> You lot, who preach restraint and watch your waist as well
> Should learn for once the way the world is run:
> However much you twist, whatever lies you tell
> Food is the first thing. Morals follow on.
> So first make sure that those who now are starving
> Get proper helpings when we all start carving. . . . .

VOICE (off): What keeps mankind alive?

JENNY (*sings*):

> What keeps mankind alive? The fact that millions
> Are daily tortured, stifled, punished, silenced, oppressed.
> Mankind can keep alive thanks to its brilliance
> In keeping its humanity repressed.

CHORUS:
  For once you must try not to shirk the facts:
  Mankind is kept alive by bestial acts.
          Curtain.

ACT III

Scene 7

That night, Peachum is readying his beggars for a demonstration of human misery to disrupt the Coronation, when Jenny enters with the whores. She wants her payment for turning Macheath over to the police, but Peachum refuses it.

PEACHUM: . . . . . Our transaction stipulates that Mr. Macheath should be behind bars. Mr. Macheath has slipped through them like butter.

JENNY: Don't talk to me about Mr. Macheath. You're not fit to black his boots. Last night I had to let a customer go because it made me cry into my pillow to think how I had sold that gentleman to you. Yes, ladies, and what do you think happened this morning? Less than an hour ago, just after I had cried myself to sleep, I heard somebody whistle, and out on the street stood the very gentleman I'd been crying about, asking me to throw down the key.

PEACHUM: Mr. Macheath?

JENNY: He wanted to lie in my arms and make me forget the wrong I had done him. Ladies, he's the last gentleman left in London. And if our friend Suky Tawdry isn't here with us now, it's because he went on from me to her to comfort her too.

Peachum sends Filch to tip off the police about Macheath's whereabouts. But the police, commanded by Tiger Brown, are already here at Peachum's, in force. Peachum finds it hard to believe that Brown has come, not for Macheath, but for him and his beggars. Peachum tells Brown: "The law was made for one thing only, for the exploitation of those who don't understand it, or are prevented by naked misery from obeying it." But Brown means to lock Peachum and all his crew in the Old Bailey on suspicion of intending to embarrass the Queen—and incidentally to take the pressure off Macheath.

Peachum argues that his pitiful cripples are harmless, and bolsters his argument with "Song of the Insufficiency of Human Endeavor."

PEACHUM (*sings*):
  A man lives by his head
  His head won't see him through
  Inspect your own. What lives off that?
  At most a louse or two.

For this bleak existence
Man is never sharp enough.
Hence his weak resistance
To its tricks and bluff . . . . .

(*Speaks.*) Your plan, Brown, was brilliant, but hardly realistic. All you can arrest here, Mr. Brown, are a few young fellows celebrating their Queen's Coronation by arranging a little fancy dress party. When the real paupers come along—there will be thousands of them. You've forgotten what an immense number of poor people there are. When you see all those cripples at the Abbey door, it won't be a festive sight. Do you know what the rose is, Brown? Yes, but how about a hundred thousand faces all flushed with the rose? Our young Queen's path should be strewn with roses, not with the rose. It will look bad. It will look disgusting. Nauseating. I feel faint at the thought of it, Brown. A small chair, if you please.

BROWN: That's a threat. See here, you, that's blackmail. We can't touch the man, in the interests of public order we simply can't touch him. I've never seen the like of it.

PEACHUM: You're seeing it now. Let me tell you something. You can treat the Queen of England as you please, but tread on the toes of the poorest man in England and you'll be brought down, Mr. Brown.

Peachum's threat puts Brown in a corner from which there is no escape. When Peachum then tells him to arrest Macheath at Suky Tawdry's, Brown has no alternative but to comply. As Brown departs, Peachum demands to see Macheath on the gallows by 6 o'clock.

Peachum celebrates his triumph with another chorus of "Song of the Insufficiency of Human Endeavor." Jenny then sings "Solomon Song," about how Solomon and Caesar were destroyed, the one by his own wisdom and the other by his own courage, as Macheath is to be betrayed and destroyed by his own sexual urges.

Scene 8

In the death cell at Newgate at 5 a.m., Macheath is awaiting execution. He offers Constable Smith, who is guarding him, a thousand pounds to let him go. Smith goes out to think it over. Macheath sings to himself a verse of "Call From the Grave."

MACHEATH (*sings*):
Hark to the voice that's calling you to weep.
Macheath lies here, not under open sky
Not under treetops, no, but good and deep.
Fate struck him down in outraged majesty.
God grant his dying words may reach a friend
The thickest walls encompass him about.
Is none of you concerned to know his fate?

Once he is gone the bottles can come out
But do stand by him while it's not too late.
D'you want his punishment to have no end?

Matthew and Jake come down the corridor, and Smith lets them in to see Macheath, who asks them to bring him the whole sum in the joint savings account—400 pounds. They must hurry—it's already 5:30. They go out.

Smith asks what Macheath would like for his last meal, and Macheath tells him asparagus. Macheath asks to see Brown, then sings another verse of his "Call From the Grave."

Brown comes in, apologetic and forlorn. Macheath, who is single-mindedly trying to raise enough money to bribe the Constable, demands an accounting of their transactions. "Oh, Mack, you're turning the knife in the wound," Brown cries, but he complies and gives Macheath a run-down of rewards and loot which the thief has shared with the sheriff.

There's still not enough to make up the sum of the bribe, and Jake and Matthew haven't yet come back with their share.

A group of people are admitted, including Jenny, Peachum and Polly, who goes to the cage and assures Macheath she'll be all right, as the business is doing well.

> *Matthew and Jake pass the cage and take up positions on the right.*

MATTHEW: We couldn't get through because of the terrible crush. We ran so hard I was afraid Jake was going to have a stroke. If you don't believe us . . .

MACHEATH: What do my men say? Have they got good places?

MATTHEW: You see, Captain, we thought you'd understand. You see, a Coronation doesn't happen every day. They've got to make some money when there's a chance. They send you their best wishes.

JAKE: Their very best wishes.

> *Mrs. Peachum steps up to the cage.*

MRS. PEACHUM: My dear Mr. Macheath, who would have expected this a week ago when we were dancing at a little hop at the Cuttlefish Hotel.

MACHEATH: A little hop.

MRS. PEACHUM: But the ways of destiny are cruel here below.

BROWN (*at the rear, to the Vicar*): And to think that I stood shoulder to shoulder with this man in Azerbaijan under a hail of bullets.

JENNY (*approaches the cage*): We Drury Lane girls are frantic. Nobody's gone to the Coronation. Everybody wants to see you.

MACHEATH: To see me.

SMITH: All right. Let's get started. Six o'clock.

> *He lets Macheath out of the cage.*

MACHEATH: We mustn't keep them waiting. Ladies and gentlemen. You see before you a declining representative of a declining social group. We lower middle class artisans who work with humble jemmies on small shopkeepers' cash registers are being swallowed up by big corporations backed by the banks. What's a jemmy compared with a share certificate? What's breaking into a bank compared with founding a bank? What's murdering a man compared with hiring a man? Fellow citizens, I hereby take my leave of you. I thank you for coming. Some of you were very close to me. That Jenny should have turned me in amazes me greatly. It is proof positive that the world never changes. A convergence of several unfortunate circumstances has brought about my fall. So be it—I fall. (*Sings "Ballad in which Macheath Begs All Men for Forgiveness"*):

> The rain washes away and purifies.
> Let it wash down the flesh we catered for
> And we who saw so much, and wanted more—
> The crows will come and peck away our eyes.
> Perhaps ambition used too sharp a goad
> It drove us to these heights from which we swing
> Hacked at by greedy starlings on the wing
> Like horses' droppings on a country road.
> O brothers, learn from us how it begins
> And pray to God that He forgives our sins. . . . .

Macheath makes his peace with Polly and Lucy as he is led to the gallows over a red carpet. He struggles with police for a moment, then raises his arms in surrender, is released and walks to the trap under the noose, which is placed around his neck.

Peachum cries "Stop!" and the action freezes.

PEACHUM (*recites*):

> Dear audience, we now are coming to
> The point where we must hang him by the neck
> Because it is the Christian thing to do.
> To prove that men must pay for what they take.
>
> But as we want to keep our fingers clean
> And you are people we can't risk offending
> We thought we'd better do without this scene
> And substitute instead a different ending . . . . .

Tiger Brown enters as a messenger on horseback to announce, in the Third Threepenny Finale, that the Queen, on the occasion of her Coronation, has pardoned Macheath and raised him to a peerage worth ten thousand pounds a year. "Reprieved!" cries Macheath, "I was sure of it." Polly, Jenny and Lucy happily echo "Reprieved!"

MRS. PEACHUM (*sings*):

> So it all turned out nicely for the ending.
> How grand it all would be if our saviors on horseback
> Always appeared when they were needed.

PEACHUM:

> Now please remain all standing where you're standing
> And join in the hymn of the poorest of the poor,
> Whose most arduous life you have seen portrayed here today,
> For in fact the poor always come to very sticky ends.
> The saviors on horseback are far from frequent in practise.
> And when a man gets kicked he often kicks back

(*Speaks.*) Which all means

> One shouldn't persecute wrongdoing too much.

ALL:

> Don't punish our wrongdoing too much. Never
> Will it withstand the frost, for it is cold.
> Think of the darkness and the bitter weather
> The cries of pain that echo through this world.

BALLAD SINGER (*"The Ballad of Mack the Knife"*):

> So we reach our happy ending
> Rich and poor can now embrace.
> Once the cash is not a problem!
> Happy endings can take place. . . . .
>
> Some in light and some in darkness
> That's the kind of world we mean.
> Those you see are in the daylight.
> Those in darkness don't get seen.
>> *Music alone. Curtain.*

A GRAPHIC GLANCE

PAMELA PAYTON-WRIGHT AND MAUREEN STAPLETON IN THE CIRCLE IN THE
SQUARE REVIVAL OF "THE GLASS MENAGERIE" BY TENNESSEE WILLIAMS

WALTER ABEL, MARYBETH HURT, MANDY PATINKIN AND ALINE MAC MAHON IN
THE REVIVAL OF "TRELAWNY OF THE 'WELLS'" BY ARTHUR WING PINERO

CURTIS RAYAM AND CARMEN BALTHROP IN "TREEMONISHA"

CELESTE HOLM, KRISTOFFER TABORI, JEAN MARSH, RACHEL ROBERTS,
JUNE HAVOC AND DONALD SINDEN IN "HABEAS CORPUS"

EVA LE GALLIENNE

VIVIAN REED IN "BUBBLING BROWN SUGAR"

GEORGE ROSE AS ALFRED P. DOOLITTLE
IN THE REVIVAL OF "MY FAIR LADY"

COLLEEN DEWHURST IN THE REVIVAL OF
"WHO'S AFRAID OF VIRGINIA WOOLF?"

RICHARD KILEY AND JANE ALEXANDER IN THE REVIVAL OF "THE HEIRESS"

PENNY FULLER AND NICOL WILLIAMSON IN "REX"

EMILY YANCY, PATRICIA ROUTLEDGE, KEN HOWARD
AND GILBERT PRICE IN "1600 PENNSYLVANIA AVENUE"

JASON ROBARDS AND ZOE CALDWELL IN THE REVIVAL OF
"LONG DAY'S JOURNEY INTO NIGHT"

PLAYS PRODUCED
IN NEW YORK

PLAYS PRODUCED ON BROADWAY

Figures in parentheses following a play's title indicate number of performances. The figures are acquired directly from the production offices in each case and do not include previews or extra non-profit performances.

Plays marked with an asterisk (*) were still running on June 1, 1976. Their number of performances is figured from opening night through May 31, 1976.

In a listing of a show's numbers—dances, sketches, musical scenes, etc.— the titles of songs are identified by their appearance in quotation marks (").

HOLDOVERS FROM PREVIOUS SEASONS

Plays which were running on June 2, 1975 are listed below. More detailed information about them appears in previous *Best Plays* volumes of appropriate years. Important cast changes since opening night are recorded in the "Cast Replacements" section of this volume.

*Grease (1,763). Musical with book, music and lyrics by Jim Jacobs and Warren Casey. Opened February 14, 1972.

*Pippin (1,512). Musical with book by Roger O. Hirson; music and lyrics by Stephen Schwartz. Opened October 23, 1972.

Raisin (847). Musical based on Lorraine Hansberry's *A Raisin in the Sun;* book by Robert Nemiroff and Charlotte Zaltzberg; music by Judd Woldin; lyrics by Robert Brittan. Opened October 18, 1973. (Closed December 7, 1975)

Candide (740). Musical revival with new book by Hugh Wheeler adapted from Voltaire; music by Leonard Bernstein; lyrics by Richard Wilbur; additional lyrics by Stephen Sondheim and John Latouche. Opened December 11, 1973 off Broadway at the Chelsea Theater Center where it played 48 performances through January 20, 1974; transferred to Broadway March 10, 1974 matinee. (Closed January 4, 1976)

*The Magic Show (837). Musical with book by Bob Randall; music and lyrics by Stephen Schwartz; magic by Doug Henning. Opened May 28, 1974.

Absurd Person Singular (592). By Alan Ayckbourn. Opened October 8, 1974. (Closed March 6, 1976)

*Equus (666). By Peter Shaffer. Opened October 24, 1974.

Sherlock Holmes (471). Revival of the play by Arthur Conan Doyle and William Gillette. Opened November 12, 1974. (Closed January 4, 1976 matinee)

All Over Town (233). By Murray Schisgal. Opened December 29, 1974. (Closed July 20, 1975)

*The Wiz (556). Musical based on L. Frank Baum's *The Wonderful Wizard of Oz;* book by William F. Brown; music and lyrics by Charlie Smalls. Opened January 5, 1975.

*Shenandoah (557). Musical based on the original screen play by James Lee Barrett; book by James Lee Barrett, Peter Udell and Philip Rose; music by Gary Geld; lyrics by Peter Udell. Opened January 7, 1975.

The Ritz (400). By Terrence McNally. Opened January 20, 1975. (Closed January 4, 1976)

Dance With Me (396). Revival of the comedy with music by Greg Antonacci. Opened January 23, 1975. (Closed January 4, 1976)

*Same Time, Next Year (509). By Bernard Slade. Opened March 13, 1975.

Bette Midler's Clams on the Half Shell (67). Revue devised as a showcase for Bette Midler. Opened April 17, 1975. (Closed June 21, 1975)

Rodgers & Hart (111). Musical revue with music by Richard Rodgers; lyrics by Lorenz Hart; concept by Richard Lewine and John Fearnley. Opened May 13, 1975. (Closed August 16, 1975)

PLAYS PRODUCED JUNE 1, 1975—MAY 31, 1976

*Chicago (388). Musical based on the play by Maurine Dallas Watkins; book by Fred Ebb and Bob Fosse; music by John Kander; lyrics by Fred Ebb. Produced by Robert Fryer and James Cresson in association with Martin Richards, Joseph Harris and Ira Bernstein at the Forty-Sixth Street Theater. Opened June 3, 1975.

Velma Kelly	Chita Rivera	Martin Harrison	Michael Vita
Roxy Hart	Gwen Verdon	Matron	Mary McCarty
Fred Casely	Gary Gendell	Billy Flynn	Jerry Orbach
Sgt. Fogarty	Richard Korthaze	Mary Sunshine	M. O'Haughey
Amos Hart	Barney Martin	Go-to-Hell Kitty	Charlene Ryan
Liz	Cheryl Clark	Harry	Paul Solen
Annie	Michon Peacock	Aaron	Gene Foote
June	Candy Brown	Judge	Ron Schwinn
Hunyak	Graciela Daniele	Court Clerk	Ross Miles
Mona	Pamela Sousa		

The Band: Sy Berger, Harry Divito, Hank Freeman, Karen Gustafson, John Monaco, Tony Pagano, Waymon Reed, James Sedlar, Chuck Spies, William Stanley, Art Wagner, Frank Wess, Tony Posk.

Dance Alternates: Hank Brunjes, Monica Tiller. Standbys: Miss Verdon—Lenora Nemetz; Mr. Orbach—Steve Elmore; Miss McCarty—Laura Waterbury; Miss O'Haughey—Marsha Bagwell. Understudies: Miss Rivera—Michon Peacock; Mr. Martin—Richard Korthaze.

Directed and choreographed by Bob Fosse; musical direction, Stanley Lebowsky; scenery, Tony Walton; costumes, Patricia Zipprodt; lighting, Jules Fisher; orchestrations, Ralph Burns; dance music arrangements, Peter Howard; sound, Abe Jacob; production stage manager, Phil Friedman; stage managers, Robert Corpora, Paul Phillips; press, The Merlin Group, Ltd., Cheryl Sue Dolby, Harriett Trachtenberg, Harold Lubin.

Time: The late 1920s. Place: Chicago, Ill.

A self-styled "musical vaudeville" of molls, mobsters and murderesses in a jazzed-up version of the Jazz Age, based on the satirical comedy of the same title which was produced on Broadway 12/30/26 for 172 performances and was named a Best Play of its season.

Leonora Nemetz replaced Gwen Verdon 7/30/75. Liza Minnelli replaced Leonora Nemetz 8/8/75. Gwen Verdon replaced Liza Minnelli 9/15/75. Rex Everhart replaced Barney Martin 2/20/76-2/28/76.

A Best Play; see page 146

ACT I

"All That Jazz" .... Velma, Company
"Funny Honey" .... Roxie
"Cell Block Tango" .... Velma, Girls
"When You're Good to Mama" .... Matron
"Tap Dance" .... Roxie, Amos, Boys
"All I Care About" .... Billy, Girls
"A Little Bit of Good" .... Mary Sunshine
"We Both Reached for the Gun" .... Billy, Roxie, Mary Sunshine, Company
"Roxie" .... Roxie, Boys
"I Can't Do It Alone" .... Velma
"Chicago After Midnight" .... The Band
"My Own Best Friend" .... Roxie, Velma

ACT II

"I Know a Girl" .... Velma
"Me and My Baby" .... Roxie, Gene, Paul
"Mister Cellophane" .... Amos
"When Velma Takes the Stand" .... Velma, Boys
"Razzle Dazzle" .... Billy, Company
"Class" .... Velma, Matron
"Nowadays" .... Roxie
"Nowadays" (Reprise), "R.S.V.P., "Keep It Hot" .... Roxie, Velma

The First Breeze of Summer (48). By Leslie Lee. Produced by The Negro Ensemble Company, Douglas Turner Ward artistic director, Robert Hooks executive director, Frederick Garrett administrative director, in association with Woodie King Jr. at the Palace Theater. Opened June 10, 1975; see note. (Closed July 20, 1975)

Gremmar	Frances Foster	Sam Greene	Carl Crudup
Nate Edwards	Charles Brown	Briton Woodward	Anthony McKay
Lou Edwards	Reyno	Reverend Mosely	Lou Myers
Aunt Edna	Barbara Montgomery	Hope	Petronia
Milton Edwards	Moses Gunn	Joe Drake	Peter DeMaio
Hattie	Ethel Ayler	Gloria Townes	Bebe Drake Hooks
Lucretia	Janet League	Harper Edwards	Douglas Turner Ward

Directed by Douglas Turner Ward; scenery, Edward Burbridge; costumes, Mary Mease Warren; lighting, Thomas Skelton; production stage manager, Horacena J. Taylor; press, Howard Atlee, Clarence Allsopp.

Time: The present. Place: A small city in the Northeast. Act I: Thursday afternoon through Friday night in June. Act II: The following Saturday afternoon through Sunday night.

A black family is moving into the middle class and beyond, while its matriarch remembers her difficult past, taking pleasure in the memory of the three men who fathered her children, as she helps to ease her grandson's emotional tensions in the present.

NOTE: This production of *The First Breeze of Summer* was presented off Broadway from 3/2/75 through 4/27/75 for 80 performances (see its entry in the "Plays Produced off Broadway" section of *The Best Plays of 1974-75*) before being transferred to Broadway for an additional run.

Circle in the Square. 1974-75 schedule of four programs ended with **Death of a Salesman** (64). Revival of the play by Arthur Miller. Produced by Circle in the

Square, Theodore Mann artistic director, Paul Libin managing director, at Circle in the Square Theater. Opened June 26, 1975. (Closed August 24, 1975)

Linda Loman	Teresa Wright	Howard Wagner	Pirie MacDonald
Willy Loman	George C. Scott	Jenny	Helen Harrelson
Happy	Harvey Keitel	Stanley	Mordecai Lawner
Biff	James Farentino	Miss Forsythe	Bara-Cristin Hansen
Bernard	Chuck Patterson	Letta	Joanne Jonas
1st Woman	Patricia Quinn	2d Woman	Julie Garfield
Charley	Arthur French	Waiter	Craig Wasson
Uncle Ben	Ramon Bieri		

Standby: Mr. Scott—Roy Poole. Understudies: Miss Wright—Helen Harrelson; Messrs. Keitel, Farentino—Bruce Weitz; Mr. French—Maxwell Glanville; Mr. Patterson—Les Roberts; Messrs. MacDonald, Lawner—Michael Durrell; Misses Hansen, Jonas—Katherine De Hetre.

Directed by George C. Scott; scenery, Marjorie Kellogg; costumes, Arthur Boccia; lighting, Thomas Skelton; incidental music, Craig Wasson; production stage manager, Randall Brooks; stage manager, James Bernardi; press, Merle Debuskey, Susan L. Schulman.

The play was presented in three acts.

Death of a Salesman was first produced on Broadway 2/10/49 for 742 performances, when it was named a Best Play and won the Critics Award and the Pulitzer Prize. This is its first New York revival.

Martin Sheen replaced Harvey Keitel 8/5/75.

*A Chorus Line (326). Musical conceived by Michael Bennett; book by James Kirkwood and Nicholas Dante; music by Marvin Hamlisch; lyrics by Edward Kleban. Produced by Joseph Papp in association with Plum Productions in the New York Shakespeare Festival production at the Sam S. Shubert Theater. Opened July 25, 1975; see note.

Roy	Scott Allen	Don	Ron Kuhlman
Kristine	Renee Baughman	Bebe	Nancy Lee
Sheila	Carole Bishop	Connie	Baayork Lee
Val	Pamela Blair	Diana	Priscilla Lopez
Mike	Wayne Cilento	Zach	Robert LuPone
Butch	Chuck Cissel	Mark	Cameron Mason
Larry	Clive Clerk	Cassie	Donna McKechnie
Maggie	Kay Cole	Al	Don Percassi
Richie	Ronald Dennis	Frank	Michael Serrecchia
Tricia	Donna Drake	Creg	Michel Stuart
Tom	Brandt Edwards	Bobby	Thomas J. Walsh
Judy	Patricia Garland	Paul	Sammy Williams
Lois	Carolyn Kirsch	Vicki	Crissy Wilzak

The Orchestra: Jerry Goldberg associate conductor; Fran Liebergall keyboards; George Davis guitars; Roland Wilson bass guitar; Jaime Austria upright base; Bernice Horowitz harp; Allen Herman drums; Benjamin Herman percussion; Joseph Maggio, Buzz Brauner, Norman Wells, Marvin Roth reeds; Bob Millikan, James Morreale, Al Mattaliano trumpets; Vincent Forchetti, Gordon Early Anderson trombones; Blaise Turi bass trombone.

Understudies: Messrs. Percassi, Cilento—John Mineo; Messrs. Williams, Dennis—Chuck Cissel; Misses Baughman, Baayork Lee, Cole—Donna Drake; Messrs. Kuhlman, Mason—Brandt Edwards; Misses McKechnie, Bishop—Carolyn Kirsch; Misses Lopez, Lane—Carole Schweid; Messrs. Clerk, Stuart, Walsh—Michael Serrecchia; Misses Blair, Garland—Crissy Wilzak; Mr. LuPone—Clive Clerk.

Directed and choreographed by Michael Bennett; co-choreographer, Bob Avian; musical direction and vocal arrangements, Don Pippin; scenery, Robin Wagner; costumes, Theoni V. Aldredge; lighting, Tharon Musser; sound, Abe Jacob; orchestrations, Bill Byers, Hershy Kay, Jonathan Tunick; music coordinator, Robert Thomas; associate producer, Bernard Gersten; production stage manager, Jeff Hamlin; stage manager, Frank Hartenstein; press, Merle Debuskey, Bob Ullman, Bruce Cohen.

Time: Now. Place: Here, an audition. The play was presented without intermission.

A Broadway director is selecting a chorous for his show; he narrows the applicants down to 17 dancers, of whom he must pick eight.

The list of musical numbers in *A Chorus Line* appears on pages 360-361 of *The Best Plays of 1974-75.*

NOTE: This production of *A Chorus Line* was presented off Broadway from 4/15/75 through 7/13/75 for 101 performances and was named a Best Play and won the 1975 Critics Award (see its entries in *The Best Plays of 1974-75*) before being transferred to Broadway for an additional run. It opened on Broadway 7/25/75 but did not hold its press date until 10/19/75, following the musicians' strike.

Cookie Vasquez replaced Renee Baughman, Barbara Monte-Britton replaced Pamela Blair, Lauree Berger replaced Kay Cole, Winston DeWitt Hemsley replaced Ronald Dennis, Sandhal Bergman replaced Patricia Garland, Vicki Frederick replaced Carolyn Kirsch, David Thomé replaced Ron Kuhlman, Gillian Scalici replaced Nancy Lee, Lauren Kayahara replaced Baayork Lee, Barbara Luna replaced Priscilla Lopez, Joe Bennett replaced Robert LuPone, Ann Reinking replaced Donna McKechnie, Bill Nabel replaced Don Percassi, Justin Ross replaced Michel Stuart, George Pesaturo replaced Sammy Williams 4/20/76. Carole Bishop changed her name to Kelly Bishop during this season's run.

The Skin of Our Teeth (7). Revival of the play by Thornton Wilder. Produced by Ken Marsolais with Kennedy Center-Xerox American Bicentennial Theater at the Mark Hellinger Theater. Opened September 9, 1975. (Closed September 13, 1975)

Announcer; Professor;	Doctor; Fred Bailey ....Lee Sherman
Mr. Tremayne ....Alexander Reed	Judge ....Joseph C. Davies
Sabina ....Elizabeth Ashley	Homer; Broadcast
Mr. Fitzpatrick ...............F.J. O'Neil	Announcer ....Norman Michael Chase
Mrs. Antrobus ....Martha Scott	Miss E. Muse;
Dinosaur ....Roi Petersen	Conveener's Wife ....Eda Seasongood
Mammoth; Monkey Man .....Denny Dillon	Miss T. Muse ....Josephine Nichols
Telegraph Boy; Asst. to	Miss M. Muse ....Betty Lynd
Broadcast Announcer ....Barry Livingston	Fortune Teller ....Charlotte Jones
Gladys ....Janet Grey	Defeated Candidate ....Douglas Fisher
Henry ....Steve Railsback	Hester ....Yuye Fernandes
Mr. Antrobus ....Alfred Drake	Ivy ....Gertrude Jeannette

Drum Majorettes: Betty Lynd, Kristina Callahan, Kate Kellery, Yuye Fernandes. Chair Pushers: Philip Lindsay, Roi Petersen. Conveeners: Richard DeFabees, Joseph C. Davies, Douglas Fisher, J.F. Hall, Steven Kelly, Lee Sherman, Alexander Reed, Barry Livingston.

Understudies: Misses Ashley, Seasongood, Nichols—Kristina Callahan; Mr. Drake—Alexander Reed; Misses Scott, Jeanette—Eda Seasongood; Misses Jones, Fernandes—Josephine Nichols; Messrs. Railsback, Livingston—Richard DeFabees; Messrs. Reed, Petersen—Philip Lindsay; Misses Grey, Lynd—Kate Kellery; Messrs. O'Neil, Sherman—J.F. Hall; Mr. Dillon—Betty Lynd; Mr. Reed—Douglas Fisher.

Directed by José Quintero; scenery, Eugene Lee; costumes, Franne Lee; lighting, Ken Billington; produced for Kennedy Center by Roger L. Stevens and Richmond Crinkley; production stage manager, Martin Herzer; stage manager, David Taylor; press, Betty Lee Hunt, Maria Cristina Pucci, William Evans.

Act I: Home, Excelsior, N.J. Act II: Atlantic City Boardwalk. Act III: Home, Excelsior, N.J. *The Skin of Our Teeth* was first produced on Broadway 11/18/42 for 359 performances. It was named a Best Play of its season and was awarded the Pulitzer Prize. Its only previous professional New York revival was by ANTA 8/17/55 for 22 performances. This 1975 production was previously produced in Birmingham, Ala., Washington, D.C. and Boston.

Circle in the Square. Schedule of four revivals. **Ah, Wilderness!** (77). By Eugene O'Neill. Opened September 18, 1975. (Closed November 23, 1975) **The Glass Menagerie** (78). By Tennessee Williams. Opened December 18, 1975. (Closed February 22, 1976) **The Lady From the Sea** (77). By Henrik Ibsen; translated by Michael Meyer. Opened March 18, 1976. (Closed May 23, 1976) And *Pal Joey,* musical with book by John O'Hara, music by Richard Rodgers, lyrics by Lorenz Hart, scheduled to open 6/28/76. Produced by Circle in the Square, Theodore Mann artistic director, Paul Libin managing director, at Circle in the Square Theater.

AH, WILDERNESS!

Tommy Miller	Glenn Zachar	David McComber	Ralph Drischell
Mildred Miller	Christina Whitmore	Norah	Linda Hunt
Arthur Miller	Paul Rudd	Wint Selby	Sean G. Griffin
Essie Miller	Geraldine Fitzgerald	Belle	Suzanne Lederer
Lily Miller	Teresa Wright	Bartender	Stephen Mendillo
Sid Davis	John Braden	Salesman	Don Gantry
Nat Miller	William Swetland	Muriel	Swoosie Kurtz
Richard Miller	Richard Backus		

Standbys: Miss Fitzgerald—Shirley Bryan; Messrs. Rudd, Backus, Griffin—Thomas Leopold; Misses Lederer, Whitmore, Kurtz, Hunt—Alexandra Stoddart.

Directed by Arvin Brown; produced in association with The Long Wharf Theater; scenery, Steven Rubin; costumes, Bill Walker; lighting, Ronald Wallace; production stage manager, Nina Seely; stage manager, James Bernardi; press, Merle Debuskey, Susan L. Schulman.

Time: July 4, 1906. Place: The Miller home, a small Connecticut town. Act I, Scene 1: That morning. Scene 2: Evening of the same day. Act II, Scene 1: Back room of a small hotel bar, that night. Scene 2: The Miller home, later that night. Act III, Scene 1: The Miller home, the following afternoon. Scene 2: A strip of beach by the harbor that night. Scene 3: The Miller home, later that night.

Ah, Wilderness! was first produced on Broadway by the Theater Guild 10/2/33 for 289 performances and was named a Best Play of its season. Broadway revivals took place 10/2/41 for 29 performances and in the musical version *Take Me Along* 10/22/59 for 448 performances. The 1975 production was previously produced in New Haven, Conn.

THE GLASS MENAGERIE

Amanda	Maureen Stapleton	Laura	Pamela Payton-Wright
Tom	Rip Torn	Jim	Paul Rudd

Standbys: Miss Stapleton—Nancy Marchand; Messrs. Torn, Rudd—Marco St. John. Understudy: Miss Payton-Wright—Sharon Morrison.

Directed by Theodore Mann; scenery, Ming Cho Lee; costumes, Sydney Brooks; lighting, Thomas Skelton; incidental music, Craig Wasson; production stage manager, Randall Brooks; stage manager, James Bernardi; press, Merle Debuskey, Susan L. Schulman.

Time: Now and the past. Place: An alley in St. Louis. Part I: Preparation for a gentleman caller. Part II: The gentleman calls.

The Glass Menagerie was first produced on Broadway 3/31/45 for 561 performances and was named a Best Play of its season and won the Critics Award. Professional New York revivals have taken place 11/21/56 for 15 performances and 5/4/65 for 32 performances.

THE LADY FROM THE SEA

Ballested	George Ede	Dr. Wangel	Pat Hingle
Bolette	Kimberly Farr	Professor Arnholm	John Heffernan
Lyngstrand	Kipp Osborne	Ellida	Vanessa Redgrave
Hilde	Allison Argo	The Stranger	Richard Lynch

Directed by Tony Richardson; scenery and costumes, Rouben Ter-Arutunian; lighting, Thomas Skelton; music and sound, Richard Peaslee; production stage manager, Randall Brooks; stage manager, James Bernardi; press, Merle Debuskey, Susan L. Schulman.

Place: A small town by a fjord in Norway, summer.

The Lady From the Sea had its first New York production of record 11/6/11. It was last revived on Broadway 9/7/50 for 16 performances with Luise Rainer and was done off Broadway during the 1956-57 season.

The Acting Company. Schedule of four programs. **The Robber Bridegroom** (15). Musical based on the novella by Eudora Welty; book and lyrics by Alfred Uhry; music by Robert Waldman. Opened October 7, 1975. (Closed October 18, 1975). **Edward II** (8). Revival of the play by Christopher Marlowe. Opened October 21, 1975 (Closed October 25, 1975) **The Time of Your Life** (8). Revival of the play by William Saroyan. Opened October 28, 1975. (Closed November 1, 1975) **Three Sisters** (8). Revival of the play by Anton Chekhov; translated by Tyrone Guthrie and Leonard Kipnis. Opened November 4, 1975. (Closed November 8, 1975)

Produced by The Acting Company, John Houseman artistic director, Margot Harley producing director, at the Harkness Theater.

PERFORMER	"THE ROBBER BRIDEGROOM"	"EDWARD II"	"THE TIME OF YOUR LIFE"	"THREE SISTERS"
Robert Bacigalupi	Goat	Spencer	Dudley	
Brooks Baldwin	Kyle Nunnery	Warwick; Berkeley	Harry	Householder
Glynis Bell	Goat's Mother		Lorene; Killer's Sidekick	Anfisa
Cynthia Dickason	Queenie Sue	Beggar II; Lady in Waiting	Killer	Householder
Peter Dvorsky	Ernie Summers	Gaveston	Gentleman	Vershinin
Gerald Gutierrez			Wesley	
Sandra Halperin	Airie	Lady in Waiting	Elsie	Natasha
J.W. Harper	Little Harp	Baldock	Blick	Householder
Elaine Hausman	Raven	Lady Margaret	Newsboy	Dounyasha
Benjamin Hendrickson		(Lancaster; Lightborn)	Nick	Prozorov
Alan Kaufman	The Fiddler			
Kevin Kline	Jamie Lockhart	(Lancaster; Lightborn)	McCarthy	
Patti LuPone	Rosamund	Prince Edward	Kitty Duval	Irina
Anderson Matthews	Big Harp	Beggar I; Gurney	Sailor; (Drunkard)	Householder
Mary-Joan Negro		Queen Isabella	Lady	Masha
Richard Ooms	Tom Plymale	Elder Mortimer; Abbott	Arab	Kulygin
Mary Lou Rosato	Salome		Mary L.	Olga
David Schramm	Clemment Musgrove	Kent	Kit Carson	Chebutykin
Norman Snow	Mike Fink	Edward II	Tom	Tusenbach
Roy K. Stevens	John Oglesby	Matrevis; Beggar III	Krupp	Ferapont
Nicolas Surovy	Billy Brenner	Canterbury	Joe	Lt. Fedotik
Michael Tolaydo	Herman McLaughlin	Leicester; Coventry	(Willie; Drunkard)	Lt. Rode
Sam Tsoutsouvas		Young Mortimer	(Willie)	Capt. Solyony

(Parentheses indicate roles in which the performers alternated)

ALL PLAYS—Executive director, Porter Van Zandt; scenery, Douglas W. Schmidt; lighting, David F. Segal; production stage manager, Howard Crampton-Smith; stage manager, Sam Clester; press, Gifford/Wallace, Inc.

THE ROBBER BRIDEGROOM—Directed by Gerald Freedman; arranged by Robert Waldman; choreography, Donald Saddler; costumes, Jeanne Button.

Understudies: Messrs. Kline, Snow—Nicolas Surovy; Mr. Harper—Norman Snow; Mr. Schramm—Richard Ooms; Mr. Bacigalupi—Brooks Baldwin; Miss Rosato—Glynis Bell; Miss LuPone—Sandra Halperin; Miss Bell—Elaine Hausman; Misses Halperin, Hausman—Cynthia Dickason; Neighbors—Benjamin Hendrickson.

The Wretched Refuse: Bob Jones guitar, Alan Kaufman fiddle and mandolin, David Markowitz bass, Richard Shulberg fiddle, Steve Tannenbaum banjo.

Place: Legendary Mississippi. The play was presented without intermission.

Folk tale of the farmer's pretty daughter and a handsome brigand in disguise.

MUSICAL NUMBERS

"With Style" ....Jamie Lockhart, Company
"The Real Mike Fink" ....Jamie, Clemment Musgrove, Mike Fink
"The Pricklepear Bloom" ....Salome
"Nothin Up" ....Rosamund
"Deeper in the Woods" ....Company
"Riches" ....Musgrove, Jamie, Salome, Rosamund
"Love Stolen" ....Jamie
"Poor Tied Up Darlin" ....Little Harp, Goat
"Goodbye Salome" ....Company
"Sleepy Man" ....Rosamund

EDWARD II—Directed by Ellis Rabb; music and sound, Bob James; costumes, Nancy Potts.
Attendants: Cynthia Dickason, Peter Dvorsky, Sandra Halperin, J.W. Harper, Elaine Hausman, Anderson Matthews, Richard Ooms, Roy K. Stevens, Michael Tolaydo.

Understudies: Miss Dickason—Glynis Bell; Miss LuPone—Sandra Halperin; Miss Hausman—Cynthia Dickason; Miss Negro—Mary Lou Rosato; Messrs. Tolaydo, Surovy, Stevens, Matthews—Gerald Gutierrez; Messrs. Tsoutsouvas, Hendrickson, Kline—J.W. Harper; Mr. Dvorsky, Alternate—Kevin Kline; Mr. Bacigalupi—Anderson Matthews; Mr. Snow—David Schramm; Mr. Harper—Roy K. Stevens; Messrs. Ooms, Baldwin—Michael Tolaydo; Mr. Schramm—Richard Ooms.

Edward II is believed to have been first performed about 1592 by the Earl of Pembroke's Company. Its only previous New York productions of record were a college production in 1947-48 and an Equity Library Theater staging in 1957-58.

THE TIME OF YOUR LIFE—Directed by Jack O'Brien; costumes, Nancy Potts.

Understudies: Mr. Surovy—David Schramm, Miss LuPone—Sandra Halperin; Mr. Hendrickson—J.W. Harper; Messrs. Ooms, Bacigalupi—Michael Tolaydo; Messrs. Stevens, Baldwin—Anderson Matthews; Miss Halperin—Cynthia Dickason; Mr. Harper—Sam Tsoutsouvas; Mr. Kline—Peter Dvorsky; Miss Rosato—Mary-Joan Negro; Messrs. Snow, Dvorsky, Gutierrez—Kevin Kline; Misses Negro, Dickason—Glynis Bell.

Time: Afternoon and night of a day in October, 1939. Place: Nick's Pacific Street Saloon, Restaurant and Entertainment Palace at the foot of Embarcadero in San Francisco. The play was presented in three parts.

The Time of Your Life was first produced on Broadway by the Theater Guild at the Booth Theater 10/25/39 for 185 performances and was named a Best Play of its season and won both the Pulitzer Prize and Critics Award (for Best American Play). Its most recent revival was by the Repertory Theater of Lincoln Center 11/6/69 for 52 performances. Others were by the Theater Guild 9/23/40 for 32 performances, off Broadway by Associated Playwrights, Inc. during the 1946-47 season, and by the New York City Center Theater Company 1/19/55 for 15 performances.

THREE SISTERS—Directed by Boris Tumarin; musical direction, Gerald Gutierrez; dances staged by Elizabeth Keen; costumes, John David Ridge.

Understudies: Miss Rosato—Glynis Bell; Misses Halperin, Hausman—Cynthia Dickason; Miss Negro—Mary Lou Rosato; Misses LuPone, Bell—Elaine Hausman; Messrs. Tolaydo, Tsoutsouvas—Robert Bacigalupi; Messrs. Baldwin, Matthews, Harper, Surovy—Gerald Gutierrez; Mr. Schramm—J.W. Harper; Messrs. Snow, Dvorsky—Kevin Kline; Mr. Ooms—Nicolas Surovy; Mr. Stevens—Michael Tolaydo; Mr. Hendrickson—Sam Tsoutsouvas.

Time: The turn of this century. Place: The Prozorov home in a provincial town of Russia. Act I: The drawing room, noonday in spring. Act II: The same, two days later, a winter evening. Act III: Olga and Irina's room, two years later, 3 a.m. in early spring. Act IV: The garden of the house, noonday in autumn of the same year. The play was presented in two parts with the intermission following Act II.

Three Sisters was first performed by the Moscow Art Theater in 1901. This is the production presented by the Acting Company on Broadway 12/19/73 for 7 performances, and on a national tour.

The 5th Season (122). Musical version of the play by Sylvia Regan; adapted by Luba Kadison in Yiddish and English; music and lyrics by Dick Manning. Produced by Harry Rothpearl and Jewish Nostalgic Production, Inc. at the Eden Theater. Opened October 12, 1975. (Closed January 25, 1976)

Mr. Katz	Elias Patron	Benny Goodwin	Stan Porter
Shelly	Gerri-Ann Frank	Frances Goodwin	Evelyn Kingsley
Laurie	Raquel Yossifson	Marty Goodwin	Gene Barrett
Perl	David Carey	Miriam Oppenheim	Miriam Kressyn
Max Pincus	Joseph Buloff	Mr. Lewis	Jack Rechtzeit

Models: Franceska Fischler, Cathy Carnevale, Barbara Joan Frank.

Directed by Joseph Buloff; Yiddish adaptation of lyrics by Isaac Dogim; musical numbers staged by Sophie Maslow; musical direction, Renee Solomon; scenery and costumes, Jeffrey B. Moss; lighting, Bob McCarthy; production stage manager, Jay S. Hoffman; press, Max Eisen, Barbara Glenn.

Time: The present. Place: A Seventh Avenue fashion showroom. Act I, Scene 1: The showroom. Scene 2: Two hours later. Scene 3: Six weeks later. Act II, Scene 1: That evening. Scene 2: The same evening. Scene 3: A few days later.

Comedy about a romantically and financially beleaguered dress businessman, originally produced on Broadway 1/23/53 for 654 performances, now adapted as a Yiddish-English musical.

ACT I

"Believe in Yourself" ....Benny, Laurie
"My Son, the Doctor" ....Benny, Frances, Marty
"Goodbye" ....Benny, Laurie
"The Fifth Season" ....Ensemble

ACT II

"Friday Night" ....Pincus, Miriam
  (Lyrics by Luba Kadison)
"Mom! You Don't Understand!" ....Marty, Frances
"How Did This Happen to Me" ....Benny
"From Seventh Avenue to Seventh Heaven" ....Benny, Ensemble

* **New York Shakespeare Festival at Lincoln Center.** Schedule of four revivals. **Trelawny of the "Wells"** (47). By Arthur Wing Pinero. Opened October 15, 1975. (Closed November 23, 1975) **Hamlet** (47). By William Shakespeare. Opened December 17, 1975. (Closed January 25, 1976) **Mrs. Warren's Profession** (55). By George Bernard Shaw. Opened February 18, 1976. (Closed April 4, 1976) * **Threepenny Opera** (35) Musical with book and lyrics by Bertolt Brecht; lyrics by Kurt Weill; new translation by Ralph Manheim and John Willett. Opened May 1, 1976. Produced by New York Shakespeare Festival, Joseph Papp producer, at the Vivian Beaumont Theater.

ALL PLAYS—Associate producer, Bernard Gersten; director of play development, Gail Merrifield; production manager, Andrew Mihok; press, Merle Debuskey, Faith Geer.

TRELAWNY OF THE "WELLS"

Mrs. Mossop	Helen Verbit	Sarah	K.T. Baumann
Mr. Ablett	Merwin Goldsmith	Clara De Foenix	Ann McDonough
Tom Wrench	Michael Tucker	Capt. De Foenix	Jeffrey Jones
Imogen Parrott	Meryl Streep	Justice William Gower	Walter Abel
James Telfer	Jerome Dempsey	Trafalgar Gower	Aline MacMahon
Ferdinand Gadd	John Lithgow	Charles	Walter Gorney
Augustus Colpoys	Ben Slack	O'Dwyer	Christopher Hewett
Mrs. Telfer	Anita Dangler	Mr. Denzil	Jerry Mayer
Avonia Bunn	Sasha Von Scherler	Miss Brewster	Suzanne Collins
Rose Trelawny	Marybeth Hurt	Mr. Hunston	Tom Blank
Arthur Gower	Mandy Patinkin		

Understudies: Messrs. Tucker, Patinkin—Tom Blank; Messrs. Abel, Dempsey, Gorney—Thomas Barbour; Miss McDonough—K.T. Baumann; Misses Von Scherler, Streep, Baumann—Suzanne Collins; Messrs. Lithgow, Hewett—Jeffrey Jones; Messrs. Slack, Goldsmith, Jones—Jerry Mayer; Miss Hurt—Ann McDonough; Misses MacMahon, Dangler, Verbit—Elsa Raven.

Directed by A.J. Antoon; scenery, David Mitchell; costumes, Theoni V. Aldredge; costume supervision, Hal George; lighting, Ian Calderon; music, Peter Link; production stage manager, Louis Rackoff; stage manager, Richard S. Viola.

Time: Around the turn of the century. Place: New York City. Act I: The Telfers' apartment at Mrs. Mossop's boarding house, late spring. Act II: The mansion of Justice William Gower, Gracie Square, early summer. Act III: Miss Trelawny's room at Mrs. Mossop's boarding house, six months later. Act IV: The stage of the Lyric Theater, spring. The play was presented in three parts with intermissions following Acts I and II.

Trelawny of the "Wells" was first presented in New York by Daniel Frohman at the Lyceum Theater 11/22/98 for 131 performances. Its most recent revival took place off Broadway at

New York Shakespeare Festival Public Theater 10/11/70 for 48 performances; its last Broadway production was 1/31/27 for 56 performances.

HAMLET

Claudius ....Charles Cioffi
Gertrude ....Jane Alexander
Hamlet ....Sam Waterston
Polonious; 1st Gravedigger.......Larry Gates
Laertes ....James Sutorius
Ophelia ....Maureen Anderman
Horatio ....George Hearn
Voltemand ....James Gallery
Rosencrantz ....David Ackroyd
Guildenstern ....John Heard
Marcellus; Murderer ....Richard Brestoff
Francisco; Player Queen ....David Naughton
Bernardo; Priest; Dumb Show
Murderer ....Stephen Lang

Reynaldo ....Erik Fredricksen
2nd Gravedigger ....Jack R. Marks
Fortinbras; Dumb Show
King ....Mandy Patinkin
Capt. to Fortinbras;
Dumb Show Queen ...Hannibal Penney Jr.
Ghost ....Robert Burr
Osric ....Bruce McGill
Player King ....James Hurdle
Prologue; Apprentice Actor..Nancy Campbell
Company Manager ....Vance Mizelle
Technical Director ....Ernest Austin

Stagehands: Michael Cutt, Ronald Hunter, Reginald Vel Johnson, Jack R. Marks, David Howard. Ensemble: Ernest Austin, Richard Brestoff, Michael Cutt, Erik Fredricksen, David Howard, Ronald Hunter, Reginald Vel Johnson, Henson Keys, Stephen Lang, Jack R. Marks, Vance Mizelle, Bruce McGill, David Naughton, Richard Sanders.

Understudies: Mr. Naughton—Ernest Austin; Messrs. Heard, Hurdle—Richard Brestoff; Miss Anderman—Nancy Campbell; Messrs. Brestoff, Marks—Michael Cutt; Mr. Gates—James Gallery; Mr. Waterston—John Heard; Miss Alexander—Ruby Holbrook; Mr. Penney—Davis S. Howard; Messrs. Hearn, Austin—Ronald Hunter; Mr. Cioffi—James Hurdle; Mr. Mizelle—Reginald Vel Johnson; Mr. Lang—Henson Keys; Mr. Ackroyd—Stephen Lang; Mr. Gallery—Jack R. Marks; Mr. Sutorius—Bruce McGill; Mr. McGill—David Naughton; Mr. Patinkin—Hannibal Penny Jr.; Mr. Burr—Richard Sanders.

Directed by Michael Rudman; scenery, Santo Loquasto; costumes, Hal George; lighting, Martin Aronstein; music, John Morris; production stage manager, D.W. Koehler; stage manager, Michael Chambers.

The play was presented in two parts. This production of *Hamlet* was first mounted in Central Park this season by New York Shakespeare Festival 6/18/75 for 28 performances (see its entry in the "Plays Produced Off Broadway" section of this volume).

MRS. WARREN'S PROFESSION

Vivie Warren ....Lynn Redgrave
Praed ....Ron Randell
Mrs. Kitty Warren ....Ruth Gordon

Sir George Crofts ....Philip Bosco
Frank Gardner ....Edward Herrmann
Rev. Samuel Gardner ....Milo O'Shea

Understudies: Messrs. O'Shea, Bosco—John Carpenter. Miss Redgrave—Donna Isaacson; Mr. Randell—Edmund Lyndeck; Mr. Herrmann—John Schak.

Directed by Gerald Freedman; scenery, David Mitchell; costumes, Theoni V. Aldredge; lighting, Martin Aronstein; production stage manager, Mary Porter Hall.

Time: 1894. Act I: A summer afternoon in a cottage garden in Haslemere, Surrey. Act II: Inside the cottage later that evening. Act III: The Rectory garden the next morning. Act IV: Honoria Fraser's chambers in Chancery Lane, London, two days later. The play was presented in three parts with intermissions following Acts II and III.

Mrs. Warren's Profession was first produced in New York the weeks of 10/23/05 and 10/30/05 and was revived for 25 performances 3/11/07. Subsequent Broadway revivals took place 3/11/18 and 2/22/22. It was also revived off Broadway in 11/51 and 4/24/63 for 14 performances.

THREEPENNY OPERA

Ballad Singer ....Roy Brocksmith
Mack The Knife ....Raul Julia
Jenny Towler ....Ellen Greene

Jonathan Peachum ..........C.K. Alexander
Samuel ....Tony Azito
Charles Filch ....Ed Zang

Mrs. Peachum	Elizabeth Wilson	Jimmy	Robert Schlee
Matt	Ralph Drischell	Walt	Max Gulack
Polly Peachum	Caroline Kava	Tiger Brown	David Sabin
Jake	William Duell	Smith	Glen Kezer
Bob	K.C. Wilson	Lucy Brown	Blair Brown
Ned	Rik Colitti		

Beggars and Policemen: Pendleton Brown, M. Patrick Hughes, George McGrath, Rick Petrucelli, John Ridge, Craig Rupp, Armin Shimerman, Jack Eric Williams, Ray Xifo. Whores: Penelope Bodry, Nancy Campbell, Gretel Cummings, Brenda Currin, Mimi Turque.

Standby: Mr. Julia—Keith Charles. Understudies: Misses Kava, Brown—Penelope Bodry; Mr. Gulack—Pendleton Brown; Miss Wilson—Gretel Cummings; Mr. Alexander—Ralph Drischell; Ensemble Swing—Frank di Filia; Mr. Sabin—Glenn Kezer; Ensemble Swing—Liza Kirchner; Messrs. Azito, Wilson—George McGrath; Mr. Drischell—John Ridge; Mr. Schlee—Craig Rupp; Messrs. Zang, Colitti—Armin Shimerman; Miss Greene—Mimi Turque; Mr. Brocksmith—Jack Eric Williams; Mr. Duell—Ray Xifo.

Directed by Richard Foreman; musical director, Stanley Silverman; scenery, Douglas W. Schmidt; costumes, Theoni V. Aldredge; lighting, Pat Collins; production stage manager, D.W. Koehler; stage manager, Michael Chambers.

Time: The time of Queen Victoria's coronation. Place: London, rearranged in Brecht's imagination. The play was presented in three parts.

A new translation of the Brecht-Weill material more akin to the rough, anti-social original than the smoothed-out Marc Blitzstein adaptation which as *The Threepenny Opera* was produced at the Theater de Lys the season of 1953-54 for 2,611 performances, second only to *The Fantasticks* as off-Broadway's longest-running production.

Special citation as Best Revival; see page 283

Lamppost Reunion (77). By Louis LaRusso II. Produced by Joe Garofalo at the Little Theater. Opened October 16, 1975. (Closed December 21, 1975)

Biggie	Danny Aiello	Jobby	George Pollock
Mac	Frank Quinn	Fred	Gabriel Dell
Tommy	Frank Bongiorno		

Directed by Tom Signorelli; scenery, Robert U. Taylor; costumes, Judy Dearing; lighting, Spencer Mosse; production stage manager, Paul Austin; press, Max Eisen, Carl Samrock.

Time: The present. Place: Hoboken. Act I: The Lamppost Bar, 3:30 a.m. Act II: Sometime later. Act III: Near dawn.

A play self-described as "about a kid from Hoboken" who has become a singing superstar and returns to visit his old haunts and cronies.

Tom Signorelli replaced Frank Quinn 11/24/75.

The Leaf People (8). By Dennis J. Reardon. Produced by New York Shakespeare Festival, Joseph Papp producer, at the Booth Theater. Opened October 20, 1975. (Closed October 26, 1975)

The Fishbellies:		Mayteemo	James Sbano
1st Interpreter	Grayson Hall	Monkey Man	Ernesto Gonzalez
2nd Interpreter	Anthony Holland	Keerah	Denise Delapenha
Shaughnessy	Tom Aldredge	Yawahlapeetee	Joanna Featherstone
Meatball	Ernesto Gonzalez	Kreetahshay	Susan Batson
P. Sigmund Furth	Lane Smith	Green Father	Roy Brocksmith
Steven	Ted LePlat	Jeeshoom	Francisco Blackfeather
Michelle	Denise Delapenha	Kahleemshoht	Ron Capozzoli
Anna Ames	Margaret Hall	Choolkahnoor	Jeffrey David-Owen
The Leaf People:		Lahbayneezh	Jelom Viera
Sutreeshay	Geanine-Michele Capozzoli	Treekah	Josevaldo Machado
Gitaucho	Raymond J. Barry	Zhahbahroosh	Ric Lavin
The Sound	Leon Morenzie	Lohzhoodish	Soni Moreno
Leeboh	William Parry	Lohmohheetet	Jeannette Ertelt

Musicians: Joel Kaye, Donald Hettinger, Efstratios Vavagiakis, Ruben Rivera, Michael Lamont.

Understudies: Messrs. Gonzalez, Parra, Sbano—Ron Capozzoli; Messrs. Smith, Morenzie—

Jeffrey David-Owen; Misses Hall, Batson, Featherstone—Jeannette Ertelt; Mr. Aldredge—Ric Lavin; Misses Delapenha, Capozzoli—Soni Moreno; Mr. Barry—William Parry; Mr. LePlat— James Sbano.

Directed by Tom O'Horgan; scenery, John Conklin; costumes, Randy Barcelo; lighting, John McLain; sound, Roger Jay; original music, Xantheus Roh Leempoor; associate producer, Bernard Gersten; production stage manager, Galen McKinley; stage manager, William Schill; press, Merle Debuskey, Leo Stern.

Time: Early October, 1973. Place: The Amazon Rain Forest. Act I. Scene 1: Shaughnessy's clearing. Scene 2: Furth's place. Scene 3: A dark place. Scene 4: Inside Anna's airplane. Scene 5: Gitaucho's tukul. Scene 6: The jungle. Scene 7: Gitaucho's tukul. Scene 8: Green Father's camp. Scene 9: The proclamation. Act II. Scene 1: The Sound's tukul. Scene 2: Gitaucho's tukul. Scene 3: The jungle. Scene 4: Gitaucho's tukul. Scene 5: Green Father's camp. Scene 6: Gitaucho's tukul. Scene 7: In front of the Maloca.

Singer's search for a missing missionary leads him to the discovery of a new breed of intelligent creatures with strange language and lifestyle.

Treemonisha (64). Opera in two acts by Scott Joplin; libretto by Scott Joplin. Produced by Adela Holzer, James Nederlander and Victor Lurie in the Huston Grand Opera Association production at the Palace Theater. Opened October 21, 1975. (Closed December 14, 1975)

Zodzetrick	Ben Harney	Andy	Kenneth Hicks
Ned	Willard White	Lucy	Cora Johnson
(Monisha)	Betty Allen, Lorna Myers	Parson Alltalk	Edward Pierson
(Treemonisha)	Carmen Balthrop, Kathleen Battle	Simon	Raymond Bazemore
		Cephus	Dwight Ransom
Remus	Curtis Rayam	Luddud	Dorceal Duckens

(Parentheses indicate roles in which the performers alternated)

Treemonisha Dancers: Clyde-Jacques Barrett, Thea Barnes, Dwight Baxter, Renee Brailsford, Karen Burke, Veda Jackson, Reggie Jackson, Julia Lema, Anita Littleman, Rick Odums, Dwayne Phelps, Ivson Polk, Mabel Robinson, Martial Roumain, Katherine Singleton, James Thurston, Bobby Walker, Pamela Wilson.

Treemonisha Chorus: Earl L. Baker, Kenneth Bates, Barbara Christopher, Steven Cole, Ella Eure, Gregory Gardner, Melvin Jordan, Patricia McDermott, Janette Moody, Marion Moore, Vera Moore, Lorna Myers, Glover Parham, Patricia Pates, William Penn, Dwight Ransom, Cornel Richie, Patricia Rogers, Christine Spencer, Walter Turnbull, Gloria Turner, Peter Whitehead, Arthur Williams, Barbara Young.

Production conceived and directed by Frank Corsaro; choreography, Louis Johnson; musical direction, supervision and orchestration, Gunther Schuller; scenery and costumes, Franco Colavecchia; lighting, Nananne Porcher; artistic consultant, Vera Brodsky Lawrence; production stage manager, Ben Janney; stage managers, Elizabeth Caldwell, Clinton Davis; press, Michael Alpert, Marilynn LeVine, Joshua Ellis, Warren Knowlton.

Time: The 1880s. Place: A plantation in the state of Arkansas, northeast of the town of Texarkana and three or four miles from the Red River.

The legend of an orphan girl found under a tree working through education to improve the lot of the people of her black community. Composed by its author in 1907, *Treemonisha* was never produced in New York except in a rehearsal-hall run-through. Previously produced in the 1970s in Atlanta, Houston and Washington, D.C.

ACT I

Scene 1: Morning

Overture	Orchestra, Zodzetrick, Dancers
"The Bag of Luck"	Treemonisha, Monisha, Remus, Ned, Zodzetrick
"The Corn-Huskers"	Treemonisha, Chorus
"We're Goin' Around"	Treemonisha, Monisha, Lucy, Remus, Ned, Chorus, Dancers
"The Wreath"	Treemonisha, Monisha, Lucy
"The Sacred Tree"	Monisha
"Surprise"	Treemonisha
"Treemonisha's Bringing Up"	Treemonisha, Monisha
"Good Advice"	Parson Alltalk, Chorus

"Confusion" ....Monisha, Lucy, Remus, Ned
Scene 2: Afternoon of the same day
"Superstition" ....Simon, Cephus
"Treemonisha in Peril" ....Zodzetrick, Simon, Luddud, Cephus
"The Frolic of the Bears" ....Dancers
"The Wasp Nest" ....Simon, Cephus
"The Rescue" ....Treemonisha, Remus
"We Will Rest Awhile" ....Quartet
"Going Home" ....Treemonisha, Remus, Foreman
"Aunt Dinah Has Blowed de Horn" ....Chorus, Dancers.

ACT II

Scene 1: That evening
Prelude ....Orchestra
"I Want to See My Child" ....Monisha, Ned
"Treemonisha's Return" ....Treemonisha, Monisha, Remus, Ned, Andy
"Wrong Is Never Right" ....Remus, Chorus
"Abuse" ....Treemonisha, Andy
"When Villains Ramble Far and Near" ....Ned
"Conjuror's Forgiven" ....Treemonisha, Andy
"We Will Trust You As Our Leader" ....Treemonisha, Monisha, Lucy, Ned,
                                                         Remus, Andy, Chorus
"A Real Slow Drag" ....Company
"Aunt Dinah Has Blowed de Horn" (Reprise) ....Company

* **Me and Bessie** (252). Conceived and written by Will Holt and Linda Hopkins. Produced by Norman Kean in the Center Theater Group/Mark Taper Forum and Lee Apostoleris production at the Ambassador Theater. Opened October 22, 1975.

Bessie Smith ....Linda Hopkins   Woman ....Gerri Dean
Man ....Lester Wilson

The Band: Howlett Smith piano; Bob Bushnell bass; Ray Mosca drums; Dick Griffin trombone; Lenny Hambro clarinet, saxophone.
Understudies: Mr. Wilson—Larry Low; Miss Dean—Alfre Woodard.
Directed by Robert Greenwald; musical direction, Howlett Smith; scenery, Donald Harris; costumes, Pete Menefee; lighting, Tharon Musser; special dance sequences, Lester Wilson; production stage manager, Martin Herzer; stage manager, Landi Sundsten; press, Les Schecter Associates.
Memories of Bessie Smith evoked in the story of her life and in songs she sung, in a third-person concept stopping short of actual impersonation of the noted blues singer.
Thomas M. Pollard replaced Lester Wilson 11/17/75.
MUSICAL NUMBERS: Act I—"I Feel Good," "God Shall Wipe All Tears Away," "Moan You Mourners," "New Orleans Hop Scop Blues," "Romance in the Dark," "Preach Them Blues," "A Good Man Is Hard to Find," "T'Ain't Nobody's Business If I Do," "Gimme a Pigfoot," "Put It Right Here," "You've Been a Good Ole Wagon," "Trombone Cholly," "Jazzbo Brown," "After You've Gone." Act II—"There'll Be a Hot Time in the Old Town Tonight," "Empty Bed Blues," "Kitchen Man," "Mama Don't 'Low," "Do Your Duty," "Fare Thee Well," "Nobody Knows You When You're Down and Out," "Trouble," "The Man's All Right."

Yentl (224). Return engagement of the play by Leah Napolin and Isaac Bashevis Singer. Produced by Cheryl Crawford, Moe Septee and The Chelsea Theater with Mrs. Victor H. Potamkin in the The Chelsea Theater Center of Brooklyn production (Robert Kalfin artistic director, Michael David executive director, Burl Hash production director) at the Eugene O'Neill Theater. Opened October 23, 1975. (Closed May 2, 1976)

CAST: Yentl—Tovah Feldshuh; Reb Todrus, Fulcha, Laibish, Cantor, Messenger, Musician—Bernie Passeltiner; Rivka, Necheleh, Chambermaid—Mary Ellen Ashley; Lemmel, Yussel, Wedding Jester, Dr. Solomon, Mohel, Musician—Leland Moss; Reb Nata, Shamus, Zelig—Reuben Schafer; Nehemiah, Rabbi, Sheftel—Albert M. Ottenheimer; Mordecai, Feitl—Hy Anzell; Shmuel, Zisheh, Musician—Stephen De Pietri; Moishe, Gershon, Chaim, Musician—

David Eric; Dovid, Yitzhok, Musician—Michael James Stratford; Treitl, Reb Alter—Herman O. Arbeit; Avigdor—John V. Shea; Raizeleh, Avram—Robin Bartlett; Finkl, Berel—Diane Tarlton; Zelda-Leah, Shimmel—Madeline Shaw; Hadass—Lynn Ann Leveridge; Frumka—Natalie Priest; Pesheh—Blanche Dee; Yachna—Rita Karin; Zlateh—Elaine Grollman.

Principal understudies: Miss Feldshuh—Robin Bartlett; Mr. Shea—Michael James Stratford; Misses Leveridge, Ashely, Bartlett—Diane Tarlton; Misses Karin, Dee, Priest—Mary Ellen Ashley; Messrs. Passletiner, Anzell—Herman O. Arbeit; Mr. Moss—Stephen De Pietri; Mr. Schafer—Leland Moss; Messrs. Ottenheimer, Arbeit—Bernie Passeltiner; Miss Grollman—Madeline Shaw; Messrs. Stratford, De Pietri, Eric—Richard Manheim.

Conceived and directed by Robert Kalfin; scenery, Karl Eigsti; costumes, Carrie F. Robbins; lighting, William Mintzer; music, Mel Marvin; associate producer, Paul B. Berkowsky; production stage manager, Clint Jakeman; stage manager, Richard Manheim; press, Betty Lee Hunt, Maurice Turet, Maria Cristina Pucci.

Time: 1873. Place: The villages of Yanev, Zamosc, Bechev and Lublin, Poland. The play was presented in two parts.

Dramatization of Singer's story *Yentl the Yeshiva Boy* about a young Jewish girl disguising herself as a boy in order to pursue learning and maintaining the masquerade in marriage. This production of *Yentl* was presented off Broadway last season by The Chelsea Theater of Brooklyn for 48 performances.

Arn Weiner replaced Herman O. Arbeit 3/76. Jonathan Greenman replaced David Eric 4/76.

Summer Brave (16). Revised version of *Picnic* by William Inge. Produced by Barry M. Brown, Burry Fredrik, Fritz Holt and Sally Sears in association with Robert V. Straus in the American Bicentennial Theater production at the ANTA Theater. Opened October 26, 1975. (Closed November 9, 1975)

Millie Owens	Sheila K. Adams	Hal Carter	Ernest Thompson
Newsboy	Bill Barrett	Rosemary Sydney	Alexis Smith
Bomber	Mark Kologi	Mrs. Helen Potts	Martha Greenhouse
Beano	Miles Chapin	Irma Kronkite	Patricia O'Connell
Madge Owens	Jill Eikenberry	Christine Schoenwalder	Alice Drummond
Alan Seymour	Peter Weller	Howard Bevans	Joe Ponazecki
Flo Owens	Nan Martin		

Standbys: Miss Smith—Patricia O'Connell; Misses Greenhouse, Martin, O'Connell—Alice Drummond; Mr. Ponazecki—F.J. O'Neil; Misses Eikenberry, Adams, Drummond—Stephanie Kurz; Messrs. Weller, Thompson—Richard DeFabees; Messrs. Kologi, Chapin—Bill Barrett; Mr. Barrett—Jason La Padura.

Directed by Michael Montel; scenery, Stuart Wurtzel; costumes, Donald Brooks; lighting, David Segal; dance staged by Michel Stuart; produced for Kennedy Center and Xerox Corporation by Roger L. Stevens and Richmond Crinkley; production stage manager, Dyanne Hochman; stage manager, Jason LaPadura; press, Shirley Herz.

Time: The early 1950s. Place: A small Kansas town. Act I: Labor Day morning. Act II: Late that day. Act III: Early the next morning.

Inge's play *Picnic* about the impact of a handsome male visitor on small-town characters was first produced 2/19/53 for 477 performances, when it was named a Best Play and won the Critics Award and Pulitzer Prize. The rewrite under the new title *Summer Brave* was previously produced off off Broadway by Equity Library Theater 4/5/73. The present production was previously staged in Washington, D.C.

Travesties (155). By Tom Stoppard. Produced by David Merrick, Doris Cole Abrahams, Burry Fredrik in association with S. Spencer Davids and Eddie Kulukundis in the Royal Shakespeare Company production at the Ethel Barrymore Theater. Opened October 30, 1975. (Closed March 13, 1976)

Tristan Tzara	Tim Currry	Nadezhda Krupskaya	Frances Cuka
Cecily Carruthers	Beth Morris	Vladimir Ilyich Ulyanov (Lenin)	Harry Towb
James Joyce	James Booth	Henry Carr	John Wood
Gwendolen Carr	Meg Wynn Owen	Bennett	John Bott

Standby: Mr. Wood—David Dukes. Understudies: Misses Owen, Morris—Kate McGregor-Stewart; Mr. Booth—John Bott/Edward Earle; Messrs. Towb, Bott—John Clarkson; Miss Cuka—Leila Martin.

Directed by Peter Wood; scenery and costumes, Carl Toms; lighting, Robert Ornbo; movement, William Chappell; musical supervision, Grant Hossack; slide drawings, Robert P. Vannutt; production stage manager, Alan Hall; stage manager, Susie Cordon; press, Solters & Roskin, Inc., Bud Westman.

Time: 1917. Place: Zurich, in two locations: a section of the public library and the drawing room of Henry Carr's apartment. The play was presented in two parts.

Fanciful, egocentric reminiscences of a semi-senile minor British official who served in Zurich while Joyce and Lenin were there. A foreign play previously produced in London.

David Dukes replaced John Wood 3/1/76.

A Best Play; see page 149

Kennedy's Children (72). By Robert Patrick. Produced by Michael Harvey in association with Robert Colby at the John Golden Theater. Opened November 3, 1975. (Closed January 4, 1976)

Wanda	Barbara Montgomery	Mark	Michael Sacks
Bartender	Douglas Travis	Rona	Kaiulani Lee
Sparger	Don Parker	Carla	Shirley Knight

Understudies: Misses Montgomery, Lee, Knight—Giulia Pagano; Messrs. Sacks, Parker—Douglas Travis; Mr. Travis—Robert T. O'Rourke.

Directed by Clive Donner; design, Santo Loquasto; lighting, Martin Aronstein; associate producer, Ramon Getzov; production stage manager, Mark Wright; press, David Powers, William Schelble.

Time: a rainy February afternoon in 1974. Place: A bar on the lower East Side of New York. The play was presented in two parts.

Interlocking monologues by leftover 1960s characters (a flower child, a sex goddess, a Vietnam soldier, etc.) who have grown out of their era and their emotional orientations. Previously presented off off Broadway in 1973 and in London in 1974.

Hello, Dolly! (51). Revival of the musical based on *The Matchmaker* by Thornton Wilder; book by Michael Stewart; music and lyrics by Jerry Herman. Produced by Robert Cherin in association with Theater Now, Inc. at the Minskoff Theater. Opened November 6, 1975. (Closed December 21, 1975)

Mrs. Dolly Gallagher Levi	Pearl Bailey	Barnaby Tucker	Grenoldo Frazier
Ernestina	Bessye Ruth Scott	Irene Molloy	Mary Louise
Ambrose Kemper	Howard Porter	Minnie Fay	Chip Fields
Horse	Kathy Jennings, Karen Hubbard	Mrs. Rose	Birdie M. Hale
Horace Vandergelder	Billy Daniels	Rudolph	Jonathan Wynne
Ermengarde	Karen Hubbard	Judge	Ted Goodridge
Cornelius Hackl	Terrence Emanuel	Court Clerk	Ray Gilbert

Townspeople, Waiters, etc.: Sally Benoit, Terry Gene, Pat Gideon, Ann Givin, Birdie M. Hale, Karen Hubbard, Gwen Humble, Eulaulá Jennings, Francie Mendenhall, Bessye Ruth Scott, Sachi Shimizu, Guy Allen, Don Coleman, Richard Dodd, Ray Gilbert, Charles Goeddertz, Ted Goodridge, Clark James, James Kennon-Wilson, Richard Maxon, Charles Neal, Howard Porter, Jimmy Rivers, Ken Rogers, David Staller, Teddy Williams, Jonathan Wynne.

Understudies: Miss Bailey—Birdie M. Hale; Mr. Daniels—Ted Goodridge; Miss Louise—Pat Gideon; Mr. Emanuel—Jonathan Wynne; Miss Fields—Gwen Humble; Mr. Frazier—Teddy Williams; Miss Hubbard—Eulaulá Jennings; Misses Scott, Hale—Lisa Brown; Messrs. Wynne, Judge—Guy Allen; Mr. Porter—Ken Rogers; Mr. Gilbert—Don Coleman; Dance Alternates—Ron Crofoot, Lisa Brown.

Directed by Lucia Victor; original production directed and choreographed by Gower Champion; musical direction, Al Cavaliere; scenery, Oliver Smith; costume supervision, Robert Pusilo; lighting, John Gleason; dances recreated by Jack Craig; production stage manager, Kenneth Porter; stage manager, Robert Vandergriff; press, Betty Hunt Associates, Maria Cristina Pucci, William Evans, Maurice Turet.

Time: The 1880s. Place: Yonkers and New York City.

Hello, Dolly! was first produced 1/16/64 for 2,844 performances, the fourth longest run in Broadway history, and was named a Best Play of its season and won the Critics Award. This is its first New York revival.

In the following synopsis of scenes and musical numbers, The Polka Contest in Act II in this revival (see below) replaces the number "Come and Be My Butterfly" in the original production, whose song numbers are listed on page 320 of *The Best Plays of 1963-64*.

ACT I

Scene 1: Along Fourth Avenue, New York City
Scene 2: Grand Central Station
"I Put My Hand In" ....Dolly, Company
Scene 3: A street in Yonkers
Scene 4: Vandergelder's Hay and Feed Store, Yonkers
"It Takes a Woman" ....Vandergelder, Glee Club
"Put on Your Sunday Clothes" ....Cornelius, Barnaby, Dolly, Ambrose, Ermengarde
Scene 5: Grand Central Station
"Put on Your Sunday Clothes" (Reprise) ....Passengers
Scene 6: Outside Mrs. Molloy's Hat Shop, Water Street, New York City
Scene 7: Inside the Hat Shop
"Ribbons Down My Back" ....Mrs. Molloy
"Motherhood" ....Dolly, Vandergelder, Mrs. Molloy, Minnie Fay, Cornelius, Barnaby
"Dancing"..................Dolly, Cornelius, Barnaby, Minnie Fay, Mrs. Molloy, Dancers
Scene 8: A quiet street
Scene 9: 14th Street
"Before the Parade Passes By" ....Dolly, Vandergelder, Company

ACT II

Scene 1: In front of the Hoffman House Hotel on Fifth Avenue
"Elegance" ....Mrs. Molloy, Cornelius, Minnie Fay, Barnaby
Scene 2: Outside the Harmonia Gardens Restaurant, on the Battery
Scene 3. Inside the Harmonia Gardens Restaurant
"The Waiter's Gallop" ....Rudolph, Waiters
"Hello, Dolly!" ....Dolly, Rudolph, Waiters, Cooks.
Scene 4: The Polka Contest ....Ambrose, Ermengarde, Mrs. Molloy, Cornelius,
Minnie Fay, Barnaby, Contestants
Scene 5: A courtroom on Centre Street
"It Only Takes a Moment" ....Cornelius, Mrs. Molloy, Prisoners, Policeman
"So Long Dearie" ....Dolly, Vandergelder
Scene 6: The Hay and Feed Store, Yonkers
"Hello, Dolly!" (Reprise) ....Dolly, Vandergelder
Finale ....Company

A Musical Jubilee (92). Musical devised by Marilyn Clark and Charles Burr; continuity by Max Wilk. Produced by the Theater Guild and Jonathan Conrow at the St. James Theater. Opened November 13, 1975. (Closed February 1, 1976)

Lillian Gish   John Raitt
Tammy Grimes   Cyril Ritchard
Larry Kert   Dick Shawn
Patrice Munsel

Ensemble: Steven Boockvor, Eric Brotherson, Marcia Brushingham, Igors Gavon, Nana, David King, Jeanne Lehman, Bettye Malone, Estella Munson, Julie Pars, Dennis Perren, Leland Schwantes, Craig Yates.

Understudies: Mr. Raitt—Igros Gavon; Miss Munsel—Estella Munson; Miss Grimes—Jeanne Lehman; Mr. Shawn—David King; Mr. Ritchard—Eric Brotherson; Mr. Kert—Craig Yates; Miss Gish—Marcia Brushingham.

Directed by Morton Da Costa; musical supervision, Lehman Engel; musical direction, John Lesko; choreography, Robert Tucker; scenery, Herbert Senn; costumes, Donald Brooks; lighting, Thomas Skelton; dance arrangements and musical continuity, Trude Rittman; orchestrations, Philip J. Lang, Hershy Kay, Elman Anderson; associate producer, Merle D. King; production stage manager, William Dodds; stage manager, Marnel Sumner; press, Joe Wolhandler associates, Sol Jacobson.

The evolution of the Broadway musical expressed in show tunes, folk songs and other musical numbers by various composers and lyricists, selected from the decades of development. The play was presented in two parts.

ACT I

Opening: "Happy Days" (music by Johann Strauss, lyrics by Howard Dietz)—Company.
American Frontier: "Whoa-Haw"—Larry Kert; "Lorena" (music, J.P. Webster, lyrics, Rev. H.D.L. Webster)—John Raitt; "Sweet Betsy From Pike"—Tammy Grimes; "Skip to My Lou" —Patrice Munsel, Kert; "Whoa-Haw" (Reprise)—Company.
American Military: "Hold on Abraham" (by William B. Bradbury)—Ensemble; "Bonnie Blue Flag" (music by Valentine Vousden, lyrics by Harry Macarthy)—Kert, Steven Bookvor, Igors Gavon, David King, Dennis Perren, Leland Schwantes, Craig Yates; "Tipperary" (by Jack Judge and Harry Williams)—Miss Grimes, Male Ensemble; "I Didn't Raise My Boy To Be a Soldier" (music by Al Piantadosi, lyrics by Alfred Bryan)—Lillian Gish; "Mademoisell From Armentiers" (by Howard Ross)—Cyril Ritchard, Dick Shawn; "Battle Hymn of the Republic" (lyrics by Julia Ward Howe)—Raitt, Company.
Old Vienna: "Wien, Wien, You're Calling Me" (music by Sieczynski), "I'm in Love With Vienna" (music by Johann Strauss)—Miss Munsel, Raitt, Ensemble; "Der Shimmy" (music, Emmerich Kalman)—Miss Grimes; "I've Got Something" (music by Franz Lehar, lyrics by Harry B. and Robert B. Smith)—Richard, Marcia Brushingham, Nana, Jeanne Lehman, Bettye Malone, Julie Pars, Estella Munson. "Oh, the Women" (music by Franz Lehar)—Kurt, Gavon, Perren; "Gypsy Love" (music by Franz Lehar) Miss Munsel, Ensemble.
Britain: "And Her Mother Came Too" (music by Ivor Novello, lyrics by Dion Titheradge) —Ritchard.
Early Broadway: "Song of the Vagabonds" (music by Rudolf Friml, lyrics by Brian Hooker and W.H. Post)—Raitt, Male Ensemble; "Totem Tom-Tom" (music by Rudolf Friml, lyrics by Otto Harbach and Oscar Hammerstein II)—Miss Grimes, Female Ensemble; "Serenade" (music by Sigmund Romberg, lyrics by Dorothy Donnelly)—Kert; Violetta (sketch)—Ritchard, Kert, Brotherson, Miss Grimes; "Moonstruck" (music by Ivan Caryll and Lionel Monckton, lyrics by James T. Tanner)—Miss Gish, Male Ensemble; "You Are Love" (music by Jerome Kern, lyrics by Oscar Hammerstein II)—Miss Munsel, Raitt; "I've Told Ev'ry Little Star" (music by Jerome Kern, lyrics by Oscar Hammerstein II)—Shawn, Female Ensemble; "Why Was I Born?" (music by Jerome Kern, lyrics by Oscar Hammerstein II)—Miss Munsel; "The Best Things in Life Are Free" (music by Ray Henderson, lyrics by Lew Brown and B.G. DeSylva)—Kert, Ensemble; "They Didn't Believe Me" (music by Jerome Kern, lyrics by Herbert Reynolds)—Miss Grimes; "The Song Is You" (music by Jerome Kern, lyrics by Oscar Hammerstein II)—Raitt; "Something Seems Tingle Ingleing" (music by Rudolf Friml, lyrics by Leo Dietrichstein and Otto Harbach)—Ritchard, Female Ensemble; "Yankee Doodle Tune" (by George M. Cohan)—Shawn, Company.

ACT II

The Smart Set: "We're Blasé" (music by Ord Hamilton, lyrics by Bruce Sievier)—Raitt, Ritchard, Shawn, Misses Munsel, Grimes; "Poor Little Rich Girl" (music and lyrics by Noel Coward)—Miss Grimes; "You Go to My Head" (music by J. Fred Coots, lyrics by Haven Gillespie)—Raitt; "Find Me a Primitive Man" (music and lyrics by Cole Porter)—Misses Munsel, Grimes; "I Guess I'll Have to Change My Plan" (music by Arthur Schwartz, lyrics by Howard Dietz)—Shawn; "Sophisticated Lady" (music by Duke Ellington, lyrics by Mitchell Parish and Irving Mills)—Kert; "Love Me or Leave Me" (music by Walter Donaldson, lyrics by Gus Kahn)—Miss Munsel; "Gilbert the Filbert" (music by Herman Finck, lyrics by Arthur Wimperis)—Ritchard; "We're Blasé" (Reprise)—Raitt, Ritchard, Shawn, Kert, Misses Munsel, Grimes.
Vaudeville: "At the Moving Picture Ball" (music by Joseph Santly, lyrics by Howard Johnson)—Ensemble; "Miss Annabelle Lee" (music by Lew Pollack, lyrics by Sidney Clare and Harry Richman)—Shawn; "I Wanna Be Loved by You" (music by Harry Ruby, lyrics by Bert Kalmar)—Misses Munsel, Grimes, Gish; The Green Eye of the Little Yellow God (sketch by Reginald Purdell, based on the poem by Milton Hayes)—Ritchard, Shawn, Brotherson.
Jazz: "How Jazz Was Born" (music by Fats Waller, lyrics by Andy Razaf and Henry Creamer)—Kert, Ensemble; "Ain't Misbehavin' " (music by Fats Waller, lyrics by Andy Razaf) —Kert; "I'm Just Wild About Harry" (music by Eubie Blake, lyrics by Noble Sissle)—Miss Grimes; "Me and My Shadow" (music by Al Jolson and Dave Dreyer, lyrics by Billy Rose)— Shawn; "Sometimes I'm Happy" (music by Vincent Youmans, lyrics by Irving Caesar)—Miss Munsel; "Great Day" (music by Vincent Youmans, lyrics by Billy Rose and Edward Eliscu) —Raitt; "How Jazz Was Born" (Reprise)—Raitt, Shawn, Kert, Misses Munsel, Grimes, Ensemble.
Late Broadway: "Lullaby of Broadway" (music by Harry Warren, lyrics by Al Dubin)—

Ensemble; "Lucky Day" (music by Ray Henderson, lyrics by B.G. DeSylva and Lew Brown)—Shawn; "If You Knew Susie" (by B.G. DeSylva and Joseph Meyer)—Ritchard; " 'S Wonderful" (music by George Gershwin, lyrics by Ira Gershwin)—Miss Gish; "Fascinating Rhythm" (music by George Gershwin, lyrics by Ira Gershwin)—Kert; "Liza" (music by George Gershwin, lyrics by Ira Gershwin and Gus Kahn)—Miss Grimes; "Where or When" (music by Richard Rodgers, lyrics by Lorenz Hart)—Miss Munsel; "Hallelujah" (music by Vincent Youmans, lyrics by Clifford Grey and Leo Robin)—Raitt, Company.

Boccaccio (7). Musical based on stories from *The Decameron* by Giovanni Boccaccio; book and lyrics by Kenneth Cavander; music by Richard Peaslee. Produced by Rita Fredricks, Theater Now, Inc. and Norman Kean at the Edison Theater. Opened November 24, 1975. (Closed December 30, 1975)

Beltramo (Egano) ....Michael Zaslow	Isabella (Sister Angelica) ..D'Jamin Bartlett
Giletta (Abbess) ....Virginia Vestoff	Alibech (Sister Makaria) ....Jill Choder
Masetto (Ferondo) ......Armand Assante	Rustico (Leonetto, Brother
Beatrice (Sister Teresa,	Perdurabo) ....Munson Hicks
Ferondo's Wife) ....Caroline McWilliams	Anichino (Nuto, Abbot) ....Richard Bauer

(Parentheses indicate roles the characters play while acting out the stories)

Standbys: Female Roles—Sheilah Rae; Male Roles—Michael Forella.
Directed by Warren Enters; musical staging, Julie Arenal; scenery, Robert U. Taylor; costumes, Linda Fisher; lighting, Patrika Brown; orchestrations and arrangements, Walt Levinsky, Richard Peaslee; production stage manager, Ron Abbott; stage manager, John Beven; press, Les Schecter Associates.
Time: 1348. Place: A villa outside Florence.
Refugees from the plague flee the city and pass the time in the country telling stories, usually of a ribald nature. Previously produced at Arena Stage, Washington, D.C.

ACT I

Introduction ....Company

The Stories

Masetto
"Masetto's Song" ....Masetto, Nuto
"Nuns's Song" ....Abbess, Nuns
"God Is Good" ....Masetto, Nuns
"Now My Season's Here" ....Company
Anichino
"Only in My Song" ....Anichino
"Egano D'Galluzzi" ....Anichino, Egano
"The Men Who Have Loved Me" ....Beatrice
"In the Garden" ....Anichino, Egano
"Lucky Anichino" ....Company
Pretend You're Living ....Isabella
Devil in Hell ....Alibech, Rustico, Company

ACT II

The Stories (continued)

The She Doctor
"She Doctor" ....Giletta, Beltramo
"Lover Like a Blind Man" ....Giletta
"If You Had Seen" ....Giletta
"Love Was Just a Game" ....Beltramo
Madonna Isabella ....Isabella, Company
Ferondo
"My Holy Prayer" ....Abbot, Monks
"Hold Me Gently" ....Ferondo's Wife
Finale ....Company

Habeas Corpus (95). By Alan Bennett. Produced by James M. Nederlander, Victor Lurie and Michael Codron at the Martin Beck Theater. Opened November 25, 1975. (Closed February 15, 1976)

Arthur Wicksteed ....Donald Sinden	Sir Percy Shorter ....Ian Trigger
Mrs. Swabb ....June Havoc	Lady Rumpers ....Celeste Holm
Mrs. Wicksteed ....Rachel Roberts	Felicity Rumpers ....Constance Forslund
Dennis ....Kristoffer Tabori	Mr. Shanks ....Richard Gere
Constance Wicksteed ....Jean Marsh	Mr. Purdue ....Stephen D. Newman
Canon Throbbing ....Paxton Whitehead	Patient ....Leo Leyden

The Hove Palm Court Trio: Dorothea Freitag piano, Judith Martin cello, Roberta Hankin violin.

Standby: Mr. Trigger—Leo Leyden. Understudies: Messrs. Sinden, Whitehead—Stephen D. Newman; Misses Roberts, Havoc, Holm—Joyce Worsley; Misses Marsh, Forslund—Holly Villaire; Messrs. Tabori, Gere, Newman—Tom Everett.

Directed by Frank Dunlop; scenery and costumes, Carl Toms; lighting, Jennifer Tipton; musical arrangements, Dorothea Freitag; dances, Riggs O'Hara; production stage manager, Frank Bayer; stage manager, Louis Pulvino; press, Michael Alpert, Marilynn LeVine.

Time: The present. Place: A refined English seaside resort, in the Wicksteeds' home, and occasionally at the end of the West Pier. The play was presented in two parts.

Farcical treatment of a restless resort doctor and his equally restless family, friends and patients. A foreign play previously produced in London.

Paxton Whitehead replaced Donald Sinden, Mark Baker replaced Kristoffer Tabori, Stephen D. Newman replaced Paxton Whitehead, Tom Everett replaced Stephen D. Newman, Joyce Worsley replaced Leo Leyden 1/26/76. Kristoffer Tabori replaced Stephen D. Newman 1/29/76.

* **The Norman Conquests.** Repertory of three plays by Alan Ayckbourn: * **Table Manners** (69), * **Living Together** (68) and * **Round and Round the Garden** (68). Produced by Robert Fryer, James Cresson and Michael Codron in association with Martin Richards and Victor D'Arc at the Morosco Theater. All three plays opened December 7, 1975.

ALL PLAYS

Norman ....Richard Benjamin	Sarah ....Estelle Parsons
Annie ....Paula Prentiss	Reg ....Barry Nelson
Tom ....Ken Howard	Ruth ....Carole Shelley

Standbys: Mr. Benjamin—Donegan Smith; Miss Prentiss—Donna Wandrey; Mr. Howard—Richard Altman; Miss Parsons—Laura Stuart; Mr. Nelson—Richard Seff; Miss Shelley—Elaine Hyman.

Directed by Eric Thompson; scenery and lighting, Robert Randolph; costumes, Noel Taylor; stage manager, Milt Commons; press, Betty Lee Hunt, Maria Cristina Pucci, William Evans.

Time: A weekend in July. Place: An English country house.

TABLE MANNERS—The dining room. Act I, Scene 1: Saturday, 6 p.m. Scene 2: Sunday, 9 a.m. Act II, Scene 1: Sunday, 8 p.m. Scene 2: Monday, 8 p.m.

LIVING TOGETHER—The living room. Act I, Scene 1: Saturday, 6:30 p.m. Scene 2: Saturday, 8 p.m. Act II, Scene 1: Sunday, 9 p.m. Scene 2: Monday, 8 a.m.

ROUND AND ROUND THE GARDEN—The garden. Act I, Scene 1: Saturday, 5:30 p.m. Scene 2: Saturday, 9 p.m. Act II, Scene 1: Sunday, 11 a.m. Scene 2: Monday, 9 a.m.

Three full-length comedies interlocking in time and taking place in different areas of the same house during the same weekend with the same set of characters, one of whom, Norman, manages to seduce all three of the women. A foreign play previously produced in London and Los Angeles.

Don Murray replaced Ken Howard 2/10/76. Elaine Hyman replaced Carole Shelley 5/19/76. A Best Play; see page 168

* **Very Good Eddie** (193). Revival of the musical based on a farce by Philip Bartholomae; book by Guy Bolton; revised by Guy Bolton; music by Jerome Kern; lyrics by Schuyler Greene, Elsie Janis, P.G. Wodehouse, Anne Caldwell, Frank

Craven, Harry Graham, Harry B. Smith, John E. Hazzard and Herbert Reynolds.
Produced by David Merrick, Max Brown and Byron Goldman in the Goodspeed
Opera House production at the Booth Theater. Opened December 21, 1975.

Steward; Al Cleveland .... James Harder
Mr. Dick Rivers .... David Christmas
Mme. Matroppo .... Travis Hudson
Miss Elsie Lilly .... Cynthia Wells
M. de Rougemont .... Joel Craig
Mrs. Georgina Kettle ...... Spring Fairbank
Mr. Eddie Kettle .... Charles Repole
Mr. Percy Darling .... Nicholas Wyman
Mrs. Elsie Darling .... Virginia Seidel

Miss Lily Pond .... Wendy Young
Miss Chrystal Poole .... Karen Crossley
Miss Carrie Closewell .... Gillian Scalici
Miss Alwys Innit .... Robin Herbert
Mr. Tayleurs Dumme .... Russ Beasley
Mr. Dayr Thurst .... John Engstrom
Mr. Dustin Stacks .... Larry McMillian
Mr. Rollo Munn .... Hal Shane

Directed by Bill Gile; dances and musical numbers staged by Dan Siretta; musical direction
and arrangements, Russell Warner; scenery and lighting, Fred Voelpel; costumes, David Toser;
produced for the Goodspeed Opera House by Michael P. Price; special consultant, Alfred
Simon; production stage manager, Don Judge; stage managers, Mark Potter, Pat Trott; press,
Max Eisen, Warren Pincus, Judy Jacksina.

Time: June 1913. Act I: A Hudson River Dayliner. Act II, Scene 1: Lobby of Honeymoon
Inn in the Catskills, that evening. Scene 2: The same, the next morning.

Ill-assorted young couples are shuffled and re-paired happily after many adventures afloat
and ashore. This musical was first produced at the Princess Theater 12/23/15 for 341 performances. This revival was previously presented in July and October of this year at the Goodspeed Opera House, East Haddam, Conn.

ACT I

(Lyrics are by Schuyler Greene unless otherwise noted)
"We're on Our Way" .... Company
"Some Sort of Somebody" .... Elsie Lilly, Dick
(Lyrics by Elsie Janis)
"Thirteen Collar" .... Eddie
"Bungalow in Quogue" .... Elsie Darling, Percy
(Lyrics by P.G. Wodehouse)
"Isn't It Great To Be Married" .... Elsie Darling, Georgina, Eddie, Percy
"Good Night Boat" .... Company
(Lyrics by Anne Caldwell and Frank Craven)
"Left All Alone Again Blues" .... Elsie Darling
(Lyrics by Anne Caldwell)
"Hot Dog!" .... Company
(Lyrics by Anne Caldwell)
"If You're a Friend of Mine" .... Elsie Darling, Eddie
(Lyrics by Harry Graham)
"Wedding Bells Are Calling Me" .... Company
(Lyrics by Harry B. Smith)

ACT II

"Honeymoon Inn" .... Elsie Lilly, Company
(Lyrics by P.G. Wodehouse)
"I've Got to Dance" .... de Rougemont, Company
"Moon of Love" .... Mme. Matroppo, Company
(Lyrics by Anne Caldwell)
"Old Boy Neutral" .... Elsie Lilly, Dick
"Babes in the Wood" .... Elsie Darling, Eddie
"Katy-did" .... Mme. Matroppo
(Lyrics by Harry B. Smith)
"Nodding Roses" .... Elsie Lilly, Dick
(Lyrics by Schuyler Greene and Herbert Reynolds)
"Finale" .... Company
(Lyrics by John E. Hazzard and Herbert Reynolds)

Angel Street (52). Revival of the play by Patrick Hamilton. Produced by Shepard Traube at the Lyceum Theater. Opened December 26, 1975. (Closed February 8, 1976)

Mrs. Manningham	Dina Merrill	Elizabeth	Bette Henritze
Mr. Manningham	Michael Allinson	Rough	Robert E. Thompson
Nancy	Christine Andreas		

Understudies: Misses Merrill, Andreas, Henritze—Eleanor Tauber; Mr. Allinson—Alfred Karl.

Directed by Shepard Traube; scenery, Douglas W. Schmidt; costumes, Patricia Adshead; lighting, Leon Di Leone; lighting supervision, Douglas W. Schmidt; production stage manager, Audrey Koran; stage manager, Rick Ralston; press, Lenny Traube.

Time: 1880: Place: A house on Angel Street, located in the Pimlico district in London. Act I: Late afternoon. Act II: Immediately afterwards. Act III later the same night.

Angel Street was first produced on Broadway 12/5/41 for 1,295 performances and was named a Best Play of its season. It was revived on Broadway 1/22/48 for 14 performances and off Broadway the same season.

Christine Ebersole replaced Christine Andreas 1/27/76.

Murder Among Friends (17). By Bob Barry. Produced by R. Tyler Gatchell Jr. and Peter Neufeld in association with Barnard S. Straus at the Biltmore Theater. Opened December 28, 1975. (Closed January 10, 1976)

Angela Forrester	Janet Leigh	Gertrude Saidenberg	Jane Hoffman
Ted Cotton	Lewis Arlt	Marshall Saidenberg	Richard Woods
Palmer Forrester	Jack Cassidy	Larry	Michael Durrell

Standbys: Miss Leigh—Holland Taylor; Mr. Cassidy—John Aniston; Mr. Durrell—Andrew Bloch; Mr. Arlt—Ted Shackelford.

Directed by Val May; scenery, Santo Loquasto; costumes, Joseph G. Aulisi; lighting, Jennifer Tipton; associate producers, Erv Tullman, Barry Potashnick; production supervisor, Pat Tolson; press, Betty Lee Hunt Associates, Maria Cristina Pucci, Bill Evans.

Time: The present, New Year's Eve. Place: The Palmer Forrester townhouse. Act I, Scene 1: 10 p.m. Scene 2: 11 p.m. Act II, Scene 1: 3 a.m. Scene 2: 4:30 a.m.

Cat and mouse games of blackmail and murder played by a Broadway stage star and his friends and associates, often in a vein of ironic comedy.

Sweet Bird of Youth (48). Revival of the play by Tennessee Williams. Produced by Michael Harvey and Harvey Frand in the Kennedy Center-Xerox Corporation American Bicentennial Theater production at the Harkness Theater. Opened December 29, 1975. (Closed February 7, 1976)

Chance Wayne	Christopher Walken	Miss Lucy	Cathryn Damon
Princess Kosmonopolis	Irene Worth	Stuff	Tom Stechschulte
Fly	Flloyd Ennis	The Heckler	David Gale
Maid	Bunny Kacher	Violet	Linda Martin
George Scudder	Christopher Bernau	Scotty	Lanny Flaherty
Hatcher	Richard Kuss	Edna	Susan Logan
Boss Finley	Pat Corley	Bud	Eric Loeb
Tom Junior	Matthew Cowles	Men in Bar	Richard Babcock,
Charles	Philip Lindsay		Frank Rohrbach
Aunt Nonnie	Eugenia Rawls	Trooper	George Bamford
Heavenly Finley	Lisa Richards	Baton Twirler	Alicia Enterline

Understudies: Mr. Walken—Christopher Bernau; Mr. Corley—Richard Kuss; Misses Damon, Rawls, Martin, Logan—Bunny Kacher; Misses Richards, Kacher—Susan Logan; Mr. Cowles—Tom Stechschulte; Messrs. Kuss, Lindsay, Ennis—Richard Babcock; Messrs. Gale, Flaherty, Bernau—Eric Loeb; Messrs. Stechschulte, Loeb—George Bamford; Mr. Bamford—Frank Rohrbach.

Directed by Edwin Sherin; scenery, Karl Eigsti; costumes, Laura Crow; lighting, Ken Billington; produced for Kennedy Center by Roger L. Stevens and Richmond Crinkley; produced for

Academy Festival Theater by William Gardner; production stage manager, Mark Wright; stage manager, Andrea Wilson; press, David Powers, William Schelble.

Time: Modern, an Easter Sunday, from morning till late night. Place: Somewhere on the Gulf Coast. Act I, Scene 1: A bedroom in the Royal Palms Hotel, morning. Scene 2: The same, afternoon. Act II, Scene 1: The terrace of Boss Finley's house in St. Cloud, evening. Scene 2: The Palm Garden Cocktail Lounge of the Royal Palms Hotel, night. Act III: The bedroom again.

Sweet Bird of Youth was first produced on Broadway 3/10/59 for 375 performances and was named a Best Play of its season. This is its first commercial New York revival. This production was previously presented in Lake Forest, Ill., Washington, D.C. and at the Brooklyn Academy of Music (see its entry in the "Plays Produced Off Broadway" section of this volume).

Elena Karam replaced Eugenia Rawls and Susan Logan changed her name to Susan Kay Logan during the Broadway run of this revival.

* The Royal Family (176). Revival of the play by George S. Kaufman and Edna Ferber. Produced by Barry M. Brown, Burry Fredrik, Fritz Holt and Sally Sears in the American Bicentennial Theater production at the Helen Hayes Theater. Opened December 30, 1975.

Della	Rosetta LeNoire	Fanny Cavendish	Eva Le Gallienne
Jo	John Remme	Oscar Wolfe	Sam Levene
Hallboy; Gunga	James C. Burge	Julie Cavendish	Rosemary Harrris
McDermott	Sherman Lloyd	Tony Cavendish	George Grizzard
Herbert Dean	Joseph Maher	Chauffeur; Hallboy	Miller Lide
Kitty Dean	Mary Louise Wilson	Gilbert Marshall	Donald Barton
Gwen Cavendish	Mary Layne	Hallboy	Mark Fleischman
Perry Stewart	Forrest Buckman	Miss Peake	Eleanor Phelps

Understudies: Misses Harris, LeNoire, Wilson, Phelps—Maria Cellario; Miss Le Gallienne—Eleanor Phelps; Messrs. Grizzard, Buckman—James C. Burge; Messrs. Levene, Barton, Maher—Miller Lide; Misses Layne, Phelps—Pat De Rousie; Messrs. Remme, Lloyd—Mark Fleischman.

Directed by Ellis Rabb; scenery, Oliver Smith; costumes, Ann Roth; lighting, John Gleason; original music, Claibe Richardson; produced for Kennedy Center and Xerox Corporation by Roger L. Stevens and Richmond Crinkley, in association with the McCarter Theater Company; production stage manager, Helaine Head; stage manager, Andrea Love; press, Shirley Herz.

Time: 1927. Place: The duplex apartment of the Cavendishes, in the East Fifties, New York City. Act I: A Friday in November, early afternoon. Act II: Saturday, between matinee and evening. Act III: A year later.

The Royal Family was first produced on Broadway 12/28/27 for 345 performances and was named a Best Play of its season. It was revived at the City Center 1/10/51 for 15 performances. This production was previously represented in Princeton, N.J., Washington, D.C. and the Brooklyn Academy of Music (see its entry in the "Plays Produced Off Broadway" section of this volume).

Ellis Rabb replaced George Grizzard 1/12/76. Richard Council replaced Ellis Rabb 5/76.

Home Sweet Homer (1). Musical based on Homer's *Odyssey;* book by Roland Kibbee and Albert Marre; lyrics by Charles Burr and Forman Brown; music by Mitch Leigh. Produced by The John F. Kennedy Center for the Performing Arts at the Palace Theater. Opened and closed at the evening performance, January 4, 1976.

Odysseus	Yul Brynner	Melios	Bill Nabel
Penelope	Joan Diener	Polybos	Les Freed
Telemachus	Russ Thacker	King Alkinoos	Shev Rodgers
Antinous	Martin Vidnovic	Nausikaa	Diana Davila
Pilokrates	Ian Sullivan	Therapina	Suanne Sponsler
Ktesippos	Bill Mackey	Melantho	Cecile Santos
Eurymachus	Daniel Brown	Hippodameia	Christine Uchida
Leokritos	Brian Destazio	Kerux	Darel Glaser
Pimteus	John Aristides	Dekati Evdomi	P.J. Mann

Directed by Albert Marre; musical direction, Ross Reimueller; scenery and lighting, Howard Bay; costumes, Howard Bay, Ray Diffen; orchestrations, Buryl Red; choreographic assistant, Michael Mann; press, Betty Lee Hunt, Ruth Cage.

Musical adaptation of the Homeric epic formerly entitled *Odyssey* on a ten-month cross-country tour. The play was presented without intermission.

MUSICAL NUMBERS

"The Sorceress" ....Penelope, Suitors
"The Departure" ....Odysseus, Dekati Evdomi
"Home Sweet Homer" ....Odysseus
"The Ball" ....Nausikaa, Handmaidens
"How Could I Dare to Dream" ....Odysseus, Telemachus
"I Never Imagined Goodbye" ....Penelope
"Love Is the Prize" ....Odysseus
"Penelope's Hand" ....Antinous
"He Will Come Home Again" ....Telemachus
"Did He Really Think" ....Penelope
"I Was Wrong" ....Odysseus
"The Rose" ....Penelope
"Tomorrow" ....Antinous, Suitors
"The Contest" ....Odysseus, Telemachus, Antinous, Suitors

The Poison Tree (5). By Ronald Ribman. Produced by Emanuel Azenberg, William W. Bradley, Marvin A. Krauss and Irving Siders at the Ambassador Theater. Opened January 8, 1976. (Closed January 11, 1976)

Albert Heisenman ....Danny Meehan
Walter Turner ....Daniel Barton
Officer Lowery ....Gene O'Neill
Officer DiSantis ....Peter Masterson
Sgt. Coyne ....Robert Symonds
Officer Lloyd ....Charles Brown
Officer Friezer ....Arlen Dean

Officer Rollock ....Pat McNamara
Willy Stepp ....Cleavon Little
Bobby Foster ....Dick Anthony Williams
Benjamin Hurspool ....Moses Gunn
Charles Jefferson ......Northern J. Calloway
Smiling Man ....Dennis Tate

Understudies: Messrs. Little, Gunn—Arthur French; Mr. Williams—Charles Brown; Mr. Masterson—Arlen Dean; Messrs. Symonds, Meehan—Frank Hamilton; Messrs. Dean, McNamara, O'Neill—Steven Shaw; Messrs. Calloway, Brown, Barton, Tate—Charles Douglass.

Directed by Charles Blackwell; scenery, Marjorie Kellogg; costumes, Judy Dearing; lighting, Martin Aronstein; production manager, Henry Velez; stage managers, Robert St. Clair, Steven Shaw, Gene O'Neill; press, Merle Debuskey, Leo Stern.

Time: The present. Place: A Western state prison. Act I, Scene 1: The Adjustment Center, a maximum security area. Scene 2: Sgt. Coyne's office. Scene 3: A cell. Scene 4: The guards' locker room. Scene 5: The guards' locker room. Scene 6: A cell. Act II, Scene 1: A holding cell area. Scene 2: Guards' lounge. Scene 3: A cell. Scene 4: The yard.

The modern prison as a breeding ground for inhumanity. Previously produced at Playhouse-in-the-Park in Philadelphia.

* **Pacific Overtures** (161). Musical with book by John Weidman; music and lyrics by Stephen Sondheim; additional material by Hugh Wheeler. Produced by Harold Prince in association with Ruth Mitchell at the Winter Garden. Opened January 11, 1976.

Cast: Reciter, Shogun, Jonathan Goble—Mako; Abe, 1st Councillor—Yuki Shimoda; Manjiro—Sab Shimono; 2d Councillor, Old Man, French Admiral—James Dybas; Shogun's Mother, Observer, Merchant, American Admiral—Alvin Ing; 3d Councillor, Samurai's Daughter—Freddy Mao; Kayama—Isao Sato; Tamate, Samurai, Storyteller, Swordsman—Soon-Teck Oh; Samurai, Adams, Noble—Ernest Abuba; Samurai, Thief, Soothsayer, Warrior, Russian Admiral, British Sailor—Mark Hsu Syers; Servant, Commodore Matthew Galbraith Perry—Haruki Fujimoto; Observer—Ricardo Tobia; Fisherman, Sumo Wrestler, Lord of the South—Jae Woo Lee; Son, Priest, Girl, Noble, British Sailor—Timm Fujii; Grandmother, Sumo Wrestler, Japanese Merchant—Conrad Yama; Williams, Lord of the South—Larry Hama; Shogun's Wife—Freda Foh Shen; Physician, Madam, British Admiral—Ernest Harada; Priest, Girl, Boy—Gedde

Watanabe; Shogun's Companion, Girl, Dutch Admiral, British Sailor—Patrick Kinser-Lau; Girl—Leslie Watanabe; Imperial Priest—Tom Matsusaka.

Proscenium Servants, Sailors, Townspeople: Susan Kikuchi, Diane Lam, Kim Miyori, Freda Foh Shen, Kenneth S. Eiland, Timm Fujii, Joey Ginza, Patrick Kinser-Lau, Tony Marinyo, Kevin Maung, Dingo Secretario, Mark Hsu Syers, Ricardo Tobia, Gedde Watanabe, Leslie Watanabe.

Musicians: Fusako Yoshida shamisen, Genji Ito percussion.

Understudies: Mr. Mako—Jae Woo Lee; Mr. Soon-Teck Oh—Gedde Watanabe, Freddy Mao, Ernest Abuba; Mr. Shimoda—Ernest Abuba; Mr. Shimono—Patrick Kinser-Lau; Mr. Sato— Tom Matsusaka; Mr. Dybas—Ricardo Tobia; Mr. Mao—Tony Marinyo.

Directed by Harold Prince; choreography, Patricia Birch; musical direction, Paul Gemignani; scenery, Boris Aronson; costumes, Florence Klotz; lighting, Tharon Musser; orchestrations, Jonathan Tunick; dance music, Daniel Troob; Kabuki consultant, Haruki Fujimoto; makeup and wigs, Richard Allen; masks and dolls, E.J. Taylor; production stage manager, George Martin; stage manager, John Grigas; press, Mary Bryant, Randy Kaplan.

Time: Act I—July, 1853. Act II—From then on. Place: Japan.

Highly Japanese-stylized musical version of the impact on Japan of Commodore Perry's arrival there with four ships in 1853, following 250 years of Japan's total isolation.

A Best Play; see page 121

ACT I

"The Advantages of Floating in the Middle of the Sea" .... Reciter, Company
"There Is No Other Way" .... Tamate, Observers
"Four Black Dragons" .... Fisherman, Thief, Reciter, Townspeople
"Chrysanthemum Tea" ...... Shogun (Reciter), Shogun's Mother, Soothsayer, Shogun's Wife, Priests, Shogun's Companion, Physician, Sumo Wrestlers
"Poems" .... Kayama, Manjiro
"Welcome to Kanagawa" .... Madam, Girls
"Someone in a Tree" .... Old Man, Reciter, Boy, Warrior
Lion Dance .... Commodore Perry

ACT II

"Please Hello" .... Abe, Reciter; American, British, Dutch, Russian and French Admirals
"A Bowler Hat" .... Kayama, Manjiro
"Pretty Lady" .... British Sailors
"Next" .... Reciter, Company

The Phoenix Theater. Two repertory schedules of four revival programs. **27 Wagons Full of Cotton** by Tennessee Williams and **A Memory of Two Mondays** by Arthur Miller (33). Program of two one-act plays. Opened January 26, 1976. **They Knew What They Wanted** (30). By Sidney Howard. Opened January 27, 1976. (First repertory schedule closed March 21, 1976) **Secret Service** (13). By William Gillette. Opened April 12, 1976. **Boy Meets Girl** (10). By Bella and Sam Spewack. Opened April 13, 1976. (Second repertory schedule closed May 2, 1976). Produced by The Phoenix Theater, T. Edward Hambleton managing director, Marilyn S. Miller executive director, Daniel Freudenberger producing director, at the Playhouse.

PERFORMER	"27 WAGONS FULL OF COTTON"	"A MEMORY OF TWO MONDAYS"	"THEY KNEW WHAT THE WANTED"
Barry Bostwick			Joe
Leonardo Cimino		Jim	Father McKee
Joel Colodner		Jerry	Giorgio
Alice Drummond		Agnes	
Pierre Epstein		Raymond	
Clarence Felder		Mechanic	Angelo
Joe Grifasi		Frank	
Thomas Hulce		Bert	
Calvin Jung		William	Ah Gee

PERFORMER	"27 WAGONS FULL OF COTTON	"A MEMORY OF TWO MONDAYS"	"THEY KNEW WHAT THE WANTED"
Ben Kapen		Mr. Eagle	The RFD
John Lithgow		Kenneth	
Tony Musante	Silva Vicarro	Larry	
Lois Nettleton			Amy
Roy Poole	Jake Meighan	Gus	
Rex Robbins		Tom	Doctor
Meryl Streep	Flora Meighan	Patricia	
Louis Zorich			Tony

PERFORMER	"SECRET SERVICE"	"BOY MEETS GIRL"
Lenny Baker	Henry Dumont	Robert Law
Gwendolyn Brown		Studio Nurse
Frederick Coffin	Lt. Maxwell	Larry Toms
Alice Drummond	Mrs. Varney	Miss Crews
Joe Grifasi	Cpl. Matson	Green; Announcer
David Harris	Jonas	Studio Officer
Marybeth Hurt	Caroline Mitford	Susie
Jeffrey Jones	Sgt. Wilson	Maj. Thompson
Charles Kimbrough	Benton Arrelsford	J. Carlyle Benson
John Lithgow	Capt. Thorne	
Ann McDonough		Peggy
Arthur Miller		Cutter
Moultrie Patten	Orderly	Slade
Jonathan Penzner	Lt. Allison	
Roy Poole	Maj. Gen. Randolph	Mr. Friday
Rex Robbins	Lt. Foray	Rosetti
Hansford Rowe	Messenger	
Don Scardino	Wilfred Varney	Rodney Bevan
Meryl Streep	Edith Varney	
Louise Stubbs	Martha	Nurse
Stuart Warmflash	Pvt. Eddinger	Young Man

ALL PLAYS—Scenery and lighting, James Tilton; production manager, Robert Beard; stage managers, Jonathan Penzner, Peter DeNicola; press, Gifford/Wallace, Inc.

27 WAGONS FULL OF COTTON—Directed by Arvin Brown; costumes, Albert Wolsky.
Understudies: Mr. Poole—Rex Robbins; Miss Streep—Fiddle Viracola; Mr. Musante—Joel Colodner.
Place: The front porch of the Meighans' cottage near Blue Mountain, Mississippi. This one-act play was first produced on Broadway 4/19/55 for 47 performances on a bill with *Trouble in Tahiti* and Paul Draper. This is its first professional New York revival.

A MEMORY OF TWO MONDAYS—Directed by Arvin Brown; costumes, Albert Wolsky.
Understudies: Messrs. Hulce, Lithgow—Joel Colodner; Messrs. Poole, Cimeno—Ben Kapen; Messrs. Epstein, Musante—Clarence Felder; Miss Streep—Linda Carlson; Miss Drummond—Fiddle Viracola; Mr. Robbins—Joe Grifasi.
Time: A hot Monday morning in summer just before 9 in a bygone year; and a morning in winter. Place: The shipping room of a large auto parts warehouse in Manhattan. This one-act play was first produced on Broadway 9/29/55 for 149 performances on a bill with *A View From the Bridge*. This is its first professional New York revival.

THEY KNEW WHAT THEY WANTED—Directed by Stephen Porter; costumes, Albert Wolsky.
Understudies: Mr. Zorich—Clarence Felder; Miss Nettleton—Linda Carlson; Mr. Bostwick—Joel Colodner; Messrs. Cimino, Robbins—Pierre Epstein.
Place: Tony's farmhouse in the Napa Valley, California. Act I: Morning in early summer. Act II: Evening of the same day. Act III: Three months later. *They Knew What They Wanted* was first produced on Broadway 11/24/24 for 414 performances and was named a Best Play of its season and won the Pulitzer Prize. It was revived on Broadway 10/2/39 for 24 performances and 2/16/49 for 61 performances; and in its musical adaptation *The Most Happy Fella* 5/3/56 for 676 performances, winning the Critics Award for best musical, 2/10/59 for 16 performances and 5/11/66 for 15 performances.

SECRET SERVICE—Directed by Daniel Freudenberger; costumes, Clifford Capone; audio, David Rapkin; banjo, autoharp, harmonica and musical direction, Arthur Miller.

Understudies: Misses Drummond, Streep—Gwendolyn Brown; Mr. Scardino—Stuart Warmflash; Miss Hurt—Ann McDonough; Mr. Lithgow—Rex Robbins; Mr. Kimbrough—Frederick Coffin; Messrs. Coffin, Baker—Jeffrey Jones; Mr. Robbins—Joe Grifasi; Messrs. Poole, Penzner—Moultrie Patten.

Act I, Scene 1: Drawing room at Gen. Varney's house, Franklin St., Richmond, an evening in October 1864. 8 o'clock. Scene 2: The same, 9 o'clock. Act II, Scene 1: Telegraph office, War Department, 10 o'clock. Scene 2: Drawing room of the Varney house, 11 o'clock. *Secret Service* was first produced on Broadway 10/5/96 for 176 performances and was named a Best Play of its season in the retrospective 1894-99 *Best Plays* volume. Later Broadway productions of record took place in 1897 and 1898 at the Empire Theater, 1899 at the Harlem Opera House, 1910 and 1915 at Empire.

BOY MEETS GIRL—Directed by John Lithgow; costumes, Clifford Capone; film sequences produced by David Fallon, directed by John Lithgow, edited by Steve Brand.

Understudies: Mr. Baker—Joe Grifasi; Messrs. Coffin, Jones—Moultrie Patten; Messrs. Kimbrough, Robbins—Jeffrey Jones; Messrs. Scardino, Patten—Stuart Warmflash; Miss Hurt—Ann McDonough; Miss Drummond—Gwendolyn Brown; Miss McDonough—Louise Stubbs; Mr. Grifasi—David Harris; Mr. Poole—Hansford Rowe.

Place: The Royal Studios in Hollywood. Act I: Mr. Friday's office. Act II, Scene 1: The screen of Your Neighborhood Theater, seven months later. Scene 2: Mr. Friday's office. Scene 3: The same, several hours later. Act III, Scene 1: A hospital corridor, three weeks later. Scene 2: A Station KNX radio broadcast. Scene 3: Mr. Friday's office. *Boy Meets Girl* was first produced on Broadway 11/27/35 for 669 performances and was named a Best Play of its season. It was revived 6/22/43 for 15 performances.

A Matter of Gravity (79). By Enid Bagnold. Produced by Robert Whitehead, Roger L. Stevens and Konrad Matthaei at the Broadhurst Theater. Opened February 3, 1976. (Closed April 10, 1976)

Dubois	Charlotte Jones	Shatov	Elizabeth Lawrence
Estate Agent	Robert Moberly	Herbert	Paul Harding
Mrs. Basil	Katharine Hepburn	Elizabeth	Wanda Bimson
Nicky	Christopher Reeve	Tom	Daniel Tamm

Understudies: Misses Jones, Lawrence—Maggie Task; Mr. Harding—Robert Moberly; Miss Bimson—Kathleen Heaney; Mr. Moberly—Bill Becker.

Directed by Noel Willman; scenery, Ben Edwards; costumes, Jane Greenwood; lighting, Thomas Skelton; production stage manager, Ben Strobach; stage manager, Bill Becker; press, Seymour Krawitz, Patricia McLean Krawitz.

Place: A room in an old English country house. Act I: An afternoon in summer. Act II: A short time afterwards. Act III: Eight years later, November.

Comedy, an old lady bears up as bravely and as long as she can under the burden of tolerating the sexual and other foibles of her grandson and his acquaintances. A foreign (British) play in its professional world premiere in this production.

Rockabye Hamlet (7). Musical based on *Hamlet* by William Shakespeare; book, music and lyrics by Cliff Jones. Produced by Lester Osterman Productions and Joseph Kipness in association with Martin Richards, Victor D'Arc and Marilyn Strauss at the Minskoff Theater. Opened February 17, 1976. (Closed February 21, 1976)

Horatio	Rory Dodd	Ophelia	Beverly D'Angelo
Hamlet	Larry Marshall	Laertes	Kim Milford
Claudius	Alan Weeks	Rosencrantz	Christopher Chadman
Gertrude	Leata Galloway	Guildenstern	Winston DeWitt Hemsley
Priest	Meat Loaf	Player	Irving Lee
Polonius	Randal Wilson	Playeress; Honeybelle Huckster	Judy Gibson

Acolytes, Swordsmen, Nobles, Courtesans: Tommy Aguilar, Steve Anthony, Terry Calloway, Prudence Darby, George Giraldo, Larry Hyman, Kurt Johnson, Clinton Keen, Paula Lynn, Joann Ogawa, Sandi Orcutt, Merel Poloway, Joseph Pugliese, Yolanda Raven, Michelle Stubbs, Dennis Williams.

Singers: James Braet, Judy DeAngelis, B.G. Gibson, Judy Gibson, Pat Gorman, Suzanne Lukather, Bruce Paine, William Parry. Roadies: Chet D'Elia, David Fredericks, David Lawson, Jeff Spielman.

Rockabye Hamlet Band: Bill Schneider associate conductor; Allen Herman, Michael Levinson, Peter Phillips, Phil Davis, Billy Schwartz, Richie Resnicoff, Erik Frandsen, Ron McClure; Lowell Hershey, Peter Yellin, Bruce Shaffel, Gene Lowinger, Marc Horowitz; arrangements, Alan Ralph, Thomas Pierson, Horace Ott, Bill Brohn, Jim Tyler.

Standbys: Messrs. Marshall, Milford—Philip Casnoff; Swing Dancer—Chuck Thorpe.

Directed and Choreographed by Gower Champion; co-choreographer, Tony Stevens; musical direction and vocal arrangements, Gordon Lowry Harrell; scenery, Kert F. Lundell; costumes, Joseph G. Aulisi; lighting, Jules Fisher; sound, Abe Jacob; swordplay, Larry Carpenter; dance music arrangements, Douglas Katsaros; production stage manager, David Taylor; stage managers, Bethe Ward, Tony Manzi; press, Betty Lee Hunt Associates, Maria Cristina Pucci.

Very free adaptation of the *Hamlet* drama in an operatic form with a hard rock score. A foreign play previously produced at the Charlottetown Festival, Prince Edward Island under the title *Kronberg 1582*.

ACT I

Prologue
"Why Did He Have to Die?" ....Horatio, Chorus
Scene 1: Chapel
  "The Wedding" ....Hamlet, Claudius, Gertrude, Priest, Chorus
  "That It Should Come to This" ....Hamlet
Scene 2: Throne Room
  "Set It Right" ....Claudius, Hamlet, Gertrude, Chorus
  "Hello-Hello" ....Ophelia, Hamlet
  "Don't Unmask Your Beauty to the Moon" ....Hamlet, Laertes
  "If Not to You" ....Ophelia, Chorus
  "Have I Got a Girl for You" ....Rosencrantz, Guildenstern, Hamlet, Chorus
  "Tis Pity, Tis True" ....Polonius, Claudius, Gertrude
Scene 3: Queen's Bedchamber
  "Shall We Dance" ....Hamlet, Gertrude
  "All My Life" ....Gertrude
Scene 4: The Disco
  "Something's Rotten in Denmark" ....Hamlet, Player, Playeress, Chorus
  "Denmark Is Still" ....Hamlet, Ophelia, Chorus
  "Twist Her Mind" ....Horatio, Hamlet, Ophelia, Chorus
  "Gentle Lover" ....Ophelia
  "Where Is the Reason" ....Hamlet
Scene 5: The Great Hall
  "The Wart Song" ....Players, Chorus
  "He Got It in the Ear" ....Honeybelle
  "It Is Done" ....Hamlet, Horatio

ACT II

Scene 1: The Chapel
  "Midnight—Hot Blood" ....Hamlet
  "Midnight Mass" ....Hamlet, Gertrude, Claudius, Priest, Choir
  "Hey . . . !" ....Rosencrantz, Guildenstern, Claudius
  "Sing Alone" ....Hamlet
Scene 2: Limbo
  "Your Daddy's Gone Away" ....Horatio
  "Rockabye Hamlet" ....Ophelia
  "All By Yourself" ....Laertes
  "The Rosencrantz & Guildenstern Boogie" ....Claudius, Chorus Girls
  "Laertes Coercion" ....Claudius, Laertes, Gertrude, Chorus Girls
  "The Last Blues" ....Gertrude
Scene 3: The Graveyard
  "Didn't She Do It for Love" ....Priest, Claudius, Hamlet, Laertes, Chorus
  "If My Morning Begins" ....Hamlet
Scene 4: The Great Hall
  "Swordfight" ....Claudius, Hamlet, Laertes, Gertrude, Horatio, Chorus

* Knock Knock (104). By Jules Feiffer. Produced by Terry Allen Kramer and Harry Rigby by arrangement with the Circle Repertory Company at the Biltmore Theater. Opened February 24, 1976.

Cohn .... Daniel Seltzer	Wiseman; Messenger; Gambler;	
Abe .... Neil Flanagan	Judge; Joan's Voices .... Judd Hirsch	
	Joan .... Nancy Snyder	

Standbys: Men—Herman O. Arbeit; Joan—Kristin Van Buren.

Directed by Marshall W. Mason; scenery, John Lee Beatty; costumes, Jennifer Von Mayrhauser; lighting, Dennis Parichy; sound, Charles London, George Hansen; special effects, Robert E. McCarthy; stage manager, Dan Hild; press, Henry Luhrman Associates.

Time: The present. Place: A small house in the woods. The play was presented in three parts.

Feiffer's comedy-fantasy about Joan of Arc moving in with a couple of men living in disarray in an isolated cottage was previously produced off Broadway 1/18/76 by Circle Repertory Company for 41 performances before transferring to Broadway (see its entry in the "Plays Produced Off Broadway" section of this volume).

Leonard Frey replaced Judd Hirsch 4/6/76. Lynn Redgrave replaced Nancy Snyder, Charles Durning replaced Daniel Seltzer, John Heffernan replaced Neil Flanagan under new direction by José Quintero 5/25/76, played a week of previews and "reopened" 6/2/76.

A Best Play; see page 195

* Bubbling Brown Sugar (104). Musical revue based on a concept by Rosetta LeNoire, book by Loften Mitchell, music and lyrics by various authors (see below), original music by Danny Holgate, Emme Kemp and Lillian Lopez. Produced by J. Lloyd Grant, Richard Bell, Robert M. Cooper and Ashton Springer in association with Moe Septee, Inc. in the Media House production at the ANTA Theater. Opened March 2, 1976.

Skip; Young Checkers ...... Lonnie McNeil	Marsha; Young Irene .... Vivian Reed
Bill; Time Man; Bumpy;	Tony; Waiter; Dutch ... Anthony Whitehouse
Emcee .... Vernon Washington	Irene Paige .... Josephine Premice
Ray; Young Sage .... Newton Winters	John Sage; Rusty .... Avon Long
Carolyn; Gospel Lady; Female	Checkers; Dusty .... Joseph Attles
Nightclub Singer .... Carolyn Byrd	Jim; Male Nightclub Singer .... Chip Garnett
Norma .... Karen Grannum	Ella .... Ethel Beatty
Gene; Gospel Lady's Son ..... Alton Lathrop	Judy; Dutch's Girl ...... Barbara Rubenstein
Helen .... Dyann Robinson	Charlie; Count .... Barry Preston
Laura .... Charlise Harris	

The Solitunes: Alton Lathrop, Lonnie McNeil, Newton Winters. Chorus: Murphy Cross, Nedra Dixon, Emme Kemp, Stanley Ramsey.

Musicians: Neil Tate conductor, piano; Joseph Marshall associate conductor, drums; Rudy Stevenson contractor, guitar, flute.

Standby: Mr. Long—Vernon Washington. Understudies: Misses Premice, Byrd—Emme Kemp; Miss Reed—Karen Grannum, Carolyn Byrd; Messrs. Attles, Washington—David Bryant; Miss Beatty—Nedra Dixon; Chip Garnett—Stanley Ramsay; Miss Robinson—Charlise Harris; Miss Rubenstein—Murphy Cross; Messrs. Whitehouse, Preston—E. Lynn Nickerson; Mr. Lathrop—Millard Hurley; Dance Alternates—Carol Pennyfeather, Millard Hurley.

Directed by Robert M. Cooper; choreography and musical staging, Billy Wilson; musical direction, Danny Holgate; scenery, Clarke Dunham; costumes, Bernard Johnson; lighting, Barry Arnold; projections, Lucie D. Grosvenor, Clarke Dunham; sound, Joel S. Eichman; choral arrangements, Chapman Roberts; production stage manager, Sam Ellis; stage manager, E. Lynn Nickerson; press, Max Eisen.

A nostalgic revisiting of the Harlem of the 1920s, 30s and 40s in the form of a musical revue combining old and new musical numbers. Previously produced off off Broadway at the Amas Repertory Theater.

MUSICAL NUMBERS

(Titles of new numbers appear below in *italics*)

Act I, Scene 1, Harlem today: *"Harlem '70"* (music by Danny Holgate)—Company; *"Bubbling Brown Sugar"* (music by Danny Holgate, lyrics by Lillian Lopez and Emme Kemp)—

Company; "That's What Harlem Is to Me" (by Andy Razaf)—Josephine Premice; Bill Robinson Specialty—Vernon Washington; *"Harlem Sweet Harlem"* (music by Danny Holgate, lyrics by Emme Kemp)—Company; "Nobody" (by Axel Rogers and Bert Williams)—Avon Long; *"Goin' Back in Time"*—Washington.

Scene 2 (this and the rest of the action takes place in old Harlem between 1920 and 1940), Downtown speakeasy: "Some of These Days" (by Shelton Brooks)—Barbara Rubenstein; *"Moving Uptown"* (music by Danny Holgate, lyrics by Loften Mitchell)—Washington.

Scene 3, 125th Street and Seventh Avenue: *"Strolling"* (music by Danny Holgate)—Alton Lathrop, Charlise Harris, Lonnie McNeil, Karen Grannum, Newton Winters, Dyann Robinson.

Scene 4, 135th Street and Lenox Avenue: "I'm Gonna Tell God All My Troubles"—Lathrop; "His Eye Is on the Sparrow" and "Swing Low, Sweet Chariot" medley—Carolyn Byrd, Company; "Sweet Georgia Brown" (by Maceo Pinkard)—McNeil, Winters, Vivian Reed; "Honeysuckle Rose" (by Andy Razaf and Thomas "Fats" Waller)—Long, Miss Premice.

Scene 5, Harlem night spots: "Stormy Monday Blues" (by Earl "Fatha" Hines)—Miss Byrd; "Rosetta" (by Earl "Fatha" Hines)—Lathrop, McNeil, Winters; "Sophisticated Lady" (by Irving Mills, Mitchell Parish and Duke Ellington)—Chip Garnett, Washington, Miss Robinson; "In Honeysuckle Time, When Emaline Said She'd Be Mine" (by Noble Sissle and Eubie Blake)—Long, Attles; "Solitude" (by Duke Ellington, Eddie DeLange and Irving Mills)—Lathrop, McNeil, Winters, Miss Reed.

Scene 6, At the Savoy: *"C'mon Up to Jive Time"*—Washington; "Stompin' at the Savoy" (by Andy Razaf, Benny Goodman, Edgar Sampson and Chick Webb) and "Take the 'A' Train" (by Duke Ellington and Billy Scrayhorn) medley—Company.

Act II, Scene 1, Lenox Avenue a few minutes later: *"Harlem-Time"*—Washington; "Love Will Find a Way" (by Noble Sissle and Eubie Blake)—Garnett, Ethel Beatty; *"Dutch's Song"* (music and lyrics by Emme Kemp)—Anthony Whitehouse; "Brown Gal" (by Avon Long and Lil Armstrong)—Long; "Pray for the Lights to Go Out" (by Renton Tunnan and Will Skidmore)—Attles.

Scene 2, Another street in Harlem: "I Got It Bad" (by Duke Ellington and Paul Webster)—Miss Beatty; *"Harlem Makes Me Feel!"* (music and lyrics by Emme Kemp)—Barry Preston.

Scene 3, Small's Paradise: "Jim, Jam, Jumpin' Jive" (by Cab Calloway)—Washington, McNeil, Winters; "There'll Be Some Changes Made" (by W. Benton Overstreet and Billy Higgins)—Miss Premice; "God Bless the Child" (by Arthur Herzog Jr. and Billie Holiday)—Miss Reed; "It Don't Mean a Thing" (by Duke Ellington and Irving Mills)—Garnett, Whitehouse, Miss Premice, Company.

Zalmen or The Madness of God (22). By Elie Wiesel; adapted by Marion Wiesel. Produced by Moe Septee at the Lyceum Theater. Opened March 17, 1976. (Closed April 4, 1976)

Zalmen .... Richard Bauer	Nina .... Polly Adams
The Rabbi .... Joseph Wiseman	Mischa .... Rodman Flender
Chairman, Synagogue Council ... Paul Sparer	Alexei .... David Little
Members of the Synagogue Council:	Cantor; 2nd Guard .... John B. Jellison
Shmuel .... Edwin Bordo	Commissar .... Jack Hollander
Srul .... Sanford Seeger	1st Guard .... Michael Haney
Motke .... Carl Don	3d Guard .... Irwin Atkins
Chaim .... David Reinhardsen	Secretary .... Nancy Dutton
Zender .... Warren Pincus	Avrom .... Michael Gorrin
Doctor .... David Margulies	Feige .... Zviah Igdalsky
Inspector, Ministry of	
Religious Affairs .... Lee Wallace	

Understudies: Messrs. Bauer, Seeger—John B. Jellison; Mr. Wiseman—Irwin Atkins; Messrs. Sparer, Margulies—Edwin Bordo; Mr. Wallace—Jack Hollander; Misses Adams, Igdalsky—Nancy Dutton; Mr. Little—David Reinhardsen; Mr. Gorrin—Carl Don; Mr. Reinhardsen—Michael Haney; Mr. Hollander—Sanford Seeger.

Directed by Alan Schneider; scenery, William Ritman; costumes, Marjorie Slaiman; lighting, Richard Nelson; assistant director, Susan Einhorn; production stage manager, R. Derek Swire; stage manager, Ted Harris; press, Max Eisen, Barbara Glenn, Judy Jacksina.

Time: The late 1950s. Place: A small town somewhere in Russia. Act I: The synagogue. Act II: The same, the next day, night.

Russian authorities investigate a supposed incident of inflammatory protest by a rabbi goaded by his mad but inspired beadle, Zalmen. A foreign (French) play previously produced at the Arena Stage, Washington, D.C.

* **My Fair Lady** (75). Revival of the musical adapted from George Bernard Shaw's *Pygmalion;* book and lyrics by Alan Jay Lerner; music by Frederick Loewe. Produced by Herman Levin at the St. James Theater. Opened March 25, 1976.

Mrs. Eynsford-Hill ....Eleanor Phelps	Jamie; Ambassador ....Richard Neilson
Freddy Eynsford-Hill ....Jerry Lanning	Alfred P. Doolittle ....George Rose
Eliza Doolittle ....Christine Andreas	Mrs. Pearce ....Sylvia O'Brien
Col. Pickering ....Robert Coote	Mrs. Hopkins; Lady
Henry Higgins ....Ian Richardson	Boxington ....Margaretta Warwick
1st Cockney ....Kevin Marcum	Butler; Bartender ....Clifford Fearl
2d Cockney ....Jack Starkey	Mrs. Higgins ....Brenda Forbes
3d Cockney; Flunkey ....William James	Chauffeur ....Jack Karcher
4th Cockney; Footman ....Stan Page	Constable ....Timothy Smith
Bartender; Footman ...Kevin Lane Dearinger	Flower Girl ....Dru Alexandrine
Harry; Lord Boxington;	Queen of Transylvania ....Karen Gibson
Zoltan Karpathy .... John Clarkson	Mrs. Higgin's Maid ....Sonja Stuart

Buskers: Debra Lyman, Stan Picus, Ernie Pysher. Servants: Sonja Anderson, Lynn Fitzpatrick, Karen Gibson, Vickie Patik, Kevin Lane Dearinger.

Singing Ensemble: Sonja Anderson, Alyson Bristol, Lynn Fitzpatrick, Karen Gibson, Cynthia Meryl, Vickie Patik, Kevin Lane Dearinger, Clifford Fearl, William James, Kevin Marcum, Stan Page, Jack Starkey.

Dancing Ensemble: Dru Alexandrine, Sally Benoit, Marie Berry, Debra Lyman, Mari McMinn, Gina Ramsel, Catherine Rice, Sonja Stuart, Bonnie Walker, Richard Ammon, Jeremy Blanton, David Evans, Jack Karcher, Richard Maxon, Stan Picus, Ernie Pysher, Rick Schneider, Timothy Smith.

Standbys: Mr. Richardson—Patrick Horgan; Miss Andreas—Vickie Patik. Understudies: Mr. Rose—John Clarkson; Mr. Coote—Richard Neilson; Miss Forbes—Eleanor Phelps; Mr. Lanning—William James; Miss O'Brien—Margaretta Warwick; Mr. Clarkson—Kevin Marcum; Mr. Neilson—Stan Page; Miss Warwick—Cynthia Meryl; Miss Phelps—Karen Gibson.

Directed by Jerry Adler (based on the original by Moss Hart); choreography and musical numbers by Crandall Diehl (based on the original by Hanya Holm); musical direction, Theodore Saidenberg; scenery, Oliver Smith; costumes, Cecil Beaton; lighting, John Gleason; special costume assistant, W. Robert Lavine; musical arrangements, Robert Russell Bennett, Philip J. Lang; dance music arrangements, Trude Rittman; production stage manager, Nicholas Russiyan; stage manager, Alisa Jill Adler; press, Seymour Krawitz, Ted Goldsmith, Patricia McLean Krawitz.

My Fair Lady was first produced 3/15/56 for 2,717 performances (fifth longest run in Broadway history) and was named a Best Play of its season and won the Critics Award for best musical. It was revived 5/20/64 for 47 performances and 6/13/68 for 22 performances, both times by the City Center Light Opera Company.

The synopsis of scenes and list of musical numbers in *My Fair Lady* appear on pages 378-9 of *The Best Plays of 1955-56*.

* **Who's Afraid of Virginia Woolf?** (69). Revival of the play by Edward Albee. Produced by Ken Marsolais and James Scott Productions, Inc. in association with MPL, Ltd. at the Music Box. Opened April 1, 1976.

Martha ....Colleen Dewhurst	Honey ....Maureen Anderman
George ....Ben Gazzara	Nick ....Richard Kelton

Standbys: Miss Dewhurst—Betty Miller; Mr. Gazzara—James Karen; Miss Anderman—Katherine Bruce; Mr. Kelton—Josef Warik.

Directed by Edward Albee; scenery and lighting, William Ritman; costumes, Jane Greenwood; produced by arrangement with Richard Barr and Clinton Wilder; production stage manager, Mark Wright; stage manager, Wayne Carson; press, Betty Lee Hunt Associates, Maria Cristina Pucci.

Act I: Fun and games. Act II: Walpurgisnacht. Act III: The exorcism.

Who's Afraid of Virginia Woolf? was first produced 10/13/62 for 664 performances and was named a best play of its season. Its only previous New York revival was 7/3/68 by Atelje 212 for 7 performances in a Serbo-Croatian translation.

Monty Python Live! (23). Revue conceived and written by the "Monty Python" team. Produced by Artist Consultants at the City Center 56th Street Theater. Opened April 14, 1976. (Closed May 2, 1976)

The "Monty Python" team:
Graham Chapman
John Cleese
Terry Gilliam
Eric Idle

Terry Jones
Michael Palin
and
Carol Cleveland
Neil Innes

Directed by the "Monty Python" team; American scenic supervision, Karl Eigsti; sound, Abe Jacob; lighting, John Gleason; stage manager, Molly Kirkland; press, the Wartoke Concern Inc., Jane Friedman.

A foreign show made up of comedy sketches featuring the original team members of the BBC-TV series *Monty Python's Flying Circus,* seen in the U.S. on public broadcasting stations.

Shirley MacLaine (14). One-woman revue performed by Shirley MacLaine; written by Fred Ebb; additional material by Bob Wells; music composed and arranged by Cy Coleman. Produced by HMT Associates at the Palace Theater. Opened April 19, 1976. (Closed May 1, 1976)

With Shirley's Gypsies: Candy Brown, Gary Flannery, Adam Grammis, Jo Ann Lehmann, Larry Vickers. Drummer: Tom Duckworth.

Directed by Tony Charmoli: special choreography, Alan Johnson; lighting design, Richard Winkler; lighting consultant, Graham Large; sound consultant, Steve Wooley; stage manager, Earl Hughes; press, Michael Alpert Public Relations, Marilynn LeVine, Warren Knowlton, Carl Samrock.

Solo show of singing, dancing and informal monologue, with a background of five "gypsies," or chorus performers, presented without intermission.

MUSICAL NUMBERS (Shirley MacLaine performed all the following numbers assisted by members of the chorus as noted): "If My Friends Could See Me Now"—Adam Grammis, Gary Flannery; "Personal Property"; "Remember Me?"; "Hey Big Spender"—Candy Brown, Jo Ann Lehmann; "I'm a Person Too"; "Irma La Douce"; "Gypsy in My Soul"—Gypsies; "It's Not Where You Start"—Gypsies; "Every Little Movement Has a Meaning All Its Own"—Gypsies; "The Hustle"—Gypsies; "Star"; "I'm a Brass Band"—Gypsies.

The Heiress (23). Revival of the play by Ruth and Augustus Goetz; based on the novel *Washington Square* by Henry James. Produced by Steven Beckler and Thomas C. Smith in the American Bicentennial Theater production at the Broadhurst Theater. Opened April 20, 1976. (Closed May 9, 1976)

Maria	Sharon Laughlin	Arthur Townsend	Roger Baron
Dr. Austin Sloper	Richard Kiley	Marian Almond	Cecilia Hart
Lavinia Penniman	Jan Miner	Morris Townsend	David Selby
Catherine Sloper	Jane Alexander	Mrs. Montgomery	Toni Darnay
Elizabeth Almond	Dorothy Blackburn	Coachman	William Gibberson

Understudies: Mr. Kiley—William Gibberson; Misses Alexander, Hart—Sharon Laughlin; Miss Miner—Diana Mathews, Toni Darnay; Mr. Selby—Roger Baron; Messrs. Baron, Gibberson—Joe Lorden; Misses Hart, Darnay, Laughlin—Diana Mathews.

Directed by George Keathley; scenery, Oliver Smith; costumes, Ann Roth; lighting, David F. Segal; produced for Kennedy Center and the Xerox Corporation by Roger L. Stevens and Richmond Crinkley; associate producer, Ken Morse; stage manager, Joe Lorden; press, Betty Lee Hunt Associates, Maria Cristina Pucci.

Time: 1850. Place: The front parlor of Dr. Sloper's house in Washington Square. Act I, Scene 1: An October evening. Scene 2: An afternoon two weeks later. Scene 3: The next morning. Act II, Scene 1: An April night six months later. Scene 2: Two hours later. Scene 3: A morning three days later. Scene 4: A summer evening almost two years later.

The Heiress was first produced on Broadway 9/29/47 for 410 performances and was named a Best Play of its season. It was revived at the City Center 2/8/50 for 16 performances.

* Rex (41). Musical with book by Sherman Yellen; music by Richard Rodgers; lyrics by Sheldon Harnick. Produced by Richard Adler in association with Roger Berlind and Edward R. Downe Jr. at the Lunt-Fontanne Theater. Opened April 25, 1976.

Norfolk	Charles Rule	Will Somers	Tom Aldredge
Cardinal Wolsey	William Griffis	Henry VIII	Nicol Williamson

Mark Smeaton ....Ed Evanko
Queen Catherine ....Barbara Andres
Princess Mary ....Glenn Close
Lady Jane Seymour ....April Shawhan
Francis I ....Stephen D. Newman
English Herald; Herald .....Danny Ruvolo
French Herald ....Jeff Phillips

Queen Claude; Katharine Parr;
    Lady Margaret ....Martha Danielle
Anne Boleyn; Princess
    Elizabeth ....Penny Fuller
Dauphin ....Keith Koppmeier
Comus ....Merwin Goldsmith
Nursemaid ....Melanie Vaughan
Prince Edward ....Michael John

Ladies and Gentlemen of the Courts: Dennis Daniels, Harry Fawcett, Paul Forrest, Pat Gideon, Kim Henley, Dawn Herbert, Robin Hoff, Don Johanson, Jim Litten, Craig Lucas, Carol Jo Lugenbeal, Valerie Mahaffey, Eugene Moose, Jeff Phillips, Charles Rule, Danny Ruvolo, Lillian Shelby, Jo Speros, Gerald R. Teijelo Jr., Candice Tovar, John Ulrickson, Melanie Vaughan.

Sword Dancers: Dennis Daniels, Ken Henley, Don Johanson, Jim Litten, Jeff Phillips, Danny Ruvolo.

Understudies: Mr. Williamson—Stephen D. Newman; Miss Fuller—Martha Danielle; Mr. Aldredge—Jeff Phillips; Miss Shawhan—Carol Jo Lugenbeal; Miss Andres—Lillian Shelby; Miss Close—Pat Gideon; Miss Danielle—Valerie Mahaffey, Pat Gideon, Candace Tovar; Mr. Evanko—Craig Lucas; Messrs. Goldsmith, Newman—Gerald R. Teijelo Jr.; Mr. Griffis—Charles Rule; Master John—Keith Koppmeier; Master Koppmeier—Michael John.

Directed by Edwin Sherin; choreography, Dania Krupska; musical direction, Jay Blackton; scenery and costumes, John Conklin; lighting, Jennifer Tipton; orchestrations, Irwin Kostal; dance arrangements, David Baker; production stage manager, Bob Bernard; stage manager, Jack Timmers; press, Jeffrey Richards, James Storrow, Barbara Shelley.

Musical biography of Henry VIII as a husband and father.

ACT I

Scene 1: Greenwich Palace
Scene 2: Henry's tent
    "No Song More Pleasing" ....Smeaton
Scene 3: Field of Cloth of Gold
    "The Field of Cloth of Gold" ....Company
    "Where Is My Son?" ....Company
Scene 4: French pavilion
    Basse Dances ....Company
Scene 5: Comus's chambers
Scene 6: Hever Castle
    "The Chase" ....Comus, Will, Smeaton, Gentlemen
Scene 7: Hampton Court Palace
    "Away From You" ....Henry
Scene 8: Chapel
    "As Once I Loved You" ....Catherine
Scene 9: Palace hallway
Scene 10: The throne room
    "Away From You" (Reprise) ....Anne, Henry
Scene 11: Hampton Court corridor
Scene 12: Queen Anne's bedroom
    "Elizabeth" ....Smeaton, Lady Margaret, Lady in Waiting
Scene 13: Comus's Lab
Scene 14: The palace
    "No Song More Pleasing" (Reprise) ....Jane, Henry
    "So Much You Loved Me" ....Anne
    "So Much You Loved Me"(Reprise) ....Anne
Scene 15: The Tower of London
Scene 16: The coronation
Scene 17: The City of London
    "Te Deum" ....Company

ACT II

Scene 1: Hampton Court Palace
    "Christmas at Hampton Court" ....Elizabeth, Edward, Mary
Scene 2: The great hall at Hampton Court Palace
    "The Wee Golden Warrior" ....Will, Edward, Elizabeth, Mary, Ladies, Gentlemen

"The Masque" ....Will, Edward, Elizabeth, Mary, Ladies, Gentlemen
Sword Dance ....Sword Dancers
Scene 3: The throne room
"From Afar" ....Henry
Scene 4: Hampton Court corridor
"In Time" ....Elizabeth, Will
Scene 5: Comus's lab
Scene 6: Henry's bedroom
Scene 7: The throne room
"In Time" (Reprise) ....Elizabeth, Edward
"Te Deum" (Reprise) ....Company

So Long, 174th Street (16). Musical based on Joseph Stein's *Enter Laughing* from the novel by Carl Reiner; book by Joseph Stein; music and lyrics by Stan Daniels. Produced by Frederick Brisson in association with the Harkness Organization and Wyatt Dickerson at the Harkness Theater. Opened April 27, 1976. (Closed May 9, 1976)

David ....Robert Morse	Wanda ....Loni Ackerman
Stage Manager ....Joe Howard	Marvin ....Lawrence John Moss
Girl ....Freda Soiffer	Miss B.......................Sydney Blake
Barrymore; Waiter; Pike;	Don Baxter ....Chuck Beard
Ziegfeld ....Gene Varrone	Don Darwin ....Michael Blue Aiken
Pope; Harry Hamburger ......Robert Barry	Angela ....Barbara Lang
King; Peabody ....Richard Marr	Marlowe; Butler; Judge ....George S. Irving
Roosevelt ....David Berk	Papa ....Lee Goodman
Eleanor Roosevelt ....Nancy Killmer	Soda Jerk; Man ....James Brennan
Mr. Foreman ....Mitchell Jason	

Ensemble: Jill Cook, Nancy Killmer, Meribeth Kisner, Denis Mauthe, Rita Rudner, Freda Soiffer, Michael Blue Aiken, Chuck Beard, David Berk, Joe Howard, Richard Marr, William Swiggard.

Standby: Mr. Morse—James Brennan. Understudies: Miss Ackerman—Rita Rudner; Swing Girl—Claudia Asbury; Swing Boy—Jack Magradey.

Directed by Burt Shevelove; choreography, Alan Johnson; musical direction, John Lesko; scenery, James Riley; costumes, Stanley Simmons; lighting, Richard Nelson; orchestrations, Luther Henderson; dance music arrangements, Wally Harper; production supervisor, Stone Widney; production stage manager, Mortimer Halpern; stage manager, Bryan Young; press, Solters & Roskin, Inc., Lee Solters, Bud Westman, Stanley F. Kaminsky.

Time: The present and the late 1930s. Place: New York City. The play was presented without intermission.

Bronx high school boy struggles to escape his destiny as a pharmacist and become an actor.

ACT I

"David Kolowitz, the Actor" ....David, Ensemble
"It's Like" ....David, Wanda
"Undressing Girls With My Eyes" ....David, Marvin, Girls
"Bolero on Rye" ....David, Miss B, Waiter
"Whoever You Are" ....David
"You" ....David, Marlowe, Angela, Ziegfeld, Ensemble
"My Son the Druggist" ....Papa
"You Touched Her" ....David, Marvin, Men
"Men" ....Wanda, Soda Jerk, Girls
"Boy Oh Boy" ....David, Company
"The Butler's Song" ....Butler
"Being With You" ....Wanda, David
"If You Want to Break Your Father's Heart" ....David, Papa, Judge, Jury
"So Long, 174 Street" ....David, Family, Friends, Neighbors
"David Kolowitz, the Actor" (Reprise) ....Company
Finale ....Company

* The Belle of Amherst (38). One-woman performance by Julie Harris in a play by William Luce; compiled by Timothy Helgeson. Produced by Mike Merrick and Don Gregory at the Longacre Theater. Opened April 28, 1976.

Directed by Charles Nelson Reilly; scenery and lighting, H.R. Poindexter; costumes, Theoni V. Aldredge; production stage manager, George Eckert; stage manager, Benny Baker; press, Seymour Krawitz, Patricia McLean Krawitz, Ted Goldsmith.
Time: 1845-1886. Place: The Dickinson home in Amherst, Mass. The play was presented in two parts.
The character and life of Emily Dickinson portrayed by Julie Harris, with reference to the following additional characters: Maggie Maher, Austin Dickinson, James Francis Billings, Abby Wood, Jennie Hitchcock, Uriah Crowell, Edward Dickinson, Mary Lyon, Lavinia Dickinson, Buffy, Susan Gilbert Dickinson, Thomas Wentworth Higginson, Charles Wadsworth, Emily Norcross Dickinson.

1600 Pennsylvania Avenue (7). Musical with book and lyrics by Alan Jay Lerner; music by Leonard Bernstein. Produced by Roger L. Stevens and Robert Whitehead at the Mark Hellinger Theater. Opened May 4, 1976. (Closed May 8, 1976)

The President . . . . Ken Howard	Coley . . . . Carl Hall
The President's Wife . . . . . . Patricia Routledge	Joby . . . . Janette Moody
Lud . . . . Gilbert Price	Broom . . . . Howard Ross
Seena . . . . Emily Yancy	Jim . . . . Cornel J. Richie
Little Lud . . . . Guy Costley	Sally . . . . Louise Heath
Stage Manager . . . . David E. Thomas	The British:
The Thirteen Delegates:	Ordway . . . . Walter Charles
Massachusetts . . . . Howard Ross	Pimms . . . . John Witham
New York . . . . Reid Shelton	Barker . . . . Lee Winston
Pennsylvania . . . . Ralph Farnworth	Gleig . . . . Raymond Cox
New Hampshire . . . . J.T. Cromwell	Maitland . . . . Alexander Orfaly
Rhode Island . . . . Lee Winston	Ross . . . . Edwin Steffe
Connecticut . . . . Richard Chappell	Pratt . . . . Richard Chappell
New Jersey . . . . Walter Charles	Scott . . . . J.T. Cromwell
Virginia . . . . Edwin Steffe	Budgen . . . . Richard Muenz
North Carolina . . . . John Witham	Cockburn; Sen. Conkling . . . . Reid Shelton
South Carolina . . . . Richard Muenz	Rev. Bushrod . . . . Bruce A. Hubbard
Delaware . . . . Alexander Orfaly	Auctioneer; Mr. Henry;
Maryland . . . . Raymond Cox	Babcock . . . . Lee Winston
Georgia . . . . Randolph Riscol	James Hoban; Judge . . . . Edwin Steffe
The Staff:	Royal Visitor . . . . Randolph Riscol
Henry . . . . Raymond Bazemore	Sec. of the Senate . . . . Howard Ross
Rachel . . . . Urylee Leonardos	

Singers: Raymond Bazemore, Elaine Bunse, Nancy Callman, Richard Chappell, Walter Charles, Raymond Cox, J.T. Cromwell, Beth Fowler, Carl Hall, Louise Heath, Bruce A. Hubbard, Kris Karlowski, Urylee Leonardos, Joyce MacDonald, Janette Moody, Richard Muenz, Sharon Powers, Cornel J. Richie, Randolph Riscol, Martha Thigpen, Lee Winston.
Dancers: Jo-Ann Baldo, Clyde-Jacques Barrett, Joella Breedlove, Allyne DeChalus, Linda Griffin, Bob Heath, Michael Lichtefeld, Diana Mirras, Hector Jaime Mercado, Cleveland Pennington, Al Perryman, Renee Rose, Juliet Seignious, Thomas J. Stanton, Clayton Strange, Mimi B. Wallace.
Swings: Leah Randolph, Martial Roumain. Understudies: Mr. Howard—Richard Chappell; Miss Routledge—Beth Fowler; Mr. Price—J. Edwards Adams; Miss Yancy—Louise Heath; Mr. Costley—Karl M. Horton.
Directed and choreographed by Gilbert Moses and George Faison; musical direction, Roland Gagnon; scenery, Kert Lundell; lighting, Tharon Musser; costume supervision, Whitney Blausen, Dona Granata; orchestrations, Sid Ramin, Hershy Kay; sound, John McClure; produced by arrangement with Saint Subber; production stage manager, William Dodds; stage managers, Marnel Sumner, Michael Turque; press, Seymour Krawitz, Patricia McLean Krawitz, Ted Goldsmith.
Series of episodes about the White House and its occupants above and below stairs from George Washington to Theodore Roosevelt, subtitled "A musical about the problems of housekeeping."

ACT I

"Rehearse!" ....President, First Lady, Lud, Seena, Company
"If I Was a Dove" ....Little Lud
"On Ten Square Miles by the Potomac River" ....Washington, Delegates
"Welcome Home Miz Adams" ....Henry, Rachel, Staff
"Take Care of This House" ....John and Abigail Adams, Little Lud, Staff
"The President Jefferson Sunday Luncheon Party March" ....Jefferson, Little Lud, Guests
"Seena" ....Lud
"Sonatina" (The British) ....Cockburn, Officers, Citizens
   1. Allegro con brio. 2. Tempo di menuetto (including an authentic harmonization of "To Anacreon in Heav'n," 1740, later known as "The Star Spangled Banner." 3. Rondo.
Lud's Wedding
"I Love My Wife" ....Lud, Seena, Staff
"Auctions" ....Auctioneer, Buyers
"The Little White Lie" ....James and Eliza Monroe
"We Must Have a Ball" ....Buchanan
The Ball ....Company

ACT II

"Forty Acres and a Mule" ....Staff
"Bright and Black" ....Seena, Staff
"Duet for One" (The First Lady of the Land) ....Julia Grant, Lucy Hayes, Company
"The Robber-Baron Minstrel Parade" ....Minstrels
"Pity the Poor" ....Minstrels
"The Red White and Blues" ....Minstrels
"I Love This Land" ....President
"Rehearse!" (Reprise) ....Company

D'Oyly Carte. Repertory of three musical revivals by W.S. Gilbert and Arthur Sullivan. **The Mikado** (10). Opened May 5, 1976. **The Pirates of Penzance** (8). Opened May 6, 1976. **H.M.S. Pinafore** (4). Opened May 16, 1976. (Repertory closed May 23, 1976). Produced by James M. Nederlander by arrangement with The D'Oyly Carte Opera Trust Ltd. and Dame Bridget D'Oyly Carte at the Uris Theater.

PERFORMER	"THE MIKADO"	"THE PIRATES OF PENZANCE"	"H.M.S. PINAFORE"
John Ayldon	Mikado	Pirate King	Dick Deadeye
Caroline Baker		Kate	
Patricia Ann Bennett		Isabel	
Michael Buchan			Bob Beckett
James Conroy-Ward		Maj. Gen. Stanley	
Jon Ellison	Go-To	Samuel	Bill Bobstay
Julia Goss	Yum-Yum	Mabel	
Lyndsie Holland	Katisha	Ruth	Buttercup
Patricia Leonard	Peep-Bo		Hebe
Barbara Lilley			Josephine
Jane Metcalfe	Pitti-Sing	Edith	
Michael Rayner	Pish-Tush	Sergeant	Capt. Corcoron
John Reed	Ko-Ko		Joseph Porter
Meston Reid		Frederic	Ralph Rackstraw
Kenneth Sandford	Pooh-Bah		
Geoffrey Shovelton	Nanki-Poo		

ALL PLAYS—Chorus and understudies: Paul Burrows, Barry Clark, Malcolm Coy, Gareth Jones, Guy Matthews, William Palmerley, Edwin Rolles, Thomas Scholey, Alan Spencer, William Strachan, Paul Waite, Michael Westbury, Gillian Burrows, Lorraine Dulcie-Daniels, Anne Egglestone, Josephine Hinchley, Beti Lloyd-Jones, Elsie McDougall, Roberta Morrell, Helen Moulder, Suzanne O'Keefe, Andrea Phillips, Glynis Prendergast, Patricia Rea, Vivian Tierney.

Musical director, Royston Nash; production director, Michael Heyland; production supervisor, Ben Janney; press, Michael Alpert, Marilynn LeVine.

All three operettas were previously presented this season by the Light Opera of Manhattan (see its entry in the "Plays Produced Off Broadway" section of this volume). All were performed during the last visit to New York of D'Oyly Carte 10/29/68 for 23 performances.

THE MIKADO—Scenery, Disley Jones; costumes, Charles Ricketts, Nanki-Poo in Act I, Disley Jones.

Act I: Courtyard of Ko-Ko's official residence. Act II: Ko-Ko's garden.

THE PIRATES OF PENZANCE—Act I: A rocky seashore on the coast of Cornwall. Act II: A ruined chapel by moonlight.

H.M.S. PINAFORE—Back cloth, Joseph and Phil Harker.

Place: Quarterdeck of H.M.S. Pinafore off Portsmouth. Act I: Noon. Act II: Night.

Des Journées Entières Dans les Arbres (Days in the Trees) (11). Play in the French language by Marguerite Duras. Produced by Le Tréteau de Paris and Jean de Rigault in association with the French Institute and Alliance Française, under the sponsorship of L'Association Française D'Action Artistique of the Government of the French Republic, in the Compagnie Renaud-Barrault production at the Ambassador Theater. Opened May 6, 1976. (Closed May 15, 1976)

Mother ....Madeleine Renaud	Marcelle ....Françoise Dorner
Son (Jacques) ....Jean-Pierre Aumont	Bartender ....Jean Martin

Directed by Jean-Louis Barrault; stage manager, Dominique Ehlinger; press, Michael Alpert Public Relations, Marilynn LeVine.

Time: The spring. Place: A two-room apartment, on the street, and in a nightclub, somewhere in Paris. Act I: Mid-day. Act II, Scene 1: Later the same afternoon. Scene 2: Late evening the same day. Act III: 2 o'clock the next morning.

An old woman losing her grip on life visits her one ne'er-do-well son—"one son in reserve for when the bad times come"—in a play which tries to explore life's hidden meanings. A foreign play first presented by the Compagnie Renaud-Barrault at the Odeon Theater in Paris 12/1/65. The present revised version was first done by the same company at the Théâtre d'Orsay 10/15/75 and was brought to New York for a limited engagement as "a French contribution to the Bicentennial celebrations."

Legend (5). By Samuel Taylor. Produced by Gladys Rackmil and Kennedy Center at the Ethel Barrymore Theater. Opened May 13, 1976. (Closed May 15, 1976)

Quince ....Robert Anthony	Jesse Lymburner ....F. Murray Abraham
Tumbleweed ....James Carrington	Judah Lymburner ....George Parry
Alkali ....Ben Slack	Betsey-No-Name ....Elizabeth Ashley
Barney-One-Ball ....Ron Max	Virgil Biggers ....Stephen Clarke
Mahogany Brown ....Shev Rodgers	Frankie Scruggs ....Wayne Maxwell
Muley ....'......Munson Hicks	Freddie Scruggs ....Sebastian Stuart
Kettle-Belly ....Bill McIntyre	Lacy Underwood; McNally ......J.J. Quinn
William F.P. Morgan ......George Dzundza	Clarence; Stranger ....Tom Flagg

Standby: Miss Ashley—Tricia O'Neil. Understudies: Mr. Abraham—Robert Anthony; Mr. Clarke—James Carrington; Mr. Dzundza—Ben Slack; Messrs. Max, Maxwell, Stuart—Tom Flagg; Mr. Flag—J.J. Quinn; Mr. Parry—Donald Kehr; General Understudy—Valentine Mayer.

Directed by Robert Drivas; scenery, Santo Loquasto; costumes, Florence Klotz; lighting, Thomas Skelton; original music, Dan Goggin; production supervisor, Larry Forde; produced for Kennedy Center by Roger L. Stevens; stage manager, Valentine Mayer; press, Betty Lee Hunt Associates, Maria Cristina Pucci, Maurice Turet.

Time: Somewhere in the past. Place: Somewhere in Western America. The play was presented in two parts.

Lady bank robber must choose between the sheriff who captured her and her outlaw lover in a romantic comedy Western.

* The Runner Stumbles (16). By Milan Stitt. Produced by Wayne Adams and Willard Morgan by special arrangement with the Hartman Theater Company at the Little Theater. Opened May 18, 1976.

Amos	Morrie Piersol	Mrs. Shandig	Sloan Shelton
Father Rivard	Stephen Joyce	Prosecutor	Craig Richard Nelson
Erna Prindle	Katina Commings	Monsignor Nicholson	Joseph Mathewson
Toby Felker	James Noble	Louise	Marilyn Pfeiffer
Sister Rita	Nancy Donohue		

Understudies: Male Roles—David Lile; Misses Commings, Pfeiffer, Shelton—Monica Guglielmina; Miss Donohue—Marilyn Pfeiffer.

Directed by Austin Pendleton; scenery, Patricia Woodbridge; costumes, James Barton Harris; lighting, Cheryl Thacker; production stage manager, Peggy Peterson; press, Howard Atlee, Becky Flora.

Time: April 1911. Place: A cell and courtroom in Solon, Mich. The play was presented in two parts.

A priest is tried for the murder of a nun under his supervision, in a drama of loneliness and commitment based on an actual case history. Previously produced by the Hartman Theater, Stamford, Conn., the Manhattan Theater Club and others.

A Best Play; see page 263

* **Something's Afoot** (5). Musical with book, music and lyrics by James McDonald, David Vos and Robert Gerlach; additional music by Ed Linderman. Produced by Emanuel Azenberg, Dasha Epstein and John Mason Kirby at the Lyceum Theater. Opened May 27, 1976.

Lettie	Neva Small	Nigel Rancour	Gary Beach
Flint	Marc Jordan	Lady Grace Manley-Prowe	Liz Sheridan
Clive	Sel Vitella	Col. Gillweather	Gary Gage
Hope Langdon	Barbara Heuman	Miss Tweed	Tessie O'Shea
Dr. Grayburn	Jack Schmidt	Geoffrey	Willard Beckham

Standbys: Misses O'Shea, Sheridan—Lu Leonard; Messrs. Gage, Schmidt, Jordan, Vitella—Bryan Hull; Messrs. Beach, Beckham—Sal Mistretta; Misses Heuman, Small—Meg Bussert.

Directed and choreographed by Tony Tanner; musical direction, Buster Davis; scenery, Richard Seger; costumes, Walter Watson, Clifford Capone; lighting, Richard Winkler; orchestrations, Peter M. Larson; production stage manager, Robert V. Straus; stage manager, Marilyn Wilt; press, The Merlin Group, Ltd., Sandra Manley, Harriett Trachtenberg.

Time: Late spring, 1935. Place: Rancour's Retreat—a country estate in the English lake district. Act I: The entrance hall of Rancour's Retreat. Act II: The same, immediately following.

A group of ten house guests and servants marooned on an island estate is threatened with murder one by one, in the manner of Agatha Christie's *Ten Little Indians* converted into a musical farce. Previously produced at Goodspeed Opera House, East Haddam, Conn. and elsewhere in regional theater.

MUSICAL NUMBERS—Act I: "A Marvelous Weekend," "Something's Afoot," "Carry On," "I Don't Know Why I Trust You (But I Do)," "The Man With the Ginger Moustache," "Suspicious." Act II: "The Legal Heir," "You Fell Out of the Sky," "Dinghy," "I Owe It All," "New Day."

PLAYS WHICH CLOSED
PRIOR TO BROADWAY OPENING

Plays which were organized by New York producers for Broadway presentation, but which closed during their tryout performances, are listed below.

The Red Devil Battery Sign. By Tennessee Williams. Produced by David Merrick, Doris Cole Abrahams and Robert Colby in a pre-Broadway tour at the Shubert Theater, Boston. Opened June 18, 1975. (Closed June 28, 1975)

Woman Downtown ....Claire Bloom	La Nina ....Annette Cardona
Man at the Bar;	Perla ....Katy Jurado
1st Policeman ....Pat Corley	McCabe ....Stephen McHattie
Charlie; 2d Policeman ....John Ramsey	Drummer ....Alfred Karl
King Del Rey ....Anthony Quinn	Hotel Manager ....Tom Noel
Julio ....Frank C. Martinez	Pharmacist ....Will Hussung

The King's Men: Agustin Bustamente, Paul Cohen, Juan De Sanctis, Dick Dia, Ford Harrison, Paul La Tirenta, Frank C. Martinez, Emilio Prados, Sal Rainone.

Directed by Edwin Sherin; scenery, Robin Wagner; costumes, Ruth Wagner; lighting, Marilyn Rennagel; music, Sidney Lippman; musical arrangements and supervision, Horace Diaz, Robert Colby; production stage manager, Marnel Sumner; stage manager, Eugene Stuckman; press, Solters/Roskin, Inc., Stanley F. Kaminsky.

Time: Shortly after the John F. Kennedy assassination. Place: Dallas. Act I, Scene 1: The cocktail lounge of the Yellow Rose Hotel. Scene 2: The penthouse bedroom. Scene 3: The penthouse bedroom, a while later. Scene 4: King's house in Crestview and a bedroom in Chicago. Scene 5: The Chicago bedroom. Scene 6: The cocktail lounge of the Yellow Rose Hotel, a month later. Scene 7: The penthouse bedroom. Scene 8: The penthouse bedroom. Act II, Scene 1: King's house, the cocktail lounge and a drugstore. Scene 2: The drugstore and an unspecified place near Crestview, some time later.

Drama of a bandleader, his family and associates in the sickened atmosphere following the assassination in Dallas.

The Soft Touch. By Neil Cuthbert. Produced by Gene Persson with Samuel J. Schwartz, Ted Chapin and Pangloss Productions in a pre-Broadway tryout at the Wilbur Theater, Boston. Opened September 1, 1975. (Closed September 13, 1975)

Wilfred ....Bob Harper	Harry Crisp ....Richard Libertini
Mom ....Ruth Jaroslow	Beatrice Crisp ....Jo Anne Meredith
Harvey ....Joshua Mostel	Landlord ....Michael Granger
Blinkey ....Lenny Baker	Emile ....Robert Lesser

Directed by Alan Arkin; scenery, Kert Lundell; costumes, Albert Wolsky; lighting, Roger Morgan; press, Arthur Rubine, Ted Goldstein.

Comedy about the tribulations of a young man in the big city. The 1974 American Theater Association playwrighting award winner, previously produced in Washington, D.C.

Truckload. Musical with book by Hugh Wheeler, music by Louis St. Louis, lyrics by Wes Harris. Produced by Adela Holzer, The Shubert Organization, Inc. and Dick Clark at the Lyceum Theater. Opened September 6, 1975. (Closed September 11, 1975)

Driver ....Louis St. Louis	Leon ....Doug McKeon
Heustis ....Kelly Ward	Lee Wu ....Kenneth S. Eiland
Bonnie ....Ilene Graff	Whitfield ....Ralph Strait
Horace ....Donny Burks	Rosa ....Deborah Allen
Amelia ....Laurie Prange	Ricardo ....José Fernández
Glory ....Cheryl Barnes	Carlos ....René Enriquez
Darleen ....Sherry Mathis	

The All Nite Drivers: Richard Weinstock keyboards, Jimmy Young drums, Steve Mack bass, Dickie Frank and Jack Cavari guitars, Luther Rix Latin percussion.

Directed and choreographed by Patricia Birch; scenery, Douglas W. Schmidt; costumes, Carrie F. Robbins; lighting, John Gleason; sound design, Robert Minor; orchestrations, Michael Gibson, Bhen Lanzaroni; vocal arrangements, Flamin' Mama Music, Carl Hall; assistant to director, James Dybas; Spanish translation, Roberto Fernandez; production stage manager, T. Schuyler Smith; stage managers, William H. Batchelder, Lani Sundsten; press, Betty Lee Hunt Associates, Maria Cristina Pucci, Bill Evans, Maurice Turet.

Time: Last night. Place: Any open road. The play was presented without intermission.

About hitch-hiking across the country on trucks.

MUSICAL NUMBERS

The Highway
"Truckload" ....Driver, Company
"Find My Way Home" ....Glory, Driver, Company
The Come On Inn
Cumbia/Wedding Party ....Rosa, Carlos, Ricardo, Company
"Step-Mama" ....Darleen, Heustis, Company
"Look at Us" ....Rosa, Ricardo
"Standing in This Phonebooth" ....Mr. Whitfield
All Night Driving
"Amelia's Theme" ....Amelia
"I Guess Everything Will Turn Out All Right" ....Heustis, Mr. Whitfield, Company
"Rest Stop" ....Darleen, Driver
Plaza Truck Stop
"Boogie Woogie Man" ....Horace, Lee Wu, Bonnie, Darleen, Heustis
"Ricardo's Lament" ....Ricardo, Rosa, Carlos
"Hash House Habit" ....Lee Wu
"Dragon Strikes Back" ....Lee Wu, Company
"Bonnie's Song" ....Bonnie
"Pour Out Your Soul" ....Glory, Company
"Jesus Is My Main Man" ....Glory, Company
"There's Nothing Like Music" ....Driver
"Hello Sunshine" ....Driver, Company
"Truckload" (Reprise) ....Company

An Evening With Romberg. Revue of musical numbers by Sigmund Romberg. Produced by Contemporary Artists Management in a pre-Broadway tryout. Opened at Orrie De Nooyer Auditorium, Hackensack, N.J., October 5, 1976. (Closed at Fulton Opera House, Lancaster, Pa., October 25, 1976)

With Allan Jones, J. Edward Adams. Gary Barker, Joan B. Duffin, Gary Reese Holcombe, Gail Malmuth, Kevin Marcum, Donna Monroe, Jacqueline Rohrbacker, Dean Russell, Melanie Vaughan.

Directed by Jeffrey B. Moss; musical direction, Peter Michael Sozio; press, Max Eisen, Carl Samrock.

Nostalgic collection of numbers from the works of Sigmund Romberg.

Souvenir. By George Axelrod and Peter Viertel. Produced by Arthur Cantor and E.E. Fogelson in association with Eric Friedheim in a pre-Broadway tryout at the Shubert Theater in Los Angeles. Opened October 29, 1975. (Closed November 9, 1975)

Julie's Stand-in	Jillian Lindig	William Swanson	Edmund Lyndeck
Jack's Stand-in	Bryce Holman	Ben	Laurence Hugo
Fritz Tauber	John Carpenter	Larry Stevens	Reno Roop
Mark Sanders	Tony Musante	Edith	Emmy Nance Grise
Assistant Director	Joseph Hill	French Bellboy	Gary Farr
Camera Operator	Bruce Brighton	Italian Bellboy	John Michalski
Jack Robson	Edward Easton	Guy Holstein	Arthur Ed Forman
Eunice Blaustein	Donna Isaacson	Rick Townsend	Art Burns
Julie Stevens	Deborah Kerr		

Directed by Gerald Freedman; scenery, William Pitkin; costumes, Theoni V. Aldredge; lighting, Martin Aronstein; sound sequences, Pia Gilbert; production manager, Mitchell Erickson; stage manager, Charles Kindl; press, Stanley F. Kaminksy, C. George Willard.

Time: The present. Place: Hollywood. Act I: A Wednesday afternoon. Act II: Three weeks later.

Romantic comedy about a movie star's love affair with a younger man.

Together Tonight by Norman Corwin. Produced by Gordon Crowe in cooperation with the Open View Society in a pre-Broadway tryout. Opened February 9, 1976 at the Hanna Theater, Cleveland. (Closed at the Walnut Street Theater, Philadelphia, May 2, 1976)

John Lenox	Alan Manson	Alexander Hamilton	Howard Duff
Aaron Burr	Monte Markham	Thomas Jefferson	Dana Andrews

Directed by Norman Corwin; scenery and lighting, C. Murawski; press, Bill Watters.
Discussion in a town-hall framework of the political peccadillos of the election of 1800.

Me Jack, You Jill by Robes Kossez. Produced by Adela Holzer in previews at the John Golden Theater. Opened March 2, 1976. (Closed March 16, 1976)

Bibi	Lisa Kirk	Tessie	Sylvia Sidney
Annie	Barbara Baxley	Young Man	Russ Thacker

Directed by Harold J. Kennedy; scenery and costumes, Lawrence King, Michael H. Yeargan; lighting, Jane Reisman; special effects, Ronald Vitelli, Neil Schazt; production stage manager, Tom Porter; press, Michael Alpert, Marilynn LeVine, Joshua Ellis, Warren Knowlton.
Time: The present. Place: The empty stage of a Broadway theater. Act I: Afternoon. Act II, Scene 1: Immediately after. Scene 2: A few minutes later.
Family happenings during a lunch catered by Sardi's on the stage of a theater.

Weekend With Feathers by Romeo Muller. Produced by Don Saxon, Don Kaufman and Lesley Savage in a pre-Broadway tryout. Opened April 12, 1976 at the Shubert Theater, New Haven, Conn. (Closed April 24, 1976 at the Playhouse, Wilmington, Del.)

Bellhop	Nick Malekos	Sparky	Robert R. Kaye
Millie Burroughs	Cara Duff-MacCormick	Mr. Warhold	Truman Gaige
Danny Stone	Donald O'Connor	Mary Jones	Lee Meredith
Maid	Gloria Irizarry		

Directed by Morton Da Costa; scenery, James Hamilton; costumes, Gloria Gresham; lighting, Thomas Skelton; press, Marvin Cohn.
Farce about a mid-Western widower and a call girl.

PLAYS PRODUCED
OFF BROADWAY

Some distinctions between off-Broadway and Broadway productions at one end of the scale and off-off-Broadway productions at the other were blurred in the New York theater of the 1970s. For the purposes of this *Best Plays* listing the term "off Broadway" is used to distinguish a professional from a showcase (off off Broadway) production and signifies a show which opened for general audiences in a mid-Manhattan theater seating 299 or fewer during the time period covered by this volume and 1) employed an Equity cast, 2) planned a regular schedule of 7 or 8 performances a week and 3) offered itself to public comment by critics at designated opening performances.

Occasional exceptions of inclusion (never of exclusion) are made to take in selected Brooklyn productions, visiting troupes, borderline cases and a few non-qualifying productions which readers might expect to find in this list because they appear under an off-Broadway heading in other major sources of record.

Figures in parentheses following a play's title indicate number of performances. These figures are acquired directly from the production office in each case and do not include previews or extra non-profit performances.

Plays marked with an asterisk (*) were still running on June 1, 1976. Their number of performances is figured from opening night through May 31, 1976.

In a listing of a show's numbers—dances, sketches, musical scenes, etc.— the titles of songs are identified by their appearance in quotation marks (").

Most entries of off-Broadway productions which ran fewer than 20 performances are somewhat abbreviated.

HOLDOVERS FROM PREVIOUS SEASONS

Plays which were running on June 1, 1975 are listed below. More detailed information about them appears in previous *Best Plays* volumes of appropriate years. Important cast changes since opening night are recorded in a section of this volume.

* **The Fantasticks** (6,699; longest continuous run of record in the American theater). Musical suggested by the play *Les Romantiques* by Edmond Rostand; book and lyrics by Tom Jones; music by Harvey Schmidt. Opened May 3, 1960.

* **Godspell** (2,100). Musical based on the Gospel according to St. Matthew; conceived by John-Michael Tebelak; music and lyrics by Stephen Schwartz. Opened May 17, 1971.

The Hot l Baltimore (1,166). By Lanford Wilson. Opened March 22, 1973. (Closed January 4, 1976)

* Let My People Come (1,122). Musical revue with music and lyrics by Earl Wilson Jr. Opened January 8, 1974.

Diamond Studs (232). Musical based on the life of Jesse James; book by Jim Wann; music and lyrics by Bland Simpson and Jim Wann. Opened January 14, 1975. (Closed August 3, 1975)

The National Lampoon Show (180). Cabaret revue with words and lyrics by the cast, overlooked by Sean Kelly; music by Paul Jacobs. Opened March 2, 1975. (Closed July 6, 1975)

Be Kind to People Week (100). Musical with book, music and lyrics by Jack Bussins and Ellsworth Olin. Opened March 23, 1975. (Closed June 29, 1975)

A Chorus Line (101). Musical conceived by Michael Bennett; book by James Kirkwood and Nicholas Dante; music by Marvin Hamlisch; lyrics by Edward Kleban. Opened April 15, 1975. (Closed July 13, 1975 and transferred to Broadway; see its entry in the "Plays Produced on Broadway" section of this volume)

Bluebeard (53). By Charles Ludlam. Opened April 18, 1975. (Closed June 29, 1975)

Women Behind Bars (54). By Tom Eyen. Opened May 1, 1975. (Closed June 15, 1975)

The Taking of Miss Janie (42). By Ed Bullins. Opened May 4, 1975. (Closed June 15, 1975)

Rubbers and **Yanks 3 Detroit 0 Top of the Seventh** (145). Program of one-act plays by Jonathan Reynolds. Opened May 16, 1975. (Closed September 21, 1975)

Waiting for Mongo (33). By Silas Jones. Opened May 18, 1975. (Closed June 15, 1975)

What Every Woman Knows (71). Revival of the play by James M. Barrie. Opened May 28, 1975. (Closed July 27, 1975)

PLAYS PRODUCED JUNE 1, 1975—MAY 31, 1976

New York Shakespeare Festival. Summer schedule of outdoor programs of two revivals of plays by William Shakespeare. **Hamlet** (28). Opened June 18, 1975; see note. (Closed July 19, 1975) **The Comedy of Errors** (28). Opened July 24, 1975; see note. Closed August 24, 1975. Produced by New York Shakespeare Festival, Joseph Papp producer, at the Delacorte Theater in Central Park.

BOTH PLAYS—Associate producer, Bernard Gersten; scenery, Santo Loquasto; lighting, Martin Aronstein; produced in cooperation with City of New York, Hon. Abraham D. Beame mayor, Hon. Edwin L. Weisl administrator of parks; press, Merle Debuskey, Bob Ullman, Norman L. Berman.

HAMLET

Claudius ....Robert Burr	Horatio ....James Cahill
Gertrude ....Ruby Dee	Voltemand ....James Gallery
Hamlet; Ghost ....Sam Waterston	Rosencrantz;
Polonius; 1st Gravedigger .....Larry Gates	2nd Gravedigger ....Douglas Stender
Laertes; Player King ....John Lithgow	Guildenstern; Priest ....John Heard
Ophelia ....Andrea Marcovicci	Marcellus; Dumb Show King ..Mark Metcalf

Francisco ....Richard Brestoff
Reynaldo ....Bruce McGill
Fortinbras; Player Queen ....Franklin Seales
Capt. to Fortinbras;
    Dumb Show Queen ...Hannibal Penney Jr.

Murderer; Dumb Show
    Murderer ....Ralph Byers
Prologue ....Stephen Lang
Company Manager ....Vance Mizelle
Technical Director ....Ernest Austin
Apprentice Actor ....Nancy Campbell

Military Aides to the King: Richard Brestoff, Graham Beckel, Ray Munro, Cleveland O'Neal III, John Rowe. Stagehands: Michael Cutt, Reggie Johnson, Jack R. Marks, Ken Marshall, Peter Van Norden.

Understudies: Mr. Penney—Graham Beckel; Mr. Lithgow—Mark Metcalf, Richard Brestoff; Miss Marcovicci—Nancy Campbell; Mr. Stender—Michael Cutt, Stephen Lang; Mr. Burr—Erik Fredricksen; Mr. Gates—James Gallery; Mr. Waterston—John Heard; Mr. Cahill—Reggie Johnson; Mr. Metcalf—Ken Marshall; Mr. McGill—Ray Munro; Mr. Gallery—Peter Van Norden.

Directed by Michael Rudman; costumes, Albert Wolsky; fight sequences, Erik Fredricksen; percussion score, Herbert Harris; Danish anthem, Norman L. Berman.

The play was presented in two parts. This production of *Hamlet* was transferred to Broadway at the Vivian Beaumont Theater (see its entry in the "Plays Produced on Broadway" section of this volume). The most recent New York *Hamlet* was the New York Shakespeare Festival's at the Delacorte 6/20/72 for 21 performances with Stacy Keach in the title role.

THE COMEDY OF ERRORS

Bodyguard #1 ....Ted Danson
Bodyguard #2 ....Peter Iacangelo
Egeon ....Leonardo Cimino
Solinus ....John Seitz
Merchants ....Laurie Faso, Paul Kreppel
Antipholus of Syracuse ....Don Scardino
Dromio of Syracuse ....Michael Tucker
Dromio of Ephesus ....Larry Block
Adriana ....June Gable

Luciana ....Blair Brown
Antipholus of
    Ephesus ....John Christopher Jones
Balthazar ....Danny DeVito
Luce ....Susan Peretz
Angelo ....Pierre Epstein
Courtesan ....Linda Lavin
Dr. Pinch ....Jeffrey Jones
Emilia ....Anita Dangler

Townspeople, Vendors, Prostitutes, etc.: Maggie Askew, Roxanne Hart, Terri King, Charles McCaughan, Thom McCleister, Harlan Schneider, Kas Self.

Musicians: Peter Phillips conductor, tack piano, concertina, trombone, organ; Henry Jaramillo drums, percussion, vibes; Richard Meldonian flute, clarinet, saxophone; Max Ellen violin; Austin Wallace string bass, tuba.

Understudies: Misses Lavin, Dangler—Maggie Askew; Mr. Jones—Ted Danson; Mr. Seitz—Danny DeVito; Mr. Cimino—Pierre Epstein; Mr. Epstein—Laurie Faso; Miss Brown—Roxanne Hart; Mr. DeVito—Peter Iacangelo; Miss Peretz—Terri King; Mr. Danson—Paul Kreppel; Messrs. Jones, Scardino—Charles McCaughan; Mr. Iacangelo—Thom McCleister; Messrs. Tucker, Block—Harlan Schneider; Miss Gable—Kas Self.

Directed by John Pasquin; music, Peter Link; costumes, Santo Loquasto; choreography, Elizabeth Keen; production stage manager, Richard S. Viola; stage manager, Peter Von Mayrhauser.

The play was presented without intermission. *The Comedy of Errors* was last produced in New York by New York Shakespeare Festival in Central Park 6/7/67 for 22 performances.

NOTE: In this volume, certain programs of off-Broadway companies like New York Shakespeare Festival in Central Park are exceptions to our rule of counting the number of performances from the date of the press coverage. When the official opening night takes place late in the run of a play's public or subscription performances (after previews) we count the first performance of record, not the press date, as opening night. Press date for *Hamlet* was 6/24/75; for *The Comedy of Errors* 8/7/75.

Roundabout Theater Company. Schedule of four programs. **Summer and Smoke** (64). Revival of the play by Tennessee Williams. Opened September 16, 1975; see note. (Closed November 9, 1975) **Dear Mr. G.** (46). By Donna de Matteo. Opened November 25, 1975; see note. (Closed January 4, 1976) **Clarence** (64). Revival of the play by Booth Tarkington. Opened December 23, 1975; see note. (Closed February 15, 1976) **The Cherry Orchard** (56). Revival of the play by Anton Chekhov. Opened April 2, 1976; see note. (Closed May 23, 1976) And *The*

World of Sholom Aleichem, revival of the play by Arnold Perl based on the writings of Sholom Aleichem, scheduled to open 6/11/76. Produced by Roundabout Theater Company, Gene Feist producing director, Michael Fried executive producer. Name of this organization was changed to Roundabout Theater Center at beginning of 1976-77 season.

SUMMER AND SMOKE

Mrs. Winemiller .... Sara Lou Cooper	Roger Doremus .... William Newman
Rev. Winemiller .... Wyman Pendleton	Dr. John Buchanan Sr. ...... Edward Holmes
Alma Winemiller .... Debra Mooney	Mrs. Bassett .... Eda Reiss Merin
Dr. John Buchanan Jr. ...... Michael Storm	Rosemary .... Nancy Donovan
Rosa Gonzales .... Livia Genise	Dusty .... Lewis Mead
Nellie Ewell .... Robin Pearson Rose	Gonzales .... John Seitz
Chloe .... Katharine Stanton	Archie Kramer .... Howard Schechter

Directed by Gene Feist; scenery, Holmes Easley; costumes, Christina Giannini; lighting, Ian Calderon; sound, T. Richard Fitzgerald; score, Philip Campanella; angel sculpture, Debra Schechter; production stage manager, Douglas F. Goodman; press, Gerald Siegal, Valerie Warner.

Time: The turn of the century. Plcae: Glorious Hill, Miss. Part I: Summer. Part II: Winter.

Summer and Smoke was first produced on Broadway 10/6/48 for 100 performances. It was revived off Broadway in the 1951-52 season.

DEAR MR. G.

Tommy Giordano .... Anthony Ponzini	Roscoe Nigera .... Frank Nastasi
Marlene Giordano .... Karen Leslie	Carmella Giordano .... Mildred Clinton
Louis Polaski .... Chip Zien	

Directed by Gene Feist; produced with McGraw-Lyttle Productions, Inc.; scenery, Holmes Easley; costumes, Christina Giannini; lighting, Dan Koetting; lighting supervision, Ian Calderon; production stage manager, J.R. Grant.

Time: The present. Place: The home of Mr. and Mrs. Thomas Giordano in a suburban town in Queens. Act I: Early morning. Act II: Immediately following.

A Queens mafia boss viewed in the context of a family situation comedy. Previously produced by HB Playwrights Foundation Workshop Series.

CLARENCE

Mrs. Martyn .... Lorraine Spritzer	Violet Pinney .... Marian Clarke
Mr. Wheeler .... Sonny Fox	Clarence .... Stephen Keep
Mrs. Wheeler .... Barbara Britton	Della .... Carolyn Lagerfelt
Bobby Wheeler .... Sam McMurray	Dinwiddie .... John Neville-Andrews
Cora Wheeler .... Nancy Addison	Hubert Stem .... Anthony McKay

Directed by Gene Feist; scenery, Holmes Easley; costumes, Christina Giannini; lighting, Ian Calderon; musical supervision, Philip Campanella; production stage manager, Douglas F. Goodman.

Time: 1919. Act I: The anteroom to Mr. Wheeler's private office in New York, an autumn morning. Act II: Living room of Mr. Wheeler's home in Englewood, N.J., afternoon, three weeks later. Act III: the same, that evening. Act IV: The same, next morning. The play was presented in three parts.

Clarence was first produced on Broadway 9/20/19 and was named a Best Play of its season. This is its first professional New York revival of record.

THE CHERRY ORCHARD

Lopahin .... Paul Benedict	Gaev .... William Roerick
Dunyasha .... Regina Baff	Pishtchik .... Kurt Knudson
Epidohov .... Roy K. Stevens	Yasha .... Christopher Curry
Firs .... Fred Stuthman	Trofimov .... Stephen Keep
Mme. Ranevskaya .... Kim Hunter	Wayfarer .... Michael Kolba
Anya .... Patricia Conwell	Station Master .... Paul Pape
Varya .... Verna Bloom	Post Office Clerk .... Mark Blum
Charlotta .... Sudie Bond	

Directed by Robert Mandel; scenery, Holmes Easley; costumes, Christina Giannini; lighting, Arden Fingerhut; dances, Penny Stahlnecker; music, Robert Dennis; production stage manager, Douglas F. Goodman; press, David Guc.

Time: 1904. Place: The estate of Mme. Ranevskaya, Russia. Act I: Early morning in May. Act II: Late afternoon, June. Act III: Early evening, Aug. 22. Act IV: Morning, October. The play was presented in two parts with the intermission following Act II.

The Cherry Orchard was last revived in New York by New York Shakespeare Festival at the Public Theater, 12/7/72 for 86 performances.

The Roundabout's Stage One housed *Summer and Smoke, Clarence* and *The Cherry Orchard.* Stage Two housed *Dear Mr. G.* 1975-76 workshop programs at the Roundabout Theater appear under its heading in the "Plays Produced off off Broadway" section of this volume.

NOTE: In this volume, certain programs of off-Broadway companies like Roundabout Theater Company are exceptions to our rule of counting the number of performances from the date of the press coverage. When the official opening night takes place late in the run of a play's public or subscription performances (after previews) we count the first performance of record, not the press date, as opening night. Press date for *Summer and Smoke* was 10/6/75, for *Dear Mr. G.* 12/4/75, for *Clarence* 1/5/76, for *The Cherry Orchard* 4/25/76.

* **Boy Meets Boy** (295). Musical with book by Billy Solly and Donald Ward; music and lyrics by Billy Solly. Produced by Edith O'Hara in association with Lee Barton and Christopher Larkin at the Actors Playhouse. Opened September 17, 1975.

Casey O'Brien	Joe Barrett	Bruce	Bobby Reed
Andrew	Paul Ratkevich	Head Waiter	Gene Borio
Guy Rose	David Gallegly	Asst. Hotel Manager; Porter	Richard King
Bellboy; Alphonse	Bobby Bowen	Rosita	Kathy Willinger
Clarence Cutler	Raymond Wood	Lolita	Mary-Ellen Hanlon
Lady Rose; Josephine		Pepita	Jan Crean
La Rosa	Rita Gordon	Jane	Monica Grignon

Reporters: Richard King, Bobby Reed, Dan Rounds. Photographers: Jan Crean, Monica Grignon. The Van Wagners: Bobby Bowen, Kathy Willinger.

Dylan Hartman electric keyboards; Jim Fradrich piano.

Directed by Ron Troutman; musical numbers staged by Robin Reseen; musical direction and vocal arrangements, David Friedman; scenery and lighting, David Sackeroff; costumes, Sherry Buchs; music and dance arrangements, James Fradrich; production stage manager, Gene Borio; press, Sol Jacobson, Lewis Harmon.

Time: December 1936. Place: London and Paris.

An American foreign correspondent and an English nobleman find each other.

ACT I

Opening	Boys and Girls
"Boy Meets Boy," "Party in Room 203"	
"Giving It Up for Love"	Casey, Andrew
"Me"	Clarence, Chorus
"The English Rose"	Reporters, Photographers
"Marry an American"	Girls and Boys
"It's a Boy's Life"	Casey, Guy
"Does Anybody Love You?"	Guy
"You're Beautiful"	Guy
"Let's"	Casey, Chorus
Dance	Casey, Guy
"Giving It Up for Love" (Reprise)	Casey
Finaletto	Clarence, Chorus

ACT II

"Just My Luck"	Casey, Clarence, Girls
"It's a Dolly"	Josephine, Boys, Girls
"What Do I Care?"	Guy
"Clarence's Turn"	Clarence
"Does Anybody Love You?" (Reprise)	Casey, Guy
Finale	Company

Classic Stage Company. Repertory of five programs. **Measure for Measure** (28). Revival of the play by William Shakespeare. Opened September 18, 1975. **Hedda Gabler** (48). Revival of the play by Henrik Ibsen; translated by William Archer. Opened September 20, 1975. **A Country Scandal** (28). Revival of the play by Anton Chekhov; translated by Alex Szogyi. Opened September 25, 1975. **Antigone** (40). Revival of the play by Jean Anouilh; based on the play by Sophocles; translated by Alex Szogyi. Opened December 9, 1975. **The Hound of the Baskervilles** (42). By Christopher Martin; adapted from the story by Arthur Conan Doyle. Opened March 14, 1976. (Repertory closed May 16, 1976) Produced by CSC Repertory Company, Christopher Martin director, William Glass managing director, Stuart Vaughan associate director, at the Abbey Theater.

PERFORMER	"MEASURE FOR MEASURE"	"HEDDA GABLER"	"A COUNTRY SCANDAL"	"ANTIGONE"
Lisa Carling	Sister; Mariana	Thea Elvsted	Sofia	Ismene
Edward Cicciarelli	Angelo		Dr. Triletski	
Deborah Dennison	Juliet	Juliana Tesman	Maria	Eurydice
Tom Donaldson	Provost	George Tesman	Platonov	
John Fitzgibbon	Claudio		Markov	
Carol Flemming				Nurse
Edward S. Gero	1st Soldier; Barnadine		Yakov	
Sheila Grenham	Mistress Over-Done; Kate Keepdown	Berta	Sacha	
Christopher Martin	The Duke	Judge Brack	Ossip	Creon
Ronald Perlman	Lucio	Lovborg	Vengerovich	
Jose Rodriguez				Haemon
Noble Shropshire				Messenger
Karen Sunde	Isabella	Hedda	Anna	Antigone
Alberto Tore	2d Soldier; Froth; Abhorson		Petrin	Jonas
Earl Trussell	Friar; Elbow		Voinitzev	Chorus
Debora Valle			Katya	
Peter Van Norden	Escalus		Glagolaev	Durand
Wayne Wofford	Pompey		Kiryl	Boudousse

THE HOUND OF THE BASKERVILLES

Sherlock Holmes ....Tom Donaldson
Doctor John H. Watson ...Peter Van Norden
Mrs. Hudson ....Carol Flemming
Dr. James Mortimer ....Earl Trussell
Sir Henry Baskerville ....Wayne Wofford
Wiggins ....Deborah Dennison
John Clayton;
    Jack Stapleton ....Noble Shropshire

(Barrymore) ....Jose Rodriguez, Christopher Martin
Mrs. Barrymore ....Karen Sunde
Perkins ....Sam Blackwell
Beryl Stapleton ....Lisa Carling
(Frankland) ....Christopher Martin, Sam Blackwell
Mrs. Laura Lyons ....Deborah Dennison
Inspector Lestrade.............Alberto Tore

(Parentheses indicate role in which the performers alternated)

MEASURE FOR MEASURE—Directed by Christopher Martin; scenery, Clay Coyle; costumes, Kristina Watson; lighting, Joel Grynheim; sound, Joel Grynheim; stage manager, Victor Gelb; press, Sharon Block.

The play was presented in two parts. *Measure for Measure* was last revived by City Acting Company 12/26/73 for 7 performances.

HEDDA GABLER—Directed by Christopher Martin; scenery, Clay Coyle; costumes, Donna Meyer; lighting, Joel Grynheim; sound, Joel Grynheim; stage manager, John Shannon.

The play was presented in two parts. Hedda Gabler was last revived on Broadway in a Christopher Hampton adaptation 2/17/71 for 56 performances.

A COUNTRY SCANDAL—Directed by Stuart Vaughan; scenery, Clay Coyle; costumes, Donna Meyer; lighting Joel Grynheim; sound, Joel Grynheim; stage manager, Victor Gelb.

The only professional New York revival of record of Chekhov's *A Country Scandal* was off Broadway at the Greenwich Mews in this Szogyi translation 5/5/60.

ANTIGONE—Directed by Christopher Martin; assistant director, Rene Buch; design, Christopher Martin; stage manager, John Shannon.

This production of *Antigone* was performed on a bare stage in rehearsal costume. The Anouilh play was first produced on Broadway 2/18/46 for 64 performances in the Lewis Galantière adaptation and was named a Best Play of its season.

THE HOUND OF THE BASKERVILLES—Directed by Christopher Martin; design, Christopher Martin; costumes, Linda Shannon; stage manager, John Shannon.

The play was presented in two parts. This adaptation of the story "is all but exclusively the words of Conan Doyle," derived from *Hound* and other stories.

Classic Stage Company also produced the following programs in previews but did not open them in 1975-76 repertory: *School for Buffoons* by Michel de Ghelderode, translated by Kenneth S. White, and *Escurial* by Michel de Ghelderode, translated by George Hauger, directed by Christopher Martin, 10/25/75-1/4/76; *Tartuffe* by Molière, directed by Christopher Martin, 1/10/76-3/7/76; *The Homecoming* by Harold Pinter 3/6/76-5/16/76; *La Celestina* (or The Old Whore) by Fernando de Rojas 3/21/76-5/16/76.

Finn MacKool, the Grand Distraction (1). By Frank Hogan. Produced by Rudi Golyn and Lee D. Sankowich at the Theater de Lys. Opened and closed at the evening performance September 29, 1975.

Directed by Lee D. Sankowich; scenery, David Chapman; costumes, Jane Greenwood; lighting, Richard Nelson; sound, Abe Jacob; visual projections, Jack Coddington; production stage manager, Paul Bennett; press, Howard Atlee, Clarence Allsopp. With Michael J. Hume, Valerie French, Eulalie Noble, Peter MacLean, Patti Walker, William Hickey.

A tragic Irish-American political family in parallels suggestive of the Kennedys.

The Collected Works of Billy the Kid (10). By Michael Ondaatje; music by Alan Laing; lyrics by Michael Ondaatje. Produced by the Canadian Department of External Affairs and the Canada Council Touring Office in association with the Brooklyn Academy of Music in the Neptune Theater Company of Nova Scotia production at The Lepercq Space of the Brooklyn Academy of Music. Opened October 13, 1975. (Closed October 19, 1975)

Billy the Kid (William Bonney) . .	Neil Munro	Manuela Bowdre	Suzanne Ristic
Charlie Bowdre	John Sweeney	Sallie Chisum	Carole Galloway
Tom O'Folliard	P.M. Howard	John Chisum	David Renton
Angela Dickinson	Patricia Collins	Pat Garrett	Ivar Brogger

Musicians: Alan Laing harmonicas, piano, vibes, organ; David Mazurek violin; Dean Meredith guitars; David Morgan banjo, guitar; Arthur Lang bass, electronic bass; John Bird recorder, autoharp, percussion; taped segments, Alan Laing; technical assistance, Roger Gaskell.

Directed by John Wood; design, John Ferguson; lighting design for original production, Gil Weschler, interpreted for this production by Robert A. Elliott; stage manager, Catherine McKeehan; press, Kate MacIntyre, Deborah Ann Williams

Time: The last few years of William Bonney's life. Place: The Southwest, particularly West Texas and New Mexico. Act I: Professional secrets. Act II: In rude state.

Homespun version of the Billy the Kid story with a background of folk music, originally, written as a poem and subsequently adapted by its author into a play. A foreign play previously produced in Canada.

Christy (40). Musical based on John Millington Synge's *The Playboy of the Western World;* book and lyrics by Bernie Spiro; music by Lawrence J. Blank. Produced by Joseph Lillis in association with Joan Spiro at the Bert Wheeler Theater. Opened October 14, 1975. (Closed November 16, 1975)

Pegeen Flaherty	Betty Forsyth	Philly Cullen	Brian Pizer
Widow Quin	Bea Swanson	Sara Malone	Martha T. Kearns
Shawn Keogh	John Canary	Susan Brady	Lynn Kearney
Michael James Flaherty . .	Alexander Sokoloff	Maggie Tansey	Marie Ginnetti
Old Mahon	Bruce Levitt	Honor Blake	Bebe Sacks Landis
Jimmy Farrell	Bill Hedge		

Directed by Peter David Heth; musical direction, vocal arrangements and incidental music, Robert Billig; lighting, Marc Surver; choreography, Jack Estes; design, Peter David Heth; production stage manager, Amy Schecter; press, John Ross.

Synge's *Playboy* was last revived by the Repertory Theater of Lincoln Center 1/7/71 for 52 performances.

ACT I

"Christy" ....Christy
"To Please the Woman in Me" ....Pegeen, Sara, Susie, Maggie, Honor
"To Please the Woman in Me" (Reprise) ....Pegeen
"Grain of the Salt of the Earth" ....Michael James, Jimmy, Philly, Pegeen, Christy
"Until the Likes of You" ....Christy, Pegeen
"Picture Me" ....Christy
"The Morning After" ....Pegeen
    (Music by Robert Billig)
"Rumors" ....Sara, Susan, Maggie, Honor, Widow Quin
"One Fell Swoop" ....Christy, Sara, Susan, Maggie, Honor, Widow Quin
"All's Fair" ....Widow Quin, Shawn
"Picture Me" (Reprise) ....Sara, Susan, Maggie, Honor, Widow Quin, Pegeen, Christy

ACT II

"The Heart's a Wonder" ....Pegeen, Christy
"Down the Hatch" ....Michael James, Jimmy, Philly, Widow Quin
"Gallant Little Swearers" ....Michael James, Pegeen, Christy, Ensemble
"Christy" (Reprise) ....Christy
"Until the Likes of You" (Reprise) ....Pegeen

* **New York Shakespeare Festival Public Theater.** Schedule of six programs. **Jesse and the Bandit Queen** (155). By David Freeman. Opened October 17, 1975; see note. (Closed February 29, 1976) **Rich & Famous** (78). By John Guare. Opened January 13, 1976; see note. (Closed April 25, 1976) **Apple Pie** (64). Musical with libretto by Myrna Lamb; music by Nicholas Meyers. Opened January 27, 1976; see note. (Closed March 21, 1976) * **So Nice, They Named it Twice** (31). By Neil Harris. Opened May 5, 1976; see note. * **For Colored Girls Who Have Considered Suicide/When the Rainbow Is Enuf** (16). By Ntozake Shange. Opened May 17, 1976; see note. * **Rebel Women** (40). By Thomas Babe. Opened May 6, 1976; see note. Produced by New York Shakespeare Festival, Joseph Papp producer, at the Public Theater.

ALL PLAYS—Associate producer, Bernard Gersten; director of play development, Gail Merrifield; press, Merle Debuskey, Bob Ullman, Bruce Cohen.

JESSE AND THE BANDIT QUEEN

Belle ....Pamela Payton-Wright   Jessie ....Kevin O'Connor

Standbys: Miss Payton-Wright—Laurie Heineman; Mr. O'Connor—Stephen Keep.

Directed by Gordon Stewart; scenery, Richard J. Graziano; costumes, Hilary M. Rosenfeld; lighting, Arden Fingerhut; production stage manager, Penny Gebhard.

Time: Just after the Civil War till the early 1880s. Place: Missouri, Kansas and the Indian Territories. The play was presented in two parts.

Fantasy intertwining the lives of Jesse James and Belle Starr and portraying America's love-fear relationship with some of its folk heroes. Previously produced in workshop at the Public Theater immediately prior to its off-Broadway run.

Dixie Carter replaced Pamela Payton-Wright 11/25/75. Barry Primus replaced Kevin O'Connor 12/30/75.

A Best Play; see page 105

RICH & FAMOUS

Cast: Bing Ringling—William Atherton; Dante Alighieri, Beatrice, Virgil, The Spirit of the Entire Divine Comedy, The People of the Inferno, Purgatorio and Paradisi, Black People, White

People, Straight People, Gay People, Actors, Actresses, Producers, Directors, Composers, Mothers, Fathers, Boy Friends, Girl Friends, Old Friends, New Friends, Failures, Fans, Stars— Ron Leibman, Anita Gillette.

Musicians: Herbert Kaplan conductor, organ; Morty Lewis saxophone, woodwinds; Aaron Bell bass.

Directed by Mel Shapiro; scenery, Dan Snyder; costumes, Theoni V. Aldredge; lighting, Arden Fingerhut; music and lyrics, John Guare; musical direction and arrangements, Herbert Kaplan; production stage manager, Peter Von Mayrhauser; stage manager, Jean Weigel.

Time: The opening night of Bing Ringling's first play. The play was presented without intermission.

The fantasy life of a playwright the night of his first opening.

APPLE PIE

Lise .... Stephanie Cotsirilos	Doctor .... Joseph Neal
The Mirror .... Ilsebet Anna Tebesli	Boss .... John Watson
Mother Marlene .... Lucille Patton	Marshall .... Robert Guillaume
Streicher .... Spain Logue	Harry; Father .... Lee Allen
American .... Robert Polenz	

Musicians: Bill Grossman keyboards, Brian Kunin guitar, Joel Kaye reeds, David Cox percussion, Ross Konikoff trumpet, Sam Burtis trombone, John Carbone bass.

Understudies: Messrs. Allen, Watson—Virgil Curry; Messrs. Logue, Neal, Polenz—Will Sharpe Marshall; Mr. Guillaume—Ra Joe Darby; Misses Cotsirilos, Patton, Tebesli—Dorothea Joyce.

Directed by Joseph Papp; musical direction, Liza Redfield; scenery, David Mitchell; costumes, Timothy Miller; lighting, Pat Collins; paintings, Richard Lindner; visuals, Thom Lafferty, David Mitchell; movement, Lynn Weber; production stage manager, Richard S. Viola; stage manager, Jane E. Neufeld.

The play was presented without intermission. Drama of a woman hounded out of Nazi Germany only to be degraded by American anti-feminist attitudes and actions.

Alan Weeks replaced Robert Guillaume 3/76.

MUSICAL NUMBERS

Overture: "Yesterday Is Over"	
"I'm Lise" .... Lise, Company
"Waltz of Lise's Childhood" .... Lise, Mirror, Company
"Father's Waltz" .... Father, Company
"Men Come With Guns" .... Lise, Company
"Hundsvieh" .... Lise, Company
"Mother's March" .... Mother Marlene, Company
"The Trial" .... Mother Marlene, Mirror, Company
"Marshall's Blues" .... Marshall
"The Counterman" .... Father, Harry
"America—We're in New York" .... Company
"The Victim Dream" .... Lise, Father, Harry
"The Stockboy Blues" .... Marshall, Lise
"The Too Much Motet" .... Mother Marlene, Company
"The Mating Dance" .... Harry, Lise
"Love Scene" .... Marshall, Lise
"The Doctor" .... Doctor, Lise, Mother Marlene, Mirror
"Lise Dear" .... Mother Marlene, Lise, Company
"The Wedding" .... Lise, American, Mother Marlene, Company
"Gun Scene" .... Marshall, Lise
"Harry's Rag" .... Harry, Company
"Freedom Anthem" .... Marshall, Lise, Company
"Reified Expression" .... Marshall, Henry
"Yesterday Is Over" .... Mother Marlene, Company
"Break-up Rag" .... Harry, Lise, Marshall
"Marshall's Reply" .... Marshall
"Survival Song" .... Lise
"Survival" (Reprise) .... Lise, Company
"Final Judgment" .... Company
"Yesterday Is Over" (Reprise) .... Company
"I'm Lise" (Reprise) .... Lise

SO NICE, THEY NAMED IT TWICE

Abe	Bill Jay	Henrietta	Starletta DuPois
Betty	Veronica Redd	Kitty	Robbie McCauley
Doris	Dianne Kirksey	Larry	Brent Jennings
Dr. Harris	Nick Smith	Lee	Taurean Blacque
Mrs. Jones	Joanna Featherstone	Terry	Alfre Woodard
Go-Go Dancer	Terrie Taylor	Miji	Allen Ayers
Reggie	Neil Harris	Country Bill	Hank Ross
Gunn	J.W. Smith		

Passers-by: War Hawk Tanzania, Nadyne Spratt, Hank Frazier.

Understudies: Messrs. Jay, Smith—Gerry Black; Messrs. Smith, Ayers, Ross—Hank Frazier; Misses McCauley, Woodard—Nadyne Spratt; Messrs. Harris, Blacque, Jennings—War Hawk Tanzania; Misses Kirksey, DuPois—Cheryl Jones; Misses Redd, Featherstone—Sundra Jean Williams.

Directed by Bill Lathan; scenery, lighting and visual format, Clarke Dunham; costumes, Mary Mease Warren; projections, Lucie Grosvenor; stage manager, Martha Knight.

Time: The present. Place: New York, New York. The play was presented in two parts.

Ironic comedy about black life in New York, New York.

FOR COLORED GIRLS WHO HAVE CONSIDERED
SUICIDE/WHEN THE RAINBOW IS ENUF

Lady in Rose	Janet League	Lady in Purple	Risë Collins
Lady in Yellow	Aku Kadago	Lady in Blue	Laurie Carlos
Lady in Red	Trazana Beverley	Lady in Orange	Ntozake Shange
Lady in Green	Paula Moss		

Directed by Oz Scott; choreography, Paul Moss; costumes, Judy Dearing; lighting, Victor En Yu Tan; mural, Ifa Iyaun; music for "I Found God in Myself," Diana Wharton; stage manager, John Beven.

Black woman's exploration of inner space in seven facets of herself with poetry, dance, stories. Previously produced by the Henry Street Settlement.

REBEL WOMEN

Tussie	Deloris Gaskins	3d Soldier; Civilian	David Dean
Katharine King	Deborah Offner	Maj. Robert Steele Strong	Mandy Patinkin
Mrs. Mary E. Law	Leora Dana	Dr. Samuel Sutler	John Glover
Mrs. Mary Law Roberts	Kathryn Walker	Gen. Sherman	David Dukes
1st Soldier	Eric Anthony Roberts	Lt. Henry Hitchcock	Peter Weller
2d Soldier	Mark Kologi	Soldiers	Ralph Byers, Tracey Walter

Directed by Jack Hofsiss; scenery, John Lee Beatty; costumes, Carrrie F. Robbins; lighting, Neil Peter Jampolis; lyrics, Barbara Bonfigli; music, Catherine MacDonald; production stage manager, Peter Von Mayrhauser; stage manager, Penny Gebhard.

Time: December 5-6, 1864. Place: The summer home of the Law family in Vidalia, Ga. Act I: Late afternoon. Act II: Evening of the same day. Act III: Dawn, the following day.

Three Southern women stand in opposition to Sherman's march to the sea.

A Best Play; see page 249

In Joseph Papp's Public Theater there are many separate auditoriums. *Jesse and the Bandit Queen* and *So Nice, They Named It Twice* played The Other Stage, *Rich & Famous* and *Rebel Women* played the Estelle R. Newman Theater, *Apple Pie* and *For Colored Girls*, etc. played the Florence S. Anspacher Theater.

NOTE: In this volume, certain programs of off-Broadway companies like New York Shakespeare Festival Public Theater are exceptions to our rule of counting the number of performances from the date of the press coverage. When the official opening takes place late in the run of a play's public or subscription performances (after previews) we count the first performance of record, not the press date, as opening night. Press date for *Jesse and the Bandit Queen* was 11/2/75, for *Rich & Famous* was 2/19/76, for *Apple Pie* was 2/12/76, for *So Nice They Named It Twice* was 5/26/76, for *For Colored Girls*, etc. was 6/1/76, for *Rebel Women* was 6/3/76.

The American Place Theater. Schedule of three programs. **Gorky** (44). By Steve Tesich; music by Mel Marvin; lyrics by Steve Tesich. Opened October 24, 1975; see note. (Closed November 30, 1975) **Every Night When the Sun Goes Down** (45). By Phillip Hayes Dean. Opened January 16, 1976. (Closed February 22, 1976) **The Old Glory.** Revival of **Endecott and the Red Cross** and **My Kinsman, Major Molineux** (41) and **Benito Cereno** (39) By Robert Lowell. Opened April 9, 1976; see note. (Closed May 23, 1976) Produced by The American Place Theater, Wynn Handman director, Julia Miles associate director, at The American Place Theater.

ALL PLAYS—Literary advisors, Joel Schechter, Cassandra Medley; press, David Roggensack.

GORKY

Gorky .... Philip Baker Hall	Gorky as a Young Man ...... Douglas Clark
Doctor; Gypsy; Mathew .... Richard Ramos	Peasant; Party Man .... J. Kevin Scannell
Grandma; Old Peasant Woman ... Lilia Skala	Chaliapin; Cement Man .... Monte Jaffe
Grandpa; Old Peasant Man .... Fyvush Finkel	Gavrillo .... Stuart Pankin
Gorky as a Boy .... John Gallogly	Peasant Woman .... Jacque Dean
Mother; Peasant's Wife;	Young Peasant Girl;
Electric Lady .... Tanny McDonald	Party Dancer .... Diane Duffy
Becky .... Caroline Kava	Young Peasant Man;
Priest; Nikita; Stalin .... Lloyd Battista	Party Dancer .... Robert Petersen

Understudy: Mr. Gallogly—Steve Deshler.

Directed by Dennis Rosa; scenery, David Jenkins; lighting, Roger Morgan; costumes, Shadow; orchestrations, Mel Marvin, Ken Guilmartin; production stage manager, Franklin Keysar; stage manager, Mary E. Baird.

Musicians: Stan Free conductor, accordion; Ian Finkel percussion, drums; Artie Kruger clarinet, flute; Ben Mortell guitar, mandolin; Denise Semenovich violin; Doug Shear bass.

Act I: Old Russia. Act II: Pre-revolution and into Soviet Union.

Maxim Gorky, on the eve of a surgical "operation" intended to kill him, looks back over his life, in a play with music.

EVERY NIGHT WHEN THE SUN GOES DOWN

Sneeky Pete .... Joe Seneca	Ballerina .... Marki Bey
Blood .... Frank Adu	Clean Sam .... Richard Ward
Caldonia .... Marge Eliot	Jericho .... Norman Matlock
Pretty Eddie .... Roscoe Orman	Cockeyed Rose .... Billie Allen

Directed by Gilbert Moses; scenery, Kert Lundell; costumes, Judy Dearing; lighting, Richard Nelson; sound, Jerry Kornbluth; instrumental musical arranged and adapted by Howard Roberts; hymns performed by the Metropolitan AME Church Choir; production stage manager, Franklin Keysar; stage manager, Mary E. Baird.

Time: The recent past. Place: Moloch, Michigan. The play was presented in two parts.

Barroom habitues are persuaded to reexamine their escapist lives and join forces for change and betterment.

Les Roberts replaced Richard Ward at many performances beginning the week of 2/9/76.

THE OLD GLORY

Endecott and the Red Cross

Assawamset .... Manu Tupou	Drummer .... George Simson
Thomas Morton .... Jerome Dempsey	Gov. Endecott .... Kenneth Harvey
Assawamset's Daughter ...... Joan Jacklin	Standard Bearer .... Josh Clark
Mr. Blackstone .... Richard Clarke	Wolf's Head .... Colter Rule
Stag's Head .... Andre Bishop	Palfrey .... J.T. Walsh
Edward .... Noah Manne	Witch .... George Hall
Edith .... Elisabeth Price	Woman .... Barbara Le Brun
Indian Whore .... Gloria Rossi	Bear .... Rene Mainguy
Sergeant .... Thomas O'Rourke	Girl .... Sallyanne Tackus
Private .... Bruce Bouchard	Executioner .... Frank Askin

Merry Mount Men: James Cromar, George Hall, Rene Mainguy, Colter Rule. Indians: Frank Askin, George Simson, Gerard Wagner. Soldiers: James Cromar, Rene Mainguy, Robert Rigley.

My Kinsman, Major Molineux

Ferryman	Manu Tupou	Tavern Keeper; Watchman	J.T. Walsh
Boy	Scott Sorrel	2d Barber	Bruce Bouchard
Robin	Josh Clark	Clergyman	George Hall
1st Redcoat	Rene Mainguy	Prostitute	Gloria Rossi
2d Redcoat	Colter Rule	Col. Greenough	Jerome Dempsey
1st Barber	Thomas O'Rourke	Man in Periwig	Richard Clarke
		Major Molineux	Kenneth Harvey

Citizens of Boston: Frank Askin, Andre Bishop, James Cromar, Joan Jacklin, Barbara Le Brun, Noah Manne, Elisabeth Price, Robert Rigley, George Simson, Sallyanne Tackus, Gerard Wagner.

Benito Cereno

Capt. Amasa Delano	Nicolas Coster	Babu	Roscoe Lee Browne
John Perkins	John Getz	Artuful	Paul Benjamin
Don Benito Cereno	Alan Mixon	Francesco	Darryl Croxton

American sailors: Bill Conway, Mark A. French, Steven Pally, Stephen Lawrence Smith, Daniel Stern. Spanish Sailors: Peter B. Gelblum, Peter Lownds, Negro Slaves: Make Bray, Edythe Davis, Sandra Harris, Gregory Jackson, Llewellyn Jones, Bob Long, Gavin Moses, Jarrett Smithwrick, Sidney Strong, Anthony Wayne.

ALL PLAYS—Scenery, John Wulp; costumes, Willa Kim; lighting, Neil Peter Jampolis. Each of the plays was presented without intermission, with *Endecott and the Red Cross* and *My Kinsman, Major Molineux* on the same program. All three works were previously produced at American Place Theater: *My Kinsman, Major Molineux* and *Benito Cereno* on a single program entitled *The Old Glory* 11/1/64 for 36 performances and *Endecott and the Red Cross* 5/7/68 for 15 performances.

ENDECOTT AND THE RED CROSS—Directed by Brian Murray; music, Herbert Kaplan; choreography, Eileen Lawlor.

Time: The 1630s. Place: Merry Mount, the settlement of Thomas Morton near Wollaston, Mass.

MY KINSMAN, MAJOR MOLINEUX—Directed by Brian Murray; music, Herbert Kaplan.

Time: Just before the American Revolution. Place: Boston.

BENITO CERENO—Directed by Austin Pendleton; associate director, John Parks.

Time: About the year 1800. Place: Aboard the ships *President Adams* and *San Domingo*.

In addition to its regular schedule, American Place presented a program in its *American Humorists* series in their theater's Sub-Plot Cafe: *Conversations With Don B* drawn from the writings of Donald Barthelme, with music by John Rubins, directed by Caymichael Patten, January 23, 1976 for 12 performances.

Other special programs at American Place included Ed Bullins's *I Am Lucy Terry*, subtitled *An Historical Fantasy for Young Americans*, in 12 morning performances 2/11/76–2/20/76.

Other experimental and workshop productions presented during the season by The American Place Theater appear under its heading in the "Plays Produced off off Broadway" section of this volume.

NOTE: In this volume, certain programs of off-Broadway companies like The American Place Theater are exceptions to our rule of counting the number of performances from the date of the press coverage. When the official opening takes place late in the run of a play's public or subscription performances (after previews) we count the first performance of record, not the press date, as opening night. Press date for Gorky was 11/16/75 matinee, for *The Old Glory* 4/16/76.

Circle Repertory Company. Schedule of six programs. **The Elephant in the House** (32). By Berrilla Kerr. Opened October 28, 1975; see note. (Closed November 23, 1975 matinee) **Dancing for the Kaiser** (24). By Andrew Colmar. Opened December 14, 1975. (Closed January 4, 1976) **Knock Knock** (41). By Jules Feiffer. Opened January 18, 1976. (Closed February 22, 1976 and transferred to Broadway; see its entry in the "Plays Produced on Broadway" section of this volume) **Who Killed Richard Cory?** (31) By A.R. Gurney Jr. Opened March 10, 1976. (Closed March 28, 1976) **Serenading Louie** (33). By Lanford Wilson. Opened May 2, 1976; see note. (Closed May 30, 1976) And *Mrs. Murray's Farm* by Roy London scheduled to open 6/30/76. Produced by the Circle Repertory Company, Marshall W. Mason artistic director, Jerry Arrow executive director, at the Circle Theater.

THE ELEPHANT IN THE HOUSE

Mary Elizabeth Adams	Helen Stenborg	Molly	Conchata Ferrell
Francesca	Lisa Pelikan	Jennny	Stephanie Gordon
Mr. Johnson	Neil Flanagan	Horace	Bob Thirkield
Timothy	Terence Foley	Gwenyth	Henrietta Bagley

Directed by Marshall W. Mason; scenery, John Lee Beatty; costumes, Jennifer Von Mayrhauser; lighting, Dennis Parichy; original music, Jonathan Horgan; sound, Charles London, George Hansen; stage manager, Susana Meyer; press, Rima Corben.

Bedridden New York lady opens her house to a multitude of strange visitors including a lunatic scientist, in a revised version of the play produced in 1972 off off Broadway by this company. The play was presented in two parts.

DANCING FOR THE KAISER

Douglas North Wicksteed	Douglass Watson	Mrs. Willow	Maryellen Flynn
Walter Skendal	Peter Burnell	Father Bernard Buller;	
Willimot; Maurice;		Judge Sweet	George Hall
Court Clerk	Hy Mencher	Leo Kroonenberg	Peter Walker
Lionel Buckmaster;		Sir Osmon Pryor	Peter Murphy
Dr. Alfred Brey	Tom McDermott	Annie	Patricia Roberts
Erica Kroonenberg	Jacqueline Bertrand	The Man	Jean-Pierre Stewart
Martha Willow	Joanna Miles		

Directed by Marshall Oglesby; scenery, Atkin Pace; costumes, Jennifer Von Mayrhauser; lighting, Dennis Parichy; choreography, Gilda Mullette; sound, George Mansen, Charles London; stage manager, Richard Kilberg.

Scandals and intrigue in the London of 1918.

KNOCK KNOCK

Cohn	Daniel Seltzer	Wiseman	Judd Hirsch
Abe	Neil Flanagan	Joan	Nancy Snyder

Joan's Voices, Other Apparitions: Judd Hirsch.

Directed by Marshall W. Mason; scenery, John Lee Beatty; costumes, Jennifer Von Mayrhauser; lighting, Dennis Parichy; sound, Charles London, George Hansen; production stage manager, Dan Hild; stage manager, Dave Clow.

Time: The present. Place: A small house in the woods. The play was presented in three parts. Absurdist comedy-fantasy, Joan of Arc moves in with a couple of men living in disarray in an isolated cottage.

A Best Play; see page 195

WHO KILLED RICHARD CORY?

Howard; Joe; Chip	Roger Chapman	Elsie; Mrs. Baker; Mother	Joyce Reehling
Piano Player	Charles Greenberg	Eddie; Father; Anarchist	Larry Rosler
Prostitute; Librarian; Emily	Jane Hallaren	Doctor; William;	
Alice; Louise; Bessie	Sharon Madden	Chester	M. Jonathan Steele
Rose; Charlotte;		Frank; Rev. Davis; Ted Babcock	Robb Webb
Grandmother	Patricia O'Connell	Richard Cory	Bruce Gray

Directed by Leonard Peters; scenery, Joan Ferenchak; costumes, Gary Jones; lighting, Arden Fingerhut; musical direction, Charles L. Greenberg; choreography, Bridget Leicester; production stage manager, Marjorie Horne; stage manager, Amy Schecter.

The play was presented in two parts. An exploration of reasons why Richard Cory, the subject of Edward Arlington Robinson's poem, "one calm summer night went home and put a bullet through his head."

SERENADING LOUIE

Mary	Tanya Berezin	Gabrielle	Trish Hawkins
Carl	Edward J. Moore	Alex	Michael Storm

Directed by Marshall W. Mason; scenery, John Lee Beatty; costumes, Jennifer Von Mayrhauser; lighting, Dennis Parichy; production stage manager, David Clow; stage manager, Amy Schecter.

Time: The present. Place: A suburban home, north of Chicago, with the action alternating between the homes of Carl and Alex. Act I: Friday afternoon and evening, at the end of October. Act II: A week later, Saturday night and Sunday morning.

A pair of college chums' marriages are breaking up after about ten years, one explosively.

A Best Play; see pages 368-370

Experimental and workshop productions presented during the season by Circle Repertory Company appear under its heading in the "Plays Produced off off Broadway" section of this volume.

A children's play, *Cavern of the Jewels* by John Heuer, was produced by Circle Repertory Company in a limited engagement of 16 performances 4/2/76-4/11/76.

NOTE: In this volume, certain programs of off-Broadway companies like Circle Repertory Company are exceptions to our rule of counting the number of performances from the date of the press coverage. When the official opening takes place late in the run of a play's public or subscription performances (after previews) we count the first performance of record, not the press date, as opening night. Press date for *The Elephant in the House* was 11/2/75, for *Serenading Louie* was 5/7/76.

Conversations With an Irish Rascal (19). Adapted from the works of Brendan Behan by Kathleen Kennedy with David O. Frazier. Produced by Elliot Martin in the Cleveland Playhouse Square Association production at the Top of the Gate. Opened October 29, 1975. (Closed November 16, 1975)

Directed by Joseph J. Garry; press, Frank Goodman/Seymour Krawitz. With David O. Frazier, Gusti.

Reminiscences of Brendan Behan in songs and stories.

And So to Bed (7). Revival of the play by J.B. Fagan. Produced by Catherine Ellis at Stage 73. Opened November 5, 1975. (Closed November 9, 1975)

Directed by Eugenie Leontovich; scenery, Kristine Haugan; costumes, Patricia Britton; lighting, Barry Arnold; musical arrangements and supervision, Jason McAuliffe; production stage manager, Peter Lawrence; press, David Powers, William Schelble. With Michael Oakes, David Macenulty, Pawnee Sills, Ellen Farran, Jane Altman, Christopher Wynkoop, Jason McAuliffe, Laura May Lewis, Sharon Talbot, Catherine Ellis, Cam Cornman, Randall Robbins, John Bergstrom.

Comedy about Samuel Pepys and his wife, originally produced in London in 1926 and on Broadway in 1927. This is its first New York revival of record.

* The Light Opera of Manhattan. Repertory of nine operetta revival programs. **Iolanthe** (18). Book and lyrics by W.S. Gilbert; music by Arthur Sullivan. Opened November 5, 1975. **Naughty Marietta** (12). Book and lyrics by Rida Johnson Young; music by Victor Herbert. Opened November 12, 1975. **The Mikado** (24). Book and lyrics by W.S. Gilbert, music by Arthur Sullivan. Opened November 19, 1975. **The Vagabond King** (42). Musical version of Justin Huntly McCarthy's *If I Were King*; book and lyrics by Brian Hooker and W.H. Post; music by Rudolf Friml. Opened December 3, 1975. **The Pirates of Penzance** (12). Book and lyrics by W.S. Gilbert; music by Arthur Sullivan. Opened January 7, 1976. **H.M.S. Pinafore** (24). Book and lyrics by W.S. Gilbert; music by Arthur Sullivan. Opened January 14, 1976. **The Gondoliers** (12). Book and lyrics by W.S. Gilbert; music by Arthur Sullivan. Opened February 25, 1976. **Patience** (12). Book and lyrics by W.S. Gilbert; music by Arthur Sullivan. Opened March 10, 1976 (Repertory closed May 1, 1976) *** The Student Prince** (18). Book and lyrics by Dorothy Donnelly; music by Sigmund Romberg. Opened May 11, 1976. Produced by The Light Opera of Manhattan, William Mount-Burke producer-director, at the Eastside Playhouse.

PERFORMER	"IOLANTHE"	"NAUGHTY MARIETTA"	"THE MIKADO"	"THE VAGABOND KING"
Raymond Allen	Chancellor	Silas Slick	Ko-Ko	Louis XI
Stephen Anderson				Thibaut
Diane Armistead			(Katisha)	Lady Mary
Jeanne Beauvais		Adah		
Paul Bufano				DeMontigny
Maureen Burns				1st Lady
Roger Owen Childs			Nanki-Poo	
Rebecca Dorman				Johanneton
Lynn Greene	Iolanthe		(Pitti-Sing)	Huguette
Susan Greenleaf				(2d Lady)
Paul Huck				4th Guardsman
Edwin Hustwit				Casin; Herald
Joanne Jamieson		Felice		Jehan
Joan Lader			(Pitti-Sing)	Margot
Michael McBride				3d Guardsman
Georgia McEver	Phyllis	Marietta	(Yum-Yum)	Katherine
Valerie Mondini	Leila	Nanette	Peep-Bo	(2d Lady)
Mary Moore				3d Lady
Joanne Morris				Trios
John Palmore				1st Guardsman
Nancy Papale			(YumYum)	
Vashek Pazdera	Pvt. Willis	Governor	Mikado	Captain
Gary Pitts	Tolloller	Warrington		Noel
Steven Polcek				Rogati
Frank Prieto				Hangman
Gary Ridley		Florenze	Pish-Tush	Villon
Julio Rosario	Strephon	Grandet	Pooh-Bah	Tabarie
Cheryl Savitt	Celia	Fanchon		
Martha Schut				Blanche
Richard Smithies		Blake		Tristan
Rhanda Spotton	Fleta			Queen
Jack Sweeney				2d Guardsman
James Weber	Mountararat	Rudolfo		Oliver
Eleanor Wold	Fairy Queen	Lizette	(Katisha)	

(Parentheses indicate role in which the performer alternated)

PERFORMER	"THE PIRATES OF PENZANCE"	"H.M.S. PINAFORE"	"THE GONDOLIERS"	"PATIENCE"
Raymond Allen	Stanley	Porter	Plaza-Toro	Bunthorne
Diane Armistead	(Ruth)	Buttercup		(Lady Jane)
Dennis Britten				Dunstable
Paul Bufano			Antonio	
Maureen Burns			Fiametta	Lady Ella
Roger Owen Childs		Rackstraw	Marco	
Rebecca Dorman			Inez	
Lynn Greene			Tessa	(Angela)
Paul Huck			Annibale	
Joan Lader	Isabel	Hebe	Giulia	(Angela)
Georgia McEver	(Mabel)	(Josephine)	Casilda	(Patience)
Valerie Mondini	Kate		Vittoria	Lady Saphir
John Palmore	Samuel		Francesco	
Nancy Papale	(Mabel)	(Josephine)	Gianetta	(Patience)
Vashek Pazdera	Sergeant	Deadeye	DeBolero	Calverly
Gary Ridley	Frederic	Boatswain	Luiz	Grosvenor
Julio Rosario	Pirate King	Corcoran	Giuseppe	Murgatroyd
Cheryl Savitt	Edith			
Richard Smithies				Solicitor
James Weber		Carpenter	Giorgio	
Eleanor Wold	(Ruth)		Duchess	(Lady Jane)

(Parentheses indicate role in which the performer alternated)

THE STUDENT PRINCE

Von Mark	Richard Smithies	Von Asterberg	Julio Rosario
Dr. Engel	Lloyd Harris	Lucas	Vashek Pazdera
Prince Karl Franz	Dennis Britten	Kathie	Georgia McEver
Gretchen	Joan Lader	Anastasia	Eleanor Wold
Ruder	James Weber	Princess Margaret	Elizabeth Tanner
Toni	Frank Prieto	Capt. Tarnitz	Gary Ridley
Lutz	Raymond Allen	Baron Arnheim	John Palmore
Hubert	Cleveland Kingston	Countess Leyden	Rebecca Dorman
Detlef	Gary Pitts		

Others in all plays: Elizabeth Devine, Sally Ann Swarm, David Vodenichar, Gerald Bruce.

Dance Ensemble: Beth Campbell, Mary Lou Crivello, Elizabeth Devine, Gina Fisher, Barbara Guerard, Marilyn Komisar, Vicki Piper, Fina Rogers, Gabrielle Taylor.

ALL PLAYS—Artistic director and conductor, William Mount-Burke; associate director, Raymond Allen; assistant musical director and piano, Brian Molloy; stage manager, Jerry Gotham; press, Michelle Yules, Mark Somers.

IOLANTHE—The last professional New York production of *Iolanthe* as well as *The Mikado, The Pirates of Penzance, H.M.S. Pinafore* and *Patience*—other than previous stagings in The Light Opera of Manhattan repertory—was during the visit of the D'Oyly Carte Opera Company to Broadway 10/29/68-11/17/68.

NAUGHTY MARIETTA—This operetta was first produced on Broadway 11/7/10 for 136 performances. Major revivals included 10/21/29 for 16 performances and 11/16/31 for 24 performances.

THE MIKADO—Scenery, William Schroder; costumes, George Stinson.

THE VAGABOND KING—Choreography, Jerry Gotham; scenery and costumes, William Schroder; duels, Michael A. Maurice.

Time: The time of Louis XI. Place: Old Paris. Act I, Scene 1: The tavern. Scene 2: A corridor. Scene 3: The court, next morning. Act II, Scene 1: The masque. Scene 2: The procession. Scene 3: The gibbet.

The Vagabond King was first produced on Broadway 9/21/25. A major New York revival took place 6/29/43 for 56 performances.

ACT I

"Gaudeo"	Ensemble
"Love for Sale"	Huguette
"Drinking Song"	Tabarie
"Song of the Vagabonds"	Villon, Ensemble
"Someday"	Katherine
"Only a Rose"	Katherine, Villon
"Finaletto Scene 1"	Ensemble
"Scotch Guardsmen's Song"	Captain, Guardsmen
"Only a Rose" (Reprise)	Katherine
"Tomorrow"	Katherine, Villon
"Finale Act I"	Ensemble

ACT II

"Nocturn (In the Night)"	Ensemble
Ballet (Tarantella)	Dance Ensemble
"Serenade"	Tabarie, Oliver, Lady Mary
"Huguette Waltz"	Huguette
"Love Me Tonight"	Katherine, Villon
"Song of the Vagabonds" (Reprise)	Ensemble
"Te Deum Laudamus!"	Ensemble
"The Victory March"	Ensemble
Finale	Ensemble

THE PIRATES OF PENZANCE—Scenery, William Schroder; costumes, George Stinson.

THE GONDOLIERS—Scenery and costumes by William Schroder.

PATIENCE—Costumes by George Stinson.

THE STUDENT PRINCE—Choreography, Jerry Gotham; scenery, Eloise Meyer; costumes, George Stinson; lighting, Peggy Clark.

Time: Spring 1860. Act I, Scene 1: Antechamber in the palace at Karlsberg. Scene 2: Garden of the inn of the "Three Golden Apples" at the University of Heidelberg. Act II, Scene 1: Sitting room of Prince Karl at the inn, four months later. Scene 2: A room of state in the royal palace at Karlsberg, two years later. Scene 3: Garden of the inn, the next day.

The Student Prince was first produced on Broadway 12/2/24. The most recent of its professional New York revivals were off Broadway, at the Greenwich Mews 7/13/61 for 13 performances and by the American Savoyards 12/21/61 for 14 performances. A revival produced for Broadway closed out of town 10/21/73.

ACT I

Prologue ....Lackeys
"Golden Days" ....Prince, Engel
"To the Inn We're Marching" ....Students
"Drinking Song" ....Students
"Come Boys" ....Kathie, Students
"Heidelberg" ....Prince, Engel
"Gaudeamus Igitur" ....Students
"Golden Days" (Reprise) ....Engel
"Deep in My Heart, Dear" ....Kathie, Prince
Finale: Serenade

ACT II

"Student Life" ....Students
"Thoughts Will Come to Me" ....Prince
"Gavotte" ....Ensemble
"Just We Two" ....Prince, Tarnitz
"The Flag That Flies Above Us" ....Ensemble
"Just We Two" (Reprise) ....Ensemble
"What Memories" ....Prince
"Drinking Song" (Reprise) ....Students
"Gaudeamus Igitur" (Reprise) ....Students
"Deep in My Heart, Dear" (Reprise) ....Prince, Kathie

Bil Baird's Marionettes. Schedule of marionette programs. **Alice in Wonderland** (87). Revival of the musical based on the story by Lewis Carroll; book by A.J. Russell; music by Joseph G. Raposo; lyrics by Sheldon Harnick. And **Bil Baird's Variety.** Opened November 2, 1975. (Closed January 18, 1976). **Winnie the Pooh** (111). Revival of the musical based on the stories by A.A. Milne; adapted by A.J. Russell; music by Jack Brooks; lyrics by A.A. Milne and Jack Brooks. And **Bil Baird's Variety.** Opened January 24, 1976. (Closed April 30, 1976) Produced by the American Puppet Arts Council, Arthur Cantor executive producer, at the Bil Baird Theater.

ALICE IN WONDERLAND

Performer: Alice—Olga Felgemacher.

Puppeteers: White Rabbit, Tweedledee, Frog Footman, 1st Creature, Lobster, Violet—Peter Baird; Alice, Turtle, Cheshire Cat, Dormouse, 2d Creature, Snail—Rebecca Bondor; Alice, Queen, Tiger Lily, Caterpillar, Turtle, 3d Creature—Olga Felgemacher; Duchess, Walrus, Knave of Hearts, Humpty Dumpty, March Hare, Five of Spades, Mock Turtle—Brian Stashick; Fish Footman, Tweedledum, Mad Hatter, King, Lobster, Violet—William Tost; Three of Spades, Executioner, Cook, Carpenter, Violet—Steven Widerman. (All voices except Alice spoken by Puppeteers.)

Singing Voices: Alice—Mary Case; Duchess—George S. Irving; White Rabbit, March Hare, Tweedledee—Sheldon Harnick; Violet Trio—Rose Mary Jun, Ivy Austin, Margery Gray; Mad Hatter, Tweedledum, Whiting—William Tost; Dormouse—Margery Gray; Mock Turtle, Walrus, Caterpillar—Bil Baird.

Directed by Paul Leaf; designed and produced by Bil and Susanna Baird; scenery, Howard Mandel; lighting, Peggy Clark; artistic associate, Frank Sullivan; production manager, Douglas Gray; press, C. George Willard.

The marionette play was presented in two parts, followed by *Bil Baird's Variety*. It was last produced by Bil Baird's Marionettes 3/1/75 for 51 performances.

BIL BAIRD'S VARIETY

Scene 1: Bill Tost and Purseface. Scene 2: Introducing Slugger Ryan. Scene 3: Froggy piano. Scene 4. The rain forest. Scene 5: The Bughouse Band. Scene 6: Finale.

Perennial exhibition of "puppet virtuosity embodying many styles and types" performed without intermission.

WINNIE THE POOH

Puppeteers: Winnie the Pooh—William Tost; Piglet—Peter Baird; Eeyore—Brian Stashick; Kanga—Rebecca Bondor; Roo, Christopher Robin, Tigger, Owl-Olga Felgemacher; Tigger—Steven Widerman; Bee—Madeleine Gruen; Moles, Spiders, Cows, Butterflies, Raccoons, Bees—Members of the Company.

Singing Voices: Eeyore, Owl—Bil Baird; Winnie the Pooh—Bill Marine; Mice—Carly Simon, Lucy Simon.

Directed by Bil Baird; designed and produced by Bil and Susanna Baird; scenery, Howard Mandel; lighting, Peggy Clark; musical direction and arrangements, Alvy West; production manager, Douglas Gray.

Place: In and around the 100-acre wood. The marionette play was presented in two parts, followed by *Bil Baird's Variety*. It was last produced by Bil Baird's Marionettes 10/29/72 for 44 performances.

The Homecoming (9) Revival of the play by Harold Pinter. Produced by Wayne Adams in association with Willard Morgan and Michael Condon in the Alive Theater Production at Wonderhorse. Opened November 6, 1975. (Closed November 14, 1975)

Directed by Jack Chandler; scenery, Jack Chandler; costumes, Betty Martin; music design, Gary Burke, Dede Washburn; production stage manager, Victor Amerling; press, Howard Atlee, Clarence Allsopp, Meg Gordean. With John Neville-Andrews, Jack Eric Williams, Tim Cahill, Darrell Ziegler, Brad Russell, Gail Cook.

The Homecoming had its New York premiere on Broadway 1/5/67 for 324 performances, when it was named a Best Play and won the Critics Award. Its last professional New York revival took place off Broadway 5/18/71 for 32 performances.

The Chelsea Theater Center. Series of three Manhattan programs. **The Family, Parts 1 and 2** (23). By Lodewijk de Boer; translated by Albert Maurits. Opened November 12, 1975. (Closed November 30, 1975) **By Bernstein** (17). Musical cabaret by Betty Comden and Adolph Green; music by Leonard Bernstein; lyrics by Leonard Bernstein, Betty Comden and Adolph Green, John Latouche, Jerry Leiber and Stephen Sondheim. Opened November 23, 1975. (Closed December 9, 1975) * **Vanities** (80). By Jack Heifner. Produced with The Lion Theater Company and Playwrights Horizons. Opened March 22, 1976. Produced by The Chelsea Theater Center of Brooklyn, Robert Kalfin artistic director, Michael David executive director, Burl Hash production director, at the Westside Theater.

THE FAMILY, Parts 1 and 2

Doc	David Selby	Cabot	Joe Palmieri
Kil	Brent Spiner	Brigit	Diane Kagan
Gina	Dale Soules	Man	Ed Preble

Directed by Barry Davis; scenery, Lawrence King; costumes, Jeanne Button; lighting, Daniel Flannery; videography, Alan Shulman, Mediatrics; production stage manager, Julia Gillett; press, Betty Lee Hunt.

Two full-length plays separated by a dinner break (there are two more plays in this series, Parts 3 and 4) in a soap opera-like treatment of a family living on the outskirts of Amsterdam. A foreign play previously produced in Holland and recipient of the Dutch National Award for best play.

BY BERNSTEIN

Jack Bittner
Margery Cohen
Jim Corti
Ed Dixon

Patricia Elliott
Kurt Peterson
Janie Sell

Musicians: Bob Steen woodwinds, Dean Kelso cello, Joe Bongiomo bass, Paul Pizzuti percussion, Clay Fullum piano.

Directed by Michael Bawtree; conceived by Betty Comden and Adolph Green with Michael Bawtree, Norman L. Berman and the Chelsea Theater Center; musical direction and vocal arrangements, Clay Fullum; scenery and costumes, Lawrence King, Michael H. Yeargan; lighting, Marc B. Weiss; orchestrations, Thomas Pierson; assisting director, Norman L. Berman; production stage manager, Fred Reinglas; press, Betty Lee Hunt Associates, Bill Evans.

Collection of Leonard Bernstein theater musical numbers written for various shows but dropped in production.

MUSICAL NUMBERS: "Welcome" (lyrics by Betty Comden and Adolph Green)—Company; "Gabey's Comin'" (lyrics by Comden and Green)—Kurt Peterson, Company; "Lonely Me" (lyrics by Comden and Green)—Peterson; "Say When" (lyrics by Comden and Green)—Patricia Elliott; "Like Everybody Else" (lyrics by Stephen Sondheim)—Janie Sell, Ed Dixon. Jim Corti; "I'm Afraid It's Love" (lyrics by Comden and Green)—Peterson; "Another Love" (lyrics by Comden, Green and Leonard Bernstein)—Miss Elliott; "I Know a Fellow" (lyrics by Bernstein)—Corti; "It's Gotta Be Bad To Be Good" (lyrics by Bernstein)—Miss Sell, Corti; "Dream With Me" (lyrics by Comden, Green and Bernstein)—Miss Cohen, Dixon, Company; "Another Love" (reprise) Company; "Ringaroundarosy" (lyrics by John Latouche)—Dixon, Corti, Company; "Captain Hook's Soliloquy" (lyrics by Bernstein)—Jack Bittner, Company; "The Riobamba" (lyrics by Bernstein)—Misses Elliott, Sell, Cohen, Company; "The Intermission's Great" (lyrics by Comden and Green)—Company; "The Story of My Life" (lyrics by Comden and Green)—Miss Sell; "Ain't Got No Tears Left" (lyrics by Comden, Green and Bernstein)—Miss Elliott; "The Coolie's Dilemma" (lyrics by Jerry Leiber)—Corti, Company; "In There" (lyrics by Sondheim)—Bittner, Company; "Spring Will Come Again" (lyrics by Comden and Green)—Miss Cohen, Company; "Here Comes the Sun" (lyrics by Comden and Green)—Company.

VANITIES

Kathy ....Jane Galloway
Mary ....Susan Merson

Joanne ....Kathy Bates

Directed by Garland Wright; scenery, John Arnone; costumes, David James; lighting, Patrika Brown; production stage manager, Ginny Freedman; press, Maria Cristina Pucci.

Scene 1: A gymnasium, fall, 1963. Scene 2: A sorority house, spring, 1968. Scene 3: The garden of an apartment, summer, 1974.

The changing relationships of three women from their high school days to a reunion as adults.

In addition to its own schedule of programs, the Chelsea Westside Theater housed the T. Schreiber Studio off-off-Broadway production of Lanford Wilson's *Lemon Sky* 3/2/76-3/14/76.

The Chelsea Theater Center of Brooklyn. Schedule of two Brooklyn programs. **Ice Age** (32). By Tankred Dorst in cooperation with Ursula Ehler; English version by Peter Sander. Opened November 18, 1975; see note. (Closed December 14, 1975) **The Boss** (24). Revival of the play by Edward Sheldon. Opened February 24, 1976; see note. (Closed March 14, 1976) Produced by The Chelsea Theater Center of Brooklyn, Robert Kalfin artistic director, Michael David executive director, Burl Hash production director, at the Brooklyn Academy of Music.

ICE AGE

Old Man ....Roberts Blossom
Fragile Lady ....Anne Ives
Cleaning Lady; Diva ....Sonia Zomina
Gardener; Man With Camera ..Curt Williams

Spinster ....Eleanor Cody Gould
Major's Widow ....Frances Pole
Oswald ....Nicholas Hormann
Prof. Jenssen ....Jerrold Ziman

Male Assistant ....Robert Einenkel	Vera ....Ruth Hunt
Female Assistant ....Janice Fuller	Woman in Wheelchair ....Frances Bay
Paul ....George Morfogen	Old Soldier ....William Robertson
Holm; Man in Mask ....Larry Swansen	Berend ....Charles Mayer
Reich; Fat Man in Mask ....K. Lype O'Dell	Cook ....Renos Mandis
Bank Director; Blind Man .....Gary Allen	Kristian ....Roger DeKoven

Understudies: Misses Hunt, Ives, Pole, Zomina—Frances Bay; Mr. Blossom—Roger De-Koven; Messrs. O'Dell, Morfogen, Hormann—Robert Einenkel; Mr. Mandis—K. Lype O'Dell; Messrs. DeKoven, Ziman, Mayer—Curt Williams; Messrs. Allen, Swansen—Jerrold Ziman; Miss Gould—Sonia Zomina.

Directed by Arne Zaslove; scenery, Wolfgang Roth; costumes, Ruth Morley; lighting, Daniel Flannery; production stage manager, Sherman Warner; press, Joel Wald.

Time: 1947-48. Place: An old people's home and the adjoining park, Norway. The play was presented in two parts.

A play of reflection suggested by the life of a noted Norwegian author who supported the Nazis during the occupation and was later interned for treason. A foreign play previously produced in West Germany.

THE BOSS

James D. Griswold ....Allan Frank	Mrs. Cuyler; Cook ....Pamela Burrell
Donald Griswold ....Gregory Abels	Gates ....James Eames
Emily Griswold ....Louise Shaffer	"Porky" McCoy ....Tom-Patrick Dineen
Mitchell; Police Lieutenant ......John Genke	Scanlon; Police Officer ....Chris Carrick
Lawrence Duncan ....Dennis Lipscomb	Archbishop Sullivan ....Igors Gavon
Michael R. Regan ....Andrew Jarkowsky	French Maid ....Catherine Henry Lamm
Davis ....Richard K. Sanders	Police Officer ....Chip Lucia

Understudies: Mr. Eames—Allan Frank; Mr. Genke—Igors Gavon; Messrs. Sanders, Jarkowsky, Gavon—John Genke; Misses Shaffer, Burrell—Catherine Henry Lamm; Mr. Carrick—Dennis Lipscomb; Messrs. Abels, Lipscomb, Dineen—Chip Lucia.

Directed by Edward Gilbert; scenery, Lawrence King; costumes, Carrie F. Robbins; lighting, William Mintzer; production stage manager, Bob Jaffe.

Time: 1910-1911. Place: One of the Eastern lake-ports. Act I: Mr. Griswold's drawing room the afternoon of Oct. 28, 1910. Act II: Mr. Regan's library the evening of April 29, 1911. Act III: The following evening. Act IV: a Room at the police station three days later. The play was presented in two parts with the intermission following Act II.

The Boss was first presented on Broadway 1/30/11 for 88 performances. This is its first professional New York revival of record.

NOTE: In this volume, certain programs of off-Broadway companies like The Chelsea Theater Center of Brooklyn are exceptions to our rule of counting the number of performances from he date of the press coverage. When the official opening takes place late in the run of a play's public or subscription performances (after previews) we count the first performance of record, not the press date, as opening night. Press date for Ice Age was 11/26/75, for The Boss was 3/4/76.

Gift of the Magi (48). Musical based on the O. Henry short story; book, music and lyrics by Ronnie Britton. Produced by Wayne Clark and Joseph Tiraco in association with Larry J. Pontillo at the Players Theater. Opened December 1, 1975. (Closed January 11, 1976)

Her ....Mary Saunders	Jim ....Bill March
Della ....Paige O'Hara	Him ....William Brockmeier

Musicians: James Fradrich piano, Beth Tulchin harp, Hal Onserud bass, Richard Keene flute.

Directed by M.T. Knoblauh; musical direction and arrangements, James Fradrich; scenery, Michael Dulin; costumes, Neil Cooper; lighting, Jerryn Michaels; production coordinator, David M. Clark; stage manager, Schorling Schneider.

Time: December, 1906. Place: Greenwich Village in New York City. Musical adaptation of O. Henry short story about a penurious husband and wife who sacrifice their most cherished possessions to give each other a Christmas present.

ACT I

The Magi Waltz ....Orchestra
"There You Go Again" ....Her
"The Gift" ....Della
"Della's Desire" ....Her
"Mr. James Dillingham Young" ....Jim, Della
"Day After Day" ....Jim
"Kids Are Out" ....Jim, Della
"Sullivan Street Flat" ....Jim, Della, Him, Her
"The Beautiful Children" ....Della
"You'd Better Tell Her!" ....Him
"Washington Square" ....Jim
"Till Tomorrow" ....Him, Her, Jim, Della

ACT II

Entr'acte ....Orchestra
"Quiet Morning" ....Him, Her
"Brave You" ....Della
"A Penny Saved" ....Della
"Day After Day" (Reprise) ....Della
"I've Got Something Better" ....Jim
"Pretty Lady" ....Jim, Della, Him, Her
"He Did It, She Did It!" ....Him, Her
"Make Him Think I'm Still Pretty" ....Della
Finale ....Jim, Della, Him, Her

* **Tuscaloosa's Calling Me . . . but I'm Not Going!** (205). Musical revue by Bill Heyer, Hank Beebe and Sam Dann; music by Hank Beebe; lyrics by Bill Heyer. Produced by Jerry Schlossberg, Arch Lustberg and Bruce Nelson in the Quintal production at the Top of the Gate. Opened December 1, 1975.

Len Gochman
Patti Perkins
Renny Temple

Directed by James Hammerstein and Gui Andrisano; musical direction, Jeremy Harris; scenery, Charles E. Hoefler; costumes, Rome Heyer; audio, Donald P. Smith; production manager, Xane Weiner; press, Michael Alpert Associates, Warren Knowlton.

The case for living in New York City, in songs and sketches.

Ted Pritchard replaced Len Gochman 3/31/76. Paul Kreppel replaced Ted Pritchard and Chip Zien replaced Renny Temple 4/7/76.

MUSICAL NUMBERS AND SKETCHES—Act I: "Only Right Here in New York City"—Company; "I Dig Myself"—Renny Temple; "Gold Cash"—Company; "Things Were Out"—Patti Perkins; "Central Park on a Sunday Afternoon"—Company. "New York From the Air" —Miss Perkins; The Old Man—Miss Perkins, Len Gochman; "Backwards"—Gochman; "Delicatessen"—Miss Perkins, Ccmpany; The Out of Towner—Gochman, Temple; "Everything You Hate Is Right Here"—Company. Act II: "Fugue for a Ménage à Trois"—Company; The Purse Snatch—Miss Perkins, Temple; "Poor"—Miss Perkins, Temple; "Graffiti"—Company; "Singles Bar"—Miss Perkins, Temple; "Astrology"—Gochman; "New York '69"—Company; "Tuscaloosa's Calling Me, but I'm Not Going"—Company.

Brooklyn Academy of Music. Series of three revivals in the Kennedy Center-Xerox Corporation American Bicentennial Theater Productions. **Sweet Bird of Youth** (15). By Tennessee Williams. Opened December 3, 1975 (Closed December 14, 1975; see note) **The Royal Family** (15). By George S. Kaufman and Edna Ferber. Opened December 17, 1975. (Closed December 28, 1975; see note) **Long Day's Journey Into Night** (11). By Eugene O'Neill. Opened January 28, 1976. (Closed February 8, 1976) Produced by the Brooklyn Academy of Music at the Brooklyn Academy of Music.

NOTE: These American Bicentennial Theater productions of *Sweet Bird of Youth* and *The Royal Family* transferred to Broadway following their off-Broadway runs; for casts and other production credits and details, see their individual entries in the "Plays Produced on Broadway" section of this volume.

Eugenia Rawls (Aunt Nonnie), Pamela Lewis (Violet) and John B. Jellison (Trooper) appeared in the off-Broadway cast of *Sweet Bird of Youth*.

LONG DAY'S JOURNEY INTO NIGHT

James Tyrone . . . . Jason Robards	Edmund Tyrone . . . . Michael Moriarty
Mary Cavan Tyrone . . . . Zoe Caldwell	Cathleen . . . . Lindsay Crouse
James Tyrone Jr. . . . . Kevin Conway	

Standbys: Mr. Robards—Ernest Graves; Miss Caldwell—Carol Teitel; Mr. Conway—Paul Thomas. Understudies: Mr. Moriarty—W.T. Martin; Miss Crouse—Dyanne Hochman.

Directed by Jason Robards; scenery, Ben Edwards; costumes, Jane Greenwood; lighting, Ken Billington; produced for Kennedy Center by Roger L. Stevens and Richmond Crinkley; production stage manager, Murray Gitlin; stage manager, Dyanne Hochman; press, Kate MacIntyre, Deborah Ann Williams.

Place: The living room of the Tyrones' summer home. Act I, Scene 1: 8:30 a.m. of a day in August, 1912. Scene 2: Around 12:45 that afternoon. Scene 3: About half an hour later. Act II: Around 6:30 that evening. Act III: Around midnight.

Long Day's Journey Into Night was first produced on Broadway 11/7/56 for 390 performances and was named a Best Play of its season and won the Critics Award for best play and the Pulitzer Prize. It was revived on Broadway 5/14/62 for 2 performances by the Royal Dramatic Theater of Sweden, off Broadway 4/21/71 for 121 performances and off off Broadway in each of the last two seasons.

Phèdre (9) Revival of the play by Racine in the French language. Produced by Le Tréteau de Paris, l'Association Française d'Action Artistique of the French Government and Institute/Alliance Française in the New Theater 9 production at The American Place Theater. Opened December 8, 1975. (Closed December 15 1975)

Directed by Michel Hermon; scenery, Michel Hart; costumes, Michel Hermon; masks, Jean Herbin; lighting, Pollux; press, David Roggensack. With Jeanne David, Didier Sandre, Olivier Picq, Anita Plessner, Michel Hart, Lawrence Fevrier, Michel Hermon.

Phèdre was last produced in New York off Broadway by IASTA in an English version 2/10/66 for 100 performances.

Dear Piaf (74). Musical revue with music adapted by Ken Guilmartin; lyrics translated and adapted by Lucia Victor. Produced by Ira Rubin at Mama Gail's. Opened December 19, 1975. (Closed February 14, 1976 and transferred to off off Broadway)

Michael Calkins	Lou Rodgers
Irene Datcher	Michael Tartel
Linda Fields	Norman Carey, pianist

Directed by Dorothy Chernuck; musical direction and arrangements, Ken Guilmartin; scenery and lighting, T. Winberry; costumes, Adri; press, Lewis Harmon.

A revue of songs Edith Piaf sang, translated from the original French.

MUSICAL NUMBERS: Overture; "Life Cry" (Cri du Coeur, by Prevert and Crolla)—Ensemble; "Words, Words, Words" (Les Mots d'Amour, by Rivgauche and Dumont)—Linda Fields, Michael Tartel; "Music of Love" (La Belle Histoire d'Amour, by Piaf and Dumont)—Lou Rodgers, Tartel; "Lucien" (Mon Vieux Lucien, by Rivgauche and Dumont)—Michael Calkins; "Grenadiers" (Les Grognards, by De la Noe and Giraud)—Ensemble; "Hurdy-Gurdies" (Les Orgues de Barbarie, by Moustaki)—Miss Fields; "You're Beautiful" (T'Es Beau, Tu Sais, by Contet and Moustaki)—Irene Datcher; "Non, Je Ne Regrette Rien" (by Vaucaire and Dumont)—Ensemble; "Snow From Finland" (Les Neiges de Finlande, by Contet and Monnot)—Rodgers; "I'm Yours Alone" (Je Suis a Toi, by Boquet and Chauvigny)—Miss Datcher, Calkins; "Running" (Dans la Ville Inconnue, by Vaucaire and Dumont)—Calkins; "Every Day That Passes" (Tant Qu'il y Aura des Jours, by Rivgauche and Monnot)—Ensemble; "Lovers of Teruel" (Les Amants de Teruel, by Plante and Theodorakis)—Tartel, Rodgers; "Mon Dieu"

(by Vaucaire and Dumont)—Miss Datcher; "Carnival" (La Foule, by Rivgauche and Dumont)
—Miss Fields; "Bravo for the Clown" (Bravo Pour le Clown, by Contet and Louigny)—Tartel;
"The Ones in White" (Les Blouses Blanches, by Rivgauche and Monnot)—Rodgers; "C'Est
l'Amour Qui Fait Qu'on S'Aime" (by Piaf and Monnot)—Ensemble; "Life Cry" (Reprise)—
Ensemble.

From Sholom Aleichem With Love (31). One-man show adapted from the works
of Sholom Aleichem by and with Elliot Levine. Produced by Charles Woodward
at the Marymount Manhattan Theater. Opened January 7, 1976. (Closed February
1, 1976)

Directed by Elliot Levine; lighting, Rick Claflin; associate producer, Jerry Sirchia; press,
Betty Lee Hunt Associates, Maurice Turet.
Time: 1915. Place: New York City. Act I, *The Old Country:* The Shake-Out, The Clock,
Rothschild and the Kasrilik, Two Anti-Semites. Act II, *In America:* Regards from Berel-Ayzik,
Meeting Mark Twain, Adventures of Mottle the Cantor's Son, The Triangle Fire.
Adaptation in English of Sholom Aleichem material, with Elliot Levine playing "the Jewish
Mark Twain."

New York Shakespeare Festival Public Theater. Schedule of two programs of
resident companies. **Jinxs Bridge** (11). By Michael Moran; in the Manhattan Project production. Opened January 21, 1976. (Closed February 2, 1976) **Woyzeck**
(22). Revival of the play by Georg Buechner; translated by Mira Rafalowicz; in
The Shaliko Company production, Leonardo Shapiro director. Opened March 24,
1976. (Closed April 25, 1976) Produced by New York Shakespeare Festival Public Theater, Joseph Papp producer, at the Public Theater.

BOTH PLAYS—Associate producer, Bernard Gersten; press, Merle Debuskey, Bob Ullman,
Bruce Cohen.

JINXS BRIDGE

Ghost of Capt. Ogden Leroy Jinxs;	Maeve Zant ....Kate Weiman
Mendelsohn Wilkes-Jinxs ....Tom Costello	Vito Benelli ....John Ferraro
Charlie ....John P. Holmes	Elmo Durke ....Larry Pine
Alvin Dimple ....Himself	Fred E. Metzman ....David Laden
Carl ....Michael Moran	Maria Louise Bianci .....Angela Pietropinto

Conceived, directed and designed by members of the Manhattan Project, Andre Gregory
artistic director.
Time: The present. Place: A room under a bridge on the Harlem River, New York City.
Comedy, an oil-rich Iranian wants to buy a New York bridge.

WOYZECK

Cast: Drum Major, Grandmother, Cop—Ray Barry; Idiot—James Carrington; Woyzeck—
Joseph Chaikin; Dancing Child, Doctor, Soldier, Child—Jake Dengel; Captain, Barker, Soldier,
Student, Pawnbroker—Ron Faber; Andres, Old Man Singing, Soldier, Student, Child—Christo-
pher McCann; Maria—Jane Mandel; Announcer, Sergeant, Soldier, Student—Arthur Strimling;
Margaret, Monkey, Horse, Kathy, Child—Maria Zakrzewski.
Conceived by Mira Rafalowicz; directed by Leonardo Shapiro; costumes, Patricia McGourty;
lighting, Nicholas Wolff Lyndon; design coordinator, Ronald Antone; music, Peter Golub;
production manager, DeLoss Brown.
The last professional New York revivals of *Woyzeck* were in German by the German theater
group called Die Brücke 12/5/72 for 7 performances, and in English off Broadway 5/25/71 for
8 performances.

New York Shakespeare Festival at Lincoln Center. Schedule of two programs.
The Shortchanged Review (46). By Michael Dorn Moody. Opened January 22,
1976. (Closed February 29, 1976) * **Streamers** (39). By David Rabe. Opened April
21, 1976. Produced by New York Shakespeare Festival, Joseph Papp producer, at
the Mitzi E. Newhouse Theater.

BOTH PLAYS—Associate producer, Bernard Gersten; director of play development, Gail Merrifield; production manager, Andrew Mihok; press, Merle Debuskey, Faith Geer.

THE SHORTCHANGED REVIEW

Ed Squall	Herbert Braha	Jane Sloat Shanningan	Virginia Vestoff
Nicky Shannigan	Mason Adams	Darrell Shannigan	T. Miratti
Vanessa Sloat	Tricia Boyer	Peter Cope	William Russ

Understudies: Messrs. Braha, Adams—Raleigh Bond; Messrs. Miratti, Russ—Robert Burke; Miss Boyer—Mie Dillon; Miss Vestoff—Janet Sarno.

Directed by Richard Southern; scenery, Marsha L. Eck; costumes, Hilary M. Rosenfeld; lighting, Cheryl Thacker; sound, Samuel E. Platt; music, Clouds; production stage manager, Louis Rackoff.

Time: 1975. Place: Suburban New York. Act I: Late May. Act II: September.

Melodrama of conflicting modern convictions personified by family and friends of a liberal, middle-aged radio station owner. Previously presented off off Broadway at Ensemble Studio Theater.

STREAMERS

Martin	Michael Kell	Sgt. Cokes	Dolph Sweet
Richie	Peter Evans	M.P. Officer	Arlen Dean Snyder
Carlyle	Dorian Harewood	Hinson, M.P.	Les Roberts
Billy	Paul Rudd	Clark, M.P.	Mark Metcalf
Roger	Terry Alexander	M.P.	Miklos Horvath
Sgt. Rooney	Kenneth McMillan		

Understudies: Messrs. Metcalf, Roberts, Snyder—Miklos Horvath; Mr. Evans—Michael Kell; Messrs. Rudd, Kell—Mark Metcalf; Messrs. Harewood, Alexander—Les Roberts; Messrs. McMillan, Sweet—Arlen Dean Snyder.

Directed by Mike Nichols; scenery, Tony Walton; costumes, Bill Walker; lighting, Ronald Wallace; production stage manager, Nina Seely.

Time: 1965. Place: An Army Barracks in Virginia. The play was presented in two parts.

Study of violence taking the form of impulsive murder, heavily overlaid with symbols of racism, homosexuality, the Vietnam war and other American tensions.

A Best Play; see page 212

Fire of Flowers (38). Musical with words and lyrics by Peter Copani, music by Peter Copani, David McHugh, Lawrence Pitilli, Christian Staudt, Bob Tuthill and Ed Vogel. Produced by The Peoples Performing Company, Inc. at the Provincetown Playhouse. Opened January 29, 1976. (Closed February 29, 1976)

Larry Campbell	Val Reiter
Sylvia Miranda	Gwen Sumter

Musicians: Cisco Carire drums, Michael LeVasseur piano, Christian Staudt guitar, Ed Vogel trumpet.

Directed by Don Signore; musical direction, Ed Vogel; scenery and lighting, Richard Harper; production stage manager, John Copani; press, Lewis Harmon.

Revue-style musical agglomeration of songs on varying subjects of contemporary interest. The play was presented without intermission.

MUSICAL NUMBERS: "Today Will Be"—Company; "Keep Hope Alive"—Company; "Poppy Fields"—Val Reiter; "A Special Man"—Gwen Sumter; "If Jesus Walked"—Company; "Instant Hate"—Reiter; "One of Us"—Sylvia Miranda; "I Need to Know"—Larry Campbell; "In the Name of Love"—Company; "I'm Afire"—Miss Sumter; "God Is in the People"—Campbell, Company; "A Lover's Dream"—Reiter, Miss Miranda; "Who Can Say?"—Campbell, Miss Sumter; "Strawberries, Pickles and Ice Cream"—Miss Miranda; "Down on Me"—Campbell; "The Blind Junkie"—Miss Sumter, Company; "Riot"—Reiter, Company; "I Love the Sun"— Miss Miranda, Company; "Pairs of One"—Campbell, Reiter; "Verily, Verily"—Misses Miranda, Sumter; "More Than Love"—Miss Sumter, Company; "Make Them Hate"—Reiter, Miss Miranda; "Street Jesus"—Company; "L'America Ha Fato per Te"—Miss Miranda; "Love Comes and Goes"—Reiter; "Drug Free"—Campbell, Company; "Wait and See"—Miss Sumter; "When We Are Together"—Company; "God Is in the People" (Reprise)—Company.

Cracks (1) By Martin Sherman. Produced by Adela Holzer at the Theater de Lys. Opened and closed at the evening performance, February 10, 1976.

Directed by Tony Giordano; music, Carlos Holzer; scenery, Peter Larkin; costumes, Randy Barcelo; lighting, Marc B. Weiss; presented by special arrangement with Lucille Lortel Productions, Inc.; production stage manager, Robert Vandergriff; press, Michael Alpert, Marilynn LeVine, Warren Knowlton. With Jeremy Lucas, Victor Garber, Gale Garnett, Mary Elaine Monti, Donald Linahan, Christopher Lloyd, Meg Myles, Louis Giambalvo, Jane Lowry.

Comedy about the murder of a rock star.

The Primary English Class (120). By Israel Horovitz. Produced by Jack Schlissel, Joseph Kipness and Steven Steinlauf at the Circle in the Square. Opened February 16, 1976. (Closed May 16, 1976)

Smiednik	Tom Kubiak	Mrs. Pong	Lori Tan Chinn
Patumiera	Robert Libertini	Translator	Christine Von Dohln
LaPoubelle	Jean-Pierre Stewart	Yoko Kuzukago	Atsumi Sakato
Translator	Robert Picardo	Debbie Wastba	Diane Keaton
Mulleimer	Sol Frieder		

Understudies: Miss Keaton—Christine Von Dohln; Messrs. Libertini, Stewart, Frieder—Robert Picardo.

Directed by Edward Berkeley; scenery supervision, Fredda Slavin; lighting, Andrea Wilson; costume coordination, Patricia McGourty; associate producer, Irving Welzer; production stage manager, Rober Shear; press, Solters & Roskin, Milly Schoenbaum, Bud Westman.

Jill Eikenberry replaced Diane Keaton 4/20/76.

Time: Night. Place: Classroom. The play was performed without an intermission.

Comedy, a neurotically impatient night school teacher turns her classroom full of pupils trying to learn English into a frustrating Babel of voices each speaking a different language.

The Polish Mime Theater (5). Mime program inspired by Frank Wedekind's *Die Kaiserin von Neu Funland*; adapted by Henryk Tomaszewski. Produced by Kazuko Hillyer at the Beacon Theater. Opened February 23, 1976. (Closed February 25, 1976)

Empress Phylissa	Danuta Kisiel Drzewinska	Dark-Skinned	Czeslaw Bielski
Major Domo	Ewa Czekalska	Rappo Eugene; Athlete	Ryszard Staw
Page	Anatol Krupa	Molly	Elzbieta Orlow
Marquis; Arranger	Janusz Pieczuro	Hidalla; Hypnotist	Zygmunt Rozlach
Ludovica; Illusionist	Jerry Reterski	Medium	Krzysztof Szwaja
Napoleon the Greater;		Black Angel;	
Stunt Man	Jerzy Stepniak	Motorcyclist	Feliks Kudakiewicz
Max-Pipifax; Juggler	Jerzy Koztowski	White Angel; Guitarist	Wojciech Hankiewicz
Mr. Adison; Tamer	Marek Olesky	Court Physician	Zbigniew Zukowski

Maids of Honor: Grayzyna Bielawska, Urszula Hosiej. Courtiers: Julian Hasiej, Marek Oleksy, Zbigniew Papis, Zygmunt Rozlach, Ludovico's Company: Wojciech Hankiewicz, Wojciech Misiuro, Feliks Kudakiewicz, Krzysztof Szwaja. Napoleon's Company: Andrzej Musiat, Zbigniew Zukowski. Hidalla's Company: Julian Hasiej, Jerzy Stepniak.

Directed by Henryk Tomaszewski; choreography, Henryk Tomaszewski; scenery, Kasimierz Wisniak; costumes, Wladyslaw Wigura; music, Zbigniew Karnecki; assistant director, Jerzy Koztowski; lighting, Kazimierz Doniec; musical supervision and sound, Mieczyslaw Gawronski; press, The Merlin Group, Ltd., Elizabeth Rodman.

A prologue, eight scenes and an apotheosis, enacting a fairy tale translated as "The Menagerie of the Empress." This Polish troupe specializes in combining mime, ballet and theater in performance.

* The Negro Ensemble Company. Schedule of three programs. *** Eden** (95). By Steve Carter. Opened March 3, 1976; transferred to the Theater de Lys May 14, 1976. **A Season-Within-a-Season** (32). Four one-week limited engagements of new plays from The Negro Ensemble Company Playwrights Workshop. Opened April 6, 1976. (Closed May 2, 1976). And *Livin' Fat* by Judi Ann Mason scheduled to open 6/1/76. Produced by The Negro Ensemble Company, Douglas Turner Ward artistic director, Robert Hooks executive director, Frederick Garrett administrative director, Gerald S. Krone director of special projects, at the St. Marks Playhouse.

EDEN

Eustace	Samm-Art Williams	Agnes	Ramona King
Nimrod	Nate Ferrell	Annetta	Shirley Brown
Solomon	Laurence Fishburne III	Florie	Ethel Ayler
Aunt Lizzie	Barbara Montgomery	Joseph Barton	Graham Brown

Directed by Edmund Cambridge; scenery, Pamela S. Peniston; costumes, Edna Watson; lighting, Sandra L. Ross; production stage manager, Clinton Turner Davis; press, Howard Atlee, Clarence Allsopp, Meg Gordean.

Time: 1927. Place: The Phipps Houses (interior of the Bartons' apartment, hallway landing, the roof) on the upper West Side of New York City in the Sixties. Act I, Scene 1: A summer afternoon in July. Scene 2: A short time later that same day. Scene 3: Later that evening. Act II: Several days later. Scene 2: a few evenings later. Scene 3: Later that same night. Scene 4: Later that same night. Act III, Scene 1: Some months later in December. Scene 2: The following Sunday afternoon.

Haughty West Indian immigrants clash with American-born blacks.

James Warden Jr. replaced Laurence Fishburne III 5/14/76.

A SEASON-WITHIN-A-SEASON

This annual showcase project consisted this season of the following four programs for 8 performances each: *The Trap Play* by Reginald Vel Johnson, directed by Edmund Cambridge, 4/6/76-4/11/76; *A Love Play* by Samm Williams, directed by Frances Foster, 4/13/76-4/18/76; *A Fictional Account of the Lives of Richard and Sarah Allen* by Sylvia-Elaine Foard, directed by Horacena J. Taylor, 4/20/76-4/25/76; *Sunshine, Moonbeam* by Alberta Hill and *Kingdom* by Ali Wadud, 4/27/76-5/2/76.

Medal of Honor Rag (41). By Tom Cole. Produced by Paul B. Berkowsky, Woodie King Jr. and Lucille Lortel at the Theater de Lys. Opened March 28, 1976. (Closed May 2, 1976)

Doctor	David Clennon	Military Guard	John Robert Yates
Dale Jackson	Howard E. Rollins Jr.		

Directed by David Chambers; scenery, Raymond C. Recht; costumes, Carol Oditz; lighting, Marshall S. Spiller; production stage manager, Dan Early; press, The Merlin Group, Ltd., Sandra Manley, Elizabeth Rodman.

Time: The afternoon of April 23, 1971. Place: An office of the Valley Forge Army Hospital, Valley Forge, Pa. The play was presented without intermission.

A Medal of Honor winner reveals to a sympathetic psychiatrist his uncontrollable rage at the enemy when his buddies were killed in Vietnam, followed by crippling feelings of guilt.

Caprice (26). By Charles Ludlam. Produced by Ridiculous Theatrical Company at the Provincetown Playhouse. Opened April 15, 1976. (Closed May 9, 1976)

Directed by Charles Ludlam; press, Alan Eichler. With Charles Ludlam, Lola Pahalinski, Black-Eyed Susan, John D. Brockmeyer, Bill Behr, Richard Currie, Mario Montez.

Stylized play about competing fashion houses, previously entitled *Fashion Bound* and previously produced at Connecticut College, New London, and The Performing Garage.

Royal Shakespeare Company. Repertory of two revivals. **Henry V** (23). By William Shakespeare. Opened April 22, 1976. **The Hollow Crown** (2) Anthology devised by John Barton. Opened May 1, 1976. (Repertory closed May 9, 1976) Produced by the Brooklyn Academy of Music in the Royal Shakespeare Company production, by arrangement with the governors of the Royal Shakespeare Theater, Stratford-Upon-Avon, England, Trevor Nunn artistic director and chief executive, Peggy Ashcroft and Peter Brook directors, at the Brooklyn Academy of Music.

HENRY V

Chorus	Emrys James	Nym; Orleans	Philip Dunbar
Canterbury; Gower	Jeffery Dench	Pistol	Richard Moore
Ely; Fluellen	Trevor Peacock	Boy	Peter Bourke
Henry V.	Alan Howard	Mistress Quickly	Brenda Bruce
Gloucester	Stephen Jenn	Jamy	Ken Stott
Clarence	Anthony Naylor	Court	Richard Derrington
Exeter	Philip Brack	Charles VI	Clement McCallin
Cambridge; Macmorris	Barrie Rutter	Dauphin	Geoffrey Hutchings
Scroop; Williams	Charles Dance	Katharine	Carole Rousseau
Grey; Bates	Arthur Whybrow	Constable of France	Bernard Brown
Westmoreland; Erpingham	Reginald Jessup	Montjoy; French Bishop	Oliver Ford-Davies
Bardolph; M. le Fer	Tim Wylton	Alice	Yvonne Coulette

Musicians: Colin Clague, William Grant, Roger Hellyer, Andrew Hepton, David Hissey, Gordon Kember, Tony McVey, Brian Newman, Ian Reynolds, David Statham, Robin Weatherall.

Directed by Terry Hands; music, Guy Woolfenden; design, Farrah; lighting, Stewart Leviton; assistant to the director, Ian Judge; musical director, Gordon Kember; stage manager, Tim Richards; press, Kate MacIntyre, Clint Brownfield.

The play was presented in two parts. *Henry V* was last produced professionally in New York by ANTA 11/10/69 for 16 performances.

THE HOLLOW CROWN

Cast: Brenda Bruce, Jeffrey Dench, Oliver Ford-Davies, Richard Moore. Guitarist-singer, Bill Homewood.

Directed by John Barton; stage manager, Tim Richards.

The two performances of *The Hollow Crown* in this repertory took place 5/1/76 and 5/8/76. This "entertainment by and about the kings and queens of England—music, poetry, speeches, letters and other writings from the chronicles, from plays and in the monarchs' own words; also music concerning them and by them" was last presented off Broadway 4/18/74 for 7 performances and on Broadway 1/29/63 for 46 performances. A listing of its contents appears on pages 399-400 in *The Best Plays of 1973-74.*

* **Women Behind Bars** (41). Return engagement of the play by Tom Eyen. Produced by R. Paul Evans Jr. and Otto Grun Jr. at the Truck and Warehouse Theater. Opened April 25, 1976.

Matron	Divine	Ada	Jana Schneider
Louise	Sweet William	Guadalupe	Vira Colorado
Blanche	Lori Saveriano	Mary-Eleanor	Lisa Jane Persky
Jo-Jo	Beverly Bonner	Granny	Virginia Barrie
Cheri	Brenda Bergman	The Man	Zarco Kalmic
Gloria	Ellie Schadt		

Directed by Ron Link; title song by Tom Eyen, sung by Larry Paulette; scenery, Sturgis Warner; costume supervision, Ron Link; lighting, Michael Lodick; stage manager, John Cook; press, Terry Lilly.

Time: 1952-1960. Place: The Women's House of Detention. The play was presented without intermission.

This take-off of women's prison movies was first produced last season 5/1/75 for 54 performances. This production was previously presented at the Washington, D.C. Theater Club.

Tickles by Tucholsky (16). Cabaret musical conceived by Moni Yakim; original material by Kurt Tucholsky; translated and adapted by Louis Golden and Harold Poor. Produced by Norman Stephens and Primavera Productions, Ltd. in association with Max Weitzenhoffer at Theater Four. Opened April 26, 1976. (Closed May 9, 1976)

Helen Gallagher
Jerry Jarrett
Joe Masiell

Joseph Neal
Jana Robbins

Directed by Moni Yakim; music arranged and conducted by Wolfgang Knittel; scenery, Don Jensen; costumes, Christina Giannini; lighting, Spencer Mosse; production stage manager, Philip Price; stage manager, Steve Helliker; press, Sandra Manley, Harriett Trachtenberg.

A compendium of songs and sketches written by Kurt Tucholsky for Berlin cabaret in the 1920s and 1930s.

Titanic (8). By Christopher Durang. And **Das Lusitania Songspiel.** Produced by John Rothman at the Van Dam Theater. Opened May 10, 1976. (Closed May 16, 1976)

Directed by Peter Mark Schifter; scenery and costumes, Ernie Smith; lighting, Mitchell Kurtz; press, Betty Lee Hunt Associates, Maria Cristina Pucci, Fred Hoot. With Kate Mc-Gregor-Stewart, Stafan Hartman, Richard Peterson, Sigourney Weaver, Jeff Brooks, Ralph Redpath.

Titanic is a black comedy of absurdities aboard the doomed liner.

Das Lusitania Songspiel was a curtain-raising concert of songs by various composers, original lyrics by Christopher Durang, directed by Peter Mark Schifter, with Christopher Durang and Sigourney Weaver accompanied by Jack Gaughan.

Josef Szajna's Studio Theater. Schedule of two programs. **Dante** (8). By Josef Szajna; music by Krzysztof Penderecki; based on Dante's life and his *The Divine Comedy.* Opened in The Opera House May 25, 1976. (Closed May 30, 1976) **Replika** (8). By Joseph Szajna. Opened in The Lepercq Space June 1, 1976. (Closed June 6, 1976) Produced by The Slavic Cultural Center, Inc. in the Josef Szajna Studio Theater production at the Brooklyn Academy of Music.

Choreography, Josef Szajna; press, Kate MacIntyre, Clint Brownfield. With Tomasz Marzecki.

Dante is a dramatization—mostly in pantomime but partly in the Polish and English languages—of Dante's exploration of hell, purgatory and heaven, commissioned by the International Festival of Theater in Florence and performed with a cast of 22 members of this Polish group. Previously produced at Studio Arena Theater, Buffalo, N.Y.

Replika is a pantomime described by its author as "A wordless odyssey through the holocaust, depicting the indomitable spirit of man tempered by the inhumanity directed against him by himself."

OFF OFF BROADWAY
AND ADDITIONAL PRODUCTIONS

Here is a comprehensive sampling of off off Broadway and other experimental or peripheral 1975-76 productions in New York, compiled by Camille Croce. There is no definitive "off-off-Broadway" area or qualification. To try to define or regiment it would be untrue to its fluid, exploratory purpose. The listing of more than 600 programs below is as inclusive as reliable sources will allow, however, and takes in almost all Manhattan-based, new-play-producing, English-language organizations listed by the Off Off Broadway Alliance and the Theater Development Fund—plus many others.

The more active and established producing groups are identified in **bold face type,** in alphabetical order, with artistic policies and the name of the managing director(s) given whenever these are a matter of record. Examples of their 1975–76 programs—and in many cases a group's whole 1975–76 schedule—are listed with play titles in CAPITAL LETTERS. Often these are works in progress with changing scripts, casts and directors, usually without an engagement of record (but an opening or early performance date is included when available).

Authors' credits are not included in entries of revivals of obvious classics. A large selection of other groups and shows that made appearances during the season appears under the "miscellaneous" heading at the end of this listing.

A report on the highlights of the off-off-Broadway season by Marion Fredi Towbin appears in "The Season in New York" section of this volume.

The Actors Studio. Development of talent in productions of new and old works. Arthur Penn and Lee Strasberg, artistic directors.

> ECONOMIC NECESSITY by John Hopkins. March 25, 1976. Directed by Arthur Sherman; with Paul Gleason, Carlin Glynn, Michael Hadge, Michael Heart, Geoffrey Horne, Nick La-Padula, J.J. Quinn, Joseph Ragno, Maximillia Scheider, Sandra Seacat, Ann Wedgeworth.

Afro-American Studio. Express the black experience in terms of theater. Ernie McClintock, artistic director.

> TO BE YOUNG, GIFTED AND BLACK by Lorraine Hansberry. November 27, 1975. Directed by Richard Gant. (Re-opened May 21, 1976; directed by Ernie McClintock).
> SHANGO By Pepe Carril. January 11, 1976. Directed by Ernie McClintock.
> TABERNACLE by Paul Carter Harrison. January 15, 1976. Directed by Ernie McClintock.
> A HAND IS ON THE GATE-'76 by Roscoe Lee Browne. March 5, 1976. Directed by Ernie McClintock.

Afro-American Total Theater. Developing and producing the work of black artists. Hazel Bryant, artistic director.

> SISYPHUS AND THE BLUE-EYED CYCLOPS written and directed by Garland Lee Thompson. July, 1975.
> FRANK SILVERA'S PLAYWRIGHTS' WORKSHOP: new script by Dan Owens. November 3, 1975. Directed by Garland Thompson. New script by Ivy McCrae. November 24, 1975.

Amas Repertory Theater. Creative arts as a powerful instrument of peaceful change, towards healthier individuals. Rosetta LeNoire, founder and artistic director.

> THE MAN WITH THE RAGTIME BLUES (musical) book, music, lyrics and performed by Mitch Douglas. October 16, 1975. Directed by Jay Binder.
> THE BIG KNIFE by Clifford Odets. January 9, 1976. Directed by Conrad McLaren.
> GODSONG (musical) adapted and directed by Tad Truesdale from J.W. Johnson's *God's Trombones*. March 4, 1976. With Ernie Adano, Ruth Brisbane, Leslie Foglesong, Dee Dee Lavant, Rudy Lowe.

American Center for Stanislavski Theater Art (ACSTA I) Development of the Stanislavski method in the American Theater. Sonia Moore, artistic director.

> A DEED FROM THE KING OF SPAIN by Joseph Baldwin. November 21, 1975. Directed by Sonia Moore; with Darell Brown, Stephen Hunter, Phyllis Gibbs, Cathy Brady, David Herman, Peter Sherayko, Len Silver.
> STANISLAVSKI's FINAL CONCLUSIONS (five discussions). December, 1975.
> DESIRE UNDER THE ELMS. January 9, 1976. Directed by Sonia Moore.
> THIS PROPERTY IS CONDEMNED by Tennessee Williams; THE SLAVE by Imamu Amiri Baraka; directed by Sonia Moore; THE INDIAN WANTS THE BRONX by Israel Horovitz, directed by Len Silver. February 27, 1976. With Stephen Hunter, Roberta Manners, David Herman, Linda Chapman, Ray Matthews, John Ambrose, Thomas Napolitano.
> A STREETCAR NAMED DESIRE. April 9, 1976. Directed by Sonia Moore.

American Ensemble Company. Interested in literary value of plays; concerned with entertaining as well as stimulating thoughts of audiences. Robert Petito, artistic director.

DON JUAN IN HELL. September 18, 1975. Directed by George Callahan.
THE CHALK GARDEN by Enid Bagnold. January 8, 1976. Directed by Robert Petito.
BREAK-A-LEG (revue) staged by Robert Petito. February, 1976.
THE DESK SET by William Marchant. April 29, 1976. Directed by Robert Petito.
NO EXIT by Jean Paul Sartre. May 21, 1976. Directed by Robert Schwager.

The American Place Theater Basement Space. Presents completely developed new plays (usually short) by American writers, not presented as part of the regular subscription season. David Roggensack, director.

THE DOMINO COURTS by William Hauptman. December 12, 1975. Directed by Barnet Kellman; with Regina Baff, Guy Boyd, Conard Fowkes, Mary Elaine Monti.
CONVERSATIONS WITH MY WIFE by Steven Shea. January 23, 1976. Directed by Paul Cooper; with Robyn Goodman, Leon Russom.

American Theater Company. New works done, but accent on the American theater's heritage. Richard Kuss, artistic director.

WHY AM I HERE by Barbara de la Cuesta. December, 1975. Directed by Ellis Santone.

Bicentennial Repertory Season:
THE FALL OF BRITISH TYRANNY OR AMERICAN LIBERTY TRIUMPHANT by John Leacock. February 15, 1976. Directed by Richard Kuss.
PATRIOTS, ETC. by Robert Munford. April 30, 1976. Directed by Richard Kuss.
THE BATTLE OF BROOKYLN (anonymous). May 1, 1976. Directed by Richard Kuss.

Association of Theater Artists. Presents classical and modern plays, including new and experimental works. Roderick Nash, artistic director and director of all plays.

A LITTLE NIGHT MUSIC (musical) book by Hugh Wheeler, music and lyrics by Stephen Sondheim. September 18, 1975.
SMALL CRAFT WARNINGS by Tennessee Williams. November 6, 1975.
THE CHERRY ORCHARD. January 22, 1976.
TWELFTH NIGHT. March, 1976.

Byrd Hoffman Foundation. Company dedicated to production of new and experimental works in the theater. Robert Wilson, director.

DIA LOG. August, 1976. With Robert Wilson and Christopher Knowles. TO STREET. September, 1976. With Robert Wilson.
SPACEMAN (video/performance) by Robert Wilson and Ralph Hilton. January, 1976.

Central Arts Ministry of Central Presbyterian Church. An open community of artists. Bill Silver, director of Arts Ministries.

THE EPICENE OR THE SILENT WOMAN by Ben Jonson. June 5, 1975. Directed by Maurice Edwards.
ENTERTAINING MR. SLOANE by Joe Orton. September, 1975. Directed by J.P. Duffy.
MARY TUDOR by Victor Hugo. November 6, 1975. Directed by Maurice Edwards.
RING ROUND THE MOON by Jean Anouilh. December, 1975. Directed by John Perry McDonald.
LA RONDE by Arthur Schnitzler. January, 1976. Performed by the Public Players.
THE CO-OP by Barbara Garson and Fred Gardner. February, 1976. Directed by Jerry Heymann.
A MIDSUMMER NIGHT'S DREAM. March 11, 1976. Directed by John Perry McDonald; with the Public Players.
REPORT TO THE ACADEMY by Gert Staub.
THE INSECT COMEDY. May 17, 1976. Directed by Sande Shurin.

Circle Repertory Company Projects in Progress. Developmental program for playwrights and directors. Marshall W. Mason, director.

SPRING'S AWAKENING by Frank Wedekind. June 12, 1975. Directed by Jan Eliasberg.
OVERRULED by George Bernard Shaw. November, 1975. Directed by Bill Ludel.

THE LESSON OF THE MASTER by Richard Howard. May 18, 1976. Directed by Michael Feingold; with Nancy Marchand, Lenny Baker.
WHEN I DYED MY HAIR IN VENICE by Helen Duberstein, directed by Alice Rubenstein, with Nancy Reardon; SOLO FOR TWO by Juliette Bowles, directed by Hiram Taylor, with Joanne Jacaruso, David Swatling; THE MAGIC FORMULA by Sidney Morris, directed by Alan Coleridge, with Bob Whiting, Ronald Hunter, Sharon Madden. May 19, 1976.
TERMINAL and NIGHT THOUGHTS by Corinne Jacker. May 26, 1976. Directed by Steven Gomer, with Jacqueline Brooks, Patricia O'Connell.

City Playworks. A new company with varied ambitions and a first-year schedule of two Equity-approved showcases. Linda Brumfield, Christopher Cara, Gus Kaikkonen, Jonathan Sand, directors.

IVANOV. Translated by Alex Szogyi. August 14, 1975. Directed by Gus Kaikkonen; produced with ETC Theater; with Christopher Cara, Joe Endes, Susan Krebs, Parler McCormick, Robb Webb.
IN THE BOOM BOOM ROOM by David Rabe. December 18, 1975. Directed by Terry Grossman; with Corie Sims, Randy Danson, Mike Scott, Mark Kologi, Gloria Lord.

Colonnades Theater Lab. Resident repertory company with an in-training program for actors. Emphasis on new playwrights. Michael Lessac, artistic director.

SECOND WIND by David Morgan. December 2, 1975. Directed by Michael Lessac.
A MONTH IN THE COUNTRY by Ivan Turgenev, adapted by David Morgan. December 4, 1975. Directed by Michael Lessac.
CINEMA SOLDIER by Paavo Tammi. December 6, 1975. Directed by Tom Tammi.
REFLECTIONS (musical) book by David Morgan, music and lyrics by Miriam Moses. December 9, 1975. Directed by Michael Lessac.

The Comedy Stage Company. Actors, directors and audiences interested in the revival of modern and traditional comedies. Tim Ward, director (and director of all productions).

THE MISER by Molière. September 18, 1975.
EVERYMAN and ACT WITHOUT WORDS I by Samuel Beckett. December 4, 1975.
JOE EGG by Peter Nichols. February 12, 1976.
LOOT by Joe Orton. April 29, 1976.

Counterpoint Theater Company. Maintain high standards of excellence in the service of plays of distinction, through theatrical productions of enduring value. Howard Green, artistic director.

MISS JULIE and THE STRONGER. October 3, 1975. Directed by Gonzalo Madurga.
CHILDREN OF DARKNESS by Edwin Justus Mayer. November 21, 1975. Directed by Howard Green.
A CHEKHOV PORTFOLIO (four one-act-plays): On the Harmfulness of Tobacco, The Boor, Summer in the Country, Swan Song. January 16, 1976. Directed by Howard Green.
ROCKET TO THE MOON by Clifford Odets. March 5, 1976. Directed by Joel Friedman; with Len Auclair, Sylvia Gassell, Sam Gray, Howard Green, Elek Hartman, John J. Martin, Fanny McDonald.
THE REHEARSAL by Jean Anouilh. April 23, 1976. Directed by Howard Green.

The Courtyard Playhouse Foundation. Eclectic policy of searching for "a good play", new ones preferred but not exclusively. Houses Little People's Theater Company for quality in children's theater. Kenneth R. Eulo, artistic director.

UNINVITED by Peter Dee. July 17, 1975. Directed by William McKitrick; with Vincent McNally, Michael Oakes, Freda Scott, Sara Sullivan.
BIRDBATH and HALLOWEEN by Leonard Melfi. Directed by Micci Johnson.
FINAL EXAMS written and directed by Kenneth R. Eulo. November, 1975.
PORNO STARS AT HOME by Leonard Melfi. January 28, 1976. Directed by Kenneth R.

Eulo; with Rebecca Stanley, Michael Lamont, Jody Catlin, Richard Hayes, Grace Woodward, Philip Adelman.
DETECTIVE STORY by Sidney Kingsley. March 26, 1976. Directed by Marvin Kahan.

The Cubiculo and **Cubiculo III.** Experiments in the use of theater, dance, music, etc. housed in four studios and two stages. Phillip Meister, artistic director.

FESTIVAL OF NEW PLAYS from Israel Horovitz's workshop at Brandeis University: RAPPAPORT by William Weshta, directed by Will Weiss; THE PRIMARY ENGLISH CLASS by Israel Horovitz, directed by Stephen Drewes. June 4, 1975.
THE MAN ON THE MONKEY BARS and THE BRIDGE AT BELHARBOUR by Janet L. Neipris. June 6, 1975. Directed by James Clay; with Valerie Marino.
EXHIBITION by Janet L. Neipris, TO SKIN A CAT by Liz Coe and MOVING DAY by Linda Segal. June 6, 1975.
SWING/SLIDE by Patricia Gibson, directed by Nancy Alexander and TANGLEWOOD by David Cohen, directed by Moneer Zarou. June 8, 1975.
THE MEMOIRS OF CHARLIE POPS by Joseph Hart. September 19, 1975. Directed by John Bettenbender; with Frank Ammirati, Robin Siegel, Rita Bascari.
WEEKS by Nancy Heiken. September 25, 1975. Directed by Heiner Stadler; with Susan Topping.
SURVIVING THE BARBED WIRE CRADLE by Francine Marie Storey and TERRIBLE JIM FITCH by James Leo Herlihy (one-act plays). November 1, 1975. Directed by Dana Roberts.
THE DEVIL'S DISCIPLE by George Bernard Shaw. November 6, 1975. Directed by Robert Elston.
A GOOD OLD FASHIONED REVUE conceived by Les Barkdull. November 12, 1975. With Carleton Carpenter, Sue Lawless.
PEOPLE FROM DIVISION STREET adapted by Alexandra Devon from Studs Terkel's *Division Street: America.*
BENSON AND CISSY, CISSY AND BENSON, BOXES/BOXES GOING TO SALEM and TWO SEE BESIDE THE SEA (one-act plays) by Gary Martin. December, 1975. Directed by Gene Becker.
SPOON RIVER ANTHOLOGY by Edgar Lee Masters, adapted by John Franceschina. December, 1975. Directed by Sue Lawless.
WHAT IS DON GIOVANNI DOING IN SUE'S BEDROOM by and with Sue Sheehy. December, 1975. Directed by David Nunemaker.
REFLECTIONS by David Nunemaker. January 22, 1976.
DUETS OF DRAMA (one-act plays): I HATE THE SITUATION MORE THAN I LOVE YOU by Bob Banov and Te Revesz and YOU AND ME AND THE REST OF THE WORLD by Jacqueline Berger. January 28, 1976. Directed by Sol Weinstein; performed by Inscape Company.
THE HOME (improvisation) by Kent Andersson and Bengt Bratt. January 28, 1976. Directed by Robert Horen.
HOLY GHOSTS by Romulus Linney. February, 1976. Directed by John Olon-Scrymgeour.
THE BEDBUG by Vladimir Mayakovsky, adapted and directed by John Merensky. April 1, 1976. With Ron Klein.
DR. HERO by Israel Horovitz. April 5, 1976. Directed by Lee Rachman.
FOUNDING FATHER by Amlin Gray. April 22, 1976. Directed by Constance Clarke; with Jeffrey DeMunn.
CLYTEMNESTRA by Elaine Sulka. May 11, 1976. Directed by Phillip Meister.
OH by Sandro Key-Aberg. May 20, 1976. Directed by Bob Horen. STAUF written and directed by Michael Sahl and Eric Salzman. May 25, 1976.

Direct Theater. A professional company of actors and other stage artists exploring new techniques. Allen R. Belknap, artistic director.

DISCOVERING BODIES (two plays) written and directed by Richard Ohanesian. June, 1975.
TIGERS by Andrew Lascelles, directed by John Loven; THE LADY OF LARKSPUR LOTION by Tennessee Williams, directed by Edmund Bradley, JACK, OR THE SUBMISSION by Eugene Ionesco, directed by David Dean. September, 1975.
THE AFFECTIONATE CANNIBALS by Ross Alexander. October 8, 1975. Directed by Ross Alexander and Edmund Bradley; with Justin Rashid, Beth Ellen Keyes, Amanda Davis.

COLUMBUS (musical) adapted and directed by Allen R. Belknap from Michel de Ghel-derode's *Christophe Colombe*, music by Gary Levinson, lyrics by Beth Bowden. December 4, 1975. With Susan J. Baum, Jeff Brooks, Bob DelPazzo, Debra Dickinson, Gene Lindsey, George Maguire, Lilene Mansell, Milledge Mosley, Diana Schuster, Ted Wass.

RICHARD II. January 15, 1976. Directed by Charle Bright and Ann Occhiogrosso; with Randall Duk Kim, Ric Lavin, David Darlow, Dana Mills, John Tatlock, Danny Watkins.

ICARUS'S MOTHER by Sam Shepard, directed by Ted Snowdon; SOLO FOR TWO by Juliette Bowles, directed by Hiram Taylor. March, 1976.

BACK BOG BEAST BAIT by Sam Shepard. March, 1976. Directed by Matthew Bullock.

NOON and SWEET EROS by Terrence McNally. April 14, 1976. Directed by David Dean; with James Paige Morrison, Leslie Ritter, Jessica James, Peter Frederic Steinberg, Henson Keys.

THE TRANSFIGURATION OF BENNO BLIMPIE by Albert Innaurato. April 22, 1976. Directed by Peter Mark Schifter; with Anne DeSalvo, Henry Ferrentino, Kathy McKenna, Jon Polito, Vic Polizos.

HOW HE LIED TO HER HUSBAND by George Bernard Shaw and THE WHITE LIARS by Peter Shaffer. May 15, 1976. Directed and performed by Glynis Bell, Michael Tolaydo, Richard Ooms, Sam Tsoutsouvas.

11:00 After-Theater Series:

THE NATURE AND PURPOSE OF THE UNIVERSE by Christopher Durang. September 3, 1975. Directed by Allen R. Belknap and Yannis Simonides; with James Nisbet Clark, Anne DeSalvo, Lynnie Godfrey, Justin Rashid, Nick Mariano, David Wilborn.

JACK, OR THE SUBMISSION by Eugene Ionesco. December 6, 1975. Directed by David Dean; with Linda Burt, Barry Couillard, Janet Cover, F. Kenneth Freedman, James Paige Morrison, Brian Newberg.

TITANIC by Christopher Durang. March 3, 1976. Directed by Peter Mark Schifter; with Jeff Brooks, Stefen Hartman, Richard Peterson, Ralph Redpath, Kate McGregor Stewart, Sigourney Weaver.

Drama Committee Repertory Theater. Performs 19th and 20th century classics of all nations. Arthur Reel, artistic director.

CAMINO REAL by Tennessee Williams. August, 1975. Directed by Arthur Reel.

STREET SCENE by Elmer Rice. September, 1975. Directed by Arthur Reel.

THE MAN WHO CAME TO DINNER by George S. Kaufman and Moss Hart. October, 1975. Directed by Zachary D. Silver.

THE CHERRY ORCHARD. November 1, 1975. Directed by Arthur Reel.

THE RESPECTFUL PROSTITUTE by Jean-Paul Sartre, directed by Arthur Reel; THE RED DEVIL adapted from Maxim Gorki and directed by Arthur Reel. November 5, 1975.

BLUE HOTEL and MAGGIE adapted from Stephen Crane by Arthur Reel. November 12, 1975. Directed by Eli Ask.

MISS LONELYHEARTS by Nathanael West. January 16, 1976. Directed by Arhtur Reel.

SEPARATE TABLES by Terence Rattigan. January, 1976. Directed by Arthur Reel.

SUMMER AND SMOKE by Tennessee Williams. February, 1976. Directed by Laura Darius.

THE CHILDREN'S HOUR by Lillian Hellman. March 28, 1976. Directed by Zachary D. Silver.

PEER GYNT. April 23, 1976. Directed by Zachary D. Silver.

A THURBER CARNIVAL. May 16, 1976. Directed by Arthur Reel.

Drama Ensemble Company. Devoted to experimental plays, as outgrowths of on-going workshops; open to new writers and directors. Peter Ehrman, artistic director.

THE MISUNDERSTANDING by Albert Camus. October 9, 1975. Directed by Stephen Yarian.

TARTUFFE. November 28, 1975. Directed by Stephen Yarian.

NEXT by Terrence McNally; ANSWERS by Tom Topor; STEPHEN by Alice Cooper. April, 1976. Directed by Joseph Criscoli.

MANY LOVES by William Carlos Williams. April 29, 1976. Directed by Robert Feinstein.

CONVENTION written and directed by Alan Ehrman. May 28, 1976.

Elysian Playhouse/The Mufson Company. To stage exciting, truthful and imagina-tive productions of naturalistic and realistic plays, both comedy and drama, origi-nals and revivals. Ken Mufson, artistic director.

THE LAST OF THE RED HOT LOVERS by Neil Simon. June, 1975. Directed by Ken Mufson.

A THOUSAND CLOWNS by Herb Gardner. October 1, 1975. Directed by Ken Mufson.

A MASS MURDER IN THE BALCONY OF THE OLD RITZ-RIALTO (musical) book by Ed Kuczewski, music, lyrics and directed by Bill Vitale. December, 1975.

THE CARPENTERS by Steve Tesich. January 9, 1976. Directed by Ken Mufson; with Frank A. Ammirati, Fran Carlon, Richard Weiss, Harry Browne, Robin Groves.

I NEVER SANG FOR MY FATHER by Robert Anderson. Directed by Ken Mufson.

A STRAWBERRY GREW AN APPLE TREE (musical) by Irving Reed. Directed by Pat Carmichael.

Encompass Theater. Dedicated to finding, developing and producing new playwrights. Special emphasis on new and rarely performed plays and musicals by and about women. Nancy Rhodes, artistic director.

THE MOTHER OF US ALL by Gertrude Stein, music by Virgil Thomson, adapted and directed by Nancy Rhodes. May 24, 1975 (new production reopened March 20, 1976). With Anne Collins, Joanne Picone, Cardiff M. Williams, Karen Bradicich, Ray Romain, Timothy Lafontaine.

Ensemble Studio Theater. Nucleus of 26 playwrights-in-residence dedicated to supporting individual theater artists and developing new works for the stage. 40-50 projects each season, initiated by E.S.T. members. Curt Dempster, artistic director.

THE SHORTCHANGED REVIEW by Michael Dorn Moody. November 6, 1975. Directed by Richard Southern.

GETTING THROUGH THE NIGHT by John Ford Noonan. February 12, 1976. Directed by James Hammerstein; with Lynne Lipton, Jean DeBaer, Melodie Somers, Pamela Reed.

POSSESSION by Lyle Kessler. March 25, 1976. Directed by James Hammerstein.

MONEY by Arthur Giron. April 29, 1976. Directed by Jan Eliasberg.

THE SOFT TOUCH by Neil Cuthbert. May, 1976. Directed by Jerry Zaks.

Equity Library Theater. Actors' Equity produces a series of revivals each season as showcases for the work of its actor-members. George Wojtasik, managing director.

THE PURSUIT OF HAPPINESS by Armina Marshall and Lawrence Langner. October 16, 1975. Directed by Tisa Chang.

TENDERLOIN (musical) book by Jerome Weidman and George Abbott, music by Jerry Bock, lyrics by Sheldon Harnick. November 6, 1975. Directed by Robert Brink; with Brad Blaisdell, Pamela McLernon, Stan Page, Suzanne Ford, Alan Abrams, Sherry Rooney.

ANOTHER LANGUAGE by Rose Franken. December 4, 1975, Directed by Leonard Peters; with Margaret Whitton, Mildred Dana, James Doerr, Robert Bonds, Marjorie Lovett, Ron Frazier.

PANAMA HATTIE (musical) book by Herbert Fields and B.G. DeSylva, music and lyrics by Cole Porter, adapted by Charles Abbott and Frederic Dehn. January 15, 1976. Directed by Charles Abbott; with Mary Ellen Ashley, Lynn Martin, Douglas Hayle, Michael Davis, May Keller, Diana Barrows.

MISSOURI LEGEND by E.B. Ginty. February 12, 1976. Directed by Thom Molyneaux; with Bill Tatum, Earl Wentz, Michael Oakes, Sofia Landon, Jeanne Schlegel, Todd Drexel.

MAGGIE FLYNN (musical) book, music and lyrics by Hugo Peretti, Luigi Creatore and George D. Weiss. March 4, 1976. Directed by William Koch; with Austin Colyer, Deborah Combs, Paul A. Corman, Mike Dantuono, Bette Glenn, Richard Halpern.

THE RIMERS OF ELDRITCH by Lanford Wilson. April 1, 1976. Directed by Cyprienne Gabel; with Kender Jones, Virginia Downing, Joan G. Gilbert, Martha Miller, Rose Lischner, Daniel Landon.

FOLLIES (musical) book by James Goldman, music and lyrics by Stephen Sondheim. May 6, 1976. Directed by Russell Treyz; with George Maguire, Lois Ann Saunders, Andrew Roman, Joan Ulmer, Kurt Johnson, Spence Ford, Margaret Goodman.

ETC Theater. Produces plays by American playwrights. Improvisational techniques utilized in all shows. J.J. Barry, Frank Bongiorno, Ron Comenzo, artistic directors.

JOHNNY MANHATTAN (musical) by Danny Coggin and Robert Lorick. November, 1975. Directed by Robert Lorick.

RELATIVES by Meir Z. Ribalow. December 9, 1975. Directed by Lou LaMonte; with J.J. Barry, Carole Barry, Neil Flanagan, Aaron Freeman, Tom Kleh.

DUCKSONG by David Mercer. February, 1976. Directed by Barry Cornet.

THE COMEBACK and THE COMPETITORS by Jack Gilhooley. February 26, 1976. Directed by Michael Vale.

THE LOOKING GLASS by Joseph MacLaren. April 1, 1976. Directed by Stephen James.

ZEN BOOGIE by J.J. Barry. May 6, 1976.

Gene Frankel Theater Workshop. Development of new works and revivals for the theater. Gene Frankel, artistic director, executive producer.

THE CRUCIBLE by Arthur Miller. November 26, 1975. Directed by Robert Cusack.

MIDSUMMER adapted and directed by Nancy Zala from *A Midsummer Night's Dream*. March 4, 1976.

SARAH BERNHARDT and ECHOES OF . . . (mime). March 22, 1976. With Stephanie Rich.

THE BLACK SWAN by Anne Marie Sapse. April 3, 1976. Directed by Alexander Sokoloff.

THE LION IS A SOUL BROTHER written and directed by Joseph A. Walker. April 24, 1976.

THE FATHER by August Strindberg. May 13, 1976. Directed by Alexander Sokoloff.

Hudson Guild Theater. American classics interspersed with original and experimental plays. Craig Anderson, artistic director.

CEREMONIES IN DARK OLD MEN by Lonne Elder III. October 2, 1975. Directed by Craig Anderson.

WHO'S HAPPY NOW? by Oliver Hailey. December 11, 1975. Directed by Craig Anderson.

WORKING OUR WAY DOWN by Bette Craig. January 10, 1976. Directed by Chuck Portz; performed by The Labor Theater.

THE DISINTEGRATION OF JAMES CHERRY by Jeff Wanshel. February 26, 1976. Directed by David Kerry Heefner.

YESTERDAY AND TODAY (musical revue). April, 1976.

WHERE'S MY LITTLE GLORIA? By Hector Troy. May 13, 1976. Directed by Ernest Martin.

Playwright's Program: staged readings:
CURTAINS by Gloria Gonzalez. A CHARMING AFTERNOON by Howard Singer. BREEDING GREAT ORCHIDS by Lionel Chetwynd. WRITER'S CAMP by Albert Lynch and Peter Dee. WHERE'S MY LITTLE GLORIA? by Hector Troy.

Impossible Ragtime Theater (IRT). Dedicated to exploration of the director's role in all aspects of theater. Ted Story, George Ferencz, artistic directors.

DIAL M FOR MURDER by Frederick Knott. June, 1975. Directed by George Ferencz; with Doug Day, Jonathan Foster, David Forsyth, Steve Randolph, Kate Zentall.

AMERICAN STICKBALL LEAGUE by Howard Kuperberg. September 20, 1975. Directed by George Ferencz; with Al Cowing, Henry Ferrentino, David Forsyth, David Kerman, Stuart Rudin, Oliver J. Wyman, Jr.

ROUNDELAY by Peter Swet, based on Arthur Schnitzler's *La Ronde* November 8, 1975. Directed by Ted Story; with Catharine Boyd, Peter Brooks-Jackson, Stan Edelman, Eva Galan, Edward Gallardo, David Garcia, Lorey Hayes, Hansford Rowe, Roz Vallero, Basil A. Wallace.

THE RATS by Agatha Christie, directed by Stephen Zuckerman and THE LONG CHRISTMAS DINNER by Thornton Wilder, directed by Jonathan Foster. December 11, 1975. With Francois De La Giroday, Penelope Hirsch, William Turner, Lottie Ward, Margaret Flanagan, Ann Freeman.

THE HAIRY APE by Eugene O'Neill. January 10, 1976. Directed by George Ferencz; with Ray Wise, Annette Kurek, Cynthia Crane, Greg Fabian.

THE FRIENDS ROADSHOW. March 19, 1976.

IVANOV. April 24, 1976. Directed by Ted Story.

JULIUS CAESAR adapted and directed by George Ferencz. May 21, 1976.

IRT East
TELEMACHUS CLAY by Lewis John Carlino. October 16, 1975. Directed by Jonathan Foster.
SHADOW OF A GUNMAN by Sean O'Casey. February 5, 1976. Directed by Ron Daley.
NOT ENOUGH ROPE by Elaine May, directed by Jude Schanzer; HELLO FROM BERTHA and TALK TO ME LIKE THE RAIN by Tennessee Williams, directed by Jonathan Foster. March 26, 1976. With Jean Campbell, Chris Wallace, Missie Zollo, Bonni Leu Banyard, Darby Louis, Phyllis Ward.
THE GREAT RAGE OF PHILIP HOTZ by Max Frisch, directed by Ron Daley; with Larry Carr, Cynthia Crane, Tim Flanagan, Annette Kurek, John Del Regno, Mike Zettler; LUNCHTIME by Leonard Melfi. May 28, 1976. Directed by Alison Mackenzie; with Don Klecak, Johanna Leister.

Lunchtime Theater
THE BOOR, adapted from Anton Chekhov. October 14, 1975. Directed by James DiPaola.
THE PATIENT by Agatha Christie. December 8, 1975. Directed by David William Kitchen.
BEDTIME STORY by Sean O'Casey. February 9, 1976. Directed by Alison Mackenzie; with Kathleen Coyne, Con Roche.
THE GYPSYS (musical by Bob Jewett. March 29, 1976. Directed by Stephen Zukerman; with Ziva Flomenhaft, Jonathan Frakes, Michael Huber, Bob Jewett, Denny McCormick, Jim Ragland.
THE LAST STRAW by Charles Dizenzo. May 24, 1976. Directed by Stephen Zuckerman; with Lee Wilkof, David Wilborn.

Interart Theater. Showcase opportunities which provide a professional environment for women playwrights, directors, designers and performers to participate in theatrical activity. Margot Lewitin, Joyce Aaron, Susan Kellermann, coordinators.

THE FIRST OF APRIL and MATUSHKA-BARYSHNYA (one-act plays) by Nina Voronel. October 23, 1975. Directed by Margot Lewitin; with Rose Lischner, Helen Ludlam, Dwight Marfield, Judith Elder, Mary Boylan, Maurice Braddell.
CO-RESPONDENTS. October 28, 1975. Performed by Woman's Troupe.
ACROBATICS written and directed by Luna Tarlo and Joyce Aaron. March, 1976. With Jacqueline Barnett, Joyce Aaron.

Workshop Productions
GARDEN VARIETY (mime) with Marcy Arlin, Lynn Cataldo, Susan Goldbetter, Marge Helenchild, Elizabeth Roth, Hank Smith; ON THE HARMFULNESS OF TOBACCO. Directed by Muriel Stursberg; with Lucille Saint-Peter. June 11, 1975.
PANDORA'S BOX (Poetry-drama) written and directed by Lucille Saint-Peter. February 19, 1976.
MOTHER'S DAY written and directed by Judith Morley. May 6, 1976.

The Irish Rebel Theater (An Claidheamh Soluis). Dedicated to establishing an awareness among people of all ethnic backgrounds of the artistic expression of the Irish people. Larry Spiegel, artistic director.

THE FLATS by John Boyd. November 7, 1975. Directed by Larry Speigel.
LOVERS by Brian Friel, directed by Tom Connelley; THE RISING OF THE MOON by Lady Gregory, directed by James F. Olwell; THE DARK MOON AND THE FULL by Joseph Hart, directed by Georgia Freemoor. April 2, 1976.
THE FIELD by John B. Keane. May, 1976. Directed by Larry Speigel.

Jean Cocteau Repertory. Located in the historic Bouwerie Lane Theater, the Jean Cocteau Repertory presents vintage and modern classics on a rotating repertory schedule. Eve Adamson, artistic director.

ORPHÉE by Jean Cocteau. June 13, 1975. Directed by Eve Adamson.
TWELFTH NIGHT. September 19, 1975. Directed by Eve Adamson; with Craig Smith, Coral S. Potter, Barbara Slone.
BRECHT ON BRECHT by George Tabori. September 21, 1975. Directed by Eve Adamson.
DESIRE UNDER THE ELMS. October 11, 1975. Directed by Eve Adamson.
THE IMPORTANCE OF BEING EARNEST. November 22, 1975.

ENDGAME by Samuel Beckett. January 17, 1976.
THE COUNT OF MONTE CRISTO dramatization by Marshall Borden. February 21, 1976. Directed by Eve Adamson; with Coral S. Potter, Jon Brooks, George Brunner, Joan Grant, Boris Kinberg, James S. Payne.
VERA, OR THE NIHILISTS by Oscar Wilde. April 15, 1976.
WINTERSET by Maxwell Anderson. May 12, 1976.
THE LESSON by Eugene Ionesco. May 26, 1976.

Jones Beach Marine Theater. Each summer a musical classic is presented in this huge outdoor theater on Long Island. Guy Lombardo, producer.

OKLAHOMA (musical) book and lyrics by Oscar Hammerstein II, music by Richard Rodgers. June 26, 1975. Directed by John Fearnley; with Thomas McKinney, Judith McCauley, Harvey Evans, Nancy Andrews, Will Ray, Bruce Adler.

Joseph Jefferson Theater Company. Performs solely American plays, both revivals and new works largely drawn from their playwrights' workshop. Cathy Roskam, founder.

GETTING GERTIE'S GARTER by Wilson Collison and Avery Hopwood. June 5, 1975. Directed by Robert Moss; with Carole Doscher, Peter Simpson, Cathy Roskam, Maria Cellario, Robert McFarland, Dana Gladstone.
RIP VAN WINKLE (Dion Boucicault version). July 14, 1975. Directed by William Koch; with Reathel Bean, Suzanne Osborne, Nita Novy, Jennifer Thompson, James Newell, Peter Simpson.
THUNDER ROCK by Robert Ardrey. October 23, 1975. Directed by William Koch; with Reathel Bean, Peter Alzado, Madeline Gorman, Richard Marr, Paul Meacham, Frank Miazga, Nita Novy, Suzanne Osborne, Bill Tatum, Tracey Walter.
APRIL FISH (one-act play) by Ted Pezzulo, directed by Christopher Cox; with Jo Flores Chase, Richard Zavaglia, Antonino Pandolfo, Jason Howard, Michael Brindisi, Dwight Marfield; and THE WOOING OF LADY SUNDAY (one-act Play) by Ted Pezzulo, directed by Bill Herndon; with Susan Walker, Frank Cascio, Henry Ferrentino, Marjorie Austrian, Jason Howard, Rachel Milder. December 2, 1975.
MEMORY OF A LARGE CHRISTMAS by Lillian Smith. December 18, 1975. Directed by William Koch; narrated by Eugenia Rawls.
MORNING'S AT SEVEN by Paul Osborn. February 11, 1976. Directed by Cathy Roskam; with Anita Bayless, Bill Daprato, Eleanor Cody Gould, Melanie Hill, I.W. Klein, Rose Lischner, George Lloyd, Frances Pole, William Robertson.
JOHN by Philip Barry. May 5, 1976. Directed by Cyril Simon; with Armand Assante, Elizabeth Hubbard, James Carruthers, Richard Cox, Natalia E. Chuma.

The Judson Poets' Theater. The theater arm of Judson Memorial Church and its pastor, Al Carmines, who creates a series of new, unconventional musicals which are sometimes transferred to the commercial theater. Al Carmines, director.

WHY I LOVE NEW YORK (musical) by Al Carmines. October 10, 1975. Directed by Leonard Peters.
CHRISTMAS RAPPINGS by Al Carmines. December, 1975. With Lee Guilliatt, Essie Borden.
THREE EVENINGS ON A REVOLVING STAGE conceived and directed by Jean DuPuy. January, 1976.
THE BONUS ARMY (musical) book by David Epstein, music and lyrics by Al Carmines. February 20, 1976. Directed by Jacques Levy; with Reathel Bean, Gordon Hammett, Daniel Keys, William Knight, Anne Korzen, Peter Lombard, Richard Miller, Leslie Ann Ray, Rick Warner, Ronald Willoughby, Alex Wipf.
CAMP MEETING: 1840 by Al Carmines. May 20, 1976.

La Mama Experimental Theater Club (ETC). A busy workshop for experimental theater of all kinds. Ellen Stewart, director.

C.O.R.F.A.X. (DON'T ASK) (musical) written and directed by Wilford Leach, music by William Elliott. October 20, 1975.
COTTON CLUB GALA (revue). December 5, 1975. With Aaron Bell, the Original Hoofers,

the Ellington Alumni, Lari Becham and La Soubrettes, Tony Azito, Denise Rogers, Eric Concklin.

STAR FOLLOWERS IN AN ANCIENT LAND written and directed by H.M. Koutoukas, music by Tom O'Horgan, additional songs by Gale Garnett. December 15, 1975. Performed by The School for Gargoyles.

MYTHS OF AMERICA SMITH AND HIS SON by Greg Antonacci, music by Ronnie B. Baker. December 18, 1975. Directed by Joel Zwick.

FRAGMENTS OF A TRILOGY: THE TROJAN WOMEN and ELECTRA conceived and directed by Andrei Serban, music by Elizabeth Swados. December 27, 1975. With Priscilla Smith, Jane Lind, Valois Mickens, Joanna Peled, Peter Jon DeVries, Joyce Hanley.

WATER PLAY by Kikuo Saito. January 15, 1976.

GAUNTLET, OR, THE MOON'S ON FIRE written and directed by John Braswell. January 22, 1976. With Helen Stenborg.

THE GOOD WOMAN OF SETZUAN by Bertolt Brecht, English version by Eric Bentley, music by Elizabeth Swados. January 23, 1976. Directed by Andrei Serban; with Jane Lind, Jerry Cunliffe, Justin Rashid, Priscilla Smith, Valois Mickens, Richard Jackiel.

HUMAN ARTS ENSEMBLE (workshop). February 12, 1976. With Melvin Smith, Phillip Wilson.

REPORT TO THE COMMITTEE ON PORNOGRAPHY and SERVICE IN TIME OF LOVE (work-in-progress) by Tevye Abrams. February, 1976. Directed by Lindsay Huffman.

ZAINAMOH written and directed by Hassin Wakrim. February 25, 1976.

CRACKER CLUB COUNTRY FAIR GALA (revue). February 27, 1976. With Hoe-Downs Square, Piute Pete. Contributing playwrights and composers: Greg Antonacci, Ronnie B Baker, John Braden, William Elliott, Paul Foster, Leonard Melfi, Elizabeth Swados.

THE CHINESE SCREEN by China Clark, directed by Darryl Croxton and RUNNING FAST THRU PARADISE by Calva Duridy, directed by Owa. February 27, 1976. (Works-in-progress).

A RAT'S MASS/PROCESSION IN SHOUT by Adrienne Kennedy and Cecil Taylor. March, 1976. Directed by Cecil Taylor.

CARMILLA adapted from J.S. LeFanu's novella by Wilford Leach, music by Ben Johnston. March, 1976. Directed by Wilford Leach.

ROLLS OF GOLD written and directed by Josef Bush. March 4, 1976.

THE SOLEDAD TETRAD, PARTS I and II written and directed by Owa. March, 1976.

THE FALL OF MASADA written and directed by Amnon Ben Nomis. March 23, 1976.

LA BOUTIQUE by Jeannine Worms. March 25, 1976. With Marthe Mercadier.

PHANTOM DANCE by Edward Evans. March 26, 1976.

WORLD THEATER CELEBRATION: TWITAS (A Third World Cultural Perspective). March 27, 1976.

SOUNDS IN MOTION by Diane McIntyre. March 28, 1976.

QUARRY conceived and directed by Meredith Monk. April 2, 1976. Performed by The House.

THE WONDERFUL BEAST by Louisa Rose. April 8, 1976. Directed by John Braswell.

GODSONG by James Weldon Johnson, music and directed by Tad Truesdale. April 23, 1976.

BROTHERS (musical) by Christopher Gore, music and directed by David Spangler. April 29, 1976.

DR. JEKYLL AND MR. HYDE adapted by Charles Peters. May 19, 1976. Directed by David McKenna.

THE ORPHAN OF CHAO. May 20, 1976. Directed by Tisa Chang; performed by The Chinese Theater Group.

THE ARCHITECT AND THE EMPEROR OF ASSYRIA by Fernando Arrabal. May 27, 1976. Directed by Tom O'Horgan.

Lion Theater Company. Actors' company with an eclectic repertory. Gene Nye, Garland Wright, artistic directors.

TWELFTH NIGHT, with music by Mac McKinney. July 23, 1975. Directed by Garland Wright; with Jack Heifner, John Arnone, William Metzo, Bob Machray, Gene Nye, John Guerrasio.

THE DOCTOR IN SPITE OF HIMSELF. July 31, 1975. Directed by Gene Nye; with Ron Van Lieu, Jane Galloway, Jack Heifner, John Guerrasio, David Gallagher, Rick Salome.

END AS A MAN by Calder Willingham. September, 1975. Directed by Garland Wright.

VANITIES by Jack Heifner (cooperative venture with Playwrights Horizons). December, 1975. Directed by Garland Wright; with Kathy Bates, Jane Galloway, Susan Merson.

Manhattan Theater Club. A producing organization with three stages for productions, readings, workshop activities and cabaret. Lynne Meadow, artistic director.

Upstairs:
SEA MARKS by Gardner McKay. November 1, 1975. Directed by Steven Robman.
A SLIGHT ACHE and THE BASEMENT by Harold Pinter. November 13, 1975. Directed by David Kerry Heefner.
GEOGRAPHY OF A HORSE DREAMER by Sam Shepard. December, 1975. Directed by Jacques Levy; with Rick Warner, Robert Lesser, J. Zakkal, John Mitchell, Gordon Hammett, Paul Andor.
PATRICK HENRY LAKE LIQUORS by Larry Ketron. February, 1976. Directed by Ronald Roston; with Jay Devlin, James Hilbrandt, Ed Seamon, Regina Baff, Christine Lauren, Donna Emmanuel, Toni Kalem.
THE VOICE OF THE TURTLE by John Van Druten. March, 1976. Directed by Julianne Boyd.
DEARLY BELOVED by John Raymond Hart. April, 1976. Directed by Paul Schneider.
THE POKEY by Stephen Black. May, 1976. Directed by Lynne Meadow.
TRANSFORMATIONS (opera) libretto by Ann Sexton, music by Conrad Sousa. May, 1976. Directed by David Shookoff.

Downstairs
GOLDEN BOY by Clifford Odets. October 16, 1975. Directed by Lynne Meadow.
LIFE CLASS by David Storey. December, 1975. Directed by Robert Mandel, with Kevin Conway, Christopher Curry, William Carden, Veronica Castang, Lenny Baker, Dale Hodges.
THE BLOOD KNOT by Athol Fugard. February 11, 1976. Directed by Thomas Bullard, with David H. Leary, Robert Christian.
THE SON by Gert Hofmann, translated by Jon Swan. March, 1976. Directed by Stephen Pascal.
IN THE WINE TIME by Ed Bullins. April 21, 1976. Directed by Robert Macbeth.

Cabaret
MARVIN'S GARDEN, music by Mel Marvin. June 12, 1975.
SONGS FROM RUBY'S PLACE. November 1, 1975. With Alaina Reed, Andre deShields, Larry Moss, Sarah Harris.
KANDER AND EBB CABARET. February, 1976.
PINS AND NEEDLES (songs) by Harold Rome. February 26, 1976. Musical direction by Jez Davidson; with Cynthia Bostick, Margery Cohen, Margaret Warneke, Jonathan Hadary, Marc Gass.
CRACKED TOKENS (improvisation group).
AN EVENING WITH SHOLOM ALEICHEM with Murray Horwitz. March, 1976. Directed by Richard Maltby Jr.
PEOPLE SONGS (three-man show of songs). March, 1976.
MUSICAL PERFORMANCE by Stephanie Cotsirilos. April 17, 1976.
JAZZ BABIES (songs of the 20's). May 13, 1976. With Seth Glassman.

Medecine Show Theater Ensemble. Develops works that juggle incongruities of style and form, mingle wit and high physical energy. Barbara Vann, director.

GLOWWORM conceived and directed by Barbara Vann, text by Carl Morse and Susan Wilkins, music by Jim Milton. February, 1976. Developed by the company.

National Arts Theater. To present revivals and re-adaptations of classical works. Robert Sterling, Robert Stocking, co-producers, co-artistic directors.

THE MOUSETRAP by Agatha Christie. June, 1975. Directed by Robert Sterling.
A STREETCAR NAMED DESIRE by Tennessee Williams. September, 1975. Directed by Robert Stocking.
THE REFLECTIONS OR THE INDICTMENT by Neville Aurelius. November 1, 1975. Directed by Robert Stocking.
CALIGULA by Albert Camus. November 20, 1975. Directed by Robert Sterling.
THE SEAGULL. May 26, 1976. Directed by Robert Sterling.

National Black Theater. Developing a new form of theater as a ritualistic revival to present new and positive images for audiences. Barbara Ann Teer, founder.

SOULJOURNEY INTO TRUTH (musical) written and directed by Barbara Ann Teer. Performed by the company (ongoing, changing production).

The New Dramatists. An organization devoted to playwrights; member writers may use the facilities for anything from private cold readings of their material to workshop stagings. Jeff Peters, Program Director.

Workshop Stagings
NEVER A SNUG HARBOUR by David Ulysses Clarke. September 23, 1975. Directed by Tom Ligon; with Joseph Regalbuto, Richard Brestoff, Robert Boardman, Paul Andor, Mora Dunfee, Peter Dee.
THE LAST CHRISTIANS by Jack Gilhooley. October 7, 1975. Directed by Clinton J. Atkinson; with Alan Brasington, Robert Lydiard, Steve Vinovich, Marianne Muellerleile, Libby Lyman, Joseph Alaskey.
THE WOLVES AND THE LAMBS by Frieda Lipp. October 21, 1975. Directed by Christopher Adler; with Marvyn Haines, Jr., Edith Greenfield, Peter Anlyan, Lane Binkley, Beth Holland, Stephen Weyte.
SISTER SADIE written and directed by Clifford Mason. November 4, 1975. With Virginia Capers, Ernest Harden, Jr., Fred Morsell, Ellwoodson Williams, Henry Hayward, Maurice Watson.
FATHER UXBRIDGE WANTS TO MARRY written and directed by Frank Gagliano. November 18, 1975. With Barbara Coggin, Steve Vinovich, Bill McIntyre, Valerie Mahaffey, Robert Christian.
THE ENCHANTED HUDSON by Eric Thompson. December 9, 1975. Directed by Thom Molyneaux; with Ellen Cameron, Bernard Pollock, Marina Thompson, Barbara Cohen, Carrie Rubio, Haskell V. Anderson III.
THE BEACH CHILDREN by John von Hartz. January 14, 1976. Directed by Ronald Roston; with Maia Danziger, Mark Metcalf, Roger Omar Serbagi, Nancy Franklin, Martin Marinaro, Tanny McDonald.
THE RESURRECTION OF JACKIE CRAMER by Frank Gagliano, music by Raymond Benson. April 20, 1976. Directed by J. Ranelli; with David Berman, Mary Testa, Jerry McGee, Kenith Bridges, Nancy Foy, Joseph White.

Readings
THE WOLVES AND THE LAMBS by Frieda Lipp. June 5, 1975.
HALFWAY TREE BROWN by Clifford Mason. June 11, 1975. Directed by Stan Lachow.
THE CORRIDOR by Diane Kagan. June 19, 1975.
THE ENCHANTED HUDSON by Eric Thompson. September 14, 1975.
AMOUREUSE by Anne and Stuart Vaughan, from the French play by Georges de Porto-Riche. January 19, 1976.
A NICE GIRL LIKE YOU by Aldo Giunta. January 28, 1976.
THE ELUSIVE ANGEL by Jack Gilhooley. February 17, 1976. Directed by Peter Maloney.
APRIL by John Wolfson. February 27, 1976.
THE FAR-OFF SWEET FOREVER by Conn Fleming. March 5, 1976.
THE MAN WHO DREW CIRCLES by Barry Berg. March 8, 1976. Directed by Cliff Goodwin.
A SAFE PLACE by C.K. Mack. March 16, 1976.
EVEN THE WINDOW IS GONE by Gene Radano. April 2, 1976. Directed by Shan Covey.
THE HOUSE OF SOLOMON by Allen Davis III. May 5, 1976.
LUST by Steven Somkin. May 13, 1976. Directed by Rhoda Feuer.

New Federal Theater. The Henry Street settlement's training and showcase unit for new playwrights, mostly black and Puerto Rican. Woodie King Jr., director.

THE COMMITMENT by Joseph Lizardi. June 19, 1975. Directed by Carla Pinza.
COTILLION by John Oliver Killens. July, 1975. Directed by Allie Woods. (Also ran September 11-22, 1975 at Harlem Performing Center).
SECTION D by Reginald Vel Johnson. October 9, 1975. Directed by Anderson Johnson.
TOE JAM by Elaine Jackson. October, 1975. Directed by Anderson Johnson.
TRANSITION conceived and directed by Ken Rubenstein. December 11, 1975. With Reinaldo Arana, Roderick Hinds, Diane Johnson.
GILBEAU written and directed by Clayton Riley. January 15, 1976. With Graham Brown, Saundra McClain, Novella Nelson, Shauneille Perry, Walter Steele, Kim Sullivan.
THE MYSTERY OF PHYLLIS WHEATLEY by Ed Bullins. February, 1976. Directed by

Elizabeth Van Dyke; with Marzetta Jones, Norman Mizell Wilkerson III, Edward Schiff, James Shearwood, Terria Joseph, Susan Sherman.
SHOWDOWN by Don Evans. February, 1976. Directed by Shauneille Perry; with Charles Brown, Sherman Jones, Herman Jones, R.T. Vessels, Kirk Kirsey, Arthur French.
THE GREATEST MAN ON EARTH by Val Coleman. March 5, 1976. Directed by Ed Rombola.
FOR COLORED GIRLS WHO HAVE CONSIDERED SUICIDE/WHEN THE RAIN-BOW IS ENUF by Ntozake Shange. March 30, 1976. Directed by Oz Scott; with Trazana Beverly, Laurie Carlos, Judy Dearing, Lorey Hayes, Aku Kadogo, Thea Martinez, Ntozake Shange.
BARGAININ' THING by Dan Owens. April, 1976. Directed by Harold Scott.
MONDONGO by Ramiro Ramirez. May, 1976. Directed by Dean Irby.

New York Shakespeare Festival Public Theater. Schedule of experimental work-shop or work-in-progress productions and guest residencies, in addition to its regu-lar productions. Joseph Papp, producer.

THE CONJURER words and music by Michael Sahl and Eric Salzman. June 1, 1975. Di-rected by Tom O'Horgan.
JESSE AND THE BANDIT QUEEN by David Freeman. October 3, 1975.
THE SUN ALWAYS SHINES FOR THE COOL by Miguel Piñero. December 9, 1975. Di-rected by Marvin Felix Camillo.
SO NICE THEY NAMED IT TWICE by Neil Harris. December 27, 1975. Directed by Bill Lathan.
THE LOCAL STIGMATIC by Heathcote Williams. March 18, 1976.
GOGOL written and directed by Len Jenkin. May 28, 1976. With Richard Bright, Carol Kane, Frederick Neumann.

New York Theater Ensemble. Organization of participating artists to encourage new theater artists and playwrights. Lucille Talayco, artistic director.

ARIA DA CAPO and MURDER OF LIDICE by Edna St. Vincent Millay. June 18, 1975. Directed by Ron Nash.
BETWEEN TIME AND TIMBUKTU by Kurt Vonnegut Jr. August 6, 1975.
RALPH NADER IS NOT SORRY by Gene Ruffini; TOP SECRET by Neil Berger; THE TAKEOVER by Francis McDonald. August 13, 1975.
TONIGHT'S THE NIGHT, DURING THE WAR, THE RETURN OF NOCTURNAL STROLLS and BETTIE AND WILL by Michael Shurtleff. September 4, 1975. Directed by Richard Roberts; with Patricia Mertens, Cynthia David, James Ramsey, Dina Walden.
THE PRINCESS PRUZZIA, THE ROGUE and THE ALMOND NIGHTINGALE written and directed by Jackie Berger, songs by Roseanne Sheridan.
THE MUTILATED by Tennessee Williams. September 17, 1975. Directed by Ron Nash.
THE LOWER DEPTHS. October, 1975. Directed by Robert Pace.
1984 by George Orwell, adapted and directed by Steven Lieb. November 5, 1975.
TANIA (muscial) book by Mario Fratti, music and lyrics by Paul Dick. November, 1975. Directed by Ron Nash.
A NICE TRY by Hal Craven, music and lyrics by Arthur Rosen and Oswald Daljord. De-cember, 1975. Directed by Oswald Daljord.
BLACK BREAD AND ONIONS (one-man revue) written and performed by Martin Bard. January, 1976.
WABASH CANNONBALL by Thelma Moss, directed by Camille Monte and THE SECRE-TARIES by Thelma Moss, directed by Howard Lipson. February, 1976.
WELCOME TO THE MONKEY HOUSE by Kurt Vonnegut Jr., adapted by Christopher Sergel. February, 1976. Directed by Rich Samuelson.
ZIP! ! by Marc Sirinsky. February, 1976. Directed by Hal Muchnik and Marc Sirinsky.
INSIDE by Gloria Horowitz, based on Sylvia Plath's works. March 11, 1976. Directed by Steve Brant.
THE BEARD by Michael McClure. March, 1976. Directed by Lucille Talayco.
THE MISUNDERSTANDING by Albert Camus. May, 1976. Directed by Bob Duncan.
HAIL, HAIL THE GANG! by James de Jongh and Charles Cleveland. May 13, 1976. Di-rected by Regge Life.

New York Theater Strategy. Organization of playwrights for the production of their works. Maria Irene Fornes, president.

A BLACK HOLE IN SPACE by Murray Mednick. June 19, 1975. Directed by David Schweitzer.
SHE WHO WAS HE by Rosalyn Drexler, music by John Herbert McDowell. March 24, 1976. Directed by William Prosser.
TAXES written and directed by Murray Mednick. March 1, 1976.
BABES IN THE BIG HOUSE by Megan Terry. May 15, 1976. Directed by JoAnn Schmidman.

The Nighthouse. Eclectic policy of outreaching theater. David Gaard, producer, T. Bolick manager.

MS. HOOD OR EWES AFRAID OF THE BIG BAD WOLF conceived and performed by Hot Peaches. October, 1975.
MERRY XMAS, AMERICA (Christmas pageant) by Hot Peaches. December, 1975.
THE BALCONY by Jean Genet. January 2, 1976. Directed by Michael Nee.

No Smoking Playhouse. Eclectic producing policy. Norman Thomas Marshall, artistic director.

THE TROJAN WOMEN by Euripides, adapted and directed by Lou Trapani. December, 1975.
PRESTER JOHN by Gene Ruffini. February 5, 1976. Directed by Norman Thomas Marshall.
THE MERRY WIVES OF WINDSOR. March. 1976. Directed by Lou Trapani.
NO SALE by Michael McGrinder; DAISY SNAPS by Chryse Maile; BOX AND COX by J. Madison Morton. March, 1976. Directed by Norman Thomas Marshall.
THE KNIGHT OF THE BURNING PESTLE adapted and directed by George Wolf Reilly. May 13, 1976.

Ontological-Hysteric Theater. Avant garde theater productions written, directed and designed by the group's founder, Richard Foreman.

RHODA IN POTATOLAND (HER FALL STARTS) conceived and directed by Richard Foreman. December 18, 1975; with Kate Manheim, Bob Fleischner.

The Open Eye. Total theater involving actors, dancers, musicians and designers working together, each bringing their own talents into a single project. Jean Erdman, artistic director.

ORPHEE by Jean Cocteau. April, 1976. Directed by Albert Takazauckas.
MOON MYSTERIES by William Butler Yeats, conceived and directed by Jean Erdman. April, 1976.
PRIMORDIAL VOICES: IN THE TIME OF MOULTING SWANS composed and directed by Dan Erkkila; HAITIAN SUITE conceived and directed by Teiji Ito. April 27, 1976.
SUN DOOR conceived and directed by Dan Erkkila, choreographed by Andrea Stark. May, 1976.

The Open Space in Soho. Focus on presenting new plays and developing new playwrights through workshops; through acting workshops, they prepare and perform one revival each season. Lynn Michaels, Harry Baum, directors.

PANORAMA by Frank Biancamano. November 7, 1975. Directed by Richard Ward.
THE ALL AMERICAN SWEEPSTAKES by George Sibbald. January, 1976. Directed by Aleta Reeson; with Richard Corley, Nicholas Mele, Charles Harper, Stephen J. Liska, Rod Britt, Thomas Cappadonna.
THE LAST CHRISTIANS by Jack Gilhooley. March 25, 1976. Directed by Clinton Atkinson; with Lillah McCarthy, Nancy Barber, Celia Howard, Nick Francisco, Sheryl King, Philip Le Strange.
STUCK by Sandra Scoppettone. April 29, 1976. Directed by Camilla Clay.
OLD TIMES by Harold Pinter. May 13, 1976. Directed by Paul Schneider.

The People's Performing Company. New, socially significant musicals. Peter Copani, Vince Gugliotti, Denise Bonenfant, directors.

THE BLIND JUNKIE (musical) by Peter Copani. October, 1975. Directed by David Morrow.

FIRE OF FLOWERS (musical) book and lyrics by Peter Copani, music by Peter Copani, Christian Staudt, Bob Tuthill, Lawrence Pitilli, David McHugh, Ed Vogel. January, 1976. Directed by Don Signore.

The Performance Group. Experiments with new, collaborative and non-verbal creative techniques. Richard Schechner, director.

SAKONNET POINT by Spalding Gray. June 17, 1975. Directed by Elizabeth LeCompte.
THE TOOTH OF CRIME by Sam Shepard. November, 1975. Directed by Richard Schechner.
THE MARILYN PROJECT. November 14, 1975. Directed by Richard Schechner; with Joan MacIntosh, Elizabeth LeCompte.

Playwrights Horizons. Purpose is to give playwrights the opportunity to see their work produced by professionals in an atmosphere devoid of commercial pressure. Robert Moss, executive director.

Manhattan Full Productions (asterisk indicates also performed at Queens Theater in the Park):
LEANDER STILLWELL by David Rush. June, 1975. Directed by Joseph Kavanaugh.
PELICAN DINER by Fred Cerwin. June 13, 1975. Directed by Caymichael Patten.
THE COMPLAINT DEPT. CLOSES AT FIVE by Edward M. Cohen. June 21, 1975.
CLAIR AND THE CHAIR written and directed by Marsha Sheiness and PROFESSOR GEORGE by Marsha Sheiness. September 25, 1975. Directed by Hillary Wyler; with Victoria Boothby, Maria Cellario, Paul Lieber, Robert Burke.*
THE IMPORTANCE OF BEING EARNEST. October 6, 1975. Directed by Paul Cooper.*
A QUALITY OF MERCY by Roma Greth. Directed by Anita Khanzadian.*
THE LYMWORTH MILLIONS by David Shumaker. November 8, 1975. Directed by Alfred Gingold; with Cathy Roskam.*
A REPORT TO THE STOCKHOLDERS by Kevin O'Morrison. December, 1975. Directed by Robert Livingston.*
JULIUS CAESAR. Directed by Paul Schneider.*
THE PUBLIC GOOD by Susan Dworkin. February 19, 1976. Directed by Leonard Peters; with Earl Hendran, Martin Shakar, Jane Squibb, Marsha Wischhusen, Anne Murray, Sharron Shayne.*
THE SPELLING BEE by Marsha Sheiness. March, 1976. Directed by Harold Scott; with John Wylie, Joel Brooks, Chevi Colton, Robyn Goodman, Robert Burke, Patricia Stewart.*
PERCHED ON A GABARDINE CLOUD by Steven Braunstein. Directed by Frank Cento.*
TWO FOR THE SEESAW by William Gibson. April, 1976. Directed by Michael Heaton.*
MAGRITTE SKIES by Yale M. Udoff. April 22, 1976. Directed by Richard Place.
THE CASEWORKER by George Whitmore. May 13, 1976. Directed by Leland Moss.
CAKES WITH THE WINE by Edward M. Cohen. May 27, 1976. Directed by Thomas Grunewald.*

Manhattan Workshops
GLANCE AT A LANDSCAPE by Steven Yaffee. November 17, 1976. Directed by Bill Shorr.
GUY GAUTHIER'S EGO PLAY by Guy Gauthier. December 18, 1975. Directed by Kent Wood; with Robert Burke, Laurie Copland, Sheldon Feldner, Paul Lieber.
VANITIES by Jack Heifner. January 15, 1976. Directed by Garland Wright; with Kathy Bates, Jane Galloway, Susan Merson.*
OCEAN WALK by Philip Magdalany. February, 1976. Directed by Michael Flanagan.
THE CHEKHOV COMEDIES (four one-act plays) by Anton Chekhov. Directed by Jonathan Alper, Robert Moss, Kent Wood, Philip Himberg, Dennis Pearlstein.*
MATT, THE KILLER by Howard Pflanzer. Directed by Paul Cooper.
WINNER TAKE ALL by Meir Z. Ribalow. December 17, 1975. Directed by Michael Heaton; with Linda Carlson, Paul Geier, Lin Shaye.
THE TEACHERS' ROOM by Howard Pflanzer. February 11, 1976. Directed by Carol Corwen.
PUP by Iris Rosofsky. Directed by Anita Khanzadian.
SWEETBIRD by The Iowa Theater Lab. Directed by Ric Zanc.*

Queens Theater in the Park
MISALLIANCE. January 8, 1976. Directed by Robert Moss.

THE BOSS by Edward Sheldon. March, 1976. Directed by Edward Gilbert.
GEORGE WASHINGTON SLEPT HERE by George S. Kaufman and Moss Hart. April 29, 1976. Directed by Paul Cooper.

Quaigh Theater. Primarily a playwrights' theater, devoted to the new playwright, the established contemporary playwright and the modern (post-1920) playwright. William H. Lieberson, artistic director.

NEW YORK FESTIVAL II (one-act plays) 4 CORNERS by Helen Duberstein, directed by Bill Lentsch; 15 MINUTES OF EVIDENCE by Richard Foreman, directed by Kate Davy; INCREDIBLE JULIA by Jean Reavey, directed by John Clarkson; ONE PIECE SMASH by Arthur Sainer, directed by Geraldine Lust; PAY ATTENTION TO THE RAVEL by Donald Kvares, directed by Curtiss W. Sayblack; LORD TOM GOLDSMITH by Victor Lipton, directed by Thom Molyneaux; BIRDS by William Kushner, directed by Curtiss W. Sayblack. May, 1975. With Lynn Webster, Bill Wiley, Bill Cuikowski, Jacqueline King, J.R. Home.
STREET SCENE by Elmer Rice. July 9, 1975. Directed by Will Lieberson.
OUT CRY (rewrite) by Tennessee Williams. August, 1975. Directed by Bill Lentsch.
CAST THE FIRST STONE by Nishan Parlakian. September 4, 1975. Directed by Vincent Arto.
MEMPHIS ASIDE by Gayther Myers. September, 1975. Directed by Martin Donegan.
OUR BETTERS by W. Somerset Maugham. December, 1975. Directed by Martin Oltarsh; with Lois Young.
NIGHT OWL THEATER (late-night cabaret). December 3, 1975. With Nancy Parker, Garrett Nichols.
LIKE IT adapted from *As You Like It*. December 12, 1975. Directed by Geraldine Court; with Anna Stuart, Dana Coen, Charles Lutz, Richard Crook, Elise Hunt.
THE CLIMATE OF EDEN by Moss Hart. February 18, 1976. Directed by Will Lieberson.
JIGSAW (sketches, lyrics) by Jean Reavey, music by John Wallowitch. March, 1976. Directed by Bertram Ross.
QUIET CARAVANS by Barry Dinerman. May 4, 1976. Directed by Martin Oltarsh.

Richard Morse Mime Theater. To create a home for a permanent mime theater in America. Richard Morse, artistic director.

MOBY DICK REHEARSED (Orson Welles's adaptation). July 17, 1975. Directed by Richard Morse; with Jerome Dempsey.
MIME FOR A SUMMER NIGHT. August, 1975. With Richard Morse and Pilar Garcia.
SHAW FOR A SUMMER NIGHT: OVERRULED, directed by Richard Morse and VILLAGE WOOING, directed by Edward Townley. August 21, 1975.
MIME FOR A WINTER NIGHT and SHAW FOR A WINTER NIGHT. October 22, 1975.
DUET and VOYAGES. March 1976. With Rasa Allen, Tony Curry, Richard Hall, David McGee, Miko, Tina Sakai, K.C. Schulberg.

Roundabout Theater Stage II. Workshop program of the noted off-Broadway producing group. Gene Feist producing director, Michael Fried executive producer.

THE AWAKENING OF SPRING by Frank Wedekind. June 11, 1975. Directed by Jan P. Eliasberg.
SCHOOL FOR BUFFOONS and ESCURIAL (one-act plays) by Michel de Ghelderode. June 25, 1975. Directed by Gavin Cameron Webb.
A MUSICAL MERCHANT OF VENICE music by Jim Smith, lyrics by Tony Tanner. June, 1975. Directed by Tony Tanner; with Cara Duff-MacCormick, Phyllis Ward.
LOVE AND INTRIGUE by Friedrich von Schiller. May 6, 1976.

Shelter West. Company of artists working to bring challenging and enlightened theater to the community. Judy Joseph, founder.

THE RATS by Gerhardt Johann Robert Hauptmann. November 5, 1975. Directed by Dan Mason.
HUNTING SCENES FROM LOWER BAVARIA by Martin Sperr, translated by Christopher Holme. March, 1976. Directed by Dan Mason.
THE TOTEM POLE by Paul Smith. May, 1976. Directed by Dan Mason.

Shirtsleeve Theater. Concentration on new works and works previously performed which are felt not to have had a "fair" production. John Vaccaro, Jimmy Wisner, artistic directors.

HOCUS POCUS DOMINOCUS! by Jim Doyle. June 23, 1975. Directed by Micheal Posnick.
THE REBIRTH CELEBRATION OF THE HUMAN RACE AT ARTIE ZABALA'S OFF-BROADWAY THEATER by William Saroyan, July 10, 1975. Directed by Roger Hendricks Simon; with Dick Shawn, David Margulies, Jerrold Ziman, Lucy Lee Flippin, William Newman, Dana Gladstone.
AN EVENING OF BANANAS AND DRUMS (one-man show) with Dick Shawn. July 22, 1975. With the New World Consort.
THE STRAIGHT MAN, THE COMIC and THE TALKING LADY (sketches). August, 1975. Directed by Michael Posnick; with Lee Meredith, Joseph Elic, Luis Avalos, Carol Jean Lewis, Mike Moran.
WINNIE'S NOODLE SURPRISE by William Thut. March 25, 1976. Directed by Ron Abbott.

Soho Rep. Primarily classical plays in repertory. Marlene Swartz, Jerry Engelbach, artistic directors.

KEY LARGO by Maxwell Anderson. September 25, 1975. Directed by Jerry Engelbach.
THE MASTER BUILDER. October 4, 1975. Directed by Marlene Swartz.
CORIOLANUS. November 16, 1975. Directed by Jerry Engelbach.
THE CONGRESSWOMEN by Aristophanes, adapted by William W and Billie Snow. November 20, 1975. Directed by Marlene Swartz; with Murphy Guyer.
ANNA CHRISTIE by Eugene O'Neill. January 30, 1976. Directed by Marlene Swartz.
THE INFERNAL MACHINE by Jean Cocteau. February 6, 1976. Directed by Michael Wright.
HEARTBREAK HOUSE. March 6, 1976. Directed by Jerry Engelbach.
THE FATHER. March 19, 1976. Directed by Jonathan Furst.
THE IMAGINARY INVALID, translated by Frances Kosbab. April 17, 1976. Directed by Marlene Swartz.
ABELARD AND HELOISE by Ronald Duncan. April 9, 1976. Directed by Chuck Conwell.
BIMBOS IN PARADISE by B. Prune. May 1, 1976. Directed by Michael Wright.
CANDIDA. May 29, 1976. Directed by Jerry Engelbach.

St. C American Repertory. New plays, play readings, workshops, Music Theater Lab, full musical productions, on a highly professional level (some programs originally performed at St. Clement's Church). Larry Goossen, executive producer.

PRINCIPAL OF THE MATTER (reading) by Barry Rehfeld. June, 1975.
KING ARTHUR by Richard Peaslee and Kenneth Cavander. June 13, 1975.
SEXUAL PERVERSITY IN CHICAGO by David Mamet. September 29, 1975. Directed by Albert Takazauckas.
CHILE, CHILE (staged documentary). September, 1975. Directed by Joseph Chaikin; performed by Theater of Latin America.
DOWNRIVER by Jeff Tambornino, music and lyrics by John Braden, adapted from Mark Twain. December 19, 1975. Directed by Brian Murray.
AMERICAN BUFFALO by David Mamet. January 23, 1976. Directed by Greg Mosher; with Michael Egan, J.T. Walsh, Mike Kellin.
THE SORROWS OF FREDERICK by Romulus Linney. February, 1976. Directed by Elinor Renfield; with Austin Pendleton.
FEEL FREE (staged reading) by Nancy Henderson and Charlotte Kraft.
WAR BABIES (improvisation). February 20, 1976.
JOE'S OPERA (rock opera) music and lyrics by Tom Mandel. February, 1976. Directed by Robert Ackerman.

The Shaliko Company. Environmental theater group based on the primacy of the audience-actor relationship. Leonardo Shapiro, director.

GHOSTS by Ibsen and THE MEASURES TAKEN by Bertolt Brecht. November, 1975.

South Street Theater. Developing an outdoor environmental theater on Pier 17 at the South Street Seaport Museum. Michael Fischetti, artistic director.

MOBY DICK, adapted and directed by Michael Fischetti. June 26, 1975.
SPOON RIVER ANTHOLOGY adapted from Edgar Lee Masters. July, 1975. Directed by Michael Fischetti.

Stage Directors and Choreographers Workshop Foundation. Experimental showcase. Madolin Cervantes, director.

RAINBOWS FOR SALE and CONCERNING THE EFFECTS OF TRIMETHYLCHLORIDE (one-act plays) by John Ford Noonan. November, 1975. Directed by Dick Gaffield.
EVER SO HUMBLE (one-man show) written and directed by Warren Kliewer. December, 1975.
THE APOLLO OF BELLAC by Jean Giraudoux. January 12, 1976. Directed by Tisa Chang.
THE GREEN BAY TREE by Mordaunt Shairp. Directed by Madolin Cervantes.

T. Schreiber Studio. Establishing a close bond with the audience with all productions, with the widest range possible. Original scripts and plays deserving a second chance produced. Terry Schreiber, artistic director.

THE TRIP BACK DOWN by John Bishop. October 1, 1975. Directed by Terry Schreiber; with Gene Rupert, Jill Andre, Ellen Olian-Bate, J.P. Dooley, Ian Cadenhead, Gordon Oas-Heim.
MY THREE ANGELS by Sam and Bella Spewack. November 21, 1975. Directed by Don Lamb; with Eve Johnson, Fred Morsell, Norman Parker, Daniel Pollack, George Riddle, Robert Tennenhouse.
LEMON SKY by Lanford Wilson. February 4, 1976. Directed by Peter Thompson; with Jill Clements, Penny Peyser, Mike Brown, David Garber.
CLEAN AS A WHISTLE by Michael Norell and Richard Lenz. March 24, 1976. Directed by Alfred Gingold; with Bob Arcaro, George Curley, Bob DeFrank, Elise Hunt, Philip Oxnam, Marilyn Redfield, Jane Roberts, Gene Thompson.
WHERE DO WE GO FROM HERE? by John Ford Noonan. May 5, 1976. Directed by Terry Schreiber.

Theater at Noon. Dedication to the idea that there is a place for the arts in the midst of everyday life. David Donadio, managing and artistic director.

SKRONTCH (program of music) by Duke Ellington. October, 14, 1975. Directed by Michael Posnick.
OVERRULED by George Bernard Shaw. October 27, 1975. Directed by Bill Ludel; with Tanya Berezin, Roger Chapman, Bruce Gray, Anne C. Twomey.
THE DRAPES COME by Charles Dizenzo. November 11, 1975. Directed by Kent Paul.
THE RICHEST GIRL IN THE WORLD FINDS HAPPINESS (pop opera) libretto by Robert Patrick, music and lyrics by Gregory Sandow. December 1, 1975. Directed by Michael Feingold; with Stephanie Cotsirilos, Michael Hume, Gail Johnston, Charlie Leipart.
FOREPLAY, DOOR PLAY by Robert Auletta. December 15, 1975. Directed by Peter Mark Schifter; with Robert Burke, Peter Evans, Kathy K. Gerber, Stefan Hartman, Rose Lischner.
WOMEN IN MOTION (revue) by Marcia Jean Kurtz and Rae Tattenbaum. January 5, 1976. Directed by Rae Tattenbaum; with Marcia Jean Kurtz, Amandina Lihamba, Kathrin King Segal.
ARTISTSOLO (one-person shows) January 19, 1976. With Clamma Dale, Steven Hansen, David Ignatow, Michael Sahl, Paul Tracey.
DR. KHEAL by Maria Irene Fornes. Directed by Robert Gainer; with Richard Hamburger; I LOVE MY VOICE (opera) libretto by Stephen Holt, music by Brenda Berman. January 26, 1976.
CABARET PROGRAM by Carole Schweid, David Summers. March 1, 1976.
PROGRAM by Tony Watkins and Paul Knopf. March 8, 1976.
CRACKED TOKENS (improvisation group). March 22, 1976.
PIMPINONE (opera by Georg Philipp Telemann. March 29, 1976. Directed by Harvey E. Phillips; with Marilyn Brustadt, William Pell.
THE FROG PRINTS and PUNCH AND JUDY (puppet show) by Steven Hansen. April 19, 1976.
NOT ENOUGH ROPE by Elaine May. April 26, 1976. Directed by Bill Ludel.
BUT NOT FOR ME by Tom Topor. May 10, 1976. Directed by John Margulis; with Pat Elliott, Pirie Macdonald, Brandon Maggart.

Theater for the New City. Specializing in experimental productions. Crystal Field, artistic director.

SENSUAL SAVAGES. June 6, 1975. Performed by Hot Peaches.
STEWART SHERMAN SPECTACLE. June 9, 1975.
FEAST FOR FLIES by Stanley Seidman. June 26, 1975. Directed by William Perley.
MAMA LIBERTY'S BICENTENNIAL PARTY (street theater program) by Crystal Field and George Bartenieff. August 2, 1975.
THE CUTTLEFISH OR THE HYRCANIAN WORLD VIEW by Stanislaw Witkiewicz. August 7, 1975. Directed by Jaroslaw Strzimien.
THE TRAGEDY QUEEN by Arthur Williams, music by David Tice. September 1, 1975. Directed by James Waving.
MEMPHIS IS GONE by Dick Hobson. September, 1975. Directed by Susan Gregg; with John Pielmeill, Catherine Ramey, William Grady, James Maxwell.
IN THE SABBATH QUEEN by Avrana Patt. September 18, 1975. Performed by the Barking Rooster Company.
THE LOST ONES and WAITING FOR GODOT by Samuel Beckett. October 16, 1975. Performed by Mabou Mines.
THE PENALTY FOR BEING SLOW by Ralph Seymour. October 21, 1975. Directed by Bert Schneider.
ANDY HARDY. November 13, 1975. Performed by Inner Transit Theater.
JESUS IS A JUNKIE by Leo Rutman. November 13, 1975. Directed by Ron Roston.
THE ONLY GOOD INDIAN by Mario Fratti and Henry Salerno. December 18, 1975. Directed by Crystal Field.
BAGGAGE (1-woman show) written and performed by Deborah Forstan. January, 1976.
AXLE GROSS (adult puppet show). January, 1976.
THE BABY ELEPHANT by Bertolt Brecht and BRECHT MEETS HUAC by Larry Heit. January, 1976.
CAP-A-PIE written and directed by Maria Irene Fornes. January, 1976.
EMMA by Howard Zinn. February 12, 1976. Directed by Jeff Zinn.
THE COUNTRY WIFE by William Wycherly. February, 1976. Directed by David Burr.
THE WARRINGHAM ROOF by Donald Kvares. March 5, 1976. Directed by Curtiss W. Sayblack.
DAY OLD BREAD by Arthur Sainer. Directed by Crystal Field.
WHALE HONEY by Diane DiPrima. May, 1976. Directed by John Herbert McDowell.

Theater Genesis. Writers' theater; production of new American plays. Walter Hadler, artistic director.

SONATA written and directed by Bill Duke. July 3, 1975.
THE MEASURES TAKEN by Bertolt Brecht. January 2, 1976. Performed by Shaliko Company.
THE GROWL and SPIDER RABBIT by Michael McClure, directed by Tony Barsha; THE MEATBALL by Michael McClure, directed by Walter Hadler. February, 1976. With Maxine Albert, Sharon Ann Barr, Michael Brody, Taylor Mead, Larry Mintz, Scott Redman.
CARS AND GUITARS written and directed by Michael Winsett. April, 1976.
BLUE HEAVEN and TECHNOCRACY (ensemble pieces) conceived and performed by The Quena Company. May, 1976. Directed by Ray Barry.

Theater of the Riverside Church. Maintains high professional standards. Arthur Bartow, artistic director.

PROMETHEUS, PRUFROCK & FRIENDS (mime) by Richard Clairmont. June 12, 1975. With Ching Valdes, Peter Lobdell, Charles Stahl.
THE SHOESHINE PARLOR by James Lee. October 19, 1975. Directed by Marvin Felix Camillo.
MORNING'S AT SEVEN by Paul Osborn. November 6, 1975. Directed by Arthur Bartow.
OLD TIMES, GOOD TIMES by James P. Farrell. February 12, 1976. Directed by Bret Lyon, with Max Cole, Robert Davis, Chet Doherty, Dorothi Fox, Glen Kezer, Vera Visconti-Lockwood.
THE BIG REWARD by Brian O'Connor and Rosemary Foley. March 11, 1976. Directed by Brian O'Connor.
THE CAT AND THE FIDDLE (musical) by Jerome Kern and Otto Harbach. May 6, 1976. Directed by Jack Lee.

Theater Off Park. Theater for the community, attempting to reach as wide an audience as possible through as wide a variety of productions as possible. Martin deMaat, executive director.

SMOKING PISTOLS by Donald Kvares. September, 1975. Directed by Ernest Martin; with Monica May, Douglas Andros.
THE LARK by Jean Anouilh, adapted by Lillian Hellman. November 10, 1975. Directed by Eve Brandstein.
DIARIES OF ADAM AND EVE, adapted from Mark Twain. January, 1976. Directed by Mary Allyn-Raye.
THE PIMIENTA PANCAKES by Sally Dixon Wiener. March 12, 1976. Directed by Monica May; with Ned Austin, Garret M. Brown.
COWBOYS 2 by Sam Shepard. March 15, 1976. Directed by David Avcollie; with Vinny Guastaferro, Marty Levy.
SMALL WAR ON MURRAY HILL by Robert E. Sherwood. May, 1976. Directed by Frank Marino.

Theater 77. New plays preferred. Purpose is to provide opportunities for playwrights and actors to entertain in needful institutions, to find appropriate commercial vehicles for the productions. Rod Clavery, Dolores McCullough, artistic directors.

THE WALRUS SAID by Cary Pepper; LAUGHS, ETC. by James Leo Herlihy; DEPARTING FLIGHTS (one-act plays) by Charles Wilbert. March, 1976.

Thirteenth Street Repertory Company. The city's only musical company focusing on new work; also children's programs. Edith O'Hara, artistic director.

THE BLIND JUNKIE (musical) by Peter Copani. September, 1975. Directed by Jim Payne.
LINE and SHOOTING GALLERY by Israel Horovitz. February, 1976. Directed by Carol Ilson; with Phil Levy, Ann Bronston, Michael Sharrow, Tony DiBenedetto, Hiram Kastenbaum, Jacklyn Maddux.
RIP! (musical based on *Rip Van Winkle*) music and lyrics by Julius Adams. Directed by Brad Lutz.
RATS by Israel Horovitz. Directed by Jim Payne (workshop).

Time and Space, Ltd. Experiments in writing and production. Linda Mussman, artistic director.

THE DEVIL'S DISCIPLE. September 11, 1975. Directed by Linda Mussman.
THE WILD DUCK. November 6, 1975. Directed by Linda Mussman.
UNCLE VANYA. January 15, 1976. Directed by Linda Mussman.
GERTRUDE STEIN'S THE MAKING OF AMERICANS conceived and directed by Linda Mussman. March 18, 1976. Performed by Robert Balderson, Ronald Harrington, Donna Inglima, Margie Burman. (Reopened May 27, 1976 at St. Clement's Church.)

Triad Playwrights Company. Non-profit playwrights' theater that develops and produces new plays in existing performance spaces. Milan Stitt, executive director, Richard Tirotla, managing director.

TRIAD SINGLES (one-acters): PAINTING DISTANT MEN by Richard Greene, directed by Don Price; EDIE'S HOME by Milan Stitt, directed by Bill Herndon; I USED TO BE A ROCK 'N' ROLL STAR by D.B. Gilles, directed by William Martin; ON THE BRIDGE by Ross Alexander, directed by Alan Mixon. August 20, 1975 (at Stage One).

At Direct Theater
WHEN I LIVED IN BATON ROUGE by D.B. Gilles. October, 1975. Directed by Alan Mixon.
TWOSOMES (one-acters): SINGER TO THE LUTE by Robert Esposito, directed by Kimothy Cruse; PAINTING DISTANT MEN by Richard Greene, directed by Austin Pendleton. October, 1975.
COCONUT BEACH by Richard Greene. February 12, 1976. Directed by Bill Herndon.

Urban Arts Corps. Dedicated to the development of theater arts and craft skills in the black community. Vinnette Carroll, artistic director.

PLAY MAS by Mustafa Matura. March 24, 1976. Directed by Vinnette Carroll; with Jayant Blue, Marie Thomas, Neville Richen, Every Hayes, Russ Gustafson, Jeffrey Anderson-Gunter.
THE MUSIC MAGIC conceived and directed by Shauneille Perry, music by Neal Tate. April, 1976.
I'M LAUGHIN' BUT I AIN'T TICKLED conceived and directed by Vinnette Carroll, music by Micki Grant. May, 1976.

West Side Community Repertory Theater. Contemporary approaches to classical plays. Andres Castro, director (and director of all productions).

ARMS AND THE MAN. October 31, 1975. With James Haston, Jennifer Underwood, Patrick Hanratty.
RIDERS TO THE SEA, IN THE SHADOW OF THE GLEN and THE TINKER'S WEDDING by John Millington Synge. March, 1976.

Wonderhorse Theater. Eclectic policy of producing. Wayne Adams, Gary Burke, Ken Graham, DeDe Washburn, associates.

WITNESS FOR THE PROSECUTION by Agatha Christie. August, 1975. Directed by Michael Hartig and Christopher Cox; with Madeline Gorman.
DEATHWATCH by Jean Genet. September, 1975. Directed by JoAnn Green; with Frank Licato, Paul D'Amato, Tony Pernicone, David Dula.
THE HOMECOMING by Harold Pinter. November 6, 1975. Directed by Jack Chandler; with John Neville-Andrews, Jack Eric Williams, Tim Cahill, Darrell Ziegler, Brad Russell, Gail Cook.
POE IN PERSON (one-man show). December, 1975. With Conrad Pomerleau.
THE MASTER PSYCHOANALYST by Stanley Nelson. December, 1975. Directed by Joseph Lazarus.

Workshop of the Players Art (WPA). 200-member company presenting works of quality, both traditional and experimental. Harry Orzello, artistic director; Daniel P. Dietrich, co-producer.

FOURTH ANNUAL NEW PLAYS FESTIVAL schedule included: THE ANNUAL SEDUCTION OF EMERSON FITZGERALD McWAD by Jeannine O'Reilly, directed by Neil Flanagan; AREATHA IN THE ICE PALACE by Tom Eyen, directed by Jamie Brown; ASIE (ASIA) mime directed and performed by Gabriel Oshen; 'CAUSE MAGGIE'S AFRAID OF THE DARK by Howard Ashman, directed by James Nicola; CHARLIE McDEATH by Lars Forssell, directed by Bob Horan; DOLLY MAN AND HIS WOMAN by Michael Shurtleff, directed by Michael Dennis Moore; THE FORCEPS by Roman Chalbaud, directed by Ruis Woertendyke; HALFWAY by Roma Greth, directed by Pat Mullen; THE INFANCY OF THE TELEPHONE by Allan Knee, directed by Cyprienne Gabel; JOIN THE DANCE by Stephen Poliacoff, directed by Craig Barish; KID'S GAMES by Allan Bates, directed by Dick Gaffield; LOUISIANA BOUND by Stephen Holt, directed by Joseph Siracuse; TIRA by Michael Weller, directed by Ron Max; TWO LADIES TALKING by Gary Martin, directed by C. David Barrett; UGLY AND THE BEAST by Joseph Renard, directed by Robert Barger; WHEN I DYED MY HAIR IN VENICE by Helen Duberstein, directed by Alice Rubenstein. June 11, 1975.
PHILADELPHIA, HERE I COME! by Brian Friel. November 12, 1975. Directed by Jamie Brown; with Virginia Downing, Larry Rosler, Kelly Monaghan, Joseph Warren, Cheryl Meguire, P.L. Carling.
IF THIS AIN'T IT! (revue) music, lyrics and directed by Don Arrington. December, 1975. With Jean Andalman, Frank Juliano, Dinah Day, Audrey Lavine, Lynnie Godfrey, Bruce Robinson, Steve Patterson.
THE CHRONICLE OF NINE by Florence Stevenson. January 16, 1976. Directed by Otto Maximilian; with Valerie Beaman, Kathleen Tremaine, Todd Drexel, Janice Fuller, Mary Jennings-Dean, Thomas Sminkey.
COCK-A-DOODLE DANDY by Sean O'Casey. February 18, 1976. Directed by Ronald Frazier; with S.C. Benzall, Terence M. Sullivan, Bonnie Brewster, John O'Keefe, E.J. Hyland, Armin Shimmerman.
DREAMSTUFF (musical) book by Howard Ashman, music by Marsha Malamet, lyrics by

Dennis Green, based on *The Tempest*. April 2, 1976. Directed by James Nicola; with Pat Lavalle, Thomas Callaway, Dick Latessa, Betty Maul, Barabara Niles, Kitty Rea. EAST LIBERTY, PA. by Allan Bates. May 7, 1976. Directed by Richard Gaffield.

The York Players. Each season, three or four productions of classics are mounted with professional casts; concerned with bringing classics to neighborhood residents. Janet Heyes Walker, artistic director.

THE CONTRAST by Royall Tyler. October 14, 1975. Directed by Janet Hayes Walker.
OUR AMERICAN COUSIN by Tom Taylor, adapted by Lowell Swortzell. November 18, 1975. Directed by Janet Hayes Walker.
A TOUCH OF THE POET by Eugene O'Neill. February 17, 1976. Directed by Janet Hayes Walker.
ROMEO AND JULIET. March 26, 1976. Directed by Robert W. Smith.

Miscellaneous

In the additional listing of 1975-76 off-off-Broadway productions below, the names of the producing groups or theaters appear in CAPITAL LETTERS and the titles of the works in *italics*. This list consists largely of new or reconstituted works and excludes most revivals, especially of classics.

AMERICAN JEWISH ENSEMBLE. *The Theater of Peretz* adapted from I.L. Peretz by Isaiah Sheffer. February, 1976. Directed by Stanley Brechner.

ASTOR PLACE THEATER SUMMER FESTIVAL OF NEW AMERICAN PLAYWRIGHTS. July 23-August 31, 1975. *Orfeo for Me* by Albert Fiorella; *Home Is Where You Hang Yourself* and *The New Man* by Jon von Hartz; *Rites of Passage* by Rose Leiman Goldemberg.

BACK EAST. *This Is the Rill Speaking* by Lanford Wilson. September, 1975. Performed by Actors Ensemble. *Raft* by Martin Zuria, Shelby Buford Jr. and William Rolleri. December, 1975. Directed by William Rolleri. *The Four Seasons of Salt* by Daniel Gabriel. March, 1976. Directed by Anna Antaramian.

BARI & BENNETT PRODUCTIONS. *M. Gorky: A Portrait* conceived and performed by Michael DelMedico. September, 1975.

BERT WHEELER THEATER. *The Tavern* by George M. Cohan. December, 1975. Directed by Davis Hall. *The Big Apple* by Abe Einhorn. March, 1976. Directed by Lewis J. Stadlen.

BILLY MUNK THEATER. *The Love Death Plays of William Inge (Part I)*. July 10, 1975. Directed by Barbara Loden; with Lane Smith, Jack Aaron, Morgan Donohue, Judy Fields, Gayle Greene. *(Part II)* July 17, 1975. Directed by Barbara Loden; with Janet Ward, Robert Giber, Al Herter, Joseph Jamrog, Molly McCarthy, Michael Nader.

BOTTOM LINE. *The Telltale Heart* adapted from Edgar Allen Poe and *The Damned Thing* adapted from Ambrose Bierce by Patricia Cooper. April, 1975.

THE BROOK. *Dwight Night* (one-man show) by Dwight Marfield. March 5, 1976. *Macbeth.* May, 1976. Directed by A. Bogart.

CAMARIS. *Hi Mom; What's New?* (musical) by Maria Brescio, Isabel Kaskel, Camille McCabe. April 2, 1976. Directed by Daniel Lanning.

CAMBRIDGE ENSEMBLE. *Deathwatch* by Jean Genet. October, 1975. Directed by Joann Green.

CECIL ALONZO PLAYERS. *1999* written and directed by Cecil Alonzo. November 7, 1975.

CHURCHYARD PLAYHOUSE. Festival of New Italian Plays: *Law and Order* by Ada Bindi Caminiti and *Parallel Streets* by Carmen Scano. December, 1975. Directed by Pietro Sia. *Minions of the Race* and *Incident at the Great Wall* by Anne Paolucci. January 13, 1976. *The Guardian of the Tomb* by Franz Kafka and *After a Hard Day's Work Everybody Has the*

Right To Be Brutal by Franco Zardo, directed by Luigi Butera; *Mellon's* by Alan F. Levine, directed by George Walsh. February 10, 1976.

CIRCLE IN THE SQUARE WORKSHOP. *Tango* by Slawomir Mrozek. December, 1975. Directed by Steven Rotoman.

THE CLASSIC THEATER. *Badvi Hamar* (For the Sake of Honor) by Alexandre Shirvanzade. January 18, 1976. Directed by Maurice Edwards. *The Apocalypse According to Jean-Jacques (Rousseau)* by Mario Apollonio, translated by Anne Paolucci. March, 1976. Directed by Maurice Edwards; with John Michalski, Kristina Callahan, Joseph Frisari, Tom Jarus, Ellen Kelly, Robert Milton, The Loyola Boys Choir.

CRICKET THEATER. *Rip* (musical version of *Rip Van Winkle*) music and lyrics by Julius Adams. December 20, 1975. Directed by Brad Lutz; with Daniel Holberg. *It's Only Temporary* by Patricia M. Reedy. February 18, 1976.

CUTTING EDGE. *Croon* conceived and directed by Andrea Balis, text by Elizabeth Levy. March, 1976. With Sara Christiansen, Abigail Costello.

DI PINTO DI BLU CAFE. *Just Keep Listening* by John Kendrick. December, 1975. Directed by Mel Winkler. *A Perfect Analysis Given by a Parrot* by Tennessee Williams and *Dutchman* by LeRoi Jones. *The Dreamy Kid* by Eugene O'Neill; *The Best Part* by Frank Biancamano; *The Priest and High John the Conqueror* by Warren Goodson. May 29, 1976.

THE DRAMA TREE. *Into Love and Out Again* (works by Dorothy Parker). October 10, 1975. Directed by Bruce Adams. *Bloody Mary* written and directed by Robert Dey. January 30, 1976. With John Benson.

DUO THEATER. *Rasputin* conceived and directed by Manuel Martin. December, 1975. The Capoeiras Conta Voodoo (musical narrative of Brazilian folklore). January, 1976.

EIGHTEENTH STREET PLAYHOUSE. *An Evening of Gershwin and Odets.* January, 1976. Directed by Michael Dinelli. *A Hatful of Rain* by Michael V. Gazzo. February 12, 1976. Directed by Mercedes Ruehl. *Testimonies* by James Edward Shannon. March, 1976. Directed by Michael Bass.

ETI. Festival of New Italian Plays in English: *Natural Persons* and *Eccentrics* by Giuseppe Patroni Griffi, directed by Walter Burns; *The Liar* by Diego Fabbri; *Natural Histories: 1* by Edoardo Sanguinetti; *The Trial of Giordano Bruno* by Mario Moretti; *In Spite of Gramsci* by Adele Cambria; *Chronicle From the Other World* by Alessandro Antonio; *Salvatore Vaccaro's Inheritance* by Marcello di Benedetto; *Vestal Rite* by Ernesto Sfriso; *It's Not a Crime to Put Spectacles on Pheasants* by Franco Zardo. September-October, 1975.

EXCHANGE FOR THE ARTS. *Citadel* (musical) based on Stendahl's *La Chartreuse de Parme* book by David Schiller, music, lyrics and directed by Keith Baker. December, 1975.

FIRST MORAVIAN CHURCH. *Ever So Humble* adapted and directed by Warren Kliewer. May 29, 1976.

FRANKLIN THOMAS REPERTORY THEATER. *Something for Jamie* by Gertrude Greenidge, music and lyrics by Holly Hamilton. October, 1975. Directed by Franklin Thomas.

GALAXY 21. *Time Remembered of a Moon and Star* by Jean Anouilh, adapted by Dan Crugnale. January, 1976. Directed by Helen Guditis.

GAP THEATER COMPANY. *Hadrian's Hill* by Richard Vetere. December, 1975. Directed by Anthony Napoli; with Steven Edwards, Russ Banham.

THE GLINES. *The Soft-Core Kid* by Frank Hogan and Walter Kubran. May, 1976. Directed by John Glines. *The Jumping Place* written and directed by Glyn O'Malley. May 12, 1976.

GREENWICH HOUSE. *In Rachel's House* by Martha Urnston. March 12, 1976. Directed by Alan Wynroth.

GREENWICH MEWS THEATER. *In Need of Care* by David E. Rowley, *A Day for Surprises* by John Guare and *Winners* by Brian Friel. June 13, 1975. Directed by John Merensky; with Eileen Brady, Tom-Patrick Dineen, Kaiulani Lee, Sandy Martin, Larry Rosler. *Night Must Fall* by Emlyn Williams, August 8, 1975. Directed by Alan Gabor.

GUILD STUDIO. *Benjie, Where Are You Going?* by Nomi Rubel. December 14, 1975.

HANSEN GALLERY. *Balances* by Mel Yosso. March, 1976. Directed by David Morrow.

HARTLEY HOUSE. *Gerald Piper's Portfolio* by Martin Minsky, directed by David Willinger and *The Golden Fleece* by A.R. Gurney Jr., directed by Norma Kaplan. January 9, 1976. *Something About an Oyster* by Arnold Colbath. March, 1976. Directed by Robert Engstrom.

ICON COMPANY. *Black Robe Entry* by Donald Kvares and *Information Please* by Clarence Locke. February, 1976.

INTERNATIONAL THEATER SOCIETY. *Hair '75* (musical) by James Rado, Gerome Ragni, Galt MacDermot. September 17, 1975. Directed by Bruce Macheim-Rashid.

JEWISH REPERTORY COMPANY. *A Night in May* by Avraham Yehoshua. October 1, 1975. Directed by Ann Raychel; with Ann Pitoniak, Dorothy Fielding. *The Closing of Mendel's Cafe* and *Relatives* (one-act plays) by Eve Able. November 13, 1975. Directed by Ran Avni.

LAB THEATER. *The Bear* and *The Proposal* by Anton Chekhov. January, 1976. *Who Killed Ida Lupino* by Albert Fiorella. March 24, 1976. Directed by Matt Conley. *The Reconciliation* by Albert Evans. May 7, 1976. Directed by Elly Burke.

LITTLE THEATER ON WEST 26TH STREET. *Address to the Academy* by Franz Kafka; *Krapp's Last Tape* by Samuel Beckett. September, 1975. Directed by Andrew Loucka. *The Killing Game* (premiere) by Eugene Ionesco. November 1, 1975. Directed by Andrew Loucka. *The Owl and the Pussycat* by Bill Manhoff. December, 1975. Directed by Andrew Loucka. *Abstract Stills* by Candide Cummings. February, 1976. Directed by Alex Iglesias. *Act Without Words* and *Happy Days* by Samuel Beckett. February 19, 1976. Directed by Vanya Cassal and Andrew Loucka. *Don Juan in Hell*. May, 1976. Directed by Andrew Loucka.

LOFT CABARET THEATER. *Another Way to Love* presented by The Project. February, 1976. *Orbits* by Errol Strider and *The Surrealistic Light Movie Machine* by Douglas and Rose Lavery.

MABOU MINES. *The Lost Ones* by Samuel Beckett. Performed by Mabou Mines. *The Saint and the Football Players* conceived and directed by Lee Breuer. February 7, 1976. Performed by Mabou Mines. *Cascando* by Samuel Beckett, music by Philip Glass. April, 1976. Directed by JoAnne Akalaitis; with Frederick Neumann, Thom Cathcurt, David Hardy, Ellen McElduff, William Raymond, David Warrilow.

THE MALACHY COMPANY. *Variety Flight* (musical) by Annie M. Taylor. September, 1975. Directed by Anthony Osnato. *The Curious Savage* by John Patrick. October 17, 1976. Directed by Ray Vanderwood. *The Cocktail Party* by T.S. Eliot. November 21, 1975. Directed by Nicholas Sean Austin. *Sarah and the Sax* by Lewis John Carlino, directed by Annie Taylor; *Have a Nice Life* written and directed by Jerry Wehking; *Even Among the Thorns* by Nicholas Sean Austin, directed by Veronica Stone. February 6, 1976. *Talk to Me Like the Rain* by Tennessee Williams, directed by Aldo Vigliardo; *Triumph of Love* by Beaumont and Fletcher, directed by Richard Heifer; *The Ugly Duckling* by A.A. Milne, directed by Nicholas Sean Austin. February 13, 1976. *The Crystal* by Nicholas Sean Austin. March, 1976.

MAMA GAIL'S. *Victoria* by Christian and Marcia Hamilton. September, 1975. Directed by Bruce Graham. *The Purification* by Tennessee Williams. November 26, 1975. Directed by Paul Kielar; with Peter Kingsley. *Dear Piaf* (revue) lyrics translated and adapted by Lucia Victor. December, 1975. Directed by Dorothy Chernuck. *Behind the Bar In Front of the Mirror* by C. Lester Franklin. February, 1976. *Freed From the Met* by Walter Corwin. April, 1976. Directed by Robert Barger.

MANHATTAN LAMBDA PRODUCTIONS. *Cupid Is a Bum . . . Is a Bum . . . Is a Bum* by John Kirkpatrick. November 1, 1975. Directed by Eric Neilsen. *One Mad Night* by James Reach. December 5, 1975. Directed by Edmund W. Trust. *What Can You Buy for a Token?* by Eddy Allen. March, 1976. Directed by Stanley Bonk. *The Great Divide* by William Vaughan Moody. May 1, 1976. Directed by Vivian Paszamant.

MINOR LATHAM PLAYHOUSE. *Shufflings* written and directed by Kenneth James. February 17, 1976.

MUSIC THEATER PERFORMING GROUP. *Fable* (musical) by Jean-Claude van Itallie, music by Richard Peaslee. October, 1975. Directed by Joseph Chaikin.

NAMELESS THEATER. *Bedtime Story* and *The End of the Beginning* by Sean O'Casey. March, 1976. *Fellarella* by Chris Andretta. May, 1976. Directed by Tom Ribbank.

NAT HORNE THEATER. *Look, We've Come Through!* by Hugh Wheeler. March 4, 1976. Directed by Susan Schulman; with Christine Sinclair, Nita Angeletti, Bruce Detrick, Jared Sakren, Ian Stulberg, David Dangler. *The Great Caper* by Ken Campbell. May, 1976. Directed by Jerry Heymann. *The Late Late Show* (revue) by Freda Scott. May, 1976.

NEW GENESIS PRODUCTIONS. *A Trio of Vignettes* by Ed Bullins; *Just Keep Listening* by John Kendrick; *Interesting* by JoAnn Tedesca; *The Reachers* by Mel Winkler. February, 1976.

NEW HERITAGE REPERTORY THEATER. *Fat Tuesday* (musical) book and directed by Roger Furman, music and lyrics by Dee Robinson.

NEW MEDIA STUDIO. *Thunder in the Index* by Phillip Hayes Dean and *Paper Dolls* by Miranda McDermott. August, 1975. Directed by Mary Hayden. *City Clowns* by Miranda McDermott. February, 1976. Directed by Franklin Engel.

NEW YORK CO-OP. *The Tent Show Queen* written and directed by Myra R. Quigley. January, 1976. *An Autumn Afternoon in a Suburban Backyard* and *It's the Music That's Driving You Crazy* by Richard Taylor. February, 1976.

NEW YORK PUBLIC LIBRARY PROGRAMS. *Triage* by Richard Cavalier. November, 1975. *Hey Death, Here's Looking at You* (one-act plays) by William Lederer. December, 1975. *Love on a Dark Night* by Neal Black. *Despite All Odds* (one-woman show) by Maureen Hurley. February, 1976.

NUYURICAN POETS' CAFE. *Flamingo* by Lucky Clen Fuegos. May 27, 1976. Directed by Richard August.

PAINTERS' THEATER COMPANY. *In Praise of Falling* by Shirley Kaplan, music by William Obrecht. March 12, 1976. Directed by June Ekman.

THE PERFORMING GARAGE. *Council of Love* adapted from *Das Liebeskonzil* by Oskar Panizza. September 4, 1975. Directed by Andreas Nowara. *Sly Mourning.* October, 1975. Directed by Stephen Borst; performed by Shaman Company. *Scales* composed and directed by Spalding Gray. December 10, 1975. *Burning Daylight* (one-man show) written and performed by William Shephard. January 8, 1976. *Electra* by Robert Montgomery. January, 1976. Directed by Joseph Chaikin. *Okay Doc* (one-man show). May, 1976. *Kuku Ryku* (workshop). May 27, 1976.

PERSONA CAFE THEATER. *Portable Radio Circus.* July 2, 1975. Directed by Louis Hetler. *Lip Service* (revue). Directed by Ronald Marquette.

SHARED FORMS THEATER. *Memories of the Saltimbanques* conceived and performed by Rob McBrien, Wendy Washdahl, Duncan Kegerreis. March, 1976.

SOBOSSEK'S. *Comedy at 10 and 11:30* (musical revue) by Martin Calabrese, Jason McAuliffe and Leon Odenz. March, 1976. *First Amendment Musical Comedy Group.* March, 1976. *Louisiana Bound* by Stephen Holt, Alice Carey and Jeffrey Knox. March, 1976. Directed by Joseph Siracuse. *Democrats!* (revue). May, 1976. With Amelia Haas, James Hornbeck, Gene Lindsey, Dick Bonelle, Joy Garrett.

SOHO ARTISTS. *Out of Sight* by Aleen Malcolm. May, 1976. Directed by Dino Narizzano.

SPIDERWOMAN THEATER WORKSHOP. *Woman in Violence.* January 8, 1976. (Ensemble piece). *Firesticks.* March, 1976. (Ensemble piece).

STAGE 73. *Grass Widows* by Mary Orr. January 15, 1976. Directed by Reginald Denham; with Patricia Barry, William Gibberson, Javotte Sutton Greene, Richard Sale, Patricia Wheel, Mary Orr.

STRUCTURALIST WORKSHOP. *Eight People* by Michael Kirby. December, 1975.

STUDIO 17. *Romantica* by Richard Hoffman. March, 1976. Directed by Louis Mascolo; with Paul Brennan, Chiri Couture, Jerry Oliver, Ceal Phelan, Richard Witkowski.

STUDIOS 59 PLAYHOUSE. *The Springtime of Others* by Jean-Jacques Bernard, translated and directed by Thomas Luce. May, 1976.

STUYVESANT OPERA COMPANY. *The Window Game* by Cecil Bentz; *The Last Game* by Mildred Kayden. February 20, 1976.

THE THEATER (31 Perry Street). *Twelfth Night.* May, 1976. Directed by Mark Harrison; with Russ Banham. *Faust* conceived and directed by Vasek Shimek. May, 1976. *Indulgences in the Louisville Harem* by John Orlock. *Van Gogh!* by Phillip Rod Stevens (one-man show). May 21, 1976. Directed by Jim O'Connor; with Lou Malandra.

TITLE THEATER. *Help Wanted* by William Rolleri. January, 1976. Directed by Martin Zuria. *Raft* by Martin Zuria, Shelby Buford Jr. and William Rolleri. Directed by William Rolleri; with Shelley Mitchell. *Women in Black* by Shelby Buford Jr. March, 1976. Directed by Martin Zuria. *The Illusionist* presented by Raft Theater. May, 1976.

TOSOS (THE OTHER SIDE OF SILENCE). *Now She Dances* adapted and directed by Doric Wilson from Oscar Wilde's *Salome.* September 11, 1975. Directed by Doric Wilson; with Sally Eaton. *The Rape of Bunny Stunte* by A.R. Gurney Jr. December, 1975. Directed by Douglas Popper.

TRIANGLE THEATER COMPANY. *Rosewood* (musical) book by Joel Gross, music and lyrics by Brian Hurley. December, 1975. Directed by David Black; with Harold Davis, Don Detrick, Andrew Gale, Rebecca Hoodwin, William McClary, Jane Smulyan, Jeanne Walsh.

TRUCK AND WAREHOUSE THEATER. *Dirtiest Show II* (musical) music by Henry Krieger, lyrics and directed by Tom Eyen. December 9, 1975.

UNIT 453. *L'Amour en Visites* by Alfred Jarry. July 9, 1975. Directed by Richard Vos; with Gail Ryan, Marilyn Meyers, Denise Moses, Barbara Winkler, Grace Woodward, George Sanders.

U.T.O. *The Mortality Game* conceived and directed by Robert Monticello. December, 1975.

VANDAM THEATER. *Cubistique* by Thomas Cone, Directed by J. van der Veen and *Herringbone* by Thomas Cone, directed by Sheldon Rosen; with Jack Davidson. February 25, 1976.

WALDEN THEATER. *The Night Thoreau Spent in Jail* by Jerome Lawrence and Robert E. Lee. November 6, 1975. Directed by Bruce Cornwell.

WASHINGTON MARKET PLAYHOUSE. *Comings and Goings* by Megan Terry. December 6, 1975. Directed by Fred Gorelick. *Cornucopia, a Christmas Cabaret* written and directed by Stuart Warmflash. December, 1975. *Small Craft Warnings* by Tennessee Williams. January 8, 1976. Directed by Jeff Chambers. *Noel and Cole—Just One of Those Things* (revue) by David Rubinstein, Richard Bower, Jolly Nelson. March, 1976. *The Dodo Bird* by Emanuel Fried. March 30, 1976. Directed by John Gillick.

WEST PARK THEATER. *Masks of Love and Death* (three plays) by William Butler Yeats. February, 1976. Directed by Gray McKee. *What the Butler Saw* by Joe Orton. February, 1976. Directed by Gray McKee. *The Lewis and Clark Expedition* by Ron Mangravite. May 21, 1976. Directed by Joe Wald.

WOOD THEATER. *Alley Cats* (one-man show) by, with and directed by Tom Coble. January 12, 1976.

CAST REPLACEMENTS AND TOURING COMPANIES

Compiled by Stanley Green

The following is a list of the more important cast replacements in productions which opened in previous years, but were still playing in New York during a substantial part of the 1975–76 season; or were still on a first-class tour in 1975–76; or opened in New York in 1975–76 and went on tour during the season (casts of first-class touring companies of previous seasons which were no longer playing in 1975–76 appear in previous *Best Plays* volumes of appropriate years).

The name of each major role is listed in *italics* beneath the title of the play in the first column. In the second column directly opposite appears the name of the actor who created the role in the original New York production (whose opening date appears in *italics* at the top of the column). Indented immediately beneath the original actor's name are the names of subsequent New York replacements, together with the date of replacement when available.

The third column gives information about first-class touring companies, including London companies (produced under the auspices of their original Broadway managements). When there is more than one roadshow company, #1, #2, etc., appear before the name of the performer who created the role in each company (and the city and date of each company's first performance appears in *italics* at the top of the column). Their subsequent replacements are also listed beneath their names, with dates when available.

A note on bus-truck touring companies appears at the end of this section.

ABSURD PERSON SINGULAR

	New York 10/8/74	*Wilmington 9/29/75*
Marion	Geraldine Page Sheila MacRae 8/25/75 Geraldine Page 9/8/75	Sheila MacRae
Ronald	Richard Kiley Fritz Weaver 3/10/75 Dalton Dearborn 8/4/75 Scott McKay 8/25/75	Patrick MacNee
Eva	Sandy Dennis Carol Lynley 6/26/75 Sandy Dennis 11/12/75 Betsy Von Furstenberg 1/12/76 Sandy Dennis 1/19/76	Betsy Von Furstenberg
Sidney	Larry Blyden Paul Shyre 5/19/75 Dalton Dearborn 10/74/75 Paul Shyre 11/5/75	Michael Callen Paul Shyre Gene Rupert
Jane	Carole Shelley Marilyn Clark 8/4/75	Judy Carne
Geoffrey	Tony Roberts Curt Dawson 5/12/75	David Watson

ALL OVER TOWN

	New York 12/29/74	*Toronto 8/14/75*
Lewis	Cleavon Little Ron O'Neal 5/26/75	Ron O'Neal
Dr. Lionel Morris	Barnard Hughes George S. Irving 3/11/75 Thomas Toner 7/10/75	Thomas Toner

CANDIDE

	Brooklyn 12/11/73 New York 3/10/74
Dr. Pangloss	Lewis J. Stadlen Charles Kimbrough 1/75
Candide	Mark Baker Kelly Walters 9/17/75
Cunegonde	Maureen Brennan
Old Lady	June Gable Niki Flacks 7/3/75 Joanne Jonas 9/75
Paquette	Deborah St. Darr Paula Cinko 9/75
Maximilian	Sam Freed

A CHORUS LINE

	N.Y. Off-Bway 4/15/75 N.Y. Bway 7/25/76	#1 Toronto 5/3/76 #2 San Francisco 5/11/76
Roy	Scott Allen	#1 Donn Simeone #2 Tim Cassidy
Kristine	Renee Baughman Cookie Vasquez 4/26/76	#1 Christine Baker #2 Renee Baughman
Sheila	Carole Bishop (name changed to Kelly Bishop 3/76)	#1 Jane Summerhays #2 Charlene Ryan
Val	Pamela Blair Barbara Monte-Britton 4/26/76	#1 Mitzi Hamilton #2 Pamela Blair
Mike	Wayne Cilento	#1 Don Correia Jeff Hyslop #2 Don Correia
Butch	Chuck Cissel	#1 Ken Rogers #2 Sam Tampoya
Larry	Clive Clerk	#1 T. Michael Reed #2 Roy Smith
Maggie	Kay Cole Lauree Berger 4/26/76	#1 Jean Fraser #2 Kay Cole
Richie	Ronald Dennis Winston DeWitt Hemsley 4/26/76	#1 A. William Perkins #2 Ronald Dennis
Tricia	Donna Drake	#1 Nancy Wood #2 Rebecca York
Tom	Brandt Edwards	#1 Mark Dovey #2 Danny Taylor
Judy	Patricia Garland Sandhal Bergman 4/26/76	#1 Yvette Mathews #2 Patricia Garland
Lois	Carolyn Kirsch Vicki Frederick 4/26/76	#1 Wendy Mansfield #2 Carolyn Kirsch

Don	Ron Kuhlman	#1 Ronald Young
	David Thomé 4/26/76	#2 Ron Kuhlman
Bebe	Nancy Lane	#1 Miriam Welch
	Gillian Scalici 4/26/76	#2 Nancy Lane
Connie	Baayork Lee	#1 Jennifer Ann Lee
	Lauren Kayahara 4/26/76	#2 Baayork Lee
Diana	Priscilla Lopez	#1 Loida Iglesias
	Barbara Luna 4/26/76	#2 Priscilla Lopez
	Carole Schweid 5/7/76	
Zach	Robert LuPone	#1 Elvind Harum
	Joe Bennett 4/26/76	#2 Robert LuPone
Mark	Cameron Mason	#1 Timothy Scott
		#2 Paul Charles
Cassie	Donna McKechnie	#1 Sandy Roveta
	Ann Reinking 4/26/76	#2 Donna McKechnie
Al	Don Percassi	#1 Steve Baumann
	Bill Nabel 4/26/76	#2 Don Percassi
Frank	Michael Serrecchia	#1 Troy Garza
		#2 Claude R. Tessier
Greg	Michel Stuart	#1 Andy Keyser
	Justin Ross 4/26/76	#2 Michel Stuart
Bobby	Thomas J. Walsh	#1 Ron Kurowski
		#2 Scott Pearson
Paul	Sammy Williams	#1 Tommy Aguilar
	George Tesaturo 4/26/76	#2 Sammy Williams
Vicki	Crissy Wilzak	#1 Nancy Dafgek
		#2 Mary Ann O'Reilly

DANCE WITH ME

New York 1/23/75

| Honey Boy | Greg Antonacci |
| | Peter Riegert 7/10/75 |

EQUUS

New York 10/24/74   *Boston 11/18/75*

Dr. Martin Dysart	Anthony Hopkins	Brian Bedford
	Anthony Perkins 6/30/75	
	Richard Burton 2/16/76	
	Anthony Perkins 5/11/76	
Alan Strang	Peter Furth	Dai Bradley
	Thomas Hulce 6/30/75	
	Jacob Milligan 1/6/76	
	Keith McDermott 2/16/76	

THE FANTASTICKS

New York 5/3/60

El Gallo	Jerry Orbach
	Gene Rupert
	Bert Convy

John Cunningham
Don Stewart 1/63
David Cryer
Keith Charles 10/63
John Boni 1/13/65
Jack Metter 9/14/65
George Ogee
Keith Charles
Tom Urich 8/30/66
John Boni 10/5/66
Jack Crowder 6/13/67
Nils Hedrick 9/19/67
Keith Charles 10/9/67
Robert Goss 11/7/67
Joe Bellomo 3/11/68
Michael Tartel 7/8/69
Donald Billett 6/70
Joe Bellomo 2/15/72
David Rexroad 6/73
David Snell 12/73
Hal Robinson 4/2/74
Chapman Roberts 7/30/74
David Brummel 2/18/75
David Rexroad 8/31/75
Roger Brown 9/30/75

Luisa   Rita Gardner
Carla Huston
Liza Stuart 12/61
Eileen Fulton
Alice Cannon 9/62
Royce Lenelle
B. J. Ward 12/1/64
Leta Anderson 7/13/65
Carole Demas 11/22/66
Leta Anderson 8/7/67
Carole Demas 9/4/67
Anne Kaye 5/28/68
Carolyn Magnini 7/29/69
Virginia Gregory 7/27/70
Leta Anderson
Marty Morris 3/7/72
Sharon Werner 8/1/72
Leilani Johnson 7/73
Sharon Werner 12/73
Sarah Rice 6/24/74
Cheryl Horne 7/1/75
Sarah Rice 7/29/75
Betsy Joslyn 3/23/76

Matt   Kenneth Nelson
Gino Conforti
Jack Blackton 10/63
Paul Giovanni
Ty McConnell
Richard Rothbard
Gary Krawford
Bob Spencer 9/5/64
Erik Howell 6/28/66
Gary Krawford 12/12/67
Steve Skiles 2/6/68
Craig Carnelia 1/69
Erik Howell 7/18/69
Samuel D. Ratcliffe 8/5/69

Michael Glenn-Smith 5/26/70
Jimmy Dodge 9/20/70
Geoffrey Taylor 8/31/71
Erik Howell 3/14/72
Michael Glenn-Smith 6/13/72
Phil Killian 7/4/72
Richard Lincoln 9/72
Bruce Cryer 7/24/73
Phil Killian 9/11/73
Michael Glenn-Smith 6/17/74
Ralph Bruneau 10/29/74
Bruce Cryer 9/30/75

NOTE: As of May 31, 1976, 24 actors have played the role of El Gallo, 18 actresses had played Luisa, and 19 actors had played Matt.

GOOD EVENING

New York 11/14/73	*Washington 2/4/75*
Peter Cook	Peter Cook
Dudley Moore	Dudley Moore

GREASE

New York 2/14/72

Danny Zuko

Barry Bostwick
  Jeff Conaway 6/73
  John Lansing 11/74
  Treat Williams 12/75

Sandy Dumbrowski

Carole Demas
  Ilene Graff 3/73
  Candice Earley 6/17/75

Betty Rizzo

Adrienne Barbeau
  Elaine Petrikoff 3/73
  Randee Heller 5/74
  Karren Dille 12/1/75

Kenicke

Timothy Meyers
  John Fennessy
  Jerry Zaks
  Timothy Meyers
  Danny Jacobson 12/75

Vince Fontaine

Gardner Hayes
  Jim Weston
  John Holly
  Walter Charles
  Jim Weston 1/76

THE HOT L BALTIMORE

New York 3/22/73

Jackie

Mari Gorman
  Jennifer Harmon 10/24/73
  Lisa Jacobson
  Joyce Reehling 8/75

Bill

Judd Hirsch
  David Groh
  Joseph Stern
  William Wise 7/30/74

Mr. Katz	Antony Tenuta
	Larry Spinelli 11/74
	Jack Davidson 12/75

Girl	Trish Hawkins
	Faith Catlin
	Heather MacRae 10/1/74
	Trish Hawkins
	Penny Peyser 5/27/75

Suzy	Stephanie Gordon
	Jane Lowry 1/14/75
	Stephanie Gordon
	Corie Sims 6/75
	Sharon Madden 8/75

Mrs. Oxenham	Louise Clay
	Maryellen Flynn
	Molly Adams 7/1/75

April	Conchata Ferrell
	Jane Cronin
	Sarallen 11/11/75

Jamie	Zane Lasky
	Chip Zien
	Ron Paul Little
	John Shuman
	Harry Brown 12/75

KENNEDY'S CHILDREN

	New York 11/3/75	*San Francisco 3/2/76*
Wanda	Barbara Montgomery	Bobo Lewis
		Barbara Rush 4/1/76
		Shelley Winters 5/6/76
Sparger	Don Parker	Don Parker
		Farley Granger 5/6/76
Mark	Michael Sacks	Michael Sacks
		Al Freeman Jr. 5/6/76
Rona	Kaiulani Lee	Kaiulani Lee
		Sally Kirkland 5/6/76
Carla	Shirley Knight	Shirley Knight
		Ann Wedgeworth 5/6/76

THE MAGIC SHOW

	New York 5/28/74	*Boston 12/17/74*
Doug*	Doug Henning	Peter DePaula
	Joe Abaldo 3/30/76	
Cal	Dale Soules	Pippa Pearthree
	Dara Norman 10/29/75	
	Dale Soules	
Charmin	Anita Morris	Hester Lewellen
	Loni Ackerman 8/75	
	Louisa Flaningam 3/76	

Feldman	David Ogden Stiers	Paul Keith
	Kenneth Kimmins 1/75	
	Timothy Jerome 8/75	
	Steve Vinovich 4/76	

* Name of character changed to Joe when Mr. Abaldo played role, to Peter in the touring company.

A MUSICAL JUBILEE

	New York 11/13/75	*Toronto 5/31/76*
	John Raitt	Howard Keel
	Patrice Munsel	Patrice Munsel
	Tammy Grimes	Eartha Kitt
	Cyril Ritchard	Cyril Ritchard
	Larry Kert	Larry Kert

PIPPIN

	New York 10/23/72
Pippin	John Rubinstein
	Michael Rupert 11/74
	Dean Pitchford 12/1/75
	Michael Rupert 12/8/75
Charles	Eric Berry
Catherine	Jill Clayburgh
	Betty Buckley 6/11/73
	Joy Franz 3/76
Fastrada	Leland Palmer
	Priscilla Lopez 1/6/74
	Patti Karr 8/5/74
	Antonia Ellis 1/5/76
Berthe	Irene Ryan
	Lucie Lancaster 4/73
	Dorothy Stickney 6/11/73
	Lucie Lancaster 7/74
	Fay Sappington 8/18/75
	Lucie Lancaster 9/1/75
	Fay Sappington 12/75
Leading Player	Ben Vereen
	Northern J. Calloway 2/18/74
	Ben Vereen 5/7/74
	Samuel E. Wright 12/74
	Irving Lee 6/75
	Ben Harney 1/12/76
	Northern J. Calloway 5/24/76

RAISIN

	New York 10/18/73	*Wilmington 12/9/75*
Lena Younger	Virginia Capers	Virginia Capers
Walter Lee Younger	Joe Morton	Autris Paige
	Autris Paige 11/11/75	
Ruth Younger	Ernestine Jackson	Mary Seymour
	Mary Seymour 11/11/75	

Travis Younger	Ralph Carter	Darren Green
	Paul Carrington 9/3/74	
	Darren Green 11/74	
Bobo Jones	Ted Ross	Irving D. Barnes
	Irving D. Barnes 10/1/74	

THE RITZ

	New York 1/20/75	
Gaetano Proclo	Jack Weston	
	George Dzundza 3/3/75	
	Jack Weston 3/17/75	
	Stubby Kaye 9/1/75	
Googie Gomez	Rita Moreno	
	June Gable 10/28/75	
Carmine Vespucci	Jerry Stiller	
	Mike Kellin 7/28/75	
Claude Perkins	Paul B. Price	
	Rik Colitti 9/1/75	

SAME TIME, NEXT YEAR

	New York 3/13/75	*Toronto 12/1/75*
Doris	Ellen Burstyn	Joyce Van Patten
	Joyce Van Patten 10/20/75	
	Loretta Swit 12/1/75	
George	Charles Grodin	Conrad Janis
	Conrad Janis 10/20/75	
	Ted Bessell 12/1/75	

SCAPINO

	Brooklyn 3/12/74	
	New York 5/18/74	
	New York 9/27/74	*Los Angeles 4/27/75*
Scapino	Jim Dale	Jim Dale

SHENANDOAH

	New York 1/7/75	
Charlie Anderson	John Cullum	
Jenny	Penelope Milford	
	Maureen Silliman 9/8/75	
James	Joel Higgins	
	Wayne Hudgins 2/76	
Robert	Joseph Shapiro	
	Mark Perman	
Gabriel	Chip Ford	
	Brent Carter	
	David Vann 4/76	

SHERLOCK HOLMES

	New York 11/12/74	*Toronto 1/14/76*
Sherlock Holmes	John Wood Patrick Horgan 4/22/75 John Neville 5/13/75 Robert Stephens 8/19/75	Robert Stephens Leonard Nimoy 2/9/76
Prof. Moriarty	Philip Locke Clive Revill 2/4/75 Alan Sues 11/4/75	Alan Sues
Dr. Watson	Tom Pigott-Smith Dennis Cooney 2/4/75 Michael Hawkins Robert Stattel 11/4/75	Robert Stattel
Alice Faulkner	Mel Martin Lynne Lipton 2/4/75 Diana Kirkwood 9/23/75	Diana Kirkwood
Madge Larrabee	Barbara Leigh-Hunt Christina Pickles 2/4/75	Christina Pickles
Sidney Prince	Trevor Peacock Tony Tanner 2/4/75 Geoff Garland 9/2/75	Geoff Garland
James Larrabee	Nicholas Selby Ron Randell 2/4/75	Ron Randell
John Forman	Harry Towb Richard Lupino 2/4/75	Richard Lupino

SIZWE BANZI IS DEAD and THE ISLAND

	New York 11/13/74	*Los Angeles 6/5/75*
Styles; Buntu; John	John Kani	John Kani
Sizwe Banzi; Winston	Winston Ntshona	Winston Ntshona

VERY GOOD EDDIE

	New York 12/21/75	*London 3/23/76*
Elsie Darling	Virginia Seidel	Prue Clarke
Eddie Kettle	Charles Repole	Richard Freeman
Georgina Kettle	Spring Fairbank	Cookie Weymouth
Percy Darling	Nicholas Wyman	Nigel Williams
Mme. Matroppo	Travis Hudson	Gita Denise
Dick Rivers	David Christmas	Robert Swann
Elsie Lilly	Cynthia Wells	Mary Barrett
*Al Cleveland**	James Harder	John Blythe
De Rougement	Joel Craig	Teddy Green

* Name of character changed to Al Dallas in London.

WHAT THE WINE-SELLERS BUY

	New York 2/14/74	*Chicago 3/11/75*
Rico	Dick A. Williams	Gilbert Lewis
Steve Carlton	Glynn Turman	Herb Rice Ron Trice 6/2/75
Mae Harris	Loretta Greene	Loretta Greene Debbie Morgan 6/2/75

THE WIZ

	New York 1/5/75
Tinman	Tiger Haynes
Lion	Ted Ross James Wigfall 5/11/76
Scarecrow	Hinton Battle
Dorothy	Stephanie Mills
Glinda	DeeDee Bridgewater Deborah Burrell 4/12/76
Evillene	Mabel King Theresa Merritt 4/12/76
The Wiz	Andre De Shields Alan Weeks 5/4/76

BUS-TRUCK TOURS

These are touring productions designed for maximum mobility and ease of handling in one-night and split-week stands (with occasional engagements of a week or more). The one-man show is increasingly an attraction, because it is not required to give eight performances weekly (per Equity rules) and thus can be played for only one or two stands per week. The number of large-scale bus-truck tours has tended to diminish in recent seasons because 1) there have been fewer Broadway hits available and 2) the obligatory stars have been slow to commit themselves the necessary many months in advance for college and commercial bookings.

Among shows on tour in the season of 1975-76 were the following bus-truck troupes, listed in alphabetical order of titles:

Ben Franklin, Citizen (one-man show) with Fredd Wayne, intermittent dates 12/5/75-4/15/76.
Charley's Aunt with Roddy McDowall, Vincent Price, Coral Browne, 5/11/76-6/27/76.
Don't Bother Me, I Can't Cope, 9/17/75-2/1/76.
Gene Kelly's Salute to Broadway (revue) with Howard Keel, Mimi Hines, Lainie Nelson, 9/16/75-12/6/75.
Give 'Em Hell, Harry (one-man show) with James Whitmore, later Ed Nelson, intermittent bookings 8/25/76-4/11/76.
The Great American Nut Show (one-man show) with Michael Brown, intermittent bookings 9/30/75-2/10/76.
Irene with Patsy Kelly, later Virginia Graham, Meg Bussert, 10/3/75-2/23/76.
Jack Aranson in Repertory (one-man show), intermittent bookings 12/12/75-5/15/76.
Man of La Mancha with David Atkinson, 1/14/76-4/4/76.
Mark Twain Tonight (one-man show) with Hal Holbrook, intermittent bookings 9/12/75-5/23/76.
The Odd Couple with Jack Klugman, Tony Randall, 6/2/75-8/10/75 and 5/10/76-5/17/76.
Royal Shakespeare Company (*The Hollow Crown* and *Pleasures and Repentances*), 9/29/75-11/19/75.
1776 with Don Perkins,, 9/13/75-5/23/76 (plus special Bicentennial summer engagement in Philadelphia).
Together Tonight with Howard Duff, Monte Markham, Dana Andrews, Alan Manson, 1/15/76-3/28/76.
William Windom Plays Thurber (one-man show), intermittent bookings 9/19/75-5/6/76.
Words and Music (one-man show) with Sammy Cahn. 9/26/75-1/11/76.

FACTS AND
FIGURES

LONG RUNS ON BROADWAY

The following shows have run 500 or more continuous performances in a single production, usually the first, not including previews or extra non-profit performances, allowing for vacation layoffs and special one-booking engagements, but not including return engagements after a show has gone on tour. Where there are title similarities, the production is identified as follows: (p) straight play version, (m) musical version, (r) revival.

THROUGH MAY 31, 1976

(PLAYS MARKED WITH ASTERISK WERE STILL PLAYING JUNE 1, 1976)

Plays	Number Performances	Plays	Number Performances
Fiddler on the Roof	3,242	Guys and Dolls	1,200
Life With Father	3,224	Cabaret	1,165
Tobacco Road	3,182	Mister Roberts	1,157
Hello, Dolly!	2,844	Annie Get Your Gun	1,147
My Fair Lady	2,717	The Seven Year Itch	1,141
Man of La Mancha	2,328	Butterflies Are Free	1,128
Abie's Irish Rose	2,327	Pins and Needles	1,108
Oklahoma!	2,212	Plaza Suite	1,097
South Pacific	1,925	Kiss Me, Kate	1,070
Harvey	1,775	Don't Bother Me, I Can't Cope	1,065
* Grease	1,763	The Pajama Game	1,063
Hair	1,750	The Teahouse of the August	
Born Yesterday	1,642	Moon	1,027
Mary, Mary	1,572	Damn Yankees	1,019
The Voice of the Turtle	1,557	Never Too Late	1,007
Barefoot in the Park	1,530	Any Wednesday	982
* Pippin	1,512	A Funny Thing Happened on	
Mame (m)	1,508	the Way to the Forum	964
Arsenic and Old Lace	1,444	The Odd Couple	964
The Sound of Music	1,443	Anna Lucasta	957
How To Succeed in Business		Kiss and Tell	956
Without Really Trying	1,417	Bells Are Ringing	924
Hellzapoppin	1,404	The Moon Is Blue	924
The Music Man	1,375	Luv	901
Funny Girl	1,348	Applause	896
Oh! Calcutta!	1,314	Can-Can	892
Angel Street	1,295	Carousel	890
Lightnin'	1,291	Hats Off to Ice	889
Promises, Promises	1,281	Fanny	888
The King and I	1,246	Follow the Girls	882
Cactus Flower	1,234	Camelot	873
Sleuth	1,222	The Bat	867
1776	1,217	My Sister Eileen	864

Plays	*Number Performances*	*Plays*	*Number Performances*
No, No, Nanette (r)	861	Peg o' My Heart	692
Song of Norway	860	The Children's Hour	691
A Streetcar Named Desire	855	Purlie	688
Comedy in Music	849	Dead End	687
Raisin	847	The Lion and the Mouse	686
That Championship Season	844	White Cargo	686
* The Magic Show	837	Dear Ruth	683
You Can't Take It With You	837	East Is West	680
La Plume de Ma Tante	835	Come Blow Your Horn	677
Three Men on a Horse	835	The Most Happy Fella	676
The Subject Was Roses	832	The Doughgirls	671
Inherit the Wind	806	The Impossible Years	670
No Time for Sergeants	796	Irene	670
Fiorello!	795	Boy Meets Girl	669
Where's Charley?	792	Beyond the Fringe	667
The Ladder	789	* Equus	666
Forty Carats	780	Who's Afraid of Virginia	
The Prisoner of Second Avenue	780	Woolf?	664
Oliver	774	Blithe Spirit	657
State of the Union	765	A Trip to Chinatown	657
The First Year	760	The Women	657
You Know I Can't Hear You		Bloomer Girl	654
When the Water's Running	755	The Fifth Season	654
Two for the Seesaw	750	Rain	648
Death of a Salesman	742	Witness for the Prosecution	645
Sons o' Fun	742	Call Me Madam	644
Candide (mr)	740	Janie	642
Gentlemen Prefer Blondes	740	The Green Pastures	640
The Man Who Came to Dinner	739	Auntie Mame (p)	639
Call Me Mister	734	A Man for All Seasons	637
West Side Story	732	The Fourposter	632
High Button Shoes	727	Two Gentlemen of	
Finian's Rainbow	725	Verona (m)	627
Claudia	722	The Tenth Man	623
The Gold Diggers	720	Is Zat So?	618
Jesus Christ Superstar	720	Anniversary Waltz	615
Carnival	719	The Happy Time (p)	614
The Diary of Anne Frank	717	Separate Rooms	613
I Remember Mama	714	Affairs of State	610
Tea and Sympathy	712	Star and Garter	609
Junior Miss	710	The Student Prince	608
Last of the Red Hot Lovers	706	Sweet Charity	608
Company	705	Bye Bye Birdie	607
Seventh Heaven	704	Irene (r)	604
Gypsy (m)	702	Broadway	603
The Miracle Worker	700	Adonis	603
Cat on a Hot Tin Roof	694	Street Scene (p)	601
Li'l Abner	693	Kiki	600

Plays	Number Performances	Plays	Number Performances
Flower Drum Song	600	Let's Face It	547
A Little Night Music	600	Milk and Honey	543
Don't Drink the Water	598	Within the Law	541
Wish You Were Here	598	The Music Master	540
A Society Circus	596	Pal Joey (r)	540
Absurd Person Singular	592	What Makes Sammy Run?	540
Blossom Time	592	The Sunshine Boys	538
The Me Nobody Knows	586	What a Life	538
The Two Mrs. Carrolls	585	The Unsinkable Molly Brown	532
Kismet	583	The Red Mill (r)	531
Detective Story	581	A Raisin in the Sun	530
Brigadoon	581	The Solid Gold Cadillac	526
No Strings	580	Irma La Douce	524
Brother Rat	577	The Boomerang	522
Show Boat	572	Follies	521
The Show-Off	571	Rosalinda	521
Sally	570	The Best Man	520
Golden Boy (m)	568	Chauve-Souris	520
One Touch of Venus	567	Blackbirds of 1928	518
Happy Birthday	564	Sunny	517
Look Homeward, Angel	564	Victoria Regina	517
The Glass Menagerie	561	Half a Sixpence	511
I Do! I Do!	560	The Vagabond King	511
Wonderful Town	559	The New Moon	509
Rose Marie	557	* Same Time, Next Year	509
* Shenandoah	557	The World of Suzie Wong	508
Strictly Dishonorable	557	The Rothschilds	507
A Majority of One	556	Sugar	505
The Great White Hope	556	Shuffle Along	504
Toys in the Attic	556	Up in Central Park	504
Sunrise at Campobello	556	Carmen Jones	503
* The Wiz	556	The Member of the Wedding	501
Jamaica	555	Panama Hattie	501
Stop the World—I Want to Get Off	555	Personal Appearance	501
Florodora	553	Bird in Hand	500
Ziegfeld Follies (1943)	553	Room Service	500
Dial "M" for Murder	552	Sailor, Beware!	500
Good News	551	Tomorrow the World	500

LONG RUNS OFF BROADWAY

Plays	Number Performances	Plays	Number Performances
* The Fantasticks	6,699	* Godspell	2,100
The Threepenny Opera	2,611	Jacques Brel	1,847

Plays	Number Performances	Plays	Number Performances
You're a Good Man		Oh! Calcutta!	704
Charlie Brown	1,597	Scuba Duba	692
The Blacks	1,408	The Knack	685
The Hot l Baltimore	1,166	The Balcony	672
Little Mary Sunshine	1,143	America Hurrah	634
* Let My People Come	1,122	Hogan's Goat	607
El Grande de Coca-Cola	1,114	The Trojan Women (r)	600
One Flew Over the		Krapp's Last Tape &	
Cuckoo's Nest (r)	1,025	The Zoo Story	582
The Boys in the Band	1,000	The Dumbwaiter &	
Your Own Thing	933	The Collection	578
Curley McDimple	931	Dames at Sea	575
Leave It to Jane (r)	928	The Crucible (r)	571
The Mad Show	871	The Iceman Cometh (r)	565
The Effect of Gamma Rays on		The Hostage (r)	545
Man-in-the-Moon Marigolds.	819	Six Characters in Search of an	
A View From the Bridge (r) ..	780	Author (r)	529
The Boy Friend (r)	763	The Dirtiest Show in Town ..	509
The Pocket Watch	725	Happy Ending & Day of	
The Connection	722	Absence	504
Adaptation & Next	707	The Boys From Syracuse (r) ..	500

DRAMA CRITICS CIRCLE VOTING, 1975–76

The New York Drama Critics Circle voted the British play *Travesties* by by Tom Stoppard the best play of the season on the first ballot by the required majority of first choices of the 21 critics present and voting. *Travesties* received 11 votes (from Clive Barnes, John Beaufort, Brendan Gill, Ted Kalem, Emory Lewis, Norman Nadel, George Oppenheimer, William Raidy, Marilyn Stasio, Richard Watts Jr. and Edwin Wilson) to 9 for *Streamers* (from Harold Clurman, William H. Glover, Martin Gottfried, Henry Hewes, Jack Kroll, Edith Oliver, John Simon, Allan Wallach and Douglas Watt) and one for *Knock Knock* (from Walter Kerr). The other two Circle members—Hobe Morrison and Julius Novick—were not present and not voting.

Having named a foreign play bests of bests, the Circle voted *Streamers* by David Rabe the best American play on the first ballot by an even larger majority of 16 votes (from Barnes, Clurman, Gill, Glover, Gottfried, Hewes, Kroll, Lewis, Nadel, Oliver, Raidy, Simon, Stasio, Wallach, Watt and Wilson) to 3 for *Knock Knock* (from Beaufort, Kerr and Watts) and one for *Lamppost Reunion* (from Kalem), with one abstention (Oppenheimer).

The critics then named *Pacific Overtures* by John Weidman, Stephen Sondheim and Hugh Wheeler the year's best musical on a weighted second ballot, after no show received the necessary majority on the first, whose first choices were distributed as follows: *Pacific Overtures* 6 (Beaufort, Glover, Gottfried, Kroll, Oppenheimer, Wallach), *Tuscaloosa's Calling Me . . . but I'm Not Going* 4 (Clurman, Kerr, Lewis, Oliver), *The Robber Bridegroom* 1 (Hewes), *Chicago* 1 (Stasio) and 9 abstentions (Barnes, Gill, Kalem, Nadel, Raidy, Simon, Watt, Watts, Wilson). On the second ballot, weighted to produce a consensus by points (with 3 points given to a critic's first choice, 2 for second and 1 for third), the scoring was as follows: *Pacific Overtures* 27, *Tuscaloosa, etc.* 13, *The Robber Bridegroom* 10, *Chicago* 9, *Very Good Eddie* 4, *Rex* 2, *So Long, 174th Street* 1. The new translation of *Threepenny Opera* produced by Joseph Papp at Lincoln Center had been voted ineligible (as a revival) before this best-musical balloting started, accounting for at least one of the relatively large number of abstentions.

Here's the way the votes were distributed on the second, weighted ballot for best musical:

SECOND BALLOTT FOR BEST MUSICAL

Critic	1st Choice (3 pts.)	2d Choice (2 pts.)	3d Choice (1 pt.)
Clive Barnes *Times*	Abstain		
John Beaufort *Monitor*	Pacific Overtures	Tuscaloosa's Calling Me . . . but I'm Not Going	The Robber Bridegroom
Harold Clurman *The Nation*	Tuscaloosa	Very Good Eddie	Pacific Overtures
Brendan Gill *New Yorker*	Abstain		
William H. Glover AP	Pacific Overtures	Chicago	Tuscaloosa
Martin Gottfried *Post*	Pacific Overtures	Robber Bridegroom	Chicago
Henry Hewes *Saturday Review*	Robber Bridegroom	Pacific Overtures	So Long, 174th Street
Ted Kalem *Time*	Abstain		
Walter Kerr *Times*	Abstain		
Jack Kroll *Newsweek*	Pacific Overtures	Chicago	Robber Bridegroom
Emory Lewis *Bergen Record*	Tuscaloosa	Pacific Overtures	Robber Bridegroom
Hobe Morrison *Variety*	Absent		
Norman Nadel Scripps-Howard	Abstain		
Julius Novick *Village Voice*	Absent		
Edith Oliver *New Yorker*	Tuscaloosa	Very Good Eddie	Pacific Overtures
George Oppenheimer *Newsday*	Pacific Overtures	Rex	Robber Bridegroom
William Raidy Newhouse	Abstain		
John Simon *New Leader*	Abstain		
Marilyn Stasio *Cue*	Pacific Overtures	Chicago	Robber Bridegroom

Allan Wallach *Newsday*	Pacific Overtures	Chicago	Tuscaloosa
Douglas Watt *Daily News*	Abstain		
Richard Watts Jr. *Post*	Abstain		
Edwin Wilson *Wall St. Journal*	Abstain		

CHOICES OF SOME OTHER CRITICS

Critic	*Best Play*	*Best Musical*
Judith Crist	Travesties	Pacific Overtures
Stewart Klein WNEW-TV	Streamers	Bubbling Brown Sugar
Hobe Morrison *Variety*	The Belle of Amherst	Chicago
Joseph Porter *Cue*	Travesties	Pacific Overtures
Leonard Probst WNBC	Travesties	Abstain

NEW YORK DRAMA CRITICS CIRCLE AWARDS

Listed below are the New York Drama Critics Circle Awards from 1935–36 through 1975–76 classified as follows: (1) Best American Play, (2) Best Foreign Play, (3) Best Musical, (4) Best, regardless of category (this category was established by new voting rules in 1962–63 and did not exist prior to that year).

1935–36—(1) Winterset
1936–37—(1) High Tor
1937–38—(1) Of Mice and Men, (2) Shadow and Substance
1938–39—(1) No award, (2) The White Steed
1939–40—(1) The Time of Your Life
1940–41—(1) Watch on the Rhine, (2) The Corn Is Green
1941–42—(1) No award, (2) Blithe Spirit
1942–43—(1) The Patriots
1943–44—(2) Jacobowsky and the Colonel
1944–45—(1) The Glass Menagerie
1945–46—(3) Carousel
1946–47—(1) All My Sons, (2) No Exit, (3) Brigadoon
1947–48—(1) A Streetcar Named Desire, (2) The Winslow Boy
1948–49—(1) Death of a Salesman, (2) The Madwoman of Chaillot, (3) South Pacific
1949–50—(1) The Member of the Wedding (2) The Cocktail Party, (3) The Consul
1950–51—(1) Darkness at Noon, (2) The Lady's Not for Burning, (3) Guys and Dolls
1951–52—(1) I Am a Camera, (2) Venus Observed, (3) Pal Joey (Special citation to Don Juan in Hell)
1952–53—(1) Picnic, (2) The Love of Four Colonels, (3) Wonderful Town

1953–54—(1) Teahouse of the August Moon, (2) Ondine, (3) The Golden Apple
1954–55—(1) Cat on a Hot Tin Roof, (2) Witness for the Prosecution, (3) The Saint of Bleecker Street
1955–56—(1) The Diary of Ann Frank, (2) Tiger at the Gates, (3) My Fair Lady
1956–57—(1) Long Day's Journey Into Night, (2) The Waltz of the Toreadors, (3) The Most Happy Fella
1957–58—(1) Look Homeward, Angel, (2) Look Back in Anger, (3) The Music Man
1958–59—(1) A Raisin in the Sun, (2) The Visit, (3) La Plume de Ma Tante
1959–60—(1) Toys in the Attic, (2) Five Finger Exercise, (3) Fiorello!
1960–61—(1) All the Way Home, (2) A Taste of Honey, (3) Carnival
1961–62—(1) The Night of the Iguana, (2) A Man for All Seasons, (3) How to Succeed in Business Without Really Trying
1962–63—(4) Who's Afraid of Virginia Woolf? (Special citation to Beyond the Fringe)
1963–64—(4) Luther, (3) Hello, Dolly! (Special citation to The Trojan Women)
1964–65—(4) The Subject Was Roses, (3) Fiddler on the Roof

1965–66—(4) The Persecution and Assassination of Marat as Performed by the Inmates of the Asylum of Charenton Under the Direction of the Marquis de Sade, (3) Man of La Mancha

1966–67—(4) The Homecoming, (3) Cabaret

1967–68—(4) Rosencrantz and Guildenstern Are Dead, (3) Your Own Thing

1968–69—(4) The Great White Hope, (3) 1776

1969–70—(4) Borstal Boy, (1) The Effect of Gamma Rays on Man-in-the-Moon Marigolds, (3) Company

1970–71—(4) Home, (1) The House of Blue Leaves, (3) Follies

1971–72—(4) That Championship Season, (2) The Screens, (3) Two Gentlemen of Verona (Special citations to Sticks and Bones and Old Times)

1972–73—(4) The Changing Room, (1) The Hot 1 Baltimore, (3) A Little Night Music

1973–74—(4) The Contractor, (1) Short Eyes, (3) Candide

1974–75—(4) Equus, (1) The Taking of Miss Janie, (3) A Chorus Line

1975–76—(4) Travesties, (1) Streamers, (3) Pacific Overtures

PULITZER PRIZE WINNERS, 1916–17 TO 1975–76

1916–17—No award

1917–18—Why Marry?, by Jesse Lynch Williams

1918–19—No award

1919–20—Beyond the Horizon, by Eugene O'Neill

1920–21—Miss Lulu Bett, by Zona Gale

1921–22—Anna Christie, by Eugene O'Neill

1922–23—Icebound, by Owen Davis

1923–24—Hell-Bent fer Heaven, by Hatcher Hughes

1924–25—They Knew What They Wanted, by Sidney Howard

1925–26—Craig's Wife, by George Kelly

1926–27—In Abraham's Bosom, by Paul Green

1927–28—Strange Interlude, by Eugene O'Neill

1928–29—Street Scene, by Elmer Rice

1929–30—The Green Pastures, by Marc Connelly

1930–31—Alison's House, by Susan Glaspell

1931–32—Of Thee I Sing, by George S. Kaufman, Morrie Ryskind, Ira and George Gershwin

1932–33—Both Your Houses, by Maxwell Anderson

1933–34—Men in White, by Sidney Kingsley

1934–35—The Old Maid, by Zoë Akins

1935–36—Idiot's Delight, by Robert E. Sherwood

1936–37—You Can't Take It With You, by Moss Hart and George S. Kaufman

1937–38—Our Town, by Thornton Wilder

1938–39—Abe Lincoln in Illinois, by Robert E. Sherwood

1939–40—The Time of Your Life, by William Saroyan

1940–41—There Shall Be No Night, by Robert E. Sherwood

1941–42—No award

1942–43—The Skin of Our Teeth, by Thornton Wilder

1943–44—No award

1944–45—Harvey, by Mary Chase

1945–46—State of the Union, by Howard Lindsay and Russel Crouse

1946–47—No award.

1947–48—A Streetcar Named Desire, by Tennessee Williams

1948–49—Death of a Salesman, by Arthur Miller

1949–50—South Pacific, by Richard Rodgers, Oscar Hammerstein II and Joshua Logan

1950–51—No award

1951–52—The Shrike, by Joseph Kramm

1952–53—Picnic, by William Inge

1953–54—The Teahouse of the August Moon, by John Patrick

1954–55—Cat on a Hot Tin Roof, by Tennessee Williams

1955–56—The Diary of Anne Frank, by Frances Goodrich and Albert Hackett

1956–57—Long Day's Journey Into Night, by Eugene O'Neill

1957–58—Look Homeward, Angel, by Ketti Frings

1958–59—J. B., by Archibald MacLeish

1959–60—Fiorello!, by Jerome Weidman, George Abbott, Sheldon Harnick and Jerry Bock

1960–61—All the Way Home, by Tad Mosel

1961–62—How to Succeed in Business Without Really Trying, by Abe Burrows, Willie Gilbert, Jack Weinstock and Frank Loesser

1962–63—No award

1963–64—No award

1964–65—The Subject Was Roses, by Frank D. Gilroy

1965–66—No award

1966–67—A Delicate Balance, by Edward Albee

1967–68—No award

1968–69—The Great White Hope, by Howard Sackler

1969-70—No Place to Be Somebody, by Charles Gordone
1970-71—The Effect of Gamma Rays on Man-in-the-Moon Marigolds, by Paul Zindel
1971-72—No award
1972-73—That Championship Season, by Jason Miller

1973-74—No award
1974-75—Seascape, by Edward Albee
1975-76—A Chorus Line, by Michael Bennett, James Kirkwood, Nicholas Dante, Marvin Hamlisch and Edward Kleban

THE TONY AWARDS

The Antoinette Perry (Tony) Awards are voted by members of the League of New York Theaters, the governing bodies of the Dramatists Guild, Actors' Equity, the American Theater Wing, the Society of Stage Directors and Choreographers, the United Scenic Artists Union and members of the first and second-night press, from a list of nominations in each category.

Nominations are made by a committee serving at the invitation of the League of New York Theaters, which sponsors the awards under an agreement with the American Theater Wing, with nominating committee personnel changing every year. The 1975-76 nominating committee was composed of Peter Bailey of *Ebony* and *Jet,* Martin Gottfried of the New York *Post,* Otis L. Guernsey Jr. of *Best Plays,* Francis Herridge of the *Post,* Paul Myers of the New York Public Library Theater Collection, Seymour Peck of the New York *Times,* Joan Rubin of *Playbill,* Marilyn Stasio of *Cue,* Allan Wallach of *Newsday* and Edwin Wilson of the *Wall Street Journal.*

Nominations were made from a list of nominees eligible in each category, provided by the Tony administration's Eligibility Committee whose personnel included Ruth Green of the League of New York Theaters, Stuart W. Little of the American Theater Wing and Hobe Morrison of *Variety.*

The list of nominees follows, with winners in each category listed in **bold face type:**

BEST PLAY. *The First Breeze of Summer* by Leslie Lee, produced by Negro Ensemble Company; *Knock Knock* by Jules Feiffer, produced by Harry Rigby and Terry Allen Kramer; *Lamppost Reunion* by Louis LaRusso II, produced by Joe Garofalo; *Travesties* by **Tom Stoppard,** produced by **David Merrick, Doris Cole Abrahams** and **Burry Fredrik.**

BEST MUSICAL. *Bubbling Brown Sugar* produced by J. Lloyd Grant, Richard Bell, Robert M. Cooper and Ashton Springer; *Chicago* produced by Robert Fryer and James Cresson; *A Chorus Line* produced by **Joseph Papp;** *Pacific Overtures* produced by Harold Prince.

BEST BOOK OF A MUSICAL. *Chicago* by Fred Ebb and Bob Fosse; *A Chorus Line* by **James Kirkwood** and **Nicholas Dante;** *Pacific Overtures* by John Weidman, additional material by Hugh Wheeler; *The Robber Bridegroom* by Alfred Uhry.

BEST SCORE. *Chicago,* music by John Kander, lyrics by Fred Ebb; *A Chorus Line,* music by **Marvin Hamlisch,** lyrics by **Edward Kleban;** *Pacific Overtures,* music and lyrics by Stephen Sondheim; *Treemonisha,* music and lyrics by Scott Joplin.

BEST ACTOR—PLAY. Moses Gunn in *The Poison Tree;* George C. Scott in *Death of a Salesman;* Donald Sinden in *Habeas Corpus;* **John Wood** in *Travesties.*

BEST ACTRESS—PLAY. Tovah Feldshuh in *Yentl;* Rosemary Harris in *The Royal Family;* Lynn Redgrave in *Mrs. Warren's Profession;* **Irene Worth** in *Sweet Bird of Youth.*

BEST ACTOR—MUSICAL. Mako in *Pacific*

Overtures; Jerry Orbach in *Chicago*; Ian Richardson and **George Rose** in *My Fair Lady*.

BEST ACTRESS—MUSICAL. **Donna McKechnie** in *A Chorus Line*; Vivian Reed in *Bubbling Brown Sugar*; Chita Rivera and Gwen Verdon in *Chicago*.

BEST FEATURED ACTOR—PLAY. Barry Bostwick in *They Knew What They Wanted*; Gabriel Dell in *Lamppost Reunion*; **Edward Herrmann** in *Mrs. Warren's Profession*; Daniel Seltzer in *Knock Knock*.

BEST FEATURED ACTRESS—PLAY. Marybeth Hurt in *Trelawny of the "Wells"*: **Shirley Knight** in *Kennedy's Children*; Lois Nettleton in *They Knew What They Wanted*; Meryl Streep in *27 Wagons Full of Cotton*.

BEST FEATURED ACTOR—MUSICAL. Robert LuPone and **Sammy Williams** in *A Chorus Line*; Charles Repole in *Very Good Eddie*; Isao Sato in *Pacific Overtures*.

BEST FEATURED ACTRESS—MUSICAL. **Carole (Kelly) Bishop** and Priscilla Lopez in *A Chorus Line*; Patti LuPone in *The Robber Bridegroom*; Virginia Seidel in *Very Good Eddie*.

BEST DIRECTOR—PLAY. Arvin Brown for *Ah, Wilderness*; Marshall W. Mason for *Knock Knock*; **Ellis Rabb** for *The Royal Family*; Peter Wood for *Travesties*.

BEST DIRECTOR—MUSICAL. **Michael Bennett** for *A Chorus Line*; Bob Fosse for *Chicago*; Bill Gile for *Very Good Eddie*; Harold Prince for *Pacific Overtures*.

BEST SCENIC DESIGNER. **Boris Aronson** for *Pacific Overtures*; Ben Edwards for *A Matter of Gravity*; David Mitchell for *Trelawny of the "Wells"*; Tony Walton for *Chicago*.

BEST COSTUME DESIGNER. **Theoni V. Aldredge** for *A Chorus Line*; Florence Klotz for *Pacific Overtures*; Ann Roth for *The Royal Family*; Patricia Zipprodt for *Chicago*.

BEST LIGHTING DESIGNER. Ian Calderon for *Trelawny of the "Wells"*; Jules Fisher for *Chicago;* **Tharon Musser** for *A Chorus Line* (and *Pacific Overtures*).

BEST CHOREOGRAPHER. **Michael Bennett** and **Bob Avian** for *A Chorus Line*; Patricia Birch for *Pacific Overtures*; Bob Fosse for *Chicago*; Billy Wilson for *Bubbling Brown Sugar*.

SPECIAL AWARDS (voted by the Tony Administration Committee): First Lawrence Langner Award for lifetime achievement in the theater to **George Abbott**; Theater Wing Actor's Award to **Richard Burton**; special Tony Awards to the **Arena Stage**, Washington, D.C. as a pioneer of regional theater, **Thomas H. Fitzgerald** (posthumous) as lighting technician, **Mathilde Pincus** as musical score preparation supervisor and **Circle in the Square** as a pioneer of off-Broadway theater.

ADDITIONAL PRIZES AND AWARDS, 1975–76

The following is a list of major prizes and awards for theatrical achievement. In all cases the names of winners—persons, productions or organizations—appear in **bold face type**.

VILLAGE VOICE OFF-BROADWAY (OBIE) AWARDS for excellence selected by a committee of judges whose members were Michael Feingold, Francoise Kourilsky, Erika Munk, Julius Novick, Arthur Sainer, Carll Tucker and Ross Wetzsteon. Best theater piece—**Rhoda in Potatoland** by Richard Foreman. Best new playwright—**David Mamet** for *American Buffalo* and *Sexual Perversity in Chicago*. Direction—**Joanne Akalaitis** for *Cascando*; **Marshall W. Mason** for *Knock Knock* and *Serenading Louie*. Special citations—**Michael Bennett, James Kirkwood, Nicholas Dante, Marvin Hamlisch** and **Edward Kleban** as creators of *A Chorus Line*; Edward Bond's **Bingo** (in the Yale Repertory Theater production); **Meredith Monk** for *Quarry*; **Morton Lichter** and **Gordon Rogoff** for *Old Timers' Sexual Symphony*; **Chile! Chile!;** **Santo Loquasto** for the sets and costumes of *The Comedy of Errors;* **Philip Glass** for the music for Mabou Mines; **Donald Brooks** for the set of *The Tempest*; **Neil Flanagan** for distinguished contribution to off-Broadway theater.

Performance Obies—**Joyce Aaron** in *Acrobatics*; **Roberts Blossom** in *Ice Age*; **Robert Christian** in *Blood Knot*; **Crystal Field** in *Day Old Bread*; **June Gable** in *The Comedy of Errors*; **Mike Kellin** in *American Buffalo*; **Tony Lo Bianco** in *Yanks 3 Detroit 0 Top of the Seventh*; **Priscilla Lopez** and **Sammy Williams** in *A Chorus Line*; **Kate Manheim** in *Rhoda in Potatoland*; **T. Miratti** in *The Shortchanged Review*; **Pamela Payton-Wright** in *Jesse and the Bandit Queen*; **Priscilla Smith** in *The Good Woman of Setzuan*; **David Warrilow** in *The Lost Ones*.

1975 MARGO JONES AWARD for the professional producer and theater deemed to have made the most significant contribution to the American theater. **Robert Kalfin** and the **Chelsea Theater Center of Brooklyn.**

1976 JOSEPH MAHARAM FOUNDATION AWARDS for distinguished New York theatrical design by American designers. Scenery design—**Boris Aronson** for *Pacific Overtures*; **John Lee Beatty** for *Knock Knock*. Costume design—**Florence Klotz** for *Pacific Overtures*.

CLARENCE DERWENT AWARDS for the most promising female and male actors on the metropolitan scene. **Nancy Snyder** for *Knock Knock*; **Peter Evans** for *Streamers*.

ELIZABETH HULL-KATE WARRINER AWARD to the playwright whose work produced within the 1974–75 season dealt with controversial subjects involving the fields of political, religious or social mores of the time, selected by the Dramatists Guild Council. **Edward Albee** for *Seascape*.

32d ANNUAL THEATER WORLD AWARDS for the outstanding new performers in Broadway and off-Broadway productions during the 1975–76 season. **Danny Aiello** in *Lamppost Reunion*; **Christine Andreas** in *My Fair Lady*; **Dixie Carter** in *Jesse and the Bandit Queen*; **Tovah Feldshuh** and **John Shea** in *Yentl*; **Chip Garnett** and

Vivian Reed in *Bubbling Brown Sugar*; **Richard Kelton** in *Who's Afraid of Virginia Woolf?*; **Charles Repole** and **Virginia Seidel** in *Very Good Eddie*; **Daniel Seltzer** in *Knock Knock*; **Meryl Streep** in Phoenix Theater productions.

DRAMA DESK AWARDS for outstanding contribution to the 1975–76 theater season. New play—**David Rabe** for *Streamers*. Book of a musical—**James Kirkwood** and **Nicholas Dante** for *A Chorus Line*. Music and lyrics—**Marvin Hamlisch** and **Edward Kleban** for *A Chorus Line*. Revival—**Barry M. Brown, Burry Fredrik, Fritz Holt** and **Sally Sears** for *The Royal Family*. Director of a play—**Ellis Rabb** for *The Royal Family*. Director of a musical and choreographer—**Michael Bennett** for *A Chorus Line*. Actor in a play—**John Wood** in *Travesties*. Actress in a play—**Rosemary Harris** in *The Royal Family*. Actor in a musical—**Ian Richardson** in *My Fair Lady*. Actress in a musical—**Kelly Bishop** and **Donna McKechnie** (tie) in *A Chorus Line*. Supporting actor in a play—**Judd Hirsch** in *Knock Knock*. Supporting actress in a play—**Rachel Roberts** in *Habeas Corpus*. Supporting actor in a musical—**George Rose** in *My Fair Lady*. Supporting actress in a musical—**Vivian Reed** in *Bubbling Brown Sugar*. Scenery—**Boris Aronson** for *Pacific Overtures*. Costumes—**Florence Klotz** for *Pacific Overtures*. Lighting—**Jules Fisher** for *Chicago*. Unique evening in the theater—**The Norman Conquests**. Special commendations—Playwrights Horizons' new **Queens Theater in the Park** and the **Hartman Theater**, Stamford, Conn., as new theaters; the **Hudson River Museum** for its exhibition of theater items.

1975–76 PUBLICATION OF RECENTLY-PRODUCED PLAYS

Action/The Unseen Hand. Sam Shepard. Faber & Faber.
Arbuckle's Rape. Louis Phillips. Colonnades Theater Lab (paperback).
Ascent of Mount Fuji, The. Chingiz Aitmatov and Kaltai Mukhamedzhanov. Farrar, Straus and Giroux (also paperback).
Bacchae of Euripides, The; A Communion Rite. Wole Soyinka. Norton (paperback)
Black Man's Country. Desmond Forristal. Proscenium Press (paperback).
Black Picture Show. Bill Gunn. Reed, Cannon and Johnson.
Brassneck. Brenton, Howard and David Hare. Eyre Methuen (paperback).
Cannibals, The. George Tabori. Davis-Poynter (paperback).
Children's Crusade, The. Paul Thompson. Heinemann (paperback).
Churchill Play, The. Howard Brenton. Eyre Methuen (paperback).
Cromwell. David Storey. Jonathan Cape (paperback).
Da. Hugh Leonard. Proscenium Press (paperback).
Death and the King's Horsemen. Wole Soyinka. W.W. Norton (also paperback).
Dodo Bird, The. Emanual Fried. Labor Arts Books.
End of Me Old Cigar, The/Jill and Jack. John Osborne. Faber & Faber.
Enemy Within, The. Brian Friel. Proscenium Press (paperback).
Farm, The. David Storey. Jonathan Cape (paperback).

Freeway, The. Peter Nichols. Faber & Faber (paperback).
Gentle Island, The. Brian Friel. Davis-Poynter (paperback).
Give 'Em Hell Harry. Samuel Gallu. Avon (paperback).
God's Favorite. Neil Simon. Random House.
Hell of a Mess, A. Eugene Ionesco. Grove (paperback).
In the Boom Boom Room. David Rabe. Knopf (paperback).
Kennedy's Children. Robert Patrick. Random House.
Life Class. David Storey. Jonathan Cape (paperback).
Lulu. Peter Barnes. Heinemann (paperback).
Miles and Playboy. Mark Dunster. Linden.
Miracle Play. Joyce Carol Oates. Black Sparrow Press.
Neffie/In Sorrow's Room. China Clark. ERA Publishing (paperback).
No Man's Land. Harold Pinter. Grove (also paperback).
Old Ones, The. Arnold Wesker. Jonathan Cape (paperback).
Orphans, The. Thomas Murphy. Proscenium Press (paperback).
Pignight/Blowjob. Snoo Wilson. John Calder.
Pippin. Roger O. Hirson and Stephen Schwartz. Drama Book Service.
Same Time, Next Year. Bernard Slade. Delta (paperback).
Statements: Three Plays. Athol Fugard, John Kani and Winston Ntshona. Oxford (paperback).
Sylvia Plath: A Dramatic Portrait. Barry Kyle. Faber & Faber (paperback).
Travesties. Tom Stoppard. Grove Press (also paperback).
Wager, The and *Two Short Plays.* Mark Medoff. James T. White (paperback).
Watch It Come Down. John Osborne. Faber & Faber (paperback).
When the Rattlesnake Sounds. Alice Childress. Coward, McCann & Geoghegan.

A SELECTED LIST OF OTHER PLAYS PUBLISHED IN 1975–76

America on Stage. Stanley Richards, editor. Doubleday.
Bedbug, The. Vladimir Mayakovsky. Davis-Poynter.
Best Short Plays, The: 1975. Stanley Richards, editor. Chilton.
Chekhov Plays: Uncle Vanya, The Cherry Orchard, The Wood Demon. Anton Chekhov. Oxford (paperback).
Children of the Sun, The. Maxim Gorky. Davis-Poynter (paperback).
Dramas of Testimony. August Strindberg. University of Washington Press.
Gertrude Stein: Last Operas and Plays. Gertrude Stein. Vintage (paperback).
Last Days of Mankind, The. Karl Kraus. Unger (paperback).
Mandate, The/The Suicide. Nikolai Erdman. Ardis Publishers.
Rise and Fall of the City of Mahagonny. Bertolt Brecht. David R. Godine.
Samson Riddle, The. Wolf Mankowitz. Valentine, Mitchell.
Sweet Bird of Youth. Tennessee Williams. New Directions.
Three Plays. M. J. Molloy. Proscenium Press.
Trip to the Exposition of 1889, A. Henri Rousseau. Cafe Farrago.

MUSIC AND DRAMATIC RECORDINGS OF NEW YORK SHOWS

Title and publishing company are listed below. Each record is an original New York cast unless otherwise indicated. An asterisk (*) indicates recording is also available on cassettes. Two asterisks (**) indicate it is available on eight-track cartridges. Three asterisks (***) indicate is available in Quad-compatible.

Black Mikado, The. (Original London cast). Translantic.
Blithe Spirit. (Original touring cast). Beastly Hun.
Bubbling Brown Sugar. (*) (**). (H & L).
Hair (Re-issue). (*) (**). RCA.
Little Night Music, A. (*) (**). (Original London cast.) RCA.

Me and Bessie. Columbia.
My Fair Lady. (*) (**) (***). (Original cast 20th anniversary). Columbia.
Pacific Overtures. (*) (**). RCA.
Philemon. Galley.
Rex. RCA.
Rodgers & Hart. London.
Show Boat. (London cast). Stanyan (2 albums).

THE BEST PLAYS, 1894–1975

Listed in alphabetical order below are all those works selected as Best Plays in previous volumes in the *Best Plays* series. Opposite each title is given the volume in which the play appears, its opening date and its total number of performances. Those plays marked with an asterisk (*) were still playing on June 1, 1976 and their number of performances was figured through May 31, 1976. Adaptors and translators are indicated by (ad) and (tr), the symbols (b), (m) and (l) stand for the author of the book, music and lyrics in the cast of musicals and (c) signifies the credit for the show's conception.

NOTE: A season-by-season listing, rather than an alphabetical one, of the 500 Best Plays in the first 50 volumes, starting with the yearbook for the season of 1919–1920, appears in *The Best Plays of 1968–69.*

PLAY	VOLUME	OPENED	PERFS.
ABE LINCOLN IN ILLINOIS—Robert E. Sherwood	38–39	Oct. 15, 1938	472
ABRAHAM LINCOLN—John Drinkwater	19–20	Dec. 15, 1919	193
ACCENT ON YOUTH—Samson Raphaelson	34–35	Dec. 25, 1934	229
ADAM AND EVA—Guy Bolton, George Middleton	19–20	Sept. 13, 1919	312
ADAPTATION—Elaine May; and NEXT—Terrence McNally	68–69	Feb. 10, 1969	707
AFFAIRS OF STATE—Louis Verneuil	50–51	Sept. 25, 1950	610
AFTER THE FALL—Arthur Miller	63–64	Jan. 23, 1964	208
AFTER THE RAIN—John Bowen	67–68	Oct. 9, 1967	64
AH, WILDERNESS!—Eugene O'Neill	33–34	Oct. 2, 1933	289
AIN'T SUPPOSED TO DIE A NATURAL DEATH—(b,m,l) Melvin Van Peebles	71–72	Oct. 7, 1971	325
ALIEN CORN—Sidney Howard	32–33	Feb. 20, 1933	98
ALISON'S HOUSE—Susan Glaspell	30–31	Dec. 1, 1930	41
ALL MY SONS—Arthur Miller	46–47	Jan. 29, 1947	328
ALL OVER TOWN—Murray Schisgal	74–75	Dec. 12, 1974	233
ALL THE WAY HOME—Tad Mosel, based on James Agee's novel *A Death in the Family*	60–61	Nov. 30, 1960	333
ALLEGRO—(b, l) Oscar Hammerstein II, (m) Richard Rodgers	47–48	Oct. 10, 1947	315
AMBUSH—Arthur Richman	21–22	Oct. 10, 1921	98
AMERICA HURRAH—Jean-Claude van Itallie	66–67	Nov. 6, 1966	634
AMERICAN WAY, THE—George S. Kaufman, Moss Hart	38–39	Jan. 21, 1939	164
AMPHITRYON 38—Jean Giraudoux, (ad) S. N. Behrman	37–38	Nov. 1, 1937	153
ANDERSONVILLE TRIAL, THE—Saul Levitt	59–60	Dec. 29, 1959	179
ANDORRA—Max Frisch, (ad) George Tabori	62–63	Feb. 9, 1963	9
ANGEL STREET—Patrick Hamilton	41–42	Dec. 5, 1941	1,295
ANIMAL KINGDOM, THE—Philip Barry	31–32	Jan. 12, 1932	183
ANNA CHRISTIE—Eugene O'Neill	21–22	Nov. 2, 1921	177
ANNA LUCASTA—Philip Yordan	44–45	Aug. 30, 1944	957
ANNE OF THE THOUSAND DAYS—Maxwell Anderson	48–49	Dec. 8, 1948	286
ANOTHER LANGUAGE—Rose Franken	31–32	Apr. 25, 1932	344
ANOTHER PART OF THE FOREST—Lillian Hellman	46–47	Nov. 20, 1946	182
ANTIGONE—Jean Anouilh, (ad) Lewis Galantière	45–46	Feb. 18, 1946	64
APPLAUSE—(b) Betty Comden and Adolph Green, (m) Charles Strouse, (l) Lee Adams, based on the film *All About Eve* and the original story by Mary Orr	69–70	Mar. 30, 1970	896

NECROLOGY

MAY 1975–MAY 1976

PERFORMERS

Ague, James W. (75)—Summer 1975
Akar, John (48)—June 23, 1975
Albright, Hardie (71)—December 7, 1975
Allyn, Alyce—February 11, 1975
Allen, Kenneth (72)—January 15, 1976
Anderson, Ruth (64)—November 1975
Arbuckle, Minta Durfee (85)—Sept. 10, 1975
Arlen, Richard (75)—March 28, 1976
Arno, Sig (79)—August 17, 1975
Atkinson, Howard T. (75)—July 29, 1975
Aubrey, Georges (47)—November 1, 1975
Baddeley, Angela (71)—February 22, 1976
Baker, George (90)—January 8, 1976
Ballard, Florence (32)—February 22, 1976
Bannerman, Margaret (79)—April 25, 1976
Baragrey, John (57)—August 4, 1975
Barclay, Don Van Tassel (83)—Oct. 16, 1975
Bare, Carl (15)—December 19, 1975
Barringer, Ned (87)—February 13, 1976
Baxter, Alan (67)—May 8, 1976
Becker, Ned M. (82)—August 4, 1975
Belarsky, Sidor (77)—June 7, 1975
Bell, Nolan D. (55)—February 27, 1976
Belmonte, Herman (84)—September 15, 1975
Belson, Edward (77)—December 1, 1975
Benham, Earl (89)—March 21, 1976
Berger, Victoria Sherry (67)—June 23, 1975
Bertenshaw, Betty Jane—November 14, 1975
Blair, David (43)—April 1, 1976
Blaise, Pierre (24)—August 31, 1975
Blyden, Larry (49)—June 6, 1975
Bode, Allan (69)—October 9, 1975
Bolan, Jeanne (49)—April 17, 1976
Borzage, Daniel (78)—June 17, 1975
Bosl, Heinz (29)—June 12, 1975
Bossick, Bernard B. (57)—Nov. 10, 1975
Bradford, Reuben A. (82)—June, 1975
Brent, Evelyn (74)—June 4, 1975
Bretherton, Dorothea M. (79)—Feb. 6, 1976
Brisson, Cleo (81)—November 28, 1975
Brokaw, Charles (77)—October 23, 1975
Brown, Pamela (58)—September 18, 1975
Bruce, David (60)—May 3, 1976
Brunner, Heinrich (22)—September 9, 1975
Brunton, Garland Lewis (72)—July 24, 1975
Bryant, Robin (50)—January 18, 1976
Buckley, Tim (28)—June 29, 1975
Burgette, William L. (64)—January 23, 1976

Burnett, Chester A. (65)—January 10, 1976
Burnside, William Jr. (49)—March 25, 1976
Burr, Marion (67)—February 12, 1976
Butsova, Hilda (78)—March 21, 1976
Cairns, Angus (65)—October 14, 1975
Callega, Joseph (78)—Autumn, 1975
Calvin, Henry (57)—October 6, 1975
Cameron, Retta (49)—July 19, 1975
Cammans, Jan (84)—January 6, 1976
Carroll, Louise—August 1, 1975
Case, Nelson (66)—March 24, 1976
Cavendish, June—February 22, 1976
Chaliapin, Lydia Feodorovna (74)—December 15, 1975
Chandler, Christine (30)—July 21, 1975
Charlton, Alethea (43)—May 11, 1976
Charon, Jacques (55)—October 15, 1975
Cobb, Lee J. (64)—February 11, 1976
Cochran, Eddie—February 19, 1975
Coffee, Andrew J. (74)—Summer 1975
Colby, Barbara (36)—July 24, 1975
Collier, Cecil (67)—August 22, 1975
Cone, Thomas George (85)—May 1976
Conley, Harry J. (90)—June 23, 1975
Collins, Jerry (50)—January 26, 1976
Coons, Johnny (58)—July 6, 1975
Cooper, Clancy (68)—June 14, 1975
Cotton, George (72)—May 26, 1975
Coughlin, Kevin (30)—January 19, 1976
Crawford, Nan (82)—July 4, 1975
Crosby, Wade (65)—October 1, 1975
Cross, Wellington (88)—October 12, 1975
Curzon, George (77)—May 10, 1976
Daggett, Robert True (71)—July 20, 1975
Dalla Rizza, Gilda (82)—July 4, 1975
Davenport, Davis (42)—July 23, 1975
Davis, Clatie Polk—Autumn 1975
Day, Dorothy (77)—July 24, 1975
De Groot, Gerry—July 29, 1975
de Tolly, Deena—January 23, 1976
Deen, Nedra—December 28, 1975
Delevanti, Cyril (86)—December 13, 1975
Delight, June (77)—October 3, 1975
DeMont, Charles (84)—February 21, 1976
Din, Dulce S. (39)—July 29, 1975
Ditson, Lenny (63)—November 6, 1975
Dixon, Aland (65)—February 22, 1976
Dixon, Madelyn (81)—September 20, 1975
Donaldson, Jack (65)—June 20, 1975
Dorkin, Jack (81)—June 4, 1975

Dowling, Eddie (81)—February 18, 1976
Downing, Robert (61)—June 14, 1975
Dresdel, Sonia (67)—January 18, 1976
Duncan, Lisa (76)—January 24, 1976
Dunn, Liam (59)—April 11, 1976
Eckles, Robert (55)—August 9, 1975
Edmondson, Edward E. (65)—Jan. 29, 1976
Edwards, Julia (93)—April 16, 1976
Ellington, Evie Ellis (64)—April 7, 1976
Ellis, Charles (83)—March 11, 1976
Enright, Josephine (72)—February 24, 1976
Espinda, David (61)—June 7, 1975
Faulkner, Edith Jane (81)—July 29, 1975
Faye, Irma (63)—May 17, 1976
Fender, Doris (75)—July 24, 1975
Fisk, Edith (67)—April 20, 1976
Flanagan, Ann (60's)—June 1, 1975
Flavin, James (69)—April 23, 1976
Flosso, Al (80)—May 13, 1976
Foltz, Jane—May 28, 1975
Ford, Paul (74)—April 12, 1976
Fordyce, Marie D. (83)—April 7, 1976
Fort, Syvilla (58)—November 8, 1975
Franklin, Alberta (79)—March 14, 1976
Franklyn, Leo (78)—September 17, 1975
Franks, Ollie (56)—January 29, 1976
Franks, Percy (83)—February 10, 1976
Freed, Barboura M. (43)—October 23, 1975
Frizzell, William Orville (47)—July 19, 1975
Frome, Barbara (54)—March 17, 1976
Fuerheerd, Josephine B. (84)—April 26, 1976
Gilbert, Paul (58)—February 12, 1976
Giles, Paul Kirk (80)—April 23, 1976
Gilmore, Ruth—February 12, 1976
Gioi, Vivi (58)—July 12, 1975
Glover, Carrie (49)—January 13, 1976
Glyn, Neva Carr—August 10, 1975
Goodlife, Michael (61)—March 22, 1976
Griffies, Ethel (97)—September 9, 1975
Griner, Geunie (47)—July 21, 1975
Grosskurth, Kurt (66)—May 29, 1975
Haberfield, Graham (34)—October 17, 1975
Hall, Jeannette F. (77)—May 28, 1976
Halle, Cliff (57)—April 3, 1976
Hansen, William (64)—June 23, 1975
Harvey, Edward (82)—August 5, 1975
Hearn, Julia Knox (92)—May 1, 1976
Hill, Jane (95)—October 13, 1975
Hillery, Mable (46)—April 27, 1976
Holbrook, Ruby (63)—October 9, 1975
Hope, Douglas (82)—November 10, 1975
Hope, Francis James (84)—July 27, 1975
Howard, Johnny (70's)—January 21, 1976
Howerton, Clarence (62)—Nov. 18, 1975
Hunter, Susan (39)—January 18, 1976
Inescourt, Frieda (75)—February 21, 1976
Izumi, Edward I. (63)—August 1, 1975
Jackson, Jennie (54)—March 14, 1976
Jaffe, Michael (71)—January 29, 1976
James, Sidney (62)—April 26, 1976
Jonay, Roberta (50's)—April 19, 1976
Joslin, Howard (67)—August 1, 1975
Justice, James Robertson (70)—July 2, 1975
Kahan, Evelyn K. (72)—May 19, 1976

Kahanu, Archie (59)—October 29, 1975
Karger, Ann (89)—November 12, 1975
Kaufman, Irving (85)—January 3, 1976
Kaye, Deborah (83)—May 3, 1976
Keaton, Georgia (65)—June 24, 1975
Keller, Nan—December 10, 1975
Kelly, Margot (82)—March 10, 1976
Kenner, Chris (46)—January 25, 1976
Kiernan, James (35)—July 24, 1975
Knight, Fuzzy (74)—February 23, 1976
Knott, Else (63)—August 10, 1975
Koop, Mary Jane (57)—September 4, 1975
Kramer, Lawrence (66)—August 26, 1975
Kriza, John (56)—August 18, 1975
Krueger, Emmy (89)—March 13, 1976
Lackey, Kenneth (74)—April 16, 1976
Landis, Cullen (79)—August 26, 1975
Lapauri, Aleksandr (49)—August 5, 1975
Lee, Valerie (52)—July 12, 1975
Leider, Frida (87)—June 4, 1975
Leighton, Margaret (53)—January 13, 1976
LeRoy, Loretta (77)—December 2, 1975
Leslie, Scott—Winter 1975
Letteri, Al (47)—October 18, 1975
Licht, David (71)—July 31, 1975
Likely, Patricia (52)—February 24, 1976
Livesey, Roger (69)—February 5, 1976
Livingstone, Kay (55)—July 25, 1975
Lloyd, Jack (53)—May 21, 1976
Losch, Tilly (70's)—December 24, 1975
Lundigan, William (61)—December 20, 1975
MacGill, Moyna (80)—November 25, 1975
Mackenzie, George (74)—September 4, 1975
Malcolm, Edith Fisk (67)—April 20, 1976
Mardo, Charles (80)—March 8, 1976
Marshall, Horace (73)—February 24, 1976
Martinec, Lee A. (49)—September 4, 1975
Matz, Walter J. (81)—June 24, 1975
Maus, Arthur (70)—October 2, 1975
May, Marty (77)—November 11, 1975
McBride, Mary Margaret (76)—April 7, 1976
McCabe, Mary (73)—December 24, 1975
McCallum, Neil (46)—April 26, 1976
McCann, Dora (60)—August 13, 1975
McDevitt, Ruth (80)—May 27, 1976
McGiver, John (62)—September 9, 1975
McGonicle, Margaret (66)—Aug. 27, 1975
McGrath, Michael—January 16, 1976
McGurk, Harriet (72)—December 19, 1975
McIntyre, Marion (90)—November 19, 1975
Merande, Doro (70's)—November 1, 1975
Merrill, Fred R. (87)—March 16, 1976
Mihail, Alexandra (28)—December 17, 1975
Miller, Ruby (86)—April 2, 1976
Mineo, Sal (37)—February 12, 1976
Modley, Sidney Allen (73)—Winter 1976
Moncrieff, Gladys (83)—February 8, 1976
Moore, Chris (55)—June 6, 1975
Moor-Jones, Edna (84)—December 19, 1975
Morgan, George (50)—July 7, 1975
Morton, Clive (71)—September 24, 1975
Moscona, Nicola (68)—September 17, 1975
Mulvaney, John (45)—April 24, 1976
Myers, Beverly H. (49)—May 31, 1976

Mylong, John (82)—September 8, 1975
Naughton, Charlie (89)—February 11, 1976
Neil, Jimmy (58)—Winter 1976
Neligan, Donal (27)—December 14, 1975
Nelson, Ozzie (69)—June 3, 1975
Nervo, Jimmy (78)—December 5, 1975
Nickel, Paul (35)—June 24, 1975
Nielsen, Karl (85)—September 8, 1975
Nord, Betty (69)—April 29, 1976
Norins, Leslie H. (59)—June 19, 1975
Norman, Bruce (73)—January 11, 1976
Ochs, Phil (35)—April 9, 1975
Ody, Mel (62)—March 10, 1976
O'Malley, Rex (75)—May 1, 1976
O'Niel, Colette (80)—October 6, 1975
Orkin, Harvey (57)—November 3, 1975
Ornellas, Norman (36)—May 31, 1975
Ornstein, Honora (92)—June 19, 1975
Ort, Izzy (84)—October 13, 1975
Ortega, Santos (76)—April 10, 1976
Osnath-Halevy, Sarah (62)—Oct. 12, 1975
Palmer, Charles (46)—March 21, 1976
Pardee, C.W. (90)—July 17, 1975
Parker, Bob—June 28, 1975
Parker, Lester (43)—October 6, 1975
Patterson, Elmer C. (86)—August 23, 1975
Patterson, Troy (49)—November 1, 1975
Pavlos, Anthony E. (44)—June 30, 1975
Payne, Ben Iden (94)—April 6, 1976
Perez, Pepito (79)—July 13, 1975
Phillips, Eleanor Hyde (94)—June 4, 1975
Polan, Lou (71)—March 8, 1976
Pons, Lily (71)—February 13, 1976
Powell, Jack (75)—April 6, 1976
Powell, Ken (61)—March 11, 1976
Proctor, Jessie (102)—July 6, 1975
Puglia, Frank (83)—October 25, 1975
Pyle, Thomas F. (58)—January 22, 1976
Radd, Ronald (47)—April 23, 1975
Ray, Jack (58)—October 31, 1975
Red Fox, Chief William (105)—March 1, 1976
Reed, Lewis (80)—March 22, 1976
Regan, Daniel T. (60's)—September 28, 1975
Reif, Keith (33)—May 14, 1976
Rhodes, Ruth (79)—August 3, 1975
Ricci, Nora (51)—April 15, 1976
Riggs, Glenn E. (68)—September 12, 1975
Rivero, Julian (85)—February 24, 1976
Robbins, Archie (62)—September 26, 1975
Roberts, Roy (69)—May 28, 1975
Robeson, Paul (77)—January 23, 1976
Rose, Kathleen (83)—November 7, 1975
Rose, Rufus C. (70)—May 29, 1975
Rosenbloom, Maxie (71)—March 6, 1976
Ross, Danny (45)—Winter 1976
Ross, Lenny (71)—January 25, 1976
Rouvaun (36)—December 29, 1975
Roy, John (77)—May 31, 1975
Ruiz, Enrique (67)—November 5, 1975
Ruskin, Shimen (69)—April 23, 1976
Russell, Evelyn (49)—February 4, 1976
Ryan, James E. (35)—January 6, 1976
Ryan, Sheila (54)—November 4, 1975

Sample, Forrest (76)—September 19, 1975
Sanders, Betty (53)—August 21, 1975
Schwartz, Ida (80's)—March 27, 1976
Servais, Jean (65)—February 22, 1976
Shaub, Edna E. (98)—October 7, 1975
Shelton, James (62)—September 2, 1975
Shiro, James A.—October 14, 1975
Shutta, Ethel (79)—February 5, 1976
Simon, Michel (80)—May 30, 1975
Sizemore, Asher (69)—Autumn 1975
Slate, Syd (68)—May 2, 1976
Smith, Tom (84)—February 23, 1976
Snyder, Bert N.—June 12, 1975
Sowell, Ione M. (62)—July 29, 1975
Sritange, Mahdee (25)—August 31, 1975
Stark, Harold W. (61)—August 21, 1975
Steele, Vickie (28)—December 13, 1975
Strasser, Ilona (55)—March 19, 1976
Sullivan, Annette Kellerman (87)—November 5, 1975
Sullon, Paul (55)—October 3, 1975
Sully, Frank (67)—December 17, 1975
Taulbee, Gladys—June 1975
Teal, Ray (74)—April 2, 1976
Tetley, Walter (60)—September 4, 1975
Teyte, Maggie (88)—May 26, 1976
Thidblad, Inga (73)—Summer 1975
Thor, Larry (59)—March 15, 1976
Tierney, Agnes (60's)—January 1975
Tooker, Guy (83)—September 15, 1975
Traver, Lee (70)—July 26, 1975
Travis, Jan R. (23)—July 19, 1975
Treacher, Arthur (81)—December 14, 1975
Troy, John J. (56)—November 31, 1975
Tyson, Davey (73)—February 23, 1976
Upton, Frances (71)—November 27, 1975
Van Leer, Arnold (80)—June 3, 1975
Varvaro, Gloria (61)—April 8, 1976
Vazquez, Vicente (60)—December 15, 1975
Venkataramaya, Relangi (65)—Autumn 1975
Villa, Alba (55)—Spring 1976
Walker, Betty (81)—Winter 1976
Walker, Lillian (88)—October 10, 1975
Walker, Wally (74)—August 7, 1975
Walsh, Miriam Cooper (84)—April 12, 1976
Ward, Winifred (95)—December 27, 1975
Weed, Leland T. (74)—August 29, 1975
Weidman, Charles (73)—July 15, 1975
Wendell, Howard David (67)—Aug. 11, 1975
Wesson, Gene (54)—August 22, 1975
West, Billy (82)—July 21, 1975
Whipper, Leigh (98)—July 26, 1975
White, Princess (95)—March 20, 1976
White, Valerie (59)—December 3, 1975
Widom, Leonard (58)—April 18, 1976
Wiley, Lee (60)—December 11, 1975
Williams, Audrey—November 4, 1975
Williams, O. T. (68)—March 13, 1976
Wise, Patricia Doyle (60)—Sept. 22, 1975
Young, Gladys (70)—August 18, 1975
Young, James L. (58)—August 28, 1975
Zacchini, Hugo (77)—October 20, 1975
Zimmerl, Christl (36)—March 18, 1976
Zorran (60's)—January 4, 1976

PLAYWRIGHTS

Armstrong, Anthony (79)—February 10, 1976
Bigelow, Joe (66)—February 20, 1976
Bjorneboe, Jens (55)—May 10, 1976
Buchman, Sidney (73)—August 23, 1975
Casey, Rosemary (70)—March 22, 1976
Christie, Agatha (85)—January 12, 1976
Davin-Power, Maurice (66)—Dec. 16, 1975
Derman, Lou (61)—February 15, 1976
Fields, Sid (77)—September 28, 1975
Giltinan, Donal (67)—March 1976
Graham, Joseph (83)—April 29, 1976
Horne, Kenneth (75)—June 5, 1975
Houser, Mervin (65)—March 23, 1976
Hughes, Richard (76)—April 28, 1976
Johnson, Clint (60)—December 9, 1975
Klausner, Margot (70)—Autumn 1975
Kober, Arthur (74)—June 12, 1975
Kraft, Hyman S. (75)—July 29, 1975
Laver, James (76)—June 3, 1975
Laws, Frederick (65)—January 26, 1976
Lederer, Charles (65)—March 5, 1976
Lever, J. W. (62)—November 11, 1975
Lloyd, John (38)—March 30, 1976
Lord, Phillips H. (73)—October 19, 1975
Lord, Robert (75)—April 5, 1976
Maas, Audrey Gellen (40)—July 2, 1975
Marx, Marvin (50)—December 23, 1975
McCarthy, Joseph A. (53)—Nov. 7, 1975
McGrath, Frank (72)—January 24, 1976
Mulligan, Eugene (47)—March 17, 1976
Pearl, Hal (61)—December 17, 1975
Provo, Frank (62)—November 20, 1975
Riley, Lawrence (78)—November 29, 1975
Robinson, Jack (65)—October 3, 1975
Rose, Tom (51)—February 19, 1976
Russo, Sarett Rude (58)—April 16, 1976
Seelin, Elpha (62)—December 27, 1975
Segall, Harry (78)—November 25, 1975
Serling, Rod (50)—June 28, 1975
Seymour, James (80)—January 29, 1976
Sherriff, Robert C. (79)—November 13, 1975
Snow, Davis (62)—December 5, 1975
Steen, Marguerite (81)—August 4, 1975
Storm, Lesley (71)—October 19, 1975
Tarn, Adam (73)—Summer 1975
Welch, William Addams (61)—Feb. 2, 1976
Wilder, Thornton (78)—December 7, 1975
Wylie, Max (71)—September 21, 1975

COMPOSERS, LYRICISTS

Baird, Tom—Winter 1976
Bellow, Alexander (63)—March 12, 1976
Bloom, Rube (73)—March 30, 1976
Brandon, Arthur F. (50)—June 27, 1975
Brooks, Shelton L. (89)—September 6, 1975
Burman, S. D. (76)—Autumn 1975
Carr, Leon (65)—March 27, 1976
Cook, Jean Lawrence (76)—April 2, 1976
Dominguez, Alberto (73)—September 1, 1975
Dunlap, Louis M. (64)—May 3, 1976
Edwards, Darrell Darwin (56)—June 10, 1975

Espla, Oscar (96)—January 6, 1976
Frisch, Albert (60)—April 11, 1976
Gaynor, Charles (66)—December 18, 1975
Gesensway, Louis (70)—March 13, 1976
Gilbert, Ray (63)—March 3, 1976
Green, Bernard (66)—August 8, 1976
Guaraldi, Vince (47)—February 7, 1976
Herrmann, Bernard (64)—December 24, 1975
Hollander, Friedrich (79)—January 18, 1976
Jackson, Al (39)—October 1, 1975
James, Philip (85)—November 1, 1975
Leslie, Edgar (90)—January 22, 1976
Liebrecht, Max (59)—July 31, 1975
Mainardi, Enrico (78)—April 11, 1976
Marcus, Sol (63)—February 5, 1976
Nelson, Oliver (43)—October 27, 1975
Orr, Charles W. (82)—Winter 1976
Palmer, Jack (75)—March 17, 1976
Roberts, Paddy (65)—August 24, 1975
Schmerts, Robert W. (77)—June 7, 1975
Seeberg, Dr. Harry (61)—May 27, 1975
Sherman, James B. (67)—October 11, 1975
Shostakovich, Dimitri (68)—August 9, 1975
Siday, Eric (71)—March 25, 1976
Smith, Frank M. (70)—May 8, 1976
Steininger, Franz (69)—December 28, 1975
Sternberg, Ann (42)—June 12, 1975
Stolz, Robert (94)—June 27, 1975
Tamkin, David (68)—June 21, 1975
Taube, Evert (85)—January 31, 1976
Ugarte, Floro M. (91)—July 11, 1975
Varma, Vayalar Rama (46)—Autumn 1975
Weathers, Roscoe (55)—April 18, 1976
Windsor, John Peter (60)—February 3, 1976

PRODUCERS, DIRECTORS, CHOREOGRAPHERS

Abraham, Louis (51)—June 8, 1975
Anderson, Linda (36)—December 24, 1975
Baker, Ray (35)—January 12, 1976
Belasco, William (41)—February 26, 1976
Benesh, Rudolf F. (59)—May 3, 1975
Berkeley, Busby (80)—March 14, 1976
Blakely, Don F. (49)—February 22, 1976
Blechman, Marcus (67)—October 2, 1975
Brown, Danny (63)—March 1, 1976
Burnley, Fred (41)—July 7, 1975
Byers, Charles A. (72)—October 25, 1975
Carpenter, Louisa d'A. (68)—Winter 1976
Carrington, Frank (73)—July 3, 1975
Carroll, Edward Linus (68)—June 4, 1975
Choate, Edward (67)—July 23, 1975
Code, Reginald F. (78)—June 13, 1975
Cohan, William (66)—February 12, 1976
Collins, Ernest S. (84)—October 13, 1975
Costil, William Jr. (63)—April 19, 1976
Cutler, Robert Frye (75)—February 24, 1976
Dancigers, Oscar (74)—February 27, 1976
Daubeny, Peter (54)—August 6, 1975
Davidson, Norris West (69)—Sept. 11, 1975
Diskin, Marshall (62)—December 5, 1975
Dodge, Wendell P. (92)—May 26, 1976
Donovan, Frank R. (69)—September 26, 1975

Duff, Gordon (66)—December 4, 1975
Edelman, Louis F. (75)—January 6, 1976
Eisenstat, Jacob (33)—December 9, 1975
Essex, Tony (49)—May 16, 1975
Farnell, Jack (61)—May 1, 1976
Felsenstein, Walter (74)—October 8, 1975
Fenno, Ada V. (90)—June 24, 1975
Fishman, Melvin A. (46)—February 18, 1976
Ford, Philip (73)—January 12, 1976
Franks, Lorraine (58)—January 5, 1976
Fried, Walter (69)—May 28, 1975
Furrer, Urs B. (41)—August 30, 1975
Goodman, Bernard R. (64)—August 5, 1975
Gorham, Maurice (73)—August 9, 1975
Grajales, Fernando Felix (32)—Sept. 4, 1975
Guenther, Dorothee (79)—September 29, 1975
Hays, Jack (76)—May 30, 1975
Heller, Robert P. (60)—July 29, 1975
Henabery, Joseph E. (88)—February 18, 1976
Hillie, Edward (56)—July 1, 1975
Horn, Leonard (48)—May 25, 1975
James, Cyril (63)—August 27, 1975
Jewell, James (69)—August 5, 1975
Johnstone, Paul (55)—March 13, 1976
Jordan, Glenn R. (56)—July 22, 1975
Kane, Joseph (81)—August 25, 1975
Lampe, Gus (74)—August 19, 1975
Larsen, Niels (49)—December 13, 1975
Lee, Rowland V. (84)—December 21, 1975
Lynn, Dane W. (56)—October 16, 1975
Mathews, Cicely (65)—August 4, 1975
Meyer, Johannes—January 25, 1976
Moguy, Leonide (77)—April 1976
Pasolini, Pier Paolo (53)—November 2, 1975
Prager, Gerhard (55)—July 17, 1975
Rackin, Martin Lee (58)—April 13, 1976
Rao, A. Venkata Subba (67)—Summer 1975
Reed, Carol (69)—April 25, 1976
Rees, Edward (57)—March 10, 1976
Remond, Fritz (73)—March 31, 1976
Richter, Hans (87)—February 1, 1976
Rodakiewicz, Henwar (73)—Feb. 12, 1976
Roewade, Paul (39)—March 10, 1976
Rogers, Budd (84)—August 13, 1975
Rossin, Alfred A. (57)—February 19, 1976
Sagal, Sara Macon (47)—September 1, 1975
Salmaggi, Alfredo (89)—September 5, 1975
Savage, David D. (62)—November 1, 1975
Serneau, Gunther (51)—January 8, 1976
Shah, Chandulal J. (77)—November 25, 1975
Shainmark, Lou (75)—January 5, 1976
Sharpe, Don—November 20, 1975
Smith, Susan (34)—August 17, 1975
South, Barbara (45)—August 26, 1975
Steinman, Harold (70)—August 23, 1975
Streit, Pierre (52)—October 5, 1975
Thiele, William J. (85)—September 7, 1975
Twist, John (77)—February 11, 1976
Virsky, Pavel (70)—Summer 1975
Visconti, Luchino (69)—March 17, 1976
Votion, Jack (75)—October 16, 1975
Waring, James (53)—December 2, 1975
Weitzel, Thomas (50)—September 30, 1975
Wellman, William A. (79)—December 9, 1975

Willat, Irvin V. (84)—April 17, 1976
Willig, Steven (30)—August 14, 1975
Yakobson, Leonid (71)—October 20, 1975
Young, Christopher B. (67)—Dec. 1, 1975
Young, Felix (80)—February 12, 1976
Zimbalist, Al (59)—August 28, 1975
Zimmer, Dolph M. (75)—October 23, 1975

CONDUCTORS

Baum, Oscar Frederick (84)—July 26, 1975
Broad, Harry (72)—July 27, 1975
Budney, Chester B. (54)—September 30, 1975
Campbell, George (72)—April 13, 1976
Carter, Alan (71)—September 21, 1975
Chichester, Edward (71)—May 24, 1975
Clarke, Vera (79)—January 29, 1976
Cocoros, Constantine (47)—Sept. 15, 1975
Dale, Ted (65)—July 25, 1975
D'Amato, Noel (78)—March 13, 1976
Davis, Meyer (83)—April 5, 1975
DePolis, Joseph (52)—October 4, 1975
Desai, Vasant (61)—Winter 1976
Durso, Michael (70)—December 26, 1975
Faith, Percy (67)—February 9, 1976
Farber, Nat (53)—September 13, 1975
Fodor, Jerry (64)—November 26, 1975
Gerun, Tom (74)—June 12, 1975
Gorham, James H. (73)—January 11, 1976
Gui, Vittorio (90)—October 16, 1975
Hanson, Lloyd (68)—April 19, 1976
Hurt, Hervey Pugh (72)—September 3, 1975
Kozma, Tibor (66)—March 24, 1976
Kumpfe, Rudolph (65)—May 11, 1976
Kuttner, Michael (57)—October 10, 1975
Le Winter, David (61)—January 22, 1976
Linton, Theodore Moore (59)—Nov. 26, 1975
Lopez, Vincent (80)—September 20, 1975
Mann, Bernie (61)—January 31, 1976
Martinon, Jean (66)—March 1, 1976
Mathieson, Muir (64)—August 2, 1975
Mendoza, David (81)—May 23, 1975
Middleman, Herman (70's)—Nov. 6, 1975
Nelson, Harmon O. Jr. (68)—Sept. 28, 1975
Norris, Arthur—December 15, 1975
Oliver, Eddie (69)—March 19, 1976
Porter, Hughes (69)—June 22, 1975
Robinson, Nathan (86)—May 4, 1976
Romanoff, Boris (78)—October 12, 1975
Russo, Charles A. (64)—May 28, 1975
Swarowsky, Hans (75)—September 10, 1975
Trotter, John Scott (67)—October 29, 1975
Valinote, Merrick D. (78)—February 24, 1976
Vinton, Stanley (63)—February 17, 1976
Wayne, Roger (66)—October 12, 1975
Whitmer, Kenneth—February 5, 1976
Williams, Fess (81)—December 17, 1975

DESIGNERS

Ayrton, Michael (54)—November 17, 1975
Boxhorn, Jerome (55)—September 11, 1975
Carpenter, Claude E. (71)—February 18, 1976
Dawson, Beatrice (68)—April 16, 1976

Devaney, Thomas (67)—December 18, 1975
Emert, Oliver (73)—August 13, 1975
Heinrich, Rudolf (49)—December 1, 1975
Holm, Dolores (69)—January 20, 1976
Irvine, Richard F. (65)—March 30, 1976
Ktenavea, Stamatia (77)—December 12, 1975
Levy, Leon Ralph (75)—May 27, 1975
Matthew, Sir Robert (68)—June 21, 1975
McQuinn, Robert (92)—June 24, 1975
Merritt, Guy E. (49)—October 20, 1975
Mielziner, Jo (74)—March 15, 1976
Oenslager, Donald M. (73)—June 21, 1975
Pond, John (72)—November 27, 1975
Pye, Merrill (73)—November 17, 1975
Sylos, Frank Paul (75)—April 16, 1976

CRITICS

Arceo, Romeo J. (45)—June 8, 1975
Baker, William K. (50)—May 12, 1976
Balbo, Giuseppe C. (88)—January 30, 1976
Barney, Phil (81)—December 2, 1975
Betts, Ernest (79)—June 9, 1975
Callaghan, J. Dorsey (80)—October 9, 1975
Donnelly, Tom (57)—February 10, 1976
Douglas, Jeff (32)—Autumn 1975
Gleason, Ralph J. (58)—June 3, 1975
Grant, Elspeth (60's)—November 13, 1975
Greenlees, Leslie M. (68)—July 23, 1975
Grosbayne, Benjamin (82)—January 24, 1976
Herring, Robert (72)—November 4, 1975
Kaye, Joseph (77)—June 9, 1975
Kean, J. Harold (79)—October 21, 1975
Kenny, Nick (80)—December 1, 1975
Lewitan, Joseph (82)—April 9, 1976
Malcolm, Donald (43)—August 15, 1975
McIntyre, Dave (52)—June 7, 1975
McLaughlin, Russell (81)—Summer 1975
Melven, Charles Jr. (53)—February 15, 1976
Mountjoy, John (61)—May 21, 1975
Rosenfeld, Jay C. (80)—October 21, 1975
Solano, Solita (86)—November 22, 1975
Stern, Harold S. (53)—May 25, 1976
Swan, Bradford F. (68)—February 20, 1976
Taylor, Weston (47)—October 1, 1975
Yates, Peter B. (66)—February 25, 1976

MUSICIANS

Adams, Michael James (23)—May 3, 1976
Adderley, Julian (47)—August 8, 1975
Alexander, Sam (56)—February 29, 1976
August, Jan (71)—January 17, 1976
Barclay, Chester A. (72)—July 21, 1975
Basilevsky, Ivan (84)—December 5, 1975
Benoric, Stephen P. J. (63)—March 17, 1976
Brailowsky, Alexander (80)—April 25, 1976
Brave, Charles (81)—April 27, 1976
Briglia, Joseph (91)—November 28, 1975
Brunious, John (55)—May 7, 1976
Busch, Hermann (77)—June 3, 1975
Chenault, David W. (56)—March 18, 1976
Corigliano, John (74)—September 1, 1975

Dawson, David P. (62)—November 16, 1975
Delaney, Jack (45)—September 22, 1975
Donath, Paul L. (97)—February 1, 1976
Duffy, Eugene (58)—June 2, 1975
Duncan, Ted (74)—March 9, 1976
Elkan, Ida (81)—March 17, 1976
Everly, Ike (67)—October 22, 1975
Fellowes, Horace (100)—Autumn 1975
Fiedler, Elsa (84)—September 25, 1975
Forte, Frank (79)—December 1, 1975
Frey, Nathan (95)—November 10, 1975
Fuller, Jesse (79)—January 1975
Geraghty, Tony (33)—July 31, 1975
Gibbs, Thomas Parker (70)—August 7, 1975
Glassman, Karl (92)—October 11, 1975
Hawes, John (59)—June 29, 1975
Herz, Otto (81)—January 5, 1976
Jacobson, Berthe Poncy (81)—Oct. 2, 1975
Johnson, Clifford (67)—April 24, 1976
Kass, Harry (87)—October 7, 1975
Klatzkin, Dr. Arthur (83)—May 5, 1976
Kossoff, Paul (25)—March 18, 1976
Lampley, Claude L. (79)—May 31, 1975
Lannuit, Charles (78)—March 21, 1976
Law, Hayward Earl (24)—May 3, 1976
Lipscomb, Mance (80)—January 30, 1976
Luck, Walter H. E. (79)—June 7, 1975
Mack, Theodore (65)—September 26, 1975
Madden, Doris (90)—May 12, 1976
Martin, Charles—Autumn 1975
Maury, Lowndes (64)—December 11, 1975
McCoy, Brian (33)—July 31, 1975
McGee, Sam (81)—August 21, 1975
Monroe, Charlie (72)—September 27, 1975
Munrow, David (32)—May 15, 1976
Nance, Ray (62)—January 28, 1976
Oliver, Richard B. (64)—July 30, 1975
O'Toole, Francis (29)—July 31, 1975
Palazzi, Richard J. (27)—November 7, 1975
Patwardhan, Vinayakarao (78)—Summer 1975
Rabinoff, Benno (71)—July 6, 1975
Rocco, Maurice (56)—March 25, 1976
Rudnytsky, Antin (73)—November 30, 1975
Sanders, Wayne A. (64)—December 15, 1975
Sands, Eugene (21)—November 10, 1975
Schachter, Julius (67)—March 31, 1976
Schenk, Robert C. (81)—June 23, 1975
Schrader, John W. (51)—April 13, 1976
Seeger, Constance (88)—October 10, 1975
Shopnick, Mack (69)—July 18, 1975
Short, Robert (59)—April 4, 1976
Simkin, Meyer (70)—April 5, 1976
Singer, Harry (69)—February 12, 1976
Singleton, Zutty (77)—July 14, 1975
Solomon, Robert (32)—May 30, 1975
Sopkin, Stefan A. (75)—July 18, 1975
Starr, Will (53)—March 6, 1975
Summey, James Clell (61)—August 18, 1975
Tarasca, Albert G. (72)—June 20, 1975
Taylor, Theodore (59)—December 17, 1975
Thain, Tary (27)—December 15, 1975
Troila, Anibal (61)—Spring 1976
Tyson, James M. (68)—July 28, 1975
Willens, Joseph—October 26, 1975

Willis, Charles (59)—January 28, 1976
Wilson, Amis (72)—September 7, 1975

OTHERS

Arnold, Jonas (72)—November 10, 1975
  Publicist
Astaire, Ann Geilus (96)—July 29, 1975
  Mother of Fred and Adele Astaire
Bader, Merwin O. (80)—October 8, 1975
  Built The Playhouse, Wilmington, Delaware
Barker, Mike (60)—February 25, 1976
  Head of Associated Booking Corp.
Barnhart, Franklin (49)—March 2, 1976
  Labor executive of IATSE
Batt, Madeline (80)—November 23, 1975
  Leader in Philadelphia arts circles
Bau, Gordon R. (68)—July 21, 1975
  Makeup artist
Beasley, William (87)—November 20, 1975
  Chairman, Whittle Music Company, Dallas
Berman, Abraham L. (85)—October 13, 1975
  Theatrical attorney
Biow, Milton R. (83)—February 1, 1976
  Founder, Biow Company ad agency
Bogdanoff, Leonard (50)—October 6, 1975
  Financial executive
Bradley, Frankie (81)—January 8, 1976
  Philadelphia restauranteur
Brookhouser, Frank (63)—November 3, 1975
  Columnist, newsman, author
Brooks, Neil (62)—August 20, 1975
  General manager, London Palladium
Brown, Joe David (60)—April 22, 1976
  Author, newsman
Bruno, Anthony J. (82)—February 6, 1976
  Photographer of stars
Bushell, Leonard O. (78)—February 6, 1976
  Voice and music teacher
Carman, Jerry (75)—August 18, 1975
  Detroit talent agent
Chadwick, Dorothy (90)—January 17, 1976
  Active in N. Y. cultural organizations
Christy, George Washington (86)—Aug. 7, 1975
  Circus owner
Comen, Stuart (50)—July 17, 1975
  Personal manager
Considine, Bob (68)—September 25, 1975
  Journalist, columnist, author
Corcoran, Leo J. (74)—October 27, 1975
  Bartender at Artist and Writers
Crawford, Dorothy (90)—February 9, 1976
  Founder of Little Theater, New Haven
Dailey, J.W. (74)—April 27, 1976
  Publicist
de Mond, Willy (72)—February 3, 1976
  Supplied special hosiery to stars
Dewitz, Ursula (60)—November 27, 1975
  Owner of Thalia Theater, New York
Donahue, Vincent (58)—February 10, 1976
  Assistant executive director, Actors Equity
Dvorkin, Etta (77)—February 26, 1976
  Dean, High School of Music and Art

Ecker, I. Elmer (77)—July 26. 1975
  Theatrical lawyer
Eddy, Jim (50)—September 30, 1975
  Publicist
Erichs, Harold (74)—February 6, 1976
  Treasurer, financial editor, Variety
Ernst, Morris (87)—May 21, 1976
  Civil libertarian lawyer
Factor, Louis (68)—December 4, 1975
  Vice president, Max Factor & Co.
Feinberg, Joe (73)—September 18, 1975
  Agent, vaudeville booker
Feldman, Maurice (66)—May 6, 1976
  Publicist
Fine, Hank (72)—July 22, 1975
  Publicist
Fleishhacker, Mortimer (68)—Spring 1976
  San Francisco arts leader
Forrestal, Josephine Ogden (76)—Jan. 3, 1976
  Theatrical investor
Frankel, Adolph (72)—June 30, 1975
  Florida cultural leader
Gale, Joseph T. (70)—April 20, 1976
  Pioneer in entertainment
Green, Ruth (72)—May 20, 1976
  Asst. exec. director, League N. Y. Theaters
Gruskin, George (65)—August 18, 1975
  Talent agent
Gryzbowski, Walter (58)—March 8, 1976
  Personal manager
Hales, F. David (55)—January 14, 1976
  Publicist
Harbage, Alfred (74)—May 2, 1976
  American Shakespeare scholar
Hardin, John A. (88)—March 27, 1976
  Hardin Theater Supply Company, Dallas
Holzfeind, Frank (75)—June 26, 1975
  Jazz entrepreneur
Hughes, Howard R. (70)—April 5, 1976
  Former owner of RKO Studio
Hunt, Guy B. (66)—June 25, 1975
  Amusement business executive
Hunter, Ruth (74)—February 22, 1976
  Theatrical wardrobe supervisor
Jacobs, Thomas (73)—March 3, 1976
  Stand-in for brother, Danny Thomas
Jaffe, Teri (58)—September 11, 1975
  Active in theatrical charities
Johnson, Roma Burton—March 3, 1976
  Publicist
Kahn, Gilbert W. (72)—December 15, 1975
  Arts patron
Kapp, David (71)—March 1, 1976
  Pioneer, Broadway musical cast albums
Kazan, Athena Sismanoglou—Nov. 21, 1975
  Mother of Elia Kazan
Kean, Edith—August 25, 1975
  Staff member, Solters & Roskin
Keiser, David M. (69)—November 26, 1975
  President, New York Philharmonic
Kelley, Robert F. (75)—December 15, 1975
  Publicist and newspaper man
Kennedy, Kathleen M. (28)—July 28, 1975
  Publicist

King, Herbert G. (73)—July 11, 1975
Director, Metropilitan Opera Club

King, Howard (91)—September 15, 1975
Organizer of King Brothers Circus

Kingston, Vincent F. (73)—March 6, 1976
Manager, Alcazar Ballroom, York, Pa.

Kolodney, William (76)—January 18, 1976
Educational director, 92nd St. YM-YWHA

Lentz, Abraham (64)—October 30, 1975
Wrote for comedians

Leventritt, Rosalie (84)—February 28, 1976
Founder, Leventritt music prize

Loft, Solly (67)—August 2, 1975
Music publisher

Lombardo, Florence (84)—January 3, 1976
Widow of Carmen Lombardo

Luftig, Charles—August 22, 1975
Personal manager

Mandel, Bebe (50)—November 29, 1975
Booking agent

Marr, Paul (71)—February 13, 1976
Booking agent

Martin, Harry J. (82)—June 1, 1975
Promoter, theater manager

McCormick, John (82)—December 12, 1975
Owner of Dolly's, theatrical store

Melniker, William (80)—February 23, 1976
Theatrical attorney

Miessner, Benjamin E. (85)—March 25, 1976
Inventor of musical equipment

Miles, Helen Clark—March 15, 1976
Box office treasurer, Berkshire Playhouse

Mills, Jake (65)—December 29, 1975
Owner, Mlils Brothers Circus

Mittler, William H. (70's)—March 20, 1976
Personal manager

Morgan, Swifty (90)—September 19, 1975
Broadway character

Moss, Clarence H. (75)—Dec. 29, 1975
Theater executive

Newhill, Charles (82)—July 26, 1975
Katharine Hepburn's chauffeur

Nicoll, Allardyce (81)—April 17, 1976
Historian of English drama

Nidorf, Mike (60's)—May 27, 1975
Agent

Osborne, Georgia Lund (57)—June 18, 1975
Talent agency head

Owen, William (38)—November 13, 1975
Drama professor, Brooklyn College

Pirandello, Fausto (76)—November 30, 1975
Son of Luigi Pirandello

Polland, Elizabeth H. (82)—May 25, 1975
Acting teacher

Rapoport, Gene W. (36)—October 2, 1975
Agent

Rauch, Greta (74)—January 14, 1976
Publicist

Reis, Herb (66)—January 21, 1976
President, Herb Reis Music

Revson, Charles H. (68)—August 24, 1975
President, Revlon Inc.

Riffe, Bessie Tons (93)—January 2, 1976
Wardrobe mistress

Robey, Don D. (71)—June 16, 1975
Pioneer in entertainment

Roon, Al (73)—January 30, 1976
Trained Follies, Carroll dancers

Rudich, Nathan M. (56)—December 26, 1975
Executive and publicist

Sager, Max (82)—August 18, 1975
Shubert Organization employee

Saxe, Thomas Jr. (72)—Decmber 20, 1975
Shakespeare Theater, Stratford, Conn.

Schneider, Max (74)—Summer 1975
Operator, Boston Steubens Vienna Room

Schooler, Lee (52)—September 28, 1975
Publicist

Schuster, Milton (92)—July 31, 1975
Booking agent

Sciolla, Gaetano (85)—February 6, 1976
Philadelphia supper club proprietor

Sendrey, Alfred (92)—March 3, 1976
Musicologist

Shurlock, Geoffrey (81)—April 26, 1976
Production Code administrator

Simard, Robert (50)—November 29, 1975
Executive musical director

Simon, Harry (87)—January 1, 1976
Active in insuring plays

Solomon, Edward (64)—March 23, 1976
Publicist

Spar, Herbert (35)—January 16, 1976
Agent

Steinman, Morris W. (65)—January 11, 1976
Publicist

Stetler, M. Edith (86)—January 14, 1976
Piano, voice instructor

Stout, Rex (88)—October 27, 1975
Novelist

Streeter, Edward (84)—March 31, 1976
Humorist

Sullivan, Frank (83)—February 19, 1976
Humorist, author

Sulzer, Elmer G. (72)—February 15, 1976
Educator and publicist

Talley, William Edgar (64)—Winter 1975
President, Barn Dinner Theater Corp.

Taplinger, Robert (66)—November 24, 1975
Publicist

Thompson, Foster D. (63)—April 23, 1976
Production manager

Trimble, Byron A. (61)—May 12, 1976
Director of Hartford Civic Center

Ullman, S. George (82)—October 1, 1975
Agent

Wilder, Mrs. Jay L. (82)—December 1, 1975
Missouri promoter

Yeager, Robert (64)—January 19, 1976
Publicist

Zahl, Ephraim (48)—August 8, 1975
Agent

INDEX

Play titles appear in **bold face**. *Bold face italic* page numbers refer to those pages where complete cast and credit listings for New York productions may be found.

496   INDEX